Violence and Gender

Violence and Gender
An Interdisciplinary Reader

Editors

PAULA RUTH GILBERT
KIMBERLY K. EBY
George Mason University

PEARSON
Prentice
Hall

Upper Saddle River, New Jersey 07458

Library of Congress Cataloging-in-Publication Data
Violence and gender : an interdisciplinary reader / edited by Paula Ruth
Gilbert and Kimberly K. Eby.
     p. cm.
Includes bibliographical references.
  ISBN 0-13-111631-2
  1. Violence. 2. Sex role. 3. Family violence. I. Gilbert, Paula
Ruth. II. Eby, Kimberly K.
  HM886 .V5593 2003
  303.6—dc21   2003000332

Publisher: *Nancy Roberts*
Editorial Assistant: *Lee Peterson*
Production Liaison: *Joanne Hakim*
Senior Marketing Manager: *Amy Speckman*
Marketing Assistant: *Adam Laitman*
Manufacturing Buyer: *Mary Ann Gloriande*
Cover Art Director: *Jayne Conte*
Cover Design: *Bruce Kenselaar*
Cover Illustration/Photo: *Noma/Stock Illustration Source*
Cover Image Specialist: *Karen Sanatar*
Composition/Full-Service Project Management: *Patty Donovan*
Printer/Binder: *Hamilton Printing Company*

Credits and acknowledgments borrowed from other sources and reproduced, with permission, in this textbook appear on page 429.

Pearson Education LTD.
Pearson Education Singapore, Pte. Ltd
Pearson Education Canada, Ltd
Pearson Education—Japan
Pearson Education Australia PTY, Limited

Pearson Education North Asia Ltd
Pearson Educación de Mexico, S.A. de C.V.
Pearson Education Malaysia, Pte. Ltd
Pearson Education, Upper Saddle River, New Jersey

10 9 8 7 6 5 4 3 2 1

ISBN 0-13-111631-2

For Arthur, Randy, Meredith, and Chris

For José, Lisa, Kay, and Rich

*before a reading means I have reviewed it enough to make an include-or-not judgment.
comments afterward indicate usability for the course*

Contents

III   Youth Violence

IV   The Violation of Body Space

V   Violence and Sports

VI   Media Representation of Violence

VII   Preventing Violence and Revisioning the Future

Preface

When we first conceptualized this book in 1996 we wanted to create a text that would speak to the many forms of violence occurring both domestically and globally. Moreover, we believed, and continue to believe, that much public and academic discourse still largely ignores the interrelationships between the different manifestations of violence and the construct of gender. Since the social construction of our gender greatly informs how we act, how we react, and how we function in our world, it seems crucial that we begin an inquiry into how our notions of gender influence the perpetration and experience of violence.

It quickly became apparent that we had to limit our focus to the United States for two reasons: addressing issues of worldwide violence and gender demands in-depth analysis that is beyond the scope of a single volume; equally importantly—and unfortunately—given the amount of violence in the United States, we certainly have more than enough material for investigation with this defined focus. Ironically enough, since September 11, 2001, Americans have become increasingly aware of and concerned about worldwide violence in forms such as terrorism, suicide bombers, the treatment of women in Afghanistan, and biological and chemical warfare. Despite this important change in the knowledge level and subsequent outlook of many Americans, we continue to believe that the violence many Americans experience "at home"—in our homes and schools, at our work, and on our streets— *especially* as it relates to the construction of gender, needs to be at the forefront of our national dialogues and debated in our classrooms.

Like many others, our interest in issues of violence and gender grows out of personal concerns. Children, who are often the victims and perpetrators of violence, are being born and raised in a society that abhors and yet remains fascinated with violence. A minority of men, who demonstrate their manhood in hostile ways, create a general fear of men in our culture. As a result, women often need to be afraid of the men whom they meet and with whom they develop intimate relationships. Children and adults of "other" religions, ethnicities, races, sexual preferences, and cultures are being subjected to the intolerance of the dominant culture. In addition, our national conversations about violence are often driven by individual incidents that are highly publicized in the media. Once these examples fade from the media and our attention, however, it is all too easy to move on with our lives and leave these issues behind. Clearly, we need thoughtful, sustained dialogues about the causes of violence, in conjunction with examinations of their relationships to gender.

As educators, we believe that the most effective way to promote this dialogue is to facilitate life-long learning for people of all ages. All of us need to develop informed opinions in order to understand the range of reasons why violence occurs, analyze the possible causes and effects of violence on others, form our own opinions about how to prevent such violent incidents, respect the opinions of others, and work toward solutions that better our lives. We believe that intolerance of the "Other" is usually caused by a lack of knowledge and understanding, by an unawareness of a different point of view. Education remains a critically important and effective way to minimize that ignorance and to begin the journey toward mutual tolerance.

The book that we have compiled is the outgrowth of an eight-credit interdisciplinary course on violence and gender that has been taught several times. The selected readings here present a number of perspectives on issues of violence and gender: from psychology; criminology; journalism; biology; sociology; history; law; cultural studies. This collection includes selections that utilize different disciplinary methods, including scholarly analyses, case studies, and research reports. Taken together, the texts can help us understand the phenomenon of violence and its links to gender.

The selections included in the book can also be used in conjunction with primary texts that focus more on the representation of violence and gender as seen through the multiple lenses of artists: novels, poems, feature films, and documentaries. We have found that it is often the case that people can better discuss and relate to controversial and sensitive issues through an interpretation of a film, an analysis of a novelistic character, or the powerful visual images in a poem. Throughout this book, therefore, we have inserted a number of poems as examples of yet another way to approach and to understand issues of violence and gender. As for other artistic representations, we have included after our Preface a list of the documentaries, feature films, and novels we have used for each section. These are only suggestions, of course, since there are so many possibilities that relate to the issues under consideration.

Violence and Gender: An Interdisciplinary Reader is divided into seven broad sections. In order to clarify the intellectual framework of this book, we have provided section introductions that elucidate how readings within each section link to each other, how various theories of violence and gender can be applied across the issues presented, and how one topic moves into another. These introductions also serve as a point of departure for thinking about both individual readings and broader issues, as they ask questions and raise points for discussion and reflection.

The first two sections of the book set up the important groundwork for better understanding and contextualizing the remainder of the material. Section I, "Conceptualizing Violence," introduces an array of disciplinary and interdisciplinary scholarship, ranging from history to biology, policy studies, public health, medicine, and psychology. Since each of these fields has contributed to and continues to contribute to our evolving understanding of the causes of violence and violent behavior, we have included a representative sampling of some of the most prominent ideas. While not exhaustive, we expect that you will come away with a significantly greater awareness of and appreciation for the complexity of understanding violence.

After examining different theoretical perspectives, we ask you to consider the "Social Construction of Masculinities, Femininities, and the 'Other,'" the topic of the second section of the book. This section presents ideas about how we form and are formed by society: how gender itself is defined; how male and female narratives differ; how we have created cultural stereotypes and myths of manhood; how women continue—or more recently refuse to continue—to be shaped by traditional visions of femininity; how males and females respond differently to anger and aggression; and how fear and misunderstanding of "Others" can lead to hatred and violence. Raising awareness of both cultural gender stereotypes and prejudices against other people is a central goal of this section.

After these two fundamental sections, we move on to "Youth Violence" where we address the phenomenon of gangs—male and female—and incidents of school violence, both related to problems such as school safety, crime, and guns. Several of the readings also call attention to the tendency toward prejudice and stereotyping of certain groups of youth. Given the increased national focus on youth violence, we are hopeful that these selections will begin to help you understand and talk about these issues, hopefully leading to a safer environment for our youth today.

Section IV is devoted to the "Violation of Body Space." The readings deal with the physical and mental health effects of battering and sexual assault on women; acquaintance rape; the psychological impact of sexual assault and rape on boys and men, particularly around sexual identity issues; and childhood sexual abuse. Domestic violence, rape, and child sexual abuse are unfortunately not limited to any one class, sex, ethnicity, race, or age. Recognizing what constitutes the violation of one's body space and developing empathy for survivors are some of our goals for this section.

A section on "Violence and Sports," the fifth section of this book, may come as a surprise to some, as many of us tend to think of sports as mere play. However, after reading about the relationships among sports, the male body image, and the construction of "sporting masculinities" and their potential influence on attitudes toward gender, you should see the relevance of this inquiry. This section also illuminates issues of athletic privilege and entitlement and focuses on one particular case study involving gang rape.

Current discussions that attempt to predict why some people—men, women, and children—become violent, often point to the dangers of our media. Accordingly, Section VI examines "Media Representation of Violence." After opening with a text that proposes an interesting link between violent sports and the media, we then tackle the question of why many people are attracted to violent entertainment. A major focus of national debates and research studies has been the potentially deleterious effects on children of watching violence. Given this, we ask readers to consider whether or not we have become desensitized to violence in entertainment because it is not "real." We close this section with a study of some of the popular stereotypes of tough and violent women in the mass media and how they form and inform our views of "appropriate" gender roles for women.

Finally in Section VII, "Preventing Violence and Revisioning the Future," we tackle issues surrounding the development of needed prevention and intervention programs, the debates on gun control and censorship, a redefinition of masculinity and of the balance of power between women and men, and ideas for reducing violence and violent behavior. Incidents of personal and public violence have been and continue to be so prevalent in the United States that some people have come to accept them as inevitable, especially as part of our increasingly diverse society. In fact, this belief in the innate evil nature of humans leads some to believe that little can be done to eradicate or even reduce acts of violence. We, however, believe in the possibility of a less violent society but maintain that the construction of gender needs to be reexamined in order to attain such a goal. It is our hope that the selections in this concluding section of the book will stimulate you to consider a range of possible solutions.

The complex issues surrounding violence and gender in the United States cannot be covered in one book. We leave it to individuals to delve further into research on the topics here, as well as on additional topics including: violence against self; institutional violence; extremist and supremacist groups; politics, war, and nationalism; terrorism; cultural, ethnic, religious, and racial violence; female genital mutilation; pornography; and international sex trafficking. Unfortunately, the list is long, and the need to understand these issues grows more and more urgent each day.

In deciding what readings to include and how to structure material for beginning an inquiry into issues of violence and gender, we have provided as broad an overview as possible. In choosing a particular aspect of violence and gender to study and in selecting particular texts, we have sought materials that offer a solid presentation and evoke dynamic responses. The best readings, in our view, are those that will provoke you into forming, analyzing, and questioning your own opinions and then encourage you to listen to the viewpoints—both convergent and divergent—of others. We trust that the topics that we have chosen and the texts that we have selected will stimulate you to think deeply about these important issues.

ACKNOWLEDGMENTS

Many people have been instrumental in the development of this book. We would like to thank John O'Connor, Karen Oates, and Janette Muir of New Century College at George Mason University for their support of both our learning community on "Violence and Gender" and this text. Molly Dragiewicz and Jennifer Gauthier helped us with securing the permissions, as did the Copyright Office of George Mason University. Nancy Roberts and Lee Peterson of Prentice Hall have been unfailing in their support of our work from the earliest stages, and the outside reviewers, Lee H. Bowker, Humboldt State University; Dolores Davison Peterson, Foothill College; Shanta Sharma, Henderson State University; Thomas Allen, University of South Dakota; and B. Christine Shea, California Polytechnic State University, offered us excellent advice on how to strengthen our text. Lorna Irvine deserves a special thanks for having initially co-designed and co-taught the course. Numerous others have made significant contributions to the success of our learning community, including Molly Dragiewicz, Kelly Dunne, Ali Vaughan, Sarah Greenfield, Renee Vespia Jackson, Daniel Cohen, Pari Ansary, and Michelle LeBaron. All of the students who have taken our course have given us tremendous feedback, and we are extremely grateful for all we have learned from them. On a more personal level, we would like to thank Michael Randy Gabel, José Cortina, and our many family members and friends for their continued belief in our work. A hearty thank you to Arthur Gilbert for the hours that have been spent talking about and analyzing issues of violence and gender.

And finally, we would like to thank each other. We have enjoyed countless hours of productive collaboration and have achieved a truly equal partnership in this endeavor.

Representations of Violence

I Conceptualizing Violence

War and violence. (1990). Phil Donahue, dir. Princeton, NJ: Films for the Humanities (documentary).

Once were warriors (1995). Lee Tamahori, dir., with Rena Owen and Temuera Morrison. Fine Line Features.

II Social Construction of Masculinities, Femininities, and the "Other"

Tough guise: Part I (1999). Jackson Katz and Sut Jhally, dirs. Northampton, MA: Media Education Foundation (documentary).

Rambo: First blood, part II (1985). George Cosmatos, dir., with Sylvester Stallone and Richard Crenna. Carolco Pictures.

American history X (1998). Tony Kaye, dir., with Edward Norton, Edward Furlong, and Beverly D' Angelo. New Line Cinema.

Boys don't cry (1999). Kimberly Pierce, dir., with Hilary Swank and Cloe Sevigny. Twentieth-Century Fox.

The Brandon Teena story (1998). Susan Muska and Greta Olafsdottir, dirs. Zeitgeist Films (documentary).

III Youth Violence

Mi vida loca: My crazy life (1993). Allison Anders, dir., with Angel Aviles, Seidy Lopez, Jacob Vargas, and Panchito Gomez. Cineville Partners.

Rodriguez, A. Jr. (1994). *Spidertown*. New York: Penguin.

School shootings: America's tragedy (2000). CBS News Productions for the Learning Channel. Princeton, NJ: Films for the Humanities & Sciences (documentary).

Tough guise: Part II (1999). Jackson Katz and Sut Jhally, dirs. Northampton, MA: Media Education Foundation (documentary).

IV The Violation of Body Space

Against the law: Battered women fighting back (2000). CBS News. Princeton, NJ: Films for the Humanities & Sciences (documentary).

Domestic violence behind closed doors (1994). Ivanhoe Broadcast News. Princeton, NJ: Films for the Humanities & Sciences (documentary).

Family violence: Breaking the chain (1993). WBZ-TV4 (Boston, MA). Princeton, NJ: Films for the Humanities & Sciences (documentary).

Ju Dou (1990). Zhang Yi-Mou and Yang Fen Liang, dirs., with Gong Li, Li Bao-Tian, and Li Wei. Tokuma Shoten Publishing and Communications.

Allison, D. (1992). *Bastard out of Carolina*. New York: Dutton.

V   *Violence and Sports*

Wrestling with manhood (2002). Sut Jhally and Jackson Katz, dirs. Northampton, MA: Media Education Foundation (documentary).

VI   *Media Representation of Violence*

Dreamworlds II: Desire, sex, and power in music video. (1995). Sut Jhally, dir. Northampton, MA: Media Education Foundation (documentary).

Natural born killers (1994). Oliver Stone, dir., with Woody Harrelson, Juliette Lewis, Robert Downey Jr., and Tommy Lee Jones. Warner Brothers.

VII   *Preventing Violence and Revisioning the Future*

Atwood, M. (1985). *The handmaid's tale*. New York: Ballantine Books.

Bowling for Columbine (2002). Michael Moore, dir. United Artists (documentary).

Tough guise: Part II-conclusion (1999). Jackson Katz and Sut Jhally, dirs. Northampton, MA: Media Education Foundation (documentary).

Violence and Gender

—— SECTION I ——

Conceptualizing Violence

This first section introduces the reader to what we call "conceptualizing violence," that is, to different theoretical perspectives about the nature and origins of violence and violent behavior. While there is a fair amount of disagreement within scholarly communities about which theoretical perspectives *best* explain violence and violent behavior, there is general agreement about the importance of looking at multiple causal influences (e.g., biological, psychological, and sociocultural) at multiple levels (individual, community, societal). This section, therefore, aims to present the reader with a range of perspectives. These perspectives shall then be referred to in the subsequent sections, asking the reader to think back to them as we investigate different contexts for violence.

In reading the following selected texts, it is important to note how different authors use the terms "violence" and "aggression." There is often an erroneous assumption that all researchers and scholars who study violence and violent behavior are using the same definitions. In fact, we find that attempting to differentiate between violence and aggression is often a valuable exercise, since it can help us identify our own ideas and assumptions about these issues. In addition to attending carefully to terminology and definitions, it is important, as we read, to understand what is meant by group differences. In discussing group differences—something that much research does—one is saying nothing about the behavior of any specific individual. The same limitations are present when talking about risk factors for violence and violent behavior. While a risk factor indicates that membership in a specific group places one at higher risk for a particular outcome, such as perpetrating violence, it does not mean that any given member of a specific group will actually engage in a violent act. We urge readers to use caution: The tendency to misinterpret these findings can lead to dangerous stereotypes and inappropriate labeling of members of certain groups.

We open with "How to Think about Violence," by Dr. James Gilligan, former Director of the Center for the Study of Violence at Harvard Medical School and former director of mental health for the Massachusetts prison system. This is an important piece because in it, Gilligan discusses the role of theory as it relates to our ability to understand and prevent violence. He articulates a need to move away from the tendency to make value judgments about violence and violent behavior, primarily because such judgments do not help us move closer to finding explanations for violence or to address its potential causes. Gilligan asserts that our social and legal institutions, particularly our criminal justice system, have been acting on a theory of violence called the "rational self-interest theory," which assumes that rational self-interest and common sense underlie the reasons that individuals engage in violent behavior. To the contrary, Gilligan sees violent behavior as an innate human response to a loss of honor and self-respect. Ultimately, he argues, in order to prevent violence we need to adopt a public health and preventive medicine model. Using this model, violence is seen as a disease that is caused by and has effects on biological, psychological, and social systems. This selection clearly raises a host of complex issues in considering why violence and violent behavior occur.

Myriam Medzian's chapter, "Boys Will Be Boys," from her widely cited book of the same title, also examines the theoretical explanations of violence and violent behavior. Unlike Gilligan's abstract approach, Medzian, a philosopher and social worker, is more concrete in her analyses. For example, she reviews the role of testsosterone in aggressive behavior, coins the term, "masculine mystique," to explore sociocultural conditions conducive to violence, examines the relationship between abuse, neglect, and aggressive behavior, and discusses specific risk factors for violent behavior. More importantly, Medzian names aggression and violent behavior as primarily male phenomena. Answering the question, "Why are men more violent than women?" is the central question in her chapter.

While these first two pieces argue for examining multiple levels of causation in our theories of violence, the readings that follow in this section all investigate a more narrowly focused line of inquiry about the causes of violence. The chapter, "Biology, Development, and Dangerousness," by Elizabeth Susman and Jordan Finkelstein, both working in the area of biobehavioral health, presents a developmental perspective on biological factors and violence. These two researchers propose that we consider the dialectical nature of the interactions between physiological and psychological processes, along with the impact of an individual's environment. Although they offer a biopsychosocial model of dangerousness, they focus extensively in this piece on biological systems and antisocial behavior, including the role of the neurotransmitter, serotonin. In your view, should biological factors be considered as risk factors comparable to behavioral risk factors, thereby necessitating specific interventions to prevent such risks? Is there a danger in moving in this direction in order to identify and prevent violence? How can interdisciplinary teams work together to address the problem of dangerousness?

In the chapter, "The Tipping Point," an initial investigation that grew into a highly regarded and more broadly conceived book of the same title, Malcolm Gladwell encourages us to think about violence from a public health perspective, incorporating yet another different theoretical framework. He takes his lesson from epidemiologists, and he uses the notion of the "tipping point"—the point at which ordinary phenomena can turn into public health crises—to think about violence. In making his argument, he reviews research that focuses on the nonlinearity of social problems. For example, he cites one study that shows that "at the five percent tipping point neighborhoods go from relatively functional to wildly dysfunctional virtually overnight. There is no steady decline: a little change has a huge effect" (p. 37). As you read this piece, what are the implications of Gladwell's ideas for social policy?

We return to a chapter by James Gilligan, "Shame: The Emotions and Morality of Violence," to review an additional level of analysis in thinking about violent behavior and its causes. Gilligan argues that violence is a contagious disease whose pathogen is psychological and that social, economic, and cultural factors are, consequently, more responsible for the spread of this disease than are biological factors. In "Shame," therefore, Gilligan presents his thesis that feelings of shame are at the heart of violent behavior and that violence is used to replace these feelings with those of pride and self-respect. In contemplating his thesis, consider the generalizability, or universality, of his conclusions. Thinking back to some of the sociocultural issues raised by Medzian, how is this chapter relevant to how we socialize our boys? How credible do you find his arguments? Given his conclusions, how do you think we ought to prevent violence in our society?

So far, all of the readings have taken a contemporary look at the causes of violence in society. The United States, however, is one of the most violent societies in the industrialized world, whether measured by suicides, homicides, rapes, gun deaths, or other forms of assault. While some of the above theories might account for this fact (e.g., looking at the particular ways that boys and girls are socialized in the United States, observing the great disparity between the poor and the rich in the United States), the chapter by the American Studies' scholar, Richard Slotkin, "The White City and the Wild West," examines the active construction of American frontier mythology and its transformation into history. Through the creation of Buffalo Bill's Wild West shows, for example, America's frontier history was scripted by William Cody and reinforced in the public mind as reality. Although Cody did strive to present an "authentic" visual representation of the American frontier, he also presented as "moral truth" a representation of the frontier experience that suggested that "violence and savage war were the necessary instruments of American progress" (p. 77). Slotkin suggests that the link in the American psyche between violence and progress is critical to understanding our current justifications for the use of violence in asserting and preserving our dominance at home and worldwide.

In this first section, we present a number of readings that conceptualize violence in varied ways. Ranging from the biological to the psychological to public health to the sociological and finally to the historical, each of these theories can play a role in our understanding of why violence and violent behavior occurs. After reading this section, can you identify the various causes of violent behavior? Which theories or constellation of theories do you find most persuasive and on the basis of what evidence? Try to place these theories within a framework that moves from individual-level factors to societal-level factors. Can you make any recommendations for how to prevent violence at this point in your study?

How to Think About Violence 1996

James Gilligan

We live in an age in which there is a deep mistrust of theories; the very idea of theorizing itself is suspect. This powerful and widespread skepticism emanates from both ends of the current intellectual spectrum. From the more traditional, conservative wing of conventional science and scholarship—the positivist-empiricist wing—there is a common assumption that only "facts" are reliable and trustworthy, that any attempt to go beyond raw empirical data to the realm of principles or generalizations is hopelessly idealistic or fatally overambitious. The conservative criminologist, James Q. Wilson,[1] for example, has written that there is no such thing as "underlying causes" of crime; that we should abandon the attempt to discover and ameliorate or eradicate those so-called causes, and simply continue with our customary approach to crime, namely imprisonment and punishment.

Skepticism about theory emanates from the opposite wing as well, the current avant-garde or, as it calls itself, the post-modernist or deconstructionist wing, which rejects and distrusts any and all possible theories (except its own, if I understand it correctly) as inevitably being corrupted and distorted by the power interests which they unavoidably, if unconsciously, both serve and conceal, or mystify (unlike its own theory, which is presumably free from such distortions, for reasons that I am not sure I do understand). One statement of this distrust of any and all possible theories was recently articulated with reference to theories about crime by Carol Smart[2] who stated that

the [post-modernist] challenge to modernist thought . . . does not entail a denial of poverty, inequality, repression, racism, sexual violence, and so on. Rather it denies that the intellectual can divine the answer to these through the demand for more scientific activity and bigger and better theories . . . in particular, that we can establish a casual explanation which will in turn provide us with objective methods for intervening in the events defined as problematic.

Smart's essay concludes that "the continuing search for the theory, the cause, and the solution" is simply futile, misguided, and counter-productive—a hopeless waste of time and energy. Ironically, it reaches the same point of intellectual exhaustion as does the conservative view, providing a remarkable example of that well-known phenomenon, the meeting of opposites. Both approaches would have us abandon the search for causes and strategies for the prevention of crime and violence.

On the other hand, a group of behavioral scientists appointed by the National Academy of Sciences[3] found that one of the main limitations and obstacles to our ability to understand and prevent violence was the lack of an adequate general theory on the subject:

The panel found that a substantial knowledge base exists regarding some aspects of violent events and behaviors. . . . However, we were frustrated to realize that it was still not possible to link these fields of knowledge together in a manner that would provide a strong theoretical base on which to build prevention and intervention programs. . . . (p. 21)
[We are still] Lacking a testable general theory of violence. . . . (p. 39)

While there is a consensus that we lack a theory of violence adequate to enable us to explain, predict, and prevent violent behavior, disagreement concerns whether it will ever be possible to build such a theory. I believe this question can not be answered a priori. It can only be answered by attempting to create such a theory. Even to say that all existing theories are inadequate is not to say that we have no theory. In fact, my main objection to the arguments against theory that I have mentioned is the fact that it is impossible *not* to have a theory on this subject; because we cannot avoid dealing with violence, whatever assumptions we make about it constitute at least an implicit or inchoate theory of violence. So our choice is not between having a theory of violence and not having one; it is between having a conscious theory, which we can then examine, question, criticize, and improve; or an unconscious theory, which will remain forever untested, neither provable nor disprovable, and therefore unimprovable.

If we are going to outline a theory of violence, it might be worthwhile to pause for a moment, to reflect on what characteristics such a theory would need to possess in order to constitute an adequate explanation of violence. What I mean by an explanation is an account of an empirical (observable) phenomenon that is able to show the relation of cause to effect. Some common types of statements about violence, that are often made as if they were explanations of it, can be seen on closer examination to be lacking in explanatory content.

VALUE JUDGMENTS ARE NOT EXPLANATIONS

For example, I have often heard people explain a person's violence by saying, "He must just be evil." This usually happens when no one understands why the individual committed the crime, when there appears to be no obvious motive for it, or when the crime, even if there is an apparent motive, is so heinous as to defy "ordinary human understanding." But moral and legal judgments about violent behavior that deem it "bad" or "evil" or "guilty" are *value judgments* about it, not *explanations* of it.

Why do I say that? Let me suggest an analogy. In one of his plays, Molière[4] illustrates the difference between the philosophy (scholasticism) of the Middle Ages and the scientific thinking that was just beginning to be applied in the world of his time. One of his characters, a physician, "explains" why morphine makes people sleepy by attributing that property to its "dormative principle." "Dormative" (or soporific) merely means sleep-inducing; obviously, this is not an explanation, it is a tautology—morphine makes you sleepy because it is sleep-inducing. But we already know that morphine induces sleep; what we don't know is *why* morphine makes people sleepy.

In the same way, to say that the cause of a murder was the fact that the murderer was an evil person, or had an evil mind, or that the cause of the murder was the evil that existed in the mind or character of the murderer, is a tautology. To say that the cause of the evil act (actus reus) is the evil mind of the actor (mens rea) is merely to say the same thing: a tautology adds nothing to what we already know. The question of causation is: *Why* was he "evil"? Why did his personality take on the attributes we are calling evil? Why did he commit the violent act that we are calling evil? These are the kinds of questions a theory of violence should be able to answer; these are the questions I want to answer. But to do so, I think we have to remove (or at least bracket) moral language from our discussion.

I am suggesting that the only way to explain the causes of violence, so that we can learn how to prevent it, is to approach violence as a problem in public health and preventive medicine, and to think of violence as a symptom of life-threatening (and often lethal) pathology, which, like all forms of illness, has an etiology or cause, a pathogen. To think of violence as evil—if we confuse that value judgment about violence with an explanation of it—can only confuse us into thinking that we have an explanation when we do not.

The analogy of smoking and lung cancer can help us here. We know that some people get lung cancer even though they have never smoked, and that some people smoke and never get lung cancer; and yet no one (except perhaps the tobacco industry) really doubts that smoking is a "cause," in a scientifically valid and practically important sense, of lung cancer: neither necessary nor sufficient, but a cause. Nor does anyone "explain" the nonsmoker's lung cancer with the statement that he must therefore be "sinful." No theory can explain everything about the phenomenon it is explaining (and fortunately, as this example shows, it does not have to be able to, in order to generate life-saving methods of prevention—such as the recommendation to quit smoking). In the absence of complete explanation, moral condemnation need not follow.

We face another obstacle in trying to clear our thinking about violence of moral judgment. Suggesting that we avoid the categories of "evil," "guilt," or "crime" is all too often misinterpreted as being "soft on crime," as if in attempting to understand violence, we were forgiving violent behavior. My attempt to understand violent behavior should not be mistakenly interpreted as an effort to excuse or forgive people who commit heinous acts of violence.

The naturalistic, nonmoralistic approach to violence neither supports nor opposes the "forgiveness" of violent behavior—since one has not condemned in the first place. Condemning violence or forgiving it are irrelevant, once you see violence as a problem in public health and preventive medicine. No one supposes that because doctors do not waste their time and energy on "condemnations" or "punishments" of cancer and heart disease that they are somehow "soft on cancer" or "permissive" toward heart disease. They need all their time and energy to prevent and cure those diseases, which one does first and foremost by learning whatever one can about what causes them and how one might prevent them. It can be productive of knowledge to conceptualize violence as a health problem; but as long as we think of it as a moral problem, we will never be able to learn what causes it or what prevents it.

For three millennia our main social hypothesis—that the moral and legal way of thinking about and responding to violence (by calling it evil, forbidding it—"just say no"—and punishing it) will prevent violence (or at least bring it under control)—has been singularly unsuccessful in reducing the level of violence. Three thousand years should be an adequate length of time to test any hypothesis. That is why I am suggesting that it is time now to retire the moral way of thinking about violence for one capable of utilizing all the methods and concepts of the human sciences; time, in fact, to build a truly humane science, for the first time, for the study of violence.

THE RATIONAL SELF-INTEREST THEORY OF VIOLENCE

As a nation, our institutions have been acting on an underlying theory of violence, which I call the "rational self-interest" theory. This set of assumptions pervades our criminal justice system. Rational self-interest theory assumes that those who engage in violence do so for reasons of rational self-interest and common sense: Like anyone else in possession of rationality and common sense, those who commit violent acts do not want to go to prison, do not want to be subjected to physical violence themselves, and do not want to die. They will do anything to avoid any of these fates, and all we need do to prevent violence is to threaten to punish those who would commit such acts with greater violence of our own, such as imprisonment and capital punishment.

There are only four things wrong with this theory: It is totally incorrect, hopelessly naive, dangerously misleading, and based on complete and utter ignorance of what violent people are actually like. In addition, the rational self-interest theory of violence has had two disastrous and very expensive consequences. First, it has led us to shift our attention and resources from prevention to punishment. I am not saying that we do not need to use force to restrain the violent when our efforts to prevent violence by other means have failed. But this theory has distracted us from attempting to learn what actually causes violence; and what conditions would be necessary in order to reduce the need for violence; and from applying that knowledge to eliminating or ameliorating those conditions which lead to violence.

It is obvious that the policies we have adopted on the basis of this theory have led to an enormous and still escalating increase in violence. For example, the murder rate in the United States has repeatedly risen, to the point where it is now almost ten times as high as it was at the turn of the century and is still climbing. Like a macabre Dow-Jones average, it fluctuates from year to year, but the long-term trend is up. The murder rate in the United States is from five to twenty times higher than it is in any other industrialized democracy, even though we imprison proportionately five to twenty times more people than any other country on earth except Russia; and despite (or because of) the fact that we are the only Western democracy that still practices capital punishment (another respect in which we are like Russia).

To imagine that violence is "rational" and dictated by "self-interest" can only blind us to the reality of those forms of violence that have been most horrendously destructive of human life around the world in this century—the violence of Hitler, Stalin, Pol Pot, Idi Amin, Khomeini, Saddam Hussein; of the kamikaze pilots, the Baader-Meinhof gang, the Red Brigades; of Beirut, Belfast, Bogotá, and Bosnia; and of the endless legion of mass murderers and assassins, both "public" and "private," who are as ready to be killed as to kill—whose rage is so passionate and so blinding that it has caused the subjective distinction between killing and being killed to be all but obliterated and meaningless. As Dostoevsky[5] put it with uncanny prophetic power even before the terrible century through which we have just lived proved him right:

. . . one may say anything about the history of the world—anything that might enter the most disordered imagination. The only thing one can't say is that it's rational. The very word sticks in one's throat. . . . very often, and even most often, choice is utterly and stubbornly opposed to reason. . . .

TOWARD A THEORY OF VIOLENCE

In the course of this book, I hope to show how much of what appears anomalous, inexplicable, and incomprehensible about violence (whether individual or collective) is not anomalous at all, but all too ominously exactly what we might expect—given a certain set of conditions.

Let me begin with the common empirical observation that people feel incomparably more alarmed by a threat to the psyche or the soul or the self than they are by a threat to the body. The death of the self is of far greater concern than the death of the body. People will willingly sacrifice their bodies if they perceive it as the only way to avoid "losing their souls," "losing their minds," or "losing face."

In addition, a person only develops a stable, integrated, and differentiated sense of selfhood or identity through the process of interacting with other humans in the community, or culture. The pysche is as dependent on being nurtured by those modes of relationships and community, of child-rearing and education, which we call culture, as the body is on being nourished by food. The relationship between culture and character is an unavoidable sociopsychological reality.

One consequence of that fact is that a perceived threat to the integrity and survival of a person's culture is perceived as a threat to the integrity and survival of the individual's personality or character, and to the viability of one's ethical value system which is a central and essential component of both personality and culture, and is what most intimately links the self and its culture, the culture and its selves. Those are among the reasons why the death of one's culture is tantamount to the death of one's self.

The worlds I know where people have experienced the actual or threatened death of self and community are the maximum-security prisons and mental hospitals for the criminally insane—"extreme environments," where soul and mind and conscience, racial pride and self-respect, are incomparably more damaged, vulnerable, and threatened than anywhere else. Here it becomes especially clear that the priority humans place on honor and self-respect (including the honor of one's group and one's culture) over that of physical comfort and even survival is not only humanity's most unique and essential attribute, but also our most dangerous.

It is not a coincidence that our human propensity to create morality and civilization, and to commit homicide and suicide, are the two characteristics that most specifically differentiate us from all other species. These two sides of human nature are inextricably related. They are caused by the same complex of interacting emotional forces, which operate both individually and collectively in human psychology and culture—shame, pride, guilt, and innocence.

When individuals and groups feel their "honor" is at stake, and an intolerable degree of humiliation or "loss of face" would result from a failure to fight for that honor, they may act violently. The loss of self-esteem is experienced subjectively as the death of the self. People will sacrifice anything to prevent the death and disintegration of their individual or group identity.

If our primary goal is to prevent violence, we have no rational alternative but to view violence as a problem in public health and preventive medicine. We can define disease, broadly enough to include violence, as any force or process at work within an organism or species that tends to cause the death of the organism or, especially, the extinction of the species. Health refers to those forces or processes within organisms and species that tend to sustain, protect, and preserve life, individual and collective. I use the term violence to refer to the infliction of physical injury on a human being by a human being, whether oneself or another, especially when the injury is lethal, but also when it is life-threatening, mutilating, or disabling; and whether it is caused by deliberate, conscious intention or by careless disregard and unconcern for the safety of oneself or others. From the perspective of public health and preventive medicine, violence is death or disability that is inflicted by means of physical injury, or trauma, caused by human behavior and choice, and thus by the human mind or psyche. Thus, a violent, as opposed to a natural, death is one caused by an act of man (or woman), not an act of God, and by culture, rather than by nature.

Violence, then, can be seen as a symptom of individual or group psychopathology, whether it is an individual case (murder, suicide) or an epidemic (war, genocide). This is true even if we make the distinction, as J. P. Scott[6] and other students of animal behavior have done, between aggressive or offensive violence—initiated by the aggressor—and the defensive type—warding off an attack. Defensive violence can be seen as the effect of the aggressor's violence. Defense—even defensive violence—can be a necessary (though it is not always a sufficient) component of health. It can be adaptive—acting in the service of survival. The defense mechanisms of the body, the immune system, or the defense mechanisms of the individual mind, or of the group, the body politic, act in the same way.

But if some violence is defensive, and defensive violence can be healthy, then how can violence be both healthy and pathological at the same time? Not all mechanisms of defense do function adaptively, therapeutically, so as to heal illness and save life. In many physical illnesses, the natural defense can easily become maladaptive and self-defeating, as with pneumonia patients who drown in their own secretions, even though those secretions are an intrinsic part of their mechanisms of defense. The same is true of much "defensive" violence, which can easily become suicidal, rather than self-protective. However, even when it is adaptive and self-preserving, defensive violence can still be considered as a symptom of pathology; in this situation it is the aggressor's pathology, not the defender's. Human nature being what it is, one's own violence is almost always perceived as defensive, while other peoples' is likely to be seen as aggressive. This is the reason why the utility of the distinction between the two types of violence among humans has always been limited.

Modern technology has tragically made this problem of deciding whose violence is defensive and whose is aggressive a moot point. For now that weapons have become so destructive that there is no effective defense against them, and now that defensive violence utilizing nuclear weapons could destroy the defender as well as the aggressor, it is clear that defensive violence can no longer be healthy or adaptive enough to solve the problem. The only solution now is to apply the established principles of public health and preventive medicine to this type of pathology by learning how to achieve primary prevention of violence— that is, to prevent those social and psychological conditions that cause aggressive violence in the first place—so that defensive violence (secondary prevention) is not necessary.

I am not using the terms "illness' and "disease" as metaphors when I apply them to the subject of violence: I mean them literally. Violence, and also the social and psychological forces that cause violence, create biological pain, injury, mutilation, disability, and death just as literally as does any bacillus or malignancy. If violence is to be conceptualized as a biomedical problem, a problem in public health and preventive psychiatry, what structure does this imply for a theory of violence cast in these terms? What kinds of facts must such a theory of violence be capable of explaining? I believe the best answer to these questions was suggested some years ago by the American psychiatrist George Engel, when he argued that all medical problems, all diseases (and he was not even speaking specifically of violence) can only be understood and conceptualized adequately if they are seen as "bio-psycho-social" problems, as phenomena that are simultaneously caused by, and have effects on, biological, psychological, and social systems. Certainly this is true of violence, a term that refers to an enormously complex, multidetermined range of phenomena. Some of the data concerning violence can only be explained in biological terms some in psychological ones, and some in social, cultural, historical, and socioeconomic terms, such as class-stratification, and discrimination on the basis of age, sex, or race. No theory of violence could be considered adequate except to the extent that it is capable of integrating all three levels of abstraction.

In order to clarify the nature of the theory I am presenting here, it will also be helpful, I think, to point out that a comprehensive theory of violence cannot be solely a theory in criminology, nor solely in clinical or forensic psychiatry. It cannot be a theory in criminology because most crimes are not violent, and most violence is not criminal. Most of the crimes that are committed are property crimes. And most of the violent (that is, man-made, nonnatural) injuries and deaths that occur, both in the United States and throughout the world, are not caused by activities that the legal system defines as criminal. For example, in the United States and every other developed country, many more deaths are caused by suicides than by homicides. An even larger number of violent deaths are caused by carelessness. Although these deaths are usually, and often misleadingly, called "accidental" or "unintentional," most of them are actually the predictable (and preventable) effects of deliberate human choices and intentions, such as hazardous working conditions, substandard housing, violent sports, risk-taking avocations, and so on. These kill twice as many people as die from homicide and suicide combined. The collective violence called warfare is, with rare exceptions, entirely legal, not only according to the legal system of the nation on whose side any given soldier is fighting, but also according to that of the enemy nation. If one adds to all those the deaths caused by structural violence (that is, the excess death rates among the poor caused by the socioeconomic structure, i.e., class and caste stratification), which produces far more deaths than all of the previously mentioned categories combined, one begins to see why any theory of violence, if it is to deal at all with the medical reality involved, cannot limit itself to the subject matter of criminology.

But a theory of violence cannot be solely a theory of clinical psychiatry either, because most violence is not committed by the mentally ill (as either the psychiatrists or the courts of law have defined mental illness), and most mentally ill people are not violent. The vast majority of murders are committed by people with severe disorders of personality or character, not people who are "insane" in the sense of being out of touch with reality, or experiencing hallucinations or delusions; thus, it is no surprise that no more than about one percent of murderers in the United States are found "not guilty by reason of insanity." And only a fraction of the mentally ill commit either homicide or suicide (although the proportion who die by suicide is higher than in the general population).

Finally, the theory I am presenting here is not solely a theory in forensic psychiatry, that subspecialty that serves to assist the courts in deciding whether a given individual was "criminally responsible" for his violent act, or should be found "not guilty by reason of insanity"—whether he committed his violence while he was "sane" or "insane" at the time of the act. It is not just that the vast majority are "sane," as I just mentioned, but also because I am attempting to discover causes of violence that cut across "diagnostic" boundaries, and that are responsible for the resort to violence in both the "sane" and the "insane." In addition, I regard such terminology as so arbitrary as to be of limited usefulness and relevance anyway, when applied to violent behavior. For example, I tend to sympathize with the commonsense view that I think many people have when they respond to a particularly bizarre or brutal murder, or series of murders, with the expression, "Someone would have to be crazy to do such a thing." That most such murderers are not "crazy," as either law or psychiatry define "crazy," reveals the limitations in the standard legal and psychiatric vocabularies, and in the conventional approaches of both fields to both violence and "craziness"; or, at least, their limited usefulness for my purposes in this book. I think that the individuals (and groups) who committed much of the violence I discuss here (or much of the violence that one reads about in the newspapers every day) would have to be "sick" or "crazy," in some meaningful sense of those terms, to have done what they have done. To confine our discourse to the question of whether the behavior of such persons meets certain legal or psychiatric definitions of what constitutes madness versus badness, or psychosis versus perversion versus borderline personality may be a way of avoiding the more radical implications of understanding both their sickness and their violence.

I am convinced that violent behavior, even at its most apparently senseless, incomprehensible, and psychotic, is an understandable response to an identifiable, specifiable set of conditions; and that even when it seems motivated by "rational" self-interest, it is the end product of a series of irrational, self-destructive, and unconscious motives that can be studied, identified, and understood.

NOTES

1. As summarized by Charles Silberman, *Criminal Violence, Criminal Justice* (N.Y.: Random House, 1978), p. 163, quoting from James Q. Wilson, *Thinking About Crime* (N.Y.: Basic Books, 1975), p. xv:

> The lesson Wilson draws is that if our aim is to reduce street crime, we should forget about measures designed to eliminate its underlying causes. "I have yet to see a 'root cause,' " . . . Wilson writes. More important, "The demand for causal solutions is, whether intended or not, a way of deferring any action and criticizing any policy. It is a cast of mind that inevitably detracts attention from those few things that governments can do reasonably well and draws attention toward those many things it cannot do at all." In Wilson's view, what government can do is reduce crime by sending more convicted felons to jail. . . . What government cannot do at all, according to Wilson, is turn lower-class criminals into law-abiding citizens through measures to reduce poverty and discrimination.

2. Carol Smart, "Feminist approaches to criminology or postmodern woman meets atavistic man." In *Feminist Perspectives in Criminology*, eds. Loraine Gelsthorpe and Allison Morris (Milton Keynes: Open University Press, 1990).

3. *Understanding and Preventing Violence*, eds. Albert J. Reiss and Jeffrey A. Roth (Washington, D.C.: National Academy Press, 1993), pp. 21 and 39.

4. I have been unable to locate the source of this quotation, which I am quoting from memory, but there is an essentially identical passage in Molière's play *The Doctor in Spite of Himself* (Act II, scene 4), in which Sganarelle, the eponymous hero, has been summoned to treat Geronte's daughter, who has become mute: "*Sganarelle*: . . . your daughter is dumb. *Geronte.* Yes; but I wish you could tell me what it comes from, *Sganarelle.* Nothing easier: it comes from the fact that she has lost her speech, *Geronte.* Very good; but the reason, please, why she has lost her speech, *Sganarelle.* All our best authors will tell you that it's the stoppage of the action of her tongue." In Molière, *The Misanthrope and Other Plays.* Translated Donald M. Frame (New York: New American Library, 1968), p. 112.

5. Fyodor Dostoevsky, *Notes From Underground* (1864). In *The Short Novels of Dostoevsky* (New York: Dial Press, 1951), p. 148.

6. J.P. Scott, *Aggression* (Chicago: Univ. of Chicago Press, 1958).

"Boys Will Be Boys" *1991*

Myriam Medzian

The goal of this chapter is to answer the common objection that nothing much can be done to diminish male violence because it grows out of an inexorable aggressive instinct.

The research and writings of sociobiologists are often used to buttress the view that the male of the species has, through natural selection, developed highly aggressive and territorial drives that are unalterable and have led to conflict and violence throughout human history. Hormonal studies are marshaled to support this "killer instinct" view of male aggression. Here the culprit is the male hormone testosterone. Some turn to Sigmund Freud's hypothesis of an aggressive instinct to support the thesis that violence and war are inevitable.

It is a far cry from the simplifications of some of the popularized versions of these theories to what the most respected researchers in the field are saying. With the exception of a minority of psychoanalysts, there is a broad consensus that while violent behavior is based in human biology, it can in no way be considered an inexorable instinct or drive.

That males *from a very young age* act more aggressively than females is not the issue in any of this; for here agreement is almost universal. In 1973, psychologists Eleanor Maccoby and Carol Jacklin published *The Psychology of Sex Differences*. After analyzing thousands of research studies they concluded that there were only a few areas in which the evidence warranted the conclusion that male-female differences did exist. Aggression was one of them.

While studies of American children represent the bulk of their data, Maccoby and Jacklin also reviewed cross-cultural data, animal studies, and hormonal research. They found that both in the United States and in other cultures, boys from a very young age hit and insult each other more frequently, respond faster and more strongly when they are insulted or hit, and engage in more rough-and-tumble play. Studies of monkeys and rodents show that injections of testosterone increase aggressive behavior.

Maccoby and Jacklin emphasize that this male-female difference is not a dichotomy; it is a difference in tendencies. This conclusion follows quite clearly from an analysis of the ninety-four studies on aggression in children which they reviewed. While a majority (fifty-two) of these studies showed that boys are more aggressive, a substantial number (thirty-seven) showed no difference. Only five studies showed girls to be more aggressive. Males as a group are more aggressive, but many males are no more aggressive than most females.

Although aspects of *The Psychology of Sex Differences* have been subjected to considerable criticism, it is still considered the "definitive" study to date on male-female differences.

The issue, then, is *why* are men more violent than women? Is there an *inevitability* to high levels of male violence?

In this chapter I review some of the best available answers to these questions, beginning with hormonal, sociobiological, and psychoanalytic theory. After it is made clear that these theories do not buttress the view that it is hopeless to attempt to significantly diminish violence, I focus on what we can learn from psychoanalytic theory and social learning theory (the dominant school of psychology in American universities) about the causes of violent behavior. Finally, I examine some of the literature on physical disabilities that affect boys primarily and put them at higher than average risk of violent behavior.

Since the literature and research on violence is vast, I limit myself to the work of a few of the most highly respected thinkers in each field whose work is particularly relevant to the issues that concern us. *This is not to say that their positions are to be regarded as definitive*; [however,]...we must look to the best available present-day knowledge, with all its limitations and tentativeness, to help us begin to grapple with the social disease of violence. . . .

I have very consciously chosen to use the term "violence" rather than "aggression" throughout this book to refer to the use, or the threat, of physical force to hurt or gain power over another person, or to obtain another person's property.*

My decision to use the term "violence" grows out of the ambiguity of the term "aggression." This ambiguity tends to make acts of violence more acceptable when they are called "aggressive" rather than "violent." The reason for this is that the term "aggression" can be used in several highly divergent senses, some of which have a very positive connotation. . . .

Constructive aggression has much to do with assertiveness, determination, personal strength. It has nothing to do with violence unless a person, an organization or group, or a government decides to use violent means to achieve the goals it is aggressively pursuing. But there is no necessary connection between the two. . . .

When boys are encouraged to be not just assertive and determined, but almost obsessively competitive and concerned with dominance, it becomes more likely that they will eventually use violent or other antisocial means to achieve dominance. (They are also likely to be abusive verbally and intimidating in their "body language.") Nevertheless, violence and the desire for power are not inextricably linked. Most human beings are capable of extraordinary self-control with respect to acts that are considered deeply shameful and humiliating. . . .

For our purposes, it is sufficient to distinguish three different senses of the term "aggression": constructive aggression, as in assertiveness and determination; antisocial aggression, as in extreme competitiveness and concern with dominance; and destructive aggression, which is synonymous with violence.

When people talk or write about aggression, it is often not clear whether they have constructive, antisocial, or destructive aggression in mind. They are often not clear about it themselves. This lack of clarity allows for the use of the term "aggression" with all its positive connotations instead of the much more negative term "violence" when one is in fact describing violence. For example, to say that football is a very aggressive game sounds much better than to say that it

is a very violent game. If basketball and baseball were commonly described as aggressive and football as aggressive and violent, more parents might be inclined to encourage their sons to play basketball or baseball instead of football. For while many parents want their sons to play team sports so that they will learn to be assertive and determined, teaching them to be violent is not usually one of their goals.

Since the principal researchers and theorists whose work I discuss mostly use the word "aggression," I frequently use the term in this chapter in order to do justice to their work. The use of "aggression" to cover both aggression and violence facilitates the misinterpretation and misuse of their theories by the general public.

Within the category of destructive aggression, or violence, a further distinction needs to be made between defensive and offensive violence. When a person or a nation is attacked and mounts a defense against the aggressor, we look upon this as justified defensive behavior. For example, we might say of a boy who was involved in a fight, "He isn't really violent, he was just defending himself against the school bullies." My concern in this book is exclusively with offensive violence.

IS TESTOSTERONE THE CULPRIT?

In their book *Man and Woman, Boy and Girl,* a study of the influence of hormones on male and female behavior, John Money and Anke Ehrhardt are so intent on emphasizing the role of the environment in human development that they devote an entire chapter to this topic. They present both case studies and anthropological data showing the enormous culture-dependent human variability with respect to gender behavior. In several recent articles, Ehrhardt argues that behavior and environment can have a strong and direct influence on hormone levels, and suggests that testosterone levels may well be affected by environmental factors.[1]

What then is the contribution of hormones to aggressive behavior, according to Money and Ehrhardt?

Before addressing this question, a few basic definitions and facts of endocrinology have to be set forth.

The male hormone testosterone leads to the formation *in utero* of the male's sexual anatomy. If for some reason testosterone is not released, the embryo develops into a female even if it is genetically a male. This

---

*I am aware that some thinkers refer to the infliction of emotional pain as violent. Others focus on the importance of what they call "structural violence" growing out of inequality in the distribution of power. While these topics are beyond the scope of this book, it should be clear that the kinds of recommendations made in later chapters can only have very positive results with respect to both.

is the case with genetic males suffering from androgen insensitivity.

In order to determine the role of prenatal hormones in influencing male and female behavior, Money and Ehrhardt studied these genetic males who received no testosterone *in utero* and therefore looked like girls at birth and were raised as girls.*

Almost all of them scored very high in terms of "feminine" traits. They were less tomboyish than controls, and conformed to a high degree to the feminine stereotype in American culture at the time they were growing up. It seems that the complete absence of testosterone *in utero* leaves a child with dispositions that can easily be molded by society into "feminine" traits.

When Money and Ehrhardt studied a group of girls who received high levels of testosterone *in utero* (as a result of either an enzyme defect or their mothers' taking progestin), they found that the genetic males who had not been androgenized *in utero* were more "feminine" than the genetic females who had been androgenized.

Money and Ehrhardt's studies indicate that these androgenized girls who are born with ambiguous genitalia (usually a grossly enlarged clitoris; in rare cases a penis and empty scrotum which are surgically corrected shortly after birth) tend to exhibit more "tomboyish behavior" than control groups. This behavior includes more rough-and-tumble play, more interest in outdoor physical activities, and more self-assertiveness in competition for dominance.

From our perspective, one of the most interesting facts about the androgenized girls studied by Money and Ehrhardt is that while they engaged in significantly higher levels of tomboyish activities than did control groups, their behavior was not any more violent than the control groups in terms of their picking fights. This suggests that for many little boys, in order for their predisposition to rough-and-tumble play and their concerns with competition and dominance to be-

come translated into violent behavior, some form of social condoning and probably encouragement is required. While it is acceptable for girls to be tomboys, it is not acceptable for them to fight. . . .

The possibility that testosterone may be linked to characteristics that tend to be *precursors* to violent behavior rather than to violence itself is also entertained by Norwegian psychologist Dan Olweus. In discussing a study he and colleagues carried out to see what effects differences in testosterone levels had on a group of adolescent boys in terms of antisocial and violent behavior, he comments that the boys with higher levels of testosterone tended to be more easily frustrated, more impatient, and more irritable than the boys with lower levels. These traits increase the probability of these boys engaging in antisocial or violent behavior.[2]

This theorizing based on hormonal studies receives confirmation from behavioral studies. Eleanor Maccoby points to increasing evidence that males as a group, from a very young age, are more easily frustrated, and act more impulsively, than females.[3]

It may turn out that an important part of the biological base of male violence boils down to a lower threshold for frustration, greater irritability and impulsiveness, and a tendency to rough-and-tumble. While rough-and-tumble is usually not violent—boys often roughhouse as a way of establishing friendly contact—it would tend to encourage the expression of anger or frustration through physical activity rather than verbal reaction. . . .

A LEGACY FROM OUR HUNTING-GATHERING DAYS?

Sociobiology is an application of the theory of evolution to human behavior. Sociobiologists ask the same kinds of questions about social behavior that Darwin asked about physical characteristics. Why do some species exhibit highly aggressive behavior while others are very unaggressive? How did humans develop feelings of love, hate, envy? How did altruistic or aggressive behavior patterns come to be? As with anatomical traits, behavioral traits are explained largely in terms of natural selection. Individuals possessing advantageous traits have a better chance of surviving and passing them on to their offspring.

Aggression, sociobiologists argue, was advantageous for humans. As early hunting and gathering societies competed for limited resources, the more

---

*It is not clear at this point precisely how higher levels of testosterone *in utero* affect behavior. Research suggests that it may be that the release of the male hormone during the critical period of fetal brain development "masculinizes" the brain, influencing the nervous system permanently. Sex hormones produced in adulthood appear to play a role in activating behavior that was preorganized at an earlier developmental phase. In normal boys, testosterone levels increase sharply at puberty. Adult males have about ten times as much testosterone as women.

aggressive groups with better warriors tended to survive. These warriors were male—for males did the hunting and fighting while the females, frequently pregnant, stayed back tending to food-gathering and children. This, they believe, explains why males as a group are more aggressive than females.

Harvard professor Edward O. Wilson is the author of *Sociobiology: The New Synthesis,* perhaps the major work in the field, and *On Human Nature,* which won the Pulitzer Prize. Wilson stresses again and again that while human behavior is based on biology, and its origins can be traced through evolutionary theory of adaptation, it can only be fully understood through the interaction of biology and culture, and the weight of culture is enormous.

Wilson distinguishes between different categories of aggression, comprising both violent and nonviolent behavior. In the discussion below, the term "aggression" always includes violent behavior.

Wilson makes it clear that violent aggression does not grow out of an instinct or drive. He does describe aggression as being innate, but he defines innateness as referring to "the measurable probability that a trait will develop in a specified set of environments, not to the certainty that the trait will develop in all environments."[4] For example, bands of hunter-gatherers in all parts of the world act aggressively in their defense of land that contains a reliable source of food. Males fight over females when they are scarce in numbers. . . .

Wilson...tells us that we must not picture aggression as a fluid constantly applying pressure against the walls of its containers..., but rather as a preexisting mix of chemicals that can be transformed by specific catalysts if they are added at some later time. This is the "culture-pattern" model, which is based on the interaction of genetic potential and learning:

> . . . aggressive behavior, especially in its more dangerous forms of military action and criminal assault, is learned. But the learning is prepared . . . we are strongly predisposed to slide into deep, irrational hostility under certain definable conditions. With dangerous ease, hostility feeds on itself and ignites runaway reactions that can swiftly progress to alienation and violence.[5] . . .

Sociobiologists often support their generalizations about humans by pointing to similar behavior in other species. . . .

In animals, as in humans, a major cause of aggression among members of the same species is competition for vital resources. But aggression is only one competitive technique among many, and some animals don't exhibit it at all. Its existence in those species closest to humans adds weight to the argument that males have an underlying predisposition to act aggressively under certain conditions.

Wilson is fond of pointing out that radical changes in human aggressiveness have taken place within specific groups, going from nonaggressive to aggressive and vice versa. The Semai of Malaya seemed not even to have a concept of violent aggression. Murder was unknown in their society and there was no explicit word for killing. But the British colonial government recruited Semai men to fight Communist guerrillas in the early 1950s. After some of their kinsmen had been killed by Communist terrorists, the previously completely peaceful Semai men became extremely bloodthirsty and violent.

A change in the opposite direction occurred among the Maori of New Zealand, who in pre-European times were among the most violent people on earth. The introduction of European firearms in such a belligerent group was catastrophic. During the approximately twenty years of the resultant musket war, one quarter of their population died from causes related to the conflict. By 1830 the use of fighting for revenge was beginning to be questioned. Eventually the old values crumbled, and by the late 1830s and early 1840s warfare between the tribes had stopped entirely.

It is clear that in looking for the causes of war one must look not only to the combination of a genetic disposition to learn violent behavior and conditions of scarcity leading to violent competition for resources, but also to previous history and cultural conditions that can predispose a group to seek violent solutions to conflict. The Maori had a tradition of violence; the Semai had a tradition of nonviolence. Yet under changed social conditions, each group underwent radical changes in its behavior.

Wilson is telling us that sociocultural conditions conducive to violence can and must be transcended. We must consciously undertake to master and reduce "the profound human tendency to learn violence." . . .

In his book *The Biology of Peace and War* German sociobiologist Iraneus Eibl-Eibesfeldt deals at length with the kinds of social and economic changes that need to be made if we are to eliminate war. Like Edward Wilson, he believes that we must begin by recognizing those underlying biological dispositions—

xenophobia and territoriality—that lead to aggression and war, so that we can deal with them better. He argues that we must take concrete measures to help fulfill the basic economic needs of all people, so that nations will no longer resort to war in order to obtain the territories and raw materials they need for survival. We must combat xenophobia and learn to appreciate our own culture without automatically disparaging other cultures and systems of values and creating enemy stereotypes. We need education that socializes aggression so that it is not used destructively.

IS THE "DEATH INSTINCT" A DEAD END IDEA?

Many if not most schools of psychoanalysis reject the hypothesis of an aggressive drive altogether. Most Freudians accept it. I have chosen to focus primarily on Freudian theory because among the general public it is the most influential and best known of the psychoanalytic theories.

Freud does not distinguish between males and females as to aggression. As usual the model of "man" is male, but this is not recognized. What is important for our purposes is that this theory is used to justify the view that there isn't much we can do about violence, and leads to mistaken beliefs about catharsis.

Freud's "death instinct" and the "aggressive drive" postulated by some of his disciples have been subjected to such scorching criticism from within and without the Freudian movement that it is difficult to argue that they represent anything more than the very tenuous views of some Freudians. Further, an analysis of these concepts reveals that they are so broad that much of the time they have little if anything to do with violence.

The death instinct, according to Freud, is fueled by an internal energy that exists spontaneously, and is originally aimed at the self. He argues that all living matter carries within itself the desire to self-destruct. When we direct our death instinct toward the outside world rather than toward ourselves, it becomes an aggressive instinct. "The living creature preserves its own life, so to say, by destroying an extraneous one."[6]

Most contemporary Freudian psychoanalysts no longer accept Freud's concept of an inwardly directed death instinct, but many continue to adhere to the notion of an aggressive instinct directed against others, although, to distinguish human behavior from animal behavior they describe it as a drive rather than an instinct. They recognize that whereas animal instincts lead to predetermined behavioral responses, drives interact with experience and reflection in determining behavior. Nevertheless, they remain committed to the view that aggressive behavior grows out of an internal aggressive drive that creates excitation or tension in the individual and must then be released.[7]

[However, contemporary research has...] revealed that the psychoanalytic theory of a death instinct or aggressive drive fueled by psychic energy does not satisfy any of the conditions that normally corroborate theories in the social or physical sciences. It has neither predictive nor explanatory value nor is it supported by clinical or other data.

The Absence of Supporting Data

Robert R. Holt, who has written extensively on Freud, zoologist Patrick Bateson, and Edward Wilson are among those who are convinced that the underlying and mistaken model for Freudian instinct and drive theory is the hydraulic image of, as Wilson puts it, "a fluid that continuously builds pressure against the walls of its containers."[8] Holt and Bateson are even more explicit. Bateson tells us that if an aggressive drive exists "it is emphatically not like urine which builds up and has to be discharged from time to time."[9] Holt rejects the "model of urination" and points out that there is no evidence that "a psychic energy or anything else . . . accumulates when a person is peaceable and gets discharged via aggressive behavior."[10]

One obvious distinction between urination and aggression is that urination is a universal human function. Aggression is not. Nor does aggression have remotely the same level of universality as sex or hunger, to which it is often compared. Apart from those suffering from anorexia nervosa, or starvation, all human beings eat and drink regularly, and almost all engage in sexual activities for significant portions of their lives. But a large percentage of people, including males, go through life without spontaneously committing any significant acts of violence.

Yet in spite of the lack of evidence that aggressive behavior is in any way as universal as sexual behavior, eating, drinking, or the evacuative functions, Freud argues that it grows out of a universal instinct, the repression of which leads to unhappiness. In *Civilization and Its Discontents*, he states that the repression of sexuality *and aggression* required by civilization makes it "so hard for men to feel happy in it."[11]

Why the Aggressive Drive Explains Nothing

Besides a lack of behavioral data to support it, the Freudian theory of aggression also does a poor job of explaining violent behavior when it does occur.[12] It is based on the mistaken assumption that there must be an inner entity that corresponds to the concept "aggression." But in fact there is no one entity that the term "aggression" refers to. To think that there is provides us with the illusion that we are explaining the causes of violence, as if we could explain why one man is more violent than another by saying that he has a higher quantum of aggressive drive energy.

Since it is widely thought that Freud introduced the aggressive instinct in part to explain the death and destruction of World War I, I shall illustrate this point with the following analysis of that war.

Certainly men's willingness to start wars, and to fight in them, needs explanation. For while the willingness to fight can sometimes be explained in terms of genuine defense—they and their loved ones' lives would be endangered if they were conquered by invaders—it is safe to venture that this is very often not the case, as in World War I.

If we cease to deal in generalities, and get down to the specifics of what led some men to start that war and others to participate in it we find that the concept of an aggressive instinct or drive explains little. There is no reason to believe that most men volunteered for the war because they had an internally driven urge to kill and maim other human beings.

In her autobiography *Testament of Youth*, British writer Vera Brittain describes her brother and her fiancé, both of whom volunteered to fight in World War I (and lost their lives in it). There is no evidence at all that these sensitive, decent young men were driven by anything other than fantasies of glory, heroism, and excitement, as well as peer pressure and patriotism. Once these fantasies were replaced by the grim reality of war, doubts set in. . . .

Brittain's book corroborates the evidence presented in earlier chapters. Whether it be young American men like Ron Kovic going off to fight in Vietnam spurred by images of John Wayne in *Sands of Iwo*

Jima, or young Englishmen going to fight on the continent spurred, no doubt, by poems and epic stories of heroic wars, the prevailing feeling is that going to war is exciting, patriotic, and proof of courage and manhood.

Boys are raised to be soldiers. They are prepared from the youngest age to view war as a thrilling adventure. Their play with war toys is great fun without pain. The books they read (and today the TV shows and films they see) focus on exciting violence. In schools all over the world, little boys learn that their country is the greatest in the world, and the highest honor that could befall them would be to defend it heroically someday. The fact that empathy has traditionally been conditioned out of boys facilitates their obedience to leaders who order them to kill strangers.

J. Glenn Gray is a college professor who served in Europe and North Africa in World War II and later wrote a book about his own and his comrades' experiences. As Gray sees it, the intense feelings of power and excitement, the delight in destruction that many men experience in war, are often reactions to the boredom, the emptiness, the lack of meaningful goals that characterize so many men's daily lives. The sense of camaraderie is another major attraction.

Little boys are taught to be strong and brave and not to cry. The ensuing tendency to deny fear and vulnerability, as well as greater male impulsiveness, tend to make the excitement and ego rewards predominate in men's minds over the fear of death.

We must not forget that many, if not most, of the men who fight in wars are drafted. Their choice is between the most intense social disapproval and rejection, questioning of their manhood, prison or death; and fighting. But many who are drafted no doubt never question their orders because of their obedience to their leaders. . . .

When men first go to war, the enemy is abstract and distant; so are death and suffering. As the enemy and their own pain become more real, many change their attitudes. It is a well-documented fact that in World War I, once they were in the trenches, many of these men supposedly driven by a death instinct in fact established a truce with enemy soldiers. It was only after their superior officers got wind of what was happening and intervened that these truces were ended.

None of this is to deny that for some men war is an opportunity to express their anger, rage, and hostility, and to give legitimate vent to their desire to do physical harm to others.

Some may be venting chronic rage at parents who battered, neglected, abandoned, or humiliated them. Others may suffer from one of the genetic disabilities described below that can play a role in predisposing boys to violence. These men may make up the bulk of those who truly enjoy death and destruction. It also seems likely that their behavior encourages and sanctions such behavior in other men who on their own may not be so violently inclined. Their daring, recklessness, and violence make them role models of manhood.

False Predictions

We have seen so far that the aggressive drive theory is not based on data and lacks explanatory value. What about its ability to predict?

If the aggressive drive theory were correct, we would feel relief of tension after releasing aggressive energy and would not have to engage in violent behavior for a while. And indeed Freudian psychoanalysts have maintained that the catharsis of aggression either through direct acts of violence or through substitute activities such as participating in or viewing very aggressive sports, or viewing violent films, will diminish violent behavior. But this view has been proven incorrect through empirical research: these substitute activities in fact increase violence. . . .

Based on the hypothesis of the aggressive instinct or drive, one would also predict a decrease in violence in nations that have just been at war, since the war will have furnished either a direct or vicarious outlet for aggressive energy.

Social psychologist Dane Archer tested this hypothesis by comparing prewar and postwar homicide rates. Both in a study of the two World Wars and in a study of twelve other wars, he found that nations that had just been at war had increased homicide rates when compared with control nations. This was so even though the combatant nations had lost large numbers of young men, who are the group most likely to commit homicide.

Archer concluded that the catharsis hypothesis was refuted by the results of his study. Authorized wartime killing in fact legitimizes and encourages violence in peacetime.

In summary, the instinct or drive theory of aggression cannot be derived from data on human violence.

It is lacking in explanatory value. Its predictions are disconfirmed by data on sports, entertainment, and postwar violence.

The Many Meanings of "Aggression"

Besides the problems outlined above, much of what has been written on aggression by Freudians is simply irrelevant to the problem of violence, since both Freud and his successors adhere to a definition of aggression that encompasses far more than violence. Freud writes that the death instinct can also be called "the destructive instinct, the instinct for mastery, or the will to power."[13]

When Freudian psychoanalysts write about the aggressive drives and their emotional and behavioral consequences, they sometimes have a "violence drive" in mind . . . but much of the time they do not. Their writings are the epitome of the kind of ill-defined, all-encompassing and therefore potentially misleading use of the term "aggression" that was pointed out earlier.

THE ROLE OF EARLY CHILDHOOD DEPRIVATION

If there is any one kernel of agreement among various schools of psychoanalysis on the issue of violence, it may well lie in the idea, supported by considerable clinical and observational data, that a child who suffers emotional neglect, humiliation, or physical abuse in the early years of life is more likely to act violently in later life than a person whose childhood has been benign or relatively benign. This greater tendency toward violence can also express itself in support of violent leaders and governments.

A very brief survey of three psychoanalysts—Erich Fromm, Heinz Kohut, and Alice Miller—who hold such a view follows.

In *The Anatomy of Human Destructiveness,* which is probably the most systematic attempt to deal with the problem of aggression from a psychoanalytic perspective, Erich Fromm analyzes the sadistic personality. Stalin and Nazi henchman Himmler are two examples of such personalities.

Fromm asserts that the sadistic personality gets pleasure from having total life-and-death control over others in order to compensate for an extreme sense of powerlessness experienced as a child. The sadist has often been sadistically beaten as a child, and has grown up in a situation of psychic scarcity: ". . . there is an atmosphere of dullness and joylessness, the child freezes up; there is nothing upon which he can make a dent, nobody who responds or even listens, the child is left with a sense of powerlessness and impotence."[14]

Fromm is quick to qualify this statement by saying that extreme powerlessness in childhood does not necessarily result in a person's developing a sadistic character. Whether or not this happens depends on many other factors. But it is one of the main sources contributing to the development of sadism.

Heinz Kohut also believes that when a child's caretakers do not listen or respond to the child, when they neglect essential emotional needs, or show no admiration for achievements, the chances of violent behavior in later life are greatly increased. The very deep need that every child has for recognition, love, and admiration is referred to as a narcissistic need by Kohut. When such needs are not satisfied in childhood, people carry narcissistic injuries with them through their entire lives, and "narcissistic rage" often occurs in adulthood.

Kohut tells us that while narcissistic rages can take many different forms, they all share certain characteristics: "The need for revenge, for righting a wrong, for undoing a hurt by whatever means, and a deeply anchored, unrelenting compulsion in the pursuit of all these aims . . ."[15] . . . .

Swiss psychoanalyst Alice Miller is also convinced that the neglect of young children's emotional needs is connected with violent behavior in later life. In her book *For Your Own Good,* she attempts to trace Nazism and the enthusiasm with which it was embraced by so many Germans to the "poisonous pedagogy" by which many Germans had raised their children since the eighteenth century. She quotes extensively from respected German authorities on child-rearing. For them, the breaking of the child's will at a very early age was a major goal. This was achieved through physical punishment, extreme repression of spontaneity and life-affirming feelings, and by teaching unquestioning obedience to authority. It was believed that expressions of love or admiration would spoil the child and create an excessive degree of self-esteem, which was considered harmful.

Children raised in this way often grow up to be emotionally detached and incapable of empathy, as well as filled with unexpressed rage at the pain and humiliation they suffered as children. This rage, turned inward, can lead to self-denigration, masochism, and even suicide, or it can be turned outward. . . .

Throughout history, many women have supported wars and proudly sent off their husbands and sons to fight in them. But traditionally women have not served in the military or at least not in active combat, and so they have not participated directly in government-sanctioned violence. Even more significantly, their participation in criminal violence has been minimal compared to men's. (A survey of male and female arrest records for all crimes in twenty-five countries reveals that men are five to fifty times as likely to be arrested as women. The gender gap is even greater for serious crimes.[16]) Since girls suffer from emotional neglect, humiliation, and physical and sexual abuse at least as much, and probably more, than boys do, one would expect psychoanalysts to deal with the discrepancy in male and female levels of violence. In fact it has received very little attention. In recent years, several psychoanalytically oriented social scientists, among them Dorothy Dinnerstein, have begun to address it.

Dinnerstein argues that traditional child rearing, in which male children are raised from birth by females, results in a lower level of male sensitivity and caring, and a higher level of male aggression.[17] . . .

FOCUSING ON THE SOCIAL ENVIRONMENT

Social Learning Theory explains human behavior by focusing on the role that familial, communal, social, and cultural aspects of the environment play in influencing individual behavior.

One of its leading figures is Albert Bandura, professor emeritus of psychology at Stanford University, who has been researching and writing about aggression for the last thirty years. Bandura's basic definition of aggression is a broad one, but in the following discussion his primary concern is with violence.

While he believes that biological factors set the parameters of aggressive responses, and individual genetic endowment influences the propensity to learn aggressive behavior, Bandura's focus is on what he takes to be the three main sources of aggression in the social environment: the modeling and reinforcement provided by family, the subculture in which a boy grows up, and the mass media, TV in particular. . . .

Modeling oneself on parents is an important source of aggressive behavior. Studies indicate that boys whose fathers are criminals are more likely to become criminals, especially if the father is cruel and neglectful. A much higher percentage of delinquent boys have had aggressive fathers as models than nondelinquent. Abused children have a high rate of abusing their own children. But most aggressive boys do not have criminally or severely violent parents. What causes them to act violently?

Bandura and Richard Walters did a study in which the families of adolescent boys who repeatedly displayed antisocial aggressive behavior were compared with the families of boys who were neither particularly aggressive nor particularly passive.

It was found that parents of nonaggressive boys encouraged their sons to be strong in defending themselves, but they did not accept physical aggression as a method of settling quarrels. In family interaction these parents behaved considerately and relied heavily on reasoning in dealing with social problems. On the other hand, while parents of the aggressive boys did not display much antisocial aggression, they did repeatedly exhibit and reinforce combative attitudes and behavior. They did not tolerate aggression toward themselves, but almost invariably they encouraged their sons to be aggressive toward peers, teachers, and other adults.

Bandura's findings that physical abuse, parental modeling of aggression and permissiveness toward aggressive behavior encourage aggression in boys are supported by numerous studies by other researchers.[18]

Modeling and reinforcement by the family play an important role in causing aggression, but research indicates that the highest rates of aggressive behavior are found in surroundings where aggressive models are numerous and where aggression is highly valued. Growing up in a neighborhood where gangs dominate and where status is based mainly on fighting skills puts a boy at very high risk for violent behavior.

Bandura's emphasis on the importance of subcultures is shared by many of his colleagues. For example, in a 1987 interview, Eleanor Maccoby expressed her conviction that male peer groups are a more important influence on boys' behavior than their fami-

lies. Recent research, she pointed out, shows that there is a great emphasis on dominance, hierarchy, and prestige in boys' play groups, much more so than in girls' play groups. Compared to the behavior of boys alone, there appears to be a qualitative leap in the level of aggressive behavior of boys in groups.

While Maccoby agrees with Bandura that many boys who are not particularly aggressive are highly influenced by male subcultures, she believes that family pathology will predispose a boy to greater aggression. Those boys who carry with them a heavy dosage of hostility will be the quickest to be aroused and to fight. They are the more likely candidates for gangs or other groups that further reinforce aggressive behavior.

Bandura points out that the role of the environment goes far beyond providing immediate role models and reinforcement for aggression. From an early age, young children internalize the social pressures and role models they are presented with and develop a concept of the kind of behavior that is expected of them. A pattern of behavior can be stored cognitively and only acted on at a much later date when external conditions are conducive. Behavior learned in the family, from peers, or from the media may not manifest itself until years later.

PHYSICAL CONDITIONS THAT PUT BOYS AT RISK

The emphasis on numbers and statistics in this section is not accidental. It is often argued that the influence of mass media violence on boys is negligible because only a small group of disturbed boys already disposed toward violence will be affected. But, as we shall see, statistics indicate that millions of boys and men in the United States are at risk for violent behavior. The list of conditions described below is intended to give the reader an idea of the magnitude of the problem. It is not exhaustive. There are other conditions, for example, severe head injuries or psychomotor epilepsy, that also seem to put boys at greater risk for violent behavior.[19]

To say that they are at risk is in no way to suggest that all of them or even close to a majority of them are, or ever will be, violent. Most of the boys and men who suffer from these conditions lead and have led useful, productive, nonviolent lives. (Among them are Albert Einstein and Nelson Rockefeller.) Nevertheless *as a group* they are significantly more vulnerable to violent behavior than other boys and men.

Attention Deficit Disorder With Hyperactivity

Seth Maxell [fictitious name] was a difficult child from birth. By the time he was six months old he invariably woke up from naps crying and kicking. His response to cuddling was a stiffening of the body or more kicking. "It could easily take an hour to calm him down," his mother remembers.[20]

As he grew older, Seth would often lash out without warning. He might throw his toys or his spoon at people, punch his mother, or kick a door. Seth's attention span was very short and his tolerance for frustration very low. His physical energy level seemed unbounded. By the age of three Seth was having at least three major hysterical temper tantrums a day.

Mrs. Maxell emphasizes that Seth is not devoid of positive traits. He is often very generous and affectionate, but nevertheless she confesses that by the time he was three, she often would wake up in the morning "angry and not wanting to be Seth's mom."

Seth's parents are college-educated professionals. Mrs. Maxell, a former teacher, now devotes herself full-time to Seth and his sister. She is a sensitive, intelligent, high-energy person.

Seth was three years old when his mother took him to see a psychologist. I would guess that the diagnosis of attention deficit disorder with hyperactivity (ADDH a.k.a. ADHD) was not a difficult one to make, for Seth had many of the characteristic traits of this disorder, which affects at least 3 percent of American children: hyperactivity, impulsiveness, short attention span, temper outbursts, engaging in dangerous activities, low frustration tolerance.

The psychologist told Mrs. Maxell that unless something was done about it soon, Seth was very likely to develop into a violent man.

While violent behavior at a young age is not typical of all boys suffering from ADDH, the disorder is often a "predisposing factor" in the development of aggressive conduct disorder, which usually occurs around puberty and is characterized by acts of physical violence such as vandalism, rape, arson, mugging, assault.

In adolescence and adulthood, ADDH is a predisposing factor for antisocial personality disorder (sometimes referred to as sociopathic or psychopathic personality), whose distinguishing characteristics include delinquency, theft, vandalism, repeated physical fights or assaults, and repeated drunkenness or substance abuse. Approximately 9 percent of American boys under the age of eighteen suffer from aggressive conduct disorder and about 3 percent of men suffer from antisocial personality disorder. Both are far more common among males than females.

According to current research, ADDH (which until recently was referred to as "minimal brain dysfunction" or "minimal brain damage"), appears to be approximately six to nine times as prevalent among boys as among girls. Based on this, my estimate is that well over one million American boys may be afflicted. (Throughout this section estimates are intended to give the reader some sense of the magnitude of the problems described. No claim to exactitude is made.)[21]

By the time I met the Maxells, Seth was five years old. One year of work with the psychologist, which consisted mainly of receiving very concrete advice on how to handle Seth, had led to significant improvements. His mother estimated that between the ages of three and five, his violent behavior had decreased by approximately 60 percent.

Mrs. Maxell carefully monitors Seth's TV and film watching. She explains that "if he watches a violent show on TV he goes crazy, directly imitating whatever he sees." The most violent film he has ever seen is *Jaws*.

Even for the Maxells, who are able to afford whatever help they need, are informed on how best to deal with Seth, and have only one other child (who is good-natured and easy to raise), having a son who suffers from ADDH is extraordinarily trying. Mrs. Maxell admits that "every once in a while Seth gets a good whack," even though she and her husband are troubled about using violence to control his behavior.

Children with ADDH are prime candidates for child battering. If they can drive concerned, educated, patient, loving parents crazy, it is frightening to think what effect they would be likely to have on a poor teenage mother with no husband, no professional help, and no understanding of why her son behaves the way he does.

Seth Maxell provides us with an example of how a boy's symptoms, even when they are severe, can be alleviated by parents who have the emotional and financial ability to deal optimally with the situation.

Besides being fortunate in terms of his parents, Seth is also lucky in that he is very intelligent and does not suffer from any learning disabilities. . . .

While estimates vary considerably, there is a significant overlap of ADDH and learning disability, as well as ADDH and mental retardation. Each one of these conditions significantly increases the chances of violent behavior.

Learning Disability

It is estimated that approximately 32 percent of delinquent boys and 40 percent of the jail population in the United States suffer from learning disability (LD).[22]

Learning disability seems to afflict roughly 5 to 10 percent of the population. While boys are at least twice as likely to be identified by teachers as suffering from learning disability, recent research reveals that dyslexia (the most common of the learning disabilities) is in fact as prevalent in girls as in boys.* Assuming, conservatively, that boys make up no more than half of those suffering from *all* learning disabilities, I estimate that as many as six to twelve million American males may be afflicted.

According to the National Joint Committee for Learning Disabilities, learning disability refers to "a heterogeneous group of disorders manifested by significant difficulties in the acquisition and use of listening, speaking, reading, writing, reasoning, or mathematical abilities. These disorders are intrinsic to the individual and presumed to be due to central nervous dysfunction."[23]

A child can have a very specific learning disability, such as reversing letters when reading or severe difficulty with spelling, and yet be perfectly normal or even above average in every other way. In fact, the range of individuals suffering from learning disabilities goes from genius to retarded.

While many middle-class and upper-middle-class boys are afflicted, learning disability is considerably more common in lower socioeconomic classes. This may be due in part to complications at birth, which are more common among the disadvantaged.*

Mental Retardation

The incidence of mental retardation is much higher among prison inmates than among the general population. In fact, some experts have estimated that up to 30 percent of criminal offenders are mentally retarded.[24]

Approximately 3 percent of the American population suffer from mental retardation, which is nearly two times as prevalent among males as among females. Irritability, aggressiveness, and temper tantrums are often behavioral concomitants of mental retardation.

Since most extremely retarded people are either institutionalized or highly supervised if they live at home, it is safe to assume that criminal offenders come from the category of mildly retarded individuals, those with IQs of 50 to 70. About 80 percent of retarded people fall into this category. This means that as many as four million males may fall into the category of mildly retarded and be at high risk for violent behavior.

Mildly retarded children are born almost exclusively into economically disadvantaged families. The cause appears to be one or more of these factors: genetics, maternal alcohol or drug addiction during pregnancy, environmental factors such as malnutrition, and early child-rearing experiences.

Mentally retarded children are three to four times as likely to suffer from ADDH as the general population.

XYY Boys and Asperger's Syndrome

Several less common disabilities that affect only boys, or affect boys more often than girls, seem to have some link to violent behavior.

Research indicates that about 0.1 percent of males suffer from a genetic abnormality that consists of their

---

*We saw earlier in this chapter that boys are apparently more easily frustrated, act more impulsively, and are more interested in rough-and-tumble and outdoor physical activities than girls. These traits would make it more difficult for boys than for girls to deal with a learning disability. Boys would tend to concentrate less, make less effort, and act out more. Teachers are then more likely to identify them as suffering from a learning disability. An unobtrusive girl, working to the maximum of her capacity, may just be viewed as slow.

---

*According to Danish and Swedish studies, crime rates among adopted boys are more closely related to their biological parents' crime rates than to those of their adopted parents. (see S. A. Mednick et al., M. Rohman et al., and S. Sigvardsson et al.). These findings are corroborated by an American study (see R. R. Crowe). The fact that adopted children, who tend to come from deprived backgrounds, are four times as likely to suffer from learning disability than nonadopted children, may help to explain these findings.

having two Y chromosomes instead of one. This means that there are over 100,000 XYY men in the United States.

Young XYY boys are prone to severe temper tantrums and behavior problems. Their IQ is lower than average, and approximately half of them have problems with speech and reading at school.

Asperger's syndrome, according to most experts, is a mild form of autism in high-functioning individuals. Autism is characterized by a lack of interest in other human beings and a lack of empathy for them. Several specialists have suggested that the link between Asperger's syndrome and violent behavior needs to be explored.

Special Services or Incitement to Violence?

Millions of American boys and men suffer from conditions that put them at risk for violent behavior. Whether or not they engage in such behavior is to a significant degree a function of the familial, social, and cultural environment in which they are raised. Unfortunately, our society blindly encourages their worst tendencies.

Violent television programs and films, war toys, and even some sports provide boys and men with detailed role models of violence, and help desensitize them to the suffering of others.

According to at least one study, children who are mentally retarded, learning-disabled, or emotionally disturbed watch even more TV in general, and more violent programs in particular, than nonhandicapped children.[25] The values of the masculine mystique encourage violence in all men. Promoting these values among boys and men who suffer from physical conditions that put them at increased risk for violent behavior is a bit like throwing lit matches into a tank of gas.

The masculine mystique's emphasis on extreme competition and dominance can only serve to exacerbate this group's frustrations and increase their humiliation and anger in the face of their difficulties in school.

The mystique's glorification of danger and physical conflict provides highly impulsive and easily frustrated boys, many of whom are already predisposed to violence, with a legitimate arena in which they can prove their superiority. In fact, they may well become role models for some of their peers. If they can't do well in class, they can certainly assert their dominance

in school yard brawls. As they get older, depending on their socioeconomic background, they find opportunities to affirm their masculinity by joining gangs, committing violent crimes, going on joy rides, engaging in group rape. All of this is facilitated by the masculine mystique's ban on crying and "soft feelings," which discourages feelings of empathy for their victims.

Our national lack of interest in and lack of respect for child-rearing, our abysmal neglect of medical and social services for poor pregnant women and young mothers, and our failure to curtail teenage pregnancies can only serve to increase the numbers of boys suffering from these conditions and ensure that many of them will indeed become violent. Child-battering, emotional cruelty, and neglect increase the odds that any boy will grow up to be violent. Many of these boys are particularly prone to being battered—they can drive even the best, most patient, parent crazy.

The situation is now aggravated by the fact that more and more drug-addicted women are giving birth. Recent studies indicate that children born to mothers who are cocaine or crack addicts "show symptoms similar to those in children with mild autism or those with personality disorders . . ."[26] They are described as withdrawn, lacking in emotion, not interacting with other children. Their ability to concentrate is very low. In addition many addicted mothers subject their children to extreme emotional and physical neglect, or abandon them. Very few of these children have ever had any fathering.

Good summary

NATURE OR NURTURE?: A FALSE DICHOTOMY

Eleanor Maccoby and Carol Jacklin's work confirms what most of us already suspected. Boys, from a very young age, act more aggressively than girls. But the belief that "boys will be boys" and so the fighting and killing will go on regardless of what we do has no foundation in the best available knowledge. It is based on the erroneous belief that violent behavior grows out of a drive or instinct akin to hunger or sex.

But to say that violence is not an instinct or drive is not to deny that it has a biological basis. We are physical beings and so all of our behavior is grounded in biology. If we had not been biologically programmed with the ability to learn to be violent, then violent behavior could never have developed. Much as some of us may want to fly like birds, we shall never do so, because our biology forbids it. Intensive efforts have been made in recent years to teach language to chimps. The efforts failed. Chimps are not biologically wired to learn more than a few concrete terms; concepts and abstractions are beyond their potential. But we can learn concepts and abstractions. We can also learn violence.

We must begin to move beyond a simplistic view of violence in which one side contends that it is biological and therefore nothing can be done about it, while the other side asserts that human beings are naturally good and violence is caused by socialization alone.

Violence is best understood as developing out of an interaction between a biological potential and certain kinds of environments. In comparing males and females, the different treatment of boys and girls from birth makes it difficult to assess what is due to biology and what is due to socialization. It is the *combination* of evidence from such diverse and independent sources—studies in the United States, cross-cultural studies, hormonal and animal studies—which leads me to conclude that the potential for violence appears to be greater in males.*

Higher levels of testosterone seem to be a factor in greater male violence, but it may be that these are not so much linked directly to offensive violent behavior as to a lower threshold for frustration, more irritability and impatience, greater impulsiveness, a tendency to rough and tumble, and perhaps a greater concern with dominance, all of which can easily be precursors of violence. These tendencies can only be reinforced by the rougher treatment that boys receive from an early age. Hormone levels appear to be affected by the environment. A boy's involvement in a dominance- and violence-oriented group may cause increases in his testosterone levels.

The violence gap between boys and girls is enlarged by the fact that boys, more frequently than girls, suffer from physical disabilities which put them at greater risk for behaving violently. Nevertheless, when we speak of male-female differences with respect to violence we must remember that we are referring to tendencies which are more pronounced in one group than the other, not to separate, nonoverlapping groups. The fact that a majority of men lead essentially nonviolent lives, in spite of living in a society that applauds the values of the masculine mystique, testifies to the lack of any intense inclination towards violent behavior on their part.

Early childhood experiences are important. Boys who are emotionally neglected, humiliated, or battered, boys whose parents encourage combative attitudes and behaviors, are more likely to be violent.

Peer pressure is important. Concerns with dominance and proving manhood through fighting can lead boys in groups to commit acts of violence that they would not commit on their own.

Human beings easily learn xenophobia and territoriality. Governments often encourage and exploit these tendencies for their own purposes, including the waging of wars. Research indicates that wars serve to legitimize and encourage other forms of violence.

The enormous influence that government, society, and family have in terms of encouraging or discouraging the potential for violence is clear both from changes which take place within the same culture and differences in levels of violence between different societies.

Anthropologist Peggy Sanday's cross-cultural study of ninety-five societies revealed that 47 percent of them were free of rape. Robert R. Holt reports that there are at least thirty-three societies in which war as well as interpersonal violence are extremely rare.[27]

People who live in violent societies tend to assume that high levels of violence are inevitable. Now that we have, hopefully, been cured of this mistaken belief, we shall focus our attention on what can be done to make our society less violent.

---

*Many parents of boys have shared their experiences and views on the nature/nurture issue with me. A majority are convinced that nature plays an important role in their sons' high level of interest in rough play, war toys and violent entertainment. On the other hand a significant minority—perhaps as high as 40 percent—have told me that their sons have no or very little interest in these areas. A few have told me that their sons are far more gentle than their daughters. I have been struck by the similarity between these very informal findings and the data collected by Maccoby and Jacklin. While a majority of the ninety-four studies they examined showed boys to be more aggressive, a large number showed no difference and a few studies showed girls to be more aggressive.

NOTES

1. Erhardt, "The Psychobiology of Gender," in *Gender and the life Course* edited by A. S. Rossi, 1985, pp. 81–95; and "Gender Differences: A Biosocial Perspective," in Nebraska Symposium on Motivation 1984: *Psychology and Gender*, 1985, pp. 37–57. In both these articles Erhardt argues that a "dynamic interactional model," one that does not assume that one factor is the determining or predominant influence on behavior, must be used in the study of gender-related behavior.

2. Olweus, "Development of Stable Aggressive Reaction Patterns in Males," in *Advances in the Study of Aggression*, Volume I,

edited by R. J. Blanchard and C. L. Blanchard, pp. 131–34. See also his "Aggression and Hormones: Behavioral Relationship with Testosterone and Adrenaline," in *The Development of Antisocial and Prosocial Behavior*, edited by D. Olweus, J. Block, and M. Radke-Yarrow, pp. 53–59.

3. Maccoby stated this in a 1989 interview with me. She referred to several studies summarized in her book *Social Development* and to a study by Dutch psychologist Cornelius Van Lieshout in which he found that already by the age of two, boys are more easily frustrated and irritated than girls.

4. Wilson, *On Human Nature*, p. 102. (Some of the material paraphrased in this section is taken from *Sociobiology: The New Synthesis*.)

5. Wilson, *On Human Nature*, p. 108

6. Freud, "Why War?" *Standard Edition of the Complete Psychological Works of Sigmund Freud*, Vol. 22, edited by James Strachey, p. 211. See also *Civilization and Its Discontents*, pp. 85, 86.

7. For example, see Charles Brenner, *An Elementary Textbook of Psychoanalysis*, p. 18.

8. Wilson, op. cit., p. 108.

9. Bateson, "Is Aggression Instinctive?" in *Aggression and War*, edited by Jo Groebel and Robert A. Hinde, p. 41.

10. Holt, "Converting the War System to a Peace System," a paper prepared for a conference of the Exploratory Project on the Conditions of Peace, May 1987, p. 6.

For further critical analysis of Freud's death instinct, see Holt's "Drive or Wish? A Reconsideration of the Psychoanalytic Theory of Motivation," in *Psychological Issues*, Volume 9, Monograph No. 36, as well as the writings of psychoanalyst and social philosopher Erich Fromm and Freudian psychoanalyst Lawrence Kubie. They, among others, argue that this concept of an aggressive instinct or drive is not founded in any clinical evidence but is an outgrowth of nineteenth-century mechanistic psychology, which attempted to mimic the physical sciences. In *The Anatomy of Human Destructiveness*, Fromm tells us that Freud's teachers "looked on man as a machine driven by chemical processes" (p. 449). Just as physicists used the concept of quanta of physical energy, Freud wrote about psychic energy and argued that quanta of this energy (referred to as cathexes) were attached to mental representations of people or things. Analogously to engineers who worked with hydraulic pressures, psychoanalysts perceived themselves as working with pressures and tensions exerted by internal psychic forces seeking to express themselves emotionally and behaviorally.

Lawrence Kubie explains that the Freudian emphasis on psychological explanations in terms of variations in instinctual energy is "buttressed by a conviction that a science is not mature until it can count. Consequently to talk even of hypothetical and unmeasured quantitative variations gives us a feeling of scientific maturity which may in fact be premature and illusory" ("Symbol and Neurosis," *Selected Papers of Lawrence S. Kubie*, edited by Herbert J. Schlesinger, p. 44).

11. Freud, *Civilization and Its Discontents*. p. 91. There are repeated statements in the book to this effect. For example: "men clearly do not find it easy to do without satisfaction of this tendency to aggression that is in them; when deprived of satisfaction they are ill at ease" (p. 90). Freud states that with respect to happiness primitive man was better off—as long as he was not attacked by others—for "he knew nothing of any restrictions on his instincts" (p. 91).

Those familiar with psychoanalytic theory may protest that my analysis ignores the "neutralization" of aggressive drive energy which is analogous to the "sublimation" of sexual drive energy. Neutralization makes aggressive energy available to the ego and permits the latter to find gratification in activities and behaviors that

bear little resemblance to the original drive. But while Freud first introduced the concept of neutralization in 1923, the passages quoted above in which he suggests that holding back aggression can lead to unhappiness were written much later. It seems that neutralization is not enough to take care of all that aggressive energy.

The concept of neutralization is itself highly problematic. First the concept of an aggressive drive, which is not warranted by empirical data, is introduced. Since it is impossible to explain much of human behavior directly in terms of this drive (or in terms of a sex drive), it is then postulated that this drive is "neutralized" (and the sex drive sublimated) into all the various motives and behaviors that make up human existence!

12. Robert R. Holt, Lawrence S. Kubie, Benjamin B. Rubinstein, and E. Peterfreund are among the psychoanalytic theorists who argue that the concept of an aggressive drive as psychic energy which fuels motives and behavior has no explanatory value whatsoever.

13. Freud, "The Economic Problem of Masochism," in *Complete Psychological Works*, Vol. 19, p. 163.

Discussing this passage in *The Anatomy of Human Destructiveness*, Erich Fromm points out that "Freud combines here three very different tendencies. The instinct to destroy is basically different from the will for power: in the first case I want to destroy the object; in the second I want to keep and control it, and both are entirely different from the drive for mastery, whose aim it is to create and produce, which in fact is the precise opposite of the will to destroy" (p. 444).

14. Fromm, op. cit., p. 298.

15. Heinz Kohut, "Thoughts on Narcissism and Narcissistic Rage," in *The Search for the Self*, edited by Paul Ornstein, pp. 637–38.

16. The survey is reported by James Q. Wilson and Richard J. Herrnstein in *Crime and Human Nature*, pp. 104–5.

17. See also Nancy Chodorow, *The Reproduction of Mothering*; Lillian Rubin, *Intimate Strangers*; and Jessica Benjamin, *The Bonds of Love*.

18. See Dan Olweus, in Blanchard and Blanchard, op. cit., p. 126. Olweus discusses the results of his own research and lists other studies that also point to permissiveness and parental modeling as causal factors. Rejection on the part of the mother was also found to be a causal factor. Olweus discovered that the mother's rejection was often correlated with a poor emotional relationship between her and the boy's father. This point will be discussed at length in Chapter 4. See also K. A. Dodge, J. E. Bates, and G. S. Pettit, "Mechanisms in the Cycle of Violence" in *Science*, December 21, 1990, pp. 1678–83. In reporting on a study of 309 children the authors state that "this prospective study provides stronger evidence than ever before to support the hypothesis that physical abuse leads to a cycle of violence" (p. 1682). Because the children studied have only reached kindergarten age, the researchers refrain from any conclusions with respect to long range effects. They plan further longitudinal follow-ups.

19. See Dorothy Otnow Lewis et al., "Psychomotor Epilepsy and Violence in a Group of Incarcerated Adolescent Boys" in the *American Journal of Psychiatry*, July 1982, pp. 882–87, and Dorothy Otnow Lewis et al., "Intrinsic and Environmental Characteristics of Juvenile Murderers" in the *Journal of the American Academy of Child and Adolescent Psychiatry*, 1988, pp. 582–87.

20. Descriptions of Seth Maxell's behavior are based on 1988 and 1989 interviews with his mother.

21. My estimates are based on information and statistics that appear in the *Diagnostic and Statistical Manual of Mental Disorders—Revised*; in *Learning Disabilities: Proceedings of the National*

Conference, 1988; in *Learning Disabilities, A Report to the U.S. Congress*, 1987; and in the 1989 issue of *Their World*, a publication of the National Center for Learning Disabilities. These works are also a major source of the descriptive material that appears in this chapter. I am indebted to Dr. James F. Kavanagh, Associate Director of the Center for Research for Mothers and Children of the National Institute of Child Health and Human Development, and coeditor of *Learning Disabilities Proceedings of the National Conference*, for his help and guidance. However, I alone am responsible for the material presented here.

22. See U.S. Department of Justice, National Institute of Corrections, *Programming for Mentally Retarded and Learning Disabled Inmates: A Guide for Correctional Administrator*; and Senator Weinstein and Assemblyman Feldman's January 26, 1989, act to amend the correction law of New York State.

23. *Learning Disabilities: Report to the U.S. Congress*, p. 221. There is at present some controversy concerning the correct defini-

tion of "learning disability." The definition used here has been endorsed by most professional and lay organizations in the field.

24. See U.S. Department of Justice, National Institute of Corrections, *Programming Mentally Retarded and Learning Disabled Inmates: A Guide for Correctional Administrators*, p. 21, and "The Mentally Retarded Person in the Criminal Justice System," by Cecelia Ann Forget, in *Journal of Offender Counseling, Services and Rehabilitation*, Spring 1980, 285–95.

25. See Joyce Sprafkin and Kenneth Gadow, "Television Viewing Habits of Emotionally Disturbed, Learning Disabled, and Mentally Retarded Children," *Journal of Applied Developmental Psychology*, Jan–Mar 1986, pp. 45–59.

26. "Crack's Toll Among Babies: A Joyless View, Even of Toys," *New York Times*, September 19, 1989.

27. See Sanday's *Female Power and Male Dominance: On the Origins of Sexual Inequality*. Holt's report is from an unpublished paper entitled "Converting the War System to a Peace System."

Biology, Development, and Dangerousness   *2001*

Elizabeth J. Susman and Jordan W. Finkelstein

INTRODUCTION

The purpose is to present a developmental perspective on biological factors and dangerousness. The developmental perspective proposed is that biological factors and violence can only be understood by considering the dialectical nature of the interactions between physiological and psychological processes and the environmental contexts in which individuals develop. The chapter aims to define domains of behavior relevant to understanding biology and dangerousness; describe biopsychosocial models of dangerousness; present literature on the endocrine and serotonergic systems, autonomic nervous system, and dangerousness; and suggest clinical implications based on what is known about biological processes and dangerousness.

BEHAVIORAL DOMAINS OF DANGEROUSNESS AND BIOLOGICAL PROCESSES

The concept of dangerousness is difficult to define because it entails both psychological and behavioral risks that predispose to physical aggression and vio-

lent behavior. Furthermore, violence, aggression, and other forms of antisocial behavior are defined in diverse ways in the literature and tend to refer to constructs rather than specific behaviors. These constructs include antisocial behavior, externalizing behavior, norm breaking, violence, and illegal behavior. In contrast, when biological processes are included in research, measures representing one biological system tend to be considered: Hormones, neurotransmitters, or psychophysiological measures. Thus, conclusions regarding the relationships between interactive biological systems and violence are exceedingly simplistic even though multidimensional behaviors, attitudes, and various forms of violent behavior are immeasurably complex. An added layer of complexity entails the changing phenotypic nature of antisocial behavior throughout development.

Childhood physical aggression may become transformed to overt and covert forms of deviant behavior as development progresses in social, emotional, and behavioral domains. Similarly, physiological systems are changing during successive periods of development. For instance, at puberty, gonadal and adrenal hormone levels increase rapidly whereas these same hormones begin to decline in adulthood. In spite of these complexities, specific biological substances are somewhat reliably associated with various forms of antisocial behavior.

The manifestations of antisocial behavior included in biobehavioral studies are diverse. Generally accepted definitions of antisocial behavior include the following. Physical aggression refers to acts designed to injure another person and tend to be the focus of studies with children. Violence refers to acts that induce physical harm toward another individual. Domestic violence refers to aggression within a family. Antisocial behavior is a more inclusive construct that refers to relational and physical aggression, behavior problems and early and risky sex, substance use, conduct disorder, delinquency, and violence. The discussion that follows will include physical aggression and violence as components of the larger construct of antisocial behavior. We will use the term *antisocial behavior* to refer to the constructs mentioned above unless the literature cited uses a specific term like violence.

MODELS FOR CONSIDERING BIOLOGICAL PROCESSES AND ANTISOCIAL BEHAVIOR

The history of the biology of violence is short even though the need to integrate biological, psychological, and contextual (i.e., peers, family, communities) processes and antisocial behavior has been articulated for decades. The neglect of biology can partially be attributed to the arcane assumption of the primacy of biology as a causal influence on violence. Factors contributing to the current increase in research on biology and violence include the rejection of the primacy of biology. The models for considering biology and antisocial behavior now consider the complex bidirectional influences between biological, social, and contextual processes (Cairns & Stoff, 1996). The previous lack of integration of biological processes in studies of antisocial behavior is inconsistent with contemporary developmental perspectives that individuals develop and function as biologically and socially integrated organisms. Developmental theorists propose that maturational (biological), experiential, and cultural contributions are fused in ontogeny (Lerner & Foch, 1987; Magnusson & Cairns, 1996). Single aspects of development, like antisocial behavior, do not develop in isolation. Alternatively, it can be argued that antisocial behavior, similar to other developmental prob-

lems—depression (Compas & Hammen, 1994), adolescent violence, and pregnancy (Sells & Blum, 1995)—reflect exclusively social processes. To the extent that biological processes can explain individual differences in development and that behavior can explain individual differences in biology, then biological processes seem worthy of consideration in relation to antisocial behavior.

Current Developmental Models and Antisocial Behavior

For earlier developmental theorists, the concept of development was synonymous with biological change (e.g., Harris, 1957; Schneirla, 1957). "The concept of development is fundamentally biological" (Harris, p. 3). Within this early and still relevant perspective the concept of development refers to progressive changes in physical structures, systems and processes, systems of ideas and the organization of living structures and life processes that include emotional, social, and cognitive development as well as the contexts of development. Contemporary theorists consider development as successive changes that entail structural (biological change), as well as functional changes in psychological and behavioral capabilities that are molded by the contexts of development (Lerner, 1986). These contexts include the history of the individual, peers, family, and extra-familial institutions.

Two very different disciplinary paradigms are reflected in past approaches to antisocial behavior. Biologically oriented research focused on the role of evolution, genetics, endocrinology, neurobiology, and morphology. In contrast, behavioral research was concerned with processes within the person and the social environment. From the latter perspective, aggression is viewed as an atypical outcome derived from early familial and childhood experiences and learning experiences with deviant peers. These research models and methods did not traverse the multiple levels of analysis involved in complex antisocial behavior. The challenge for modern scientific paradigms is to explain how integration occurs across genetic, physiological, psychological, and social levels to influence the development of antisocial behavior (Cairns & Stoff; 1996; Brain & Susman; 1997; Magnusson & Cairns, 1996; Susman, 1997).

A biobehavioral science recognizes that behaviors are simultaneously determined by processes within the individual, in the social ecology, and in interactions between the two. A focus on either social or biological factors can yield only part of the story of aggressive and violent behaviors: integrative investigations are essential to complete the picture. (Cairns & Stoff, 1996, p. 338)

Recent studies are beginning to accomplish the aim of biobehavioral integration by incorporating indexes of physiological functioning (e.g., hormones, psychophysiological indexes, neurotransmitters) with psychological and contextual measures of antisocial behavior. Biology and antisocial behavior are consolidated at multiple levels of analysis (Cairns & Stoff, 1996). Dialectical relations exist between successive layers of development: cells, organs, organ systems, whole organisms, social environment (Hinde, 1987). There are different implications for the prevention of antisocial behavior when antisocial behavior is viewed from one level of analysis.

Specific Models for Considering Biology and Violence

Four basic models for considering biological processes and development are represented by the paths in Figure 1 (see also Susman, 1997). Model I represents the direct effects of biological influences on antisocial behavior. Model II shows the effect of antisocial behavior on biological processes. This model became increasingly popular during the last few decades as a result of studies showing the effects of challenging and stressful experiences on physiological systems, particularly the hypothalamic-pituitary-gonadal (HPG) and hypothalamic-pituitary-adrenal (HPA) axes (Booth, Shelley, Mazur, Tharp, & Kittok, 1989; Brooks-Gunn, Graber, & Paikoff, 1994; Mazur, Susman, & Edelbrock, 1997). As reviewed above, inherent in models of development are the reciprocal influences of biology and antisocial behavior as represented in Model III. Antisocial behavior may alter biological processes, which then accelerates or decelerates the probability of future antisocial behavior. Success in dominance encounters, for instance, may elevate testosterone (T), in turn, accelerating dominance (Mazur & Booth, 1998). The final model depicts the reciprocal effects of the contexts of development, biology, and antisocial behavior (Model IV). Contexts can include both biological (e.g., endocrine system) and social-environmental contexts. The models and corresponding statistical strategies can be used to simultaneously test the validity of competing hypotheses regarding biology and behavior interactions

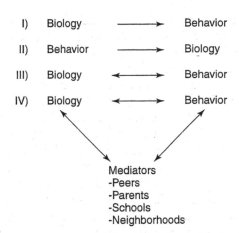

FIGURE 1　Four models of biology and behavior interactions.

(see Brooks-Gunn & Warren, 1989; Raine, Brennan, & Farrington, 1997; Susman & Ponirakis, 1997; Susman et al., 1987). Thus, the models of biological processes as influencing behavior and behavior as influencing biology gain validity if considered in conjunction but invalid if considered in isolation.

Raine et al. (1997) proposed a biosocial model of violence that includes genetics, environment, biological risks, social risks, biosocial interactions, biological and social protective factors, and violence. The Model appears in Figure 2. Genes and environmental factors are considered building blocks for influences on risk and protective factors. These factors interact to produce antisocial outcomes. Similarly, reciprocal relationships can exist between biological and social risk factors. For example, the biological risk factor of lower HPA axis arousal may stimulate an adolescent to engage in high-risk fighting in deviant peer groups. In addition, biological and social factors also can have direct effects on violence. Finally, the pathways to violence can be deterred by protective factors that interrupt the progression of certain paths. The majority of the pathways are not yet supported by empirical findings but the models described above have heuristic value for formulating hypotheses.

BIOLOGICAL SYSTEMS AND ANTISOCIAL BEHAVIOR

Multiple systems are implicated in the biology of violence: endocrine, serotonergic, dopaminergic, autonomic nervous, and other systems. Herein we consider the most frequently considered systems: endocrine,

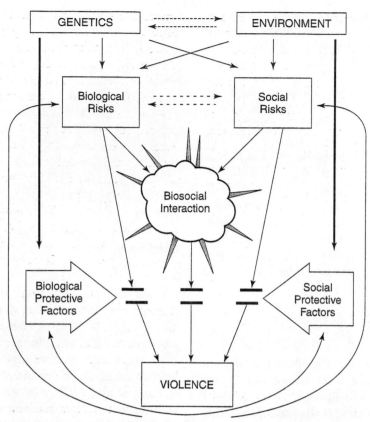

FIGURE 2 Heuristic biosocial model of violence. From Raine, A., Brennan, P., & Farrington, D. P. (1997). Biosocial bases of violence: Conceptual and theoretical issues. In A. Raine, P. A. Brennan, D. P. Farrington, & S. A. Mednick (Eds.), *Biosocial bases of violence* (pp. 1–20), New York, Plenum.

serotonergic, and autonomic nervous system (see Henry & Moffitt, 1997; Raine, Farrington, Brennan, & Mednick, 1997; Stoff & Cairns, 1996 for reviews of biological systems). Noteworthy is that interacting products of biological systems are more likely to be reliable indicators of risk for antisocial behavior than specific products.

Endocrine System and Antisocial Behavior

Products of the endocrine system, principally, the steroid hormone, T, often are implicated in physical aggression in animals and antisocial behavior in humans (see Brain, 1994 for an extensive review). The effects of gonadal steroids on antisocial behavior are hypothesized to derive from the regulatory functions

of hormones during pre- and post-natal periods as well as in later development. Speculation was that during brief, sensitive periods in pre- and early post-natal development, hormones are capable of affecting brain development such that behavior is influenced later in development. The early structural changes are referred to as organizational influences (Phoenix, Goy, Gerall, & Young, 1959). Activational influences stem from contemporaneous influences of hormones on behavior and refer to regulatory effects of previously established neural circuits. Commonly observed human sexual dimorphisms in brain structure, function, and behavioral expression are believed to originate from the differential organizational and activational effects of gonadal hormones. Recent thinking implicates hormones as having organizational influences throughout the life span as well as during the pre- and early post-natal periods of development. Adult neural circuits can respond to hormonal manipulation with structural changes in avian model studies (Gould, Woolley, & McEwen, 1991). Steroidal hormones collectively modulate brain neurochemistry and neurotransmitter functioning in multiple ways. Hormones can be viewed as substances that change the probability, versus cause antisocial behavior, that antisocial behavior will occur in certain situations in individuals with specific developmental experiences (Brain & Susman, 1997). In addition, behavior and experiences change the concentrations of specific hormones, thereby increasing or decreasing the probability of antisocial behavior.

Gonadal Steroids and Antisocial Behavior

Testosterone. Testosterone is the hormone most often linked to a variety of antisocial behaviors: physical aggression, dominance, and violence. In an extensive review of the literature, Mazur and Booth (1998) conclude that dominance is more closely linked to T than is physical aggression. Dominance may entail physical aggression with the intent of inflicting harm, although dominance also can be expressed nonaggressively such as in competitiveness.

Evidence for the role of T on antisocial behavior is derived from both correlational and experimental studies. In correlational studies in adult males, higher T is associated with aggressive behavior, dominance, and hostility (Persky, Smith, & Basu, 1971; Ehrenkranz, Bliss, & Sheard, 1974; Olweus, Mattson, Schalling, & Low, 1980; 1988). The links between relatively high T and specific antisocial acts are somewhat consistent. Dabbs, Frady, Carr, and Besch (1987) report that males with higher T committed more violent crimes, were judged more harshly by parole board members, and violated prison rules more often than men with lower T levels. Others studies have not found a relationship between T and aggressive behavior (see Archer, 1991). Inconsistencies across studies likely stem from differences in sample characteristics and measures. Developmental differences between children, adolescents, and adults add complexity to explaining relationships between T and antisocial behavior. Overall, the relationships between T and antisocial behavior are less consistent in pubertal age boys than would be anticipated given the theory that

hormones bring to expression at puberty, activational influences, behaviors such as physical aggression that have been sensitized to androgens in the pre- and perinatal period. Activational influences were not observed in the association between T and aggressive behavior in young adolescents (Susman et al., 1987) or in 4- to 10-year-old children with diagnoses of conduct problems (Constantino et al., 1993). In older adolescents, Olweus and colleagues (1988) found evidence for the causal role of T on provoked and unprovoked aggression. Testosterone at grade 9 exerted a direct causal influence on provoked aggressive behavior. Testosterone appeared to lower boys' frustration tolerance. A higher level of T appears to lead to an increased readiness to respond with vigor and assertion to provocation. For unprovoked aggressive behavior (starting fights and verbal aggression) at grade 9, the findings were somewhat different. Testosterone had no direct effects on unprovoked aggressive behavior. There was an indirect effect of T with low frustration tolerance as the mediating variable. Higher levels of T made the boys more impatient and irritable, in turn increasing readiness to engage in unprovoked aggressive behavior. It is noteworthy that the associations between antisocial behavior and T are less apparent in children and younger adolescents (Brooks-Gunn & Warren, 1989; Constantino et al., 1993; Nottelmann et al., 1987; Susman et al., 1987) than in older adolescents (Olweus, 1986; Olweus et al., 1988) and adults (Archer, 1991). These inconsistencies should be expected given the different measures of antisocial behavior. Nonetheless, some measures do capture subtle differences in adolescents with higher T levels. Adolescents with higher levels of T exhibit behaviors that are distinguishable from behavior in boys with lower T. Boy's perceptions of peer dominance were reflected in T concentrations (Schaal, Tremblay, Soussignan, & Susman, 1996). Testosterone was significantly higher in perceived leaders than in nonleaders.

The developmental differences in findings for children, adolescents, and adults indicate that elevated T and antisocial behavior may be a consequence rather than a cause of aggressive behavior during adulthood (Constantino et al., 1993; Susman, Worrall, Murowchick, Frobose, & Schwab, 1996). Model II postulates the effects of behavior on hormone concentrations. Longitudinal evidence of Model II is derived from a study of disruptive boys followed from age 6 to 13

(Schaal et al., 1996). Boys consistently displaying disruptive behavior problems across 6 years were significantly lower on T and were later in pubertal maturation compared to nondisruptive boys. The effect of antisocial behavior on suppression of gonadal steroids may result from the secretion of stress-related products of the HPA axis (corticotropin releasing hormone [CRH], adrenocorticotropin hormone [ACTH], and cortisol [Susman, Nottlemann, Dorn, Gold, & Chrousos, 1989]). Overall, the role of T in antisocial behavior is supported, but the periods of development when antisocial behavior will emerge and contextual factors that facilitate expression of T-related antisocial behavior are yet to be identified. Situations that threaten dominance may be especially notable to explore in future studies. Mazur and Booth (1998) conclude that high levels of endogenous T encourage behavior intended to dominate others.

Estrogen. The effects of estrogen on antisocial behavior only recently was considered. The lack of research on estrogen and antisocial behavior is reflective of two issues. First, males only are included in the majority of studies on hormones and antisocial behavior as physical aggression and violence are not considered a major problem in women. Second, T was considered the major hormone associated with antisocial behavior until recently when estrogen effects began to be considered as paralleling those of T. In adult males, estradiol (E_2) correlated positively with reports of physical, verbal, and impatient aggression (Gladue, 1991). Of note is that girls with higher concentrations of E_2 were likely to show greater dominance while interacting with their parents (Inoff-Germain et al., 1988). The current interest in gender phenotypic antisocial behavior (i.e., relational aggression), is likely to lead to greater specification of the role of estrogen in antisocial behavior. The role of estrogen in antisocial behavior in males also appears possible because T can be aromatized to estrogen. The extensive distribution of estrogen receptors in the brain indicates that estrogen can influence a variety of behaviors in both sexes.

Experimental studies are the preferred research design for establishing T or estrogen effects on antisocial behavior. Thus, we conducted a study in adolescents with delayed puberty who were being treated with physiological doses of T (boys) or conjugated estrogen (girls) in a placebo controlled, randomized, double-blind, cross-over design (Finkelstein et al., 1997; Finkelstein et al., 1998; Susman et al., 1998). Each

3-month treatment period was preceded and followed by a 3-month placebo period. The doses of gonadal steroids were calculated to simulate the concentrations of gonadal steroids in blood in normal early, middle, and late pubertal adolescents. Aggressive behaviors were measured by self-reports about physical and verbal aggression against peers and adults, aggressive impulses, and aggressive inhibitory behaviors. Significant increases in self-reported aggressive impulses and in physical aggression against both peers and adults were seen in girls at the low and middle dose. Significant increases in aggressive impulses and physical aggression against peers and adults were seen in boys but only at the middle dose. The findings demonstrate the influential role of gonadal steroid hormones in the initiation of aggression at puberty in adolescents with delayed puberty.

Adrenal Androgens. The adrenal androgens traditionally receive little attention in relation to antisocial behavior. Nonetheless, adrenal androgens are associated with aggressive behavior, affective expression, psychiatric disorders, and sexual behavior (Brooks-Gunn & Warren, 1989; Susman et al., 1987; Udry, Bill, Morris, Groff, & Raj, 1985; Udry & Talbert, 1988). The adrenal androgens are considered "weak" bonding androgens relative to T (Bondy, 1985). Adrenal androgen actions may parallel those of T in relation to behavior as one of the adrenal androgens, androstenedione, is a precursor of both T and estrogen. The rationale for examining antisocial behavior and adrenal androgens stems from both animal and human model studies. In the female spotted hyena, androstenedione concentrations are high and the females are highly aggressive and masculinized both anatomically and behaviorally (Glickman, Frank, Davidson, Smith, & Sitteri, 1987). High androstenedione concentrations during pregnancy may organize the sex-reversed traits of female spotted hyenas (Yalcinkaya et al., 1993). The role of androstenedione in humans is not clear beyond its role in the development of secondary sex characteristics during puberty.

In the last decade, four studies report relationships between adrenal androgens and antisocial behavior in adolescents. In pubertal age girls (Brooks-Gunn & Warren, 1989), higher dehydroepiandrosterone sulphate (DHEAS) correlated negatively with aggressive affect. The interaction between negative life events and DHEAS and aggressive affect showed that girls with lower concentrations of DHEAS and experienced negative life events had more aggressive affect than girls with fewer negative life events. The second study included 9- to 14-year-old adolescents. A consistent pattern of high adrenal androgens and low gonadal steroids was associated with problem behaviors and negative affect (Nottelmann et al., 1987; 1990; Susman et al., 1987; 1991). Adrenal androgens also correlate with dominance (Inoff-Germain et al., 1988). The third study demonstrates the contribution of adrenal androgens to sexual behavior and activities (Udry et al., 1985; Udry & Talbert, 1988). A fourth study with conduct disordered boys reported significantly higher levels of dehydroepiandrosterone (DHEA) and DHEAS and the intensity of aggression and delinquency (van Goozen, Matthys, Cohen-Kettenis, Thijssen, & van Engeland, 1998). Thus, the consistent association between adrenal androgens and antisocial behavior indicates further study.

Cortisol and Antisocial Behavior. In the 1980s, studies began to assess the relationship between products of the HPA axis, principally cortisol, and antisocial behavior. In general, antisocial behavior is associated with lower concentrations of HPA products. Virkunnen et al. (1994) showed that cerebrospinal fluid CRH was low in substance abusers and offenders and cortisol was low in habitually violent offenders. Similarly, in males with a violent history of abusing others, cortisol levels were lower than levels in comparison males (Bergman & Brismar, 1994). Lower cortisol levels are also characteristic of children who are at risk for behavior problems. Cortisol levels were lower in preadolescent sons whose fathers had conduct disorder as children and who subsequently developed antisocial personality (Vanyukov, Moss, Plail, Mezzick, & Tarter, 1993). Lower levels of cortisol also were reported in prepubertal children of parents with a psychoactive substance use disorder (PSUD) (Moss, Vanyukov, & Martin, 1995). Boys at high risk for PSUD secreted less salivary cortisol than controls in anticipation of a stressful task (Moss et al., 1995). Finally, adolescents with lower levels of plasma cortisol prior to a stressful situation (a phlebotomy procedure), but showed an increase across 40 minutes, had significantly more symptoms of conduct disorder a year later than children who decreased or those who maintained consistent levels (Susman, Dorn, Inoff-Germain & Nottelmann, Chrousos, 1997). Low HPA axis responsivity and antisocial behavior correspond to the cardiovascular system underarousal and aggres-

sive behavior relationships observed in adolescents and adults (Raine, 1996). Individuals low on HPA axis arousal may seek out stimulating and risky situations that entail antisocial behavior.

Neurotransmitters

Serotonin. The monoamines, specifically, serotonin, represent the neurotransmitter system extensively examined in relation to antisocial behavior, although a variety of neurotransmitters may be implicated in antisocial behavior (Berman, Kavoussi, & Coccaro, 1997; Virkkunen & Linnoila, 1990). Serotonin is the most widely distributed monoamine neurotransmitter in the brain, is an inhibitory neurotransmitter (Berman et al., 1997), and plays a role in sexual behavior, analgesia, appetite, sleep, and mood. The three primary methods for measuring serotonergic function are: measurement of the primary serotonin (5-HT) metabolite in cerebrospinal fluid (CSF 5-HIAA [5-hydroxyin-doleacetic acid]), endocrine responses to drug challenges, and serotonin in blood (whole blood 5-HT or platelet 5-HT uptake) (Moffitt et al., 1998). Measures of serotonin function can reflect either presynaptic availability of serotonin (e.g., reuptake) or postsynaptic neuronal sensitivity (e.g., receptor density). Studies that include assessment of serotonin tend to be carried out in clinical or forensic samples (see exception below). In these samples, the distribution of violence scores can be distorted because of a restricted range, which may reduce the sensitivity of a biological marker (Rasmusson, Riddle, Lechman, Anderson, & Cohen, 1990). The information regarding the causal role of serotonin in the development of antisocial behavior remains limited.

Dysfunctions of the serotonergic system are hypothesized to reduce the regulation of human aggression (Coccaro, 1989, Virkkunen & Linnoila, 1993). Serotonin dysregulation related disorders, such as violence and depression, are associated with low levels of serotonin. Serotonergic parameters are lower in adults with aggressive behavior (e.g., Brown et al., 1982; Brown & Linnoila, 1990; Coccaro et al., 1989; Virkkunen et al., 1994; LeMarquand, Pihl, & Benkelfat, 1994) and in suicide attempters and completers (Asberg, Schalling, Traksman-Bendz, & Wagner, 1987). The magnitude of the involvement of serotonin in antisocial behavior and psychiatric disorders varies developmentally. In children or adolescents, findings link the serotonergic system and aggression but less consistently than in adults (Zubieta & Alessi, 1993). Specifically, there was no relationship between disruptive behavior and platelet serotonin receptor density in boys at risk for delinquency but there was a negative relationship between receptor density and physically abusive family environments (Pine et al., 1996). Developmental differences may be attributed to the longevity of the antisocial behavior, psychiatric history, and interactions with family and peers may suppress serotonin synthesis, reuptake, or degradation.

Studies measuring CSF 5-HIAA generally report a negative relationship with antisocial behavior. Specifically, reduced frontal lobe serotonin turnover rate, as indexed by low CSF 5-HIAA concentrations, is reported for impulsive, violent patients with antisocial personality disorder (Berman et al., 1997; Linnoila, 1997). Children with disruptive and aggressive problems also had lower concentrations of CSF 5-HIAA (Kruesi et al., 1992). The pharmacological challenge studies also support the findings that 5-HT is inversely related to antisocial behavior. Hormone response to fenfluramine was blunted in depressed, personality-disordered subjects, and violent criminal offenders (Berman et al., 1997; O'Keane et al., 1992). The direction and magnitude of the response to fenfluramine may be affected by depression (Coccaro et al., 1989) and substance abuse (Fishbein, Lozovsky, & Jaffe, 1989). Assessing concurrently both emotional states and antisocial behavior appears essential for an accurate interpretation of challenge tests.

Pharmacological challenges also have been used to assess serotonin and familial patterns of aggression, impulsivity, and alcohol use (Coccaro, Silverman, Klar, Horvath, & Siever, 1994). Blunting of prolactin response to fenfluramine challenge was characteristic of first-degree relatives with impulsive personality traits. Questionnaire measures of aggression were not linked with problem behaviors in relatives suggesting that the challenge test may be a better predictor of problem behaviors than questionnaires. Coccaro and colleagues (Coccaro, Berman, Kavoussi, & Hauger, 1996) did find associations between self-reported aggression in personality disordered men and prolactin response to d-fenfluramine. In contrast, in children, no relationship emerged between aggression and prolactin response to fenfluramine (Stoff et al., 1992). The findings of these challenge studies and questionnaire assessments support the perspective that analysis

across biological and behavioral levels offers a more valid assessment of antisocial behavior than any analysis at one level.

Studies using whole blood 5HT or [³H] imipramine binding yield inconsistent results. Imipramine binding sites appear to be involved in the transport of serotonin from the exterior to the interior of the platelet cell surface (Berman et al., 1997). Stoff and colleagues (1987) and Birmaher et al. (1990) report a negative relationship between externalizing behavior and platelet [³H] imipramine binding in children. This relationship is not consistent across studies. Unis et al. (1997) report that whole blood 5-HT was higher in adolescents with conduct disorder, childhood type, than in others with conduct disorder, adolescent type.

Personality disorders also appear to mediate the relationship between serotonin and antisocial behavior. The often reported negative relationship between CSF 5-HIAA and aggressive behavior was not found in male or female personality-disordered patients (see Berman et al. [1997] for other instances of personality characteristics and serotonin relationships). Kruesi and Jacobsen (1997), show the importance of traits (persistent response), states (response under specified conditions), and scars (response appearing after the onset of illness or insult and then persists) as mediators of CSF 5-HIAA and human violence. The scar of early and persistent aggression related to deviant parenting represents one important environmental mediator of serotonin. The evidence for environmental scar mediation of serotonin and aggression derives from the peer-reared monkey studies. Mother-reared monkeys show significant correlations between CSF 5-HIAA, social behavior, and aggression whereas peer-reared monkeys do not exhibit this correlation (Kramer, 1997). Overall, the evidence indicates that early developmental experiences may mediate serotonin-antisocial relationships. This evidence is encouraging in that early behavioral interventions may alter the serotonergic system and thereby reduce the incidence of serotonergic-related disorders.

The problems of linking serotonin and antisocial behavior in clinical or forensic samples partially is resolved by the Moffitt et al. (1998) epidemiological study. The birth-cohort sample, measurement and analytic characteristics of the community-sample report evidence of serotonin and antisocial behavior relationships. The validity of the measures was improved over previous studies as both self-report and court records were used to assess violence. Violent men were significantly higher on serotonin than nonviolent men on both self-report and court measures even after controlling for possible confounds. Peripheral serotonin is negatively related to brain serotonin; thus, these epidemiological findings are consistent with previous findings. No relationships emerged between serotonin and violence in women.

An array of evidence supports the connections between serotonin and antisocial behavior that has been derived from clinical, forensic, and community samples of adults and children using observational and experimental methodologies. Proposed is that dysfunctions in serotonergic activity (e.g., reuptake) predispose individuals to engage in behaviors that are otherwise suppressed. In impulsive or reactive aggressive individuals, reduced central 5-HT may predispose an individual to engage in aggressive behavior that would normally not be expressed (Coccaro, 1989). The evidence that serotonin and aggressive behaviors are related in children suggests that indexes of serotonin might be a useful diagnostic tool. The mediation of serotonin by trait and state characteristics of individuals, seasonal variations, and contextual considerations indicate the need for multilevel assessments when considering a serotonin marker as a diagnostic tool.

Psychophysiology of Antisocial Behavior. The relationship between psychophysiological parameters (e.g., heart rate, skin conductance) and antisocial behavior reflects functioning of the autonomic nervous system and the brain (e.g., electroencholography). Excellent reviews of the psychophysiological correlates of antisocial behavior currently exist (Fowles, 1993; Raine, 1993; 1996; 1997). The summary here derives primarily from Raine (1996; 1997). Findings from studies of resting electroencephalograms (EEG), skin conductance (SC), and heart rate (HR) generally show characteristic underarousal in antisocial individuals. Prospective studies show a relationship between low resting heart rate and later antisocial behavior (Farrington, 1987). Low resting heart rate in children as young as 4 months predicted disinhibited behavior (Kagan, 1989). Similarly, low resting heart rate at age 3 predicted antisocial behavior at age 11 (Raine, Reynolds, Venables, & Mednick, 1997). The interpretation of these findings is that antisocial individuals are relatively fearless stimulation seekers, which entails high risk and antisocial behavior. A pattern of underarousal in children suggests that an early pattern of

autonomic underarousal may be a risk factor for antisocial behavior later in development (Kagan, 1989). Underarousal may predispose to both a disinhibited temperament and later antisocial behavior.

Deficits in attentional processes also are a risk for later antisocial and criminal behavior. Event-related potential (ERP) research reviews indicate that antisocial individuals are characterized by enhanced attentional processing to events of interest (Raine, 1993). ERPs are recorded from electrodes placed on the scalp and record electrical activity of the brain in response to experimental stimuli. Responses to stimulation vary depending on early, middle, or late latency ERPs corresponding to reduced arousal and excessive filtering of environmental stimuli (stimulus deprivation), increased ERP amplitude to stimulus intensity (sensation seeking), and enhanced P300 amplitudes to stimuli that have been selectively attended to (attention to stimulating events). The behavioral consequences of these ERP patterns are suspected to be causally linked to antisocial behavior. Individuals with chronically low levels of arousal seek out stimulating events to increase their arousal to more optimal levels. Stimulation-seeking focuses attention to events of interest, such as dangerous situations, in which violence is committed.

A prefrontal dysfunction theory summarizes the relationship between psychophysiology and antisocial behavior. The prefrontal dysfunction theory posits that damage to the frontal lobe results in arousal, orienting, and anticipatory fear deficits that predispose to antisocial behavior (Linnoila, 1997; Raine, 1997). Future studies will benefit from well conceptualized and hypothesis-driven approaches to the complexity of antisocial behavior and psychophysiology (Raine, 1996). It is likely that personality, family, and psychophysiological correlates interact to propel an individual toward or away from antisocial behavior.

CLINICAL IMPLICATIONS

Given it is not yet proven that biological substances cause antisocial behavior, the ultimate cause cannot then be assumed to be biological, experiential, or social (Brain & Susman, 1997). Biological factors might be considered risk factors comparable to behavioral risk factors. Since interventions are rarely designed on a one-to-one basis of one risk factor per intervention, it follows that interventions to prevent biological risk factors can be similar to interventions to prevent behavioral risks. Consistent with a developmental perspective, the implications that follow urge that prevention and treatment efforts be based on a multilevel and interdisciplinary level of analysis of antisocial behavior. Developmental models inherently result in assessments that go beyond the individual and consider family and community in the treatment of antisocial behavior.

How can health service providers and others prevent and manage dangerousness in the populations with which they are involved? The populations of interest include individuals of both sexes from all stages of development (birth to senescence) from differing social classes, from an increasing array of racial and ethnic groups and from groups with co-occurring mental and physical disabilities. A single group of providers will not be capable of identifying and managing dangerousness in this diverse population. Health care providers seldom learn in their academic training programs how to manage the problem of dangerousness. Academic training curricula rarely include the concept of dangerousness and those conducting research concerning dangerousness rarely have clinical experience in managing dangerousness. Thus, an important first step is to recognize inadequacies in requisite background and experience to address the problem of dangerousness. Next is the need to form interdisciplinary collaborations with professionals from a variety of disciplines who have expertise in dealing with dangerousness. These interdisciplinary teams might include professionals representing biology, criminology, psychiatry, psychology, and sociology. Professional teams could collectively recognize training shortcomings and be willing to share information and experience to deal with dangerousness. One such group in the United States are pediatricians, since violence toward and by children, adolescents, and young adults is a major clinical problem.

The role of researchers and clinicians as advocates of social policy for the prevention of dangerousness should not be underestimated. If these professional groups can influence significant others in the community to join health professionals to institute change, we will have accomplished what is needed to build prevention and intervention programs and to support the development of adequate programs for evaluations. It is essential that professionals, families, and communities be willing to collaborate to prevent antisocial behavior. If this collaboration is not accomplished, individuals will most likely continue to struggle with the problem of dangerousness, each doing important work, yet not identifying the causes, prevention, and treatment of dangerousness.

REFERENCES

ARCHER, J. (1991). The influence of testosterone on human aggression. *British Journal of Psychology, 82*, 1–28.

ASBERG, M., SCHALLING, D., TRAKSMAN-BENDZ, L., & WAGNER, A. (1987). Psychobiology of suicide, impulsivity and related phenomena. In H. Y. Melzer (Ed.), *Psychopharmacology: Third generation of progress* (pp. 655–688). New York: Raven Press.

BERGMAN, B., & BRISMAR, B. (1994). Hormone levels and personality traits in abusive and suicidal male alcoholics. *Alcoholism, Clinical and Experimental Research, 18*, 311–316.

BERMAN, M. E., KAVOUSSI, R. J., & COCCARO, E. F. (1997). Neurotransmitter correlates of human aggression. In D. M. Stoff, J. Breiling, & J. Maser (Eds.), *Handbook of antisocial behavior.* (pp. 305–313). New York: Wiley.

BIRMAHER, B., STANLEY, M., GREENHILL, L., TWOMEY, J., GAVRILESCU, A., & RABINOVICH, H. (1990). Platelet imipramine binding in children and adolescents with impulsive behavior. *Journal of the American Academy of Child and Adolescent Psychiatry, 29*, 914–918.

BONDY, P. K. (1985). Disorders of the adrenal cortex. In J. D. Wilson & D. W. Foster (Eds.), *Williams textbook of endocrinology* (pp. 816–890). Philadelphia: Saunders.

BOOTH, A., SHELLEY, G., MAZUR, A., THARP, G., & KITTOK, R. (1989). Testosterone and winning and losing in human competition. *Hormones and Behavior, 23*, 556–571.

BRAIN, P. F. (1994). Hormonal aspects of aggression and violence. In A. J. Reiss Jr, K. A., Miczek, & J. I. Roth (Eds.), *Understanding and Preventing Violence, Vol. 2 Biobehavioral Influences* (pp. 173–244). Washington, DC: National Academy Press.

BRAIN, P. F., & SUSMAN, E. J. (1997). Hormonal aspects of aggression and violence. In D. M. Stoff, J. Breiling, & J. D. Maser (Eds.), *Handbook of antisocial behavior* (pp. 314–323). New York: Wiley.

BROOKS-GUNN, J., GRABER, J., & PAIKOFF, R. (1994). Studying links between hormones and negative affect: Models and measures. *Journal of Research on Adolescence, 4*, 469–486.

BROOKS-GUNN, J., & WARREN, M. (1989). Biological and social contributions to negative affect in young adolescent girls. *Child Development, 60*, 40–55.

BROWN, G. L., EBERT, M. H., GOYER, P. F., JIMERSON, D. C., KLEIN, W. J., BUNNEY, W. E., & GOODWIN, F. K. (1982). Aggression, suicide, and serotonin: Relationships to CSF amine metabolites. *American Journal of Psychiatry, 139*, 741–746.

BROWN, G. L., & LINNOILA, M. I. (1990). CSF serotonin metabolite (5-HIAA) studies in depression, impulsivity, and violence. *Journal of Clinical Psychiatry, 51*, 42–43.

CAIRNS, R. B., & STOFF, D. M. (1996). Conclusion: A synthesis of studies on the biology of aggression and violence. In D. M. Stoff & R. B. Cairns (Eds.), *Aggression and violence: Genetic, neurobiological and biosocial perspectives*. Mahwah, NJ: Erlbaum.

COCCARO, E. F. (1989). Central serotonin and impulsive aggression. *British Journal of Psychiatry, 155*, 52–62.

COCCARO, E. F., BERMAN, M. E., KAVOUSSI, R. J., & HAUGER, R. L. (1996). Relationship of prolactin response to d-fenfluramine to behavioral and questionnaire assessments of aggression in personality-disordered men. *Biological Psychiatry, 40*, 157–164.

COCCARO, E. F., SIEVER, L. J., KLAR, H. M., MAURER, G., COCHRAN, K., COOPER, T. B., MOHS, R. D., & DAVIS, K. L. (1989). Serotonergic studies in patients with affective and personality disorders: Correlates with suicidal and impulsive aggressive behavior. *Archives of General Psychiatry, 51*, 318–324.

COCCARO, E. F., SILVERMAN, J. M., KLAR, H. K., HORVATH, T. B., & SIEVER, L. J. (1994). Familial correlates of reduced central serotonergic system function in patients with personality disorders. *Archives of General Psychiatry, 51*, 318–324.

COMPAS, B. E., & HAMMEN, C. L. (1994). Child and adolescent depression: Covariation and comorbidity in development. In R. J. Haggerty, L. R. Sherrod, N. Garmezy, & M. Rutter (Eds.), *Stress, risk, and resilience in children and adolescents: Processes, mechanisms, and interventions* (pp. 225–267). New York: Cambridge University Press.

CONSTANTINO, J. N., GROSZ, D., SAENGER, P., CHANDLER, D. W., NANDI, R., & EARLS, F. J. (1993). Testosterone and aggression in children. *Journal of the American Academy of Child and Adolescent Psychiatry, 32*, 1217–1222.

DABBS, J., JR., FRADY, R., CARR, T., & BESCH, N. (1987). Saliva testosterone and criminal violence in young adult prison inmates. *Psychosomatic Medicine, 49*, 174–182.

EHRENKRANZ, J., BLISS, E., & SHEARD, M. (1974). Plasma testosterone: Correlation with aggressive behavior and social dominance in men. *Psychosomatic Medicine, 36*, 469–475.

FARRINGTON, D. P. (1987). Implications of biological findings for criminological research. In S. A. Mednick, T. E. Moffitt, & S. A. Stack (Eds.), *The causes of crime: New biological approaches* (pp. 42–64). New York: Cambridge University Press.

FINKELSTEIN, J. W., SUSMAN, E. J., CHINCHILLI, V. M., D'ARCANGELO, M. R., KUNSELMAN, S. J., SCHWAB, J., DEMERS, L. M., LIBEN, L. S., AND KULIN, H. E. (1998). Effects of estrogen or testosterone on self-reported sexual responses and behaviors in hypogonadal adolescents. *Journal of Clinical Endocrinology and Metabolism, 83*, 2281–2285.

FINKELSTEIN, J. W., SUSMAN, E. J., CHINCHILLI, V. M., KUNSELMAN, S. J., D'ARCANGELO, M. R., SCHWAB, J., DEMERS, L. M., LIBEN, L. S., LOOKINGBILL, G., & KULIN, H. E. (1997). Estrogen or testosterone increases self-reported aggressive behaviors in hypogonadal adolescent. *Journal of Clinical Endocrinology and Metabolism, 82*, 2423–2438.

FISHBEIN, D. H., LOZOVSKY, D., & JAFFE, J. H. (1989). Impulsivity, aggression, and neuroendocrine responses to serotonergic stimulation in substance abusers. *Biological Psychiatry, 25*, 1049–1066.

FOWLES, D. C. (1993). Electrodermal activity and antisocial behavior. In J. C. Roy, W. Boucsein, D. C. Fowles, & J. Gruzelier (Eds.), *Electrodermal activity: From physiology to psychology* (pp. 223–238). New York: Plenum.

GLADUE, B. A. (1991). Aggressive, behavioral characteristics, hormones, and sexual orientation in men and women. *Aggressive Behavior, 17*, 313–326.

GLICKMAN, S., FRANK, L. G., DAVIDSON, J. M., SMITH, E. R., & SITTERI, P. K. (1987). Androstenedione may organize or activate sex-reversed traits in female spotted hyenas. *Proceedings of the National Academy of Sciences, 84*, 3444–3447.

GOULD, E., WOOLLEY, C. S., & MCEWEN, B. S. (1991). The hippocampal formation: Morphological changes induced by thyroid, gonadal, and adrenal hormones. *Psychoneuroendocrinology, 16*, 67–84.

HARRIS, D. B. (1957). *The concept of development.* Minneapolis: University of Minnesota Press.

HENRY, B., & MOFFITT, T. E. (1997). Neuropsychological and neuroimaging studies of juvenile delinquency and adult criminal behavior. In D. M. Stoff, J. Breiling, & J. D. Maser (Eds.), *Handbook of antisocial behavior* (pp. 280–288). New York: Wiley.

HINDE, R. A. (1987). *Individuals, relationships and culture: Links between ethology and the social sciences.* New York: Cambridge University Press.

INOFF-GERMAIN, G. E., ARNOLD, G. S., NOTTELMANN, E. D., SUSMAN, E. J., CUTLER, G. B., JR., & CHROUSOS, G. P. (1988). Relations between hormone levels and observational measures of aggressive behavior of early adolescents in family interactions. *Developmental Psychology, 24*, 129–139.

KAGAN, J. (1989). Temperamental contributions to social behavior. *American Psychologist, 44*, 668–674.

KRAMER, G. W. (1997). Social attachment, brain function, aggression and violence. In A. Raine, D. Farrington, P. Brennan, & S. A. Mednick (Eds.), *Unlocking crime: The biosocial key* (pp. 207–229). New York: Plenum.

KRUESI, M. J., HIBBS, E. D., ZAHN, T. P., KEYSOR C. S., HAMBURGER, S. D., BARTKO, J. J., & RAPOPORT, J. L. (1992). A 2-year prospective follow-up study of children and adolescents with disruptive behavior disorders: Prediction by cerebrospinal fluid 5-hydroxy indoleacetic acid, homovanillic acid, and autonomic measures. *Archives of General Psychiatry, 49*, 429–435.

KRUESI, M. J., & JACOBSEN, T. (1997). Serotonin and human violence: Do environmental mediators exist? In A. Raine, D. Farrington, P. Brennan, & S. A. Mednick (Eds.), *Unlocking crime: The biosocial key.* New York: Plenum.

LEMARQUAND, D., PIHL, R. O., & BENKELFAT, C. (1994). Serotonin and alcohol intake, abuse, and dependence: Findings of animal studies. *Biological Psychiatry, 36*, 395–421.

LERNER, R. M. (1986). *Concepts and theories of human development* (2nd ed.). New York: Random House.

LERNER, R. M., & FOCH, T. T. (1987). *Biological-psychosocial interactions in early adolescence.* Hillsdale, NJ: Erlbaum.

LINNOILA, M. (1997). On the psychobiology of antisocial behavior. In D. M. Stoff, J. Breiling, & J. D. Maser (Eds.), *Handbook of antisocial behavior* (pp. 336–340). New York: Wiley.

MAGNUSSON, D., & CAIRNS, R. B. (1996). Developmental science: Toward a unified framework. In R. B. Cairns, G. Elder, & J. Costello (Eds.), *Developmental Science* (pp. 7–30), New York: Cambridge University Press.

MAZUR, A., & BOOTH, A. (1998). Testosterone and dominance in men. *Behavioral and Brain Sciences, 21*, 353–397.

MAZUR, A., SUSMAN, E. J., & EDELBROCK, S. (1997). Sex difference in testosterone response to a video game contest. *Evolution and Human Behavior, 18*, 317–326.

MOFFITT, T. E., BRAMMER, G. L., CASPI, A., FAWCETT, J. P., RALEIGH, M., YUWILER, A., & SILVA, P. (1998). Whole blood serotonin relates to violence in an epidemiological study. *Biological Psychiatry, 43*, 446–457.

MOSS, H. B., VANYUKOV, M. M., & MARTIN, C. S. (1995). Salivary cortisol responses and the risk for substance abuse in prepubertal boys. *Biological Psychiatry, 38*, 546–555.

NOTTELMANN, E. D., INOFF-GERMAIN, G., SUSMAN, E. J., & CHROUSOS, G. P. (1990). Hormones and behavior at puberty. In J. Bancroft & J. M. Reinisch (Eds.), *Adolescence and puberty* (pp. 88–123), New York: Oxford University Press.

NOTTELMANN, E. D., SUSMAN, E. J., INOFF-GERMAIN, G. E., CUTLER, G. B., JR., LORIAUX, D. L., & CHROUSOS, G. P. (1987). Developmental processes in American early adolescents: Relationships between adolescent adjustment problems and chronological pubertal stage and puberty-related serum hormone levels. *Journal of Pediatrics, 110*, 473–480.

O'KEANE, V., MOLONEY, E., O'NEILL, H., O'CONNOR, A. ET AL. (1992). Blunted prolactin responses to d-fenfluramine in sociopathy: Evidence for subsensitivity of central serotonergic function. *British Journal of Psychiatry, 160*, 643–646.

OLWEUS, D. (1986). Aggressions and hormones: Behavioral relationships with testosterone and adrenaline. In D. Olweus, J. Block, & M. Radke-Yarrow (Eds.), *Development of antisocial and prosocial behavior: Research, theories, and issues* (pp. 51–72). Orlando, FL: Academic Press.

OLWEUS, D., MATTSON, A., SCHALLING, D., & LOW, H. (1980). Testosterone, aggression, physical, and personality dimensions in normal adolescent males. *Psychosomatic Medicine, 42,* 253–269.

OLWEUS, D., MATTSON, A., SCHALLING, D., & LOW, H. (1988). Circulating testosterone levels and aggression in adolescent males: A causal analysis. *Psychosomatic Medicine, 50,* 261–272.

PERSKY, H. K., SMITH, K., & BASU, G. (1971). Relation of psychologic measures of aggression and hostility to testosterone production in man. *Psychosomatic Medicine, 33,* 265–277.

PHOENIX, C. H., GOY, R. W., GERALL, A. A., & YOUNG, W. C. (1959). Organizing action of prenatally administered testosterone propionate on the tissues mediating mating behavior in the female guinea pig. *Endocrinology, 65,* 369–382.

PINE, D. S., WASSERMAN, G. A., COPLAN, J., FRIED, J. A., HUANG Y., KASSIR, S., GREENHILL, L., SHAFFER, D., & PARSONS, B. (1996). Platelet serotonin 2A (5-HT2a) receptor characteristics and parenting factors for boys at risk for delinquency: A preliminary report. *American Journal of Psychiatry, 153,* 538–544.

RAINE, A. (1993). *The psychopathology of crime: Criminal behavior as a clinical disorder.* San Diego: Academic Press.

RAINE, A. (1996). Autonomic nervous system and violence. In D. M. Stoff & R. F. Cairns (Eds.), *The neurobiology of clinical aggression* (pp. 145–168). Hillsdale, NJ: Erlbaum.

RAINE, A. (1997). Antisocial behavior and psychophysiology: A biosocial perspective and a prefrontal dysfunction hypothesis. In D. M. Stoff, J. Breiling, & J. Maser (Eds.), *Handbook of antisocial behavior* (pp. 289–304). New York: Wiley.

RAINE, A., BRENNAN, P., & FARRINGTON, D. P. (1997). Biosocial bases of violence: Conceptual and theoretical issues. In A. Raine, D. Farrington, P. Brennan, & S. A. Mednick (Eds.), *Unlocking crime: The biosocial key* (pp. 1–20), New York: Plenum.

RAINE, A., FARRINGTON, D., BRENNAN, P., & MEDNICK, S. A. (EDS) (1997). *Unlocking crime: The biosocial key.* New York: Plenum.

RAINE, A., REYNOLDS, C., VENABLES, P. H., & MEDNICK, S. A. (1997). Biosocial bases of aggressive behavior in childhood, In A. Raine, D. Farrington, P. Brennan, & S. A. Mednick (Eds.), *Unlocking crime: The biosocial key,* (pp. 107–126), New York: Plenum.

RAINE, A., VENABLES, P. H., & MEDNICK, S. A. (1997). Low resting heart rate at age 3 years predisposes to aggression at age 11 years: Evidence from the Mauritius Child Health Project. *Journal of the American Academy of Child and Adolescent Psychiatry, 36,* 1457–1464.

RASMUSSON, A. M., RIDDLE, M., LECHMAN, J. F., ANDERSON, G. M., & COHEN, D. J. (1990). Neurotransmitter assessment in neuropsychiatric disorders of childhood. In S. I. Weizman, A. Weizman, & R. Weizman (Eds.), *Applications of basic neuroscience to child psychiatry* (pp. 33–60). New York: Plenum.

SCHAAL, B., TREMBLAY, R. E., SOUSSIGNAN, R., & SUSMAN, E. J. (1996). Male testosterone linked to high social dominance but low physical aggression in early adolescence. *Journal of the American Academy of Child and Adolescent Psychiatry, 35,* 1322–1330.

SCHNEIRLA, T. C. (1957). The concept of development in comparative psychology. In D. B. Harris (Ed.), *The concept of development* (pp. 78–108). Minneapolis: University of Minnesota Press.

SELLS, C. W., & BLUM, R. W. (1995). Current trends in adolescent health. In R. J. DiClemente, W. B. Hansen, & L. B. Ponton (Eds.), *Handbook of adolescent health risk behavior* (pp. 5–34). New York: Plenum.

STOFF, D. M., & CAIRNS, R. B. (EDS.)(1996). *Aggression and violence: Genetic, neurobiological, and biosocial perspectives.* Mahwah, NJ: Erlbaum.

STOFF, D. M., PASATIEMPO, A. P., YEUNG, J., COOPER, T. C., BRIDGER, W. H., & RABINOVICH, H. (1992). Neuroendocrine responses to challenges with dl-fenfluramine and aggression in disruptive behavior disorders of children and adolescents. *Psychiatry Research, 43,* 263–276.

STOFF, D. M., POLLOCK, L., VITIELLO, B. D., & BRIDGER, W. H. (1987). Reduction of 3H-imipramine binding sites on platelets of conduct-disordered children. *Neuropsychopharmacology, 1,* 55–62.

SUSMAN, E. J. (1997). Modeling developmental complexity in adolescence: Hormones and behavior in context. *Journal of Research on Adolescence, 7,* 283–306.

SUSMAN, E. J., DORN, L. D., & CHROUSOS, G. P. (1991). Negative affect and hormone levels in young adolescents: Concurrent and longitudinal perspectives. *Journal of Youth and Adolescence, 20,* 167–190.

SUSMAN, E. J., DORN, L. D., INOFF-GERMAIN, G. E., NOTTELMANN, E. D., & CHROUSOS, G. P. (1997). Cortisol reactivity, distress behavior, and behavioral and psychological problems in young adolescents: A longitudinal perspective. *Journal of Research on Adolescence, 7,* 81–105.

SUSMAN, E. J., FINKELSTEIN, J. W., CHINCHILLI, V. M., SCHWAB, J. E., LIBEN, L. S., D'ARCANGELO, M. R., MEINKE, J., DEMERS, L. M., LOOKINGBILL, G., & KULIN, H. E. (1998). The effect of sex hormone replacement therapy on behavior problems and moods in adolescents with delayed puberty. *Journal of Pediatrics, 133,* 521–525.

SUSMAN, E. J., NOTTELMANN, E. D., INOFF-GERMAIN, G. E., DORN, L. D., & CHROUSOS, G. P. (1987). Hormonal influences on aspects of psychological development during adolescence. *Journal of Adolescent Health Care, 8,* 492–504.

SUSMAN, E. J., INOFF-GERMAIN, G. E., NOTTELMANN, E. D., CUTLER, G. B., LORIAUX, D. L., & CHROUSOS, G. P. (1987). Hormones, emotional dispositions and aggressive attributes in young adolescents. *Child Development, 58,* 1114–1134. (Reprinted in C. N. Jacklin, *The Psychology of Gender,* [1990]).

SUSMAN, E. J., NOTTELMANN, E. D., DORN, L. D., GOLD, P. W., & CHROUSOS, G. P. (1989). The physiology of stress and behavioral development. In D. S. Palermo (Ed.), *Coping with uncertainty: Behavioral and developmental perspectives* (pp. 17–37). Hillsdale, NJ: Erlbaum.

SUSMAN, E. J., & PONIRAKIS, A. (1997). Hormones-context interactions and antisocial behavior in youth. In A. Raine, D. Farrington, P. Brennan, & S. A. Mednick (Eds.), *Unlocking crime: The biosocial key* (pp. 251–269). New York: Plenum.

SUSMAN, E. J., WORRALL, B. K., MUROWCHICK, E., FROBOSE, C., & SCHWAB, J. (1996). Experience and neuroendocrine parameters of development: Aggressive behavior and competencies. In D. Stoff & R. Cairns (Eds.), *Neurobiological approaches to clinical aggression research* (pp. 267–289). Hillsdale, NJ: Erlbaum.

UDRY, J. R., BILLY, J. O., MORRIS, N. M., GROFF, T. R., & RAJ, M. H. (1985). Serum androgenic hormones motivate sexual behavior in adolescent boys. *Fertility and Sterility, 43,* 90–94.

UDRY, J. R., & TALBERT, L. M. (1988). Sex hormone effects on personality at puberty. *Journal of Personality and Social Psychology, 54,* 291–295.

UNIS, A. S., COOK, E. H., VINCENT, J. G., GJERDE, D. K., PERRY, B. D., MASON, C., & MITCHELL, J. (1997). Platelet serotonin measures in adolescents with conduct disorder. *Biological Psychiatry, 42,* 553–559.

VAN GOOZEN, S. H., MATTHYS, W., COHEN-KETTENIS, P. T., THIJSSEN, J. H., & VAN ENGELAND, H. (1998). Adrenal androgens and aggression in conduct disorder prepubertal boys and normal controls. *Biological Psychiatry, 43,* 156–158.

VANYUKOV, M. M., MOSS, H. B., PLAIL, J. A., MEZZICK, A. C., & TARTER, R. E. (1993). Antisocial symptoms in preadolescent boys and in their parents: Associations with cortisol. *Psychiatric Research, 46*, 9–17.

VIRKKUNEN, M., & LINNOILA, M. (1990). Serotonin in early onset, male alcoholics with violent behavior. *Annals of Internal Medicine, 22*, 327–331.

VIRKKUNEN, M., & LINNOILA, M. (1993). Serotonin in personality disorders with habitual violence and impulsivity. In S. Hodgins (Ed.), *Mental disorder and crime* (pp. 227–243). Newbury Park, CA: Sage.

VIRKKUNEN, M., RAWLINGS, R., TOKOLA, R., POLAND, R. E., GUIDOTTI, A., NEMEROFF, C., BISSETTE, G., KALOGERAS, K.,

KARONEN, S. L., & LINNOILA, M. (1994). CSF biochemistries, glucose metabolism, and diurnal activity rhythms in alcoholic, violent offenders, impulsive fire setters and healthy volunteers. *Archives of General Psychiatry, 51*, 20–27.

YALCINKAYA, T. M., SIITERI, P. K., VIGNE, J. L., LICHT, P., PAVGI, S., FRANK, L. G., & GLICKMAN, S. E. (1993). A mechanism for virilization of female spotted hyenas in utero. *Science, 260*, 1929–1931.

ZUBIETA, J. K., & ALESSI, N. E. (1993). Is there a role of serotonin in the disruptive behavior disorders? *Journal of Child and Adolescent Psychopharmacology, 3*, 11–35.

The Tipping Point   *1996*

Malcolm Gladwell

As you drive east on Atlantic Avenue, through the part of New York City that the Police Department refers to as Brooklyn North, the neighborhoods slowly start to empty out: the genteel brownstones of the western part of Brooklyn give way to sprawling housing projects and vacant lots. Bedford-Stuyvesant is followed by Bushwick, then by Brownsville, and, finally, by East New York, home of the Seventy-fifth Precinct, a 5.6-square-mile tract where some of the poorest people in the city live. East New York is not a place of office buildings or parks and banks, just graffiti-covered bodegas and hair salons and auto shops. It is an economically desperate community destined, by most accounts, to get more desperate in the years ahead—which makes what has happened there over the past two and a half years all the more miraculous. In 1993, there were a hundred and twenty-six homicides in the Seven-Five, as the police call it. Last year, there were forty-four. There is probably no other place in the country where violent crime has declined so far, so fast.

Once the symbol of urban violence, New York City is in the midst of a strange and unprecedented transformation. According to the preliminary crime statistics released by the F.B.I. earlier this month, New York has a citywide violent-crime rate that now ranks it a hundred and thirty-sixth among major American cities, on a par with Boise, Idaho. Car thefts have fallen to seventy-one thousand, down from a hundred

and fifty thousand as recently as six years ago. Burglaries have fallen from more than two hundred thousand in the early nineteen-eighties to just under seventy-five thousand in 1995. Homicides are now at the level of the early seventies, nearly half of what they were in 1990. Over the past two and a half years, every precinct in the city has recorded double-digit decreases in violent crime. Nowhere, however, have the decreases been sharper than Brooklyn North, in neighborhoods that not long ago were all but written off to drugs and violence. On the streets of the Seven Five today, it is possible to see signs of everyday life that would have been unthinkable in the early nineties. There are now ordinary people on the streets at dusk—small children riding their bicycles, old people on benches and stoops, people coming out of the subways alone. "There was a time when it wasn't uncommon to hear rapid fire, like you would hear somewhere in the jungle in Vietnam," Inspector Edward A. Mezzadri, who commands the Seventy-fifth Precinct, told me. "You would hear that in Bed-Stuy and Brownsville and, particularly, East New York all the time. I don't hear the gunfire anymore. I've been at this job one year and twelve days. The other night when I was going to the garage to get my car, I heard my first volley. That was my first time."

But what accounts for the drop in crime rates? William J. Bratton—who as the New York City Police

Commissioner presided over much of the decline from the fall of 1994 until his resignation, this spring—argues that his new policing strategies made the difference: he cites more coördination between divisions of the N.Y.P.D., more accountability from precinct commanders, more arrests for gun possession, more sophisticated computer-aided analysis of crime patterns, more aggressive crime prevention. In the Seven-Five, Mezzadri has a team of officers who go around and break up the groups of young men who congregate on street corners, drinking, getting high, and playing dice—and so remove what was once a frequent source of violent confrontations. He says that he has stepped up random "safety checks" on the streets, looking for drunk drivers or stolen cars. And he says that streamlined internal procedures mean that he can now move against drug-selling sites in a matter of days, where it used to take weeks. "It's aggressive policing," he says. "It's a no-nonsense attitude. Persistence is not just a word, it's a way of life."

All these changes make good sense. But how does breaking up dice games and streamlining bureaucracy cut murder rates by two-thirds? Many criminologists have taken a broader view, arguing that changes in crime reflect fundamental demographic and social trends—for example, the decline and stabilization of the crack trade, the aging of the population, and longer prison sentences, which have kept hard-core offenders off the streets. Yet these trends are neither particularly new nor unique to New York City; they don't account for why the crime rate has dropped so suddenly here and now. Furthermore, whatever good they have done is surely offset, at least in part, by the economic devastation visited on places like Brownsville and East New York in recent years by successive rounds of federal, state, and city social-spending cuts.

It's not that there is any shortage of explanations, then, for what has happened in New York City. It's that there is a puzzling gap between the scale of the demographic and policing changes that are supposed to have affected places like the Seven-Five and, on the other hand, the scale of the decrease in crime there. The size of that gap suggests that violent crime doesn't behave the way we expect it to behave. It suggests that we need a new way of thinking about crime, which is why it may be time to turn to an idea that has begun to attract serious attention in the social sciences: the idea that social problems behave like infectious agents. It may sound odd to talk about the things people do as

analogous to the diseases they catch. And yet the idea has all kinds of fascinating implications. What if homicide, which we often casually refer to as an epidemic, actually *is* an epidemic, and moves through populations the way the flu bug does? Would that explain the rise and sudden decline of homicide in Brooklyn North?

When social scientists talk about epidemics, they mean something very specific. Epidemics have their own set of rules. Suppose, for example, that one summer a thousand tourists come to Manhattan from Canada carrying an untreatable strain of twenty-four-hour flu. The virus has a two-per-cent infection rate, which is to say that one out of every fifty people who come into close contact with someone carrying it catches the bug himself. Let's say that fifty is also exactly the number of people the average Manhattanite—in the course of riding the subways and mingling with colleagues at work—comes into contact with every day. What we have, then, given the recovery rate, is a disease in equilibrium. Every day, each carrier passes on the virus to a new person. And the next day those thousand newly infected people pass on the virus to another thousand people, so that throughout the rest of the summer and the fall the flu chugs along at a steady but unspectacular clip.

But then comes the Christmas season. The subways and buses get more crowded with tourists and shoppers, and instead of running into an even fifty people a day, the average Manhattanite now has close contact with, say, fifty-five people a day. That may not sound like much of a difference, but for our flu bug it is critical. All of a sudden, one out of every ten people with the virus will pass it on not just to one new person but to two. The thousand carriers run into fifty-five thousand people now, and at a two-per-cent infection rate that translates into eleven hundred new cases the following day. Some of those eleven hundred will also pass on the virus to more than one person, so that by Day Three there are twelve hundred and ten Manhattanites with the flu and by Day Four thirteen hundred and thirty-one, and by the end of the week there are nearly two thousand, and so on up, the figure getting higher every day, until Manhattan has a full-blown flu epidemic on its hands by Christmas Day.

In the language of epidemiologists, fifty is the "tipping point" in this epidemic, the point at which an ordinary and stable phenomenon—a low-level flu outbreak—can turn into a public-health crisis. Every epidemic has its tipping point, and to fight an epidemic you need to understand what that point is. Take AIDS, for example. Since the late eighties, the number of people in the United States who die of AIDS every year has been steady at forty thousand, which is exactly the same as the number of people who are estimated to become infected with H.I.V. every year. In other words, AIDS is in the same self-perpetuating phase that our Canadian flu was in, early on; on the average, each person who dies of AIDS infects, in the course of his or her lifetime, one new person.

That puts us at a critical juncture. If the number of new infections increases just a bit—if the average H.I.V. carrier passes on the virus to slightly more than one person—then the epidemic can tip upward just as dramatically as our flu did when the number of exposed people went from fifty to fifty-five. On the other hand, even a small decrease in new infections can cause the epidemic to nosedive. It would be as if the number of people exposed to our flu were cut from fifty to forty-five a day—a change that within a week would push the number of flu victims down to four hundred and seventy-eight.

Nobody really knows what the tipping point for reducing AIDS may be. Donald Des Jarlais, an epidemiologist at Beth Israel Hospital, in Manhattan, estimates that halving new infections to twenty thousand a year would be ideal. Even cutting it to thirty thousand, he says, would probably be enough. The point is that it's not some completely unattainable number. "I think people think that to beat AIDS everybody has to either be sexually abstinent or use a clean needle or a condom all the time," Des Jarlais said. "But you don't really need to completely eliminate risk. If over time you can just cut the number of people capable of transmitting the virus, then our present behavior-change programs could potentially eradicate the disease in this country."

That's the surprising thing about epidemics. They don't behave the way we think they will behave. Suppose, for example, that the number of new H.I.V. infections each year was a hundred thousand, and by some heroic AIDS-education effort you managed to cut that in half. You would expect the size of the epidemic to also be cut in half, right? This is what scientists call a linear assumption—the expectation that every extra increment of effort will produce a corresponding improvement in result. But epidemics aren't linear. Improvement does not correspond directly to effort. All that matters is the tipping point, and because fifty thousand is still above that point, all these heroics will come to naught. The epidemic would still rise. This is the fundamental lesson of nonlinearity. When it comes to fighting epidemics, small changes—like bringing new infections down to thirty thousand from forty thousand—can have huge effects. And large changes—like reducing new infections to fifty thousand from a hundred thousand—can have small effects. It all depends on when and how the changes are made.

The reason this seems surprising is that human beings prefer to think in linear terms. Many expectant mothers, for example, stop drinking entirely, because they've heard that heavy alcohol use carries a high risk of damaging the fetus. They make the perfectly understandable linear assumption that if high doses of alcohol carry a high risk, then low doses must carry a low—but still unacceptable—risk. The problem is that fetal-alcohol syndrome isn't linear. According to one study, none of the sixteen problems associated with fetal-alcohol syndrome show up until a pregnant woman starts regularly consuming more than three drinks a day. But try telling that to a neurotic nineties couple.

I can remember struggling with these same theoretical questions as a child, when I tried to pour ketchup on my dinner. Like all children encountering this problem for the first time, I assumed that the solution was linear: that steadily increasing hits on the base of the bottle would yield steadily increasing amounts of ketchup out the other end. Not so, my father said, and he recited a ditty that, for me, remains the most concise statement of the fundamental nonlinearity of everyday life:

> Tomato ketchup in a bottle—
> None will come and then the lot'll.

What does this have to do with the murder rate in Brooklyn? Quite a bit, as it turns out, because in recent years social scientists have started to apply the theory of epidemics to human behavior. The foundational work in this field was done in the early seventies by the economist Thomas Schelling, then at Harvard University, who argued that "white flight" was a tipping-point phenomenon. Since that time, sociologists have actually gone to specific neighborhoods and figured out what the local tipping point is. A racist white neighborhood, for example, might empty out when blacks reach five per cent of the population. A liberal white neighborhood, on the other hand, might not tip until blacks make up forty or fifty per cent. George Galster, of the Urban Institute, in Washington, argues that the same patterns hold for attempts by governments or developers to turn a bad neighborhood around. "You get nothing until you reach the threshold," he says, "then you get *boom*."

Another researcher, David Rowe, a psychologist at the University of Arizona, uses epidemic theory to explain things like rates of sexual intercourse among teenagers. If you take a group of thirteen-year-old virgins and follow them throughout their teen-age years, Rowe says, the pattern in which they first have sex will look like an epidemic curve. Non-virginity starts out at a low level, and then, at a certain point, it spreads from the precocious to the others as if it were a virus.

Some of the most fascinating work, however, comes from Jonathan Crane, a sociologist at the University of Illinois. In a 1991 study in the *American Journal of Sociology,* Crane looked at the effect the number of role models in a community—the professionals, managers, teachers whom the Census Bureau has defined as "high status"—has on the lives of teenagers in the same neighborhood. His answer was surprising. He found little difference in teen-pregnancy rates or school dropout rates in neighborhoods with between forty and five per cent of high-status workers. But when the number of professionals dropped below five per cent, the problems exploded. For black school kids, for example, as the percentage of high-status workers falls just 2.2 percentage points—from 5.6 per cent to 3.4 per cent—dropout rates more than double. At the same tipping point, the rates of child-bearing for teen-age girls—which barely move at all up to that point—nearly double as well.

The point made by both Crane and Rowe is not simply that social problems are contagious—that non-virgins spread sex to virgins and that when neighborhoods decline good kids become infected by the attitudes of dropouts and teen-age mothers. Their point is that teen-age sex and dropping out of school are contagious in the same way that an infectious disease is contagious. Crane's study essentially means that at the five-per-cent tipping point neighborhoods go from relatively functional to wildly dysfunctional virtually overnight. There is no steady decline: a little

change has a huge effect. The neighborhoods below the tipping point look like they've been hit by the Ebola virus.

It is possible to read in these case studies a lesson about the fate of modern liberalism. Liberals have been powerless in recent years to counter the argument that their policy prescriptions don't work. A program that spends, say, an extra thousand dollars to educate inner-city kids gets cut by Congress because it doesn't raise reading scores. But if reading problems are non-linear the failure of the program doesn't mean—as conservatives might argue—that spending extra money on inner-city kids is wasted. It may mean that we need to spend even more money on these kids so that we can hit their tipping point. Hence liberalism's crisis. Can you imagine explaining the link between tipping points and big government to Newt Gingrich? Epidemic theory, George Galster says, "greatly complicates the execution of public policy. . . . You work, and you work, and you work, and if you haven't quite reached the threshold you don't seem to get any payoff. That's very tough situation to sustain politically."

At the same time, tipping points give the lie to conservative policies of benign neglect. In New York City, for example, one round of cuts in, say, subway maintenance is justified with the observation that the previous round of cuts didn't seem to have any adverse consequences. But that's small comfort. With epidemic problems, as with ketchup, nothing comes and then the lot'll.

Epidemic theory, in other words, should change the way we think about whether and why social programs work. Now for the critical question: Should it change the way we think about violent crime as well? This is what a few epidemiologists at the Centers for Disease Control, in Atlanta, suggested thirteen years ago, and at the time no one took them particularly seriously. "There was just a small group of us in an old converted bathroom in the sub-subbasement of Building Three at C.D.C.," Mark L. Rosenberg, who heads the Centers' violence group today, says. "Even within C.D.C., we were viewed as a fringe group. We had seven people and our budget was two hundred thousand dollars. People were very skeptical." But that was before Rosenberg's group began looking at things like suicide and gunshot wounds in ways that had never quite occurred to anyone else. Today, bringing epidemiological techniques to bear on violence is one of the hottest ideas in criminal research. "We've got a hundred and ten people and a budget of twenty-two million dollars," Rosenberg says. "There is interest in this all around the world now."

The public-health approach to crime doesn't hold that all crime acts like infectious disease. Clearly, there are neighborhoods where crime is simply endemic—where the appropriate medical analogy for homicide is not something as volatile as AIDS but cancer, a disease that singles out its victims steadily and implacably. There are, however, times and places where the epidemic model seems to make perfect sense. In the United States between the early sixties and the early seventies, the homicide rate doubled. In Stockholm between 1950 and 1970, rape went up three hundred per cent, murder and attempted murder went up six hundred per cent, and robberies a thousand per cent. That's not cancer, that's AIDS.

An even better example is the way that gangs spread guns and violence. "Once crime reaches a certain level, a lot of the gang violence we see is reciprocal," Robert Sampson, a sociologist at the University of Chicago, says. "Acts of violence lead to further acts of violence. You get defensive gun ownership. You get retaliation. There is a nonlinear phenomenon. With a gang shooting, you have a particular act, then a counter-response. It's sort of like an arms race. It can blow up very quickly."

How quickly? Between 1982 and 1992, the number of gang-related homicides in Los Angeles County handled by the L.A.P.D. and the County Sheriff's Department went from a hundred and fifty-eight to six hundred and eighteen. A more interesting number, however, is the proportion of those murders which resulted from drive-by shootings. Between 1979 and 1986, that number fluctuated, according to no particular pattern, between twenty-two and fifty-one: the phenomenon, an epidemiologist would say, was in equilibrium. Then, in 1987, the death toll from drive-bys climbed to fifty-seven, the next year to seventy-one, and the year after that to a hundred and ten; by 1992, it had reached two hundred and eleven. At somewhere between fifty and seventy homicides, the idea of drive-by shootings in L.A. had become epidemic. It tipped. When these results were published last fall in the *Journal of the American Medical Association,* the paper was entitled "The Epidemic of Gang-Related Homicides in Los Angeles County from 1979 Through 1994." The choice of the word "epidemic" was not metaphorical. "If this were a disease,"

H. Range Hutson, the physician who was the leading author on the study, says, "you would see the government rushing down here to assess what infectious organism is causing all these injuries and deaths."

Some of the best new ideas in preventing violence borrow heavily from the priniciples of epidemic theory. Take, for example, the so-called "broken window" hypothesis that has been used around the country as the justification for cracking down on "quality of life" crimes like public urination and drinking. In a famous experiment conducted twenty-seven years ago by the Stanford University psychologist Philip Zimbardo, a car was parked on a street in Palo Alto, where it sat untouched for a week. At the same time, Zimbardo had an identical car parked in a roughly comparable neighborhood in the Bronx, only in this case the license plates were removed and the hood was propped open. Within a day, it was stripped. Then, in a final twist, Zimbardo smashed one of the Palo Alto car's windows with a sledgehammer. Within a few hours, that car, too, was destroyed. Zimbardo's point was that disorder invites even more disorder—that a small deviation from the norm can set into motion a cascade of vandalism and criminality. The broken window was the tipping point.

The broken-window hypothesis was the inspiration for the cleanup of the subway system conducted by the New York City Transit Authority in the late eighties and early nineties. Why was the Transit Authority so intent on removing graffiti from every car and cracking down on the people who leaped over turnstiles without paying? Because those two "trivial" problems were thought to be tipping points—broken windows—that invited far more serious crimes. It is worth noting that not only did this strategy seem to work—since 1990, felonies have fallen more than fifty per cent—but one of its architects was the then chief of the Transit Police, William Bratton, who was later to take his ideas about preventing crime to the city as a whole when he became head of the New York Police Department.

Which brings us to North Brooklyn and the Seventy-fifth Precinct. In the Seven-Five, there are now slightly more officers than before. They stop more cars. They confiscate more guns. They chase away more street-corner loiterers. They shut down more drug markets. They have made a series of what seem, when measured against the extraordinary decline in murders, to be small changes. But it is the nature of nonlinear phenomena that sometimes the most modest of changes can bring about enormous effects. What happened to the murder rate may not be such a mystery in the end. Perhaps what William Bratton and In-spector Mezzadri have done is the equivalent of repairing the broken window or preventing that critical ten or fifteen thousand new H.I.V. infections. Perhaps Brooklyn—and with it New York City—has tipped.

Shame

1996

The emotions and morality of violence

James Gilligan

We know from past experience how effective the public health approach has been in our struggles against epidemics. In the nineteenth century, for example, strategies such as cleaning up the sewer system and the water supply were far more effective in the battle against diseases than all the doctors, medicines, and hospitals in the world. In addition, discovering the specific pathogen in the water supply that was killing people guided our preventive efforts both by clarifying what specifically needed to be removed from the contaminated water, and by enabling us to know when it had been removed. Identifying the causes of the various forms of disease is the first step in prevention.

Using what I have come to think of as a "germ theory" of violence, I will identify the pathogen that causes the most lethal form of pathology of our time, except that the pathogens under the microscope are not microorganisms but emotions. After I have examined them in this chapter, I will spend the remainder of this book illustrating the explanatory and predictive power of this theory by examining where the pathogens are to be found in our society at large. . . .

. . . Granted that the pathogen that causes violence exerts its destructive effects at the level of individual psychology (just as any microbe exerts its effects at the level of the organism—the individual body); and granted that the spread of this pathogen might best be stopped by . . . reforming our social and economic sys-tem and our criminal justice and penal system; isn't it still possible that the pathogen really and ultimately is biological? Is violence caused, for instance, by inerad-icable biological instincts, or by heredity, or brain damage (such as some forms of epilepsy), or drug abuse, or the biological differences between the differ-ent races, or sexes, or age groups? In this chapter I will argue that the public health approach is the appropriate model to show that violence is a contagious disease, not an hereditary one. The pathogen is psychological, not biological, and it is spread primarily by means of social, economic, and cultural vectors, not biological ones. Biological factors are far less important as causes of violence (in the instances in which they have some effect) than are social and psychological ones. For example, I will show that the hormonal patterns characteristic of the male sex exert a much less power-ful effect on the patterns of violent behavior than do certain cultural factors, . . . examining how the gender asymmetry which characterizes patriarchal cultures stimulates violence toward both men and women, much more powerfully than do the biological differ-ences between them. . . .

How might we discover what that pathogen is? My own approach to the study of violence has been to sit down and talk with violent people, and ask them why they have been violent. What I have discovered is that many of them tell me. Not all of them do. Some . . . do not tell me in words; and many may not understand why they committed the violence that sent them to prison. With them I have had to decode the symbolic language of their violent acts, like a cryptologist, or an anthropologist who tries to decipher the meaning of a bizarre and gruesome ritual. Still, surprisingly many men do tell me, simply and directly.

For example, the prison inmates I work with have told me repeatedly, when I asked them why they had assaulted someone, that it was because "he disrespected me," or "he disrespected my visit" (meaning "visitor"). The word "disrespect" is so central in the vocabulary, moral value system, and psychodynamics of these chronically violent men that they have abbreviated it into the slang term, "he dis'ed me."

Chester T., a very angry and violent inmate in his thirties, in prison for armed robbery, was referred to me because he had been yelling at, insulting, threatening, and assaulting another inmate. He had been doing this kind of thing for the past several weeks, and, off and on, for years. But he was usually so inarticulate and disorganized that neither I nor anyone else had been able to figure out what he wanted or what was fueling these repetitive acts of violence; nor had I had much success in persuading him to stop his endlessly self-defeating power struggles with everyone around him, which inevitably resulted in his being punished more and more severely. This very pattern is extremely common among men in prison. In prisons, the more violent people are, the more harshly the prison authorities punish them; and, the more harshly they are punished, the more violent they become, so that both the inmates and the prison authorities are engaged in a constantly repeated, counterproductive power struggle—the ultimate "vicious" cycle.

In an attempt to break through that vicious cycle with this man, I finally asked him "What do you want so badly that you would sacrifice everything else in order to get it?" And he, who was usually so inarticulate, disorganized, and agitated that it was difficult to get a clear answer to any question, stood up to his full height and replied with calm assurance, with perfect coherence and even a kind of eloquence: "Pride. Dignity. Self-esteem." And then he went on to say, again more clearly than before: "And I'll kill every motherfucker in that cell block if I have to in order to get it! My life ain't worth nothin' if I take somebody disrespectin' me and callin' me punk asshole faggot and goin' 'Ha! Ha!' at me. Life ain't worth livin' if there ain't nothin' worth dyin' for. If you ain't got pride,

you got nothin'. That's all you got! I've already got my pride." He explained that the other prisoner was "tryin' to take that away from me. I'm not a total idiot. I'm not a coward. There ain't nothin' I can do except snuff him. I'll throw gasoline on him and light him." He went on to say that the other man had challenged him to a fight, and he was afraid not to accept the challenge because he thought "I'll look like a coward and a punk if I don't fight him."

One hears this from violent men in one variation or another again and again. Billy A., a man in his mid-forties, came in to see me because he also had been involved in a running battle with most of the prisoners and correction officers on his cell block. He began his explanation as to why he was doing this by saying that he didn't care if he lived or died, because the screws and the other prisoners had treated him so badly—"worse than animals in zoos are treated"—that they had taken all his property away from him and he had nothing left to lose; but what he couldn't afford to lose was his self-respect, because that was all he had left, and "If you don't have your self-respect, you don't have nothing." One way they took his self-respect was that another man threw water on him, and the officer who saw this happen did nothing to intervene. So the only way Billy A. felt he could regain his self-respect was to throw water on the officer and the other prisoner—as a result of which they sentenced him to solitary confinement. Still, he remained implacable in his expression of defiance: "Death is a positive in this situation, not a negative, because I'm so tired of all this bullshit that death seems thrilling by comparison. I'm not depressed. I don't have any feelings or wants, but I've got to have my self-respect, and I've declared war on the whole world till I get it!"

This man had a very severe paranoid personality, and was extremely dangerous because of it, in prison and before he was sent to prison. Billy A. had attempted—with no provocation or warning—to murder a woman by whom he felt persecuted. Although he, like most of the violent mentally ill, was sentenced to prison rather than a mental hospital, he was clearly in a state of paranoid delusion. A letter he wrote to a judge illustrates how the prison system made this man even more paranoid and more dangerous by systematically humiliating him. He apparently wrote this letter more for the purpose of unburdening himself and clarifying his thoughts than with any intention of mailing it, although he did finally show it to a prison psychiatrist so that she could help get the situation described in it resolved.

He expresses in the letter his desperation, his feeling that the way he was being treated was bringing him closer and closer to his limit, and his sense that he was running out of time. He describes feeling spiritually and mentally defeated, and writes that he had no fear of anyone or anything, including death. Rather, he felt that his life in solitary confinement, subjected to the mental and physical torment of the guards and other inmates, was not worth living.

Billy A. goes on in the letter to describe a specific incident that took place over three days, days that he describes as having been "the most mentally debilitating" of his whole life, worse even than death. To begin with, eight other inmates had insulted him by calling him "all sorts of unmentionable names." When he told an officer that he wished to bring charges against those prisoners for harassing him, he was ordered to go to the visitors' room and strip. He was left there for half an hour, then was marched back to his cell "buck naked." The prisoners who had exposed him to this "humiliation" began "laughing and making catcalls" at him. He discovered that his cell had also been stripped of all his personal possessions, including his toilet articles (toothbrush, soap, washcloth). What especially distressed him about this was its effect on his self-esteem—that he had been unable to take a shower for more than a week, and "the way I keep my self-respect is by keeping my body clean." Finally, in desperation he began banging on his desk because "I really needed cosmetics." In retaliation, officers again ordered him to stand naked in the visitors' room for fifteen minutes while they laughed at him and made "snide remarks." He said "the laughter really troubled me because I did not see a damn thing funny." He thought they were "getting some untold pleasure" out of treating him this way. Eventually they gave him a pair of overalls, but no shoes.

He then described how they strapped him to a bench, tightened (too tightly) the handcuffs and leg irons that all inmates are required to wear whenever they leave a solitary confinement cell, opened all the windows, and opened his overalls so that his bare skin was exposed to the cold air. He said "that brought tears to my eyes. Not because he unzipped my jumpsuit but because he looked at the other hoodlums and winked his eye and smiled." They left him shivering there (this was in January) for three hours. Then an officer grinned and said, "I do not want to get mean"—

following which he stepped on and off his bare toes with his boots, as the other officers laughed at him as if he were "a freak." He went on to say that perhaps he was as dumb as everyone treated him as being, or as insane as everyone seemed to think he was—he no longer knew or cared. That was when he resolved to "declare war on the whole world" until he was able to restore his self-respect. While his self-esteem was already so damaged that he was already antisocial, it is also true that prison was only rendering someone who was already wounded, and therefore dangerous, even more so.

Some people think armed robbers commit their crimes in order to get money. And of course, sometimes, that is the way they rationalize their behavior. But when you sit down and talk with people who repeatedly commit such crimes, what you hear is, "I never got so much respect before in my life as I did when I first pointed a gun at somebody," or, "You wouldn't believe how much respect you get when you have a gun pointed at some dude's face." For men who have lived for a lifetime on a diet of contempt and disdain, the temptation to gain instant respect in this way can be worth far more than the cost of going to prison, or even of dying.

Should we really be so surprised at all this? Doesn't the Bible, in describing the first recorded murder in history, tell us that Cain killed Abel because he was treated with disrespect? "The Lord had respect unto Abel and to his offering: But unto Cain . . . he had not respect" (Gen. 4:4–5). In other words, God "dis'ed" Cain! Or rather, Cain was "dis'ed" because of Abel. The inextricable connection between disrespect and shame is emphasized by the anthropologist Julian Pitt-Rivers, who concluded that in all known cultures "the withdrawal of respect dishonors, . . . and this inspires the sentiment of shame."[1]

In maximum security prisons, this is the story of men's lives.

I have yet to see a serious act of violence that was not provoked by the experience of feeling shamed and humiliated, disrespected and ridiculed, and that did not represent the attempt to prevent or undo this "loss of face"—no matter how severe the punishment, even if it includes death. For we misunderstand these men, at our peril, if we do not realize they mean it literally when they say they would rather kill or mutilate others, be killed or mutilated themselves, than live without pride, dignity, and self-respect. They literally prefer death to dishonor. That hunger strikes in prison go on when inmates feel their pride has been irredeemably wounded, and they see refusing to eat as their only way of asserting their dignity and autonomy and protesting the injustices of which they perceive themselves to be the victims, suggests to me that Frantz Fanon[2] was expressing a psychological truth for many when he said "hunger with dignity is preferable to bread eaten in slavery."

Perhaps the lesson of all this for society is that when men feel sufficiently impotent and humiliated, the usual assumptions one makes about human behavior and motivation, such as the wish to eat when starving, the wish to live or stay out of prison at all costs, no longer hold. Einstein taught us that Newton's laws do not hold when objects approach the speed of light; what I have learned about humans is that the "instinct of (physiological) self-preservation" does not hold when one approaches the point of being so overwhelmed by shame that one can only preserve one's self (as a psychological entity) by sacrificing one's body (or those of others).

The emotion of shame is the primary or ultimate cause of all violence, whether toward others or toward the self. Shame is a necessary but not a sufficient cause of violence, just as the tubercle bacillus is necessary but not sufficient for the development of tuberculosis. Several preconditions have to be met before shame can lead to the full pathogenesis of violent behavior. The pathogenic, or violence-inducing, effects of shame can be stimulated, inhibited, or redirected, both by the presence or absence of other feelings, such as guilt or innocence, and by the specific social and psychological circumstances in which shame is experienced.

The different forms of violence, whether toward individuals or entire populations, are motivated (caused) by the feeling of shame. The purpose of violence is to diminish the intensity of shame and replace it as far as possible with its opposite, pride, thus preventing the individual from being overwhelmed by the feeling of shame. Violence toward others, such as homicide, is an attempt to replace shame with pride. It is important to add that men who feel ashamed are not likely to become seriously violent toward others and inflict lethal or life-threatening, mutilating or disabling injuries on others unless several preconditions are met.

The first precondition is probably the most carefully guarded secret held by violent men, which it took me years of working with them to recognize, precisely be-

cause they guard it so fiercely. This is a secret that many of them would rather die than reveal; I put it that extremely because many of them, in fact, do die in order not to reveal it. They try so hard to conceal this secret precisely because it is so deeply shameful to them, and of course shame further motivates the need to conceal. The secret is that they feel ashamed— deeply ashamed, chronically ashamed, acutely ashamed, over matters that are so trivial that their very triviality makes it even more shameful to feel ashamed about them, so that they are ashamed even to reveal what shames them. And why are they so ashamed of feeling ashamed? Because nothing is more shameful than to feel ashamed. Often violent men will hide this secret behind a defensive mask of bravado, arrogance, "machismo," self-satisfaction, insouciance, or studied indifference. Many violent men would rather die than let you know what is distressing them, or even that anything is distressing them. Behind the mask of "cool" or self-assurance that many violent men clamp onto their faces—with a desperation born of the certain knowledge that they would "lose face" if they ever let it slip—is a person who feels vulnerable not just to "loss of face" but to the total loss of honor, prestige, respect, and status—the disintegration of identity, especially their adult, masculine, heterosexual identity; their selfhood, personhood, rationality, and sanity.

The assertion that men do not kill for no reason is often truer the more "unprovoked" the killing appears to be. A man only kills another when he is, as he sees it, fighting to save himself, his own self—when he feels he is in danger of experiencing what I referred to earlier as "the death of the self," unless he engages in violence. Murderers see themselves as literally having no other choice; to them, "it's him or me" (or "her or me"). This is what I mean when I say that the degree of shame that a man needs to be experiencing in order to become homicidal is so intense and so painful that it threatens to overwhelm him and bring about the death of the self, cause him to lose his mind, his soul, or his sacred honor (all of which are merely different ways of expressing the same thought).

This should not be confused with the triviality of the incident that provokes or precipitates a man's shame, which is a completely different matter. In fact, it is well known to anyone who reads the newspapers that people often seem to become seriously violent, even homicidal, over what are patently "trivial" events. Paradoxically it is the very triviality of those precipitants that makes them overwhelmingly shameful.

The second precondition for violence is met when these men perceive themselves as having no nonviolent means of warding off or diminishing their feelings of shame or low self-esteem—such as socially rewarded economic or cultural achievement, or high social status, position, and prestige. Violence is a "last resort," a strategy they will use only when no other alternatives appear possible. But that should hardly be surprising; after all, the costs and risks of engaging in violent behavior are extremely high.

The third precondition for engaging in violent behavior is that the person lacks the emotional capacities or the feelings that normally inhibit the violent impulses that are stimulated by shame. The most important are love and guilt toward others, and fear for the self. What is most startling about the most violent people is how incapable they are, at least at the time they commit their violence, of feeling love, guilt, or fear. The psychology of shame explains this. The person who is overwhelmed by feelings of shame is by definition experiencing a psychically life-threatening lack of love, and someone in that condition has no love left over for anyone else.

With respect to guilt, being assaulted, or punished, or humiliated (the conditions that increase the feeling of shame) decreases the degree of guilt. That is why penance, or self-punishment, alleviates the feeling of sinfulness. Guilt, as Freud saw, motivates the need for punishment, since punishment relieves guilt feelings. That is also why the more harshly we punish criminals, or children, the more violent they become; the punishment increases their feelings of shame and simultaneously decreases their capacities for feelings of love for others, and of guilt toward others.

Freud commented that no one feels as guilty as the saints, to which I would add that no one feels as innocent as the criminals; their lack of guilt feelings, even over the most atrocious of crimes, is one of their most prominent characteristics. But, of course, that would have to be true, for if they had the capacity to feel guilty over hurting other people, they would not have the emotional capacity to hurt them.

With respect to fear, as we have seen, when the psyche is in danger, and overwhelmed by feelings of shame, one will readily sacrifice one's body in order to rescue one's psyche, one's self-respect. That is why so-called psychopaths, or sociopaths, or antisocial personalities have always been described as notably lacking in the capacity to experience fear.

A central precondition for committing violence, then, is the presence of overwhelming shame in the absence of feelings of either love or guilt; the shame stimulates rage, and violent impulses, toward the person in whose eyes one feels shamed, and the feelings that would normally inhibit the expression of those feelings and the acting out of those impulses, such as love and/or guilt, are absent.

These preconditions explain what would otherwise seem to be two anomalies. The first is that we all experience feelings of shame in one of its many forms (feelings of inferiority, rejection, embarrassment, etc.), and yet not everyone becomes violent. Most people do not commit any acts of significant violence in their entire lives, despite the fact that shame is experienced throughout the life cycle. The theory I am presenting here suggests that most people have nonviolent means available to them to protect or restore their wounded self-esteem. Or else the circumstances in which they find themselves are such that violent behavior would not succeed in accomplishing what they needed; and, finally, because most people possess capacities for guilt and empathy with others that will not permit them to engage in lethal violence except under extremely unlikely circumstances.

The second anomaly is that even the most violent people on earth, the most intractably, frequently, and recurrently assaultive or homicidal criminals or maniacs, are not violent most of the time. Their violence occurs in brief, acute crises, so that even though we have no trouble in identifying them as very dangerous people, most of the time even they hurt no one. It only happens when an incident occurs that intensifies their feelings of being humiliated, disrespected, or dishonored to the point that it threatens the coherence of the self, or when they find themselves in a specific situation from which they feel they cannot withdraw nonviolently except by "losing face" to a catastrophic degree.

I did not enter the world of the prisons knowing this. I had been taught none of it. I reached these conclusions, against much resistance, after the violent men with whom I worked, year after year, had presented me with so much cumulative evidence that these were the only terms in which I could understand them or make any sense of their otherwise unexplained, paradoxical, and anomalous behavior. Ironically, that process began with the very first man I saw in psychotherapy in the prisons, even though it took me at least a year to see what I was seeing.

WHY DO TRIVIAL INCIDENTS LEAD TO MAJOR VIOLENCE?

One reason why we have not up to now understood the causes of violence or taken them seriously is because the reasons given for acts of violence often seem so trivial, by any "objective," rational, comparative criterion, that it is very easy to overlook them. We find it hard to comprehend how a trivial incident could lead to or precipitate serious violence, because such explanations violate our sense of reality and rationality, and they violate our sense of morality and legality (our ethical sense).

Most people are not moved to wipe out their families by the kinds of incidents that provoke those who do, just as a little extra salt in the diet does not precipitate most people into pulmonary edema, or a little extra sugar, into diabetic acidosis; but for those who are predisposed to abnormal, life-threatening pathology murder can be precipitated by events and circumstances that in another person might simply be incorporated into the ongoing metabolism of everyday life. So-called "incomprehensible" crimes are only incomprehensible because of a failure to comprehend something about them that I will now try to explain.

The central role of shame in the causation of violence has been overlooked for two inextricably related reasons. First, because the magnitude of the resulting violence is so far out of proportion to the triviality of the precipitating cause that it becomes almost impossible for any normal, rational person who operates by the criteria of common sense to recognize that the cause could in fact precipitate it. And second, because an essential but seldom noticed characteristic of the psychology of shame is this: If we want to understand the nature of the incident that typically provokes the most intense shame, and hence the most extreme violence, we need to recognize that it is precisely the triviality of the incident that makes the incident so shameful. And it is the intensity of the shame, as I said, that makes the incident so powerfully productive of violence.

It is the very triviality of the incidents that precipitate violence, the kinds of things that provoke homicide and sometimes suicide, whether in family quarrels or those that occur among friends and lovers on the street or in barrooms, that has often been commented on, with surprise and perplexity—being given a "dirty look," having one's new shoes stepped on, being called a demeaning name, having a spouse or lover flirt with someone else, being shoved by someone at a bar, having someone take food off one's plate, or refuse to move a car that is blocking one's driveway; or, to refer to the cases I mention in this book: to have one's car broken down and have too little money and mechanical expertise to get it operating again; to not like the way a friend or spouse or daughter is looking at one, or the way they are talking about one; to have one's father refuse to postpone going to a movie, when one has just arrived at his house; to have to repeat a high-school geometry course; to have one's sister help herself to things from one's own room; and so on.

These kinds of things are often noticed and commented on in newspaper accounts of so-called "senseless" or "incomprehensible" murders. But it is the very triviality of the incident that provokes the violence. The more trivial the cause of the shame, the more intense the feeling of shame.

Everybody has experienced "trivial" insults that rankle. A child is teased for a difficult word mispronounced, a professional woman is asked to get the coffee. If these small incidents rankle people with power, prestige, and status, imagine their effect on people who don't have these advantages.[3] It is difficult for many of us to abandon our moral and legal way of thinking about violence, to abandon our habit of assuming that the most important question worth asking about violence is whether or not it was justified—in other words, whether the "cause" was of sufficient magnitude to excuse, or at least mitigate, the person's moral/legal guilt.

It is precisely because the incidents that cause shame are typically so "slight" or "trivial," and hence leave one feeling so ashamed to be ashamed about them, that they leave people feeling so "slight" and "trivial" and "unimportant" themselves; as the shame-sensitive person knows better than anyone else, only an unimportant and slight person would be vulnerable to, and upset over, an unimportant slight. And in fact most people are not overwhelmed by their shame over such incidents, to the point of becoming violent; that is precisely why it is so astonishing and shocking when some do—because in fact everyone experiences slights of greater or lesser degrees of seriousness, inevitably, as an ongoing part of life; everyone knows this, and yet only a small minority ever assault or kill others or themselves because of it.

There are other reasons why an apparently or objectively trivial incident may have the power to trigger or precipitate an act of violence that is out of all proportion, in its effects, to that apparent cause. And yet, while I would agree that these other explanations are valid, I would also argue that they do not invalidate, they are not mutually exclusive with, the analysis I have just offered.

For example, the precipitating incident—the trivial event that provokes an act of violence—may be the equivalent of the proverbial "last straw" that breaks the camel's back. In this interpretation, the final precipitant is only in the most trivial sense the "cause" of the violence; the far greater cause was the stress already placed on the camel's back prior to the last little bit. Or one could think of the trivial incident that precipitates violence as nothing more than the tiny spark that ignites the gasoline can, the match that is thrown onto the powder keg. And I would agree that analogies of this sort also have their place in the full description of the events that lead up to an act of violence. As Shervert Frazier[4] put it, murder is not an event but a process; the "event" we call murder is only one point in that process. Most people do not respond to trivial humiliations or embarrassments with explosive rages. So of course the person who does respond in that way must have been "primed" in some sense, or why else would he have been so "hypersensitive" to experiences that the average person would not respond to with violence?

But the point I am making is that events that are utterly trivial from any moral or legal point of view may be of the very greatest importance and significance from a medical and psychological perspective—literally, of life-and-death importance—for that is precisely their significance. They determine the difference between life and death for millions of human beings. The power of shame is inversely proportional to the magnitude of the precipitating cause; the more trivial the cause of feeling shame, the more shameful it becomes to acknowledge that that is what one feels so ashamed (and hence so enraged) about.

The germ theory of disease can help us here. We know now that the smaller the pathogen attacking us, the more dangerous and deadly it is, and the harder it is to ward off. But when Pasteur first proposed that microorganisms too small to be seen by the naked eye could be killing humans, who are incomparably larger and stronger, the idea seemed to violate every canon of common sense. And yet, what we have discovered over and over again in the course of our evolution is

that it was relatively easy to defend ourselves against the large animals of prey, the lions and tigers; and that the larger parasites like tapeworms did not kill nearly as many of us as did those too tiny even to be seen without a microscope. But vastly more dangerous were the even tinier microorganisms, the bacteria that caused such plagues as the Black Death, and the even deadlier White Death, tuberculosis. And yet we found effective ways to protect ourselves even against these microscopic organisms, compared with those that are smaller yet, the viruses: as the worldwide AIDS epidemic is showing us. Still the even deadlier challenge and much harder to defeat are the tiniest changes of all, those that occur in ultramicroscopic double helices of intra-cellular nucleic acids, producing cancer, aging, degenerative diseases of all sorts. But even those are enormous in size compared to the deadliest challenge of all, the one that endangers not only human but even all organic life; namely, the tiniest atoms in the universe, helium and hydrogen, and their even tinier subatomic particles, their nuclei: the ultimate mechanisms of nuclear weapons, hydrogen bombs.

Truly, the more tiny and trivial the cause, the more powerful, deadly, and violent the result. The Great Chain of Being may go from atoms to God, from the smallest to the greatest, but the Great Chain of Non-Being clearly goes in exactly the opposite direction.

NOTES

1. Julian Pitt-Rivers, "Honor," *International Encyclopaedia of Social Science*, pp. 503–511, 1968; pp. 503–4.

2. Frantz Fanon, *The Wretched of the Earth* (1961; New York: Grove Press, 1968), p. 208.

3. One author who was very perceptive about this aspect of shame (although she did not discuss its relevance to violence) was Helen Merrell Lynd, in her book *On Shame and the Search for Identity* (New York: Harcourt, Brace, 1958). As she put it, "It is peculiarly characteristic of these situations . . . that evoke shame that they are often occasioned by what seems a 'ridiculously' slight incident. An ostensibly trivial incident has precipitated intense emotion" (p. 40). I would add that this makes complete sense if we remember that shame is precisely the feeling that one is, either actually or potentially, ridiculous (in one's own eyes and/or the eyes of others), ridiculed, slight (i.e., unimportant, trivial, small, or weak), or slighted (by other people). In other words, the more slight one feels oneself to be, the more easily one will feel slighted. Thus,

What has occurred is harmless in itself and has no evil pragmatic outcome. It is the very triviality of the cause— . . . a gaucherie in dress or table manners, . . . a gift or witticism that falls flat, . . . a mispronounced word . . . —that helps to give shame its unbearable character (p. 40).

Because of the outwardly small occasion that has precipitated shame, the intense emotion seems inappropriate, incongruous, disproportionate to the incident that has aroused it. Hence a double shame is involved; we are ashamed because of the original episode and ashamed because we feel so deeply about something so slight that a sensible person would not pay any attention to it (p. 42).

Tolstoy and Dostoevsky also both recognized the same psychological fact and illustrated it repeatedly. In *Anna Karenina*, for example, Tolstoy says of Levin: "There had been in his past, as in every man's, actions recognized by him as bad, for which his conscience ought to have tormented him; but the memory of these evil actions was far from causing him so much suffering as these *trivial* but *humiliating* reminiscences. These wounds never healed." (*Anna Karenina*, New York: Modern Library, 1953, pp. 178–9, emphasis added). I would add only that those wounds were so humiliating precisely because they were so trivial.

4. Shervert Frazier (in conversation).

The White City and the Wild West

Buffalo Bill and the mythic space of American history, 1880–1917

Richard Slotkin

1992

A map of that "mythic space" was already available in the composed landscape of the World's Columbian Exposition of 1893, where Turner delivered his famous address. Visitors to the fair entered an elaborately structured space. Those who followed the paths prefigured in the Exposition's map and program were engaged by symbols, displays, and rituals that visualized the rapid course of American progress. The centerpiece of the Exposition, and the culmination of the typical itinerary, was the "White City," an architectural extravaganza in ersatz marble representing the pinnacle of Euro-American civilization, the original "alabaster city . . . undimmed by human tears," "a little ideal world" prophetic of "some far away time when the earth should be as pure, as beautiful, and as joyous as the White City itself." The main road from the railroad station to this New Jerusalem lay through the "Midway Plaisance," a street lined with restaurants and souvenir shops, "kootch-dance" palaces side by side with exhibition pavilions and "villages" displaying the wares and folkways of other nations, ethnological displays superintended by Franz Boas of the Smithsonian Institution cheek by jowl with sideshows of the "Wild Man from Borneo" variety.[1]

The antipode of the White City was Buffalo Bill's Wild West. Officially it was not a part of the Exposition, but its advertising did its best to obscure that fact. Moving up the Midway to the White City, the visitor passed from the Wild West to the metropolis of the future, and from the low culture to the high; from *caveat emptor* commercialism at its most blatant to a place of classical order; from displays of primitive savagery and exotic squalor to a utopia of dynamos and pillared façades. It was easy to construe the lesson implicit in the tour. More than one journalist observed that the exhibits featuring more "advanced" races (Celts and Teutons) tended to appear closer to the White City end of the Midway while the non-White Dahomeans and American Indians appeared at the farthest remove from utopia. "You have before you the civilized, the half-civilized, and the savage worlds to choose from—or rather, to take one after the other." The stroller "up" the Midway traces "the sliding scale of humanity" according to a Social-Darwinist program. Reporter Denton Snider advised his readers that "undoubtedly the best way of looking at these races is to behold them in ascending scale, in the progressive movement. . . . In that way we move in harmony with the thought of evolution."[2]

There actually were two ways of walking the grounds and reading the parable. The novelist and social critic William Dean Howells took the tour-program as a prophecy of the nation's eventual transcendence of the present crisis of social and industrial relations. The association of African and Indian "savages" with the rampant vulgarity of American commercialism suggested an analogy between primitive savagery and "primitive" capitalism. The "pitiless economic struggle" characteristic of the regime of *laissez-faire* was (for Howells) a commercial variant of "savage war," in which the objective is to either exterminate or utterly subjugate one's business rivals and compel the proletariat to "work or starve." In Howells' view, the aims of revolutionary socialism were no true alternative to but a vengeful mirror-image of the extermination/subjugation scenarios of monopoly capitalism. But the White City suggested a third alternative: that at the end of this course of savage war lay the potential for a utopia in which the relations of labor and capital (and of rival capitalists) would be cooperative rather than competitive.[3]

Most interpreters of the Midway/White City map did not share Howells' genteel socialism. Henry Adams saw the White City as symbolic of the ultimate and necessary triumph of capital over labor, of managerial intelligence over the licensed anarchy of democracy. The esthetic and moral "harmony" of the White City expressed the victory of capitalists as a class. In the struggles of the previous two years, "All one's friends, all one's best citizens had joined the banks to force submission to capitalism" and in the process had carried the country from a "simply industrial" condition to a fully "capitalistic, centralizing [and] mechanical" order, where democratic practices and moral imperatives were out of place. The achievement of the White City was proof that if a modern society is "to be run at all, it must be run by capital and capitalistic methods." Adams' particular targets are the constituents of the Populist and labor movements ("Southern and Western farmers in grotesque aliance with city day-laborers"); but his more general point is to discredit "democracy" and advance the claims of managerial ideology.[4]

To Frederick Douglass, the aging "Black Lion of Abolition," the White City was a "whited sepulchre," concealing the reality of the nation's abandonment of Negroes to impoverishment, social segregation, and political degradation, maintained and enforced by a re-crudescence of Reconstruction's "White terror"—the lynch mob, the Klan raid. Black labor had been excluded from the work gangs that raised the White City, and the historical presence and labor of non-Whites was represented only in the "repulsive" and degrading displays of savagery in the Midway. The American Indians in the Midway were the objects of overt hostility from the White crowds; the Dahomeans were greeted with more derision than hostility, but mass-circulation journals like *Harper's Weekly* used them to reinforce White contempt for Negroes. A series of caricatures titled "Coons at the Exposition" offered grotesque stereotypes of American Blacks in ecstasy over the antics of their "cannibal" brethren.[5]

The relation of White workingmen to the White City was little better. Although organized labor had cooperated with the Exposition's planners, its contribution was presented as an entirely dependent and morally insignificant one as measured against the contributions of capital and management. Labor leader Eugene Debs complained that while labor was "quite willing to admit the alliance between money and labor in the accomplishment of great undertakings," it was unwilling to accept the premise that the rights and deserts of capital were prior to those of labor. Debs (quoting Lincoln) asserted that labor is "prior to capital" and gives it its value, and that therefore "greater credit is due to labor, because it is the creator of capital."[6] But Debs found employers impervious to the moral claims of "free labor" republicanism and unwilling to treat labor as a negotiating partner, let alone as an "ally." The building of the White City followed two decades of slack employment, the increasing oppressiveness of workplace conditions, declining standards of living, and intensified union-busting. It coincided with the Panic of 1893 and a national business contraction, with "labor wars" in Colorado and in the Coeur d'Alenes and the Homestead steel mills, and with the Johnson County War of small ranchers against a private army hired by the big cattleman of the Wyoming Stock Growers' Association. In the year following the Exposition, Debs himself would lead the railroad workers in the greatest "labor war" of the century, the "Pullman Strike"—which would be broken by federal troops (including regiments drawn away from Indian country) sent by President Cleveland over the objections of Illinois' pro-labor governor Altgeld. During that strike the White City itself would mysteriously burn to the ground.

While it was certainly possible to imagine the White City as a utopia of civility and shared progress, it was easier, in that depression year, to dismiss its "whiteness" as a utopian illusion and to imagine the inescapable city of the future as a grim and squalid Chicago divided between its few rich and its many poor, the prospective site of an apocalyptic confrontation between "civilization" and the forces of savagery and regression—between the social imperatives that Mark Twain had called "the spirit of progress" and "the spirit of massacre."[7]

Turner and Roosevelt saw "history" as the ineluctable flow of persons and events in a single, determinate direction toward the White City. But in fact, traffic on that symbolic road flowed both ways. Frederick Remington, the painter of western scenes and journalist, was in principle as committed as his friend Theodore Roosevelt to progressive politics. But he was more like Turner in the emphasis he placed on what was lost in the passing of the Frontier. On his visit to the Exposition (which he wrote up for *Harper's Weekly*) he turned away from the modernity symbolized by the White City to walk the Midway in the direction of the "Wild West," which for him fulfilled "its mission as a great educator." What it teaches "the universal Yankee nation" is the value of "that part of the world which does not wear Derby hats and spend its life in a top-and-bottom tussel with a mortgage bearing eight per cent." Despite his contempt for non-Whites, on the Midway Remington found glimpses of a real and somehow regenerative "savagery" beneath the fakery of costumes and carnival hype. The sight of an armed Turk awakens "the sense of admiration . . . that if you were not an American you would be a savage of that type." It is contact with savagery, the White City's opposite, that Remington craves as an antidote to civilized discontents, and thus his itinerary is to do "all the savages in turn, as every one else must do who goes there, and Buffalo Bill's besides, where I renewed my first love."[8]

"Buffalo Bill's Wild West" was for more than thirty years (1883–1916) one of the largest, most popular, and most successful businesses in the field of commercial entertainment. The Wild West was not only a major influence on American ideas about the frontier past at the turn of the century; it was a highly influential overseas advertisement for the United States during the period of massive European emigration. It toured North America and Europe, and its cre-ator William F. Cody became an international celebrity on terms of friendship with European royalty and heads of state as well as with the leaders of the American military establishment. With its hundreds of animals, human performers, musicians, and workmen, its boxcars filled with equipment and supplies, it was nearly as large and difficult to deploy as a brigade of cavalry; and since it went everywhere by railroad (or steamship) it was far more mobile. The staff of the Imperial German army was said to have studied Buffalo Bill's methods for loading and unloading trains in planning their own railroad operations.[9]

William F. Cody, "Buffalo Bill," was the creator, leading manager, and until the turn of the century the chief attraction of the Wild West. Over the years he worked with a series of partners whose ideas and decisions influenced the development of the enterprise and who often assumed a greater share of control over the design of the production. But it was Cody and his ideas that provided the most coherent and continuous line of development. Certainly Cody himself was primarily responsible for establishing the Wild West's commitment to historical authenticity and to its mission of historical education.[10]

The management of Cody's enterprise declared it improper to speak of it as a "Wild West show." From its inception in 1882 it was called "The Wild West" (or 'Buffalo Bill's Wild West'), a name that identified it as a "place" rather than a mere display or entertainment. A "Salutatory" notice that was added to the Program of the 1886 Wild West and that appeared in every Program thereafter, declared:

It is the aim of the management of Buffalo Bill's Wild West to do more than present an exacting and realistic entertainment for public amusement. Their object is to PICTURE TO THE EYE, by the aid of historical characters and living animals, a series of animated scenes and episodes, which had their existence in fact, of the wonderful pioneer and frontier life of the Wild West of America.[11]

The Wild West was organized around a series of spectacles which purported to re-enact scenes exemplifying different "Epochs" of American history: "Beginning with the Primeval Forest, peopled by the Indian and Wild Beasts only, the story of the gradual civilization of a vast continent is depicted." The first "Epoch" displayed Plains Indian dancers but represented them as typical of the woodland Indians who greeted the colonists on the Atlantic shore (a tableau depicting either the Pilgrims at Plymouth Rock or John Smith and Pocahontas). The historical program then cut abruptly to the settlement of the Great Plains, displaying life on a Cattle Ranch, a grand "Buffalo Hunt," and Indian attacks on a settler's cabin and the "Deadwood Stage." Between these episodes were displays of "Cowboy Fun," of trick riding and roping, and spectacular feats of marksmanship by featured performers like Annie Oakley ("Little Sure Shot") and Buffalo Bill himself.

The historical rationale of the Wild West was carefully described in the elaborate Program; but all visitors, whether or not they purchased the Program, were admonished that "Attention to the Orator [announcer] will materially assist the spectator in his grasp of the leading episodes." The authenticity of the historical program was vouched for by letters of recommendation from leading military officers published in the Program and by the use of figures publicly recognized as actual participants in the making of history: "The hardships, daring, and frontier skill of the participants" was "a guarantee of the faithful reproduction of scenes in which they had actual experience." Over the years Buffalo Bill managed to engage such figures as Sitting Bull and Geronimo as performers, and a great number of Indians who had fought against the cavalry less than a year before, as well as the services of regular units of the U.S. Cavalry to perform opposite them. But the center of the Wild West, as both premier performer and veteran of historical reality, was Buffalo Bill himself:

The central figure in these pictures is that of THE HON. W. F. CODY (Buffalo Bill), to whose sagacity, skill, energy, and courage . . . the settlers of the West owe so much for the reclamation of the prairie from the savage Indian and wild animals, who so long opposed the march of civilization.[12]

It is the most extraordinary tribute to the skill of the Wild West's management that its performances were not only accepted as entertainment but were received with some seriousness as exercises in public education. The leading figures of American military history, from the Civil War through the Plains Indian wars, testified in print to the Wild West's accuracy and to its value as an inculcator of patriotism. Brick Pomeroy, a journalist quoted in the 1893 Program, used the newly minted jargon of the educational profession to praise Buffalo Bill with the wish that "there were more progressive educators like William Cody in this world."

He thought the show ought to be called "Wild West Reality," because it had "more of real life, of genuine interest, of positive education . . . [than] all of this imaginary Romeo and Juliet business.[13]

But despite its battery of authentications, the Wild West wrote "history" by conflating it with mythology. The re-enactments were not re-creations but reductions of complex events into "typical scenes" based on the formulas of popular literary mythology: the "Forest Primeval" Epoch reads colonial history in Fenimore Cooper's terms, the Plains episodes in terms drawn from the dime novel. If the Wild West was a "place" rather than a "show," then its landscape was a mythic space in which past and present, fiction and reality, could coexist; a space in which history, translated into myth, was re-enacted as ritual. Moreover, these rituals did more than manipulate historical materials and illustrate an interpretation of American history; in several rather complex ways, the Wild West and its principals managed not only to comment on historical events but to become actors themselves.

STAGING REALITY: THE CREATION OF BUFFALO BILL, 1869–1883

Until 1869 William F. Cody had been a minor actor on the stage of western history, a frontier jack of all trades who had been a farmer, teamster, drover, trapper, Civil War soldier in a Jayhawk regiment, Pony Express rider, stagecoach driver, posse-man, meat hunter for the Kansas Pacific Railroad, and army scout. The upsurge of interest in the Plains that accompanied construction of the transcontinental railroads brought numerous tourists to the region, along with journalists, gentlemen-hunters in search of big game, and dime novelists looking for material. There was money to be made guiding such folk on hunting trips, and fame (and more hunting clients) to be garnered when the trips were written up back east. Wild Bill Hikock and Cody both achieved early fame in this way—Hikock as the subject of an article written for *Harper's Weekly* by G. W. Nichols, Cody in a Ned Buntline dime novel published in 1869 and a stage melodrama that premiered in 1871. Cody had already acquired a word-of-mouth reputation as an excellent scout and hunting guide, but after 1869 his newly acquired dime-novel celebrity made his name familiar to a national audience while linking it with spectacular and utterly fictitious adventures.[14]

In 1871 James Gordon Bennett, Jr. editor and publisher of the New York *Herald,* hired Cody as a guide on one of the more elaborate celebrity hunting trips of the era (covered of course by a *Herald* reporter). The next year General Philip Sheridan named Cody to guide the hunting party of the Russian Grand Duke Alexis, who was in the country on a state visit. General Custer was among the American notables who accompanied the expedition, and Cody again figured prominently in the elaborate press coverage of the event. When Bennett, hoping to capitalize on this journalistic coup, urged Cody to visit him in New York, Cody, encouraged by his army superiors and friends, seized the opportunity to cash in on his celebrity. The visit was a turning point in Cody's career. In New York he took control of the commodity of his fame by forming a partnership with Ned Buntline for the production of Buffalo Bill dime novels and stage melodramas.[15]

Between 1872 and 1876 Cody alternated between his career as scout for the U.S. Cavalry and his business as star of a series of melodramas in the East. His theatrical enterprises prospered, so that by 1873 he was able to form his own "Buffalo Bill Combination" with Wild Bill Hikock and "Texas Jack" Omohundro. The plays themselves were trivial and the acting amateurish, but the success of the "Combination" was evidence of the public's deep and uncritical enthusiasm for "the West," which could best be addressed through a combination of dime-novel plots and characters with "authentic" costumes and personages identified with "the real thing."[16] A poster for the 1877 edition of the "Combination" advertises the main feature of the entertainment as a performance of *May Cody or, Lost and Won,* a melodramatic variation on the captivity narrative featuring both Indians and Mormons as villains. An actor impersonates Brigham Young, but two genuine Sioux chiefs appear in the play and in the dance performances "incidental" to the drama which "introduc[e] . . . THE RED MEN OF THE FAR WEST." The play featured a series of "THRILLING TABLEAUX" in "Panoramic Order" depicting the famous "Mountain Meadows Massacre" (in which Mormon fanatics abet Indians in wiping out a wagon train) and recreations of "Brigham Young's Temple" and his residence, the "Lion House." In addition, there was a display of marksmanship by the "Austin Brothers."[17] The mixture of elements anticipates the program of the Wild West, although these performances did not approach the scale of ambition of the Wild West.

Combinations of this kind were not unprecedented. In 1766 Major Robert Rogers, the famous commander of "Rogers' Rangers," wrote and staged in London a tragedy titled *Ponteach* based on the recently concluded Indian war and featuring authentic Indian dances, costumes, and performers. In the 1830s and 40s George Catlin's touring "Indian Gallery" combined displays of Indian dances with exhibitions of paintings. Similar authenticating devices were used by the various panoramas and cycloramas—aggregations of painted scenes with a narrative program of one sort or another—which toured the country between 1850 and 1890.[18] Cody's creative achievement was his organization of these various conventions and media around a coherent set of plot formulas drawn from a literary mythology whose structure and language were (by 1870) well developed and widely recognized.

Cody's continuing engagement with the Plains wars strengthened his claims of authenticity and in 1876 provided him with a windfall of public celebrity. The outbreak of war with the Sioux and Northern Cheyenne had been expected since the failure in 1875 of government attempts to compel the sale of the Black Hills, and preparations for three major expeditions into "hostile" territory began in the winter of 1875–76. Cody was then performing in the East, but his services as Chief of Scouts had been solicited for the column led by General Crook out of Fort Fetterman. His theatrical engagements prevented his joining Crook, whose command moved out in May, but General Carr had also been trying to recruit him for the 5th Cavalry. On the 11th of June Cody announced from the stage in Wilmington, Delaware, that he was abandoning "play acting" for "the real thing" and within the week had joined the 5th (now commanded by Merritt) in southern Wyoming. While the three main columns under Terry (with Custer), Gibbon, and Crook attempted to encircle and engage the main body of "hostiles," Merritt's command moved toward the Black Hills to prevent additional warriors from leaving the reservation to join Sitting Bull and Crazy Horse. On July 7 the command learned of Custer's disastrous defeat at the Little Big Horn (June 25). Ten days later a battalion of the 5th under Captain Charles King—a professional soldier with literary ambitions—caught up with a band of off-reservation Cheyenne which it had been tracking. In a rapid sequence of ambush and counter-ambush, Cody and his scouts engaged a small party of Cheyenne outriders. Merritt and his officers, watching from a low hill, saw Cody and one of the Cheyenne meet—seemingly in mutual surprise—and spontaneously fire. They saw Cody's horse stumble and fall (the horse had stepped in a prairie-dog hole). But Cody extricated himself from the saddle, took a kneeling position and deliberate aim, and shot the charging Indian from his horse. Then, as King's advancing troopers swept by him, he walked over to the corpse, scalped it, and waved his trophy in the air.[19]

This scene became the core of the Buffalo Bill legend and the basis of his national celebrity. Before the year was over he would be hailed as the man who took "The First Scalp for Custer." It would be claimed that the Indian he slew was a leading chief, one of the leaders at the Little Big Horn, and even that Cody had announced his intention to avenge Custer from the stage in Wilmington—an absurdity, since the Last Stand did not occur until three weeks later. Although the fight itself had elements of exciting drama, it was in fact a small skirmish in a dusty, empty place. The Signal Corps observer who had the best sight of the action said only that he saw "just a plain Indian riding a calico or a paint pony." But the dusty details were immediately transformed into melodrama by Captain King, whose literary ambitions reveal themselves in the sensational prose with which he described Cody's fight in his official report (and later in a book). King's report was given to a correspondent of Bennett's New York *Herald*, who added his own touches.[20]

But the chief mythologizer of the event was Cody himself. That winter he would star in *The Red Right Hand; or, The First Scalp for Custer*, a melodrama in which the "duel" with Yellow Hand becomes the climax of a captivity-rescue scenario. (The story also appeared as a dime novel.) Moreover, it seems that Cody approached the event itself with just such a performance in mind. On the morning of July 17, knowing that the proximity of the Indians made battle probable, Cody abandoned his usual buckskin clothing for one of his stage costumes, "a brilliant Mexican *vaquero* outfit of black velvet slashed with scarlet and trimmed with silver buttons and lace"—the sort of costume that dime-novel illustrations had led the public to suppose was the proper dress of the wild Westerner. He was preparing for that moment when he would stand before his audience, wearing the figurative laurels of the day's battle and the *vaquero* suit, able to declare with truth that he stood before them in a plainsman's authentic garb, indeed the very clothes he had worn

when he took "The First Scalp for Custer." In that one gesture he would make "history" and fictive convention serve as mutually authenticating devices: the truth of his deeds "historicizes" the costume, while the costume's conventionality allows the audience—which knows the West only through such images—to recognize it as genuine.[21]

Cody also displayed the relics of Yellow Hand—a warbonnet, shield, gun, and scabbard, and the dried human scalp itself—outside theaters in which the "Combination" performed, as indisputable evidence of his claims as a historical actor. Their impact was augmented when the display was condemned as obscene and barbaric by the self-appointed keepers of public morality. Even the anti-Indian and sensation-loving *Herald* criticized Cody; and in Boston, where Friends of the Indian were numerous and influential, the "Combination" was banned. The effect of this action was roughly the same as the banning of *Huckleberry Finn* by the Boston Library Committee—or better, the advertisement in that novel of "The Royal Nonesuch" as a show to which women and children would not be admitted. It brought sensation-seekers to the show in droves.[22]

Here the Buffalo Bill signature appears clearly, in its characteristic confusion of the theatrical and the historical or political. The deed itself is unquestionably real—blood was shed, a battle won—but the event is framed by fiction from start to finish, and its ultimate meaning is determined by its re-enactment in the theater. It soon ceased to matter that the skirmish itself was unimportant, that Yellow Hand was not a war chief, that his was not "the first scalp for Custer," and that the "revenge" symbolized by Cody's deed had no counterpart in reality (since the Indians he fought had not been at the Little Big Horn). Cody and Custer had been associated very briefly (and distantly) in the Southern Plains war of 1867–70 and the Grand Duke's buffalo hunt; but beginning in 1876 Cody (and his associates) exploited his connection with the Last Stand and Custer by every means available. In addition to *The Red Right Hand*, Cody appeared as Custer's trusty scout in a series of dime novels, figuring (in terms of the Cooper formula) as a kind of Hawkeye to Custer's Duncan Heyward, or Kit Carson to Custer's Fremont. The Yellow Hand fight was transformed from a lucky accident to the climax of a program of deliberate revenge.[23] The "duel" itself became even more sensational in Cody's 1879 autobiography, where it culminated in a hand-to-hand knife fight. The image of Cody waving the scalp in the air was reduced to a crude woodcut, which became a permanent feature of Buffalo Bill iconography. It appeared in most of the Wild West Programs, as a dime-novel cover, a poster, and—elaborated in oils—as the center piece of several heroic paintings.[24]

After 1876, the Buffalo Bill mythology developed in two forms, the dime novel and (after 1882) the Wild West. Buffalo Bill was the protagonist of more dime novels than any other character, real or fictional, with the possible exception of Jesse James.[25] But after 1883, the Wild West was the basis of his fame and of his increasingly legendary status. The early Buffalo Bill dime novels (written by Cody himself, as well as by Buntline and Prentiss Ingraham) were based (loosely) on his frontier exploits; they placed Buffalo Bill in the traditional pantheon of frontier heroes derived from Boone, Hawkeye, Carson, and Crockett. But the Wild West framed Cody in a mythic spectacle that enlarged and transformed this legend; eventually even his dime novels celebrated him as the proprietor of the Wild West rather than as an old-time plainsman.[26]

THE WILD WEST AND THE RITUALIZATION OF AMERICAN HISTORY

The Wild West itself was Buffalo Bill's most important mythmaking enterprise, the basis of his later celebrity and continuing dime-novel fame. It began in 1882 as part of a July 4th celebration in Cody's hometown of North Platte, Nebraska. Its primary features were rodeo-like displays of cowboy skills—feats of marksmanship, riding and roping, horse races—framed by an elaborate parade. To this base were added elements that would appeal to the larger audience that had been drawn to the Buffalo Bill Combination, scenes "typical" of Western life, developed around a standard melodramatic narrative scheme like the captivity/rescue. Many of these scenes were drawn from Buffalo Bill dime novels: the attack on the Deadwood Stage, the Pony Express display, the raid on the settler's cabin, the "Grand Buffalo Hunt on the Plains." As in the Combination, authentic historical celebrities were recruited to lend credibility and to exploit public curiosity: Major North and his Pawnee battalion were early favorites, Sitting Bull appeared in 1884–85, *metis* veterans of the Riel Rebellion in Canada (1886). In later years the Wild West would feature appearances by Rain-in-the-Face ("the Indian who killed Custer"), chief Joseph of the Nez Perce, Jack Red Cloud (son of a famous Sioux chief), and (over the years) assorted sheriffs and outlaws whose exploits had attracted the attention of the newspapers.

In 1886 the Wild West program was reorganized and publicized as "America's National Entertainment," an exemplification of the entire course of American history. The different scenes were now presented as typifications of the stages of frontier history, although their content remained virtually unchanged. Costumes and staging were more elaborate, and spectacular "special effects" were developed, including a prairie fire, a "sunset," and a "cyclone." The historical program, and the patriotic purpose Cody and his associates claimed for it, was intended to distinguish the Wild West from other competing circus-like displays, to give it the gloss of respectability, and thus to increase its appeal. The emphasis on the Wild West as an exemplification of American history may also have been a response to the prospect of the company's first European tour (1887–89). The appeal of the Wild West could only be enhanced by representing it as a kind of cultural embassy from the New World to the Old—an exhibition of all the exotic American types that had piqued European imaginations since Cooper, if not since Columbus.[27]

Cody's stage persona was now given a more elaborate definition designed to present him as the archetype of the American frontier hero. Buffalo Bill is presented in the 1886 program as "the representative man of the frontiersmen of the past." He is "full of self-reliance" and acquires scientific knowledge through the necessary operations of his native curiosity and engagement with nature. The history of the West is, in effect, his "lengthened shadow." "His history, in fact, would be almost a history of the middle West, and, though younger, equalling in term of service and personal adventure Kit Carson, Old Jim Bridger, California Joe, Wild Bill, and the rest of his dead and gone associates." (It is worth noting that with the exception of Bridger, all these figures were as well or better known as dime-novel heroes than as historical personages.) "Young, sturdy, a remarkable specimen of manly beauty, with the brain to conceive and the nerve to execute, Buffalo Bill *par excellence* is the exemplar of the strong and unique traits that character-ize a *true American frontiersman*."

Like Hawkeye, Cody is of plebeian and agrarian origins, and therefore knows the value of democracy and hard work. As "a child of the plains" he inevitably becomes acquainted with the wilderness and with the strife endemic to a border region. These "accident[s] of birth and early association" bring him (like Hawk-eye) into intimate knowledge of the wilderness and the "implacable Indian foe." But where Hawkeye is dis-abled by this knowledge from living a civilized life, Cody's experience prepares him "to hold positions of trust, and without his knowing or intending it made him nationally famous." Cody is able to overcome Hawkeye's limitations because he possesses an in-nately superior moral character whose powers go be-yond the primitive virtues of loyalty, truthfulness, and honor. Cody's virtues are those of the manager and commander as well as the soldier. Though "full of self-reliance" he also possesses the moral qualities as-sociated with a good ship's captain. His incipient gen-tility is attested by the certified "gentlemen" of the officer corps, particularly Generals Carr and Merritt, who praise him as "a natural gentleman in his manners as well as character." Sherman figuratively ennobles Cody as "King of them all [that is, the array's scouts]." As Cody aged and prospered, the Wild West Programs would present him as a patriarchal figure of fully achieved gentility, a natural aristocrat able and worthy to socialize with royalty.[28]

In 1886 a re-enactment of "Custer's Last Fight" was added to the Wild West's repertoire, and it even-tually became not only the most spectacular of the "epochs" but the center of a reorganized program. Un-like the "Deadwood Stage" and "Settler's Cabin" scenes, "Custer's Last Fight" referred to a struggle that was not yet concluded. Geronimo was still on the warpath, and most of the Indians who had fought Custer were still alive, living uneasily on the reserva-tion. Sitting Bull, widely regarded as the mastermind who had defeated Custer, was still regarded as a dan-gerous man.

Cody's presumption in addressing "history" so di-rectly was of course defended by his insistence that the re-creation was authentic. A visitor to his tent noted that he had only three books in his working li-brary, a scrapbook of newspaper clippings, a manual of infantry drill and tactics, and Frederick Whittaker's 1876 illustrated biography of Custer. He dressed his cowboys as cavalrymen and gave them proper drill:

the Indians he hired were Sioux and Cheyenne and in-cluded veterans of the Custer fight. But the "script" which these "genuine" performers played out ended in fictional melodrama, with Cody's appearance on the stricken field before a transparency bearing the motto, "Too late." The suggestion that Cody might have saved the Boy General had he only arrived in time was pure "dime novel": Cody never approached the battle-field in 1876 and had had no knowledge of (or concern with) Custer's column until July 7.

Cody's role in the "Last Fight" was at once self-ab-negating and self-aggrandizing. The suggestion that he might have saved Custer implicitly inflates his heroic stature. But by featuring Custer, the "Last Fight" sce-nario reduces Buffalo Bill to the role of elegiac com-mentator—he no longer acts the role of avenger taking the "first scalp for Custer." However, for this new role Cody invested himself with a new imagery and aura which suggested that he was not merely Custer's would-be savior and chief mourner, but in some sense a reincarnation of the heroic general. He had begun to cultivate a resemblance to Custer, doffing his famous *vaquero* suit for fringed buckskins, high boots, and a broad-brimmed hat, like those worn by Custer in pop-ular illustrations of the battle. He trimmed his long hair, beard, and mustache to resemble Custer's. The difference between his dark hair and Custer's famous "Long Yellow Hair" was not at all jarring in an age of black-and-white illustration, and as Cody's hair be-came gray with age the difference disappeared. The most significant testimony to this resemblance was provided by Mrs. Custer herself, who saw the Wild West in New York (probably in 1886 or 1887). In her book, *Tenting on the Plains* (1887), she endorses the observation of Eliza, the Negro maid who had served the Custers since the Civil War, "Well, if he ain't the 'spress image of Ginnel Custer in battle, I never seed anyone that was."[29]

Cody was of course well aware that his representa-tion of historical events was inaccurate, to say the least. But he seems to have been sincere in his belief that the Wild West offered something like a poetic truth in its representation of the frontier. His "truth" had two as-pects, the pictorial and the moral. Within the bound-aries of good showmanship he strove for the greatest accuracy of detail, because he wished to memorialize a period of his own life (and a regional life style) which he loved and from which time increasingly estranged him. This concern pervades both his public and private writing and shows as well in the care and consideration with which he treated his Indian performers and the wild animals used in the Wild West.

But the "moral truth" of the frontier experience, which the Wild West emphasized, was its exemplification of the principle that violence and savage war were the necessary instruments of American progress. Even the displays of marksmanship by Buffalo Bill and Annie Oakley are framed by the Program's essay on "The Rifle as an Aid to Civilization":

[While it is] a trite saying that "the pen is mightier than the sword," it is equally true that the bullet is the pioneer of civilization, for it has gone hand in hand with the axe that cleared the forest, and with the family Bible and school book. Deadly as has been its mission in one sense, it has been merciful in another; for without the rifle ball we of America would not be to-day in the possession of a free and united country, and mighty in our strength.[30]

Cody's sense of the Wild West's educational and ideological mission was sharpened during the European tours he undertook between 1887 and 1892 by the responses of European audiences and reviewers to this "typically American" display.[31] He was therefore well prepared for the opportunity presenced by the World's Columbia Exposition to place the Wild West in a strategic and profitable situation. His success is attested by the achievement of over a million dollars in profit from the 1893 season.

The show itself was larger and more spectacular than anything seen in America before, and Cody undertook an elaborate schedule of promotional activities to arouse and maintain public interest in the Wild West. The Program was far more elaborate in its framing of the Wild West's historical significance: the re-enactment of the Last Stand would feature performers on both sides who had been actual participants in the battle; other survivors, even Mrs. Custer, were "consulted" in preparing the performance.[32] Cody himself now appeared as a hero whose authenticity as "representative man" was attested in two different worlds. Wild West posters and publicity blazoned his triumphs before "The Crowned Heads of Europe" his success as an exemplar and promoter of American values and national prestige on the world stage. In addition, his reputation as a genuine Indian-fighter had been recently refreshed by his service during the Ghost Dance troubles of 1890, first as a would-be peacemaker between his friends Sitting Bull and General Miles, then (after the massacre of Ghost Dancers at Wounded Knee) as a member of Miles' staff.[33]

Cody exploited his connection with Wounded Knee in advertising posters which alternately showed him overseeing the making of the Peace Treaty and charging into a village to rescue White captives. He also reconstructed on the Wild West's grounds the cabin in which Sitting Bull lived at the time of his assassination. There Cody staged a ceremony of reconciliation between cavalry and Indian veterans of the two battles of the Little Big Horn and Wounded Knee. The Crow scout "Curly," famed as the last man to see Custer alive, shook hands with Rain-in-the-Face, the Sioux who had been unjustly accused (and immortalized by Longfellow) as the man who killed Custer and then cut out his heart and ate it. These ceremonies of reconciliation transfer to the Indian wars a species of public ritual previously associated with the reunion on Civil War battlefields of veterans of the Blue and the Gray. Of course, the Indian-war ceremony occurs not on the "real" battleground of the West, but on the fictive "battleground" of Buffalo Bill's Wild West. Nonetheless, the ideological import of the gesture was seriously intended. Cody framed the ceremony with a set of overt appeals for reconciliation between Whites and Indians. The Program now represented the "savages" as "The Former Foe—Present Friend—the *American*."[34]

This shift in the role assigned to the Indians signaled a change in the historical scenario enacted by the Wild West. In its original appearance, "Custer's Last Fight" had concluded the Wild West's first half and was followed by scenes displaying the peaceful life and labor of the ranch and mining camp.[35] In the new program, the "Last Fight" was the last act in the Wild West and served as an elegy for the *entire* period of American pioneering. What followed it was a vision of America assuming a new role on the world stage as leader of the imperial powers: the parade of the "Congress of the Rough Riders of the World."

THE RITUAL FRONTIER AND THE SANCTIFICATION OF IMPERIALISM

The term "Rough Riders" had been applied to western horsemen in dime novels before 1880, and Cody had adopted it during the European tours to characterize his White American horsemen. But the appeal of the "Last Fight" sequence had led the partners to increase the representation of military drill in the show. Military drill and trick-riding teams had been a regular feature of American fairs and circuses since the antebellum period; such teams, drawn from regular army units, performed in European nations as well. Cody had obtained the services of such units in the countries visited by the Wild West between 1887 and 1892, and he brought a selection of them back to the States to provide an exotic and appropriately international note for the Columbian Exposition edition of "America's National Entertainment." These units were added to the American cowboys and cavalrymen to form the "Congress of the Rough Riders of the World," whose grand parades opened and closed each performance and whose displays of horsemanship became featured acts between the historical scenes.[36]

But the full "Congress" included other kinds of horsemen as well. Beside each American or European unit rode representative horsemen of the non-White tribesmen recently conquered by the imperial powers. At the head of this "Congress" rode Buffalo Bill, identified in the Program and by his precedence not merely as "Prince of the Border Men" or "King of the Scouts" but as "King" of all the Rough Riders of the World. His pre-eminence was not merely personal but national, signifying the American assumption of a leading role in world affairs.[37]

The display of horseback skill by the Rough Riders was partly a development of the intervals of "Cowboy Fun" that had previously punctuated the staged "epochs." But the intensity with which the Wild West now pursued its historical program soon invested even these performances with ideological symbolism. If the "Custer's Last Fight" re-enactment was the funeral rite of the old frontier, then the Rough Rider contests and pageants were the ritual games that looked to the beginning of a new age. This suggestion was given substance in the greatly expanded text of the 1893 Program. All the standard features of earlier Programs were reprinted, but new essays were added, including one by Colonel T. A. Dodge, which declared that the warfare of the future would primarily engage civilized nations with barbarian races, and that therefore the American Indian-fighting cavalry would become the "pattern of the cavalry of the future." Cody's abortive embassy to Sitting Bull on the eve of Wounded Knee becomes the basis for an assertion that Buffalo Bill's mission offers a model for international diplomacy that might well be applied to the approaching Franco–German crisis over Alsace-Lorraine.[38]

Buffalo Bill's potential as a force for "universal peace" is attested by the ease with which he can move from the "red wastes" to the "great cities of Europe," and from the mixture of military skill and peace-making wisdom he brings to both settings. In moving rapidly between Dakota and Europe in 1890–91, Buffalo Bill had had a unique opportunity to contrast the might of industrial civilization with the lowest ebb of savagery; a similar experience (the Program suggests) is available to the visitor who passes freely between the Wild West and the White City of the Columbian Exposition. But as the essay explores the meaning of this juxtaposition, an ideological embivalence appears in the historical role assigned to violence. On the one hand, the contrast between Wild West and White City teaches us that the war-making spirit is an attribute of man in the "savage" state and that civilization requires the substitution of peace for war. But though war is denigrated as an end of civilization, it is exalted as a means to peace and progress.[39]

The basic thesis of this historical argument is essentially the same as that of Theodore Roosevelt's advocacy of American imperialism in "Expansion and Peace" (1899): that "peace" can be imposed on the "barbarian races" of the world only by the armed force of a superior race. The history of the Frontier has been one of Social-Darwinian racial warfare, "years of savage brutal wars conducted with a ferocious vindictiveness foreign to our methods." It was inevitable that the Red man's "once happy empire (plethoric in all its inhabitants needed)" be "brought thoroughly and efficiently under the control of our civilization, or (possibly more candidly confessed) under the Anglo-Saxon's commercial necessities."

[T]he practical view of the non-industrious use of nature's cornucopia of world-needed resources and the inevitable law of the *survival of the fittest* must "bring the flattering unction to the soul" of those—to whom the music of light, work, and progress, is the charm, the gauge of existence's worth, and to which the listless must harken, the indolent attend, the weak imbibe strength from—whose ranks the red man must join, and advancing with whose steps march cheerily to the tune of honest toil, industrious peace, and placid fireside prosperity.[40]

But the Wild West's historical ritual has a double effect: it signals the integration of the Indian into "American" life as "Former Foe—Present Friend"; and it re-awakens the "savagery" or warrior spirit that is latent in the civil sons and daughters of the heroes who won the West. A reporter for the Chicago *Inter-Ocean* declared that the 1893 performance of the "Deadwood Stage" and "Last Fight" scenes made him aware of "the aboriginal ancestor" that remains "in us after all the long generations of attempted civilization and education." David A. Curtis, writing in the *Criterion* in 1899, notes that the spectacle of "struggle and slaughter" produces effects like those of Roosevelt's "Strenuous Life": it awakens "the hidden savage," the "ineradicable trace of savage instinct" that lurks in the blood of all the great fighting races; it "stirs the thinnest blood and brightens the dullest eye" in the genteel Anglo-Saxon audience. The only "lack is that this . . . fighting is not real."[41]

As if anticipating Curtis' regret that its bloodshed was not "real," the publicity of the Wild West after 1893 asserted more strenuously than ever its claim to "realism" of detail. And it linked that claim to a more assertive statement of its educational mission. The copy attached to the Wild West's gigantic billboard of 1898–99 offered the clearest and most assertive definition yet of the Wild West's educational purpose. The billboard invited the viewer to "LOOK UPON THIS PICTURE" and behold "the VARIOUS EPOCHS of AMERICAN HISTORY, from the primitive days of savagery up to the memorable charge of San Juan hill," all reproduced with "remarkable fidelity." This epic image and performance is not merely a "show" but:

AN OBJECT LESSON

Differing as it does from all other exhibitions, BUFFALO BILL's WILD WEST and CONGRESS OF ROUGH RIDERS OF THE WORLD stands as a living monument of historic and educational magnificence. Its distinctive feature lies in its sense of realism, bold dash and reckless abandon which only arises from brave and noble inspiration. It is not a "show" in any sense of the word, but it is a series of original, genuine and instructive object lessons in which the participants repeat the heroic parts they have played in actual life upon the plains, in the wilderness, mountain fastness and in the dread and dangerous scenes of savage and cruel warfare. It is the only amusement enterprise of any kind recognized, endorsed and contributed to by Governments, Armies and Nations; and it lives longest in the hearts of those who have seen it most often, since it always contains and conveys intensely inspiring ideas and motives, while its programme is a succession of pleasant surprises and thrilling incidents.[42]

The function of realistic presentation is first to memorialize the real past in a "living monument," preserving not only the details of past heroism but also the moral truth that such "bold dash" can only arise "from brave and noble inspiration." Having memorialized true history, the Wild West's next task is to trans-

late history into useful instruction, conveying to the public "intensely inspiring ideas and motives." Whatever these ideas may be, they are of a kind that is "endorsed and contributed to" by the official apparatus of the modern nation-state, for the Wild West's ultimate distinction is that it is the only "amusement enterprise" to be "recognized" by "Governments, Armies and Nations"—as if the fictive "place" that was Wild West had achieved something like diplomatic recognition.

The Wild West's conflation of the Frontier Myth and the new ideology of imperialism was fully achieved in 1899 when "Custer's Last Fight" was replaced by the "Battle of San Juan Hill," celebrating the heroism of Theodore Roosevelt—whose First Volunteer Cavalry regiment was best known by its nickname, "The Rough Riders."

By incorporating Roosevelt into the Wild West, Cody would seem to have conferred the very honor Roosevelt sought through his energetic hunting, soldiering, and writing about the West: a place in the pantheon of frontier heroes whose founder is Daniel Boone and whose latest demigod is Buffalo Bill. But Roosevelt somewhat ungenerously denied his own real indebtedness to the Wild West for the regimental sobriquet of "Rough Riders." The 1899 Wild West Program reprints an exchange of letters between Cody and Roosevelt in which the latter denies having borrowed the name from Cody's Congress, asserts that it was spontaneously bestowed by local citizens, and that Roosevelt himself was unaware of its reference. This (as Cody rather modestly points out) was hardly credible, given the fame of the Wild West (which Roosevelt had certainly attended), and the presence of some of the show's cowboys and Indians among Roosevelt's recruits. Roosevelt offered a mollifying compliment to the effect that, however it had come about, he was proud to share the name with those "free fearless equestrians, now marshalled under the leadership of the greatest horseman of all."[43]

This exchange of names between the agents of real-world imperialism and the myth-makers of the Wild West defines a significant cultural and political relationship. In performances, programs, and posters "San Juan Hill" was substituted for "Custer's Last Fight." It was the climactic act of the Wild West performances in 1899, where it was hailed as a battle equal in significance to Lexington and Concord, opening a new phase of America's history. The colossal 108-sheet billboard poster that advertised the 1899 Wild West restated the point in panoramic iconography. The poster illustrations recapitulated the historical "epochs" from "Attack on the Settler's Cabin" at the extreme left, to "San Juan Hill" at the extreme right; and the whole was flanked with "bookends" of text that proclaimed the Wild West as "An Object Lesson" in American history. This substitution of an imperial triumph carried off in "Wild West" style, for a ritual re-enactment of the catastrophe that symbolized the end of the old frontier, completes the Wild West's evolution from a memorialization of the past to a celebration of the imperial future.

By the terms of this exchange, the categories of myth shape the terms in which the imperial project will be conceived, justified, and executed; and the imperial achievement is then re-absorbed into the mythological system, which is itself modified by the incorporation of the new material. One effect is clearly that of glorifying the "imperialization" of the American republic. But the use of Wild West imagery also has the effect of "democratizing" the imperial project—or rather, of investing it with a style and imagery that powerfully (if spuriously) suggests its "democratic" character. The point is visual in an 1898 Wild West poster, "Art Perpetuating Fame," which compares Buffalo Bill with Napoleon Bonaparte as "The Man on Horseback of 1796" and "The Man on Horseback of 1898." At the center of the poster is the black-cloaked figure of an old woman sitting before an easel: the French portrait painter Rosa Bonheur, who had painted well-known equestrian portraits of both the Emperor Napoleon and Buffalo Bill. The two men sit on white horses, facing away from the center. Napoleon (on the left) is in uniform, but he appears paunchy and looks sidelong out of the frame; Buffalo Bill is slightly more frontal, appears young and trim, has an erect seat, and wears civilian clothes. The identification of the two as "Men on Horseback" associates them not only as soldiers but as embodiments of the military principle in civil politics. The tag-phrase comes from French politics in the Dreyfus-case era to identify the conservative glorification of the army and hopes for a military assumption of civil power. The American version of this political type is youthful rather than decrepit, and "civilian" rather than military; his triumphs (the caption tells us) are peaceful rather than violent (Wild West show tours vs. military conquests). If Buffalo Bill is America's "Man on Horseback," then the American empire will be a peaceful and republican one, animated by youthful energy rather than depressed by tyrannical conservatism.[44]

Cody's version of the charge of Roosevelt's Rough Riders of course featured "the very heroes and horses who were a part of what they portray" and invited comparison with the Last Stand by describing the attack as a forlorn-hope assault against superior numbers. But those who followed "Roosevelt and the flag" reverse the Custer scenario and triumph over the lurking Spaniards. It is also characteristic of Cody that he emphasizes the ethnic and racial diversity of the soldiers, "white, red, and black," who followed Roosevelt. In this too the showman's generosity exceeds the politician's: Roosevelt does not emphasize the Indian presence in the regiment and denigrates the contributions of the Black regular infantry regiment that charged beside the Rough Riders.[45]

Both the historical program of the Wild West and its intricate play with racial categories were transformed by its identification with imperialism. In subsequent years the military elements of the show—the cavalry drills, the display of new-model artillery and Gatling guns (a feature of the San Juan Hill attack)—began to eclipse traditional western elements like "Cowboy Fun." The racialist ideology implicit in the inter-ethnic horse races is more sharply defined. In the 1893 Program the non-White riders had been identified by nationality; in 1894, as "primitive riders"; and in 1898 their competition (always one of the first five acts) was described in terms suggestive of Social Darwinism as "The Race of Races."[46]

Percival Pollard, writing in the *Criterion,* found that the outbreak of the war with Spain made the familiar scenes of the Wild West seem "freighted with a newer meaning." If the Spaniards doubted we were "a manly race . . . they might do themselves good by viewing Buffalo Bill and his cohorts." Wartime performances of the Wild West were announced in terms that deliberately echoed war news: the headline "City Capitulated" was used for both the surrender of Santiago and the announcement of a Wild West box-office triumph. In an interview given to the New York *World* in April 1898, Cody proposed a "Wild West" approach to the coming war: "Buffalo Bill Writes On 'How I Could Drive the Spaniards from Cuba with 30,000 Indians" assisted by such chieftains of the "noble but dying race" as Geronimo and Jack Red Cloud. Wild West performers were sought out for pro-war quotations, and Buffalo Bill made the show an instrument of propaganda by developing acts featuring Cuban and Filipino insurgents. However, these "savages" of the new frontier presented some of the same ideological difficulties as the old. When the Filipinos rebelled against an American takeover of the islands in 1899, the Filipinos in the Wild West became objects of hostility. Buffalo Bill himself was identified as "an avowed expansionist" and was quoted as declaring that the American Indian "Outranks the Filipino in the Matter of Common Honesty." His assertion that "Their Fighting Tactics Are Almost Identical" affirmed the polemical position taken by Roosevelt and other expansionists, that the Filipinos were "savages" like the "Apache." In a reversion to mythic origins, they were replaced in the San Juan Hill re-enactment by the Wild West's Indians.[47]

In 1901 San Juan Hill was replaced by a more recent imperial adventure, "The Battle of Tien-Tsin," a re-enactment of the capture of that city by the Allied army that suppressed China's "Boxer" Rebellion and rescued the "captives" in the Peking Legation Quarter. In this performance, the Indians assumed the role of the Boxers, and the Wild West's soldiers and cowboys represented all of White civilization storming the citadel, from which flew "the Royal Standard of Paganism . . . proudly defiant of the Christian world," to place there "the Banners of civilization." After running "Tien-Tsin" in 1901–2, Cody reprised "San Juan Hill" in 1903–4, taking advantage of (and perhaps assisting) Roosevelt's run for re-election.[48]

It is appropriate that Cody and Roosevelt should have benefitted materially from each other's activities because their contributions to American culture were complementary and mutually reinforcing. The Wild West's casting of its cowboys and Indians as Rough Riders and Cubans, Allies and Boxers, makes literal and visible the central tenet of Roosevelt's racialist myth of progress: that the struggle between Red Men and White on the American frontier is the archetype and precedent for the world-wide struggle between "progressive" and "savage" or "regressive" races that shaped the modern world. The Wild West performed as myth and ritual the doctrines of progressive imperialism that Roosevelt promulgated as ideology. By dramatizing the imperial frontier as the logical extension of the continental frontier, Cody lent mythological support to Roosevelt's Frontier Thesis: that the American "savage" and his Anglo-Saxon foe were the archetypes of the universal and world-wide opposition of

"progressive" and "regressive" races; and that empire was merely the continuation of Wild West democracy "by other means."[49]

After 1905 the Wild West fell on hard times: managerial errors were made, competition with other shows was keener, rising costs made the business less profitable. Cody believed that the Wild West had erred in allowing its traditional "frontier" elements to fall out of use. He revived "Custer's Last Fight" in 1905, and in 1907 offered a new frontier spectacle, "The Battle of Summit Springs," which featured Cody killing a chief named Tall Bull one year after the Little Big Horn. The plot and materials of this scene were a rehash of elements already present in the "Last Fight" and "Settler's Cabin" scenarios. In 1908 he attempted to appropriate specifically Western current events by staging a version of "The Great Train Hold-Up and Bandit Hunters of the Union Pacific"—a subject which had already been treated with great public fanfare in the new medium of moving pictures, in Edwin Porter's *The Great Train Robbery* (1903). Porter "scooped" Cody on this theme, and the success of movies would prove fatal to the Wild West, because films could provide similar excitements without having to maintain the huge stock of transportation, livestock, performers and technicians, or the geographical mobility that the Wild West required.[50]

From 1908 to its end in 1917 the Wild West suffered a marked decline in profitability and popularity. There was no longer a margin to cushion the effects of bad management. Cody lost control of the enterprise but remained obligated to it, because the failure of his other investments severely reduced his private fortune. Through the years of its commercial decline, the various managements of the Wild West persisted in following the practice established in 1899 of incorporating current events and concerns. For instance, in 1916, on the eve of Cody's death, the entire program was built around the theme of "Preparedness" for entry into the Great War. But its particular way of presenting those concerns had become hackneyed and predictable; other forms, like the movies, now had greater novelty, and the power to shock and surprise.[51]

But the ultimate financial failure of Buffalo Bill's Wild West should not obscure its unparalleled success as a myth-making enterprise. From 1885 and 1905 it was the most important commerical vehicle for the fabrication and transmission of the Myth of the Frontier. It reached large audiences in every major city and innumerable smaller ones throughout the United States. The period of its European triumph coincided with the period of massive immigration to America. As many immigrants testified, the Wild West was the source of some of their most vivid images and expectations of the new land. The Wild West also invented and tested the images, staging, and themes and provided much of the personnel for the motion-picture Western, which succeeded to its cultural mantle.

Nothing reveals Cody's skill and achievement as a myth-maker better than his manner of leaving the stage. His last years were marked by a seemingly endless cycle of "Farewell Performances." His personal motives for undertaking this long good-bye were undoubtedly financial and egotistical. But they also reveal the extent to which the Myth of the Frontier had become independent of the historical reality that produced it. In Cody's farewell tours, that nostalgia for the "Old West" that had been the basis of his first success gave way to a new form of the sentiment: a nostalgia not for the reality, but for the myth—not for the frontier itself, but for the lost glamour of Buffalo Bill's Wild West.[52]

NOTES

1. Trachtenberg, *Incorporation*, ch. 7; R. Reid Badger, *The Great American Fair: The World's Columbian Exposition and American Culture*, pp. 105–7.

2. Robert W. Rydell, "The World's Columbian Exposition of 1893: Racist Underpinnings of a Utopian Artifact," *JAC* (1978), pp. 253–75.

3. William Dean Howells, "Letters of an Altrurian Traveller," in Neil Harris, ed., *The Land of Contrasts, 1880–1901*, pp. 345–62.

4. Trachtenberg, *Incorporation*, pp. 219–20.

5. *Ibid.*, pp. 266–7; see any issue of *Harper's Weekly*, July-August, 1893.

6. Trachtenberg, *Incorporation*, p. 222.

7. Slotkin, *Fatal Environment*, pp. 523–30.

8. Frederic Remington, "A Gallop Through the Midway," *The Complete Writings of Frederic Remington*, pp. 111–3; Ben Merchant Vorpahl, *With the Eye of the Mind: Frederic Remington and the West*, p. 109. "Strange fierce-looking negroes who have evidently not felt the elevating influence of South Carolina pass you. . . . One of Diamond Dick's Indians shuffles along . . . [his] weak-kneed, intoed plod . . . speaks of the thorough horseman when he 'hits the flat.'"

9. Don Russell, *The Wild West: A History of Wild West Shows*, chs. 1–2, esp. p. 40.

10. On Cody's "authorship," see Don Russell, *The Lives and Legends of Buffalo Bill*, ch. 20, and pp. 300–2, 370.

11. "An Object Lesson" appeared at the right margin of a 108-sheet billboard poster advertising the "Wild West" of 1898. It was,

at the time, the largest poster ever displayed. See Jack Rennert, *100 Posters of Buffalo Bill's Wild West*, rear endpaper and p. 16.

12. John M. Burke, "Salutatory," *Buffalo Bill's Wild West*, 1886 and 1887 (hereafter *BBWW*, [date]). All citations from Wild West programs are from copies in the Western History Department, Denver Public Library. I am grateful to Eleanor M. Gehres and the library staff for their assistance.

13. Pomeroy quoted in "Hon. W. F. Cody—'Buffalo Bill,' " a biographical sketch which included sections on Cody as "A Legislator" and "As an Educator." The sketch and its appendices appear virtually unchanged in most Wild West Programs to 1900. See *BBWW*, 1886 for the first version; also 1887 and 1893. The encomia from Cody's former military commanders appeared in different forms over the years, although the same letters of commendation were always cited, and General Carr's praise of Cody as "the King of them all" was given special emphasis. See "Letters of Commendation from Prominent Military Men," *BBWW*, 1886; and *BBWW*, 1887, which adds letters from European royalty and American notables.

14. Russell, *Lives and Legends*, pp. 149–55, 181–4.

15. *Ibid.*, pp. 181–4 and chs. 11–13. On the Grand Duke's hunting party, see Slotkin, *Fatal Environment*, pp. 407–9.

16. Russell, *Lives and Legends*, ch. 15.

17. In Richard Slotkin, "The Wild West," in Leslie Fiedler, et al., *Buffalo Bill and the Wild West*, p. 30.

18. Slotkin, *Regeneration*, pp. 235–40; Robert Rogers, *Ponteach; or, The Savages of America* (1766); William H. Truettner, *The Natural Man Observed: A Study of Catlin's Indian Gallery*; George Catlin, *Catalogue of Catlin's Indian Gallery of Portraits, Landscapes, Manners and Customs, Costumes, etc.* (1837); Peter H. Hassrick, "The Artists," in Fiedler, *Buffalo Bill and the Wild West*, pp. 16–26; John Mix Stanley, *Scenes and Incidents of Stanley's Western Wilds* (1854); A. J. Donnelle, ed., *Cyclorama of Custer's Last Battle* (1889).

19. Russell, *Lives and Legends*, ch. 17.

20. *Ibid.*; *New York Herald*, July 23, 1876, p. 1; Charles King, *Campaigning with Crook, and Stories of Army Life*, esp. pp. 36–43.

21. Russell, *Lives and Legends*, pp. 230–2.

22. *Ibid.*, p. 254; *New York Herald*, August 11, 1876, p. 3.

23. Russell, *Lives and Legends*, pp. 407–8; William F. Cody, *The Crimson Trail; or, Custer's Last Warpath, A Romance Founded Upon the Present Border Warfare as Witnessed by Hon. W. F. Cody*, New York Weekly (1876); —— *Kansas King; or, The Red Right Hand*, Saturday Journal (1876), Beadle's Half-Dime Library, 1877; Prentiss Ingraham, *Buffalo Bill's Grip; or, Oath-Bound to Custer*, Beadle's Weekly, 1883; —— *Buffalo Bill's Big Four; or, Custer's Shadow*, Beadle's Weekly, 1887; —— *Buffalo Bill with General Custer*[?]; Grace Miller White, *Custer's Last Fight: A Thrilling Story Founded Upon the Play of the Same Name* (1905).

24. "Death of Yellow Hand . . . ," *BBWW*, 1886; Cody, *The Crimson Trail*; illustrations in Fiedler et al., *Buffalo Bill and the Wild West*, pp. 12, 31; John Rennert, *100 Posters of Buffalo Bill's Wild West*, "A Close Call," p. 56. William F. Cody, *The Life of Hon. William F. Cody, Known as Buffalo Bill, the Famous Hunter, Scout and Guide: An Autobiography* (1879), esp. pp. 343–4. Another example of the "First Scalp" woodcut is the frontispiece to [George A. Custer], *Wild Life on the Plains and Horrors of Indian Warfare . . .* (1891).

25. Russell, *Lives and Legends*, p. 413; Prentiss Ingraham, *Adventures of Buffalo Bill from Boyhood to Manhood: Deeds of Daring and Romantic Incidents in the Life of Wm. F. Cody, the Monarch of the Bordermen*, Beadle's Boys' Library No. 1; reprinted

in E. F. Bleiler, ed., *Eight Dime Novels*, pp. 91–105, esp. chs. 1, 29. Ingraham sketches the whole of this development in a single volume, moving through a standard set of dime-novel adventures (loosely based on fact) to Cody's achievement of business success with his Combination—which Ingraham treats as evidence of Cody's ability to surpass that fatal limitation of the Hawkeye-model hero. Cody prided himself on his transformation from frontiersman to modern businessman. In his introduction to Helen Cody Wetmore, *Last of the Great Scouts,* Zane Grey asserts that Cody later characterized his work for the Kansas Pacific as that of a "railroad builder" rather than a buffalo-hunter.

26. Russell, *Lives and Legends*, chs. 20, 27, pp. 494–503; and see for example Prentiss Ingraham, *Buffalo Bill and the Nihilists* (1910), in Western Americana Collection, Beinecke Library, Yale University.

27. Russell, *Lives and Legends*, chs. 21–22; —— *Wild West Shows*, pp. 1–42; Sarah J. Blackstone, *Buckskins, Bullets, and Business*, chs. 2, 3, 5.

28. "Hon. W. F. Cody—'Buffalo Bill,'" *BBWW*, 1886; and see the succeeding sections on his careers as 5th Cavalry scout; legislator, educator, etc.

29. Russell, *Wild West Shows*, p. 25; Elizabeth B. Custer, *Tenting on the Plains* (1887), pp. 46–7. Compare also the poster "Buffalo Bill to the Rescue" Rennert, *100 Posters*, p. 68) with the illustrations of "The Battle of the Washita" in Custer, *My Life on the Plains*, and Richard Irving Dodge, *Our Wild Indians: Thirty-Three Years Experience Among the Red Men of the Great West. . . .* Cody's "Last Fight" was much imitated by competing shows: see Russell, *Wild West Shows*, pp. 31–2, 45.

30. "The Rifle . . . ," *BBWW*, 1886, 1893.

31. Russell, *Lives and Legends*, ch. 23; Billington, *Land of Savagery*, pp. 48–56, 328–9. Although he returned for a brief American tour in 1888, his main purpose was to recruit more Indian performers and replenish his livestock; the program for this tour omitted the more spectacular "epochs" he had mounted in Europe. *BBWW*, 1888. A British cartoon shows Buffalo Bill as a conqueror of the Old World, leading a Roman triumph, "The Triumph of the West," *Life*, 12/15/87, in Fiedler, *Buffalo Bill and the Wild West*, p. 44.

32. Russell, *Lives and Legends*, ch. 26. Cody published a newspaper to report on his activities and publicize his promotional schemes. See *Cody Scrapbooks*, Vol. 2, esp. pp. 3, 8, 12, 21, 35, 37, 97 100, 102–7, in Denver Public Library.

33. Russell, *Lives and Legends*, ch. 25; Stanley Vestal, *Sitting Bull, Champion of the Sioux*, ch. 26.

34. *BBWW*, 1893, pp. 10, 31–4, 49–50; *Cody Scrapbooks*, Denver Public Library, Vol. 2, pp. 3, 8, 12, 21, 35, 37, 97–100, 102, 107.

35. *BBWW*, 1887.

36. Russell, *Lives and Legends*, p. 370, identifies John M. Burke as the originator of the idea.

37. *BBWW*, 1887 refers to "American Rough Riders." *BBWW*, 1893, "Programme" and "Salutatory," pp. 2, 4. See also Russell, *Lives and Legends*, 370–85; and —— *Wild West Shows*, 61–72. See also posters of the parade, Rennert, *100 Posters*, "A Perfect Illustration . . .," and "The Maze," pp. 101, 104.

38. *BBWW*, 1893, Dodge on p. 36; Cody and Wounded Knee, pp. 32–6, 38–45, 49–53; Alsace on 60–1.

39. "A Factor of International Amity—Carnot," poster of 1893, in Rennert, *100 Posters*, p. 106.

40. *BBWW*, 1893, pp. 60–2. It is worth noting that the Wild West's is a "kinder, gentler" version of the Roosevelt thesis, in that it envisions the integration of Native Americans into American life.

This relatively liberal position on racial politics is a consistent one for Cody, who incorporated both Native Americans and African Americans as "American soldiers" in his imperial pageants.

41. "At the Fair," *Chicago Inter-Ocean*, Sept. 12, 1893, p. 3; David A. Curtis, "The Wild West and What It Lacks," *Criterion*, in *Cody Scrapbook*, vol. 7, p. 183.

42. Rennert, *100 Posters*, rear endpaper.

43. *BBWW*, 1899, pp. 32–6.

44. Rennert, *100 Posters*, p. 64. The image of Cody in this poster is far more youthful than that in the Bonheur portrait, p. 63.

45. Cody and Saulsbury attempted to mount a "Black" Wild West in 1895, which toured the South as "Black America," but the experiment was a failure. Russell, *Wild West Shows*, p. 60. Cody also included African-American troopers of the 9th and 10th Cavalry in his San Juan Hill re-enactment (*BBWW*, 1899, p. vi), and treated their exploits as comparable to those of the White Rough Riders. Cody's relatively liberal treatment of this aspect of the race question contrasts with Roosevelt's account of the battle, which denigrates the achievements and character of the Negro regiments. Compare Roosevelt's attitudes toward the African-American troops who fought with his Rough Riders, below, Ch. 4, and in Dyer, *Theodore Roosevelt and the Idea of Race*, pp. 100–1. On Cody's treatment of Indians, see Vine Deloria, Jr., "The Indians," in Fiedler, *Buffalo Bill and the Wild West*, pp. 45–56; John G. Neihardt, *Black Elk Speaks*; Blackstone, *Buckskins*, pp. 85–8.

46. Rennert, *100 Posters*, "The Race of Races [1895]," p. 65; "Wild Rivalries of Savage, Barbarous and Civilized Races [1898]." It has been argued that the "Race of Races" and the imperialist theme was not Cody's idea; and certainly his control of the Wild West program was weakened after 1895. However, he remained the Wild West's featured performer, and his public statements affiliated him with the imperialist cause—though according to Russell, "his heart was not really in it," *Lives and Legends*, p. 417.

47. *Cody Scrapbooks*, Vol. 7, pp. iii, vii, xx, xxiv–v, 54–5, 65, 69, 73, 95, 97, 104, 107.

48. Ibid., *BBWW*, 1901, "Programme." See also the parallel depictions of frontier and imperial heroes in magazines published by Cody's associates, esp. *The Rough Rider* 1:1 (1900), p. 6; 3:4 (1901), cover and p. 2; *Frontier Guide* 2:3 (1901).

49. *BBWW*, 1901, "Programme." The Wild West rationalized imperialism as an extension of the old "westering" frontier by the simple method of substituting new "imperial" figures in places traditionally recognized as belonging to frontier heroes. The simplest form of this substitution appears in the covers of *The Rough Rider* magazine, published from 1899 to 1907 by Cody's associates. The first issue's cover showed "The Historic Rough Riders of the Sixties"—Sheridan, Cody, Custer and Sitting Bull—but much of the sixteen pages of text was devoted to San Juan Hill. A 1901 issue with a similar cover design replaced Sheridan, Cody and Custer with Cody, Roosevelt, and heroes representing both sides of the Boer War—Petrus Joubert, a Boer guerrilla, and Baden-Powell, the British war-hero and founder of the Boy Scouts. These were "Men Who Have Led the Rough Riders of the World in Civic and Military Conquests." Another, similar publication paired Pawnee Bill (another Wild West impresario) with figures from the Filipino insurrection—the rebel leader Aguinaldo, the American General Lawton, and Frederick Funston, the commando leader who captured Aguinaldo, *The Rough Rider* 1:1 (1900), p. 6; 3:4 (1901), cover and p. 2; *Frontier Guide* 2:3 (1901).

50. "Programme" sections in *BBWW* 1899–1902, 1904–5, 1907–8. Russell *Wild West Shows*, pp. 62, 72; Blackstone, *Buckskins*, ch. 2, details the logistics of the Wild West. In 1909 the Wild West merged with Pawnee Bill's Far East, an "oriental" spec-

tacle. Despite the Wild West's decline, its literature was updated and expanded. One of the most interesting of the Programs is that for 1909, which follows the suggestion in Roosevelt's *Wilderness Hunter* and *Winning of the West*, that we see our greatest leaders as scions of the Frontier, "scouts" who "wore the buckskin" one way or another. Cody's pantheon includes not only the predictable hunter-heroes like Boone, Crockett and Carson, but also Christopher Columbus and George Washington, and even Benjamin Church—the usually unrecognized Puritan progenitor of the type.

51. *BBWW*, 1909, 1916; Rennert, *100 Posters*, p. 93.

52. Russell, *Lives and Legends*, pp. 439–72; Rennert, *100 Posters*, pp. 63, 108–9.

Social Construction of Masculinities, Femininities, and "The Other"

Since the first section of this book deals with concepts and theories of violence, it seems appropriate that this next section focus on the second fundamental construct of the pair: gender. Like many others, we are making a distinction between sex, a biological construct,[1] and gender, a social construct, the form of which depends on a multitude of societal influences and messages. It is essential, therefore, to talk about how each person's sense of gender is highly individualized, how we need to acknowledge the range of different types of masculinities and femininities in our cultures, and how they inform and are informed by our notions of gender hierarchy and power. As Nancy Chodorow has stated it in her latest book, "an individual, personal creation and a projective emotional and fantasy animation of cultural categories create the meaning of gender and gender identity for any individual. Each person's sense of gender is an individual creation, and there are thus many masculinities and femininities" (Chodorow, 1999). We then explore why people label and fear other individuals and groups in opposition to their own social makeup, and why they conveniently see people unlike themselves as the "Other."

Given our belief that gender is a social institution, the readings in this section raise a number of questions. Why are we often uncomfortable with other people until we have successfully placed them in a gender status? To what degree are our choices of gender self-determined, and is it easy, or even possible, to resist society's expectations of gender conformity? As Judith Lorber states in the first selection of our subtopic on explanations of gender, 'Night to his Day': The Social Construction of Gender," a chapter of her important collection, *Paradoxes of Gender*: "In the social construction of gender it does not matter what men and women actually do or even if they do the same thing. The social institution insists only that what they do is perceived as different" (p. 26). What does such an attitude say about ourselves as a culture? Why do many of us need to stress these differences?

Carol Tavris, a well-known social psychologist, lecturer, and writer, continues this line of thinking as she discusses the conceptualization of gender as a culture, male as normalcy/the norm, and the intersection between gender and language in a chapter from her popular treatise, *The Mismeasure of Woman*. Why do we persist, for example, in using language that expresses differences between the sexes when the differences are not consistently demonstrated in research? Why do our speech and behaviors change when in the company of men, women, and women and men? In what ways does context change one's behavior, and does that behavior change in sex-typed ways? Perhaps most interesting in Tavris's study is the concept of male and female narratives that define and constrict the lives of both men and women. Consider whether or not we need new stories in order to portray more faithfully the changing lives of contemporary people. An example of such a newly defined narrative/story is the feature film, *Boys Don't Cry*, based on the documentary, *The Brandon Teena Story*, that presents a real case of transgender identity, gender confusion, and the negative attitudes of more traditional people toward "different" individuals—attitudes and beliefs that can lead (and do lead in this instance) to dire outcomes. We recommend these films as one way to supplement our material and to explore further the issue of gender(s)—both masculinities and femininities—particularly as it relates to the last subtopic in this section, "the Other."

Exploring some of these masculinities is the next subtopic of this section of the book. Recognizing the early violent history on which the United States was built, especially in the exploration and "conquest" of the West and its requisite glorification of the "civilizing" nature of the gun, we begin our inquiry here with the historical situation and after effects of the Vietnam War. The sociologist and historian, James William Gibson, author of

---

[1] Although most researchers and scholars refer to sex as a biological construct to differentiate sex from gender, there are examples of individuals whose sex cannot be simply categorized as either female or male.

Warrior Dreams: Violence and Manhood in Post-Vietnam America, presents his view of current American masculinity as based on this past. For Gibson, U.S. history, as the "regeneration through violence" (a term coined by Richard Slotkin), was broken with the defeat in Vietnam, thus creating a disruption of cultural identity and a self-image crisis in America. Basing much of his theories on the power of Hollywood films and actors (John Wayne and Rambo, for example, whose films provide additional opportunities for textual analysis), as well as on the growth of certain genres of print media, Gibson analyzes the relationships between the causes of the Vietnam defeat and the rise of the paramilitary and its culture. He discusses what he calls the New Warrior in a New War—a warrior who is hostile to authority, sees women as dangerous creatures, and chooses war as a cleaner alternative. Is the celebration of war and violence a primary cultural archetype in the United States? Do some men need to build their male narratives around this rite of passage?

Bruce Weigl's poem, "Song of Napalm," investigates even further the links between war and masculinity. This visual piece speaks of the haunting image of a young girl running down a road away from her burning village—an image that is forever emblazoned in the U.S. soldier's mind. What are the contrasts between the masculine ideal of the tough military man and the reality of the horrors of war? This reality is also ironically revealed in W. D. Ehrhart's poem, "Guerrilla War," in which the poetic voice admits the impossibility of distinguishing between Vietcong soldiers and the civilian population. In what ways do the emotions and actions of the American soldier represent, or not, what we expect of "real men"?

Does this persistent masculine ideal of toughness make it difficult to be a man in today's world even though men continue to be the dominant group and to dominate meaning in key institutions? This question leads many feminists to argue that any adequate theory of masculinity must consider the concept of power at its center. This is the argument put forth by Nigel Edley and Margaret Wetherell in "Masculinity, Power, and Identity," a chapter in the British collection, *Understanding Masculinities*, as they further explain how social institutions help structure the gender identities of those embedded within them. Taking us through a number of theories that attempt to define men and masculinity, the authors pose several questions. How do we define patriarchy? What tactics does any dominant group use in order to stay dominant? And finally, does socioeconomic status affect how men construct their occupational and private lives?

This investigation into the lives of men and their concepts of masculinity is likewise a major focus of the work being done by Christopher Kilmartin, a psychologist and scholar of men's studies. In a chapter from his book, *The Masculine Self*, Kilmartin explores "Men in Relationships with Others," describing father and son relationships, male and female relationships, and the fear of labeling that might hint at homosexuality. According to Kilmartin, what are the different perspectives on romantic relationships for males and females? How does he characterize the father and son relationship? And what, for Kilmartin, is "father hunger"? This fear of not being seen as a "real" man remains significant in the minds of adult males, but it is perhaps even more worrisome for young boys who are increasingly concerned about their masculine body image and sexual appeal (Hall, 1999). Do you think that this concern is more salient for boys and men now than in the past?

Paralleling these glimpses into masculinities, the third subtopic of this section is the social construction of femininities. The feminine/female has long been an image constructed by men and then imposed on, accepted by, and incorporated into the minds and self-images of some women. James William Gibson addresses this issue in his chapter, "Black-Widow Women." He argues that in the eyes of the New Warrior, women are seen as dangerous, erotic, and venomous creatures who can entrap and eventually kill men. This view is an example of a longstanding belief in the dichotomy of women's nature: They are either a virgin/Madonna/mother or a temptress/whore/vampire. To what extent do we see vestiges of this belief today?

Manipulated by this dominant culture and having "bought into" this sexual construction, many girls and women have long been concerned with both body image and sexual appeal. They have, as a result, remained the primary target of advertising, fashion, and cosmetic surgery, although men, in increasing numbers, are being targeted by these same industries. Similarly, girls and women exhibit a higher proportion of eating disorders. In order to investigate some of the myths and stereotypes of women, the manipulation of many girls and women by the fashion and beauty industries, the changing "ideal" body of women over the decades, and how such a social condition has played into and helped develop many women's anxieties and self-images, we have chosen to include a section from Susan Faludi's landmark 1991 study, *Backlash: The Undeclared War Against American Women*. Faludi raises some significant questions that need to be addressed as we explore the notion of gender. If women are encouraged to dress in a certain way, are they being manipulated? If so, by whom? Is there a difference in the way that both men and their images and women and their images are manipulated? If so, how would you describe this difference? In what ways has this focus on the "ideal" body changed over the years for women and for men?

In contrast to the situation for women that Faludi portrayed in the 1980s—although much of what she writes remains pertinent today—is the essay by the psychologist and journalist, Debbie Stoller, who wants to "bust the beauty myth." According to Stoller, current-day young women are in the process of reclaiming or recycling fashion, language, and self-image that older feminists discarded as of the 1960s. Wanting to have some fun with femininity, these young feminists like decorating themselves, but "it's not necessarily because we're trying to please you [men]. . . . it's fun, it's feminine, and . . . it's definitely feminist" (p. 47). Do you agree or disagree with this statement? Does the unisex style of clothing and the choice in fashion by many women indicate more self-confidence in themselves as women? How does one explain, therefore, the increase in the variety of fashion clothing for men? What is the significance of reclaiming sexist slurs like "slut" and "bitch" and of resurrecting the word "girl" in one's speech? Are younger women socially *re*constructing notions of femininity, as they blur distinctions among genders?

What is not blurred, however, is the poem, "Recipe," by Janice Mirikitani, in which the Asian poetic voice explains her attempt to imitate the dominant white culture by changing the shape of her eyes. How do the title and the poetic images convey the overriding tone of this poem? Does the dominant culture continue to insist on an overt or silent acknowledgment of its superiority around ideas of femininity? How do members of "other" ethnic, cultural, racial, and/or class groups react, respond to, and reconstruct these dominant cultural constructions of both masculinities and femininities?

In fact, it is this dominant white (and male, heterosexual) culture that frames the fourth and last subtopic of this section on gender construction. Persistent in a desire to label individuals and groups, some people cannot seem to accept others for who they are and for what they represent. Returning to a chapter by James William Gibson, "Who is the Enemy and What Does He Want?" we ask you to consider the difficult and disturbing topic of what we call the "Other." Gibson describes his "New Warriors" in their "New War" as men waging a battle against a necessary, sometimes undefined, and yet ever-present enemy—the government, non-whites, liberals, and women. These evil ones, in the mind of the "New Warrior," are represented in such influential works as *The Turner Diaries*, the racist volume that has become almost a religious text for many right-wing white supremacist and paramilitary groups and individuals (Timothy McVeigh of the Oklahoma City bombing, for example). Why do these men need an enemy? Why does this enemy always take the form of someone or some group that looks different or thinks differently from the warrior? Is the narrative of the "New Warrior" a narrative about male self-control or simply about intense anger and hatred?

Andrew Sullivan, in his controversial essay, "The Fight Against Hate: Why We Can't—and Shouldn't—Win It," argues that we cannot and perhaps should not fight this war against hate that many believe undermines American society. He writes that hate crimes are simply another name for crime, for we shall never eradicate hatred in a free country. We must, rather, somehow learn to coexist and become immune to the bigot's power. Sullivan's essay raises serious debates: Is hate a specific idea or belief, or a set of beliefs with a specific object or group of objects, or is it a combination of prejudice, bigotry, bias, anger, or aversion to others? What do the modern words, "sexism," "racism," "anti-Semitism," and "homophobia," tell us about the perpetrators and victims of hate crimes and about the structure of power? What are the differences between hate crimes that come from knowledge and the hate that comes from ignorance? Do you agree with Sullivan that "hate is only foiled not when the haters are punished but when the hated are immune to the bigot's power?" (p. 113). Is there any solution to the problem of hate?

Bridging the second and third sections of this book—from gender and "Other" construction to youth violence—is one final piece. Adrian Nicole Leblanc's "The Outsiders," illustrates the difficulties that male youth encounter in high school where cliques are prevalent and where those who are picked on try to cope. To what extent does our need to construct the "Other" influence the formation of cliques? Can we ever eradicate them, or should we even attempt to do so?

Fundamentally in this section we investigate how our families, our friends, our culture, and our society shape our identities, beliefs, and values, particularly around the subject of gender. Gender identities are indeed complex and often lead individuals, groups, and even nations to perpetrate violence against those "Others" who are different from them. What links do you see between theories of violence and the social construction of gender?

REFERENCES

CHODOROW, N. J. (1999). Gender as a personal and cultural construction. In *The Power of Feelings: Personal Meaning in Psychoanalysis, Gender, Culture* (pp. 69–91). New Haven, CT: Yale University Press.

HALL, S. S. (1999, August 22). The bully in the mirror. *The New York Times Magazine*, 31–35, 58, 62, 64–65.

"Night to His Day"

The social construction of gender

Judith Lorber

Talking about gender for most people is the equivalent of fish talking about water. Gender is so much the routine ground of everyday activities that questioning its taken-for-granted assumptions and presuppositions is like thinking about whether the sun will come up.[1] Gender is so pervasive that in our society we assume it is bred into our genes. Most people find it hard to believe that gender is constantly created and re-created out of human interaction, out of social life, and is the texture and order of that social life. Yet gender, like culture, is a human production that depends on everyone constantly "doing gender" (West and Zimmerman 1987).

And everyone "does gender" without thinking about it. Today, on the subway, I saw a well-dressed man with a year-old child in a stroller. Yesterday, on a bus, I saw a man with a tiny baby in a carrier on his chest. Seeing men taking care of small children in public is increasingly common—at least in New York City. But both men were quite obviously stared at—and smiled at, approvingly. Everyone was doing gender—the men who were changing the role of fathers and the other passengers, who were applauding them silently. But there was more gendering going on that probably fewer people noticed. The baby was wearing a white crocheted cap and white clothes. You couldn't tell if it was a boy or a girl. The child in the stroller was wearing a dark blue T-shirt and dark print pants. As they started to leave the train, the father put a Yankee baseball cap on the child's head. Ah, a boy, I thought. Then I noticed the gleam of tiny earrings in the child's ears, and as they got off, I saw the little flowered sneakers and lace-trimmed socks. Not a boy after all. Gender done.

Gender is such a familiar part of daily life that it usually takes a deliberate disruption of our expectations of how women and men are supposed to act to pay attention to how it is produced. Gender signs and signals are so ubiquitous that we usually fail to note them—unless they are missing or ambiguous. Then we are uncomfortable until we have successfully placed the other person in a gender status; otherwise, we feel socially dislocated. In our society, in addition to man and woman, the status can be *transvestite* (a person who dresses in opposite-gender clothes) and *transsexual* (a person who has had sex-change surgery). Transvestites and transsexuals carefully construct their gender status by dressing, speaking, walking, gesturing in the ways prescribed for women or men—whichever they want to be taken for—and so does any "normal" person.

For the individual, gender construction starts with assignment to a sex category on the basis of what the genitalia look like at birth.[2] Then babies are dressed or adorned in a way that displays the category because parents don't want to be constantly asked whether their baby is a girl or a boy. A sex category becomes a gender status through naming, dress, and the use of other gender markers. Once a child's gender is evident, others treat those in one gender differently from those in the other, and the children respond to the different treatment by feeling different and behaving differently. As soon as they can talk, they start to refer to themselves as members of their gender. Sex doesn't come into play again until puberty, but by that time, sexual feelings and desires and practices have been shaped by gendered norms and expectations. Adolescent boys and girls approach and avoid each other in an elaborately scripted and gendered mating dance. Parenting is gendered, with different expectations for mothers and for fathers, and people of different genders work at different kinds of jobs. The work adults do as mothers and fathers and as low-level workers and high-level bosses, shapes women's and men's life experiences, and these experiences produce different feelings, consciousness, relationships, skills—ways of being that we call feminine or masculine.[3] All of these processes constitute the social construction of gender.

Gendered roles change—today fathers are taking care of little children, girls and boys are wearing unisex clothing and getting the same education, women and men are working at the same jobs. Although many traditional social groups are quite strict about maintaining gender differences, in other social groups they seem to be blurring. Then why the one-year-old's earrings? Why is it still so important to mark a child as a girl or a boy, to make sure she is not taken for a boy or he for a girl? What would happen if they were? They would, quite literally, have changed places in their social world.

To explain why gendering is done from birth, constantly and by everyone, we have to look not only at the way individuals experience gender but at gender as a social institution. As a social institution, gender is one of the major ways that human beings organize their lives. Human society depends on a predictable division of labor, a designated allocation of scarce goods, assigned responsibility for children and others who cannot care for themselves, common values and their systematic transmission to new members, legitimate leadership, music, art, stories, games, and other symbolic productions. One way of choosing people for the different tasks of society is on the basis of their talents, motivations, and competence—their demonstrated achievements. The other way is on the basis of gender, race, ethnicity—ascribed membership in a category of people. Although societies vary in the extent to which they use one or the other of these ways of allocating people to work and to carry out other responsibilities, every society uses gender and age grades. Every society classifies people as "girl and boy children," "girls and boys ready to be married," and "fully adult women and men," constructs similarities among them and differences between them, and assigns them to different roles and responsibilities. Personality characteristics, feelings, motivations, and ambitions flow from these different life experiences so that the members of these different groups become different kinds of people. The process of gendering and its outcome are legitimated by religion, law, science, and the society's entire set of values.

In order to understand gender as a social institution, it is important to distinguish human action from animal behavior. Animals feed themselves and their young until their young can feed themselves. Humans have to produce not only food but shelter and clothing. They also, if the group is going to continue as a social group, have to teach the children how their particular group does these tasks. In the process, humans reproduce gender, family, kinship, and a division of labor—social institutions that do not exist among animals. Primate social groups have been referred to as families, and their mating patterns as monogamy, adultery,

and harems. Primate behavior has been used to prove the universality of sex differences—as built into our evolutionary inheritance (Haraway 1978a). But animals' sex differences are not at all the same as humans' gender differences; animals' bonding is not kinship; animals' mating is not ordered by marriage; and animals' dominance hierarchies are not the equivalent of human stratification systems. Animals group on sex and age, relational categories that are physiologically, not socially, different. Humans create gender and age-group categories that are socially, and not necessarily physiologically, different.[4]

For animals, physiological maturity means being able to impregnate or conceive; its markers are coming into heat (estrus) and sexual attraction. For humans, puberty means being available for marriage; it is marked by rites that demonstrate this marital eligibility. Although the onset of physiological puberty is signaled by secondary sex characteristics (menstruation, breast development, sperm ejaculation, pubic and underarm hair), the onset of social adulthood is ritualized by the coming-out party or desert walkabout or bar mitzvah or graduation from college or first successful hunt or dreaming or inheritance of property. Humans have rituals that mark the passage from childhood into puberty and puberty into full adult status, as well as for marriage, childbirth, and death; animals do not (van Gennep 1960). To the extent that infants and the dead are differentiated by whether they are male or female, there are different birth rituals for girls and boys, and different funeral rituals for men and women (Biersack 1984, 132–33). Rituals of puberty, marriage, and becoming a parent are gendered, creating a "woman," a "man," a "bride," a "groom," a "mother," a "father." Animals have no equivalents for these statuses.

Among animals, siblings mate and so do parents and children; humans have incest taboos and rules that encourage or forbid mating between members of different kin groups (Lévi-Strauss 1956, [1949] 1969). Any animal of the same species may feed another's young (or may not, depending on the species). Humans designate responsibility for particular children by kinship; humans frequently limit responsibility for children to the members of their kinship group or make them into members of their kinship group with adoption rituals.

Animals have dominance hierarchies based on size or on successful threat gestures and signals. These hierarchies are usually sexed, and in some species, moving to the top of the hierarchy physically changes the sex (Austad 1986). Humans have stratification patterns based on control of surplus food, ownership of property, legitimate demands on others' work and sexual services, enforced determinations of who marries whom, and approved use of violence. If a woman replaces a man at the top of a stratification hierarchy, her social status may be that of a man, but her sex does not change.

Mating, feeding, and nurturant behavior in animals is determined by instinct and imitative learning and ordered by physiological sex and age (Lancaster 1974). In humans, these behaviors are taught and symbolically reinforced and ordered by socially constructed gender and age grades. Social gender and age statuses sometimes ignore or override physiological sex and age completely. Male and female animals (unless they physiologically change) are not interchangeable; infant animals cannot take the place of adult animals. Human females can become husbands and fathers, and human males can become wives and mothers, without sex-change surgery (Blackwood 1984). Human infants can reign as kings or queens.

Western society's values legitimate gendering by claiming that it all comes from physiology—female and male procreative differences. But gender and sex are not equivalent, and gender as a social construction does not flow automatically from genitalia and reproductive organs, the main physiological differences of females and males. In the construction of ascribed social statuses, physiological differences such as sex, stage of development, color of skin, and size are crude markers. They are not the source of the social statuses of gender, age, grade, and race. Social statuses are carefully constructed through prescribed processes of teaching, learning, emulation, and enforcement. Whatever genes, hormones, and biological evolution contribute to human social institutions is materially as well as qualitatively transformed by social practices. Every social institution has a material base, but culture and social practices transform that base into something with qualitatively different patterns and constraints. The economy is much more than producing food and goods and distributing them to eaters and users; family and kinship are not the equivalent of having sex and procreating; morals and religions cannot be equated with the fears and ecstasies of the brain; language goes far beyond the sounds produced by tongue and larynx.

No one eats "money" or "credit"; the concepts of "god" and "angels" are the subjects of theological disquisitions; not only words but objects, such as their flag, "speak" to the citizens of a country.

Similarly, gender cannot be equated with biological and physiological differences between human females and males. The building blocks of gender are *socially constructed statuses*. Western societies have only two genders, "man" and "woman." Some societies have three genders—men, women, and *berdaches* or *hijras* or *xaniths*. Berdaches, hijras, and xaniths are biological males who behave, dress, work, and are treated in most respects as social women; they are therefore not men, nor are they female women; they are, in our language, "male women."[5] There are African and American Indian societies that have a gender status called *manly hearted women*—biological females who work, marry, and parent as men; their social status is "female men" (Amadiume 1987; Blackwood 1984). They do not have to behave or dress as men to have the social responsibilities and prerogatives of husbands and fathers; what makes them men is enough wealth to buy a wife.

Modern Western societies' *transsexuals* and *transvestites* are the nearest equivalent of these crossover genders, but they are not institutionalized as third genders (Bolin 1987). Transsexuals are biological males and females who have sex-change operations to alter their genitalia. They do so in order to bring their physical anatomy in congruence with the way they want to live and with their own sense of gender identity. They do not become a third gender; they change genders. Transvestites are males who live as women and females who live as men but do not intend to have sex-change surgery. Their dress, appearance, and mannerisms fall within the range of what is expected from members of the opposite gender, so that they "pass." They also change genders, sometimes temporarily, some for most of their lives. Transvestite women have fought in wars as men soldiers as recently as the nineteenth century; some married women, and others went back to being women and married men once the war was over.[6] Some were discovered when their wounds were treated; others not until they died. In order to work as a jazz musician, a man's occupation, Billy Tipton, a woman, lived most of her life as a man. She died recently at seventy-four, leaving a wife and three adopted sons for whom she was husband and father, and musicians with whom she had played and traveled, for whom she was "one of the boys" (*New York Times* 1989).[7] There have been many other such occurrences of women passing as men to do more prestigious or lucrative men's work (Matthaei 1982, 192–93).[8]

Genders, therefore, are not attached to a biological substratum. Gender boundaries are breachable, and individual and socially organized shifts from one gender to another call attention to "cultural, social, or aesthetic dissonances" (Garber 1992, 16). These odd or deviant or third genders show us what we ordinarily take for granted—that people have to learn to be women and men. Men who cross-dress for performances or for pleasure often learn from women's magazines how to "do femininity" convincingly (Garber 1992, 41–51). Because transvestism is direct evidence of how gender is constructed, Marjorie Garber claims it has "extraordinary power . . . to disrupt, expose, and challenge, putting in question the very notion of the 'original' and of stable identity" (1992, 16).

GENDER BENDING

It is difficult to see how gender is constructed because we take it for granted that it's all biology, or hormones, or human nature. The differences between women and men seem to be self-evident, and we think they would occur no matter what society did. But in actuality, human females and males are physiologically more similar in appearance than are the two sexes of many species of animals and are more alike than different in traits and behavior (C. F. Epstein 1988). Without the deliberate use of gendered clothing, hairstyles, jewelry, and cosmetics, women and men would look far more alike.[9] Even societies that do not cover women's breasts have gender-identifying clothing, scarification, jewelry, and hairstyles.

The ease with which many transvestite women pass as men and transvestite men as women is corroborated by the common gender misidentification in Westernized societies of people in jeans, T-shirts, and sneakers. Men with long hair may be addressed as "miss," and women with short hair are often taken for men unless they offset the potential ambiguity with deliberate gender markers (Devor 1987, 1989). Jan Morris, in *Conundrum*, an autobiographical account of events just before and just after a sex-change operation, described how easy it was to shift back and forth from

being a man to being a woman when testing how it would feel to change gender status. During this time, Morris still had a penis and wore more or less unisex clothing; the context alone made the man and the woman:

Sometimes the arena of my ambivalence was uncomfortably small. At the Travellers' Club, for example, I was obviously known as a man of sorts—women were only allowed on the premises at all during a few hours of the day, and even then were hidden away as far as possible in lesser rooms or alcoves. But I had another club, only a few hundred yards away, where I was known only as a woman, and often I went directly from one to the other, imperceptibly changing roles on the way—"Cheerio, sir," the porter would say at one club, and "Hello, madam," the porter would greet me at the other. (1975, 132)

Gender shifts are actually a common phenomenon in public roles as well. Queen Elizabeth II of England bore children, but when she went to Saudi Arabia on a state visit, she was considered an honorary man so that she could confer and dine with the men who were heads of a state that forbids unrelated men and women to have face to-unveiled-face contact. In contemporary Egypt, lower-class women who run restaurants or shops dress in men's clothing and engage in unfeminine aggressive behavior, and middle-class educated women of professional or managerial status can take positions of authority (Rugh 1986, 131). In these situations, there is an important status change: These women are treated by the others in the situation as if they are men. From their own point of view, they are still women. From the social perspective, however, they are men.[10]

In many cultures, gender bending is prevalent in theater or dance—the Japanese kabuki are men actors who play both women and men; in Shakespeare's theater company, there were no actresses—Juliet and Lady Macbeth were played by boys. Shakespeare's comedies are full of witty comments on gender shifts. Women characters frequently masquerade as young men, and other women characters fall in love with them; the boys playing these masquerading women, meanwhile, are acting out pining for the love of men characters.[11] In *As You Like It*, when Rosalind justifies her protective cross-dressing, Shakespeare also comments on manliness:

Were it not better,
Because that I am more than common tall,

That I did suit me all points like a man:
A gallant curtle-axe upon my thigh,
A boar-spear in my hand, and in my heart
Lie there what hidden women's fear there will,
We'll have a swashing and martial outside,
As many other mannish cowards have
That do outface it with their semblances. (I, i, 115–22)

Shakespeare's audience could appreciate the double subtext: Rosalind, a woman character, was a boy dressed in girl's clothing who then dressed as a boy; like bravery, masculinity and femininity can be put on and taken off with changes of costume and role (Howard 1988, 435).[12]

M Butterfly is a modern play of gender ambiguities, which David Hwang (1989) based on a real person. Shi Peipu, a male Chinese opera singer who sang women's roles, was a spy as a man and the lover as a woman of a Frenchman, Gallimard, a diplomat (Bernstein 1986). The relationship lasted twenty years, and Shi Peipu even pretended to be the mother of a child by Gallimard. "She" also pretended to be too shy to undress completely. As "Butterfly," Shi Peipu portrayed a fantasy Oriental woman who made the lover a "real man" (Kondo 1990). In Gallimard's words, the fantasy was "of slender women in chong sams and kimonos who die for the love of unworthy foreign devils. Who are born and raised to be perfect women. Who take whatever punishment we give them, and bounce back, strengthened by love, unconditionally" (D. H. Hwang 1989, 91). When the fantasy woman betrayed him by turning out to be the more powerful "real man," Gallimard assumed the role of Butterfly and, dressed in a geisha's robes, killed himself: "because 'man' and 'woman' are oppositionally defined terms, reversals . . . are possible" (Kondo 1990, 18).[13]

But despite the ease with which gender boundaries can be traversed in work, in social relationships, and in cultural productions, gender statuses remain. Transvestites and transsexuals do not challenge the social construction of gender. Their goal is to be feminine women and masculine men (Kando 1973). Those who do not want to change their anatomy but do want to change their gender behavior fare less well in establishing their social identity. The women Holly Devor called "gender blenders" wore their hair short, dressed in unisex pants, shirts, and comfortable shoes, and did not wear jewelry or makeup. They described their everyday dress as women's clothing: One said, "I wore jeans all the time, but I didn't wear men's clothes" (Devor 1989, 100). Their gender identity was women, but because they refused to "do femininity," they were constantly taken for men (1987, 1989, 107–42). Devor said of them: "The most common area of complaint was with public washrooms. They repeatedly spoke of the humiliation of being challenged or ejected from women's washrooms. Similarly, they found public change rooms to be dangerous territory and the buying of undergarments to be a difficult feat to accomplish" (1987, 29). In an ultimate ironic twist, some of these women said "they would feel like transvestites if they were to wear dresses, and two women said that they had been called transvestites when they had done so" (1987, 31). They resolved the ambiguity of their gender status by identifying as women in private and passing as men in public to avoid harassment on the street, to get men's jobs, and, if they were lesbians, to make it easier to display affection publicly with their lovers (Devor 1989, 107–42). Sometimes they even used men's bathrooms. When they had gender-neutral names, like Leslie, they could avoid the bureaucratic hassles that arose when they had to present their passports or other proof of identity, but because most had names associated with women, their appearance and their cards of identity were not conventionally congruent, and their gender status was in constant jeopardy.[14] When they could, they found it easier to pass as men than to try to change the stereotyped notions of what women should look like.

Paradoxically, then, bending gender rules and passing between genders does not erode but rather preserves gender boundaries. In societies with only two genders, the gender dichotomy is not disturbed by transvestites, because others feel that a transvestite is only transitorily ambiguous—is "really a man or woman underneath." After sex-change surgery, transsexuals end up in a conventional gender status—a "man" or a "woman" with the appropriate genitals (Eichler 1989). When women dress as men for business reasons, they are indicating that in that situation, they want to be treated the way men are treated: when they dress as women, they want to be treated as women:

By their male dress, female entrepreneurs signal their desire to suspend the expectations of accepted feminine conduct without losing respect and reputation. By wearing what is "unattractive" they signify that they are not intending to display their physical charms while engaging in public activity.

Their loud, aggressive banter contrasts with the modest demeanor that attracts men. . . . Overt signalling of a suspension of the rules preserves normal conduct from eroding expectations. (Rugh 1986, 131)

FOR INDIVIDUALS, GENDER MEANS SAMENESS

Although the possible combinations of genitalia, body shapes, clothing, mannerisms, sexuality, and roles could produce infinite varieties in human beings, the social institution of gender depends on the production and maintenance of a limited number of gender statuses and of making the members of these statuses similar to each other. Individuals are born sexed but not gendered, and they have to be taught to be masculine or feminine.[15] As Simone de Beauvoir said: "One is not born, but rather becomes, a woman . . .; it is civilization as a whole that produces this creature . . . which is described as feminine." (1952, 267).

Children learn to walk, talk, and gesture the way their social group says girls and boys should. Ray Birdwhistell, in his analysis of body motion as human communication, calls these learned gender displays *tertiary* sex characteristics and argues that they are needed to distinguish genders because humans are a weakly dimorphic species—their only sex markers are genitalia (1970, 39–46). Clothing, paradoxically, often hides the sex but displays the gender.

In early childhood, humans develop gendered personality structures and sexual orientations through their interactions with parents of the same and opposite gender. As adolescents, they conduct their sexual behavior according to gendered scripts. Schools, parents, peers, and the mass media guide young people into gendered work and family roles. As adults, they take on a gendered social status in their society's stratification system. Gender is thus both ascribed and achieved (West and Zimmerman 1987).

The achievement of gender was most dramatically revealed in a case of an accidental transsexual—a baby boy whose penis was destroyed in the course of a botched circumcision when he was seven months old (Money and Ehrhardt 1972, 118–23). The child's sex category was changed to "female," and a vagina was surgically constructed when the child was seventeen months old. The parents were advised that they could successfully raise the child, one of identical twins, as a girl. Physicians assured them that the child was too

young to have formed a gender identity. Children's sense of which gender they belong to usually develops around the age of three, at the time that they start to group objects and recognize that the people around them also fit into categories—big, little; pink-skinned, brown-skinned; boys, girls. Three has also been the age when children's appearance is ritually gendered, usually by cutting a boy's hair or dressing him in distinctively masculine clothing. In Victorian times, English boys wore dresses up to the age of three, when they were put into short pants (Garber 1992, 1–2).

The parents of the accidental transsexual bent over backward to feminize the child—and succeeded. Frilly dresses, hair ribbons, and jewelry created a pride in looks, neatness, and "daintiness." More significant, the child's dominance was also feminized:

The girl had many tomboyish traits, such as abundant physical energy, a high level of activity, stubbornness, and being often the dominant one in a girls' group. Her mother tried to modify her tomboyishness: ". . . I teach her to be more polite and quiet. I always wanted those virtues. I never did manage, but I'm going to try to manage them to—my daughter—to be more quiet and ladylike." From the beginning the girl had been the dominant twin. By the age of three, her dominance over her brother was, as her mother described it, that of a mother hen. The boy in turn took up for his sister, if anyone threatened her. (Money and Ehrhardt 1972, 122)

This child was not a tomboy because of male genes or hormones; according to her mother, she herself had also been a tomboy. What the mother had learned poorly while growing up as a "natural" female she insisted that her physically reconstructed son-daughter learn well. For both mother and child, the social construction of gender overrode any possibly inborn traits.

People go along with the imposition of gender norms because the weight of morality as well as immediate social pressure enforces them. Consider how many instructions for properly gendered behavior are packed into this mother's admonition to her daughter: "This is how to hem a dress when you see the hem coming down and so to prevent yourself from looking like the slut I know you are so bent on becoming" (Kincaid 1978).

Gender norms are inscribed in the way people move, gesture, and even eat. In one African society, men were supposed to eat with their "whole mouth, wholeheartedly, and not, like women, just with the lips, that is halfheartedly, with reservation and restraint" (Bourdieu [1980] 1990, 70). Men and women in this society learned to walk in ways that proclaimed their different positions in the society:

The manly man . . . stands up straight into the face of the person he approaches, or wishes to welcome. Ever on the alert, because ever threatened, he misses nothing of what happens around him. . . . Conversely, a well brought-up woman . . . is expected to walk with a slight stoop, avoiding every misplaced movement of her body, her head or her arms, looking down, keeping her eyes on the spot where she will next put her foot, especially if she happens to have to walk past the men's assembly. (70)

Many cultures go beyond clothing, gestures, and demeanor in gendering children. They inscribe gender directly into bodies. In traditional Chinese society, mothers bound their daughters' feet into three-inch stumps to enhance their sexual attractiveness. Jewish fathers circumcise their infant sons to show their covenant with God. Women in African societies remove the clitoris of prepubescent girls, scrape their labia, and make the lips grow together to preserve their chastity and ensure their marriageability. In Western societies, women augment their breast size with silicone and reconstruct their faces with cosmetic surgery to conform to cultural ideals of feminine beauty. Hanna Papanek (1990) notes that these practices reinforce the sense of superiority or inferiority in the adults who carry them out as well as in the children on whom they are done: The genitals of Jewish fathers and sons are physical and psychological evidence of their common dominant religious and familial status; the genitals of African mothers and daughters are physical and psychological evidence of their joint subordination.[16]

Sandra Bem (1981, 1983) argues that because gender is a powerful "schema" that orders the cognitive would, one must wage a constant, active battle for a child not to fall into typical gendered attitudes and behavior. In 1972, *Ms. Magazine* published Lois Gould's fantasy of how to raise a child free of gender-typing. The experiment calls for hiding the child's anatomy from all eyes except the parents' and treating the child as neither a girl nor a boy. The child, called X, gets to do all the things boys *and* girls do. The experiment is so successful that all the children in X's class at school want to look and behave like X. At the end of the story, the creators of the experiment are asked what will happen when X grows up. The scientists' answer is that by then it will be quite clear what X is, imply-

ing that its hormones will kick in and it will be revealed as a female or male. That ambiguous, and somewhat contradictory, ending lets Gould off the hook; neither she nor we have any idea what someone brought up totally androgynously would be like sexually or socially as an adult. The hormonal input will not create gender or sexuality but will only establish secondary sex characteristics; breasts, beards, and menstruation alone do not produce social manhood or womanhood. Indeed, it is at puberty, when sex characteristics become evident, that most societies put pubescent children through their most important rites of passage, the rituals that officially mark them as fully gendered—that is, ready to marry and become adults.

Most parents create a gendered world for their newborn by naming, birth announcements, and dress. Children's relationships with same-gendered and different-gendered caretakers structure their self-identifications and personalities. Through cognitive development, children extract and apply to their own actions the appropriate behavior for those who belong in their own gender, as well as race, religion, ethnic group, and social class, rejecting what is not appropriate. If their social categories are highly valued, they value themselves highly; if their social categories are low status, they lose self-esteem (Chodorow 1974). Many feminist parents who want to raise androgynous children soon lose their children to the pull of gendered norms (T. Gordon 1990, 87–90). My son attended a carefully nonsexist elementary school, which didn't even have girls' and boys' bathrooms. When he was seven or eight years old, I attended a class play about "squares" and "circles" and their need for each other and noticed that all the girl squares and circles wore makeup, but none of the boy squares and circles did. I asked the teacher about it after the play, and she said, "Bobby said he was not going to wear makeup, and he is a powerful child, so none of the boys would either." In a long discussion about conformity, my son confronted me with the question of who the conformists were, the boys who followed their leader or the girls who listened to the woman teacher. In actuality, they both were, because they both followed same-gender leaders and acted in gender-appropriate ways. (Actors may wear makeup, but real boys don't.)

For human beings there is no essential femaleness or maleness, femininity or masculinity, womanhood or manhood, but once gender is ascribed, the social order constructs and holds individuals to strongly gendered norms and expectations. Individuals may vary on many of the components of gender and may shift genders temporarily or permanently, but they must fit into the limited number of gender statuses their society recognizes. In the process, they re-create their society's version of women and men: "If we do gender appropriately, we simultaneously sustain, reproduce, and render legitimate the institutional arrangements. . . . If we fail to do gender appropriately, we as individuals—not the institutional arrangements—may be called to account (for our character, motives, and predispositions)" (West and Zimmerman 1987, 146).

The gendered practices of everyday life reproduce a society's view of how women and men should act (Bourdieu [1980] 1990). Gendered social arrangements are justified by religion and cultural productions and backed by law, but the most powerful means of sustaining the moral hegemony of the dominant gender ideology is that the process is made invisible; any possible alternatives are virtually unthinkable (Foucault 1972; Gramsci 1971).[17]

FOR SOCIETY, GENDER MEANS DIFFERENCE

The pervasiveness of gender as a way of structuring social life demands that gender statuses be clearly differentiated. Varied talents, sexual preferences, identities, personalities, interests, and ways of interacting fragment the individual's bodily and social experiences. Nonetheless, these are organized in Western cultures into two and only two socially and legally recognized gender statuses, "man" and "woman."[18] In the social construction of gender, it does not matter what men and women actually do; it does not even matter if they do exactly the same thing. The social institution of gender insists only that what they do is *perceived* as different.

If men and women are doing the same tasks, they are usually spatially segregated to maintain gender separation, and often the tasks are given different job titles as well, such as executive secretary and administrative assistant (Reskin 1988). If the differences between women and men begin to blur, society's "sameness taboo" goes into action (G. Rubin 1975, 178). At a rock and roll dance at West Point in 1976, the year women were admitted to the prestigious military academy for the first time, the school's administrators "were reportedly perturbed by the sight of mirror-image couples dancing in short hair and dress

gray trousers," and a rule was established that women cadets could dance at these events only if they wore skirts (Barkalow and Raab 1990, 53).[19] Women recruits in the U.S. Marine Corps are required to wear makeup—at a minimum, lipstick and eye shadow—and they have to take classes in makeup, hair care, poise, and etiquette. This feminization is part of a deliberate policy of making them clearly distinguishable from men Marines. Christine Williams quotes a twenty-five-year-old woman drill instructor as saying: "A lot of the recruits who come here don't wear makeup; they're tomboyish or athletic. A lot of them have the preconceived idea that going into the military means they can still be a tomboy. They don't realize that you are a *Woman* Marine" (1989, 76–77).[20]

If gender differences were genetic, physiological, or hormonal, gender bending and gender ambiguity would occur only in hermaphrodites, who are born with chromosomes and genitalia that are not clearly female or male. Since gender differences are socially constructed, all men and all women can enact the behavior of the other, because they know the other's social script: " 'Man' and 'woman' are at once empty and overflowing categories. Empty because they have no ultimate, transcendental meaning. Overflowing because even when they appear to be fixed, they still contain within them alternative, denied, or suppressed definitions" (J. W. Scott 1988a, 49). Nonetheless, though individuals may be able to shift gender statuses, the gender boundaries have to hold, or the whole gendered social order will come crashing down.

Paradoxically, it is the social importance of gender statuses and their external markers—clothing, mannerisms, and spatial segregation—that makes gender bending or gender crossing possible—or even necessary. The social viability of differentiated gender statuses produces the need or desire to shift statuses. Without gender differentiation, transvestism and transsexuality would be meaningless. You couldn't dress in the opposite gender's clothing if all clothing were unisex. There would be no need to reconstruct genitalia to match identity if interests and life-styles were not gendered. There would be no need for women to pass as men to do certain kinds of work if jobs were not typed as "women's work" and "men's work." Women would not have to dress as men in public life in order to give orders or aggressively bargain with customers.

Gender boundaries are preserved when transsexuals create congruous autobiographies of always having felt like what they are now. The transvestite's story also "recuperates social and sexual norms" (Garber 1992, 69). In the transvestite's normalized narrative, he or she "is 'compelled' by social and economic forces to disguise himself or herself in order to get a job, escape repression, or gain artistic or political 'freedom' " (Garber 1992, 70). The "true identity," when revealed, causes amazement over how easily and successfully the person passed as a member of the opposite gender, not a suspicion that gender itself is something of a put-on.

GENDER RANKING

Most societies rank genders according to prestige and power and construct them to be unequal, so that moving from one to another also means moving up or down the social scale. Among some North American Indian cultures, the hierarchy was male men, male women, female men, female women. Women produced significant durable goods (basketry, textiles, pottery, decorated leather goods), which could be traded. Women also controlled what they produced and any profit or wealth they earned. Since women's occupational realm could lead to prosperity and prestige, it was fair game for young men—but only if they became women in gender status. Similarly, women in other societies who amassed a great deal of wealth were allowed to become men—"manly hearts." According to Harriet Whitehead (1981):

Both reactions reveal an unwillingness or inability to distinguish the sources of prestige—wealth, skill, personal efficacy (among other things)—from masculinity. Rather there is the innuendo that if a person performing female tasks can attain excellence, prosperity, or social power, it must be because that person is, at some level, a man. . . . A woman who could succeed at doing the things men did was honored as a man would be. . . . What seems to have been more disturbing to the culture—which means, for all intents and purposes, to the men—was the possibility that women, within their own department, might be onto a good thing. It was into this unsettling breach that the berdache institution was hurled. In their social aspect, women were complimented by the berdache's imitation. In their anatomic aspect, they were subtly insulted by his vaunted superiority. (108)

In American society, men-to-women transsexuals tend to earn less after surgery if they change occupations; women-to-men transsexuals tend to increase their income (Bolin 1988, 153–60; Brody 1979). Men who go into women's fields, like nursing, have less prestige than women who go into men's fields, like physics. Janice Raymond, a radical feminist, feels that transsexual men-to-women have advantages over female women because they were not socialized to be subordinate or oppressed throughout life. She says:

We know that we are women who are born with female chromosomes and anatomy, and that whether or not we were socialized to be so-called normal women, patriarchy has treated and will treat us like women. Transsexuals have not had this same history. No man can have the history of being born and located in this culture as a woman. He can have the history of *wishing* to be a woman and of *acting* like a woman, but this gender experience is that of a transsexual, not of a woman. Surgery may confer the artifacts of outward and inward female organs but it cannot confer the history of being born a woman in this society. (1979, 114)

Because women who become men rise in the world and men who become women fall, Elaine Showalter (1987) was very critical of the movie *Tootsie*, in which Dustin Hoffman plays an actor who passes as a woman in order to be able to get work. "Dorothy" becomes a feminist "woman of the year" for standing up for women's rights not to be demeaned or sexually harassed. Showalter feels that the message of the movie is double-edged: "Dorothy's 'feminist' speeches . . . are less a response to the oppression of women than an instinctive situational male reaction to being treated like a woman. The implication is that women must be taught by men how to win their rights. . . . It says that feminist ideas are much less threatening when they come from a man" (123). Like Raymond, Showalter feels that being or having been a man gives a transsexual man-to-woman or a man cross-dressed as a woman a social advantage over those whose gender status was always "woman."[21] The implication here is that there is an experiential superiority that doesn't disappear with the gender shift.

For one transsexual man-to-woman, however, the experience of living as a woman changed his/her whole personality. As James, Morris had been a soldier, foreign correspondent, and mountain climber; as Jan, Morris is a successful travel writer. But socially, James was far superior to Jan, and so Jan developed the "learned helplessness" that is supposed to characterize women in Western society:

We are told that the social gap between the sexes is narrowing, but I can only report that having, in the second half of the twentieth century, experienced life in both roles, there seems to me no aspect of existence, no moment of the day, no contact, no arrangement, no response, which is not different for men and for women. The very tone of voice in which I was now addressed, the very posture of the person next in the queue, the very feel in the air when I entered a room or sat at a restaurant table, constantly emphasized my change of status.

And if other's responses shifted, so did my own. The more I was treated as woman, the more woman I became. I adapted willy-nilly. If I was assumed to be incompetent at reversing cars, or opening bottles, oddly incompetent I found myself becoming. If a case was thought too heavy for me, inexplicably I found it so myself. . . . Women treated me with a frankness which, while it was one of the happiest discoveries of my metamorphosis, did imply membership of a camp, a faction, or at least a school of thought; so I found myself gravitating always towards the female, whether in sharing a railway compartment or supporting a political cause. Men treated me more and more as junior, . . . and so, addressed every day of my life as an inferior, involuntarily, month by month I accepted the condition. I discovered that even now men prefer women to be less informed, less able, less talkative, and certainly less self-centered than they are themselves; so I generally obliged them. (1975, 165–66)[22]

COMPONENTS OF GENDER

By now, it should be clear that gender is not a unitary essence but has many components as a social institution and as an individual status.[23]

As a social institution, gender is composed of:

Gender statuses, the socially recognized genders in a society and the norms and expectations for their enactment behaviorally, gesturally, linguistically, emotionally, and physically. How gender statuses are evaluated depends on historical development in any particular society.

Gendered division of labor, the assignment of productive and domestic work to members of different gender statuses. The work assigned to those of different gender statuses strengthens the society's evaluation of those statuses—the higher the status, the more prestigious and valued the work and the greater its rewards.

Gendered kinship, the family rights and responsibilities for each gender status. Kinship statuses reflect and reinforce the prestige and power differences of the different genders.

Gendered sexual scripts, the normative patterns of sexual desire and sexual behavior, as prescribed for the different gender statuses. Members of the dominant gender have more sexual prerogatives; members of a subordinate gender may be sexually exploited.

Gendered personalities, the combinations of traits patterned by gender norms of how members of different gender statuses are supposed to feel and behave. Social expecta-

tions of others in face-to-face interaction constantly bolster these norms.

Gendered social control, the formal and informal approval and reward of conforming behavior and the stigmatization, social isolation, punishment, and medical treatment of nonconforming behavior.

Gender ideology, the justification of gender statuses, particularly, their differential evaluation. The dominant ideology tends to suppress criticism by making these evaluations seem natural.

Gender imagery, the cultural representations of gender and embodiment of gender in symbolic language and artistic productions that reproduce and legitimate gender statuses. Culture is one of the main supports of the dominant gender ideology.

For an individual, gender is composed of:

Sex category to which the infant is assigned at birth based on appearance of genitalia. With prenatal testing and sex-typing, categorization is prenatal. Sex category may be changed later through surgery or reinspection of ambiguous genitalia.

Gender identity, the individual's sense of gendered self as a worker and family member.

Gendered marital and procreative status, fulfillment or non-fulfillment of allowed or disallowed mating, impregnation, childbearing, kinship roles.

Gendered sexual orientation, socially and individually patterned sexual desires, feelings, practices, and identification.

Gendered personality, internalized patterns of socially normative emotions as organized by family structure and parenting.

Gendered processes, the social practices of learning, being taught, picking up cues, enacting behavior already learned to be gender-appropriate (or inappropriate, if rebelling, testing), developing a gender identity, "doing gender" as a member of a gender status in relationships with gendered others, acting deferent or dominant.

Gender beliefs, incorporation of or resistance to gender ideology.

Gender display, presentation of self as a certain kind of gendered person through dress, cosmetics, adornments, and permanent and reversible body markers.

For an individual, all the social components are supposed to be consistent and congruent with perceived physiology. The actual combination of genes and genitalia, prenatal, adolescent, and adult hormonal input, and procreative capacity may or may not be congruous with each other and with sex-category assignment, gender identity, gendered sexual orientation and procreative status, gender display, personality, and work and family roles. At any one time, an individual's identity is a combination of the major ascribed statuses of gender, race, ethnicity, religion, and social class, and the individual's achieved statuses, such as education level, occupation or profession, marital status, parenthood, prestige, authority, and wealth. The ascribed statuses substantially limit or create opportunities for individual achievements and also diminish or enhance the luster of those achievements.

GENDER AS PROCESS, STRATIFICATION, AND STRUCTURE

As a social institution, gender is a process of creating distinguishable social statuses for the assignment of rights and responsibilities. As part of a stratification system that ranks these statuses unequally, gender is a major building block in the social structures built on these unequal statuses.

As a *process*, gender creates the social differences that define "woman" and "man." In social interaction throughout their lives, individuals learn what is expected, see what is expected, act and react in expected ways, and thus simultaneously construct and maintain the gender order: "The very injunction to be a given gender takes place through discursive routes: to be a good mother, to be a heterosexually desirable object, to be a fit worker, in sum, to signify a multiplicity of guarantees in response to a variety of different demands all at once" (J. Butler 1990, 145). Members of a social group neither make up gender as they go along nor exactly replicate in rote fashion what was done before. In almost every encounter, human beings produce gender, behaving in the ways they learned were appropriate for their gender status, or resisting or rebelling against these norms. Resistance and rebellion have altered gender norms, but so far they have rarely eroded the statuses.

Gendered patterns of interaction acquire additional layers of gendered sexuality, parenting, and work behaviors in childhood, adolescence, and adulthood. Gendered norms and expectations are enforced through informal sanctions of gender-inappropriate behavior by peers and by formal punishment or threat of punishment by those in authority should behavior deviate too far from socially imposed standards for women and men.

Everyday gendered interactions build gender into the family, the work process, and other organizations and institutions, which in turn reinforce gender expectations for individuals.[24] Because gender is a process, there is room not only for modification and variation by individuals and small groups but also for institutionalized change (J. W. Scott 1988a, 7).

As part of a *stratification* system, gender ranks men above women of the same race and class. Women and men could be different but equal. In practice, the process of creating difference depends to a great extent on differential evaluation. As Nancy Jay (1981) says: "That which is defined, separated out, isolated from all else is A and pure. Not-A is necessarily impure, a random catchall, to which nothing is external except A and the principle of order that separates it from Not-A" (45). From the individual's point of view, whichever gender is A, the other is Not-A; gender boundaries tell the individual who is like him or her, and all the rest are unlike. From society's point of view, however, one gender is usually the touchstone, the normal, the dominant, and the other is different, deviant, and subordinate. In Western society, "man" is A, "wo-man" is Not-A. (Consider what a society would be like where woman was A and man Not-A.)

The further dichotomization by race and class constructs the gradations of a heterogeneous society's stratification scheme. Thus, in the United States, white is A, African American is Not-A; middle class is A, working class is Not-A, and "African-American women occupy a position whereby the inferior half of a series of these dichotomies converge" (P. H. Collins 1990, 70). The dominant categories are the hegemonic ideals, taken so for granted as the way things should be that white is not ordinarily thought of as a race, middle class as a class, or men as a gender. The characteristics of these categories define the Other as that which lacks the valuable qualities the dominants exhibit.

In a gender-stratified society, what men do is usually valued more highly than what women do because men do it, even when their activities are very similar or the same. In different regions of southern India, for example, harvesting rice is men's work, shared work, or women's work: "Wherever a task is done by women it is considered easy, and where it is done by [men] it is considered difficult" (Mencher 1988, 104). A gathering and hunting society's survival usually depends on the nuts, grubs, and small animals brought in by the women's foraging trips, but when the men's hunt is successful, it is the occasion for a celebration. Conversely, because they are the superior group, white men do not have to do the "dirty work," such as housework; the most inferior group does it, usually poor women of color (Palmer 1989).

Freudian psychoanalytic theory claims that boys must reject their mothers and deny the feminine in themselves in order to become men: "For boys the major goal is the achievement of personal masculine identification with their father and sense of secure masculine self, achieved through superego formation and disparagement of women" (Chodorow 1978, 165). Masculinity may be the outcome of boys' intrapsychic struggles to separate their identity from that of their mothers, but the proofs of masculinity are culturally shaped and usually ritualistic and symbolic (Gilmore 1990).

The Marxist feminist explanation for gender inequality is that by demeaning women's abilities and keeping them from learning valuable technological skills, bosses preserve them as a cheap and exploitable reserve army of labor. Unionized men who could be easily replaced by women collude in this process because it allows them to monopolize the better paid, more interesting, and more autonomous jobs: "Two factors emerge as helping men maintain their separation from women and their control of technological occupations. One is the active gendering of jobs and people. The second is the continual creation of subdivisions in the work processes, and levels in work hierarchies, into which men can move in order to keep their distance from women" (Cockburn 1985, 13).

Societies vary in the extent of the inequality in social status of their women and men members, but where there is inequality, the status "woman" (and its attendant behavior and role allocations) is usually held in lesser esteem than the status "man." Since gender is also intertwined with a society's other constructed statuses of differential evaluation—race, religion, occupation, class, country of origin, and so on—men and women members of the favored groups command more power, more prestige, and more property than the members of the disfavored groups. Within many social groups, however, men are advantaged over women. The more economic resources, such as education and job opportunities, are available to a group, the more they tend to be monopolized by men. In poorer groups that have few resources (such as working-class

African Americans in the United States), women and men are more nearly equal, and the women may even outstrip the men in education and occupational status (Almquist 1987).

As a *structure*, gender divides work in the home and in economic production, legitimates those in authority, and organizes sexuality and emotional life (Connell 1987, 91–142). As primary parents, women significantly influence children's psychological development and emotional attachments, in the process reproducing gender. Emergent sexuality is shaped by heterosexual, homosexual, bisexual, and sadomasochistic patterns that are gendered—different for girls and boys, and for women and men—so that sexual statuses reflect gender statuses.

When gender is a major component of structured inequality, the devalued genders have less power, prestige, and economic rewards than the valued genders. In countries that discourage gender discrimination, many major roles are still gendered; women still do most of the domestic labor and child rearing, even while doing full-time paid work; women and men are segregated on the job and each does work considered "appropriate"; women's work is usually paid less than men's work. Men dominate the positions of authority and leadership in government, the military, and the law; cultural productions, religions, and sports reflect men's interests.

In societies that create the greatest gender difference, such as Saudi Arabia, women are kept out of sight behind walls or veils, have no civil rights, and often create a cultural and emotional world of their own (Bernard 1981). But even in societies with less rigid gender boundaries, women and men spend much of their time with people of their own gender because of the way work and family are organized. This spatial separation of women and men reinforces gendered differentness, identity, and ways of thinking and behaving (Coser 1986).

Gender inequality—the devaluation of "women" and the social domination of "men"—has social functions and a social history. It is not the result of sex, procreation, physiology, anatomy, hormones, or genetic predispositions. It is produced and maintained by identifiable social processes and built into the general social structure and individual identities deliberately and purposefully. The social order as we know it in Western societies is organized around racial ethnic, class, and gender inequality. I contend, therefore, that the continuing purpose of gender as a modern social institution is to construct women as a group to be the subordinates of men as a group. The life of everyone placed in the status "woman" is "night to his day—that has forever been the fantasy. Black to his white. Shut out of his system's space, she is the repressed that ensures the system's functioning" (Cixous and Clément [1975] 1986, 67).

THE PARADOX OF HUMAN NATURE

To say that sex, sexuality, and gender are all socially constructed is not to minimize their social power. These categorical imperatives govern our lives in the most profound and pervasive ways, through the social experiences and social practices of what Dorothy Smith calls the "everyday/everynight world" (1990, 31–57). The paradox of human nature is that it is *always* a manifestation of cultural meanings, social relationships, and power politics; "not biology, but culture, becomes destiny" (J. Butler 1990, 8). Gendered people emerge not from physiology or sexual orientation but from the exigencies of the social order, mostly, from the need for a reliable division of the work of food production and the social (not physical) reproduction of new members. The moral imperatives of religion and cultural representations guard the boundary lines among genders and ensure that what is demanded, what is permitted, and what is tabooed for the people in each gender is well known and followed by most (C. Davies 1982). Political power, control of scarce resources, and, if necessary, violence uphold the gendered social order in the face of resistance and rebellion. Most people, however, voluntarily go along with their society's prescriptions for those of their gender status, because the norms and expectations get built into their sense of worth and identity as a certain kind of human being, and because they believe their society's way is the natural way. These beliefs emerge from the imagery that pervades the way we think, the way we see and hear and speak, the way we fantasy, and the way we feel.

There is no core or bedrock human nature below these endlessly looping processes of the social production of sex and gender, self and other, identity and psyche, each of which is a "complex cultural construction" (J. Butler 1990, 36). *For humans, the social is the natural.* Therefore, "in its feminist senses, gender cannot mean simply the cultural appropriation of biological sexual difference. Sexual difference is itself a fundamental—and scientifically contested—construction. Both 'sex' and 'gender' are woven of multiple, asymmetrical strands of difference, charged with multifaceted dramatic narratives of domination and struggle" (Haraway 1990, 140).

NOTES

1. Gender is, in Erving Goffman's words, an aspect of *Felicity's Condition:* "any arrangement which leads us to judge an individual's . . . acts not to be a manifestation of strangeness. Behind Felicity's Condition is our sense of what it is to be sane" (1983, 27). Also see Bem 1993; Frye 1983, 17–40; Goffman 1977.

2. In cases of ambiguity in countries with modern medicine, surgery is usually performed to make the genitalia more clearly male or female.

3. See J. Butler 1990 for an analysis of how doing gender *is* gender identity.

4. Douglas 1973; MacCormack 1980; Ortner 1974; Ortner and Whitehead 1981a; Yanagisako and Collier 1987. On the social construction of childhood, see Ariès 1962; Zelizer 1985.

5. On the hijras of India, see Nanda 1990; on the xaniths of Oman, Wikan 1982, 168–86; on the American Indian berdaches, W. L. Williams 1986. Other societies that have similar institutionalized third-gender men are the Koniag of Alaska, the Tanala of Madagascar, the Mesakin of Nuba, and the Chukchee of Siberia (Wikan 1982, 170).

6. Durova 1989; Freeman and Bond 1992; Wheelwright 1989.

7. Gender segregation of work in popular music still has not changed very much, according to Groce and Cooper 1989, despite considerable androgyny in some very popular figures. See Garber 1992 on the androgyny. She discusses Tipton on pp. 67–70.

8. In the nineteenth century, not only did these women get men's wages, but they also "had male privileges and could do all manner of things other women could not: open a bank account, write checks, own property, go anywhere unaccompanied, vote in elections" (Faderman 1991, 44).

9. When unisex clothing and men wearing long hair came into vogue in the United States in the mid-1960s, beards and mustaches for men also came into style again as gender identifications.

10. For other accounts of women being treated as men in Islamic countries, as well as accounts of women and men cross-dressing in these countries, see Garber 1992, 304–52.

11. Dollimore 1986; Garber 1992, 32–40; Greenblatt 1987, 66–93; Howard 1988. For Renaissance accounts of sexual relations with women and men of ambiguous sex, see Laqueur 1990a, 134–39. For modern accounts of women passing as men that other women find sexually attractive, see Devor 1989, 136–37; Wheelwright 1989, 53–59.

12. Females who passed as men soldiers had to "do masculinity," not just dress in a uniform (Wheelwright 1989, 50–78). On the triple entendres and gender resonances of Rosalind-type characters, see Garber 1992, 71–77.

13. Also see Garber 1992, 234–66.

14. Bolin describes how many documents have to be changed by transsexuals to provide a legitimizing "paper trail" (1988, 145–47). Note that only members of the same social group know which

names are women's and which men's in their culture, but many documents list "sex."

15. For an account of how a potential man-to-women transsexual learned to be feminine, see Garfinkel 1967, 116–85, 285–88. For a gloss on this account that points out how, throughout his encounters with Agnes, Garfinkel failed to see how he himself was constructing his own masculinity, see Rogers 1992.

16. Paige and Paige (1981, 147–49) argue that circumcision ceremonies indicate a father's loyalty to his lineage elders—"visible public evidence that the head of a family unit of their lineage is willing to trust others with his and his family's most valuable political asset, his son's penis" (147). On female circumcision, see El Dareer 1982; Lightfoot-Klein 1987; van der Kwaak 1992; Walker 1992. There is a form of female circumcision that removes only the prepuce of the clitoris and is similar to male circumcision, but most forms of female circumcision are far more extensive, mutilating, and spiritually and psychologically shocking than the usual form of male circumcision. However, among the Australian aborigines, boys' penises are slit and kept open, so that they urinate and bleed the way women do (Bettelheim 1962, 165–206).

17. The concepts of moral hegemony, the effects of everyday activities (praxis) on thought and personality, and the necessity of consciousness of these processes before political change can occur are all based on Marx's analysis of class relations.

18. Other societies recognize more than two categories, but usually no more than three or four (Jacobs and Roberts 1989).

19. Carol Barkalow's book has a photograph of eleven first-year West Pointers in a math class, who are dressed in regulation pants, shirts, and sweaters, with short haircuts. The caption challenges the reader to locate the only woman in the room.

20. The taboo on males and females looking alike reflects the U.S. military's homophobia (Bérubé 1989). If you can't tell those with a penis from those with a vagina, how are you going to determine whether their sexual interest is heterosexual or homosexual unless you watch them having sexual relations?

21. Garber feels that *Tootsie* is not about feminism but about transvestism and its possibilities for disturbing the gender order (1992, 5–9).

22. See Bolin 1988, 149–50, for transsexual men-to-women's discovery of the dangers of rape and sexual harassment. Devor's "gender blenders" went in the opposite direction. Because they found that it was an advantage to be taken for men, they did not deliberately cross-dress, but they did not feminize themselves either (1989, 126–40).

23. See West and Zimmerman 1987 for a similar set of gender components.

24. On the "logic of practice," or how the experience of gender is embedded in the norms of everyday interaction and the structure of formal organizations, see Acker 1990; Bourdieu [1980] 1990; Connell 1987; Smith 1987a.

REFERENCES

ALMQUIST, E. M. (1987). Labor market gendered inequality in minority groups. *Gender and Society* 1:400–14.

AMADIUME, I. (1987). *Male daughters, female husbands: Gender and sex in an African society*. London: Zed Books.

AUSTID, S. H. (1986). Changing sex nature's way. *International Wildlife*, May-June, 29.

BARKALOW, C., with A. RAAB. (1990). *In the men's house*. New York: Poseidon Press.

BEM, S. L. (1981). Gender schema theory: A cognitive account of sex typing. *Psychological Review* 88: 354–64.

BERNARD, J. (1981). *The female world*. New York: Free Press.

BERNSTEIN, R. (1986). France jails 2 in odd case of espionage. *New York Times*, 11 May.

BIERSACK, A. (1984). Paiela "women-men": The reflexive foundations of gender ideology. *American Ethnologist* 11: 118–38.

BIRDWHISTELL, R. L. (1970). *Kinesics and context: Essays on body motion communication*. Philadelphia: University of Pennsylvania Press.

BLACKWOOD, E. (1984). Sexuality and gender in certain Native American tribes: The case of cross-gender females. *Signs* 10:27–42.

BOLIN, A. (1987). Transsexualism and the limits of traditional analysis. *American Behavioral Scientist* 31: 41–65.

BOLIN, A. (1988). *In search of Eve: Transsexual rites of passage*. South Hadley, MA: Bergin & Garvey.

BOURDIEU, P. ([1980] 1990). *The logic of practice*. Stanford, CA: Stanford UP.

BRODY, J. E. (1979). Benefits of transsexual surgery disputed as leading hospital halts the procedure. *New York Times*, 2 October.

BUTLER, J. (1990). *Gender trouble: Feminism and the subversion of identity*. New York and London: Routledge.

CHODOROW, N. (1974). Family structure and feminine personality. In Rosaldo and Lamphere.

CHODOROW, N. (1978). *The reproduction of mothering*. Berkeley: University of California Press.

CIXOUS, H. and CLÉMENT, C. ([1975] 1986). *The newly born woman*, translated by N. Wing. Minneapolis, MI: University of Minnesota Press.

COCKBURN, C. (1985). *Machinery of dominance: Women, men and technical know-how*. London: Pluto Press.

COLLINS, J. L. (1990). Unwaged labor in comparative perspective: Recent theories and unanswered questions. In Collins and Gimenez.

COLLINS, J. L. and GIMENEZ, M. E. (eds.) (1990). *Work without wages: Comparative studies of domestic labor and self-employment*. Albany: State University of New York Press.

CONNEL, R. W. (1987). *Gender and power: Society, the person and sexual politics*. Stanford, CA: Stanford UP.

COSER, R. L. (1986). Cognitive structure and the use of social space. *Sociological Forum* 1:1–26.

DAVIES, M. W. (1982). *Woman's place is at the typewriter: Office work and office workers, 1870–1930*. Philadelphia, PA: Temple UP.

DE BEAUVOIR, S. (1953). *The second sex*, translated by H.M Parshley. New York: Knopf.

DEVOR, H. (1987). Gender blending females: Women and sometimes men. *American Behavioral Scientist* 31:12–40.

DEVOR, H. (1989). *Gender blending: Confronting the limits of duality*. Bloomington: Indiana UP.

DWYER, D. and BRUCE, J. (eds.) (1988). *A home divided: Women and income in the Third World*. Palo Alto, CA: Stanford UP.

EICHLER, M. (1989). Sex change operations: The last bulwark of the double standard. In Richardson and Taylor.

EPSTEIN, C. F. (1988). *Deceptive distinctions: Sex, gender and the social order*. New Haven: Yale UP.

FOUCAULT, M. (1972). *The archeology of knowledge and the discourse on language*, translated by A. M. Sheridan Smith. New York: Pantheon.

GARBOR, M. (1989). *Vested interests: Cross-dressing and cultural anxiety*. New York and London: Routledge.

GILMORE, D. D. (1990). *Manhood in the making: Cultural concepts of masculinity*. New Haven: Yale UP.

GORDON, T. (1990). *Feminist mothers.* New York: New York UP.

GRAMSCI, A. (1971). *Selections from the prison notebook*, translated and edited by Q. Hoare and G. N. Smith New York: International Publishers.

HARAWAY, D. (1978). Animal sociology and a natural economy of the body politic. Part I: A political physiology of dominance. *Signs* 4:21–36.

HARAWAY, D. (1990). Investment strategies for the evolving portfolio of primate females. In Jacobus, Keller, and Shuttleworth.

HOWARD, J. E. (1988). Crossdressing, the theater, and gender struggle in early modern England. *Shakespeare Quarterly* 39:418–41.

HWANG, D. H. (1989). *M Butterfly.* New York: New American Library.

JACOBUS, M., KELLER, E. F., & SHUTTLEWORTH, S. (eds.). (1990). *Body/politics: Women and the discourses of science.* New York and London: Routledge.

JAY, N. (1981). Gender and dichotomy. *Feminist Studies* 7:38–56.

KANDO, T. (1973). *Sex change: The achievement of gender identity among feminized transsexuals.* Springfield, ILL: Charles C. Thomas.

KINCAID, J. (1978). Girl. *The New Yorker*, 26 June.

KONDO, D. K. (1990). *M. Butterfly*: Orientalism, gender, and a critique of essentialist identity. *Cultural Critique*, no. 16 (Fall): 5–29.

LANCASTER, J. B. (1974). *Primate behavior and the emergence of human culture.* New York: Holt, Rinehart & Winston.

LÉVI-STRAUSS, C. (1956). The family. In *Man, culture, and society*, edited by H. L. Shapiro. New York: Oxford UP.

LÉVI-STRAUSS, C. ([1949]1969). *The elementary structures of kinship*, translated by J. H. Bell and J. R. van Sturmer. Boston: Beacon Press.

MATTHAEI, J. A. (1982). *An economic history of women's work in America.* New York: Schocken.

MENCHER, J. (1988). Women's work and poverty: Women's contribution to household maintenance in South India. In Dwyer and Bruce.

MONEY, B. and EHRHARDT, A. A. (1972). *Man & woman, boy & girl.* Baltimore, MD: Johns Hopkins UP.

MORRIS, J. (1975). *Conundrum.* New York: Signet.

ORTNER, S. B. (1974). Is female to male as nature is to culture? In Rosaldo and Lamphere.

ORTNER, S. B. AND WHITEHEAD, H. (1981a). Introduction: Accounting for sexual meanings. In Ortner and Whitehead (eds.).

ORTNER, S. B AND WHITEHEAD, H. (1981b). *Sexual meanings: The cultural construction of gender and sexuality.* Cambridge, England: Cambridge UP.

PALMER, P. (1989). *Domesticity and dirt: Housewives and domestic servants in the United States, 1920–1945.* Philadelphia: Temple UP.

PAPANEK, H. (1990). To each less than she needs, from each more than she can do: Allocations, entitlements, and value. In Tinker.

RAYMOND, J. G. (1979). *The transsexual empire: The making of the she-male.* Boston: Beacon Press.

RESKIN, B. F. (1988). Bringing the men back in: Sex differentiation and the devaluation of women's work. *Gender & Society* 2:58–81.

ROSALDO, M. Z. AND LAMPHERE, L. (eds.). (1974). *Woman, culture and society.* Stanford, CA: Stanford UP.

RUBIN, G. (1975). The traffic in women: Notes on the political economy of sex. In *Toward an anthropology of women*, edited by Reiter, R.R. New York: Monthly Review Press.

RUGH, A. B. (1986). *Reveal and conceal: Dress in contemporary Egypt.* Syracuse, N.Y.: Syracuse UP.

SCOTT, J. W. (1988). *Gender and the politics of history.* New York: Columbia UP.

SHOWALTER, E. (1987). Critical cross-dressing: male feminists and the woman of the year. In *Men in feminism*, edited by Jardine, A. and Smith, P. New York: Methuen.

SMITH, D. E. (1990). *The conceptual practices of power. A feminist sociology of knowledge.* Toronto: University of Toronto Press.

TINKER, I. (ed.) (1990). *Persistent inequalities: Women and world development.* New York: Oxford UP.

VAN GENNEP, A. (1960). *The rites of passage*, translated by Vizedom M. B. and Caffee, G. L. Chicago: University of Chicago Press.

WEST, C. and ZIMMERMAN, D. (1987). Doing gender. *Gender and society* 1:125–51.

WHITEHEAD, A. (1981). "I'm hungry, Mum": The politics of domestic budgeting. In Young, Wolkowitz, and McCullagh.

WILLIAMS, C. L. (1989). *Gender differences at work: Women and men in nontraditional occupations.* Berkeley: University of California Press.

YOUNG, K., WOLKOWITZ, C., and McCULLAGH, R. (eds.). (1981). *Of marriage and the market: Women's subordination in international perspective.* London: CSE Books.

Speaking of Gender

The darkened eye restored

Carol Tavris

If women are not deficient man, or better than men, or different from men, or the same as men, what are they? For that matter, if men are not deficient women, or better than women, or different from women, or the same as women, what are *they*? How can we think of gender, speak of gender, without imposing a flat uniformity on the diversity of experience and without transforming differences into deficiencies?

One problem is that many people persist in believing that men and women differ in important qualities, in spite of innumerable studies that have failed to pin these qualities down and keep them there. For instance, we've seen that former (average) differences in intellectual skills, such as mathematical, verbal, and spatial abilities, have gradually vanished or are too trivial to matter. Other differences have faded quickly with changing times, as was the fate of "finger dexterity" (when males got hold of computers) and "fear of success" (when females got hold of law schools). But people *love* sex differences, and not just the familiar anatomical ones. They love to notice and identify ways in which the sexes seem to differ psychologically, and then to complain or laugh about what "women" are or what "men" do.

It is time to break away from the old, literal emphasis on counting differences, because most of those differences, as two psychologists once observed with a tinge of exasperation, are a matter of "now you see them, now you don't."[1] What does that fact alone tell us about efforts to compare the sexes? How serious should we be about the phenomena that are here today and gone tomorrow, like "fear of success" or "the Cinderella complex"?

As I was working on this book a friend asked me where I fell on the maximalist/minimalist debate in the study of women. As we've seen, maximalists (including cultural feminists) take the view that there are major, fundamental differences between the sexes; minimalists, whom we might call material feminists, believe that there are no significant differences other than those temporarily imposed by society. My first inclination was to treat my friend's question jok-

ingly—"On some issues I'm a maximum minimalist, on others I'm a minimum maximalist"—but as I thought about it, I decided that the question itself is the problem.

The reason is that all polarities of thinking, like all dichotomies of groups, are by nature artificial, misleading, and oversimplified. In this book, I've tried to show that on some issues the differences between women and men *are* trivial. On matters of intellectual ability, brain function, competence, morality, empathy, hostility, greed, the need for intimacy and attachment, love and grief, and the capacity for sexual pleasure—on these I am a minimalist. But on some issues I am a maximalist. It is absurd to speak of "sex differences" in rape rates, for instance, as if men are merely somewhat more likely than women to rape; the rate for women is virtually zero. It is absurd to speak of sex differences in the experience of pregnancy, or even in the different consequences that parenthood has in men's and women's lives; parenthood transforms most women's lives in a way that it does not transform most men's.

It is time to ask again the old unfashionable questions: Who benefits from the official theories and private stories we tell about presumed sex differences? Who pays? What are the consequences? Who gets the jobs and promotions? Who ends up doing the housework? If a woman wishes to believe that her problem is PMS or codependency rather than an abusive or simply unresponsive husband, how does she benefit? How does she lose? If a man wishes to believe that a woman is naturally better at relationships, emotions, and caretaking, how does he benefit? How does he lose? If society promotes the view that women are less reliable than men because of their hormones and their pregnancies, what are the consequences for equity at work, in the law, in politics?

This way of thinking gets us out of the "who's better" approach that, as far as I'm concerned; goes merely in circles. Too often, questions are framed this way: "Is the pattern of traditional male development (going straight up the ladder, marching through life in ten-year stages) better or worse than the pattern of female development (following a path with twists, interruptions, and unpredictable transitions)?" Such questions are unanswerable, because "better" or "worse" depends on what a person values, chooses, and wants out of life, and what rewards or disadvantages follow from those choices.

Instead, we might examine some results of the *belief* that women's life paths do not fit them for an academic or corporate career the way men's development does. One consequence is that women were once excluded from universities and still are excluded from advancement at the highest corporate levels; another is that men who focus wholly on career are excluded from the pleasures and crises of daily family life. We might ask how it came to be that only one professional path is acceptable, and who decides which one is correct. We might observe that the very question of whether women's life paths are worse or better than men's deflects us from the fact that men are setting the standard of normalcy.

I believe that we can think about the influence of gender without resorting to false polarities. There are alternatives to the familiar goal of counting trivial differences in personality traits, skills, and mental abilities, while recognizing the profound differences that continue to divide men and women in their daily lives. The first approach looks outward, to a renewed emphasis on the external factors and contexts that perpetuate or reduce differences. The second looks inward, focusing on the ways that women and men perceive, interpret, and respond to events that befall them—the stories they tell about their lives.

THE POWER OF CONTEXT . . . AND THE CONTEXT OF POWER

Have you ever watched a roomful of four-year-olds at play? If so, you have probably been struck by how different the boys and girls are. Many of the boys will be shouting and racing around, leaping head-first off tables, punching and pummeling one another. The girls will seem far more mild-mannered, playing peacefully and patiently, giggling and whispering to one another. Some will be clinging to the teacher, eager to please, afraid to get too far from her.

Observations like these have persuaded many people that basic personality differences between the sexes must be ingrained, since they appear at so early an age. Psychologists have churned out theories of why boys are so much higher in activity level and are more independent than girls, and why girls are more passive and dependent than boys. Recently, however, developmental psychologist Eleanor Maccoby took another look at these classic studies of children and came up with some startling new interpretations of them.

Starting in early childhood, boys and girls do develop different styles of play and influence, as any parent knows. But Maccoby found that children do not differ in "passivity" or "activity" in some consistent, trait-like way; *their behavior depends on the gender of the child they are playing with*. Among children as young as three, for example, girls are seldom passive with each other; however, when paired with boys, girls typically stand on the sidelines and let the boys monopolize the toys. This gender segregation, Maccoby says, is "*essentially unrelated to the individual attributes of the children* who make up all-girl or all-boy groups" (my emphasis).[2] Instead, it is related to the fact that between the ages of $3\frac{1}{2}$ and $5\frac{1}{2}$, boys stop responding to girls' requests, suggestions, and other attempts to influence them. When a boy and girl compete for a shared toy, the boy dominates—unless there is an adult in the room. Girls in mixed classrooms stay nearer to the teacher, it turns out, not because they are more dependent as a personality trait, but because they want a chance at the toys! Girls play just as independently as boys when they are in all-girl groups, when they will actually sit *farther* from the teacher than boys in all-male groups do.

By elementary school, the interaction and influence styles of boys and girls have diverged significantly. Girls tend to form intimate "chumships" with one or two other girls; boys form group friendships organized around games and other activities. Boys in all-boy groups are more likely than girls to interrupt one another; use commands, threats, or boasts; refuse to comply with another child's wishes; heckle a speaker; call another child names; top someone else's story; and tell jokes. Girls in all-girl groups are more likely than boys to agree with another speaker verbally; to pause to give another girl a chance to speak; to acknowledge what a previous speaker said. Among boys, Maccoby concluded, "Speech serves largely egoistic functions and is used to establish and protect an individual's turf. Among girls, conversation is a more socially binding process."[3]

Of course, to many people the more interesting question is *why* boys stop responding to girls, and why these same-sex patterns develop at all. It may be that children are mimicking the adult patterns of male dominance that they observe. It may result from an average difference in a biological disposition for rough-and-tumble play; in all primate species, young males are more likely than females to go in for physical roughhousing. I think both factors are undoubtedly involved. But my point here is that, for whatever reason, one result of this early divergence between males and females is that a culture gap develops between them, and our society, which rewards and fosters this gap, assures that it becomes increasingly wide by the time children reach adulthood.

The result of this process is that gender, like culture, organizes for its members different influence strategies, ways of communicating, nonverbal languages, and ways of perceiving the world. Just as when in Rome most people do as Romans do, the behavior of women and men depends as much on the gender they are interacting with than on anything intrinsic about the gender they are. For example, my friend Elliot Aronson, who is a social psychologist, has noticed that when he watches football or violent movies with other men he reacts differently than he does when he is watching something violent with his wife. "I can tolerate violence, in sports or films, much more than my wife can," he says. "So when we saw *Raging Bull*, I knew as I watched that she found many of the violent scenes offensive. That awareness colored my own reactions. By the time we left the theater we each had accommodated to the other: I disliked the movie more than I might have if I'd seen it with my male buddies, and she disliked it less."

This kind of silent accommodation goes on all the time, in a process that Candace West and Don Zimmerman call "doing gender."[4] We "do" gender unconsciously, adjusting our behavior and our perceptions depending on the gender of the person we are working, playing, or chatting with. What research like Maccoby's shows is that men and women do not have a set of fixed masculine or feminine traits; the qualities and behaviors expected of women and men vary, depending on the situation the person is in. A token woman in a group of men will feel highly aware of her femaleness, and so will the group.[5] Almost everything she does will be attributed to her gender, which is why she is likely to be accused of being too feminine (thus not

"one of the boys") or too masculine ("trying to be something she's not")—but what's really at issue is her visible difference from the majority. A token man in a group of women will have the comparable experience.

I observed this phenomenon not long ago at a conference of women psychoanalysts, who had gathered to discuss "barriers to female achievement." Being psychoanalysts, they were naturally inclined to emphasize the unconscious barriers in the psyche. I, in contrast, spoke of the barriers in women's work environments: the difficulty of being the token, the systematic obstacles to advancement, the way that dead-end jobs themselves create dead-end dreams. (As the token social psychologist, I felt uncomfortable speaking in these terms, but proceeded anyway.) When I finished, the lone male psychoanalyst in the audience rose to comment. "As I was listening to you, I disagreed with what you were saying," he said. "But then, when I got up to speak, I felt uncomfortable, my heart began to pound, and I realized it was because I am the only man in this room." The audience laughed sympathetically, but a woman on the panel next to me said, "Just like a man—the only guy in the room and he still has to be the first person to speak." She was, of course, further supporting my argument. She was attending to the fact of his being a man, and attributing his behavior to it.

The prevalent inclination to regard masculinity and femininity as permanent personality traits has overshadowed the importance of the context in which men and women live. In their everyday lives, men and women often behave in "feminine" ways (for example, when they are playing with their children or providing a supportive shoulder for a friend to cry on) and sometimes men *and* women behave in "masculine" ways (for example, when they are competing for a promotion). But by regarding masculinity and femininity as polar opposites, with one side usually better than the other, we forget that, in practice, most of us "do" both.

My women friends, for instance, are always amazed at how macho their otherwise affectionate and doting husbands become when they go off with the guys. "It's a transformation," one friend says, "that I attribute to high concentrations of testosterone in one room." She's right about the apparent transformation—most men like to "do" masculinity, with its rules of stoicism, playfulness, and competition, when they are with other males. But my friend is a lot more "girl-ish" (or whatever the female equivalent of macho is) over lunch with her women friends than she is in planning sessions at her mostly-male advertising agency. She loves to "do" femininity with other women.

This flexibility has proven to be a good thing. People who are rigidly masculine or feminine across all situations are less healthy, mentally and physically, than people who can adopt the best qualities associated with both extremes. Under some conditions the qualities we label feminine are good for both sexes, and under some conditions the qualities we label masculine are good for both sexes. In the family, for example, the positive qualities of traditional femininity—compassion, nurturance, warmth, and so on—are associated with marital satisfaction *in both sexes*.[6] Naturally; everyone wants a spouse who is affectionate and caring. And at work, the positive qualities of masculinity—assertiveness, competence, self-confidence—are associated with job satisfaction and self-esteem *in both sexes*. Naturally; everyone wants a co-worker who is capable.

Conversely, the extremes of femininity and masculinity can be unhealthy—literally. Psychologist Vicki Helgeson who conducted an in-depth study of men and women who had had heart attacks, found that for men, negative characteristics associated with masculinity (such as arrogance, hostility, cynicism, and anger) were related to having had more severe attacks, whereas the men who were more empathic and nurturing were more likely to have had less severe heart attacks and better relationships. Yet for women, too much femininity produced a poorer prognosis; the sickest women were those who had become overinvolved with others to the exclusion of caring for themselves.[7]

Most men and women, however, are flexible about masculinity and femininity not only across situations, but over the course of their lives. It's always amused me to think of how many theories are based on studies of college students, who do not even represent all young people their age, let alone older people. Our ideas about sex differences in moral reasoning, sexual attitudes and motives, and the need for love, among other topics, have been limited by this narrow evidence. Similarly, psychoanalytic thinking has emphasized the powerful and presumably lasting effects on masculinity and femininity of unconscious perceptions of events that occur during the first five years, or the first three years, or, increasingly, the first few months.

Theories based on studies of people at one phase of their lives, like those based on unconscious infantile dynamics, overlook the ways in which people's experiences and attitudes cause them to change. Psychologist Lawrence D. Cohn analyzed 65 studies, involving more than 9,000 people, to determine the extent of sex differences in personality throughout adolescence and adulthood. He found that sex differences in ego development and personality traits were greatest among junior- and senior-high-school students, largely because girls mature earlier than boys. But these differences, he found, "declined significantly among college-age adults, *and disappeared entirely among older men and women*" (my emphasis).[8] Both sexes go through phases of egocentrism and conformity at somewhat different ages, but differences between them eventually disappear; in adulthood, men and women do not differ in "maturity of thought" and complexity of reasoning. Similarly, in moral reasoning (the centerpiece of cultural feminism) as in other dimensions of personality development, both sexes ultimately converge.

Across the many fields of psychology, context repeatedly overwhelms personality in the search for meaningful differences between men and women.[9] Context, however, refers to far more than a person's immediate situation. It includes everything in the environment of a person's life: work, family, class, culture, race, obligations, the immediate situation and its requirements, the likelihood of experiencing violence and discrimination, access to health care and education, legal status, and so on. These factors not only affect sex differences, of course; they are responsible for differences and conflicts *within* each gender. The arguments within feminism, for example, of whether black women "should" be identifying with white women or with black men are as unresolvable as debates over whether women are "like" men or different. On some issues, such as rape or fetal protection laws, gender is the unifying principle. On others, such as health delivery to the poor, class is the unifying principle. And on others, such as differing educational opportunities for blacks and whites, race is the unifying principle.[10]

These matters of context aren't very sexy, I realize. When I drew up a table to summarize what research currently shows about differences between men and women (see next page), I noticed an interesting pattern. Almost all of the public conversation and debate about differences falls in the left-hand column, home of all the hot and timely topics such as male-female differences in the brain, moral reasoning, pacifism, empathy, and the need or capacity for attachment and love. Yet, in fact, that column is precisely where the differences *aren't*. The differences of magnitude turn up in the righthand column, home of the mundane yet persistent inequities in income, power, family obligations, housework, medical and legal treatment, and so on. As the sociologist Cynthia Epstein has observed, we focus on the "deceptive distinctions" between men and women and thereby ignore the important ones.[11]

By seeing the behavior of women and men in context, as flexible capabilities rather than solely as steadfast qualities of the person, we move away from the unfathomable question of what women or men are "really, essentially" like. By seeing the worlds of men and women as cultures that can be as different as Norwegian and Brazilian, we can identify the elements of those worlds that perpetuate or eliminate differences. These cultures, however, are not merely different and equal; they are vastly unequal in power, resources, and status. As a result, it is easy to mistake a power difference for a cultural one, as many of us do in the case of language.

Deborah Tannen's deservedly popular book, *You Just Don't Understand*, advances the two-cultures theory of miscommunication: the idea that men and women have trouble understanding one another because they come from two different worlds.[12] Tannen's book is chock full of charming, "Eureka!"-style stories of recognition. For example, she contrasts men's comfort with public speaking—on radio call-in shows, at meetings, in groups of friends—with women's preference for private speaking, the domain of intimate conversation. Tannen describes this difference as that between *report-talk* and *rapport-talk*. Men, she says, use conversation "to preserve independence and negotiate and maintain status in a hierarchical social order"; women use conversation as "a way of establishing connections and negotiating relationships."[13] (This difference, as we saw, begins in childhood.)

At the same time that Tannen's book was rising on the best-seller lists, another book on language appeared that made much less of a splash. The reason, I think, is apparent in the title. It is called *Talking Power: The politics of language*. The author, linguist Robin Lakoff, agrees that there are many differences in the nature, function, and style of male and female

Do Men and Women Differ?

Where the differences aren't	Where the differences are
Attachment, connection	Care-taking
Cognitive abilities	Communication
Verbal, mathematical,[a] reasoning, rote memory, vocabulary, reading,[b] etc.	• interaction styles
	• uses of talk
Dependency	• power differences
Emotions	Emotions
• Likelihood of feeling them	• Contexts that produce them
Empathy	• Forms of expression
Moods and "moodiness"	• "Feminization of love"
Moral reasoning	• "Feminization of distress"
Need for achievement	Employment, work opportunities
Need for love and attachment	Health and medicine
Need for power	• medication and treatment
Nurturance[c]	• longevity differences
Pacifism, belligerence	Income
(e.g., depersonalizing enemies)	Life-span development
Sexual capacity, desire, interest	• effects of children
Verbal aggressiveness, hostility	• work and family sequence
	Life narratives
	Power and status at work, in relationships, in society
	Reproductive experiences
	Reproductive technology and its social/legal consequences
	"Second shift": housework, child care, family obligations
	Sexual experiences and concerns
	Violence, public and intimate
	Weight and body image

[a] Males excel at highest levels of math performance; in general population, females have slight advantage.

[b] Males are more susceptible to some verbal problems. However, many alleged sex differences seem to be an artifact of referral bias: More boys are *reported* for help than girls, but there are no sex differences in the *actual* prevalence of dyslexia and other reading disabilities (see Shaywitz et al., 1990).

[c] As a capacity; in practice, women do more of the actual care and feeding of children, parents, relatives, friends.

talk. Where she disagrees is in the origins of those differences; they aren't just quaint and amusing habits designed by the god (or goddess) in charge of Exasperating the Sexes. They aren't even just a matter of socialization and learning. They aren't even entrenched conversational styles.

"Men's language is the language of the powerful," argues Lakoff. "It is meant to be direct, clear, succinct, as would be expected of those who need not fear giving offense. . . . It is the language of people who are in charge of making observable changes in the real world. Women's language developed as a way of surviving and even flourishing without control over economic, physical, or social reality. Then it is necessary to listen more than speak, agree more than confront, be delicate, be indirect, say dangerous things in such a way that their impact will be felt after the speaker is out of range of the hearer's retaliation."[14]

What would happen to your language if you played a subordinate role in society? You would learn to persuade and influence, rather than assert and demand. You would become skilled at anticipating what others wanted or needed (hence "women's intuition"). You would learn how to placate the powerful and soothe ruffled feelings. You would cultivate communication, cooperation, attention to news and feelings about others (what men call gossip). In short, you would develop a "woman's language." But the characteristics of such a language develop primarily from a power imbalance, not from an inherent deficiency or superiority in communication skills, emotion, or nurturance. They develop whenever there is a status inequity, as can be seen in the languages of working-class Cockneys conversing with employers, blacks conversing with whites, or prisoners conversing with guards.

This power imbalance is the reason that women, far more than men, are able to do what linguists call "code-switching." That is, women learn to speak the standard Male Dialect as well as their own nonstandard Female, whereas men are less able to switch from their speech to female speech. As Lakoff observes:

Women in business or professional settings often sound indistinguishable from their male counterparts. Speakers of nondominant forms must be bilingual in this way, at least passively, to survive; speakers of the dominant form need not be. (So women don't generally complain that men's communication is impossible to understand, but the battlecry 'What do women want?' has echoed in one form or another down the centuries.)[15]

Tannen's book is appealing because it describes how women and men differ in their use of language, and it characterizes many familiar misunderstandings. Yet I had the same reaction after reading it that I had after reading Carol Gilligan's descriptions of male and female moral reasoning, or Nancy Chodorow's descriptions of male and female attachment styles. After feeling a flash of recognition, along with gratitude that the authors show that women's ways are as good as

men's and maybe better, I came away with the sense that men and women are monumentally but intrinsically different.

What Tannen's approach overlooks is that people's ways of speaking, just as Eleanor Maccoby observed with children, often *depend more on the gender of the person they are speaking with than on their own intrinsic "conversational style."* Psychologist Linda Carli demonstrated this by observing pairs of individuals—male-male, male-female, and female-female—discussing a topic on which they disagreed.[16] Women spoke more tentatively than men did, she found, only when they were speaking to men! With men, they offered more disclaimers ("I'm no expert," "I may be wrong," "I suppose," "I mean," "I'm not sure"). They used more hedges and moderating terms, like the use of *like* ("drinking and driving is, like, dangerous"). And they used more tag questions that solicit agreement ("It's unfair to prevent eighteen-year-olds from drinking when they can be drafted and killed in war, isn't it?").

Carli even discovered why many women use such hesitations and tags when they speak with men: It works. "Women who spoke tentatively were more influential with men and less influential with women," she reports.[17] Tag questions and hesitations annoyed other women, but they seemed to reassure the men. Even though the men regarded an assertive woman as being more knowledgeable and competent than a woman who said the same thing but with hesitations, they were more *influenced* by a woman who spoke tentatively. They liked her more and found her more trustworthy. When a woman uses tentative language with a man, Carli concludes, she may be communicating that she has no wish to enhance her own status or challenge his. This makes him more inclined to listen.

Indeed, whenever social scientists have looked beneath (or around) many of the apparent linguistic differences between women and men, they often find that qualities thought to be typical of women are, instead, artifacts of a power imbalance. . . . Both men and women who hold positions of authority display the nonverbal signs of authority, such as looking at you while they speak instead of shyly turning away. And women *and* men who are in the one-down position in a relationship, such as being witnesses in a courtroom, reveal the hesitations and uncertainties of so-called "women's speech" (pauses, hedges, "sort of's," and the like).[18]

"Women's language" often seems illogical to men, full of chatter about unimportant things. But because men have written the rules of language, says Lakoff, "women become by default the quintessential *they*. Women are the other, the outsider: unintelligible and therefore not needing to be heard."[19] The fact that women are the outsiders, not that they have some universal conversational style, is what creates differences between the sexes.

Lakoff offers the example of the Malagasy tribe, a closed, remote society of Madagascar. Because almost nothing happens to the Malagasy, news of any kind becomes a valued commodity, and the ability to hoard information is a sign of power. Powerful individuals therefore speak in a way that seems deliberately misleading and annoying to Westerners. "But this strategy is typical only of male Malagasy speakers," Lakoff notes. "Women do just the reverse: speak directly and to the point. . . . As a result, women are considered poor communicators: they just don't know how to behave in a conversation, don't know how to transmit information properly, and are therefore illogical."[20]

No one decides that a certain form of language is logical, notices that women happen to speak differently, and then rationally concludes that women are illogical. On the contrary, the dominant group first notices the ways in which subordinates differ from themselves; they then assume that these differences occur because the subordinates are illogical; they then conclude that there is something about the subordinates' brains, bodies, or abilities that makes them think and speak illogically. This is illogical reasoning.

As long as women are The Other, anything they do will be wrong. If they try to speak Male-Speak, as Geraldine Ferraro did when she ran for Vice President, they may be regarded as tough and unladylike. If they speak Female-Speak, in the manner of Vanna White, their language may be seen as incompetent and inconsequential. Some women respond to this dilemma by valuing "women's speech" for its subtleties and attention to feelings, its polite unwillingness to interrupt the (dominant) speaker, and its modest hesitations. I think this response is fine, as long as it doesn't deflect everyone from the long-range goal of reducing that power imbalance, improving communication, and making sure that women are *heard* in the public domain. Achieving this goal will require a critical density of women in the public sphere and in positions of authority, so that how any one woman speaks will not be the focus of everyone's attention. Lakoff herself is optimistic:

As long as there is a power imbalance, women will be in a double bind communicatively: any way they communicate that differs from the way men do will be stigmatized as different and therefore worse; any attempt they make to approximate the ways of men will be stigmatized as unfeminine, indicative of bad character, and uppity. . . . But as long as we remain aware and committed, things are likely to continue to get better. We just have to keep the faith.[21]

THE POWER OF STORY: GENDER AS NARRATIVE

The communications researcher George Gerbner once defined the human being as "the only species that tells stories—and lives by the stories we tell." This idea— that narratives that describe our lives are the key metaphor in understanding human behavior—is sweeping psychology and many other fields.[22] Our plans, memories, love affairs, hatreds, ambitions, and dreams are guided by plot outlines. "Understanding one's past, interpreting one's actions, evaluating future possibilities—each is filtered through these stories," says psychologist Mary Gergen. "Events 'make sense' as they are placed in the correct story form."[23]

Thus we say, "I am this way because, as a small child, I fell into a vat of cherry juice, and then my parents . . ." We say, "Let me tell you the story of how we fell in love." We say, "When you hear what happened, you'll understand why I was entitled to take such gruesome revenge." We say, "I can't be a neurosurgeon, because, when I was sixteen . . . and then . . ." As psychologist George Howard puts it, life is the story we live by, pathology is a story gone mad, and psychotherapy is an exercise in "story repair."[24] Stories need not be *fictions*, in the child's meaning of "tell me a story." They are narratives that provide a unifying theme to organize the events of our lives. They attempt to be true, but they are rarely the whole truth and nothing but the truth.

It is here, in the stories that men and women tell about their lives, that we find the greatest divergence between them.[25] In the classic myth of the hero, the man ventures forth from everyday life to conquer supernatural forces in the name of his quest. He returns, victorious, and is richly rewarded. "Where is the woman in this story?" asks Mary Gergen. "She is only to be found as a snare, an obstacle, a magic power, or a prize."[26] Anthropologist Marvin Harris has noted that "When the King told his knights, 'If you slay the dragon, I'll give you one of my daughters,' no one doubted that the daughters would go when given."[27] What effect does this story, endlessly repeated in its ancient and contemporary forms, have on women's identities and dreams?

And the classic woman's story, whether in ancient fairy tales like "Cinderella" and "Sleeping Beauty" or their modern equivalents in romance novels and films like *Pretty Woman*, is a narrative of passivity, chance, and fate. Horrible things, all of them beyond her control, happen to the beautiful heroine who awaits rescue by her Prince. Until he saves her, she is doomed to a life of sweeping, cleaning, struggling, prostitution, or corporate executivehood. If she isn't beautiful, pliant, and willing to give it all up for love, she doesn't get rescued. What effect does this story, endlessly repeated throughout our culture, have on women's identities and dreams?

I want to emphasize again that there is nothing essential to men's and women's natures that causes the difference in their stories. We've seen how, as women became the love experts in this century, their love stories changed. We've seen how stories of the body, of sexuality, of the brain have changed, along with the times. In the space of only a few years, social movements and economic upheavals can alter the stories that people are able to envision for themselves. And in our private lives, we frequently change explanatory themes as a result of love, tragedy, everyday experience, political conversion, or psychotherapy.

Moreover, it is not that all men tell one kind of story, and all women tell another; that men are always ruthless knights and women are willing pawns; that men value only success and woman value only people. As I have been arguing, the virtues and vices of human character are distributed across the sexes, arrogance and compassion included. Men and women differ, however, in the kinds of stories they tell, which reflect the different lives they lead. And, even more interestingly, they differ in what they feel obliged to include or leave out of their narratives, which reflects the roles they play and the faces they present to the world. We saw that men and women, in talking about their divorces, speak of their break-ups and their grief differently. They both feel pain, yet they publicly tell different stories.

Would a celebrity football player, age twenty-four, reveal his abiding and faithful love for his wife? Would a famous congresswoman reveal how she ruthlessly abandoned her husband when he was ill and savagely destroyed the careers of her opponents? Almost never. Gergen, who has been studying modern autobiographies of famous people, finds common metaphors in men's stories that are rarely found in women's. The stories of powerful white men typically fit the traditional male narrative: These authors became heroes, pursue their quest, overcome crises, and ultimately win victory. Women and children may come along for the ride, but (if they figure in the story at all) they must not interrupt it; even if they have the impertinence to get sick and die, the male narrators barely notice.

Thus, Lee Iacocca's best-selling autobiography describes his rise to the top of an automotive career, but he says little about his wife. Mary, a diabetic, had two heart attacks, each one following a crisis in Iacocca's career at Ford or Chrysler. He writes: "Above all, a person with diabetes has to avoid stress. Unfortunately, with the path I had chosen to follow, this was virtually impossible." Too bad for Mary. Gergen comments:

Obviously his description of his wife's death was not intended to expose his cruelty. It is, I think, a conventional narrative report—appropriate to his gender. The book (and his life) are dedicated to his career. It appears that Iacocca would have found it unimaginable that he should have ended his career in order to reduce his wife's ill-health. As a Manstory, the passage is not condemning; however, read in reverse, as a wife's description of the death of her husband or child, it would appear callous, to say the least.

Likewise, Chuck Yeager reveals in his autobiography—his shining tale of having the Right Stuff to be a pilot—that his wife, who had had four children in quick succession, became gravely ill during her last pregnancy. "Whenever Glennis needed me over the years, I was usually off in the wild blue yonder," Yeager wrote. Would a woman write that sentence about her husband? Would she be so cavalier—to use an appropriately sex-specific word—about her husband's needs?

And Richard Feynman the humorous, brilliant, Nobel Prize–winning physicist, was married to a woman who was ill with tuberculosis for seven years. Feynman, hard at work on the atomic bomb, borrowed a car to get to her bedside on the day she was dying. This is what he had to say:

When I got back (yet another tire went flat on the way), they asked me what happened. "She's dead. And how's the program going?" They caught on right away that I didn't want to talk about it.

Was the tire really more memorable to Feynman than his wife's death? Unlikely. The point is *the narrative of the story:* deaths, even of loved ones, are not to interfere in the Quest, the Task, the Goal.

Many men write of their Quest in a tone of hostility, aggression, and domination: the triumph of conquering impossible odds, defeating the other guy, or beating "nature's incalculable odds" (this last from John Paul Getty on the exhilaration of drilling his first oil well). Men's stories, says Gergen, "celebrate the song of the self"; men are even willing to play the "bastard." In letters, journals, and autobiographies, many eminent male writers and less-eminent celebrities sing of the self as John Cheever, in his published Journals, did in this entry:

I wake. My older son has returned safely from school. The trees are full of birds. I mount my wife, eat my eggs, walk my dogs. It is the day before Easter.[28]

My son, *my* wife, *my* eggs, *my* dogs, *my* sexual pleasure! Not a paragraph, I think, that could have been written by most female diarists. (Well . . . Katharine Hepburn did call her autobiography *Me*, refrained from revealing her emotions about private matters such as her brother's death, and unflinchingly described her independent professional accomplishments—and for this "male" narrative she was castigated by *The New York Times Book Review*.)

Pick up a typical celebrity autobiography by a male athlete, and chances are that you will learn about his sexual exploits, put-downs of women, childish tantrums, and drunken braggadocio. Writer Merrill Markoe, who read a few of these literary efforts, decided that "The parading of infantile character flaws as though they were badges of honor and distinction is a male trait. . . . The combination of arrogance without shame and insensitivity without humility or hindsight is the sole domain of attractive successful white men."[29]

Eminent women who write their autobiographies almost never tell the same narrative plot. Women enjoy their successes, press to win, and work hard to succeed; they may be as motivated, as self-absorbed, and as pushy as men, but they do not talk about these matters the same way. Beverly Sills, a star at the New York City Opera, gave up her singing career for two years to accompany her husband to Cleveland, where he worked. She writes: "My only alternative was to ask Peter to scuttle the goal he'd been working toward for almost twenty-five years. If I did that, I didn't deserve to be his wife." Gergen's analysis of women's stories—Nien Cheng, who wrote of her survival during years of imprisonment in China, Martina Navratilova on her tennis career, Sills, and others—shows that while men tell of sacrificing their lives to their careers, women tell the same story in reverse.

In the writings of accomplished women, Gergen finds, we hear about the audience response, affection for the opponent, and continuity with goals other than professional achievement, rather than seeing such goals in opposition to achievement. "I've never been able to treat my opponent as the enemy," writes Navratilova (but do we doubt what a fierce competitor she is?). "One of the things I always loved best about being an opera singer was the chance to make new friends every time I went into a new production," writes Sills (but do we doubt what a highly motivated and ambitious singer she was?). Merrill Markoe, wanting to be fair to those arrogant male celebrity athletes, read the comparable "trashy" autobiographies of female celebrities such as Joan Collins, Shelley Winters, and Tina Turner. The women wrote mainly about failed marriages and relationships, embarrassing personal foibles, and family tragedies (but do we really believe they are all soft-hearted sweeties?).

The autobiographies of famous people tell explicit stories; contemporary magazines often tell implicit ones. Popular magazines, for instance, reveal an interesting difference in one way that men and women may think about their lives. As you can see in the table opposite, most of the magazines directed to women include a horoscope, a mystic, or a numerologist; not one man's magazine does. Even newer magazines for older women, such as *Lear's* and *Mirabella*, have them. Why? The surface answer is that horoscopes are cheap to produce, advertisers compete to position their ads next to them, and readers like them.

I am not suggesting that women are more superstitious or gullible than men—or, in the cultural-feminist reinterpretation of this difference, more open-minded and spiritual! Actually, studies of the general population find that women are only slightly more likely than men to believe in astrology (some of the most popular astrology columns are written by men), and that even this difference shrinks when education is factored in.[30] But if we examine one meaning of horoscopes in women's magazines, I believe we find a subtle measure of a difference in women's and men's feelings of control over their lives, in their perception of opportunities and destinies.

It is no coincidence that the magazines called *Fame, Success, Money,* and *Fortune* (which both sexes read) do not have horoscopes, because astrology contradicts the capitalist message that anyone can become anything with enough hard work. Likewise it is significant that magazines about careers, families, and motherhood—*Working Woman, New York Woman, Family Circle, Good Housekeeping*—do not have horoscopes. Mothers and employed women, apparently, know that their fate has little to do with the stars and everything to do with time management. But the magazines for women about relationships, beauty, youth, and the pursuit of perfection—goals which women feel increasingly to be out of their control, increasingly a source of anxiety—tell women they can have it all, at least if their stars and cosmetics are in place.

What follows from the way people tell their stories, and how they interpret their challenges and destinies? What images inspire them and which ones restrict them? We develop and shape our identities in the narratives we tell about our lives, and we are as influenced by the stories we feel do *not* apply to us as by those that do. Two of our most popular cultural stories illustrate their power over our individual and collective imaginations: the struggle of the artist and the valor of the soldier, both of which rest on male narratives.

The writer Ursula Le Guin has skillfully dissected the male story of the artist, a narrative specifying that the artist must sacrifice himself to his art. (This idea is a justification for the "artist as bastard" subplot.) Given such a narrative, Le Guin observes, it follows that any attempt to combine art with housework and family is "impossible, unnatural."[31] How, then, have women writers told their stories? Often in terms of

Presence or Absence of Horoscopes in Leading Magazines

Women's magazines		Men's magazines	
Cosmopolitan	yes	Esquire[d]	no
Elle	yes[a]	Fame	no
Glamour	yes	Field & Stream	no
Harper's Bazaar	yes	Forbes	no
In Fashion	yes	Fortune	no
Lear's	yes	GQ	no
Mademoiselle	yes	Golf	no
Marie Claire	yes	M (The Civilized Man)	no
Mirabella	yes[b]	MGF	no
Moxie	yes[c]	(Men's Guide to Fashion)	
New Woman	yes	Manhattan, Inc.	no
Sassy	yes	Men's Fitness	no
Self	yes	Money	no
Seventeen	yes	Penthouse	no
Taxi	yes	Playboy	no
Vogue	yes	Popular Mechanics	no
Woman	yes	Soldier of Fortune	no
Family Circle	no	Sports Afield	no
Good Housekeeping	no	Sports Illustrated	no
Ladies' Home Journal	no	Success	no
McCall's	no	Tennis	no
New York Woman	no		
Redbook	no		
Working Woman	no		

NOTE: General-interest magazines directed at both sexes (*Atlantic, Harper's, People, Time,* etc.) have been omitted. Most of these do not have horoscopes, with the notable exception of *TV Guide.*
[a]Has a horoscope *and* a numerology column.
[b]Has a "Mystic of the month" column.
[c]Had a column by a self-proclaimed "psychic" answering reader's queries.
[d]The British edition of *Esquire* began a "Horoscope for Men" in 1991.

how to escape their families, how to find rooms of their own. The "heroic" female writers had books instead of babies, because otherwise, the story went, both the art and the children would suffer. Yet, as Le Guin points out, the "you-can't-write-if-you-procreate myth" applies to women only. Male writers may have children, as long as someone else is attending to them and they don't interrupt the basic plot of Heroic Male Writer on his Anguished Quest. Narratives about great artists, Le Guin shows, have lacked the possible vision that having a family, or merely having the experience of being female, might *enhance* writing:

It seems to me a pity that so many women, including myself, have accepted this denial of their own experience and narrowed their perception to fit it, writing as if their sexuality were limited to copulation, as if they know nothing about pregnancy, birth, nursing, mothering, puberty, menstruation, menopause, except what men are willing to hear, nothing except what men are willing to hear about housework, childwork, lifework, war, peace, living and dying as experienced in the female body and mind and imagination.[32]

Le Guin hastens to add she doesn't want to reverse the myth, arguing that you *have* to have children to be a great writer. She does not hold with the sentimental belief that motherhood puts a woman artist "in immediate and inescapable contact with the sources of life, death, beauty, growth, corruption. . . ." The point is that our vision of the artist has been based on, and limited by, a male narrative, and this story leaves out much that is important to men as well as to women.

Cultural narratives and metaphors are so powerful that when they are violated by actual human beings, many people feel momentarily dizzy. War is a male story par excellence; in the Persian Gulf War, which reflected a "man-to-man" battle between George Bush and Saddam Hussein, we were inundated with images of brave male soldiers "rescuing" an "innocent" nation that had been "raped" by evil villains. What, then, of the 30,000 women (about six percent of the total troops) who served in this war, in every way but combat? How can women do any rescuing of a damsel nation in distress?

The media solution was to emphasize repeatedly, in articles and images, all the mothers who were tearfully leaving small children at home. *People* magazine did a cover story on "Mom Goes to War." Writer Nell Bernstein, who looked, observed that "it was nearly impossible to find an article that mentioned women soldiers without also mentioning the children they left behind."[33] What the articles did not say, however, was that the majority of women in the military are not mothers, and that a higher percentage of male soldiers have children than female soldiers do. These facts do not fit the traditional story we tell, that war is male, fought by men *for* women. "When women start muscling in on the action," says Bernstein, "the ancient paradigms of war and peace are threatened." Indeed; perhaps it's time for new ones.

And so each sex deviates from its proper story at some peril. "Both seemed imprisoned by their stories," says Gergen; "both bound to separate pieces of the world, which if somehow put together, would create new possibilities—ones in which each could share the other's dreams."

We can be imprisoned by stories; or we can be liberated by them. This has been, in a way, a book about the stories that women and men tell about themselves and one another, and about the scientific stories that society favors. Interest in power and circumstance as the guiding story of human behavior has faded in favor of the individual, internal stories of biology and psychodynamic processes.[34] Of course we are influenced by biology, personality, and unconscious motives. Yet when we choose to emphasize these pieces of the human story over all others, the consequences can be significant. And the consequences differ for men and women, as we can see in the following two examples:

- *The story of depression.* Last year, a popular television show presented a report on postpartum depression.[35] Postpartum depression is nearly as popular a topic these days as PMS, and for many of the same reasons; hormones explain so *many* problems that women have.[36]

  In this case, the interviewer spoke with a woman who revealed how unhappy and teary she had been after the birth of each of her three children. She worried that she wasn't a contented mother "like other women." In fact, she confessed, at the point of her deepest depression she had fantasized about throwing her baby down an escalator in a shopping mall. Her husband was worried. His wife wasn't the "cute, fun girl" she once was. Fortunately, this woman learned that her problem was easily resolved: She was suffering from postpartum depression, a condition easily treated with antidepressants. Cut to shots of happy wife, happy husband, playing with happy children.

  Now, perhaps this woman does have an extreme chemical imbalance that is best treated with antidepressants. I am not unilaterally opposed to the use of medication, and if it helps her, all the better. Let us simply consider the possibility that there is more to this story than a tale of hormones gone awry. Not once during this show, for example, did it occur to the murmuring sympathetic interviewer, or to the woman herself, that this young mother's unhappiness might be due to having *three babies in four years and a Navy spouse who was out of town much of the time.* Three babies in diapers, with no help from another adult? Who *wouldn't* feel exhausted and weepy? What woman could be a "cute, fun girl" under such conditions?

  Moreover, not once during this show did the interviewer or a psychologist point out that feelings of incompetence are perfectly normal for mothers to have (especially in a society that doesn't much value what mothers do), and so are fantasies of throwing the baby over a banister (it doesn't mean you will actually do it). No one told this woman that depression can result from sheer fatigue and the daily relentlessness of caring for three babies. No one suggested that perhaps she would benefit by getting together with other mothers of small children; finding ways to organize and share child care; and insisting that her husband do his share around the house. No one interviewed the authors of a recent study, who found that the predictors of postpartum depression were in fact *pre*partum depression, "inadequate social support, reduced closeness to husband, and poor self-esteem."[36]

In this context, consider the 1990 report of a comprehensive three-year study of depression, conducted under the auspices of the American Psychological Association. This study made news, but rarely with the excitement of front-page headlines. The *Los Angeles Times* relegated it to a short item on page 25, with the boring headline "Study Analyzes Women's High Depression Risk." That hardly sounds newsworthy, until we begin reading:

> Women are twice as likely as men to suffer from major depression, for reasons more often cultural than biological, according to the results of a three-year study released Wednesday.
>
> Poverty, unhappy marriage, reproductive stress and sexual and physical abuse are stronger factors than biological conditions in accounting for the difference in depression rates between men and women, the American Psychological Assn. researchers reported . . .
>
> "The task force found that women truly are more depressed than men, primarily due to their experience of being female in our contemporary culture," [Ellen McGrath, chair of the research group] said.[37]

The APA study contradicted the widespread belief that the origins of clinical depression are primarily biochemical, and therefore that any difference between men and women in the prevalence of depression must likewise be due to biochemical differences between them. The APA study spoke in a currently unfashionable language, locating the origins of human misery in human experience. And so it was relegated to page 25 of my daily newspaper.

The story of success. Popular explanations of why more women have not reached the highest pinnacles of power have tended to blame women, in one way or another, for a failure of motivation or a personal inability to combine family and career. Certainly, in many professional situations, women are more likely then men to blame themselves for not succeeding, to lose self-confidence, and to lower their ambitions.

However, in a review of the research on gender and power in organizations, Belle Rose Ragins and Eric Sundstrom found that these psychological symptoms proved to be *results* of powerlessness, not causes. Men tend to develop more power as they progress through their careers, whereas most women do not. The reason, Ragins and Sundstrom learned, was "a consistent difference favoring men" in men's and women's access to power and having the resources to make use of it. "The processes involved in the development of power differ for men and women," they concluded, and "the path to

power for women resembles an obstacle course."[38] Powerlessness, in short, perpetuates powerlessness.

What are the results of the popularity of the story of hormones over life experiences, of intrapsychic fears of success over objective obstacles to success? They translate into how we treat our children and the expectations we have for ourselves; they affect our deepest emotions and visions of ourselves; they determine how we respond to adversity and the normal problems of adult life. We must be careful about the explanations and narratives we choose to account for our lives because, as we will see next, we live by the stories we tell. . . .

BRIDGES

The debates about sex differences—and about who is differing from whom, and why—are not academic. Our society is presently in the midst of an intellectual revolution that may prove to be as significant as what Copernicus, Darwin, and Freud wrought in their fields. The earth is not the centerpiece of the solar system, human beings are not the centerpiece of creation, the ego is not the centerpiece of the mind, and man is not the centerpiece of experience and knowledge—neither the generic man nor the individual man.[39]

This effort at expanding our vision seems the essence of sweet reason to me, but, as Bertrand Russell once said, all social movements go too far. This one will too. For some, the goal of dethroning the universal male means setting up a universal female in his place. It means that everything men do, have done, have written or composed, have thought or written, have invented or created, is worthless or hopelessly biased. Some academic conventions reverberate with the acronym DWEM, which stands for all the people whose hopelessly-biased work is now supposed to be expunged from the curriculum: dead white European males. Oh, dear; I'm rather fond of Beethoven, Socrates, Shakespeare, Aristotle, Renoir, Cervantes, Galileo, Oscar Wilde, George Bernard Shaw. . . .

In contrast to the contemporary impulse to pit the contributions of one group against those of another—male versus female, East versus West, black versus white—I wish to argue here on behalf of Anna Julia Cooper's vision one hundred years ago: a vision of the whole, rather than of segments. I believe it is possible to eradicate (or at least minimize) the assumption of "normal" men and "different" women. But we will not accomplish this in the movement toward particularization, in which each gender, race, or ethnicity seeks only its own validation, celebrates only itself, and rewrites its history and character in false phrases of its own superiority.

We need some new stories, and we need to be critical of many of the existing ones. For ourselves as individuals, one way we can evaluate our stories is not by whether they are "true" or "false"—most of the time, in trying to find the reasons for the complicated things we do, we can never know. But we can try to examine what the story leaves out, for all stories leave out something. Genetic stories tend to omit experience; psychoanalytic stories tend to overlook the environment; my own favorite social-psychological stories tend to ignore biology; childhood-blame stories leave out current events. We do best, I believe, by adding explanations to our quiver of life stories rather than limiting ourselves to only one.

Further, rather than trying to find the "right" story or the "official" story, we can direct our attention to the origins, contexts, and consequences of stories. What are the supports for narratives that rely heavily on a vocabulary of disease, deficiency, victimhood, and astrological destiny rather than a vocabulary of power, context, and current relationships? As I've tried to show, society has a considerable investment in promoting the former set of stories as explanations for why women are the way they are, and why they differ from men.

For example, over the years we have heard a lot about the problems of those poor Superwomen, the jugglers who strive to balance work and family. The attention goes to the woman who is doing the juggling. We hear how stressed she is, how impossible her task is, how likely she is to fail, how work is killing her (or making her sick), how much better off she will be if she quits knocking her head against a wall and goes home to raise her children.

In fact, the preponderance of the evidence utterly contradicts these popular impressions.[40] Women who juggle are better off in many ways than those who don't (though they *are* more tired!). The story of "superwomen," however, draws the heat away from anyone or any institution that might be able to make it easier on the woman who has a family and a job. It draws attention away from husbands and employers, the division of family obligations, and the structure of corporations. It places the burden of adjustment on the woman, thereby eliminating the need to make adjustments elsewhere.

In the last chapter we saw how one quarreling couple, Evan and Nancy, came up with a compromise story, a rearrangement of their family obligations based on their new narrative of Nancy's "compulsiveness" and Evan's "laziness." To sociologist Arlie Hochschild, who interviewed them, one consequence of this story was quite simply the survival of the marriage. Nancy and Evan's story allows them to maintain their belief that they have an equal marriage, even as she gives up half of her career time and even though her "half" of the housework is all of it, minus walking the dog. According to Hochschild, many women would rather have a stable marriage than risk the pursuit of an equitable one, and Nancy and Evan's resolution allows them to do it.

Nancy and Evan may live happily ever after. But their story is being multiplied thousands of times across the country, at which point it becomes a social problem, not just an individual one. A recent Roper survey found that, next to money, the issue of "how much my mate helps around the house" is the "single biggest source of resentment" in many women's lives.[41] The story that couples tell about their marriages may serve either to paper over that resentment or to move them toward a resolution that works.

Likewise, a story fails when it is sustained at great personal or social cost: when it has unforeseen long-term consequences, when the individual pays the price of living a lie, when a hidden toll is being taken, when it narrows vision instead of expanding it, or when it systematically leads to the exclusion or maltreatment of large segments of the population.

This is one reason that I am so concerned about the current fashion for cultural feminism, the appealing theories that women have a natural ability to be connected, attached, loving, and peaceful, that they speak in a different voice, have different ways of knowing, or different moral values. Of course, many of the women who promote these ideas do so with the intention of raising women's self-esteem and promoting their welfare in society. Nevertheless, the philosophy of cultural feminism has functioned to keep woman focused on their allegedly stable and innate personality qualities, instead of on what it would take to have a society based on the qualities we value in both sexes.

Further, quite apart from their lack of research validation, these ideas get men off the hook in family arrangements, ignore men's affections and attachments, and underwrite the ideology that women are best suited to certain kinds of jobs. At their worst, they distract us from the hard work we have to do, women and men together, to humanize jobs, foster children's welfare, save the environment, and combat corporate mindlessness.

Stories have consequences, but stories change, and how and why they do is the heart of the human enterprise. Our narratives can reclaim the psychological qualities historically associated with female deficiency, but within a framework of synthesis rather than opposition. Dependency, typically viewed as feminine and a sign of childish regression, is a basic human need. Women do not need to stop being conciliatory in order to be leaders, or to stop caring for others in order to be autonomous. Connection and autonomy are both necessary in human life. The goal for both sexes should be to add qualities and skills, not lose old ones.

We can tell more flexible stories, ones that recognize that our qualities, skills, and actions change over the life span. People develop, learn, have adventures and new experiences; and as they do, their notions of masculinity and femininity change too. The rules of gender are not frozen at one moment in time, whether the psychologically fashionable time is thought to be infancy, childhood, or adolescence.

We can become aware of the hidden agendas not only in old-fashioned stories but also in modern ones. It is easy to discern the political purpose of the diagnosis of drapetomania, that nineteenth-century "disease" that afflicted slaves with an uncontrollable urge to escape from slavery. Yet it is equally important to identify the uses of diagnoses such as PMS and Self-defeating Personality Disorder today. It is easy to see the bias in labeling as "sick" those women, years ago, who refused to play their traditional roles and wanted instead to be lawyers, scientists, and artists. It is equally important to recognize the bias in labeling as "sick" (e.g., "addicted") those women today who play the traditional role of caretaker too well.

We can realize that our favorite life stories may not apply to everyone in the same ways. We have learned that the male model of adult development does not apply to all women, the medical model of sexuality does not apply to all women or men, the female model of emotional expressivity does not apply to all men. Likewise, there is no one right way to have (or combine) a marriage, a baby, or career; no one right way to be straight or gay; no one right way to be a parent.

There is, in sum, no one right way to be, no single story that fits all.

Finally, we can resist the temptation to see the world in opposites. Western ways of thinking emphasize dualisms and opposites, and pose many questions of human life in fruitless either-or terms. Are we rational or emotional creatures? Will we win or lose? Is this decision good or bad? Are we uniquely human or basically mammalian? Are we shaped by nature or nurture, mind or environment? Are we masculine or feminine? As long as the question is framed this way—"What can we do about *them*, the other, the opposite?"—it can never be answered, no matter which sex is being regarded as "them." The question, rather, should be this: What shall we do about *us*, so that our relationships, our work, our children, and our planet will flourish?

NOTES

1. Deaux and Major, 1987, p. 369.

2. Maccoby, 1988, p. 755.

3. Maccoby, 1990, p. 516. Here, she is referring to the work of Maltz and Borker, 1982, among others.

4. West and Zimmerman, 1987.

5. On tokens, see Kanter, 1977; Nieva and Gutek, 1981; Tavris and Wade, 1984.

6. Antill, 1983.

7. Helgeson, 1990.

8. Cohn, 1991, p. 252. His conclusion on the "single path to maturity," p. 263.

9. On context, see Deaux and Major, 1987, 1990; Eagly, 1987; Jacklin, 1989.

10. For instructors and other individuals who are interested in issues of class and race in the field of gender studies, see Phyllis Bronstein and Kathryn Quina (Eds.), *Teaching a Psychology of People* (Washington, D.C.: American Psychological Association, 1988).

11. Epstein, 1988.

12. Tannen, 1990. Maltz and Borker, 1982, also propose a "two cultures" view of sex differences in communication patterns.

13. Tannen, 1990, p. 77.

14. Lakoff, 1990, p. 205.

15. Ibid., p. 202.

16. Carli, 1990.

17. Ibid., p. 941.

18. See Snodgrass, 1985, on "women's intuition"; O'Barr, 1983, and Erickson et al., 1978, on the courtroom research; Dovidio et al., 1988, on visual displays and power. See also McConnell-Ginet, 1983.

19. Lakoff, 1990, p. 199.

20. Ibid., p. 203.

21. Ibid., p. 214.

22. On narratives in psychology, see Howard, 1991; Mair, 1988; Sarbin, 1986.

23. Mary Gergen, 1992.

24. Howard, 1991, p. 194.

25. See Heilbrun, 1989, and Le Guin, 1989, on writing women's lives; on differences in the way men and women who have the same occupation perceive their work, see Weingarten and Douvan, 1985. Cultures too differ in the form a story might take, which is the source of much misunderstanding and conflict. For instance, when Anglo women talk about the reasons for the breakup of their marriages, they tell a linear story of events through time: "He did this, then I did that, and finally he did this intolerable last straw." But Puerto Rican women tend to describe their breakups in terms of significant episodes, in no particular historical order. Each story symbolizes to the speaker what her marital problems were, but whereas an Anglo interviewer can "hear" and understand the first woman, she remains "out of sync" with the second. Many people are "out of sync" with what other cultures, races, and genders are trying to say to them. See Riessman, 1987.

26. Gergen, 1992. All subsequent excerpts from her research on autobiographies are from this source.

27. Carol Tavris, "Male supremacy is on the way out. It was just a phase in the evolution of culture" (Interview with Marvin Harris), *Psychology Today*, January 1975, pp. 61–69. Quote, p. 66.

28. Excerpt reprinted in *The New Yorker*, January 28, 1991, p. 29.

29. Merrill Markoe, "Write Like a Man," *New York Woman*, April 1990, pp. 58ff.

30. See George H. Gallup, Jr., and Frank Newport, "Belief in Paranormal Phenomena Among Adult Americans" (Special Report/Gallup Poll), *Skeptical Inquirer, 15* (Winter 1991), pp. 137–146.

31. Le Guin, 1989, p. 222.

32. Ibid., p. 228.

33. Nell Bernstein, "Babes in Arms," *Image*, March 24, 1991, pp. 7–9.

34. For an analysis of this point, see Kahn and Yoder, 1989, and Mednick, 1989.

35. The show was *20/20,* August 2, 1991.

36. Mimia C. Logsdon, John C. Birkimer, and Angela B. McBride, "A Further Look at Predictors of Postpartum Depression." Paper presented at the annual meeting of the American Psychological Association, San Francisco, 1991. The evidence regarding postpartum depression is actually quite similar to that regarding PMS. That is, hormonal changes following childbirth are normal; most of the women who suffer extreme clinical depression, however, tend to have had a lifetime history of depressive episodes or other problems.

37. *Los Angeles Times*, December 6, 1990, p. A25. For the actual study on depression, see McGrath et al., 1990.

38. Ragins and Sundstrom, 1989, p. 51.

39. See, for example: Crawford and Marecek, 1989; K. Gergen, 1985; M. Gergen, 1988; Hare-Mustin and Marecek, 1990; Minnich, 1990; Tiefer, 1988.

40. See Crosby, 1991, for an excellent review of the research evidence on the benefits to women (physically and mentally) who combine paid work and family.

41. Roper Organization survey of 3,000 women, released September 1990. Quoted in Bettijane Levine, "Heavy-duty Anger," *Los Angeles Times*, September 23, 1990, pp. E1, E8–9.

Warrior Dreams

Introduction: Post-Vietnam Blues

James William Gibson

... The 1980s ... saw the emergence of a highly energized culture of war and the warrior. For all its varied manifestations, a few common features stood out. The New War culture was not so much military as paramilitary. The new warrior hero was only occasionally portrayed as a member of a conventional military or law enforcement unit; typically, he fought alone or with a small, elite group of fellow warriors. Moreover, by separating the warrior from his traditional state-sanctioned occupations—policeman or soldier—the New War culture presented the warrior role as the ideal identity for *all* men. Bankers, professors, factory workers, and postal clerks could all transcend their regular stations in life and prepare for heroic battle against the enemies of society.

To many people, this new fascination with warriors and weapons seemed a terribly bad joke. The major newspapers and magazines that arbitrate what is to be taken seriously in American society scoffed at the attempts to resurrect the warrior hero. Movie critics were particularly disdainful of Stallone's Rambo films. *Rambo: First Blood Part 2* was called "narcissistic jingoism" by *The New Yorker* and "hare-brained" by the *Wall Street Journal*. The *Washington Post* even intoned that "Sly's body looks fine. Now can't you come up with a workout for his soul?"

But in dismissing Rambo so quickly and contemptuously, commentators failed to notice the true significance of the emerging paramilitary culture. They missed the fact that quite a few people were not writing Rambo off as a complete joke; behind the Indian bandanna, necklace, and bulging muscles, a new culture hero affirmed such traditional American values as self-reliance, honesty, courage, and concern for fellow citizens. Rambo was a worker and a former enlisted man, not a smooth-talking professional. That so many seemingly well-to-do, sophisticated liberals hated him for both his politics and his uncouthness only added to his glory. Further, in their emphasis on Stallone's clownishness the commentators failed to see not only how widespread paramilitary culture had become but also its relation to the historical moment in which it arose.

Indeed, paramilitary culture can be understood only when it is placed in relation to the Vietnam War. America's failure to win that war was a truly profound blow. The nation's long, proud tradition of military victories, from the Revolutionary War through the century-long battles against the Indians to World Wars I and II, had finally come to an end. Politically, the defeat in Vietnam meant that the post-World War II era of overwhelming American political and military power in international affairs, the era that in 1945 *Time* magazine publisher Henry Luce had prophesied would be the "American Century," was over after only thirty years. No longer could U.S. diplomacy wield the big stick of military intervention as a ready threat—a significant part of the American public would no longer support such interventions, and the rest of the world knew it.

Moreover, besides eroding U.S. influence internationally, the defeat had subtle but serious effects on the American psyche. America has always celebrated war and the warrior. Our long, unbroken record of military victories has been crucially important both to

the national identity and to the personal identity of many Americans—particularly men. The historian Richard Slotkin locates a primary "cultural archetype" of the nation in the story of a heroic warrior whose victories over the enemy symbolically affirm the country's fundamental goodness and power; we win our wars because, morally, we deserve to win. Clearly, the archetypal pattern Slotkin calls "regeneration through violence" was broken with the defeat in Vietnam.* The result was a massive disjunction in American culture, a crisis of self-image: If Americans were no longer winners, then who were they?

This disruption of cultural identity was amplified by other social transformations. During the 1960s, the civil rights and ethnic pride movements won many victories in their challenges to racial oppression. Also, during the 1970s and 1980s, the United States experienced massive waves of immigration from Mexico, Central America, Vietnam, Cambodia, Korea, and Taiwan. Whites, no longer secure in their power abroad, also lost their unquestionable dominance at home; for the first time, many began to feel that they too were just another hyphenated ethnic group, the Anglo-Americans.

Extraordinary economic changes also marked the 1970s and 1980s. U.S. manufacturing strength declined substantially; staggering trade deficits with other countries and the chronic federal budget deficits shifted the United States from creditor to debtor nation. The post-World War II American Dream—which promised a combination of technological progress and social reforms, together with high employment rates, rising wages, widespread home ownership, and ever increasing consumer options—no longer seemed a likely prospect for the great majority. At the same time, the rise in crime rates, particularly because of drug abuse and its accompanying violence, made people feel more powerless than ever.

While the public world dominated by men seemed to come apart, the private world of family life also felt the shocks. The feminist movement challenged formerly exclusive male domains, not only in the labor market and in many areas of political and social life

---

*Richard Slotkin, *Regeneration through Violence: The Mythology of the American Frontier, 1660–1860.* (Middletown, Conn.: Wesleyan University Press, 1973).

but in the home as well. Customary male behavior was no longer acceptable in either private relationships or public policy. Feminism was widely experienced by men as a profound threat to their identity. Men had to change, but to what? No one knew for sure what a "good man" was anymore.

It is hardly surprising, then, that American men—lacking confidence in the government and the economy, troubled by the changing relations between the sexes, uncertain of their identity or their future—began to *dream*, to fantasize about the powers and features of another kind of man who could retake and reorder the world. And the hero of all these dreams was the paramilitary warrior. In the New War he fights the battles of Vietnam a thousand times, each time winning decisively. Terrorists and drug dealers are blasted into oblivion. Illegal aliens inside the United States and the hordes of non-whites in the Third World are returned by force to their proper place. Women are revealed as dangerous temptresses who have to be mastered, avoided, or terminated.

Obviously these dreams represented a flight from the present and a rejection and denial of events of the preceding twenty years. But they also indicated a more profound and severe distress. The whole modern world was damned as unacceptable. Unable to find a rational way to face the tasks of rebuilding society and reinventing themselves, men instead sought refuge in myths from both America's frontier past and ancient times. Indeed, the fundamental narratives that shape paramilitary culture and its New War fantasies are often nothing but reinterpretations or reworkings of archaic warrior myths. . . .

OLD WARRIORS, NEW WARRIORS

America has always had a war culture, and that long history of martial adventures provides a crucial background for understanding the post-Vietnam warrior. This culture has two fundamental stories, one celebrating the individual gunman who acts on his own (or in loose concert with other men); the other portraying the good soldier who belongs to an official military or police unit and serves as a representative defender of national honor. And these mythologies, sometimes overlapping, sometimes competing, have at different times defined the martial mentality of the country.

The lone gunman has the longer story to tell. Many of the earliest heroes of the American Revolution, from the Minutemen to Francis Marion (the South Carolina "Swamp Fox" guerrilla fighter), were acclaimed for their independence and willingness to fight on their own. The revolutionary army was not an army in the modern sense but a militia of mobilized citizens. That a kind of paramilitary force won the Revolution is a fact of profound consequence: the story of independent gunmen defeating evil enemies and founding a new society became America's creation myth.

The frontiersman who fought in the Indian Wars from the 1600s to the 1880s had a similarly important impact on American history and culture. He was the central figure of the mythologized West, a world neatly divided between a wilderness (or primeval chaos) full of savage Indians and wild beasts—a "frontier" zone of isolated cabins, ranches, and small towns—and an established civilization back East. In the mythology of the American West, evil Indians relish the chaos of their wilderness and violently resist efforts of Anglo pioneers and townspeople to push civilization westward. The heroes of these stories—figures such as Daniel Boone and Davy Crockett—are invariably men of great bravery and virtue who live on the frontier and fight on behalf of civilization, but who themselves never desire to live in the domesticated interior of society. They either fight the Indians or outlaws by themselves or recruit more ordinary men into posses to assist them in the struggle to defend the sacred order against evil.

After the Civil War, the U.S. Army became the most important armed force in the American West. Lone gunmen and paramilitary posses began to seem like archaic relics who had more in common with the Indians and outlaws they fought than with the disciplined forces of the emerging industrial society. Indeed, the lone warrior faced a real crisis once the Indian Wars came to a close. Within a decade after Custer and a detachment of his 7th Cavalry were killed at the Little Bighorn River in 1876, the battles to avenge him had driven the surviving Indians to reservations. With the "enemy" vanquished and the United States settled from coast to coast, there were no more battles for the warrior to fight and no more wilderness for him to conquer.

Without his historical mission, the old warrior hero found himself recast in a variety of roles, imaginary and real. William F. Cody was a genuine Western scout when, in 1869, a writer named Edward Judson sought him out as a source of fresh material. Writing under the pen name Ned Buntline, Judson used only the barest traces of Cody's life to create the first Buffalo Bill novels. Published on newsprint and costing just a dime, these serial adventures were an immediate success, spawning hundreds of sequels through the 1870s and 1880s. Other authors soon took the Buffalo Bill character as their model and renamed him in their works. Cody, on his part, used the growing national and international audience for his fictionalized exploits as a market for a new kind of theater, the Wild West Show. In these performances Cody repeatedly emphasized how he, personally, represented the boundary between chaos and order: "I stood between savagery and civilization most all of my early days."[1] The confrontations he staged between cowboys and Indians received at least as much acclaim as the novels.

Cody's greatest admirer was Theodore Roosevelt. It was Roosevelt who rescued the warrior hero from the circus and reintegrated him into history. And it was Roosevelt who first understood the potency of warrior images for inspiring the nation with military fervor. The scion of a wealthy New York family, Roosevelt was enamored of the romance of the Western myth; he dreamed as early as 1886 of leading the grandest posse of all time, a cavalry troop of "harum-scarum rough riders."[2] (Rough Riders was the nickname for the cowboys in William Cody's Wild West Show.) After the battleship *Maine* exploded in Havana harbor in February 1898, Roosevelt resigned his position as assistant secretary of the Navy and asked President McKinley for an officer's commission as second-in-command of a special volunteer cavalry unit. In April 1898, McKinley called for 125,000 volunteers to fight in Cuba and authorized the formation of the First U.S. Army Volunteer Cavalry, a special unit "to be composed exclusively of frontiersmen possessing special qualifications as horsemen and marksmen."[3] Roosevelt negotiated with William Cody to enlist all of his Rough Riders in the First Cavalry.[4] Before leaving for Cuba, the First Cavalry picked up two other important recruits—a pair of photographers from Vitagraph, one of the world's first motion-picture companies.[5]

The legend of Roosevelt's victory at San Juan Hill was in large part created by Vitagraph. When the pho-

tographers shot the battle, what they captured on film was a slow, undramatic encounter in which the Rough Riders were one unit among many. To make a more exciting newsreel, the Vitagraph photographers and the Rough Riders then staged a mock-battle at Santiago Bay after the real fight was over; they gave captured Spanish troops guns whose cartridges had gunpowder but no bullets, then choreographed an American charge against them. This fake footage became part of the official record of San Juan Hill. Vitagraph also staged a number of other battles showing U.S. troops winning glorious victories, some of which included scenes of Roosevelt and the Rough Riders.[6] Partly because of the fame he gained from these choreographed battles, Roosevelt became a national hero and vice president under McKinley in 1900. After McKinley's assassination in 1901, Roosevelt became president.

In reworking the Western myth of the frontiersman fighting Indians into one of U.S. Army troops fighting Spaniards in Cuba, Roosevelt created a rough synthesis of both American martial traditions. He also encouraged the emerging film industry to follow his lead and begin the transition from the Western into what would become the war movie. In 1915, Roosevelt joined forces with the president of Vitagraph, his friend Stuart Blackton, to promote *Battle Cry of Peace,* a fictional account of a German invasion of the United States made to encourage U.S. entry into World War I.[7] *Battle Cry of Peace* was among the world's first full-length feature films and had an immense success. (Vitagraph had previously made *Birth of a Nation*, D. W. Griffith's ode to the redemptive power of the paramilitary Ku Klux Klan to save white Southerners from black savagery after the Civil War.)

The film industry quickly emerged as the central medium for creating and communicating an American war culture. By the late 1930s, both Hollywood and the U.S. government understood that creating favorable images of soldiers and combat was essential to mobilizing the American populace for war. Hollywood began working closely with the military: for example, the Army Air Corps assigned over 110 planes to Metro-Goldwyn-Mayer for the production of *Test Pilot* (1939), a story loosely based on the development of the first major U.S. strategic bomber, the B-17.[8] MGM needed the planes to make the movie convincing to audiences, while the Air Corps wanted publicity to help persuade Congress to approve money for mass production of the B-17. The plan worked: Congress granted the requested appropriations.

Besides creating interest in advanced weaponry, the films made on the eve of World War II stressed the morality of going to war and the problems civilians faced in becoming soldiers. Jesse L. Lasky of Warner Bros. personally approached Sergeant Alvin York, the World War I fighter, for the rights to make a movie of his transformation from Christian pacifist to war hero.[9] Gary Cooper, the Western star, played York; the film was the top money-maker in 1941.[10] Among the millions of young men who saw it was a poor Texas farm boy named Audie Murphy who subsequently joined the Army and became the most decorated soldier of World War II. He later had a career as an actor in Westerns and war movies.[11]

After Pearl Harbor, the film industry and the Roosevelt administration established more formal working relationships. The armed forces had to recruit and educate millions of men from very different backgrounds. Hundreds of films were produced: training films on such subjects as basic personal hygiene; complex technical films on how to use and maintain equipment; political documentaries designed to motivate the troops. Ronald Reagan spent much of World War II making films like these, while other stars—John Wayne, for example—continued to appear in feature films on military subjects. Wayne wanted to enlist, but at thirty-four, married, and apparently suffering from an old University of Southern California football injury, he was not eligible. So instead he starred in *They Were Expendable* (1945) and other war epics.

Of the 1,700 full-length feature films made from 1941 to 1945, more than one-third were war-related. Film was the government's preferred medium to mobilize support for the war effort. In the words of Elmer Davis, director of the Office of War Information (whose Hollywood branch guided scriptwriters so that films would receive official approval), "The easiest way to inject propaganda ideas into most people's minds is to let it go in through the medium of an entertainment picture when they do not realize that they are being propagandized."[12] An estimated 85 million people went to the movies each week during these years, and the war films they saw told essentially the same story again and again.[13]

First, American forces are nearly always portrayed as virtuous defenders of a just cause. Second, U.S. soldiers typically win their fights against Germans and Japanese. A few films made in the early years of World War II—such as *Wake Island* (1942) and *Bataan* (1943)—showed American troops fighting to their deaths, but even in these rare cases American casualties are portrayed as necessary sacrifices, as a way to buy time for the coming American counteroffensive that will surely lead to victory. In the World War II films, might and right go hand in hand.

Third, in these films soldiers always fight as part of a larger military organization which has clearly defined command structure, and acts on behalf of the nation. Actual combat is almost always shown as a struggle between opposing military forces—civilians rarely get killed in cross fire.

Fourth, might and maturity are also linked: In the standard combat narrative, immature youths arrive at a training camp or the base area of the combat unit to which they have been assigned, receive harsh but loving instruction from a paternal commander, and then, in the course of battle, mature into men. War is presented as a relatively benign ritual transition from boyhood to adulthood.

Fifth, in these films war seems safe, even attractive. Bullet and shrapnel wounds are relatively painless and bloodless. No one screams in agonizing pain. Even death is discreet, signified by a small red dot on the chest. Finally, American soldiers never fight for the sheer joy of fighting. They are at war to stop the enemy and to establish or preserve the sacred order.

These genre conventions outlived the war they portrayed. From 1948 to 1968, under the shadow of the Cold War and American involvement in Korea, war movies and Westerns continued to be America's most popular entertainment. Approximately 1,200 war movies were made in those years; over 200 received major assistance from the Defense Department.[14]

From the 1950s to the late 1960s, millions of American boys—the male cohort of the baby-boomer generation—watched these films. Between 1965 and 1973, about 3.5 million men went to Vietnam, most of them from this generation. Indeed, one of the strongest themes to emerge from the hundreds of Vietnam War novels and oral histories concerns the profound influence imaginary wars had on these men as youths and young men. . . .

Once in Vietnam, some soldiers tried to reenact the film scenes they had seen or read about in war fiction. One senior sergeant at the central Military Assistance Command Vietnam (MACV) headquarters reported that in the first four months of 1968 some sixty Americans either killed themselves or killed others while playing fast-draw with their pistols.[15] Michael Herr recounts tragic cases in which soldiers acted like war-movie heroes for network television news teams during firefights with enemy forces:

I keep thinking about all the kids who got wiped out by seventeen years of war movies before coming to Vietnam to get wiped out for good. You don't know what a media freak is until you've seen the way a few of those grunts would run around during a fight when they knew there was a television camera nearby; they were actually making war movies in their heads, doing little guts-and-glory Leatherneck tap dances under fire, getting their pimples shot off for the networks.[16]

But these cases seem the exception, not the rule. For most soldiers, the realities of Vietnam led to disenchantment with war mythology. Tom Suddick, a former infantryman, discovered that "the movies lie. There are no young men in war. You're nineteen or twenty, and you become old with the first case of the Viet shits. Your youth drops purgatively out of your asshole during your first week in Vietnam."[17] Ron Kovic went into shock after he accidentally shot and killed a fellow Marine instead of the enemy. Referring to himself in third person, Kovic writes: "He'd never figured it would ever happen this way. It never did in the movies. There were always the good guys, the cowboys, and the Indians. There was always the enemy and each of them killed each other."[18] Another soldier shot a Vietcong opponent, but experienced emotional reactions very different than he expected: "I felt sorry. I don't know why I felt sorry, John Wayne never felt sorry."[19]

As the war continued, the name of John Wayne—whose war and Western films had grossed over 700 million dollars—took on many different meanings.[20] Gustav Hasford's fellow Marines found Wayne's movie on Vietnam, *The Green Berets* (1968)—the only major studio release on Vietnam made during the 1960s—hysterically funny. . . .

Others couldn't laugh at all. Charles Anderson remembers an infantry sergeant warning new soldiers against movie-style heroics: "Now, we don't want to see no John Wayne performances out here. Just do your job and listen to your fire team and squad leaders—they're the ones who'll teach you everything and help you to get through the next few months."[21] And after a few months, warning turned into invective: "There was no longer any doubt about what warfare in the modern industrial world had come to mean. The grunts—newbys, short-timers, and lifers alike—could see now that what happens to human beings in mechanized warfare has absolutely no poetic. Fuck you, John Wayne!"[22]

Some soldiers, however, clung desperately to the myth, perhaps to make their lives in the war zone more bearable. War-movie and comic-book heroes always survived their battles; identifying with these fantasy heroes may well have helped many soldiers conquer their fear of death. . . .

Only political and military leaders far removed from the battlefield were able to go through the Vietnam War without having their movie-informed fantasies of "regeneration through violence" severely shaken. President Richard Nixon watched *Patton* several times in the spring of 1970. In the film, George C. Scott portrays the general as a charming eccentric whose brilliance and valor save an American airborne division under siege from a German offensive. According to then–Secretary of State William Rogers and White House Chief of Staff H. R. Haldeman, Nixon talked incessantly about the movie as he decided that U.S. forces should invade Cambodia.[23] Nixon even ordered American military chaplains to pray for a change in the weather, just as Patton did during the Battle of the Bulge—a modern example of what anthropologist Sir James George Frazer called the archaic practice of homeopathic or imitative magic.[24]

Henry Kissinger also resorted to movie imagery to explain why he remained popular even at the height of the Vietnam War. "I've always acted alone," said Kissinger.

Americans admire that enormously. Americans admire the cowboy leading the caravan alone or astride his horse, the cowboy entering the village or city alone on his horse, without even a pistol maybe, because he doesn't go in for shooting! He acts, that's all: aiming at the right spot at the right time. A Wild West tale, if you like.[25]

But all these assertions of mythic grandeur and all the displays of American power, such as the massive B-52 bombing of North Vietnam in December 1972, could not sustain the myth that this was a country that always won its battles. In May 1975, Communist forces entered Saigon and television audiences watched in horror and disbelief as helicopters evacuated the last Americans from Vietnam.

At first, then, the trauma of the prolonged war in Vietnam, followed as it was by ignominious defeat, seemed to spell the end of the traditional war mythology. Both the Western and war-movie genres faded away in the late 1960s and 1970s. John Wayne's death in 1979 seemed to bring a symbolic closure to this cultural history. But paradoxically, the old mythology of American martial prowess and moral virtue instead assumed an even greater hold on the popular imagination. Why it did has much to say about the American way of looking at the world: defeat was incomprehensible, both morally and "scientifically."

Ever since World War II, it had been an article of faith of U.S. military policy that a country's technological sophistication and the sheer quantity of its war supplies were the decisive factors that would lead to victory. In this new model of warfare (which I call "technowar"), war was conceptualized as a kind of high-technology production process in which the officer corps were managers, the enlisted men were workers, and the final product was death: whoever had the biggest, most sophisticated apparatus was sure to produce the highest enemy body count and thus win.[26] The "soft" variables of war, such as the history, culture, and motivations of a people, were not seen as being important because they had none of the "hard" reality of weapons.

Not surprisingly, then, many military leaders and policy analysts were unwilling to rethink their conceptual approach as the war in Vietnam dragged on—or they were incapable of doing so. Any advance by the Vietcong and North Vietnamese Army was seen as only a temporary gain sure to be reversed by a further escalation of U.S. intervention. The basic assumptions of technowar were reasserted again and again even at the bitter end. Defeat in Vietnam came to be viewed as the result of what the Joint Chiefs of Staff called "self-imposed restraints." From this perspective, technowar would have inevitably produced victory if it hadn't been for the influences of liberals in Congress, the antiwar movement, and the news media, who together stopped the military from unleashing its full powers of destruction.*

Under the rational veneer of this conservative intellectual argument lay the classic mythology of the heroic American warrior who always won his battles and simply could not be defeated. U.S. defeat in Vietnam could only be explained by arguing that the full powers of the heroic American warriors of legend had not been unleashed. . . .

Conservative politicians, syndicated columnists, and military intellectuals had offered versions of the "self-imposed restraint" argument for years, both during and after the Vietnam War. By the late 1970s and early 1980s, it was not an esoteric doctrine, but a widely accepted explanation. Among those people who accepted the conservative analysis were magazine and novel editors and film producers who intuitively understood the popular desire for narratives of victory—New War stories featuring American heroes whose triumphs in battle could somehow heal the wounds of a crippled political system. As Alexander M. S. McColl editorialized in the premier issue of *Soldier of Fortune: The Journal of Professional Adventurers,* "The disastrous events of the last month in Southeast Asia are not only an appalling human tragedy for the peoples of Cambodia and South Vietnam, they are the most serious defeat of Western Christendom in a generation, and the final requiem of the United States as a great power."[27] *SOF,* of course, was among the first to call for the private warrior's redemption of Vietnam through new battles.

Many Hollywood filmmakers explicitly set out to revise and revive the old mythology. Menahem Golan, who, as president of the Cannon Group, was responsi-

---

*This is of course an extraordinary argument, a rhetorical coup d'état that completely dismisses just how great an effort the United States had made. Over 3.5 million men and women served in Vietnam. At the height of the war in 1968–69, the United States deployed more than 550,000 troops, a figure that excludes at least 200,000 to 300,000 more people serving in the Seventh Fleet off Vietnam, in U.S. Air Force bases in Thailand and Guam, and in logistic, repair, and training capacities in the United States. Roughly 40 percent of all U.S. Army divisions, more than 50 percent of all Marine Corps divisions, one-third of U.S. naval forces, half of the Air Force fighter-bombers, and between 25 and 50 percent (depending upon the year) of B-52 bombers in the Strategic Air Command fought in the war. From eight to fifteen million tons of bombs (U. S. versus Vietnamese figures) were dropped on Southeast Asia—at minimum, over four times the amount the United States dropped in World War II—along with another fifteen million tons of artillery shells and other munitions.

ble during the mid-1980s for cranking out scores of profitable action-adventure films, modeled his stock adventure films on Westerns. "What is a Western?" he asked. "A Western is basically a fairy tale of a hero who is supposedly good saving the town or saving the poor or fighting for something which is moralistically important to the family, to the human beings fighting for the good, fighting all the evils of the world, fighting all the demons of the world." Like fairy tales, his movies would have happy endings.[28]

Other Hollywood directors and novelists also saw themselves as modern mythologists. Joseph Zito, director of the Chuck Norris *Missing in Action* films (1984 and 1985), thought of Vietnam as an imaginary land, the perfect setting for new cowboy-and-Indian movies.[29] Lionel Chetwynd, who directed *Hanoi Hilton* (1987) for Cannon, claimed that as a director "you owe your allegiance to the mythic mold, as opposed to the war. We use [the war] as a landscape." Film, he insisted, was the direct descendant of myth.[30] . . .

The New War [that was thus created] is fought principally by paramilitary warriors who are most often hostile to official legal and police authorities. Their hostility usually dates from their experience in Vietnam. . . .

Post-Vietnam mythic heroes are completely enraged when they fight, and the violence they inflict is shocking. The scores of scenes featuring dismemberment, torture, and shredded bodies oozing fluids are absolutely central to the culture and are far removed from the older, dispassionate moral accounting. The New War promotes a vicious appetite for destruction that cannot be satiated.

Indeed, so great is that hunger for killing that the New War appears to be a war without end. At one level, this means New War stories can be set in widely varying historical eras. Many refight the Vietnam War, either in imaginary battles or in rescue missions to bring POWs home. A second type of story shows the heroes fighting terrorists of one kind or another, either inside the United States or abroad on a global battlefield. The third type presents post–World War III Armageddon narratives in which the surviving Americans battle Russian invaders in the rural South and West. In this scenario, the cities are destroyed and America returns to the mythical Western frontier, only this time the Russians are bad-guy cavalry and the Anglos get to be good-guy Indians.

The most important characteristic that distinguishes the New War mythology from the old, however, concerns the warrior's relationship to mainstream society. Although the Western hero often moved on into the wilderness after defeating the Indians or the rustlers or the corrupt cattle ranchers, he always left behind a stable world. The Western myth also made it clear that the hero believed in civic values, even if as a warrior he could only live on the margins of society. And, as previously noted, the warriors in World War II movies were soldiers—members of an official military—who fought to protect the American values of freedom and democracy and to liberate others from tyranny.

In contrast, the New War has nothing at all to say about what kind of society will be created after the enemy is vanquished. The sheer intensity of the violence in these stories tends to make the warrior's victories look like a definitive restoration of a fallen America. It's as if the end of gunfire must mean something good. But the defeat of chaos is not the same thing as the re-creation of a sacred order. In other words, the New War resembles those archaic creation myths that glorify the violent struggles that precede the establishment or restoration of social order, but not those that exalt the sacred order itself.

. . . Two hundred years after the ratification of the Constitution, the American mythology of war and the warrior was no longer connected to any idea of founding a sacred order. Instead, the New War culture portrayed the warrior as the epitome of masculine power and self-development, and combat as the only life worth living.

NOTES

1. Henry Nash Smith, *Virgin Land: The American West as Symbol and Myth* (New York: Vintage, 1950), 120.

2. Edmund Morris, *The Rise of Theodore Roosevelt* (New York: Coward, McCann and Geoghegan, 1979), 613.

3. Ibid.

4. Kevin Brownlow, *The War, the West, and the Wilderness* (New York: Knopf, 1979), xvi.

5. Morris, *Rise of Theodore Roosevelt*, 629.

6. Raymond Fielding, *The American Newsreel, 1911–1967* (Norman, Okla.: University of Oklahoma Press, 1972), 30.

7. Brownlow, *The War, the West, and the Wilderness*, 32.

8. Bruce W. Oris, *When Hollywood Ruled the Skies: Aviation Films of WW II* (Los Angeles, Calif.: Aero Associates, 1984), 5–6.

9. Clayton R. Koppes and Gregory D. Black, *Hollywood Goes to War: How Politics, Profits, and Propaganda Shaped World War II Movies* (New York: The Free Press, 1987), 36–37.

10. Emmanuel Levy, *John Wayne: Prophet of the American Way of Life* (Metuchen, N. J.: The Scarecrow Press, 1988), 24.

11. Don Graham, *No Name on the Bullet: A Biography of Audie Murphy* (New York: Viking, 1989), 20.

12. Koppes and Black, *Hollywood Goes to War*, 64–65.

13. David A. Cook. *A History of Narrative Film* (New York: Norton, 1981), 396–97.

14. For accounts of the relationships between Hollywood and the Defense Department after WW II, see Lawrence H. Suid, *Guts and Glory: Great American War Movies* (Reading, Mass: Addison-Wesley, 1977) and Julian Smith, *Looking Away: Hollywood and Vietnam* (New York: Scribner's, 1978).

15. Michael A. Kubkler, *Operation Baroom* (Gastonia, N.C.: TCP Publishers, 1900), 124–25.

16. Michael Herr, *Dispatches* (New York: Avon, 1978), 223.

17. Tom Suddick, *A Few Good Men* (New York: Avon, 1978), 23–24.

18. Kovic, *Born on the Fourth of July*, 181.

19. Robert Jay Lifton, *Home from the War* (New York: Simon and Schuster, 1973), 97.

20. Levy, *John Wayne*, 218.

21. Charles Anderson, *The Grunts* (San Rafael, Calif.: Presidio, 1976), 100.

22. Ibid., 145.

23. Robert Evans and Richard D. Novak, *Nixon in the White House* (New York: Summit, 1983), 506.

24. Sir James George Frazer, *The Golden Bough: A Study in Magic and Religion*, abridged edition (New York: Collier, 1922), 14–43.

25. Seymour M. Hersh, *The Price of Power: Kissinger in the White House* (New York: Summit, 1983), 506.

26. James William Gibson, *The Perfect War: Technowar in Vietnam* (New York: Atlantic Monthly Press, 1986).

27. Alexander M. S. McColl, "Requiem for Three Nations," *Soldier of Fortune*, Summer 1975, 6.

28. Interview with Menahem Golan, Los Angeles, February 13, 1987.

29. Interview with Joseph Zito, Los Angeles, October 21, 1986.

30. Interview with Lionel Chetwynd, Los Angeles, February 17, 1987.

Song of Napalm

for my wife

Bruce Weigl

After the storm, after the rain stopped pounding,
We stood in the doorway watching horses
Walk off lazily across the pasture's hill.
We stared through the black screen,
Our vision altered by the distance
So I thought I saw a mist
Kicked up around their hooves when they faded
Like cut-out horses
Away from us.
The grass was never more blue in that light, more
Scarlet; beyond the pasture
Trees scraped their voices into the wind, branches
Crisscrossed the sky like barbed wire
But you said they were only branches.

Okay. The storm stopped pounding.
I am trying to say this straight: for once
I was sane enough to pause and breathe

Outside my wild plans and after the hard rain
I turned my back on the old curses. I believed
They swung finally away from me . . .

But still the branches are wire
And thunder is the pounding mortar,
Still I close my eyes and see the girl
Running from her village, napalm
Stuck to her dress like jelly,
Her hands reaching for the no one
Who waits in waves of heat before her.

So I can keep on living,
So I can stay here beside you,
I try to imagine she runs down the road and wings
Beat inside her until she rises
Above the stinking jungle and her pain
Eases, and your pain, and mine.

But the lie swings back again.
The lie works only as long as it takes to speak
And the girl runs only as far
As the napalm allows
Until her burning tendons and crackling
Muscles draw her up

Into that final position
Burning bodies so perfectly assume. Nothing
Can change that: she is burned behind my eyes
And not your good love and not the rain-swept air
And not the jungle-green
Pasture unfolding before us can deny it.

===============

Guerrilla War

W. D. Ehrhart

It's practically impossible
to tell civilians
from the Vietcong.

Nobody wears uniforms.
They all talk
the same language,
(and you couldn't understand them
even if they didn't).

They tape grenades
inside their clothes,
and carry satchel charges
in their market baskets.

Even their women fight;
and young boys,
and girls.

It's practically impossible
to tell civilians
from the Vietcong;

after a while,
you quit trying.

Masculinity, Power and Identity [1996]

Nigel Edley and Margaret Wetherell

In recent years there has been a minor explosion of interest in men and masculinity. It seems that hardly a week can go by now without there being some kind of debate in the media about the state of the 'nineties man'. At the same time, of course, there has been a parallel rise in *academic* writing on men, spanning across the entire range of the social sciences including sociology (Hearn 1987), psychoanalytic theory (e.g. Chodorow 1978) and cultural theory (Chapman and Rutherford 1988).

Each of these different theoretical perspectives has its own contribution to make in understanding men and their experiences (see Brod and Kaufman 1994; Edley and Wetherell 1995 for reviews). For no single theory or academic approach can hope to capture and account for every facet of even a single man's life, let alone the lives of black men and white men, gay men and straight men, and men of all different socioeconomic classes. Yet while it is important to encourage an interdisciplinary perspective upon men and masculinity, this does not mean that all of the available approaches will be equally useful or insightful. Instead, it is most likely that some theories will carry a heavier explanatory burden than others.

However, one issue that an increasing number of social scientists appear to agree upon is the feminist argument that any adequate theory of men and masculinity has to have the concept of *power* at its centre (Connell 1987; Kimmel 1987; Brittan 1989; Segal 1990; Kaufman 1994). Surveys have shown, for example, that although there are very nearly as many British women in paid employment as there are men—10.53 million against 10.83 million (*Guardian* 9 April 1994)—men still occupy the most powerful positions within society. Men also enjoy significant privileges within the private realm of the family home. Generally speaking, housework is still regarded as woman's work, even in situations where both the man and the woman are involved in paid employment (Machung 1989; Sidel 1990).

The point that feminists are making, therefore, is that any adequate theory strivings shift to more obviously sexual interests. For the male child, the onset of the 'phallic' or 'Oedipal' stage is often signalled by an increased interest in the genitals. Moreover, Freud claimed, the young boy begins to develop a sexual interest in his own mother. He wants to keep her all to himself, and begins to perceive his father as a rival for her love and attention. At this point, Freud suggests, the boy encounters the incest taboo found in all human societies. Sensing that he is on dangerous ground, the boy begins to fear that his father will castrate him (particularly as he may have noticed that his sister and/or mother appear to have already 'lost' their penises). And so, in order to save his own precious organ, he 'identifies' himself with his father and redirects his sexual energies towards other, more acceptable female figures. By identification, Freud meant that the boy comes to internalize the values and standards set by his father (the 'superego'). In other words, the image of the father held by the boy, in a sense, becomes his own internal conscience.

Now according to this classical Freudian account, male dominance can be seen to be underpinned by the conditions of their own psychological development. Indeed, Freud regarded men as very much the superior sex. For instance, he argued that whereas the fear of castration encouraged the formation of a strong social conscience within men, the lack of urgency for women to resolve their own Oedipal complexes (due to the fact that they have no penis to lose) meant that they grow up with a less well-developed sense of justice. He also saw women as vain, ruled by their emotions, and unable to contribute much, if anything, to the advancement of civilized society.

Not surprisingly, Freud's ideas have met with some opposition. Almost from the moment he first published his theories there were those who took issue with his view of masculinity as the superior pattern of development (e.g. Karen Horney, Helene Deutsch and Ernest Jones). However, during the 1960s and 1970s a wholescale revision of psychoanalytic theory appeared, which suggested that perhaps it was men, not women, who were the more insecure and fragile sex.

Psychoanalysts began to point out that masculinity seems to have a permanently defensive flavour about it. Men, they argued, appear to be in a constant state of uncertainty about their own gender identities; always in a state of having to prove themselves as men.

Theorists such as Ralph Greenson (1968) argued that boys spend the first two years of their lives completely identified with their mothers. She feeds him, comforts him and tends to all his needs, and as a consequence he becomes totally absorbed in her. However, as time goes on the boy is forced to disidentify with his mother. According to Nancy Chodorow (1978) and Christiane Olivier (1989), it is the mother herself who initiates this process. The boy may yet not know that he is male, but she does, and this knowledge structures the way she relates to him. So as the boy grows up, the mother becomes simultaneously an object of exaggerated admiration and also something to be struggled against and transcended. He must love her and leave her; crave and despise her. But above all, he must show that he is nothing like her.

This imperative, psychoanalysts argue, helps shape the psychology of men in a number of important ways. Most notably, it affects the ways in which men relate to others. For if being a man means not being emotional, dependent, and caring (like his mother), then what sort of relationships will men enter into with their partners, children and friends? Moreover, if and when men begin to sense that they *do* have emotional needs and desires, how do they deal with these feelings? Some psychoanalysts claim that men simply suppress these feelings or 'project' them back on to women, saying in effect 'I don't need her. She needs me' (see Hollway 1984). Alternatively, men may turn more actively *against* women, abusing them sexually and/or physically as a way of denying their feelings of dependence (Frosh 1993).

So can male dominance be explained in terms of these more recent psychoanalytic theories? Could it be, for example, that in 'putting down' the feminine in themselves, men are inevitably drawn into also denigrating the women who surround them? Although such a theory sounds quite plausible, many contemporary psychoanalysts seem to feel that the psychological processes described above are a consequence rather than a cause of patriarchal societies. For instance, several have suggested that a boy's 'flight from femininity' is motivated not so much by the fear of castration, nor the mothers' wish for their sons to achieve an 'appropriate' gender identity, but by the fact that the boy sees, from a fairly early age, that in becoming a man he becomes a member of the most powerful half of humanity. As such, these theories are predicated upon rather than account for the existence of male power and privilege.

A ROLE PERSPECTIVE ON MEN

Role theory, as the name suggests, is based upon a theatrical metaphor in which all social behaviour is viewed as a kind of performance. Located at the intersection of psychology and sociology, role theory draws attention to the fact that most people, for most of the time, behave in ways which are socially prescribed (Hargreaves 1986). People are by no means free agents, going about their business or doing their own thing. Instead, role theorists claim, they are more like actors on a stage, playing out pre-scripted parts. To be a man, they suggest, is to play a certain role. Masculinity represents just a set of lines and stage direction which males have to learn to perform.

In their pioneering work in the 1930s Lewis Terman and Catherine Miles (1936) laid down the foundations of sex-role theory. Basically what they did was to conceive of masculinity and femininity as two opposing types of personality, located on either end of a single bipolar dimension (the 'M/F scale'). The masculine role consisted of a long list of characteristics each of which had its opposite in the feminine role—such as courage (M) versus timidity (F), roughness (M) versus tenderness (F) and self-reliance (M) versus dependence (F) (Archer and Lloyd 1985). Terman and Miles believed that, by using this measure, the gender personality of any individual could be calculated simply by seeing whether they exhibited a surplus of either masculine or feminine traits.

Since the 1930s, a number of other theorists have attempted to describe the male sex role in a more abbreviated fashion. Pleck and Sawyer (1974), for instance, suggested that it could be reduced to the dual maxims 'get ahead' and 'stay cool'. Similarly, Brannon (1976) saw the male role as consisting of four basic clusters:

- 'no sissy stuff'—the avoidance of all feminine behaviours and traits
- 'the big wheel'—the acquisition of success, status, and breadwinning competence

- 'the sturdy oak'—strength, confidence and independence
- 'give 'em hell'—aggression, violence and daring (see also Fasteau 1974; Pleck and Thompson 1987).

At the same time there have been those who have attempted to theorize how the male sex role gets taken up or internalized. Of these, the most widely known framework is that belonging to social learning theorists such as Walter Mischel and Albert Bandura (Bandura and Walters 1963; Mischel 1966; Mischel 1970; Bandura 1977). Based upon the principles of conditioning and reinforcement, Mischel and Bandura argued that people acquire and perform sex-typed behaviour, like any other kind of behaviour, through a combination of observation, imitation, indoctrination and conscious learning. For them, a young boy would simply be *taught* to be masculine in a way similar to how a dog owner would train a young puppy (the only difference being that eventually the young boy would also pick up the 'appropriate' sex role by directly imitating either his father or some other male role model).

Social learning theorists have conducted a great deal of research looking into the ways in which a number of important socializing 'agents'—such as the family, school and media—function to encourage sex-appropriate behaviour. Fagot (1974) found, for instance, that parents tend to reinforce the assertive behaviour of young boys whilst suppressing it in their daughters (see also Fling and Manosevitz 1972; Lewis 1975; Snow *et al.* 1983). He also discovered that nursery schoolteachers tended to encourage the same gender personalities by only allowing the children to play with sex-appropriate toys (Fagot 1977—see also Serbin *et al.* 1973).

So how might role theory account for men's social dominance? Perhaps the most obvious explanation is that the male sex role appears to be the dominant role. Reading down the list of stereotypical gender attributes, men are associated with traits such as confidence, ambition and strength, whereas women tend to be accorded the more negative characteristics of prudishness, frivolity, and constant complaining (Williams and Bennett 1975). Moreover, the quality of dominance is itself part of the male sex role. So it goes without saying, that if men are fulfilling their role expectations, it must be women who are the ones being dominated.

But this begs the question of *why* the two sex roles are defined as they are. Historically speaking, one of

the major 'plus points' of sex-role theory was that it, at least, appeared to have separated gender from biological sex; such that it was possible to account for the existence of a masculine female or an effeminate male. However, as a number of critics have pointed out (e.g. Connell 1987; Kimmel 1987; Brittan 1989), the only logic behind the theorization of two distinct sex roles is by analogy with men and women as two biologically distinctive categories.

Connell (1987) also points out that sex-role theorists fail to explain why anybody should be bothered to enforce sex-appropriate displays. Why should a mother or a teacher chastise a boy for playing with a toy pram? What makes them heap praise upon him when he stifles his tears after grazing his knee? As Connell himself notes, the motivation cannot be explained in terms of role theory. In other words, it cannot be that people are taught to be good 'socializers'; as this merely displaces the problem rather than solves it. So why do people do it? In the end, Connell argues, sex-role theorists have no answer. All they are left with is that, for some reason, people *choose* to do so.

Finally, Connell argues that sex-role theorists buy into too consensual an image of society. In other words, they portray the process of gender socialization as relatively smooth and harmonious, with boys and girls gradually learning to take on board those characteristics associated with their own sex. In so doing, he suggests, role theorists fail to appreciate the degree of struggle and negotiation which lies behind the construction of gender identities. In other words, they fail to grasp the extent to which the construction of gender identities is based upon the struggle for social power.

A SOCIAL RELATIONS PERSPECTIVE ON MEN

A social relations perspective on men views masculinity as a set of distinctive *practices* that emerge from men's positioning within a variety of social structures—such as work and the family. In other words, a man's identity takes its shape from the various institutions in which he is located or embedded. The researchers who adopt this kind of perspective are interested in the kinds of factors which influence how men are 'inserted' into these institutions. They are interested, therefore, in how a man's social class, race and gender affects his identity or sense of self.

Most of the work in this area has focused on social class and the consequences of capitalist working practices for working- and middle-class men. The basic argument is that if men are aggressive, competitive, emotionally inarticulate and oppressive, then this merely reflects the ways in which men are positioned within our current mode of economic production.

Marx illustrated how capitalism is based upon a fundamental clash of interests between the workers and the owners (or the managers who act as their representatives). The workers, having no capital of their own, are forced to sell their labour for as much as they can. The owners, on the other hand, are interested in employing these workers for as little as possible in order to maximize the profits—or 'surplus value'—gained from the sale of whatever is being produced. It is, therefore, an economic system based upon competition.

Marx also argued that, within the capitalist mode of economic production, men (*sic*) become 'alienated'. By this he meant that, whereas in precapitalist days a worker would produce something (such as a horseshoe or a plough) either to use himself or to sell, under capitalism he stands at a greater 'distance' from his creations. The spot welder on a car production line never owns the cars that he is making. What is more, by the fact that he only participates in a tiny part of the production process he is further alienated, sensing himself to be just a small cog in a huge and impersonal machine.

According to Tolson (1977), working-class men have a less deluded attitude to work in the sense of their being more obviously subordinated within a capitalist system. Middle-class men, on the other hand, are in a much more ambiguous position. Instead of seeing work as just something they have to do to get by, they are more likely to invest themselves in their work, and to see their public identities or working selves as much more central to who they 'really' are as people. So while working-class men might be more obviously oppressed and alienated by capitalism, the self-estrangement for middle-class men can be equally profound.

So capitalism draws men into a network of social relations that encourage sets of behaviours we would recognize as typically masculine. But how exactly might this network of social relations account for men's domination over women? It is tempting to begin our answer by saying that men dominate women because they are the chairpersons, directors and higher managers who run the companies for whom many women work. However, this explanation will not do

because, of course, it fails to explain why it is that it is nearly always men who occupy these powerful positions in the first place.

A better explanation is that the working lives of both working- and middle-class men profoundly influence the private, personal and sexual relationships which they have with their womenfolk. Tolson (1977) and Seidler (1989) argue, for example, that because working-class men experience little or no power within their occupational lives, they are more likely than middle-class men to attempt to dominate at home. They are also, in Tolson's opinion, more likely to adopt an aggressive, macho identity as a counterbalance to the powerlessness they feel at work. This is not to say, however, that middle-class men don't also exploit their partners. For while they might entertain what appear to be very much more egalitarian relationships, their careers, and the self-esteem which these bring with them, are often dependent on women acting as good 'career wives', beavering away in the background to maintain an image of middle-class respectability.

The problem with these arguments is that, once again, they do not appear to get to the heart of the matter. For sure we might be able to see how the different occupational experiences of working- and middle-class men helps to pattern the ways they behave both at work and elsewhere. But don't these behaviours represent little more than different ways of men being dominant? Middle-class men can do it at work so, unlike working-class men, there is no need for them to do it at home. But the question remains, of course, what makes most, if not all men want to dominate in the first place?

A number of feminist theorists (e.g. Hartmann 1979; Delphy 1984) have argued that men are less caring and empathetic towards others because, unlike women, their lack of involvement in childcare means that they never have to develop these qualities. But this still fails to account for *why* it has traditionally been the case that the man goes out to work while the woman looks after the kids. Why for so long have men opted out of childcare practices, and why, for that matter, have women usually opted into them? For, as Arthur Brittan (1989) has pointed out, there is no intrinsic reason why a capitalist society requires any kind of gender demarcation. As long as someone brings up the next generation of workers, and someone else produces the cars, electricity and so on and so forth, it does not matter whether they are male or female.

In conclusion, therefore, each of the above perspectives fails to provide an entirely satisfactory account of why men tend to dominate most human societies, including our own. As we have seen, psychoanalytic theories may well be able to account for how masculine identities get reproduced, but the power of men over women tends to be assumed in these analyses rather than explained. If anything, sex-role theory offers even less hope of a satisfactory answer. The best that it can do is to suggest that the characteristics which enable people to get on in society just happen to correspond more closely to those contained within the male sex role. Much more promising is the work of a number of sociologists and social theorists who have demonstrated the ways in which various social institutions help structure the gender identities of those embedded within them. Yet ultimately, however, even these more sophisticated theories require another level of explanation before they can get to the root of men's power.

Moreover, what do each of these three perspectives imply about the possibility of men relinquishing their dominant positions in society? As far as most feminists are concerned, the importance of placing power at the centre of any theory of men and masculinity is not so much academic as *political*. The point being, of course, that once the basis of male dominance is properly understood, it can then be tackled and dismantled. If, however, we consider each of the theories as set out above, there would appear to be little reason for optimism.

For instance, within psychoanalytic theory, the gender identity of each and every male is assumed to be determined, primarily at least, by the pattern of relationships that the boy enters into early in life. Well before he is old enough to make his way out into the wider world, his gender personality is as good as fixed. He has virtually no say in the matter. Furthermore, depending upon which school of psychoanalytic theory one takes, the chances of his parents having any kind of impact is either nil (according to classical Freudian theory), or entirely dependent upon a wholesale shift in men's involvement in childcare (which, it could be argued, will not happen unless men change!).

Role theory provides little scope for optimism either. For according to it, a man's identity, his personality, his very 'substance', is entirely dependent upon

the schedules of reinforcement or training to which he was exposed during his socialization as well as the more immediate set of social circumstances in which he finds himself from moment to moment. To this extent, the male here too is a kind of *victim* of circumstance, an unwitting beneficiary of a male supremacist culture.

The social relations perspective reveals a similar level of determinism. For if it is the case that a man's identity and his ways of relating to the world around him are largely dependent upon the social institutions in which he is embedded, then it is by no means an easy matter for him to change the way he is. Men, from this perspective, do not simply *choose* to oppress women. For their identities are constructed through a set of social structures which exist over and above the individual actions of any particular man.

It is important to stress the point that we are not arguing that any of the above perspectives are useless or even fundamentally flawed. Indeed, any thoroughgoing analysis of men and masculinity will have to understand that men are emotional beings with unconscious desires and fantasies and that they are profoundly affected by factors such as social class and race. Rather, our point is that when it comes to theorizing men's power as a social group, the burden of explanation is best carried by another perspective. Therefore, what we hope to do in the second part of this chapter is to sketch the outlines of this other perspective and to illustrate how it also avoids the determinism evident in the three already considered.

A CULTURAL PERSPECTIVE ON MEN

Since the 1960s, cultural theorists have understood culture as being, not just opera, ballet and other forms of 'high art', but as the whole way of life of a society or community. It represents a kind of framework, passed down from generation to generation, through which ordinary people conduct and make sense of their everyday lives. From a cultural perspective, therefore, every culture in the world must contain its own specific set of ideas or themes which relate to men and masculinity. Similar in some ways to the male sex role described earlier, these 'cults' of masculinity can be seen as providing members of a cultural community with a shared understanding of what it means to be a man: what one looks like, how one

Summary

should behave and so forth. One of the principal tasks of the cultural analyst is to pick out these themes, to be able to 'read' what a culture has to say about the meaning of masculinity. The reason why this is so important is because cultural theorists insist that men become, in a very real sense, constituted through these meanings or 'ideologies'.

However, here the similarity with the sex-role approach comes to an abrupt end. For when we begin to search around in books, films and television programmes for information about how our culture 'constructs' men and masculinity, we find that there is no single, consistent image of manhood, but a range of quite different, even contradictory representations. Consider, for a moment, the images of manhood provided by the characters typically played by the actors Arnold Schwarzenegger, Woody Allen and Sean Connery. All are supposed to be heroes, and yet one is a muscle-bound, all-action fighting machine, another is a sensitive intellectual with a wry sense of humour and the third is a charming and sophisticated gentleman with impeccable style and manners.

Yet while a culture may contain multiple theories or discourses of masculinity, this does not necessarily mean that they happily coexist. Indeed, it is often more useful to see the thoughtful intellectual, the active hard man, the chivalrous romantic and so on as competing arguments about how a man should be. Manliness, in other words, is a contested territory; it is an ideological battlefield. And what is more, if we look back in time, not only do we see that, at certain points in history, one specific discourse of masculinity has dominated over all of the other alternatives (i.e. it has been the most popular way of thinking about men), but we also find that the efforts to control the meaning of masculinity have played a central role in the struggle for power between various social groupings including classes, 'races', nations as well as men and women.

For example, there have been several periods during the course of the last 3000 years where the dominant definition of masculinity has equated manliness with physical strength and vigorous activity (see Hoch 1979). One such period occurred within British and American culture around the second half of the nineteenth century. Rotundo (1987) notes that during this time there arose an almost obsessional interest in the physical size and strength of the male body. Historical records show a tremendous upsurge of youngsters tak-

ing up programmes of exercise and closely monitoring their own physical development. Some completely abandoned the comforts of the city for a life in the wild outdoors, whilst many more became avid readers of story books about such adventures including the tales of Davy Crockett and Tom Brown.

But the significance of such a cultural development does not emerge until we look at the broader social, political and economic climates of these two countries. On both sides of the Atlantic concerns had been raised about the general state of the nations' men after the traumas of the American civil war and the Crimean war. Moreover, both nations were concerned to defend their interests abroad, and so the development of a new generation of fit and healthy young men, ready, if need be, to throw down their lives in the interests of their respective countries begins to make sense as a means of calming these national anxieties.

The equation of masculinity with physical strength and endurance has also played a significant role in the power struggles between the sexes. For example, Catherine Hall (1992) notes that in response to Mary Wollstonecraft's famous book *Vindication of the Rights of Woman* in 1792, which called for the equal treatment of middle-class men and women, evangelical preachers in many British churches began talking from their pulpits about the 'natural' inequalities between the sexes. Women, they said, were naturally more delicate, fragile and morally weak; a fact which, they suggested, made women less well suited to the cut and thrust of business and politics.

By the mid-nineteenth century, ideas about the 'natural' differences between men and women were also being used to justify the dichotomization of men and women's work. Middle-class women became increasingly concentrated into less physical trades such as dressmaking, schoolteaching and the retail industry, whereas in working-class society, similar concerns lead to the exclusion of women from working underground (Hall 1992). Not long after, the concept of the 'family wage' appeared, first in Britain and then in America. Here, being a *real* man meant being able to support a wife and family without her having to earn a single penny. So even if she wanted to work, for him it became a matter of honour that she didn't.

Over the course of the last 300 years, a symbolic equation of women with nature and men with culture or civilization (Ortner 1974) has also had a tremendous impact in terms of the structure of power relations between the sexes. Men, it is often assumed (even today), are more rational or reasonable than women, who for their part are ruled over by their hearts or their emotions. It is men, therefore, who are seen as most likely to contribute to the enlightenment project and to the advancement of knowledge (Seidler 1989). Women, on the other hand, became identified as the enemy. To some, they appeared to threaten, not only the pursuit of knowledge, but also civilized society itself. Three centuries ago, this belief resulted in the brutal practice of burning 'witches' at the stake. It has also led to the domination of women by more subtle means: for instance, by forcing them into silence on account of men's supposedly privileged access to 'the truth' (Seidler 1989).

social reproduction of inequality = ideology

Perhaps by now it is becoming clear how a cultural perspective on men and masculinity helps illuminate the issue of men's power. Men have dominated over women, by and large, because they have managed to gain a stranglehold on *meaning*. What it means to be a man, what it means to be a woman; what jobs constitute men's work and what jobs constitute women's work. It is through the ability to control the ways in which society thinks about these things that has provided men with the basis of their power. This is not to suggest for one moment that women have been entirely absent from these negotiations. Indeed, it is almost certain that they have attempted to intervene, or fight their corner, at every possible opportunity. However, the point is that because men have dominated many of the key institutions which help to produce and recycle meaning (namely, the church, schools and, more recently, the media), it is usually their 'versions' of the world which, in the words of Clarke *et al.* (1981) 'command the greatest weight and influence [and] secrete the greatest legitimacy'.

Now at first sight this argument may make the cultural approach appear to be just as tautological as some of the others we have criticized. For it would seem to be suggesting that men have achieved their privileged position in society by dominating most of its key social institutions. However, in practice the process *is* circular, in the sense of being iterative. In a crude way, it occurs like a game of football in which, whenever one side scores, they are allowed to field an additional player. This means that although the match might begin even, as soon as either team gains an advantage, its chances of going further ahead are immediately increased. For a very long time now, the state of play in the game of men versus women is that the men have so many more players on the park that they can score goals almost at will.

Yet there is a danger here, though, of overstating the level of autonomy or agency which men enjoy. Men's collective interests and their disproportionate power and influence are not maintained through active and self-conscious male conspiracies. Certainly, as far as I [NE] can recall, my father never took me aside as a young boy and whispered 'Right, I'm going to tell you how to keep your mother and your sister down.' Instead, the processes by which men maintain their dominance are much more complex, indirect and subtle.

One of the main reasons why this is the case is because patriarchy, like any culture, does not declare its own partiality. It does not offer itself as just one sense-making system amongst others. Instead it presents itself as *the* way of seeing the world; as entirely natural, normal and straightforward. Therefore, it would appear entirely understandable if each new generation of young men saw nothing particularly strange or unfair about the kinds of lives that awaited them. Men wear the trousers, men earn the money; women do the dishes and women look after the babies. 'It's just a fact of life', they say. This also helps to explain the paradoxical fact that whilst many men might accept that they live in a largely male-dominated society, a high proportion of them do not *feel* themselves to be powerful (Lips 1981; Griffin 1991; Kaufman 1994).

But while we must recognize that patriarchy naturalizes men's power and privilege (especially) in the eyes of men themselves, it is wrong to assume that they are incapable of changing the cultures that define them. After all, we have already heard how throughout history various social groups have managed to advance their own interests through the successful manipulation of the masculine ideal. The fact of the matter is, of course, that, paradoxical as it might sound, men are simultaneously the producers and the products of culture; the masters and the slaves of ideology. Furthermore, as Gramsci (1971) points out, the rule or hegemony of a dominant culture is never absolute. In other words, it never fully achieves the position of being the only available way of making sense of an event or situation. Instead, it has to be continually defended against the challenges of other subordinate cultures.

We would like to end this chapter with a brief, and in many ways quite unspectacular, illustration of what this defensive work looks like in practice. It should serve to prove the point that while women and other 'minority' groups may be in a better position to see the power of men, it is by no means impossible for men themselves. In doing this we will be drawing upon a series of interviews with a small number of 17- to 18-year-old boys from a Midlands-based single-sex independent school, conducted between October 1991 and June 1994 (Wetherell and Edley 1993).

From the very first interview it was apparent that the sixth form of the school was divided into a number of separate and somewhat antagonistic groups. At the centre of these conflicts stood two quite large collections of boys; one widely acknowledged as the 'hard lads', and another who defined themselves largely in opposition to this group. The identity of the hard boys was mainly organized around the playing of sport (particularly rugby) as well as a whole set of other loud and boisterous activities such as play fighting, drinking and small-scale vandalism. As such, they would appear to represent the articulation or inhabitation of what has variously been called 'traditional' (Christian 1994), 'retributive' (Chapman and Rutherford 1988) or 'hegemonic' (Carrigan *et al.* 1985) masculinity, with its emphasis upon certain macho values such as physical strength, courage and toughness.

At the level of discourse, the domination of the hard boys was signified by the fact that they talked about school life as being fairly unremarkable. Indeed, a phrase which kept on being repeated was that school was just a series of 'good laughs'. People got hurt during some of their break-time games, one boy even broke his arm, but basically, for them, it was 'just a bit of fun'.

In contrast, the members of the 'opposing' group had a great deal to say about these 'rough-house' games. Indeed, half of the first interview with them was spent describing the behaviour of the hard lads. For them, such macho games were experienced, not as a bit of harmless fun, but as deeply marginalizing and oppressive. The power of the hard lads was obvious to them; it confronted them almost every day of their school lives. As a consequence, it was not just easier, but positively in their interests to 'deconstruct' the hard lads' interpretations, to open out or develop a more complex discourse of power and subordination. But perhaps the most significant fact is that, as we can

see from the following extract, it was by no means impossible for members of the dominant group to accomplish this same type of deconstruction for themselves.

ADRIAN: *Actually it's good fun having the power that we do, like when we went on camp last year, you just tell them what to do and stuff and it's much better because the year before when I went on camp I was only a cadet and I went on camp and I was an NCO and I enjoyed it more because, it meant that I wasn't the one that had to get up at half five in the morning and I was the one that could lie in bed until seven and then push in front of everybody, get up in time for breakfast in front of everybody in the queue to get to the front and stuff like that. So that's what I enjoyed but then there's like some people that I think abuse it quite a lot like erm, they had the fire engines in here one day doing a fire display and they were spraying a hose, so all that corner by the chemistry rooms was completely flooded and they got like a little drain, it's like a little dip . . .*

PHILIP: *And they marched people in there and made them stop.*

ADRIAN: *Full of water yeah, they marched people in there . . . so you had one rank and you made them go at ease and go to attention and made them stamp in it as hard as they could so all the water flying up them, and then they'd move them a rank forward and do it again like that.*

PHILIP: *It's a laugh though isn't it? (laughs)*

ADRIAN: *Yeah, well the other thing they used to do . . . when I first joined, the NCOs used to make you do press-ups in puddles and stuff like that.*

Here we have Adrian talking explicitly about the pleasures of being macho. It's fun, he says, having the power to order the younger cadets around. It's fun pushing into the queue ahead of them just because you are of a more senior rank. He even starts to talk about the 'abuse' of such power, and goes on to describe an instance of where such an abuse occurred. But then look what happens. Philip attempts to re-present the episode as benign or harmless: 'It's a laugh though isn't it?' he suggests. 'Yeah' replies Adrian, accepting his reformulation before going on to describe yet another episode.

It was all over in an instant. Hardly anyone batted an eyelid. But in that moment both of these young men declined an opportunity to 'take the side of the other' (Billig 1987), to reinterpret their oppressive activities in terms of a different, more critical perspective. But the point is that an opportunity was there. They were presented with a chance of challenging the ideological system which both privileges and produces them. Had they taken that chance it would have been a small, but not insignificant, victory against the continuation of male domination. For ultimately, patriarchy rests upon the day-to-day maintenance of such understandings.

ACKNOWLEDGEMENTS

The authors would like to acknowledge two very different kinds of debt. The first goes to the Economic and Social Research Council (grant no. R000233129), the Open University Research Committee and the Psychology Department of the Open University for the financial support they have given this research. The second vote of thanks goes to the staff and students of the school (whose anonymity we shall, of course, respect). Needless to say, without their kindness, cooperation and openness, such work as this would never get done.

REFERENCES

ARCHER, J. and LLOYD, B. (1985) *Sex and Gender*. Cambridge: Cambridge University Press.

BANDURA, A. (1977) *Social Learning Theory*. Englewood Cliffs, NJ: Prentice Hall.

BANDURA, A. and WALTERS, R. H. (1963) *Social Learning and Personality Development*. New York: Holt, Rinehart and Winston.

BILLIG, M. (1987) *Arguing and Thinking: A Rhetorical Approach to Social Psychology*. London: Cambridge University Press.

BRANNON, R. (1976) The male sex role: our culture's blueprint of manhood, and what it's done for us lately, in D. David and R. Brannon (eds) *The Forty-Nine Percent Majority: The Male Sex Role*. Reading, MA: Addison-Wesley.

BRITTAN, A. (1989) *Masculinity and Power*. New York: Blackwell.

BROD, H. and KAUFMAN, M. (eds) (1994) *Theorizing Masculinities*. London: Sage.

CARRIGAN, T., CONNELL, R. and LEE, J. (1985) Towards a new sociology of masculinity, *Theory and Society*, 14: 551–604.

CHAPMAN, R. and RUTHERFORD, J. (eds) (1988) *Male Order: Unwrapping Masculinity*. London: Lawrence and Wishart.

CHODOROW, N. (1978) *The Reproduction of Mothering: Psychoanalysis and the Sociology of Gender*. Berkeley, CA: University of California Press.

CHRISTIAN, H. (1994) *The Making of Anti-Sexist Men*. London: Routledge.

CLARKE, J., HALL, S., JEFFERSON, T. and ROBERTS, B. (1981) Subcultures, cultures and class, in T. Bennett, G. Martin, C. Mercer and J. Woollacott (eds) *Culture, Ideology and Social Process*. Milton Keynes: Open University Press.

CONNELL, R.W. (1987) *Gender and Power*. Cambridge: Polity Press.

DELPHY, C. (1984) *Close to Home: A Materialist Analysis of Woman's Oppression*. London: Hutchinson.

EDLEY, N. and WETHERELL, M.S. (1995) *Men in Perspective: Practice, Power and Identity*. Hemel Hempstead: Harvester Wheatsheaf.

FAGOT, B. I. (1974) Sex differences in toddlers' behaviour and parental reaction, *Developmental Psychology*, 4: 554–8.

FAGOT, B. I. (1977) Consequences of moderate cross-gender behaviour in pre-school children, *Child Development*, 48: 902–7.

FASTEAU, M. F. (1974) *The Male Machine*. New York: McGraw-Hill.

FLING, S. and MANOSEVITZ, M. (1972) Sex typing in nursery school children's play interests, *Developmental Psychology*, 7: 146–52.

FROSH, S. (1993) The seeds of male sexuality, in J. Ussher and C. Baker (eds) *Psychological Perspectives on Sexual Problems*. London: Routledge.

GRAMSCI, A. (1971) *Selections from the Prison Notebooks*, ed. and trans. by O. Hoare and G. Nowell-Smith. London: Lawrence and Wishart.

GREENSON, R. (1968) Dis-identifying from mother: its special importance for the boy, *International Psychoanalytic Journal*, 49: 370–4.

GRIFFIN, C. (1991) Experiencing power: dimensions of gender, 'race' and class, *British Psychological Society Psychology of Women Section Newsletter*, 8: 43–58.

HALL, C. (1992) *White, Male and Middle Class: Explorations in Feminism and History*. Cambridge: Polity Press.

HARGREAVES, D. J. (1986) Psychological theories of sex-role stereotyping, in D. J. Hargreaves and A. M. Colley (eds) *The Psychology of Sex Roles*. London: Harper and Row.

HARTMANN, H. (1979) The unhappy marriage of marxism and feminism: towards a more progressive union, *Capital and Class*, 8: 1–33.

HEARN, J. (1987) *The Gender of Oppression: Men, Masculinity and the Critique of Marxism*. Brighton: Harvester Wheatsheaf.

HOCH, P. (1979) *White Hero, Black Beast: Racism, Sexism and the Mask of Masculinity*. London: Pluto Press.

HOLLWAY, W. (1984) Gender difference and the production of subjectivity, in J. Henriques, W. Hollway, C. Urwin, C. Venn and V. Walkerdine (eds) *Changing the Subject*. London: Methuen.

KAUFMAN, M. (1994) Men's contradictory experiences of power, in H. Brod and M. Kaufman (eds) *Theorizing Masculinities*. London: Sage.

KIMMEL, M. S. (ed.) (1987) *Changing Men: New Directions in Research on Men and Masculinity*. Newbury Park, CA: Sage.

LEWIS, M. (1975) Early sex differences in the human: studies of socio-emotional development, *Archives of Sexual Behaviour*, 4: 329–35.

LIPS, H. (1981) *Women, Men and the Psychology of Power*. Englewood Cliffs, NJ: Prentice Hall.

MACHUNG, A. (1989) Talking career, thinking job: gender differences in career and family expectations of Berkeley seniors. *Feminist Studies*, 15: 35–8.

MISCHEL, W. (1966) A social learning view of sex differences, in E.E. Maccoby (ed.) *The Development of Sex Differences*. Stanford, CA: Stanford University Press.

MISCHEL, W. (1970) Sex-typing and socialisation, in P.H. Musson (ed.) *Carmichael's Manual of Child Psychology*, 3rd edn, vol. 2. New York: John Wiley.

OLIVIER, C. (1989) *Jocasta's Children: The Imprint of the Mother*. London: Routledge.

ORTNER, S. B. (1974) Is female to male as nature is to culture? in M.Z. Rosaldo and L. Lamphere (eds) *Woman, Culture and Society*. Stanford, CA: Stanford University Press.

PLECK, J. H. and SAWYER, J. (eds) (1974) *Men and Masculinity*. Englewood Cliffs, NJ: Prentice Hall.

PLECK, J. H. and THOMPSON, E. H. (1987) The structure of male norms, in M.S. Kimmel (ed.) *Changing Men: New Directions in Research on Men and Masculinity*. London: Sage.

ROTUNDO, E. A. (1987) Learning about manhood: gender ideals and the middle-class family in nineteenth century America, in J.A. Mangan and J. Walvin (eds) *Manliness and Morality: Middle Class Masculinity in Britain and America 1800–1940*. Manchester: Manchester University Press.

SEGAL, L. (1990) *Slow Motion: Changing Men, Changing Masculinities*. London: Virago.

SEIDLER, V. J. (1989) *Rediscovering Masculinity: Reason, Language and Sexuality*. New York: Routledge.

SERBIN, L. A., O'LEARY, K. D., KENT, R. N. and TONICK, I. J. (1973) A comparison of teacher response to the preacademic problems and problem behaviour of boys and girls, *Child Development*, 44: 796–804.

SIDEL, R. (1990) *On Her Own: Growing up in the Shadow of the American Dream*. New York: Penguin.

SNOW, M. E., JACKLIN, C. N. and MACOBY, E. E. (1983) Sex of child differences in father-child interaction at one year of age, *Child Development*, 54: 227–32.

TERMAN, L. and MILES, C. (1936) *Sex and Personality*. New York: McGraw-Hill.

TOLSON, A. (1977) *The Limits of Masculinity*. London: Tavistock.

WETHERELL, M. and EDLEY, N. (1993) 'Men and masculinity: a socio-psychological analysis of discourse and gender identity'. ESRC grant no. R000233129.

WILLIAMS, J. E. and BENNETT, S. M. (1975) The definition of sex stereotypes via the adjective checklist, *Sex Roles*, 1: 327–37.

No Man Is an Island

2000

Men in relationships with others

Christopher Kilmartin

Independence is a central demand of the traditional masculine gender role. Rather, it might be more accurate to say that the *appearance* of independence is demanded. As members of a variety of social systems, men are dependent on others for information, resources, support, and human contact. It is difficult, if not impossible, for a "loner" to be productive or psychologically healthy. The masculine focus on hyperindependence creates relationship conflicts for many men.

From our earliest childhood interactions, we develop styles of relating to others. And social settings also encourage or discourage certain types of interactions (e.g., you might interact with your friends in very different ways than you would with your parents). A large volume of research indicates that males and females tend to evolve rather distinctive interactional patterns, and that the social pressure to behave in certain ways is somewhat different for males than it is for females. We also know that interaction patterns are strongly affected by power relationships between the people involved. Describing the effects of gendered

styles on men's relationships with others is the task of this chapter.

MALE SOCIAL DEVELOPMENT

Developmental psychologist Eleanor Maccoby (1990) has described distinct, gender-typed interactional patterns that emerge early in life. Maccoby contends that these are largely a function of children's preferences for same-sex interaction. By the age of $6^{1}/_{2}$, children are spending eleven times more of their time with same-sex children than with other-sex ones. Children will play in sex-integrated groups when adults force them to do so, but they will return to sex-segregated groups when the adults withdraw (Maccoby, 1988b). This segregation is not limited to gender-typed activities such as playing with dolls or trucks. It also occurs in gender-neutral activities (Maccoby, 1990) such as drawing or playing with clay.

Finding themselves frequently in the company of male peers, most boys develop a way of relating to others that is distinctly masculine. This style involves an orientation toward dominance, competition, and rough-and-tumble play (Humphreys & Smith, 1987). Boys also tend to play in larger (Levant, 1995), less intimate (Maccoby, 1990), and more publicly visible groups (Thorne & Luria, 1986).

In these all-male groups, we see boys interrupting each other, bragging, telling stories, ridiculing others, and using commands much more frequently than we see these behaviors in girls (Maltz & Borker, 1983). Girls' conversation involves more requests rather than demands, expressions of interest in others, and a general communication of a desire to sustain the relationship. Whereas girls' conversations are more of a give-and-take interaction, boys' conversations are more like taking turns, with one boy telling a story, followed by another boy (who often tries to "top" the first boy's story). Maccoby's (1990) view is that, while typical female speech serves the dual purpose of collaboration and self-assertion, typical male conversation is more singularly self-assertive.

These manners of relating to others begin early in childhood. By the second grade, female best friends' conversations begin to center around personally significant events, while boys' conversations focus on activities. By early adolescence, friendships are somewhat less stereotypical (Golombok & Fivush, 1994). Still, many of gender-typed communication patterns continue into adulthood (Tannen, 1990). Since interpersonal interactions serve to form and maintain relationships, men's long-established pattern of communication colors the character of their social ties with women, children, and other men.

ONE OF THE BOYS: MALE-MALE FRIENDSHIPS

Typically, boys and men have more friends than do girls and women. However, the friendships of women are characterized by deeper levels of intimacy (Claes, 1992). While women often talk about how they feel about their experiences, men's focus is usually on the sharing of activities (Lips, 1997; Seidler, 1992).

It is sometimes said that men have many "buddies," but few true friends. Buddies are people you do things with; friends are people with whom you are intimate. The formation of warm feelings between men is many times the result of an indirect process of spending time in a mutual pursuit or interest (sometimes referred to as "male bonding"), as opposed to a more direct process of emotional self-disclosure. The expression of closeness between men often takes the form of continuing to spend time with each other and helping each other with tasks, rather than more direct expressions such as touching, or saying "I like you," "I'm glad you're my friend," or "I feel close to you."

Some men lack the more collaborative relationship skills that are helpful in the formation of deeper friendships, yet many have a desire to be emotionally close to other men. Social structures like tasks and rituals enable men to affiliate with one another in cooperative ways. For example, men on athletic teams or men who work together often form close ties with one another (Messner, 1992). Maccoby (1990) argues that males usually need the structure that these settings provide in order to feel comfortable with others. On the other hand, women usually require less structure because they are more readily adaptable to affiliation for its own sake. This social structure hypothesis provides a partial explanation for the almost religious character of athletics in the lives of many men. Being involved as a sports participant or fan serves to give men something to talk about and do together. These activities mitigate the isolation that comes from hiding oneself behind a facade of masculinity. Still, men tend to experience more loneliness than women, probably because they experience lower levels of social support (Stokes & Levin, 1986).

Several aspects of the masculine gender role inhibit the formation of intimate relationships between male friends. The orientation toward competition and task completion is one. Males are socialized to believe that other men are their competitors. The establishment of intimacy rests partly on revealing one's weaknesses and vulnerabilities to another (Jourard, 1971). It is not wise to reveal these to a perceived competitor, who might well exploit the weakness. This would be like telling your opponent before a tennis match that your backhand is not very good. Men who feel competitive with other men tend to have friendships that are inhibited by an undercurrent of distrust. Adolescent boys tend to trust their friends less than girls (Berndt, 1992).

The gender role demand for self-sufficiency also inhibits self-disclosure. A "real man" is expected to solve his problems on his own. If he is hurt, he must "take it like a man." The expectations for hyperindependence and pain tolerance result in the devaluing of men who reveal weaknesses or ask for help. Derlega and Chaikin (1976) asked research participants to read stories about someone who was troubled by a personal problem. They varied the sex of the person in the story as well as the level of intimacy in this person's disclosure. Research participants rated men who disclosed at a high level as less mentally healthy than men who did not disclose. The opposite judgment was made for women.

Thus, men may face negative social consequences for revealing themselves, yet disclosing oneself to others has demonstrable positive mental health benefits (Pennebaker, 1995). Men who place a high value on traditional masculinity tend to avoid self-disclosure (Winstead et al., 1984). When a problem arises, they tend to rely solely on their own resources, even when other people are available and willing to help. The familiar situation where a man who is on a trip gets lost, but refuses to ask for directions, is a good illustration of how some men will solve problems inefficiently in order to protect a fragile sense of masculinity.

As with many areas of investigation, gender is a better predictor of behavior than sex. Androgynous men are as disclosing to their male friends as feminine or androgynous women; thus, they achieve a higher level of intimacy with their same-sex friends than gender-typed men. Undifferentiated and masculine women had similar levels of disclosure to men with the same gender characteristics (Wright & Scanlon, 1991). Gay men are more likely than heterosexual men to develop strong emotional intimacy with their male friends, many of whom also tend to be gay (Nardi, 1992).

Homophobia is perhaps the greatest barrier to friendships between men (Reid & Fine, 1992). Because men frequently have difficulty making a clear distinction between sexual and nonsexual intimacy, getting close to another man may feel similar to being sexual with him. The powerful antifemininity demand of the male gender role then rears its ugly head, and near panic sets in. To avoid the discomfort of this anxiety, men often keep other men at arm's length, both physically and psychologically. The friendships of highly homophobic men are significantly less intimate than those of other men (Devlin & Cowan, 1985). Moreover, the pattern of male interpersonal distance is relatively new historically. In the United States, it seems to have begun at about the time when the label "homosexual" moved from a definition of *behavior* to one of *identity* (Rotundo, 1993).

The handshake is symbolic of men's ambivalence around being close to one another. One scholar (R. Petrie, personal communication, 1986) asserts that the handshake began as a way of showing the other man that you did not have your hand on a weapon! Young boys whose fathers refuse to kiss, hug, or cuddle them, or tell them that they are loved, deprive their sons of the important human needs for touching and valuing. In addition, these fathers model unaffectionate behavior as a distinctive feature of masculinity. As a result, these boys may well grow up to be distant fathers to their own sons.

According to Thorne and Luria (1986), U.S. boys begin to use homophobic labels such as "queer" or "fag" by the fourth grade. These labels are terms of insult for low-status boys, thus they serve to highlight and maintain a masculine hierarchy. Thorne and Luria theorized about the impact of homophobic labeling on boys' physical contact:

As "fag" talk increases, relaxed and cuddling patterns of touch decrease among boys. Kindergarten and first-grade boys touch one another frequently and with ease, with arms around shoulders, hugs, and holding hands. By fifth grade, touch among boys becomes more constrained, gradually shifting to mock violence and the use of poking, shoving, and ritual gestures like "giving five" (flat hand slaps) to express bonding. (p. 182)

Thus, males appear to have a strong desire to maintain interpersonal contact with other males, but (historically and developmentally) the threat of homophobic labeling increasingly forces this contact to become highly ritualized and sometimes aggressive.

It is not only the childhood socialization of individual males that inhibits intimacy, it is also the social pressures of the moment. Boys who behave in gender-inconsistent ways are very likely to lose popularity, and so conforming to peer group norms for communication serves to help the boy avoid social rejection (Burn, 1996). You may recall Robert Brannon's (1985) question: What would the typical reaction be if one man were to say to another, "Mike, I've been so upset since we had that argument. I could hardly sleep last night. Are you *sure* you're really not mad at me?" (p. 307).

Social norms constrain behavior in significant ways. Both women and men behave in more gender-stereotypical ways in public than they do in private (Burn, 1996), and males typically express a desire to be more disclosing (Reisman, 1990), suggesting that masculine and feminine styles of friendship are at least partly a function of the social expectations that women and men tend to bring into interactions with others. It may not be unusual for two male friends to both have a desire for greater levels of intimacy with each other but to continue to keep each other at an emotional arm's length because both men overestimate the degree to which the other expects gender-stereotypical behavior. Masculinity inhibits them from talking about their expectations (which would be intimate in itself) and therefore their distorted views of each other's masculinity prevent the friendship from moving in the direction that both friends would like to move. Burn (1996) cites an unpublished study she undertook with a colleague indicating that, although few men thought that they should take care of their problems by themselves, they believed that most *other men* had this expectation.

There is considerable cross-cultural diversity in the character of men's friendships. In some parts of the world, same-sex best friends go through a ceremony similar to a marriage in order to formalize their commitment to each other. When one of the friends dies, people express more sympathy to his best friend than to family members. In Java and parts of Ghana, and in some native North American tribes, the man turns to his best friend for fulfillment of his primary emotional needs, and husband-wife relationships are marked by

less emotional intensity. The romantic ideal of mainstream U.S. culture dictates that a spouse meets all the emotional needs of his or her partner, an ideology that makes deep friendships more difficult (W. Williams, 1992).

Although there is considerable pressure for contemporary U.S. men to have unemotional and nondisclosing friendships, the desire for true intimate contact with other males sometimes leads men to fight against years of socialization and against the influence of masculine social settings. "Male bonding" tends to be a poor substitute for the deeper connections of intimate friendships. Many men experience relationship dissatisfaction even with their best friends (Elkins & Peterson, 1993). It is a difficult task to make a friend when one has a decades-long history of entrenched buddyship patterns. Box 1 describes techniques for doing so.

"CROSS-CULTURAL" INTERACTIONS: MEN WITH WOMEN

As we have already discussed, children spend inordinate amounts of time in same-sex groups, and male and female groups have different interpersonal styles and social norms. One could consider all-male and all-female groups to constitute gender cultures. When a person interacts with a person of the other sex, it may be

---

Box 1 *Guerilla Tactics for Making a Friend*

Letich (1991) makes some excellent, step-by-step suggestions for working on deeper friendships:

1. First, you have to want it: Breaking patterns not only causes anxiety, it is hard work. "You have to remind yourself that there's nothing weird or effeminate about wanting a friend" (p. 87).
2. Identify a possible friend: Seek someone who seems to want to question the values of traditional masculinity.
3. Be sneaky: Get involved in a comfortable, nonpressured activity. Get used to spending time with this man.
4. Invite him to stop for a beer or a cup of coffee: Try to make honest, personal conversation at these times.
5. Call just to get together.
6. Sit down and talk about your friendship.

Letich calls these suggestions "guerilla tactics" because they seem extreme and difficult for traditional men in a culture that discourages male-male intimacy. The last two suggestions are especially antithetical to male gender role norms. Men who try these "tactics" will feel awkward, but as with any skills, they improve and become more comfortable with practice.

Youniss and Haynie (1992) point out that friendships are based on reciprocity, the tendency to respond to a person as he or she has responded to you. Men who bring a different style of relating into their friendships influence other men to also change their behavior.

somewhat like meeting a person from another part of the country, another nation, or even a different world. Both men and women often complain that they have difficulty understanding the other sex (Tannen, 1990). This confusion may be due in large part to gender differences in socialization and gendered social environmental characteristics. The effects of these differences may be most salient in mixed-sex interactions.

Male-Female Friendships

Friendships between males and females are less common than same-sex friendships. However, they are on the rise. In the late 1970s, only about 18 percent of people in a U.S. sample reported having a close friend of the other sex. That figure grew to between 25 and 40 percent by the mid-1980s (Basow, 1992; Wright & Scanlon, 1991), perhaps reflecting a greater degree of contact between the sexes in the workplace and a greater flexibility in social expectations about gender.

Several factors operate as barriers to male-female friendships. First, we live in a gender-typed culture that emphasizes differences between the sexes despite the fact that men and women are much more similar than they are different. As friendships are often based on having something in common, people are not likely to pursue friendships with those whom they perceive as dissimilar.

Friendships are also based on reciprocity, or mutual influence (Youniss & Haynie, 1992). In the childhood peer culture of males, influence tends to be exerted through direct demands. Girls are more likely to use polite suggestions. While girls' style works well with adults, it is not very effective with boys. Therefore, girls may find it quite frustrating and unpleasant to interact with boys who will not respond to their influence attempts (Maccoby, 1990).

Whereas the aversive nature of boys' interactional style keeps girls away from them, the antifemininity norm keeps boys away from girls. The boy who acts like a girl in any way, including being friends with girls, risks losing his place in the male peer dominance hierarchy. When a boy falls to a low level in this hierarchy, he finds it difficult to exert any influence on his peers. As a result, his interactions with them may also become aversive.

Thus, the masculine culture does not foster egalitarian relationships with females. Boys are barraged with messages that females are inferior and have value only as sexual objects. It is not surprising, then, that men tend to perceive sexual interest in a woman when it is not present. Abbey (1982) demonstrated that men are more likely than women to label a woman "seductive" or "promiscuous." These findings were replicated by Saal, Johnson, and Weber (1989). Abbey speculated that this readiness to sexualize behavior may result in men misperceiving friendliness as flirtation, making it difficult to establish nonsexual cross-sex relationships. There may also be a connection between this misperception and sexual harassment in the workplace.

Despite the barriers to male-female friendships, some people do manage to establish them and find them satisfying (Swain, 1992). Although traditional gender roles emphasize sex differences, it is not unlikely that similarity with a person of the other sex would be perceived on occasion. Not surprisingly, androgynous men and women are more likely to have friends of the other sex (Lavine & Lombardo, 1984).

Both males and females tend to self-disclose more often to female friends, and so a cross-sex friendship frequently offers a male something that may well be lacking in his friendships with men. Not surprisingly, women have a stronger tendency than men to describe their cross-sex friendships as less satisfactory than their other friendships (Parker & De Vries, 1993), perhaps because it is difficult to establish and maintain relationship equality in the social context of gender inequality (O'Meara, 1989).

The most common developmental period for cross-sex friendships is young adulthood. This is a time of increased cross-sex interaction for many. Later in adulthood, especially after marriage, it is difficult to establish these types of relationships, perhaps because of the anxiety that the sexual possibility creates in potential friends and in spouses. Cross-sex friendships among married people are often confined to the context of friendships between couples (Fox, Gibbs, & Auerbach, 1985). As many people suspect a sexual undertone to male-female platonic relationships, it is sometimes difficult for cross-sex friends to convince their romantic partners that their friendship is authentic (O'Meara, 1989; Swain, 1992).

Romantic Relationships

Most heterosexual males feel a strong urge to approach females beginning at puberty. As they attempt to form close relationships, gender demands exert considerable influence over their behavior. Many men feel caught in a conflict between the masculine values of antifemininity, inexpressiveness, and independence on the one hand, and attraction toward women, natural intimacy needs, and demands for relationship-oriented behaviors on the other.

Beginning early in life, cultural demands require boys to put rigid boundaries between themselves and females in order to define themselves as masculine. When they get older, however, they are expected to merge and be intimate with women. Most males have little practice in the skills required for building intimate relationships, including emotional self-disclosure, reciprocity, and empathy for the other person. It is no wonder that they often feel inept in this foreign area. They are aware at some level that females are the relationship experts. Traditionally masculine expressions of love, such as sexual affection or instrumental helping, are often inadequate when not accompanied by more direct communications of caring (Cancian, 1986, 1987).

One interesting research finding is that males tend to "fall in love" faster than females (Huston & Ashmore, 1986; Rubin, Peplau, & Hill, 1981), contrary to the popular belief that women are more emotional and love-hungry. The origins of this male readiness to fall in love are not known, but we might make some guesses. First, men tend to place more value than women on a partner's physical attractiveness (Deaux & Hanna, 1984). Thus, they may be more likely to report being in love largely on the basis of this attraction, which of course happens early in the relationship (or even from across the room). Second, men have not been socialized to understand and manage their emotional lives except through repression. Feelings that are difficult to squelch may be experienced as a "flood" of emotion. Also interesting is the finding that women initiate 80 percent of breakups in heterosexual couples (Duck, 1991). Thus, men not only fall in love more quickly, they appear to fall out of love more slowly.

Third, the level of intimacy in a romantic relationship is likely to be very different from that of a male's other relationships, which are often centered on activities. This level of intimacy is likely to be less different from the intimacy level of the female's other relationships, which are often focused on feeling and disclosure. The man's hunger for intimacy is greater because he has few or no other places to get this need met. The heterosexual relationship becomes the only safe haven from the masculine demands for independence and inexpressiveness, the only place where he can show the "softer" side of himself. A man might well experience the normal feminine style of reciprocity and consideration as love.

One interesting finding is that married men tend to disclose even less to their male friends than single men do (Tschann, 1988). Perhaps men tend to rely almost solely on their wives for filling their intimacy needs. This is a heavy burden for wives, and males often have difficulty filling these needs if the relationship should break up (Nolen-Hoeksema & Girgus, 1994).

There is a considerable body of evidence indicating that the skills required to make an intimate relationship work and last are traditionally feminine ones. The couples that have the longest lasting and happiest relationships are those in which both partners are either androgynous or feminine (Antill, 1983). This is true for gay and lesbian couples as well as heterosexual ones (Kurdek & Schmitt, 1986). For men, the abilities to be caring and emotionally expressive are strongly related to the longevity of their relationships (Blumstein & Schwartz, 1983).

In contrast, some aspects of traditional masculinity are related to problems in relationships. Women tend to desire high levels of intimacy (McAdams, Lester, Brand, McNamara, & Lensky, 1988), but gender-typed men tend to be emotionally inexpressive and unempathic. Married women often describe their husbands' lack of attention and affection to be a major source of dissatisfaction (Cunningham, Braiker, & Kelley, 1982). Wives tend to report less satisfaction with their marriages when their husbands endorse traditionally masculine ideologies (Bradbury, Campbell, & Fincham, 1995).

The degree to which partners perceive that the relationship is equitable (i.e., that each partner's power in the relationship is roughly equal) is also a predictor of marital satisfaction (Aida & Falbo, 1991). A number of factors work against relationship equity. Most notable among these is a cultural climate that confers economic, social status, and other types of power disproportionately to men, and erotic power disproportionately to women. Substantial evidence also indicates that wives do a disproportionate amount of household work, even when they work outside of the home as much as their husbands do.

The aforementioned difference in interpersonal styles works against women's power in relationships. Males are often not responsive to the typical feminine influence style of polite suggestion. If this unresponsiveness is common in the context of a relationship, the woman may feel somewhat powerless. While men may view direct demands as a natural way of negotiating in a relationship, this style may feel aversive and overpowering to women.

The masculine demand for dominance may encourage men to ignore even direct influence attempts by their partners. Women are more likely than men to use unilateral strategies, such as withdrawing by becoming cold or silent, or walking out, to influence their partner's behavior. These types of strategies are characteristics of people in all types of relationships who perceive themselves as being at a power disadvantage (Falbo & Peplau, 1980).

Men are not always the most interpersonally powerful ones in the relationship. In fact, it is the partner who seems to be more attractive or less in love (the one who "needs the relationship least") who tends to have the most power (Lips, 1997). However, it is safe to say that when partners view a relationship as an adversarial power competition, it will either not last long, or it will quickly become unsatisfying for one or both partners. Maccoby's (1990) description of successful couples is that ". . . they develop a relationship that is based on communality rather than exchange bargaining. That is, they have many shared goals and work jointly to achieve them. They do not need to argue over turf because they have the same turf" (p. 518).

Gay male couples face some of the same challenges as heterosexual couples, as indicated by their similarities in the factors that most often produce dissatisfaction within the relationship: financial conflict, the intrusion of work into the relationship, lack of time together, and sexual infidelity. But gay couples also display some average differences from heterosexual couples. For instance, they tend to value financial and educational equality more than heterosexual couples (Blumstein & Schwartz, 1983). Like heterosexual couples, gay couples place high value on feelings of attachment (Kurdek & Schmitt, 1986) and the perception that they are true partners, with each holding equal levels of power within the relationship (Aida & Falbo, 1991).

Whereas heterosexual couples tend to play out traditional gender roles in many facets of their lives, gay couples are less role-bound (despite many heterosexuals' assumption that one partner in a gay couple takes on a masculine role and the other a feminine one). Gay couples face the stress of cultural prejudice against them, and often of low familial support as well (Basow, 1992). Because gay marriage is not an option (at least it is not yet an option), gay men do not have legal ties to each other, and this makes for fewer entanglements should one partner decide to dissolve the relationship (Kurdek & Schmitt, 1986). As with heterosexual couples, gay couples find the higher degrees of satisfaction when at least one partner has emotionally expressive traits, and low levels of satisfaction when one or both partners are masculine or undifferentiated (Cook, 1985).

SONS AND FATHERS

In his gender role workshops with men, John Lee (1991) asks participants to do this simple exercise: close your eyes and get a good mental picture of your father, then pay attention to your feelings as I say these words: "Father . . . my father . . . Dad . . . Daddy . . . my dad."

The emotional responses of men (and perhaps women) to this simple exercise are incredibly powerful. The experience is one of being flooded with emotions: love, anger, disappointment, grief. It is hard to underestimate the role of the father in shaping the personality of the son.

Traditional gender demands emphasize that the father's role is to be the provider and protector, involved in work outside of the home. The mother's role emphasizes being with the children and taking care of the home. . . . These roles are much more variable historically, cross-culturally, and in the ways that individual families have been structured. Most mothers work outside the home (U.S. Department of Labor, 1991), and fathers are more involved in child care than at any time in recent history, albeit still far short of equal participation (J. Pleck, 1997). The U.S. Bureau of the Census recently reported a 25 percent increase in the number of single-father households over just a three-year period. Between 1970 and 1998, the ratio of single-father households increased from one in ten to one in six (D. Cohn, 1998). Still, the man as breadwinner and woman as caregiver remain the dominant models for parental roles (E. Pleck & J. Pleck, 1997). Some households in which men are reported as single parents may well have a female dating partner, cohabitor, or hired employee who functions as primary caregiver to children.

Fathers' levels of family involvement are difficult to ascertain because of a wide variety of methodological problems (J. Pleck, 1997). Estimates range from twelve minutes per day (Hochschild & Machung, 1989) to just over two hours (Hossain & Roopnarine, 1993). In every case, however, fathers' time involvement with children pales in comparison to mothers' (J. Pleck, 1997). As Marsiglio (1995) put it, "Clearly, recent increases in mothers' workforce participation have far outstripped fathers' increased involvement in all aspects of child care" (p. 8). It is still not unusual to hear fathers speak of "baby-sitting" their own children. We also see average differences in the ways that fathers and mothers typically spend their interaction time with their children. Mothers are more likely than fathers to be involved in basic child-care activities: feeding, dressing, washing clothes, and bathing. Fathers spend more time playing with children (Lips, 1997).

Joseph Pleck (1997) has summarized the factors related to fathers' involvement with their children. Not surprisingly, men's levels of positive fathering are related to the kind of fathers they had. Fathers whose childhood experience was with a highly involved father are more likely to be actively involved themselves. Men who perceived their fathers as less than positive models, and who display a commitment to doing better also tend to be highly involved. Men who report having been involved in child-care responsibilities as boys or adolescents (and having responded positively to these experiences) are also more involved as fathers. There is some cross-cultural evidence that boys who provide early infant care tend to become involved fathers.

Pleck notes that several studies have demonstrated a connection between psychological androgyny and father involvement, and other characteristics such as high self-esteem, adaptiveness during pregnancy, egalitarian gender beliefs, belief in the importance of the father's role, and a mature understanding of children and of the parent-child relationship are also positively correlated with involved fathering. Other variables known to have a positive effect on paternal involvement are father's education, mother's education, mother's income, and mother's employment. Father's

income is negatively associated with paternal involvement (Erickson & Gecas, 1991).

Hard work and sacrifice are the traditional ways that a man has expressed his love. Although these are profoundly significant to the family, they are indirect expressions of love. It is difficult for children to understand and appreciate that their father disappears in the morning and is gone for most of the day because he loves them. It is much easier to feel loved by someone who feeds you, dresses you, comforts you, and says, "I love you."

In my experience, most men (and women) say two things about their fathers: "I know he loves me, but he rarely shows it," and "I wish I could be closer to my father." While warm, affectionate feelings for the father predominate for most men, there is also a feeling of deep disappointment for having been deprived of the father's time, affection, and approval (Garfinkel, 1985). This feeling is sometimes referred to as "father hunger" (Bly, 1991) or even as "the wound" (J. Lee, 1991). It is perhaps the central issue in the lives of many men. Reactions to father hunger include working compulsively at trying to win the father's respect, rebelling against the father by trying hard to be different from him, or acting out the rage at having to earn his love rather than being valued unconditionally.

There are several barriers to fathers' emotional involvement with their children. Sociobiologists would have us believe that emotional involvement is biologically based—that males have no "maternal instinct" and that they are unmotivated toward attachment to their young. There is a good deal of countervailing evidence to this hypothesis. Joseph Pleck (1981a) reviewed a number of studies that showed that male animals are responsive to the young when exposed to them for a sufficient period of time. When human males are allowed to interact with their children shortly after birth, they react similarly to mothers, showing strong emotional reactions and becoming enthralled with the baby (Parke & Tinsley, 1981). In these early interactions, fathers thus form a paternal "bond" that resembles the mother-child attachment (Greenberg & Morris, 1974; Parke & Sawin, 1976). While mothers may be more biologically predisposed to respond to children, this sex difference is almost totally erased by males' early and repeated exposure to the young.

Social forces inhibit men from spending time with children and performing caregiving behaviors. In industrial and postindustrial society, the breadwinner role has been a structural barrier to paternal involvement. This role prescribes that men spend most of their time away from the home and put a greater priority on task and achievement than on relationships (E. Pleck & J. Pleck, 1997; J. Pleck, 1985). Many men report feeling strong conflicts between work and family roles (O'Neil, Fishman, & Kinsella-Shaw, 1987), and employers have been slow to accommodate employed fathers (and mothers) who wish to participate more fully in family roles (Bowen & Orthner, 1991) through, for example, "flextime" arrangements that will allow a parent to synchronize the workday schedule with the school day schedule (Bem, 1993).

Another inhibitor of paternal participation is men's perceived lack of caregiving skill. In contrast to most women, many men have no childhood parent-like experience, such as baby-sitting or playing with dolls, nor were they taught the psychological skills of nurturing or empathy (Levant, 1990a). They are not likely to approach tasks that are associated with feelings of ineptness (especially considering the role demand to always be competent). Fathers who perceive themselves as skillful in child care are usually more involved with their children (McHale & Huston, 1984). A number of models for training fathers in caregiving have been proposed (see Kiselica, 1996; Levant, 1990a, 1988; Palm, 1997).

Some mothers seem to be reluctant to share the control over child-care duties with their husbands. Palkovitz (1984) found that women's negative attitudes toward their husbands' involvement were associated with low levels of paternal involvement. McHale and Huston (1984) suggest that an increase in men's caregiving to children is only possible if mothers are willing to relinquish some of their child-care duties. Not surprisingly, husbands of less traditional wives tend to be more involved in these duties than husbands of gender-typed wives (Baruch & Barnett, 1981; Nyquist, Slivken, Spence, & Helmreich, 1985).

At one time, men were usually absent during the births of their children and only peripherally involved during the first few days of the baby's life. The father's presence at this time appears to be critical in the formation of the parent-child bond (Greenberg & Morris, 1974). This is one barrier to paternal involvement that is breaking down in the United States. The proportion of men who attend the births of their children was 80 percent as of 1985, a nearly threefold increase

from 1975 (R. Lewis, 1986). Clearly, it is also critical for fathers to increase the amount of time they spend with their children during all phases of development. Frequent contact with children facilitates the father's psychological involvement. It is impossible for fathers to have "quality time" with their children unless they have "quantity time," in which they become connected with their children's physical and emotional needs (Lynch & Kilmartin, 1999).

In the United States, current problems associated with inadequate fathering can be traced back to the "separate spheres" ideology that began during the Victorian era (Stearns, 1991). The doctrine that prescribed fathers' role as outside the home and mothers' domestic role was a result of economic exigencies that arose from industrialization. But the economy has changed and it will continue to change, increasingly making the breadwinner-homemaker dichotomy untenable, and giving rise to the different kinds of child-care arrangements that we have begun to see during the last three decades. Far from being a biologically ordained necessity, historical and cross-cultural perspectives demonstrate that the protector-provider role (in fact, all of the culturally masculine role) is a historical artifact, driven by ordinary peoples' need to make a living. From this point of view, the current debates over the "natural" roles of women and men in the home (and elsewhere) are the "growing pains" that come with social change.

Coltrane (1995) makes an optimistic prediction about the future of fatherhood and the household division of labor:

> . . . many American fathers will become more involved in their children's upbringing and begin to share more of the housework. . . . Some couples will continue to follow conventional sex-segregated divisions of labor, while others will opt for virtual role reversal. Most, however, will fall somewhere in between. . . . We can predict, however, that the general direction of change will be toward more acceptance of sharing between men and women and more sharing of family work in actual practice. (p. 269)

The general character of masculine gender role demands inhibits many of the kinds of behaviors that make for good parenting. Therefore, better fathering is linked to the process of men breaking out of their rigid roles. Many men become less gender-typed as a result of trying on the nontraditional role of caregiver (Meredith, 1985), and men also feel freer to adopt this role as they reduce their gender-typed views of the world.

REFERENCES

ABBEY A. (1982). Sex differences in attributions for friendly behavior: Do males misperceive females' friendliness? *Journal of Personality and Social Psychology, 42,* 830–838.

AIDA, Y., & FALBO, T. (1991). Relationships between marital satisfaction, resources, and power strategies. *Sex Roles, 24,* 43–56.

ANTILL, J. K. (1983). Sex role complementarity vs. similarity in married couples. *Journal of Personality and Social Psychology, 45,* 145–155.

BARUCH, G., & BARNETT, R. (1981). Fathers' participation in the care of their preschool children. *Sex Roles, 7,* 1043–1055.

BASOW, S. (1992). *Gender: Stereotypes and roles* (3rd ed.). Monterey, CA: Brooks/Cole.

BEM, S. L. (1993). *The lenses of gender: Transforming the debate on sexual inequality.* New Haven, CT: Yale University Press.

BERNDT, T. J. (1992). Friendship and friends' influence in adolescence. *Current Directions in Psychological Science, 1,* 156–159.

BLUMSTEIN, P., & SCHWARTZ, P. (1983). *American couples.* New York: William Morrow.

BLY, R. (1991). Father hunger in men. In K. Thompson (Ed.), *To be a man: In search of the deep masculine* (pp. 189–192). Los Angeles: Tarcher.

BOWEN, G. L., & ORTHNER, D. K. (1991). Effects of organizational culture on fatherhood. In E. W. Bozett & S. M. H. Hanson (Eds.), *Fatherhood and families in cultural context* (pp. 187–217). New York: Springer.

BRANNON, R. (1985). Dimensions of the male sex role in America. In A. G. Sargent, *Beyond sex roles* (2nd ed., pp. 296–316). New York: West.

BRADBURY, T. N., CAMPBELL S. M., & FINCHAM, F. D. (1995). Longitudinal and behavioral analysis of masculinity and femininity in marriages. *Journal of Personality and Social Psychology, 68,* 328–341.

BURN, S. M. (1996). *The social psychology of gender.* Boston: McGraw-Hill.

CANCIAN, E. M. (1986). The feminization of love. *Signs, 11,* 692–709.

CANCIAN, F. M. (1987). *Love in America: Gender and self-development.* Cambridge, England: Cambridge University Press.

CLAES, M. E. (1992). Friendship and personal adjustment during adolescence. *Journal of Adolescence, 15,* 39–55.

COHN, D. (1998, December 11). Single-father households on rise: Census report reveals trends in custody, adoption cases. *The Washington Post,* p. A1.

COLTRANE, S. (1995). The future of fatherhood: Social, demographic, and economic influences on men's family involvement. In W. Marsiglio (Ed.), *Fatherhood: Contemporary theory, research, and social policy* (pp. 255–274). Thousand Oaks, CA: Sage.

COOK, E. P. (1985). *Psychological androgyny.* New York: Pergamon.

CUNNINGHAM, J. D., BRAIKER, H., & KELLEY, H. H. (1982). Marital-status and sex differences—in problems reported by married and cohabiting couples. *Psychology of Women Quarterly, 6,* 415–427.

DEAUX, K., & HANNA, R. (1984). Courtship in the personals column: The influence of gender and sexual orientation. *Sex Roles, 11,* 363–375.

DERLEGA, V. J., & CHAIKIN, A. L. (1976). Norms affecting self-disclosure in men and women. *Journal of Consulting and Clinical Psychology, 44,* 376–380.

DEVLIN, P. K., & COWANA G. A. (1985). Homophobia, perceived fathering, and male intimate relationships. *Journal of Personality Assessment, 49,* 467–473.

DUCK, S. (1991). *Understanding relationships.* New York: Guilford.

ELKINS, L. E., & PETERSON, C. (1993). Gender differences in best friendships. *Sex Roles, 29,* 497–508.

ERICKSON, R. J., & GECAS, V. (1991). Social class and fatherhood. In F. W. Bozett & S. M. H. Hanson (Eds.), *Fatherhood and families in cultural context* (pp. 114–137). New York: Springer.

FALBO, T., & PEPLAU, L. A. (1980). Power strategies in intimate relationships. *Journal of Personality and Social Psychology, 38,* 618–628.

FOX, M., GIBBS, M., & AUERBACH, D. (1985). Age and gender dimensions of friendship. *Psychology of Women Quarterly, 9,* 489–502.

GARFINKEL, P. (1985). *In a man's world: Father, son, brother, friend, and other roles men play.* New York: New American Library.

GOLOMBOK, S., & FIVUSH, R. (1994). *Gender development.* New York: Cambridge University Press.

GREENBERG, M., & MORRIS, N. (1974). Engrossment: The newborn's impact upon the father. *American Journal of Orthopsychiatry, 44,* 520–531.

HOCHSCHILD, A., & MACHUNG, A. (1989). *The second shift.* New York: Avon.

HOSSAIN, Z., & ROOPNARINE, J. L. (1993). Division of household labor and child care in dual-earner African-American families with infants. *Sex Roles, 29,* 571–583.

HUMPHREYS, A. P., & SMITH, P. K. (1987). Rough and tumble friendship and dominance in school children: Evidence for continuity and change in middle childhood. *Child Development, 58,* 201–212.

HUSTON, T. L., & ASHMORE, R. D. (1986). Women and men in personal relationship. In R. D. Ashmore & R. K. Del Boca (Eds.), *The social psychology of female-male relations* (pp. 167–210). New York: Academic Press.

JOURARD, S. M. (1971). *The transparent self.* New York: Van Nostrand.

KISELICA, M. S. (1996). Parenting skills training with teenage fathers: In M. P Andronico (Ed.), *Men in groups: Insights, interventions, and psychoeducational work* (pp. 283–300). Washington, DC: American Psychological Association.

KURDEK, L. A., & SCHMITT, J. P. (1986). Interaction of sex role self-concept with relationship quality and relationship beliefs in married, heterosexual cohabiting, gay, and lesbian couples. *Journal of Personality and Social Psychology, 51,* 365–370.

LAVINE, L. O., & LOMBARDO, J. P. (1984). Self-disclosure: Intimate and nonintimate disclosures to parents and best friends as a function of Bem sex-role category. *Sex Roles, 11,* 760–768.

LEE, C. C. (1990). Black male development: Counseling the "native son." In D. Moore & F. Leafgren (Eds.), *Men in conflict* (pp. 125–137). Alexandria, VA: American Association for Counseling and Development.

LEE, J. (1991). *At my father's wedding: Reclaiming our true masculinity.* New York: Bantam.

LETICH, L. (1991, May/June). Do you know who your friends are? *Utne Reader,* pp. 85–87.

LEVANT, R. P. (1988). Education for fatherhood. In P. Bronstein & C. P. Cowan (Eds.), *Fatherhood today: Men's changing role in the family* (pp. 253–275). New York: Wiley.

LEVANT, R. E. (1990a). Coping with the new father role. In D. Moore & F. Leafgren (Eds.), *Men in conflict* (pp. 81–94). Alexandria, VA: American Association for Counseling and Development.

LEVANT, R. F. (1995). *Masculinity reconstructed: Changing the rules of manhood—at work, in relationships, and in family life.* New York: Dutton.

LEWIS, R. A. (1986). Men's changing roles in marriage and the family. In R. A. Lewis (Ed.), *Men's changing roles in the family* (pp. 1–10). New York: Haworth.

LIPS, H. (1997). *Sex and gender: An introduction* (3rd ed.). Mountain View, CA: Mayfield.

LYNCH, J., & KILMARTIN, C. T. (1999). *The pain behind the mask: Overcoming masculine depression.* Binghamton, NY: Haworth.

MACCOBY, E. E. (1988b). Gender as a social construct. Paper presented at the annual meeting of the Eastern Psychological Association, Buffalo, NY.

MACCOBY, E. E. (1990). Gender and relationships: A developmental account. *American Psychologist, 45,* 513–520.

MALTZ, D. N., & BORKER, R.A. (1983). A cultural approach to male-female miscommunication. In J. A. Gumperz (Ed.), *Language and social identity* (pp. 195–216). New York: Cambridge University Press.

MARSIGLIO, W. (1995). Fatherhood scholarship: An overview and agenda for the future. In W. Marsiglio (Ed.), *Fatherhood: Contemporary theory, research, and social policy* (pp. 1–20). Thousand Oaks, CA: Sage.

MCADAMS, D. P., LESTER, R. M., BRAND, P. A., MCNAMARA, W. J., & LENSKY, D. B. (1988). Sex and the TAT: Are women more intimate than men? Do men fear intimacy? *Journal of Personality Assessment, 52,* 397–409.

MCHALE, S. M., & HUSTON, T. L. (1984). Men and women as parents: Sex role orientations, employment, and parental roles with infants. *Child Development, 55,* 1349–1361.

MEREDITH, D. (1985, June). Dad and the kids. *Psychology Today,* 63–67.

MESSNER, M. A. (1992). Like family: Power, intimacy, and sexuality in athletes' friendships. In P. M. Nardi (Ed.), *Men's Friendships* (pp. 215–236). Newbury Park, CA: Sage.

NARDI, P. M. (1992). Sex, friendship, and gender roles among gay men. In P. M. Nardi (Ed.), *Men's friendships* (pp. 173–185). Newbury Park, CA: Sage.

NOLEN-HOEKSEMA, S. (1995). Gender differences in coping with depression across the lifespan. *Depression, 3,* 81–90.

NOLEN-HOEKSEMA, S., & GIRGUS, J. S. (1994). The emergence of gender differences in depression during adolescence. *Psychological Bulletin, 115,* 424–443.

NYQUIST, L., SLIVKEN, K., SPENCE, J. T., & HELMREICH, R. L. (1985). Household responsibilities in middle-class couples: The contribution of demographic and personality variables. *Sex Roles, 12,* 15–34.

O'MEARA, J. D. (1989). Cross-sex friendship: Four basic challenges of an ignored relationship. *Sex Roles, 21,* 525–543.

O'NEIL, J. M., FISHMAN, D. M., & KINSELLA-SHAW, M. (1987). Dual-career couples transitions and normative dilemmas: A preliminary assessment model. *The Counseling Psychologist, 15,* 50–96.

PALKOVITZ, R. (1984). Parental attitudes and fathers' interactions with their 5-month-old infants. *Developmental Psychology, 20,* 1054–1060.

PALM, G. F. (1997). Promoting generative fathering through parent and family education. In A. J. Hawkins & D. C. Dollahite (Eds.), *Generative fathering: Beyond deficit perspectives* (pp. 167–182). Thousand Oaks, CA: Sage.

PARKE, R. D., & SAWIN, D. B. (1976). The father's role in infancy: A reevaluation. *The Family Coordinator, 25,* 365–371.

PARKE, R. D., & TINSLEY, B. R. (1981). The father's role in infancy: Determinants of involvement in caregiving and play. In M. Lamb (Ed.), *The role of the father in child development* (2nd ed., pp. 429–457). New York: Wiley.

PARKER, S., & DE VRIES, B. (1993). Patterns of friendship for women and men in same- and cross-sex relationships. *Journal of Social and Personal Relationships, 10,* 617–626.

PENNEBAKER, J. W. (1995). Emotion, disclosure, and health: An overview. In J. W. Pennebacker (Ed.), *Emotion, disclosure, and health* (pp. 3–10). Washington; DC: American Psychological Association.

PLECK, E. H., & PLECK, J. H. (1997). Fatherhood ideals in the United States: Historical dimensions. In M. E. Lamb (Ed.), *The role of the father in child development* (3rd ed., pp. 33–48). New York: Wiley.

PLECK, J. H. (1981a). *The myth of masculinity.* Cambridge, MA: MIT Press.

PLECK, J. H. (1985). *Working wives/Working husbands.* Beverly Hills, CA: Sage.

PLECK, J. H. (1997). Paternal involvement: Levels, sources, and consequences. In M. E. Lamb (Ed.), *The role of the father in child development* (3rd ed., pp. 66–103). New York: Wiley.

REID, H. M., & FINE, G. A. (1992). Self-disclosure in men's friendships. In P. M. Nardi (Ed.), *Men's friendships* (pp. 132–152). Newbury Park, CA: Sage.

REISMAN, J. M. (1990). Intimacy in same-sex friendships. *Sex Roles, 23,* 65–82.

ROTUNDO, E. A. (1993). *American manhood: Transformations in masculinity from the Revolution to the modern era.* New York: Basic Books.

RUBIN, Z., PEPLAU, L. A., & HILL, C. T. (1981). Loving and leaving: Sex differences in romantic attachments. *Sex Roles, 2,* 821–835.

SAAL, F. E., JOHNSON, C. B., & WEBER, N. (1989). Friendly or sexy?: It may depend on whom you ask. *Psychology of Women Quarterly, 13,* 263–276.

SEIDLER, V. J. (1992). Rejection, vulnerability, and friendship. In P. M. Nardi (Ed.), *Men's friendships* (pp. 15–34). Newbury Park, CA: Sage.

STEARNS, P. N. (1991). Fatherhood in historical perspective: The role of social change. In F. W. Bozett & S. M. H. Hanson (Eds.), *Fatherhood and families in cultural context* (pp. 28–52). New York: Springer.

STOKES, J., & LEVIN, I. (1986). Gender differences in predicting loneliness from social network characteristics. *Journal of Personality and Social Psychology, 51,* 1069–1074.

SWAIN, S. O. (1992). Men's friendships with women: Intimacy, sexual boundaries, and the informant role. In P. M. Nardi (Ed.), *Men's friendships* (pp. 153–171). Newbury Park, CA: Sage.

TANNEN, D. (1990). *You just don't understand: Women and men in conversation.* New York: Morrow.

THORNE, B., & LURIA, Z. (1986). Sexuality and gender in children's daily worlds. *Social Problems, 33,* 176–190.

TSCHANN, J. (1988). Self-disclosure in adult friendship: Gender and marital status differences. *Journal of Social and Personal Relationships, 5,* 65–81.

UNITED STATES BUREAU OF THE CENSUS (USBC). (1997). Statistical abstract of the United States: 1997 (117th ed.). Washington, DC: U.S. Government Printing Office.

UNITED STATES DEPARTMENT OF LABOR. (1991). Employment and earnings, February, 1991. Washington, DC: U.S. Government Printing Office.

WILLIAMS, W. L. (1992). The relationship between male-male friendship and male-female marriage. In P. M. Nardi (Ed.), *Men's friendships* (pp. 186–200). Newbury Park, CA: Sage.

WINSTEAD, B. A., DERLEGA, V. J., & WONG, P. T. P. (1984). Effects of sex-role orientation on behavioral self-disclosure. *Journal of Research in Personality, 38,* 541–553.

WRIGHT, P. H., & SCANLON, M. B. (1991). Gender role orientations and friendship: Some attenuation, but gender differences abound. *Sex Roles, 24,* 551–566.

YOUNISS, J., & HAYNIE, D. L. (1992). Friendship in adolescence. *Developmental and Behavioral Pediatrics, 13,* 59–66.

Black-Widow Women

James William Gibson

In April 1983, the cover of *Combat Handguns* featured a new Safari Arms .45 automatic for women. It looked like all the other clones of Colt's famous 1911 model, except for the grip. The synthetic ivory micrata sported a spiderweb with a large black-widow spider (complete with the red markings of a female) on each side. And that's what the gun was called too: "Black Widow—The Venomous Manstopper." For those who missed the 1983 debut of the Black Widow, the magazine ran a virtually identical story nine years later.

As all good schoolboys learn sometime around puberty, the female black-widow spider kills the male after mating and then eats him. At the very moment when a boy is trying harder than ever to establish his autonomy, this piece of spider lore calls up scenes of the overpowering mother from his infancy and childhood. At the same time, just when he is first beginning to feel some attraction to the girls around him, the image of dangerous female sexuality confirms his own worst fears—that no matter how he approaches one of them, the encounter will end badly. The New War never progresses beyond these adolescent fears. All women are black-widow women. To be sure, there are several different subspecies, but all are dangerous creatures, enemies of one kind or another who are to be either avoided, mastered, or killed.

The most deadly woman of all is of course the mother. Her death—or at least her permanent absence—is a prerequisite for the formation of the hero. Stable marriages and long-term relationships with women are also threatening to the warrior. "Good" women exist all right; they are women who recognize the power and wonderfulness of the hero. Sometimes they even love him deeply and are ready to make their lives and careers secondary to his. The hero, in turn, may finally be touched by a woman's loving grace and start to strip off his emotional armor. A "deep" relationship looms. But something always happens to these women.

"Ko," the Vietnamese woman who aids Rambo in his rescue of the American prisoners, is blown up by a Communist mortar round only seconds after they kiss and talk about the possibility of her returning with him to the United States. In *Lethal Weapon 2*, Mel Gibson finally recovers from his first wife's death only to have his new lover drowned by South African drug dealers—the lovers had only one night together! On *Miami Vice*, poor Sonny Crockett loses his second wife to a murderer's bullet shortly after they are married (his first wife divorced him at the beginning of the series because he was always off fighting bad men), while his buddy Enrico Tubbs sees his wife gunned down on their honeymoon.

In paramilitary novels, the suffering of good women is described in great detail. . . .

In this way, men vicariously destroy the women who get too close to them, and at the same time avoid guilt by blaming the "enemy." Indeed, the warrior will always punish those responsible for these crimes.

The overt rage against women expressed in these works is never acknowledged by those responsible for creating them. "A permanent woman is like one long kissing scene," explained one New York paperback editor when asked why the warrior's good lovers are always killed. He was referring to the pace of "action" in the action-adventure genre. In his assessment, a story of human relationships moves much more slowly than a story about adventure and killing. To maintain the genre, then, the good woman has to die.

Formal genre conventions, however, always delineate the major contours of an ideal social world. And this particular ideal obscures perverse psychological dynamics, such as the blatant appeal to repressed anger. In the New War, "good" women represent the deep domestic interior of society, where women give birth and raise children. But the warrior is a man who can only live outside society, on the frontier, exempt from the confining laws and moral codes that regulate social life. This is where he must be to fight the enemy. And so he must throw off the good woman to fulfill his destiny.

Conversely, to have a serious relationship, a man must retire as a warrior and accept the limitations of mortal men. A small number of New War films do indeed depict the hero's last battle. Typically, he fights it in an effort to gain control over some unruly woman. The notion of the knight winning the heart of the lady through valor is an old one. In the New War, however, some damsels are not exactly waiting for Prince Charming. Many are feminists who have either divorced or separated from their warrior husbands. Some, like Aggie in *Heartbreak Ridge* (1986), can't stand the anxiety of not knowing whether their men will live or die on the battlefield and, therefore, refuse to commit themselves. Others, like Holly Genera in *Die Hard* (1988), are focused on their own careers as rising corporate managers. These are basically "good" women, but like the black widow, they have a mean streak and an agenda that sometimes differs from the hero's. . . .

In all the hundreds of New War stories, the handful of heroes who want their former mates back are the only men who are in any way concerned about their relationships with women. (In contrast, modern women's romance novels depict virtually all men as obsessed with their would-be lovers.)[1] And the task these warriors have set themselves is as difficult as any paramilitary mission. To win the hearts of their alienated significant others, warriors must prove that their powers and virtues are far greater than those of ordinary men. Only death-defying risks really impress the feminists; only then do these women relent in their demands and accept their roles as normal wives.

But few New War stories tell of marital reconciliation through warfare. Instead, most concentrate on the other kinds of females available to the hero if he is willing to take the risks. Just as the war zone is full of violent male demons, so too is it filled with powerfully erotic female creatures. Although good women are usually shown as attractive, even sexual beings, their sexuality is not the center of their lives. In contrast, the image of the fully erotic woman is one of unlimited wantonness, sexual hunger, and electricity so extreme that she gains the power to dominate men. . . .

Women who are uncontrollably driven by their erotic hunger are obviously capable of doing practically anything to get their needs met. They can readily separate sex from love, friendship, or even the most modest recognition of a common humanity. These erotic women are so emotionally removed from their partners that like the black-widow spiders they can kill a man after making love with him. And many try. Quite often the erotic woman who appears to desire

the warrior so ardently is in reality an enemy agent. Beautiful enemy agents are not in themselves new. James Bond, the famous "007" of Her Majesty's Secret Service, always seemed to find one in his bed. But Bond's charm and swordsmanship inevitably won them over; these femmes fatales always wanted him warm and alive, not cold and dead.

In the New War, however, the erotic woman's desire for sex and desire to kill tend to merge into a single orgasmic death lust. . . .

The combination of lust for killing and lust for sexual pleasure is especially acute in female terrorists, who epitomize the height of erotic passion fatally conjoined with the coldest, most sadistic perversities. . . .

In the 1980s this image of the female terrorist was accepted by many as an accurate profile of actual operatives. Gayle Rivers wrote two books on fighting terrorists, *The Specialist: Revelations of a Counterterrorist* and *The War Against the Terrorists: How to Win It*.[2] Rivers claimed to have first served with the British Special Air Services and then become an elite mercenary for the United States and other NATO countries who needed secret commando services. He wrote that in his fifteen or more years of hunting and eliminating terrorists "the majority of female terrorists I've had to confront are spoiled, well-educated women from so-called good backgrounds who are turned on by aggressive acts."[3] According to Rivers, such women are also noted for their willingness to kill children.*

The clear implication is that all of these women— operatives, agents, and terrorists—generate a kind of evil sexual energy that is useful to the enemy. And when they embrace the male terrorist or criminal or Communist they fuse female erotic power with male violence into a single disease-ridden, demonic spirit. Interestingly enough, Peter G. Kokalis, the firearms editor of *Soldier of Fortune*, encountered such a con-

---

*Some writers in American paramilitary magazines did not think Rivers's books were legitimate. His tales of receiving assignments on his car phone while driving his Mercedes on the German Autobahn struck them as far-fetched, as did his accounts of extraordinary commando raids, assassinations, and kidnappings in Lebanon and other world hot spots. Rivers also made some major mistakes in his descriptions of weapons, ones that a real professional or even a more knowledgeable amateur would easily have avoided. Although the *Sunday Times* of London published a two-part article in 1985 that impugned Rivers's claims to have been an SAS veteran and mercenary, he succeeded in having American newspapers syndicate excerpts of his second book the following year.

stellation of threat, sex, and degeneracy in the behavior of the American press corps during one of his tours of duty in El Salvador. He is contemptuous of the journalists, who, he says, spend their days "sitting in the Camino Real bar, gloating over guerrilla spectaculars, sneering at the 'incompetence' of the Salvadoran Army officers."[4] What's worse than daytime drinking, though, is the press corps' nighttime whoremongering and their Commie-loving news articles. Kokalis contrasts his early-morning virtue in going to assist his comrades in the countryside with the antics of the liberal press in San Salvador:

I rolled out with the relief column at 0500 [5:00 A.M.], just about the time the press corps has finished turning the FMLN's (Farabundo Marti National Liberation Front) daily propaganda into hot, smoking poop after a rough night downing Pilsners at Gloria's, the local cathouse.[5]

In one sentence, he links the news media, Communist propaganda, excrement, alcoholic excess, and fornication—presumably from nightfall until five in the morning. All of these people and actions roll into a single enemy: Communism as shit; shit as sex; sex as Communism. It is an image of crude, orgiastic excess, perversion that subverts all that is good and orderly. In this respect, Kokalis follows the *Freikorps* tradition in Germany after World War I. When Ernst Otwald described his image of the enemy in his novel about German paramilitary life, *Peace and Order*, he wrote, "For that matter, the terms 'cathouse,' 'bar,' 'criminal,' and 'communist' are in separably connected in my mind."[6]

The division of women into the good, "pure" sister and the bad, "impure" temptress was also characteristic of *Freikorps* literature. *Freikorps* men frequently wrote about the virtues of their sisters, and the "whoring" of "red" working-class women. As Klaus Theweleit argued in his analysis of over two hundred *Freikorps* novels and memoirs, the repeated equation of erotic women with Communism meant that in some ways these men experienced both Communism and erotic women "as a direct assault on their genitals."[7] From this perspective, the "sister" is the only safe woman with whom the warrior can have a relationship—platonic, to be sure. According to Theweleit, "Anything beyond her is uncharted, dangerous territory, yet she herself is taboo."[8]

Just as his older brothers in the *Freikorps* rejected the erotic woman, the New Warrior must firmly maintain his hardened boundaries to avoid being contaminated by impure enemy women. He too must say no. And most stories in the New War contain at least one of these nay-saying scenes. . . .

The only other "safe" woman is the nurse, who, in *Freikorps* literature, is similar to the sister in that "the nurse's is a dead body, with no desires, no sexuality (no 'penis')."[9] . . .

More common than such noble and transforming refusals are the sometimes cruel scenes of men leaving women for war, a recurrent motif in *Freikorps* literature as well. Once, the comic-book hero Punisher literally has to push a woman off him while they are on a mission. "Cool it," he says. "Let's keep it business. Fate throws us together. But that doesn't mean we have to start acting like those animals down there."[10] On some occasions, a working-class warrior takes pleasure in leaving an upper-middle-class woman alone in bed, still wanting him.[11] Many men express relief when they no longer need to bear the burden of satisfying sexually insatiable women. In volume 30 of the *SOBs*, for example, two of Niles Barrabas's men nearly die on a sailboat so filled with hungry, naked women that all one can see are "buttocks and breasts in a kaleidoscope of white, black, and tan." When Niles calls the two men on the radio, they first chitchat about things. But soon the tension of waiting for the word gets to be too much. One warrior exclaims in joy, "Colonel? Thank God! Tell me you need us for a job. Please."[12]

There is obviously more than a hint of male narcissism in such scenes. The warrior considers himself so desirable to women that he can leave the one he's with and turn down new offers while preparing for war, because he is positive another woman will always want him. Niles, for example, can abandon a naked playmate, one with a "dark coffee color" tan all over, because he is bored—"His finely tuned mind and body were crying out for a challenge." Then, before he even gets to the airport, he has to turn down the advances of a sumptuous waitress—"Next time, baby. Maybe next time."[13]

In all of these instances, when men avoid or leave their women lovers, they appear to be exercising self-control. Only with their body armor fully in place can they guard the boundaries of society against all its enemies. Public duty seems to take precedence over private pleasure.

But what the New War really shows is that men are still deeply afraid of women. The erotic woman appears in so many terrible guises, in so many incarnations of projected fear and hostility: she is an insatiable animal; an evil terrorist aroused by killing and liable to destroy the warrior; a superficial, disposable playmate; a temptress who ruins careers and endangers missions. Compared to women, war is clean and good and dependable. By going off to war, then, men try to control their fears of women. War is the only means by which a man can subdue the erotic woman or avoid her dangerous entrapments. For the sad fact is that there can be no equality with black-widow women, only domination or subordination.

Finally, a few words must be said about a very rare character in the New War, the heroic woman warrior. Only three have appeared in recent years: the Sigourney Weaver character who battles space monsters in *Alien* (1979) and *Aliens* (1986); the Jodie Foster character who, as an FBI agent still training at the academy, tracks down a psychotic serial killer in *The Silence of the Lambs* (1991); and, in *Terminator 2* (1991), Linda Hamilton's character, the woman who tries to stop the future war between robots and humans. When movie directors and novel editors were asked in the late 1980s whether there would be more women warrior characters, the uniform answer was no. Some said that since there was little historical precedent for women combatants in war (which is not true), then obviously only the rare outer-space gig was possible. More frequently, though, the men interviewed seemed deeply vexed by the question. One well-known novel editor simply said, "I think women want to have men as heroes, and men want to have men as heroes."[14]

And that's exactly what they get. The women in the three films mentioned are strikingly similar to male New War heroes. If anything, they are hypermasculine. Women warriors avoid any romantic or erotic relationships with men, even more than male warriors avoid serious relationships with women. Linda Hamilton in *Terminator 2* is so obsessed with fighting the enemy that she is even distracted from caring for her son. A New Warrior, regardless of genitalia, is obviously incapable of sustaining serious relationships outside the war zone. Thus, although these films portray women as powerful, they maintain a strict gender dichotomy between those who fight the enemy and those who nurture, love, or have a distinct erotic presence. These warrior women are as one-dimensional as the men they replace. The difference is only superficial; their presence does not significantly change the basic mythology. After all, they fight the the same villains, the same insatiable evil.

NOTES

1. Tania Modleski, *Losing with a Vengeance: Mass-Produced Fantasies for Women* (Hamden, Conn.: Archon, 1982), 16.

2. Gayle Rivers, *The Specialist: Revelations of a Counterterrorist* (New York: Stein and Day, 1985); *The War Against the Terrorists: How to Win It* (New York: Stein and Day, 1986).

3. Rivers, *War Against the Terrorists*, 18–19.

4. Peter G. Kokalis, "Atlacatal Assault: *SOF* in Combat with Salvador's Elite Immediate Reaction Battalion," *Soldier of Fortune*, June 1984, 57.

5. Ibid., 58.

6. Klaus Theweleit, *Women, Floods, Bodies, History*, vol. 1 of *Male Fantasies*, trans. Stephen Conway with Erica Carter and Chris Turner (Minneapolis: University of Minnesota Press, 1987), 68.

7. Ibid., 74.

8. Ibid., 125.

9. Ibid., 134.

10. Mike Barron, "Sacrifice Play," *The Punisher*, vol. 11, no. 13 (November 1988), 13.

11. Stivers, *Ghost Train*, 80–81.

12. Hild, *Alaska Deception*, 64–65.

13. Ibid., 45, 68.

14. Interview with Andy Ettinger, the first editor of *The Executioner*, Oct. 17, 1986.

Backlash

Dressing the Dolls: The Fashion Backlash

Susan Faludi

Just ten days after the October 19, 1987, stock market collapse, French fashion designer Christian Lacroix unveiled his "Luxe" collection at a society gala on Wall Street. The setting, aptly for a postcrash event, was the ground floor of the towering World Financial Center. As brokers upstairs sorted through the shambles, hollow-cheeked models with crosses around their necks drifted down the courtyard's runway, their clothes-hanger bodies swaying under the weight of twenty pounds of crinoline and taffeta. The pushed-up breasts of "Maria, Mounia, Veronica, and Katoucha" blossomed with roses the size of cabbage heads;[1] beneath their tightly laced waists, pumpkin-shaped skirts ballooned. Three layers of bustles brought up the rear. These were clothes, Lacroix said, for women who like to "dress up like little girls."[2] The Lacroix price tags, however, were not so pint-sized; they ranged as high as $45,000—among the costliest raiments ever to come out of Paris.[3]

When the lights finally came up, the fashion writers leaped from their seats to litter the runway with pink carnations. Applause was deafening for the "Messiah" of couture, as the fashion press had anointed him a year earlier, when he displayed his first "Baby Doll" line in Paris. As fireworks burst outside in a Revlon-funded salute to the sartorial savior, the well-heeled guests adjourned to a $500-a-plate meal in the Winter Garden atrium. There, surrounded by three thousand votive candles, couture-industry boosters served up reverential testimonials in strategic earshot of the fashion press: Lacroix's bubble skirts exuded "independent strength and sensitivity";[4] it was like being "in a room full of Picassos," a designer told the *New York Times*.

The Luxe gowns went on sale at Bergdorf Goodman,[5] and, with Lacroix on hand to sign autographs, seventy-nine society matrons hurried to place their orders for $330,000 worth in two days. Maybe the Messiah would convert women after all to the look of High Femininity—or "frou-frou," as less worshipful observers dubbed the fashion world's sudden detour into frills and petticoats in the spring of 1987. At least de-

signers and retailers hoped he had converted them. After Lacroix's July 1986 Paris "fantasy fashion" debut had won rave reviews from *Women's Wear Daily*,[6] twenty-one of the twenty-four couture houses had rushed out their own versions of High Femininity; apparel makers had begun promoting "the idea of women as dressed-up dolls"; retailers had stocked up on poufs, miniskirts, party-girl gowns and body-squeezing garments that reduced the waist by three inches. And the fashion press had smoothed the way, promoting "the gamine look" and declaring 1987 "the Year of the Dress." But all the preparation was for naught. That spring, women just quit buying.

Lacroix's messianic appellation was more fitting than intended; by the end of the '80s, it would indeed have taken divine intervention to resurrect the women's apparel market. Black Monday, which dampened enthusiasm for conspicuous displays of wealth, was only the latest blow to an industry staggering from foreign competition, massive merger debts, record costs for raw materials, a declining dollar overseas—and then that final indignity, the rebuff of American women.

That so-called feminine ardor for clothes shopping had been flagging for some time. Between 1980 and 1986, at the same time that women were buying more houses, cars, restaurant dinners, and health care services, they were buying fewer pieces of clothing—from dresses to underwear.[7] The shaky economy played a role, but mostly women just didn't seem to enjoy clothes shopping as much anymore. In one poll, more than 80 percent said they hated it, double from a decade earlier.[8]

Throughout the decade, apparel makers and retailers tried to make up for a shrinking shopper base with rapidly inflating clothes prices. But the more stores marked up the tags, the less likely women were to take them to the register. Then, in the High Femininity year of 1987, dress prices jumped as much as 30 percent.[9] Women took one look at the tickets, another at the thigh-high dresses—and fled the stores. That year, even with higher prices compensating for lower volume, total sales dollars of women's apparel fell for the first time in a decade.[10] In the so-called Year of the Dress, dress sales alone dropped 4 percent. Even during the height of the Christmas season, fashion sales fell;[11] that hadn't even happened under the 1982 recession. And this was a one-gender phenomenon.[12] In fact, that same year, men's apparel sales rose 2.1 percent.

The women's "fashion revolt" and "sticker shock rebellion" of 1987, as the media came to call it, nearly decimated the fashion industry. And the more the dress merchants tried to force frills on their reluctant customers, the more their profit margins plunged. In the spring of 1988, after another season of flounces, bubble skirts, and minis, and another 40 percent price hike, apparel retailers' stocks plunged and quarterly earnings fell by 50 and 75 percent.[13] Department stores—where apparel accounts for 75 percent of sales—lost tens of millions of dollars in profits. By the second quarter of 1988, the apparel industry was drawing more than $4 billion less in annual women's clothes sales than in the period just before the High Femininity look was introduced.[14]

Perhaps the designers should have expected it. They were pushing "little-girl" dresses and "slender silhouettes" at a time when the average American woman was thirty-two years old, weighed 143 pounds and wore a size 10 or 12 dress.[15] Fewer than one-fourth of American women were taller than five foot four or wore a size smaller than 14—but 95 percent of the fashions were designed to fit these specifications. Of all the frilly and "retro" fashions introduced in 1987, only one really caught on: the peplum, an extra layer of fabric that hung from the waist and concealed broadening hips.

How could the industry make such a marketing blunder? As Goldman Sachs's retail analyst Joseph Ellis pointed out a year later in his analysis, "The Women's Apparel Retailing Debacle: Why?," demographics "have been warning of a strong population shift to older age categories for years now."[16] Yet designers, manufacturers, and retailers went "in exactly the wrong direction." Ellis charitably concluded that the industry must have lacked the appropriate consumer research studies.

But the fashion world hardly needed a marketing expert to tell them baby boomers were aging. The explosion of frills in 1987 wasn't simply a misunderstanding; it was an eruption of long-simmering frustration and resentment at the increasingly independent habits of the modern female shopper. "What's the matter with American women?" a French fashion designer snapped at John Molloy, the author of *Dress for Success*, while he was touring design houses in the mid-'80s.[17] "They don't do as they're told anymore. We tell them how to dress but they just don't listen." Or, as Lacroix would complain later, "[W]ith the women's-lib movement at the turn of the 'sixties [and in the] 'seventies, women became less fashion conscious," and so many affluent female customers deserted couture that "Arabian princesses and classical dowagers remained the only customers."[18] High Femininity was an attempt to command liberated women's attention with a counter-attack. As fashion designer Arnold Scaasi, one of High Femininity's leading architects, explains it, the new fashion edict "is reaction to the feminist movement, which was kind of a war."[19]

The mission of Lacroix and his fellow designers was to win this war, to make women "listen" and rein them in, sometimes quite literally. At a Lacroix fashion show, the designer trotted out his "cowgirl" model, bound and harnessed in a bridle rope.[20] It was not enough that women buy more clothes; they had to buy the clothes that the couturiers *told* them to buy. Designers wanted to be in charge of "dressing women," as the Council of Fashion Designers of America phrased it,[21] in its 1987 tribute to Lacroix.

What happened in 1987 had happened before, almost identically, in the 1947 fashion war. Women who had discovered pants, low-heeled shoes, and loose sweaters during World War II were reluctant to give them up in peacetime.[22] The fashion industry fell into a "frightening slump," as *Time* described it at the time, with orders shrinking by as much as 60 percent.[23] And women only rebelled when French designer Christian Dior unveiled the "New Look"—actually an old late-Victorian look—featuring crinolined rumps, corseted waists, and long ballooning skirts. More than three hundred thousand women joined "Little Below the Knee Clubs" to protest the New Look,[24] and, when Neiman Marcus gave its annual fashion award to Dior, women stood outside waving placards—DOWN WITH THE NEW LOOK—and booing the man who believed that waists wider than seventeen inches were "repulsive" on a lady. "Let the new look of today become the forgotten look of tomorrow," labor lawyer Anna Rosenberg proclaimed, and her sentiments were widely shared. In a poll that summer, a majority of women denounced the Dior style.[25]

The women's declarations, however, only strengthened the designer's resolve to silence them. "The women who are loudest," Dior retorted, ". . . will soon be wearing the longest dresses. . . . You can never stop the fashions."[26] By the end of the '40s, after a two-year promotional campaign by retailers and the fashion press, Dior won out. Women were wearing the New Look, albeit a toned-down version. And they were obeying Dior's order that they wear corsets capable of shaving two inches from their waist;[27] in fact, bustiers that reduced the waist by *three* inches were soon generating sales of $6 million a year.

In every backlash, the fashion industry has produced punitively restrictive clothing and the fashion press has demanded that women wear them. "If you want a girl to grow up gentle and womanly in her ways and her feelings, lace her tight," advised one of the many male testimonials to the corset in the late Victorian press.[28] In the last half of the 19th century, apparel makers crafted increasingly rib-crushing gowns with massive rear bustles.[29] And ridicule from the press effectively crushed a women's dress-reform campaign for more comfortable, sports-oriented clothing. The influential *Godey's Lady's Book* sneered at such "roomy and clownish apparel" and labeled its proponents dress "deformers."[30]

When the fashion industry began issuing marching orders again in the '80s, its publicists advanced a promotional line that downplayed the domineering intent and pretended to serve women's needs. Like the other contributors to backlash culture, fashion merchants latched on to the idea that contemporary women must be suffering from an excess of equality that had depleted their femininity. In fashion terms, the backlash argument became: Women's liberation has denied women the "right" to feminine dressing; the professional work outfits of the '70s shackled the female spirit. "A lot of women took the tailored look too far and it became unattractive," designer Bob Mackie says.[31] "Probably, psychologically, it hurt their femininity. You see a lot of it in New York, trotting down Wall Street." Women have realized that they are "beginning to lose some of their feminine attributes," fashion designer Arnold Scaasi says. "Women are fighting now for their own individuality"—by "going home and dressing up."[32]

In its desperation, the industry began to contradict its own time-honored conventions. Fashion's promoters have long rhapsodized that femininity is "eternal," rooted in women's very nature; yet at the same time, they were telling women that simply wearing the wrong set of clothes could obliterate this timeless female essence. This became the party line, voiced by merchants peddling every garment from poufs to panties. "We were wearing pinstripes, we didn't know what our identity was anymore!" cried Karen Bromley, spokeswoman for the Intimate Apparel Council. "We were having this identity crisis and we were dressing like men."[33]

But the only "identity crisis" that women faced when they looked inside their closets was the one the '80s fashion industry had fabricated. The apparel makers had good reason to try to induce this anxiety: personal insecurity is the great motivator to shop. Wells Rich Greene, which conducted one of the largest studies of women's fashion-shopping habits in the early '80s, found that the more confident and independent women became, the less they liked to shop;[34] and the more they enjoyed their work, the less they cared about their clothes. The agency could find only three groups of women who were loyal followers of fashion: the very young, the very social, and the very anxious.

While the fashion industry's publicists helped provoke and aggravate anxiety in aging baby-boomer women by their relentless promotion of "youthful" fashions, they certainly weren't going to claim credit for it. Instead, they blamed the usual culprit—feminism. The women's movement, they told fashion writers over and over, had generated women's sartorial "identity crisis"—by inventing a "dress-for-success" ideology and foisting it on women. This was an accusation that meshed well with the decade's conventional wisdom on women and the fashion press gladly bought it. But it was just another backlash myth. The leaders of the women's movement had about as much to do with pushing pinstripes as they did with burning bras.

FROM HOUSEHOLD RAGS TO GRAY-FLANNEL STITCHES

"You must look as if you're working, not playing," Henri Bendel's president instructed women readers in a 1978 *Harper's Bazaar* article titled "Self-Confident Dressing,"[35] one of many features at the time advising women to wear suits that projected "confidence" and "authority." "Dress for the job you want to have,"

Mademoiselle told readers in its September 1977 issue. "There's a clothing hierarchy paralleling the job hierarchy."[36] Its September 1979 cover story offered a "Dress for Success Guide," promoting gray flannel suits and fitted tweed jackets for "the woman who is doing something with her life."[37] The well-tailored suit, the late-'70s fashion press had uniformly decreed, was the ideal expression of women's rising economic and political aspirations.

The fashion press inherited these ideas not from the women's movement but from the writings of a male fashion consultant. John T. Molloy's *The Woman's Dress for Success Book* became an instant hit in 1977, remaining on the *New York Times* best-seller list for more than five months. The book offered simple tips on professional dressing for aspiring businesswomen, just as his first work, *Dress for Success*, dispensed clothing advice to men. That earlier book, published in 1975, was hugely popular, too.[38] But when the fashion media turned against "dress for success" a decade later, they directed their verbal assault solely on the women's edition.

A former prep school English teacher, Molloy turned to the study of women's business dressing in the mid-'70s for the money.[39] Corporations like AT&T and U.S. Steel, under federal pressure to hire women, were funding research and seminars that made them look like good equal opportunity employers. Unlike the High Femininity merchants, who determined fashion trends based on "feelings," Molloy actually surveyed hundreds of people in the work force. He even dispatched research assistants to spy on the dressing habits of corporate men and women and, in a four-year study, enlisted several hundred businesswomen to track changes in their dress and their career.[40]

Based on his survey results, Molloy calculated that women who wore business suits were one and a half times more likely to feel they were being treated as executives—and a third less likely to have their authority challenged by men. Clothing that called attention to sexuality, on the other hand—women's or men's—lowered one's status at the office. "Dressing to succeed in business and dressing to be sexually attractive are almost mutually exclusive."[41]

Molloy's motives were primarily commercial, but his book had a political subtext, as a primer for people disadvantaged by class and sex. A child of the lower middle class himself, Molloy addressed similarly situated readers, the "American bootstrap types," as he called them, "whose parents never went to college" and who were struggling to "overcome socioeconomic barriers when they choose their clothes."[42] The author was also an advocate for women's rising expectations—and urged them to rely on their brains rather than their bodies to improve their station. "Many women," he wrote, "still cling to the conscious or unconscious belief that the only feminine way of competing is to compete as a sex object and that following fashion trends is one of the best ways to win. It's not."[43]

When Molloy's book for women became a bestseller in the '70s, publishers immediately rushed three knockoffs into print.[44] Retailers began invoking Molloy's name and even claiming, most times falsely, that the clothing guru had personally selected their line of women's business wear.[45] *Newsweek* declared dress-for-success a trend.[46] And for the next three years, women's magazines recycled scores of fashion stories that endorsed not only the suits but the ambitions they represented—with headlines like YOUR GET-AHEAD WARDROBE, POWER! and WHAT TO WEAR WHEN YOU'RE DOING THE TALKING.[47] At first fashion makers welcomed dress-for-success, too. They issued new ads offering paeans to working women's aspirations—with, of course, the caveat that women could realize these objectives only in a suit. Apparel manufacturers had visions of exploiting a new and untapped market. "The success of suits has made the fashion industry ecstatic,"[48] *Newsweek* observed in 1979. They had good reason to feel that way: women's suit sales had more than doubled that year.[49]

But in their enthusiasm, fashion merchants overlooked the bottom line of Molloy's book: dress-for-success could save women money and liberate them from fashion-victim status. Business suits weren't subject to wild swings in fashion and women could get away (as men always have) with wearing the same suit for several days and just varying the blouse and accessories—more economical than buying a dress for every day of the week. Once women made the initial investment in a set of suits, they could even take a breather from shopping.

Between 1980 and 1987, annual sales of suits rose by almost 6 million units, while dresses declined by 29 million units.[50] The $600 million gain in suit sales in these years was nice—but it couldn't make up for the *billions* of dollars the fashion industry could have been getting in dress sales.[51] Matters worsened when manufacturers raised their suit prices to make up for the shortfall—and women just started buying cheaper suits from foreign manufacturers. Between 1981 and 1986, imports of women's suits nearly tripled.[52]

"When this uniform is accepted by large numbers of businesswomen," Molloy's book predicted, ". . . it will be attacked ferociously." The fashion industry, the clothing consultant warned, may even yank the suits off the racks: "They will see it as a threat to their domination over women. And they will be right."[53]

REQUIEM FOR THE LITTLE BOW TIE

In 1986, U.S. apparel manufacturers cut their annual production of women's suits by 40 percent; the following year, production dropped by another 40 percent.[54] Several large suit manufacturers shut down their women's lines altogether. The sudden cutback wasn't inspired by a lack of demand: in 1986, women's purchases of suits and blazers jumped 5.3 percent.[55] And this reduction wasn't gender-blind.[56] In the same two years, output of men's suits stayed the same.

Soon, department stores phased out the executive-dressing wings that they had opened for professional women in the late 1970s.[57] Marshall's shut down its Careers department; Carson Pirie Scott closed its Corporate Level division for women; Neiman Marcus removed all coordinated women's business suits from many of its stores. Paul Harris Stores switched from women's career clothes to miniskirts (and promptly lost $5.6 million). And Alcott & Andrews, the store that billed itself as a female Brooks Brothers when it opened in 1984, began stocking ruffled dresses. When Molloy toured its New York store in 1987, he couldn't find a single suit.[58] (Two years later, Alcott & Andrews went bankrupt.)

Fashion writers buried the dress-for-success concept as eagerly as they had once praised it. "Bye-bye to the Little Bow Tie," *Mademoiselle* eulogized in a 1987 article entitled "The Death of Dress for Success."[59] It was one of many such media obituaries, among them "The Death of the Dumb Blue Suit" and "A Uniform for Submission Is Finally Put to Rest."[60] As the latter headline (from the *Chicago Tribune*) suggests, these articles were now proposing that business suits, not unequal business status, posed the greatest

threat to women's opportunities. As a fashion consultant explained it in a *Los Angeles Times* feature on the same subject, "[The suit] shows you aren't successful because you have no freedom of dress, and that means you don't have power."[61] According to '80s fashion theory, bondage lurked in the little bow tie—though not in the corset ties that were soon to follow.

All the anti–dress-for-success crusade needed to be complete was a villain. John Molloy was the obvious choice. The fashion press soon served him with a three-count indictment; he was charged with promoting "that dreadful little bow tie," pushing "the boring navy blue suit," and making women look like "imitation men."[62] When his book first came out, Molloy was so popular that newspapers fought to bid on his syndicated column, "Making It." But with Molloy's name on the fashion blacklist, newspapers canceled their orders. A major daily paper, which had initially approached Molloy about publishing the column, pulled out with this explanation: "The fashion people won't allow it."[63]

The charges against Molloy were largely trumped up. In fact, Molloy's book never mentioned the bow tie; it wasn't even on the market when the book was published. His book did not champion navy suits; it recommended gray, which he believed conveyed more authority.[64] And a whole section of the book was specifically devoted to advising women how *not* to dress like an "imitation man."[65] *Dress for Success* didn't even endorse suits exclusively, as many magazine stories maintained; it suggested women diversify their professional wardrobe with blazers, tailored skirts, and dresses. The fashion press was attacking its own rigid version of dress-for-success, not Molloy's. As Molloy himself points out, a shrewder garment industry might have capitalized on his formula. "My book recommended a wide variety of styles," he says. "My prescription was not that narrow. It was the fashion industry that narrowed women's choices. They became their own worst enemy."[66]

LACROIX: THE CLOWN WHO WOULD BE KING

With the suits cleared from the racks and Molloy deposed, the fashion industry moved to install Lacroix as "The King of Couture,"[67] an exalted title in keeping with '80s fashion obsessions about class. While Molloy spoke to the "American bootstrap types," Lacroix addressed only the elite. He concerned himself with a class of people who didn't have to dress for success. His female clientele, the ornamental ladies of American high society, had already acquired their upper-class status—through marriage or inheritance, not a weekly paycheck.

Lacroix's preoccupation with the top rungs of the income ladder fit perfectly the upscaling sales policies of the decade's retailers. In the fashion equivalent of television's "quality demographics," scores of retailers turned their backs on middle-class women and courted only the "better-business" customers, as they euphemistically labeled the rich. Instead of offering a range of clothing choices and competitive pricing, they began to serve only the tastes and incomes of the most affluent. Instead of serving the needs of the many working women, they sponsored black-tie balls and provided afternoon tea service and high-priced facials to the idle few.[68] "We made a conscious decision as a store a few years back to deal primarily with better-quality, wealthy fashions," explains Harold Nelson, general manager of Neiman Marcus's Washington, D.C.,[69] store, where 90 percent of the fashions were in couture or high-priced designer categories by 1988. "Gradually, we've been removing the moderately priced merchandise."

Lacroix's fashion gaze was ideally suited to the era in an even more fundamental way. For inspiration, he looked only backward—"I love the past much more than the future"—and primarily to the wardrobes of the late Victorian and postwar eras.[70] In 1982, while chief designer at the House of Patou, he had even tried, unsuccessfully, to reintroduce the bustle.[71] (As Lacroix explains this effort later, "I must say, [the] bustle emphasizes the silhouette a way I like very much.")[72] For the next three years, his five subsequent retro-tinged fashion shows fell flat, too; as he would say later of this period, he "suffered from being considered the clown of couture." Nonetheless, he clung to these more "feminine" styles that had preoccupied him since childhood when, he recalled later, he had pored admiringly over late Victorian fashion magazines of corseted women and dreamed of being the world's next Dior, an aspiration he had announced at the family dinner table one day.[73] When he finally made it as an adult, he would dramatize this fantasy. He timed the grand opening of the House of Lacroix to coincide with the House of Dior's fortieth anniversary.[74]

While the fashion press, of course, declares its "trends" long before they reach the consumer, in Lacroix's case, the leading industry trade paper, *Women's Wear Daily*, would take fashion forecasting to a new extreme.[75] It declared Lacroix's first "baby doll" line a hit two days *before* the designer even displayed them at the Paris show in July 1986. As it turned out, the female audience that day was less than impressed by the onslaught of "fantasy fashion" on the runway by Lacroix and fellow designers. As *Women's Wear Daily* remarked, with more irritation than insight, reaction from the society women in attendance "seemed cool"; and even when one of the couturiers issued a "call to a less self-important way of dressing," the front-row ladies "failed to heed" him.[76] But the lackluster reception from the ladies didn't discourage the magazine, which hailed Lacroix and High Femininity in another front-page rave the next day. FASHION GOES MAD, the magazine's banner headline announced with self-induced brain fever.[77] Lacroix has "restored woman's right to outrageousness, fun and high spirits."[78]

But was Lacroix offering women "fun"—or just making fun of them? He dressed his runway models in dunce caps, clamped dog-collarlike disks around their necks, stuck cardboard cones on their breasts, positioned cabbage roses so they sprouted from their rear ends, and attached serving trays to their heads—the last touch suggesting its reverse, female heads on serving trays.[79] Then he sent them down the runway to tunes with lyrics such as these: "Down by the station, Early in the morning, See the little pufferbellies, All in a row."[80] *Women's Wear Daily* didn't celebrate Lacroix's High Femininity because it gave women the right to have "fun" but because it presented them as unspoiled young maidens, ready and willing to be ravished. John Fairchild, the magazine's publisher and the industry's legendary "Emperor of Fashion," said what he really loved about the Lacroix gown was "how you can see it in the middle of lavender fields worn by happy little virgins who don't want to be virgins."[81]

With Fairchild's backing, Lacroix was assured total adulation from the rest of the fashion world. The following July, three months before the stock crash, he unveiled his first signature collection at a Paris show, to "rhythmic applause" from fashion writers and merchants.[82] Afterward, retail executives stood in the aisles and worked the press into a lather with overwrought tributes. The president of Martha's predicted, "It will change every woman's wardrobe."[83] The senior vice president of Bloomingdale's pronounced it "one of the most brilliant personal statements I've ever seen on the runway." And Bergdorf Goodman's president offered the most candid assessment to reporters: "He gave us what we were looking for." Thus primed, the most influential fashion writers raced to spread the "news." Hebe Dorsey of the *International Herald Tribune* charged to the nearest phone bank to advise her editors that this was a development warranting front-page coverage.[84] The next day, the *New York Times* fashion writer Bernadine Morris nominated Lacroix to "fashion's hall of fame," declaring, "Like Christian Dior exactly forty years ago, he has revived a failing institution."[85]

The rest of the press quickly fell into line. *Time* and *Newsweek* produced enthusiastic trend stories.[86] *People* celebrated Lacroix's "high jinks" and the way he "jammed bustles up the backside."[87] And the mass media's infatuation with Lacroix involved not only his hyperfeminine clothes but the cult of his masculine personality. Lacroix, who stocked his own wardrobe with Ralph Lauren lord-of-the-manor wear,[88] was eager to market an all-brawn self-image: "Primitive people, sun and rough times," he informed the press, "this is my real side."[89] Stories on Lacroix were packed with approving allusions to his manly penchant for cowboys and matadors. *Time* offered this tribute from a fashion commentator: "He looks like Brando; he is pantheroid, catlike. He is sexy in a way that is absolutely not effete."[90] His swagger, and the press's enthusiasm for it, spoke to the real "crisis" fueling the backlash—not the concern that female professionalism and independence were defeminizing women but the fear that they were emasculating men. Worries about eclipsed manhood were particularly acute in the fashion world, where the perception of a widespread gay culture in the industry had collided in the '80s with homophobia and rising anxieties about AIDS.

With Lacroix coronated couture's king, rival designers competed fiercely to ascend the throne. From Emanuel Ungaro to Karl Lagerfeld, they caked on even more layers of frills and pumped up skirts with still bigger bustles. If High Femininity was supposed to accent womanly curves, its frenetic baroque excrescences succeeded only in obscuring the female figure. It was hard to see body shape at all through the thicket of flounces and floral sprays. Dress-for-success's shoulder pads were insignificant appendages compared with the foot-high satin roses Ungaro tacked to evening-gown shoulders.

While a few dozen rich American women had bought Lacroix's gowns from his 1987 Luxe collection, the designer was anxious to make his mark in the broader, real-world market of ready-to-wear clothes. His last effort while still at Patou in 1984 had failed miserably, after his designs proved to be too expensive for sale.[91] This time, he approached the market strategically. First, in the spring of 1988, he put the clothes "on tour" at a select three stores, Martha's, Bergdorf Goodman, and Saks Fifth Avenue. Then, that fall, having tantalized women with this fashion tease, he would ship ready-to-wear clothes across the country.

In May 1988, big ads appeared in the *Washington Post*, courtesy of Saks Fifth Avenue, welcoming the Lacroix traveling show to town—and advising women to hurry down and place their special orders before the rush.[92]

"I GUESS THEY DON'T LIKE LOOKING SUPERFLUOUS"

The day the Lacroix dresses arrive at Saks, five men in dark suits hover around the designer salon, supervising four elderly saleswomen who are easing the gowns from their garment bags, blue-veined hands trembling slightly as they lift the heavy crinoline-encrusted costumes to the racks. "Careful now, careful!" one of the suited men coaches whenever a hem threatens to touch the floor. A bell-shaped purple skirt is slipped out of its wrapper—$630. It comes with a top, $755.

About noon, a delivery man drops off a video of a Lacroix fashion show, to be installed for shoppers' viewing pleasure. The saleswomen gather around the TV set to watch the models teeter down the runway to the song the designer has selected for the occasion— "My Way." One of the models is covered, head to toe, in giant roses and bows. "It's ridiculous," mutters salesclerk Mimi Gott, who is wearing a gray tweed suit. "Our customers are older people. They aren't going to buy this stuff."[93]

About one P.M., Pandora Gogos arrives at the salon, on the arm of her daughter Georgia. They are going to "a black-tie dinner," and Gogos, who is "around seventy," can find nothing in the stores to wear. "I've been shopping here since they opened up in the 1950s," she complains, lowering her aching back into a chair. "Even in the fifties, I don't think they were crazy like this. I've gone all over town—Saks, Garfinckel's—and I can't find a dinner dress. There was one at Garfinckel's, a four-thousand-dollar jacket with a skirt up to here"—she reaches her hands to her throat—"nine thousand dollars!"

Soon after, a Mrs. Barkin, a middle-aged woman, arrives at the designer salon to return a frilly dress concocted by one of Lacroix's imitators. It is studded with huge flowers and a back bustle. "I just couldn't wear it," she says apologetically. Salesclerk Venke Loehe, who is wearing a simple Diane Von Furstenberg wraparound, gives her a sympathetic nod. "It's the return to the fifties," Loehe says. "A lot of our clothes now are like that. . . . But the classic look is still what's selling best." Mrs. Barkin decides on an exchange—she has a cocktail party to attend—and starts rummaging through the racks. She settles reluctantly on a dress with a pouf skirt; it's the only evening outfit she can find with a lower hem. "I don't know how I'll ever sit down in this," she worries.

Back by the Lacroix racks, the only items that seem to be drawing interest are a plain overcoat and a tailored jacket. Mostly, women don't even stop to look; by midafternoon, the salon has had fewer than a dozen visitors. The men in suits are wondering what happened to all the customers. "All that embellishment, the ruffles, lace and frills," says a frustrated Lawrence Wilsman, Saks's buyer of European designer imports, "women don't seem to want that much. They seem to want quieter, more realistic things. They want clothes to be taken seriously in. I guess they don't like looking superfluous."

* * *

That fall, Lacroix's full ready-to-wear collection arrived at Saks. A month later, markdown tags dangled from the sleeves.[94] Department stores from Nordstrom to Dayton Hudson dropped Lacroix's clothes after one season. "We needed to see a bit more that American women could relate to," explained a Nordstrom spokesperson. And when *Women's Wear Daily* surveyed department stores, the Lacroix label ranked as one of the worst sellers. By 1989, Lacroix's design house was reporting a $9.3 million loss.

FLOUNCING INTO WORK

Maybe Lacroix's poufs hadn't won over the high-end shoppers who frequent designer salons, but apparel makers and retailers were still hoping to woo the average female shopper with the habiliments of High Femininity. To this end, Bullock's converted 60 percent of its women's apparel to a "1950s look" by spring 1987.[95] And even more progressive designers like Donna Karan began parroting the couturier's retro edicts. "There has been a shift in saying to a woman, 'It's okay to show your derriere,' " she told the *New York Times*. "I questioned it at first. But women's bodies are in better shape."[96]

For High Femininity to succeed in the ready-to-wear market, working women had to accept the look—and wear it to the office. The apparel makers could design all the evening gowns they pleased; it wouldn't change the fact that the vast majority of women's clothing purchases were for work wear. In 1987, for example, more than 70 percent of the skirts purchased were for professional wardrobes.[97] Pushing baby-doll fashions to working women was also going to be a trickier maneuver than marketing to socialites. Not only did the designers have to convince women that frills were appropriate on the job, the persuasion had to be subtler; high-handed commands wouldn't work on the less fashion-conscious working women. The designers and merchants had to present the new look as the career woman's "choice."

"This thing is not about designers dictating," Calvin Klein proclaimed as he issued another round of miniskirts. "We're taking our cues from what women want. They're ready."[98] "Older women want to look sexy now on the job," the head of Componix, a Los Angeles apparel maker, insisted. "They want men to look at them like they're women. Notice my legs first, not my appraisals."[99] One by one, the dressing authorities got behind this new fashion line. "Gals like to show their legs," designer Bill Blass asserted.[100] "Girls want to be girls again," designer Dik Brandsma intoned.[101] The lone dissenting voice came from veteran designer John Weitz, who said it was *Women's Wear Daily*, not women, clamoring for girlish frocks. "Women change not at all, just journalism," he said, dismissing High Femininity as "a temporary derailment, based on widespread insecurity.[102] Eventually it will go away and women will look like strong decisive human beings instead of Popsicles." But then, Weitz could afford to be honest; he made *his* money designing men's clothes.

Taking their cue from the designers, retailers unfurled the same "choice" sales pitch—and draped it in seemingly feminist arguments, phrases, and imagery. These constrictive and uncomfortable clothes were actually a sign of women's advancement. As a publicist for Alcott & Andrews explained it, "Our woman has evolved to the point where she can really wear anything to the office that proclaims her femininity."[103] Bloomingdale's, which dubbed its latest dress department for women "Bloomingdale's NOW," proposed that women try "advancing at work with new credentials"—by buying the department's skimpy chemises and wearing them to the office.[104] Like the designers, retailers claimed to speak for women, sometimes literally. "Saks understands," a mythical career woman murmured in the store's ad copy. "They give me the options. . . . Showing me that 'going soft' doesn't have to mean losing your edge."[105] What was she pictured wearing to work? Shorts.

The fashion press pitched in, too, as the same publications that had urged working women to wear suits if they wanted to be taken seriously now began running headlines like DRESSING CUTE EN ROUTE and THE NEW SUCCESS LOOKS: YOUNG AND EASY.[106] *Savvy* told working women that "power dressing" in the '80s meant only "flower power"—stud your waist with $150 faux camellias, the magazine advised readers, "if you're intent on making a CEO statement."[107] Women could actually get ahead *faster* if they showed up for work in crinoline petticoats; DRESSING DOWN FOR SUCCESS, the *Los Angeles Times'* fashion editors called it.[108] The fashion press also resorted to pseudofeminist arguments to push prepubescent dressing: women should don party-doll frills, they argued, as an emblem of grown-up liberation—as a sort of feminist victory sash. Grasping for any angle, the fashion writers even tried invoking the Harvard-Yale marriage study. "A man shortage? What man shortage?" *Mademoiselle* crowed in its editorial for poufs and minis. "You'll be dated up till next July if you turn up in any of these ultrahot numbers."[109]

But no matter what argument the fashion promoters tried, women weren't buying. A 1988 New York Times/CBS News poll found only a quarter of adult women said they had worn a skirt above the knee even once in the past year.[110] Some women were becoming

as vocal in their resistance as the anti-Dior protesters a generation earlier. "I will wear the new short skirts when men wear rompers to the office," declared columnist Kathleen Fury in *Working Woman*.[111] Nina Totenberg, legal affairs reporter for National Public Radio, exhorted female listeners from the airwaves, "Hold the line. Don't buy. And the mini will die."[112]

The retailers, saddled with millions of dollars of untouched miniskirts, were ready to surrender. The miniskirt has thrown the women's apparel market into "confusion," worried a spokesperson for Liz Claiborne Inc., "and we don't see any indication that it is going to pass soon."[113] But the high-fashion designers—who make their money more through licensing their names than through actual dress sales—could afford to continue the campaign. So when retail buyers flocked to market to inspect the designers' upcoming fall fashions for 1988, they found—much to their amazement—yet another round of ruffled and rib-crunching styles.

*   *   *

"I think it's really a trend," Yvette Crosby, fashion director of California Mart, is telling everyone at the 1988 Market Week in Los Angeles, as she hands out copies of this season's "Trend Report." "It's a more romantic and Victorian look, and I really believe it's right for this season,"[114] says Crosby. She wears a suit.

The writers and buyers are crowding into the mart's auditorium for the morning show, entitled "Thirty Something." The program notes advise that these clothes are designed "for contemporary working women"—a necessary reminder, it happens. As the models revolve in up to five tiers of frills, huge bows bursting from hips and shoulders, it's easy to forget that this is nine-to-five wear. To evoke a proper career mood, one designer has armed his models with briefcases. The gaunt young women trip down the runway in stiletto heels, hands snug in dainty white gloves. Their briefcases swing like Easter baskets, feather light; they are, after all, empty.

At last, the models retire backstage and the fashion buyers are herded to the buying services' suites upstairs. In the Bob Mallard showroom, the mart's largest buying service, manufacturing representatives scurry hopefully into place. Mallard, who joined the business in the 1950s as a garment manufacturer in the East Bronx, surveys the proceedings with grim resignation; he has the leathery, bruised face of a fighter who's been in the ring awhile.

"Last year, the miniskirt was a disaster," he says. "Froufrou was no big hit either. Women still want suits. That's still the biggest seller." But he knows his observations will fall on deaf ears back at the design houses. "The average designer goes to the library and looks at pictures in a picture book. Maybe he worries about whether the dress is going to look good on the mannequin in the store window. That's it. I don't think he ever bothers to talk to a woman about it. The woman, she's the last to know."[115]

In the glass booths on either side of the long showroom corridor, Mallard's manufacturing reps are doing their best to pitch the "new-romance" fashions to doubtful buyers. Teri Jon's rep, Ruth McLoughlin, pulls one dress after another off the racks and holds it up to buyers Jody Krogh and Carol Jameson of the Portland-based Jameson Ltd. "Short didn't sell last year," Krogh keeps saying. "No, no, don't judge by what's on the hanger," McLoughlin answers, a little peevishly. "We can ship it long. Now how about this?" She holds up a dress with a plunging front, cinched waist and crinolines. "I don't know," Jameson says. "Women will love it," says McLoughlin. She is wearing a suit.

"This is my best reorder," says Joe Castle, a fast-talking Cattiva salesman across the hall. He waggles a ruffle-decked gown before a buyer with a blank order form. "It makes a great M.O.B. [mother of the bride] gown," Castle wheedles. Sounding a bit like a *Newsweek* trend story, Castle tries this last argument: "Everyone's looking for M.O.B.'s. More and more people are getting married."

*   *   *

At the fashion shows held in summer 1988 for the coming fall season, designers made a few compromises—adding pantsuits and longer skirts to their collections—but these additions often featured a puerile or retaliatory underside. Jean-Paul Gaultier showed pants and blazers—but they were skin-tight Lycra leotards and schoolgirl uniforms.[116] Pierre Cardin produced capelike wraps that fit so tightly even the *New York Times* fashion page found it "fairly alarming because the models wearing them cannot move their arms."[117] Romeo Gigli dropped his hemlines but the skirts were so tight the models could only hobble down the runway.[118] One of his models was doubly encumbered; he had tied her up in velvet ropes, straitjacket-style.

A year later, even the compromises were gone—as designers dressed up their women again in even shorter miniskirts, bonecrushing corsets, push-up cleavage and billows of transparent chiffon. The Lacroix brand of "humor" returned to the runways: models wore costumes modeled after clown suits, "court jester" jackets, molded "breastplates," and pinstripe suits with one arm and shoulder ripped to shreds.[119] By 1990, Valentino was pushing "baby dolls," Gianni Versace was featuring "skirts that barely clear the buttocks," and the Lacroix collection was offering jumpsuits with "gold-encrusted" corsets.[120]

If the apparel makers could not get women to wear poufs, they would try dictating another humbling mode of fashion. The point was not so much the content of the style as its enforcement. There was a reason why their designs continued to regress into female infantilism, even in the face of a flood of market reports on aging female consumers: minimizing the female form might be one way for designers to maximize their own authority over it. The woman who walks in tiny steps clutching a teddy bear—as so many did on the late '80s runways—is a child who follows instructions. The woman who steps down the aisle to George Michael's "Father Figure"—the most popular runway song in 1988—is a daughter who minds her elders.[121] Modern American women "won't do as they are told anymore," the couturier had complained to Molloy. But just maybe they would—if only they could be persuaded to think of themselves as daddy's little girls.

NOTES

1. The pushed-up breasts of . . . : Julie Baumgold, "Dancing on the Lip of the Volcano," *New York*, Nov. 30, 1987, p. 36.

2. These were clothes . . . : Jennet Conant, "Oh La La, Lacroix," *Newsweek*, Nov. 9, 1987, p. 60.

3. The Lacroix price tags, however . . . : "Christian Lacroix," *Current Biography*, April 1988, p. 39.

4. Lacroix's bubble skirts . . . : Bernadine Morris, "Lacroix Fever Spreads to New York," *New York Times*, Oct. 30, 1987, p. A16.

5. The Luxe gowns . . . : Martha Duffy, "Fantasy Comes Alive," *Time*, Feb. 8, 1988. "High Femininity" was one name fashion trendsetters gave to the look, "Fantasy Fashion" another.

6. After Lacroix's July 1986 . . . : Kathleen Beckett, "The Frill of It All," *Vogue*, April 1987, p. 178; "La Gamine: Fun and Flirty," *Harper's Bazaar*, April 1987, p. 86.

7. Between 1980 and 1986 . . . : Data from Market Research Corporation of America, Information Services; Trish Hall, "Changing U.S. Values, Tinged with Caution, Show Up in Spending," *New York Times*, Oct. 26, 1988, p. B1.

8. In one poll . . . : Martha Thomases, "Why I Don't Shop," *The Village Voice*, Dec. 27, 1988, p. 37.

9. Then, in the High Femininity year . . . : Trish Donnally, "Gloomy Fashion Forecast," *San Francisco Chronicle*, March 23, 1988, p. B3.

10. That year, even with . . . . : Woody Hochswender, "Where Have All the Shoppers Gone?" *New York Times*, May 31, 1988. Statistic on 4 percent drop in dress sales comes from Soft Goods Information Service, Market Research Corp. of America. As MRCA notes, total dollar sales of women's apparel increased in the first seven years of the decade only because the cost of women's clothes was rising so fast; the unit sales of apparel items ranged from flat to slightly depressed.

11. Even during the height . . . : Aimee Stern, "Miniskirt Movement Comes Up Short," *Adweek's Marketing Week*, March 28, 1988, p. 2.

12. And this was a one-gender phenomenon . . . : *Ibid.*; Jennet Conant, "The High-Priced Call of the Wild," *Newsweek*, Feb. 1, 1988, p. 56. Mail-order men's clothing catalogs profited most, boosting revenues by as much as 25 percent in this period. At Ruff Hewn, a mail-order business hawking gentrified country wear, sales rose 275 percent a year, and by 1988, this small North Carolina company had expanded production into seventeen factories and was planning a nationwide retail chain. The cast of characters in Ruff Hewn's catalog were backlash archetypes: "Barclay Ruffin Hewn," the company catalog's fictional hero, was depicted as a late-19th-century gentleman and highly decorated war veteran who rode with Teddy Roosevelt's Rough Riders. His wife, "Elizabeth Farnsworth Hampton Hewn," as company president Jefferson Rives named her, was "a very traditional and feminine lady who stays home to take care of Ruff and the children." (Ruff Hewn catalogs and brochures; personal interview with Jefferson Rives, 1988.)

13. In the spring of 1988 . . . : Hochswender, "All the Shoppers"; Donnally, "Gloomy Fashion"; Barbara Deters, "Limited Fashioning a Turnaround," *USA Today*, May 20, 1988, p. B3; Stern, "Miniskirt Movement Comes Up Short," p. 2; Susan Caminiti, "What Ails Retailing: Merchants Have Lost Touch With Older Customers," *Fortune*, Jan. 30, 1989, p. 61.

14. By the second quarter . . . : By contrast, sales of men's clothing in the same period rose by nearly $1 billion. Data from Department of Commerce, Bureau of Economic Analysis, Personal Consumption Expenditures.

15. They were pushing . . . : Blayne Cutler, "Meet Jane Doe," *American Demographics*, June 1989, p. 24; Thomases, "I Don't Shop," p. 37. By ignoring the 30 to 40 million women wearing size 16 and over, the fashion industry was passing up a $6 billion industry. See Jolie Solomon, "Fashion Industry Courting Large Women," *The Wall Street Journal*, Sept. 27, 1985.

16. As Goldman Sachs's . . . : Joseph H. Ellis, "The Women's Apparel Retailing Debacle: Why?" Goldman Sachs Investment Research, June 8, 1988.

17. "What's the matter with . . ." : Personal interview with John Molloy, 1988.

18. Or, as Lacroix . . . : Personal interview with Christian Lacroix, May 1991.

19. As fashion designer Arnold . . . : Personal interview with Arnold Scaasi, Feb. 1988.

20. At a Lacroix fashion . . . : "Lacroix Triumphant," *Women's Wear Daily*, July 27, 1987, p. 1.

21. Designers wanted to be in . . . : "Christian Lacroix," p. 38.

22. Women who had discovered . . . : Weibel, *Mirror Mirror*, p. 209.

23. The fashion industry fell into . . . : "Counter-Revolution," *Time*, Sept. 15, 1947, p. 87.

24. More than three hundred thousand women . . . : Jeanne Perkins, "Dior," *Life*, March 1, 1948, p. 84.

25. In a poll that summer . . . : Hartmann, *Home Front*, p. 203.

26. "The women who are loudest . . ." : "Counter-Revolution," p. 92.

27. And they were obeying . . . : Weibel, *Mirror Mirror*, p. xvi.

28. "If you want a girl . . ." : Valerie Steele, *Fashion and Eroticism: Ideals of Feminine Beauty from the Victorian Era to the Jazz Age* (New York: Oxford University Press, 1985) p. 182.

29. In the last half . . . : Robert E. Riegel, "Women's Clothes and Women's Rights," *American Quarterly*, XV, no. 3 (Fall 1963): 390–401; Elizabeth Ewins, *Dress and Undress* (New York: Drama Books Specialists, 1978) p. 89.

30. The influential *Godey's* . . . : Kinnard, *Antifeminism*, pp. 289, 304.

31. "A lot of women . . ." : Personal interview with Bob Mackie, 1988.

32. Women have realized . . . : Personal interview with Arnold Scaasi, Feb. 1988; Bernardine Morris, "The Sexy Look: Why Now?" *New York Times*, Nov. 17, 1987, p. 20.

33. "We were wearing pinstripes . . ." : Personal interview with Karen Bromley, July 1989.

34. Wells Rich Greene . . . : Personal interview with Jane Eastman, executive vice president of strategic planning at Wells Rich Greene, Feb. 1988.

35. "You must look as if . . ." : Bernadine Morris, "Self-Confident Dressing," *Harper's Bazaar*, November 1978, p. 151.

36. "Dress for the job you want . . ." : Amy Gross and Nancy Axelrad Comer, "Power Dressing," *Mademoiselle*, Sept. 1977, p. 188.

37. Its September 1979 . . . : "Your Dress-for-Success Guide," *Mademoiselle*, Sept. 1979, p. 182.

38. That earlier book . . . : John T. Molloy, *Dress for Success* (New York: Warner Books, 1975).

39. A former prep school . . . : Personal interview with John T. Molloy, 1988; John T. Molloy, *The Woman's Dress for Success Book* (New York: Warner Books, 1977) pp. 23–26.

40. He even dispatched . . . : Molloy, *Woman's Dress for Success*, pp. 40–48.

41. "Dressing to succeed . . ." : *Ibid.*, p. 21.

42. A child of . . . : *Ibid.*, pp. 25, 20–23.

43. "Many women . . ." : *Ibid.*, p. 22.

44. When Molloy's book . . . : Susan Cheever Cowley, "Dress for the Trip to the Top," *Newsweek*, Sept. 26, 1977, p. 76.

45. Retailers began invoking . . . : Molloy, *Woman's Dress for Success*, p. 30.

46. *Newsweek* declared . . . : Cowley, "Trip to the Top," p. 76.

47. And for the next . . . : "Your Get Ahead Wardrobe," *Working Woman*, July 1979, p. 46; "Power!" *Essence*, March 1980, p. 68; "What to Wear When You're Doing the Talking," *Glamour*, Oct. 1978, p. 250.

48. "The success of suits . . ." : "A Well-Suited Season," *Newsweek*, Nov. 5, 1979, p. 111.

49. They had good reason . . . : *Ibid.*

50. Between 1980 and 1987 . . . : Statistics from Market Research Corporation of America; personal interview with John Tugman, vice president and general manager, MRCA, Soft Goods Information Services, 1988.

51. The $600 million gain . . . : Statistics from MRCA.

52. Between 1981 and 1986 . . . : "Women's Coats, Suits, Tailored Career Wear, Rainwear and Furs," report in *Fairchild Fact File* (New York: Fairchild Publications, 1987) p. 20.

53. "When this uniform . . ." : Molloy, *Woman's Dress for Success*, p. 36.

54. In 1986, U.S. apparel . . . : "Women's Coats," in *Fairchild Fact File*, p. 12; U.S. Bureau of the Census, Current Industrial Reports, 1987, "Quantity of Production and Value of Shipments of Women's, Misses', and Juniors' Dresses and Suits: 1987 and 1986," Table 8; personal interview with Judy Dodds, analyst with Current Industrial Reports, U.S. Bureau of the Census, Commerce Department, 1988.

55. The sudden cutback . . . : "Women's Coats," *Fairchild Fact File*, p. 30.

56. And this reduction . . . : U.S. Bureau of the Census, Current Industrial Reports, 1987, "Quantity of Production and Value of Shipments of Men's and Boys' Suits, Coats, Vests, and Sports Coats: 1987 and 1986," Table 2.

57. Soon, department stores . . . : Mark Potts, "Thirteen Britches for Women Stores to Close," *Washington Post*, Dec. 9, 1989, p. 10; personal interview with Harold Nelson, vice president and general manager of Neiman Marcus's Washington, D.C., store, 1988; Cara Mason, "Paul Harris Stores Rebounds from 1988 Losses," *Indianapolis Business Journal*, March 12, 1990, p. A13.

58. When Molloy . . . : Personal interview with John T. Molloy, 1988.

59. "Bye-bye to the . . ." : Terri Minsky, "The Death of Dress for Success," *Mademoiselle*, Sept. 1987, p. 308.

60. It was one of many . . . : Patricia McLaughlin, "The Death of the Dumb Blue Suit," *Philadelphia Inquirer*, Feb. 7, 1988, p. 35; "Dumb Blue Suit: A Uniform for Submission Is Finally Put To Rest," *Chicago Tribune*, May 8, 1988, p. C5.

61. As a fashion consultant . . . : Betty Goodwin, "Fashion 88: Dressing Down for Success," *Los Angeles Times*, April 15, 1988, V, p. 1.

62. John Molloy was the obvious . . . : The defrocking of John Molloy recapitulates in many respects the attack on Gabrielle "Coco" Chanel, the original designer of the power suit in 1920. Chanel fashioned her classic boxy jacket and comfortably low-waisted skirt after the male business suit, and, like Molloy, she spoke to the aspiring New Woman on the lower rungs of the class ladder. (She was one of these struggling women herself, having been consigned to an orphanage as a teenager after her father deserted her.) Her era's backlash put her out of business, and when she tried for a comeback in the early '50s her fellow designers unleashed unmitigated scorn—most especially Christian Dior, who reportedly told her that a woman "could never be a great couturier." See Weibel, *Mirror Mirror*, pp. 201, 213–14; Lois W. Banner, *American Beauty* (New York: Alfred A. Knopf, 1983) pp. 275–76.

63. A major daily . . . : Personal interview with John T. Molloy, 1988.

64. His book did not champion . . . : Molloy, *Woman's Dress for Success*, pp. 43, 52.

65. And a whole section . . . : *Ibid.*, pp. 27–29.

66. "My book recommended . . ." : Personal interview with John T. Molloy, 1988.

67. With the suits . . . : Martha Duffy, "Fantasy Comes Alive," *Time* (International Edition), Feb. 8, 1988, p. 44.

68. Instead of serving . . . : Louis Trager, "Nordstrom Abuzz," *San Francisco Examiner*, Oct. 6, 1988, p. C1.

69. "We made a conscious decision . . ." : Personal interview with Harold Nelson, May 1988.

70. For inspiration . . . : Duffy, "Fantasy," pp. 46–47.

71. In 1982, while chief . . . : "Christian Lacroix," p. 37.

72. (As Lacroix explains . . .) : Personal interview with Christian Lacroix, May 1991.

73. Nonetheless, he clung . . . : Duffy, "Fantasy," p. 47.

74. He timed the grand opening . . . : "Christian Lacroix," p. 38.

75. While the fashion press . . . : "Patou's Baby Dolls," *Women's Wear Daily*, July 25, 1986, p. 1.

76. As *Women's Wear Daily* remarked . . . : Christa Worthington, "Fantasy Fashion Rebounds in Paris," *Women's Wear Daily*, July 29, 1986, p. 1.

77. FASHION GOES MAD . . . : "Fashion Goes Mad," *Women's Wear Daily*, July 29, 1986, p. 1.

78. Lacroix has "restored . . ." : Worthington, "Fantasy Fashion," p. 1.

79. He dressed his . . . : Videos of Lacroix's Paris and New York shows; Bernadine Morris, "For Lacroix, a Triumph; For Couture, a Future," *New York Times*, July 27, 1987, p. C14.

80. Then he sent them down . . . : Martha Duffy, "Welcome to the Fresh Follies," *Time*, Feb. 9, 1987, p. 76.

81. John Fairchild, the magazine's . . . : Baumgold, "Dancing on the Lip," p. 49.

82. The following July . . . : Morris, "For Lacroix a Triumph," p. C14.

83. The president of Martha's . . . : *Ibid.*; "Lacroix Triumphant," *Women's Wear Daily*, July 27, 1987, p. 1.

84. Hebe Dorsey of . . . : "Lacroix Triumphant," p. 3.

85. The next day, the *New York Times* . . . : Morris, "For Lacroix, a Triumph," p. C14.

86. *Time* and *Newsweek* . . . : Duffy, "Fantasy"; Conant, "Oh La La, Lacroix."

87. *People* celebrated . . . : "Paris' Daring Darling Shakes Up High Fashion with High Jinks," *People*, May 19, 1986, p. 138.

88. Lacroix, who stocked . . . : Baumgold, "Dancing on the Lip," p. 38.

89. "Primitive people . . ." : Duffy, "Fantasy," p. 46.

90. "He looks like Brando . . .": *Ibid.*, p. 46.

91. His last effort . . . : Nina Hyde, "The Real Lacroix," *Washington Post*, March 17, 1988, p. 1.

92. In May 1988, big ads . . . : "Introducing Christian Lacroix's Pret-a-porter first at Saks Fifth Avenue," *Washington Post*, May 19, 1988, p. A4.

93. "It's ridiculous . . ." : Personal interview with Mimi Gott, May 24, 1988. (The comments from Saks employees and shoppers are also from personal interviews the same day.)

94. A month later . . . : "Lacroix Avoids Markdown Blues," *Houston Chronicle*, Jan. 4, 1990, p. 5; Pete Born, "How the French Do in U.S. Stores," *Women's Wear Daily*, March 17, 1989, p. 1; "Stores Lament Designer Sales," *Women's Wear Daily*, June 12, 1990, p. 1; Bernadette Morra, "Mix Master Lacroix Designs with Gusto," *Toronto Star*, Oct. 25, 1990, p. D2.

95. To this end, Bullock's . . . : Lisa Lapin, "Jeepers! Cool Is Hot, Ralph Kramden Is a Folk Hero and Business Discovers There's Money To Be Made From Reviving the '50s," *Los Angeles Times*, Jan. 4, 1987, IV, p. 1.

96. "There has been a shift . . ." : Maureen Dowd, "The New Exec," *The New York Times Magazine*, Aug. 24, 1986, p. 145.

97. In 1987, for example, . . . : Statistics from Market Research Corp. of America.

98. "This thing is not about designers . . ." : Genevieve Buck, "Hemline Lib," *Chicago Tribune*, June 3, 1987, p. 7.

99. "Older women want . . ." : Goodwin, "Fashion 88," p. 1.

100. "Gals like to show . . ." : Buck, "Hemline Lib," p. 7.

101. "Girls want to be girls . . ." : "La Gamine," p. 86.

102. "Women change not at all . . ." : Personal interview with John Weitz, Feb. 1988; Morris, "The Sexy Look."

103. As a publicist . . . : Personal interview with Sarah O'Donnell, Alcott & Andrews publicist, 1988.

104. Bloomingdale's, which dubbed . . . : Bloomingdale's advertisement, *New York Times*, Aug. 24, 1988, p. A5.

105. "Saks understands . . ." : Saks Fifth Avenue two-page ad, *Vanity Fair*, March 1988.

106. The fashion press pitched in . . . : "Dressing Cute Enroute," *Mademoiselle*, August 1985, p. 56; "The New Success Looks: Young and Easy," *Harper's Bazaar*, Oct. 1987, p. 76.

107. *Savvy* told working women . . . : "Power Flower," *Savvy*, March 1988, p. 78.

108. Women could actually . . . : Goodwin, "Fashion 88," p. 1.

109. "A man shortage? . . ." : "Little Dating Looks," *Mademoiselle*, Nov. 1987, p. 226.

110. A 1988 New York Times . . . : Men, however, were far more enthusiastic; 71 percent said they preferred skirts that didn't drop below the knee. Trish Hall, "No Surprise Here: Men Prefer the Mini," *New York Times*, March 31, 1988, p. C1. An earlier 1982 survey by Audits and Surveys for the Merit Report found 81 percent of women and men either didn't want miniskirts to come back into style or just didn't care. See "Opinion Roundup—Light Fare: Of Legs, Locks, Love and Lancelots," *Public Opinion*, April–May 1982, p. 37.

111. "I will wear . . ." : Kathleen Fury, "Why I'm Not Wearing Miniskirts, I Think," *Working Woman*, Nov. 1987, p. 184.

112. Nina Totenberg, legal affairs . . . : For printed version, see Nina Totenberg, "Miniskirt, Maxi Blunder," *New York Times*, March 21, 1988, p. A19.

113. The miniskirt has thrown . . . : Sanford L. Jacobs, "Claiborne Says Miniskirts May Mean Mini-Increase in Earnings for 1988," *The Wall Street Journal*, Feb. 26, 1988.

114. "I think it's really a trend . . ." : Personal interview with Yvette Crosby and observations at California Mart's Market Week, April 9, 1988, p. 20.

115. "Last year, the miniskirt was . . ." : Personal interview with Bob Mallard. (Following scenes from personal interviews and observations at Mallard's showroom, April 9, 1988.)

116. Jean-Paul Gaultier . . . : Holly Brubach, "The Rites of Spring," *New Yorker*, June 6, 1988, p. 80.

117. Pierre Cardin produced . . . : Bernadine Morris, "In Paris Couture, Opulence Lights A Serious Mood," *New York Times*, July 26, 1988.

118. Romeo Gigli . . . : Brubach, "Rites of Spring," p. 81.

119. The Lacroix brand . . . : Gladys Perint Palmer, "Top to Toe at Paris Show," *San Francisco Examiner*, Oct. 29, 1989, p. E3.

120. By 1990, Valentino . . . : Marylou Luther, "Young and Restless: Haute Couture Sports a New Attitude for the '90s," *Chicago Sun-Times*, Aug. 1, 1990, II, p. 25.

121. The woman who steps down . . . : Brubach, "Rites of Spring."

Feminists Fatale: BUST-ing the Beauty Myth

1999

Debbie Stoller

It's Saturday night at my house, and all the girls are here. We're all feminists, of course, but we don't all look the part. Some of us shave our legs, some of us shave our heads; some of us wear miniskirts, some of us wear pants; some of us keep up with the latest trends, some of us wouldn't know the latest trend if it hit them upside the head. Still, when I bring out my beauty bucket, which contains about fifty colors of nail polish, in every shade imaginable from blue to bronze, all of us get to work. Passing around the little bottles from hand to hand, we make our choices and revel in these moments of total girlified glamour. It's almost a guilty pleasure. After all, we are the women who grew up during feminism's bra-burning heyday, who learned about *Roe v. Wade* while we were still reading Dick and Jane.

We've come a long way, baby. It was in 1968 that Robin Morgan and her group, New York Radical Women, handed out leaflets inviting women to attend a protest of the Miss America Pageant in Atlantic City, New Jersey. Taking aim at "the degrading mindless-boob-girlie symbol" that they felt the pageant promoted, the organizers complained that "women in our society are forced daily to compete for male approval, enslaved by ludicrous 'beauty' standards we ourselves are conditioned to take seriously." Among the many events that the pamphlet promised would take place at the rally, one stands out: "There will be . . . a huge Freedom Trash Can, into which we will throw bras, girdles, curlers, false eyelashes, wigs, and representative issues of *Cosmopolitan, Ladies Home Journal, Family Circle,* etc.—bring any such woman-garbage you have around the house." (Contrary to popular myth, no bra burning actually took place at this event; in fact, not a single item of lingerie was harmed.)

Thirty years later, it seems that we gals have rummaged through that trash can and recycled just about everything in it. Only now we call it "reclaiming." From lipstick lesbians to rouge-wearing riot girls, today's vampy visionaries believe that it *is* possible to make a feminist fashion statement without resorting to wearing Birkenstocks 24-7, or hiding our figures in power suits. We've taken out our shoulder pads and stuffed them into our bras, no longer disguising ourselves as men, but as women. Because it's as clear to us as it is to RuPaul that fashion is a costume, that femininity is a masquerade, and that sometimes we *like* to play dress-up. We want to shout out to all the nonbelievers who still think that the only true feminist is a hairy, scary feminist: "We're here, we use Nair, get used to it." Can I get a witness?

In the past few centuries, feminists have had plenty to say on the subject of fashion, most of which can be summed up by a single statement: They're against it. In 1790, women's rights vindicator Mary Wollstonecraft argued that it was women's addiction to adornment that was keeping them down. "[Women's] minds are not in a healthy state," she wrote, explaining that "[their] strength and usefulness are sacrificed to beauty." By the mid-1800s women's bodies were not in a healthy state either. To achieve the newly stylish "S-curve" silhouette, women had taken to squeezing themselves into tight-laced corsets, with little or no consideration for their internal organs. It was at this time that Elizabeth Cady Stanton began to advocate an outfit that was most likely the nineteenth-century equivalent of a muumuu and sweatpants: a midlength dress worn over puffy pantaloons. But the women who gladly donned these so-called "bloomers" quickly discovered that not everyone took kindly to the idea of women wearing the pants in the family. The bloomer

brigade soon found themselves trailed by jeering mobs of men who pelted them with sticks and stones. Ultimately, the costume was abandoned, as much for the embarrassment it caused its wearers as for how ugly it looked. As Stanton would later admit, the overall appearance of the outfit was "not artistic."

A strict, if more artistic, dress code for men and women remained in effect all the way up until Robin Morgan's day, when feminists and hippies alike once again advocated a free-to-be-you-and-me, unisex style of clothing. Men grew their hair long on their heads, women grew their hair long on their legs, and anything "unnatural" was thought to be oppressive. But for those of us born into the '60s and '70s, all was not ponchos and pantsuits. On the one hand, we could appreciate the no-frills look of people like Kristy McNichol and Patti Smith, but on the other, we were thoroughly seduced by the groovy glamour of Laurie Partridge and Cher. We understood very clearly what feminists, and our mothers, meant when they said, "It doesn't matter what you look like on the outside; it's what's *inside* that counts," but we still felt tempted by those ads that promised we could "be a model, or just look like one." And oh, how could we resist the siren song of Clairol's Herbal Essence shampoo (the original one), the sexy slickness of Bonne Bell's strawberry-scented lip gloss, or the pop-art perfection of Maybelline's pink-and-green tubes of mascara? These coveted items were our all-access passes to the exciting world of teenage girlhood, a mask that let us look older than we felt, a protective coat of war paint that gave us the confidence to go out and capture that elusive boy.

Maybe we were just being duped by Madison Avenue, who, by the '70s, had taken to selling us women's lib in the form of cosmetics and antiperspirants ("strong enough for a man, but made for a woman"). But for us, fashion had little to do with feminism, and everything to do with female bonding. After all, the land of clothing and hairstyles was where we held our all-girls, no-boys-allowed pajama parties, whether we were drooling in front of the boob tube over Farrah Fawcett's perfectly feathered 'do, or just hanging out at the local Pants Place Plus. We never thought that our pursuit of style in any way held us back from our pursuit of equality. We'd grown up with none of the clothing restrictions that had so obviously (to us) kept our mothers in the oppressive chains of patriarchy: white underwear, white gloves, tight girdles, and heels. We had Earth Shoes, jeans, and a wide variety of T-shirts in our closets hanging right next to our miniskirts and go-go boots. We had what no other generation of women before us did: a choice. And we intended to keep it.

By the time the 1980s rolled around, however, a generation of lip-gloss-wearing liberationists came to understand that being fashionable *and* feminist was still considered to be a conflict of interest. Those of us old enough to attend college in those years quickly learned, in our women's studies classes, that any woman who dressed *too* sexy was a traitor to the cause—after all, what self-respecting woman would ever *choose* to wear uncomfortable, skintight, or skin-revealing clothing? Susan Brownmiller defended her decision to swear off skirts "because the nature of feminine dressing is superficial in essence," and it was agreed that dressing like a sex object meant you were asking to be treated like—well, an object. So although we stridently claimed the freedom to wear whatever we wanted, it was the unspoken understanding that no woman could expect to be taken seriously unless she dressed like a man. Enlightened women at universities everywhere began retreating to the safe neutrality of overalls and jeans, while women in the corporate world donned pin-striped pants and blazers.

But then, when Madonna crossed the borderline from the MTV screen into our collective psyches, we suddenly had a poster girl for postmodern fashion. Whether she was wearing a bra, a midriff-revealing T-shirt or fishnet stockings, Madonna managed to transform each of these items from a scarlet letter of sexual submissiveness into a red badge of courage. She dressed like a sex object, but she acted like a sex subject—an explosive combination if ever there was one. So while the press took offense that Madonna was setting feminism back by presenting herself as a "boy toy," no one seemed to notice that her biggest fans were not straight men at all, but rather, young women. Suffocated by the high-school version of the Virgin/Whore complex (dress demurely and you're a prude; dress sexy and you're a slut), girls were happy to have at least one of these options invested with some power. And unlike previous va-va-voom girls such as Marilyn Monroe—whose shtick involved playing dumb about their own sexiness, as if they were too innocent to even know about such things— Madonna's over-the-top image was far from accidental. From Harlow to harlot, Maddona's ever-changing

sexual personae were carefully chosen, and completely under her control.

So instead of throwing out the bra with the bathwater, as earlier feminists had done, Madonna suggested that the trappings of femininity could be used to make a sexual statement that was powerful, rather than passive. It was an idea that had widespread appeal, and it convinced a nation of Madonna wannabes to say good-bye to the "natural" look and hello to a new style of feminine display that involved layers of lingerie and bottles of bleach. At the same time, women like Annie Lennox and Grace Jones were putting a seductive spin on androgynous dressing. Irony had become the must-have accessory of the decade, and feminism was finally being set free of its antifashion stance. Inspired by these and other glamour gals of the '80s—Cyndi Lauper, Exene Cervenka, the Go-Gos—many of us made pilgrimages to our local Salvation Army, buying up '50s dresses that made a pointed statement about just how different we were from prefeminist housewives, and vampy '40s gowns that allowed us to camp it up in our new role as feminists fatale. We dressed like girls, we dressed like boys, we dressed like women, we dressed like men. Every item in our wardrobes was chosen to convey our unwillingness to conform to traditional ideas about gender and sexuality. Suddenly, Simon de Beauvoir's statement that "One is not born, but rather becomes, a woman" could be heard in a new way: as a slogan for postmodern feminist fashion.

It was with this same sense of irony that Courtney Love, as Madonna's heir apparent in the '90s, burst onto the scene. In her little-girl dresses and bright red lipstick, Courtney Love gave more the impression of a child playing dress-up than of an adult rock star. Her girlie-girl style, coupled with her very unladylike, out-of-control performances, helped to convey her rebellion against the stereotype of the demure, selfless female, and won her a loyal following of young women who were grasping for a model of female adulthood and sexuality that could include anger and aggression.

Courtney also helped bring the gynocentric gestalt of the Riot Grrls front and center. The baby-doll dresses that she helped to popularize, and which soon became a mainstay of mainstream fashion, were directly descended from this loosely defined movement of young women. Gathering together in latter-day consciousness-raising groups, the Riot Grrls represented a new breed of feminists who were determined to embrace, and no longer apologize for, everything that was traditionally girlie, and therefore just as traditionally marginalized—including ultrafemmey fashion. Taking their cue from the queer movement, Riot Grrls worked to reclaim sexist slurs like "slut" and "bitch" by scrawling those words in lipstick or Magic Marker across their bodies. They even resurrected the word "girl" itself, by injecting it with a fierce, double-r growl. With their legs unshaven and their hair sprinkled liberally with baby barrettes, Riot Grrls took to the streets holding hands, wearing thrift-store dresses with combat boots, and carrying Barbie lunch boxes as purses, their look sending out a cacophony of messages about femininity, feminism, and fashion.

These days, girls everywhere are sporting clothing from companies with names like Poontang, Tart, Girly, and Label Whore. Started by a growing number of young female designers, these labels reveal a tongue-in-chic sensibility that is definitively feminist. Their influence can be found on everything from T-shirts in New York City boutiques that read "Whore" and "Girls Kick Ass," to watered-down versions appearing in malls across the country that read "Brat" and "Girls Rule." One company even makes a line of underwear that has a kitten illustration over the crotch accompanied by the words "Pussy-scented." Ironic, obnoxious, and unapologetically female, these designers have added a new meaning to the words "fashion statement."

Of course, nothing's become more synonymous with Girl Power than the colorful, sparkly nail polish that is being worn by everyone from Riot Grrls to Spice Girls. Whereas for years women could only choose from shades of red, pink, or coral for their manicures, new nail polish lines by Urban Decay, with their slogans "Does pink make you puke?" and "Look like a person, not a doll," and Hard Candy, started by a

girl just out of her teens, are staging a full-frontal assault on the idea that cosmetics are just about trying to be "pretty." Girls are snatching up colors like Roach Brown, Slime Green, and Puke Orange, and painting them on in an act that is almost as ornery as it is ornamental. "Yes," they seem to be saying, "we like decorating ourselves. But it's not necessarily because we're trying to please *you*."

Even mainstream companies are beginning to add a more brazen edge to their beauty products, with their own lines of nontraditional nail polish and makeup. The cosmetics firm M.A.C. paid lipstick service to the notion that makeup is politically incorrect when they used transvestites and lesbians as their product spokesmodels. Now it seems even the boys want a piece of the girlie action—Hard Candy recently introduced a new line of nail polish just for men, called Candy Man. So while we laugh at Cynthia Heimel's statement that "wearing makeup is an apology for our actual faces," we know that we're looking for more than just "facial improvement" when we step up to the makeup counter and plop down $12 for a tube of Viva Glam—we're looking for a way to grab glamour by the balls, and have some fun with the idea of femininity.

Unlike our feminist foremothers, who claimed that makeup was the opiate of the misses, we're positively prochoice when it comes to matters of feminine display. We're well aware, thank you very much, of the beauty myth that's working to keep women obscene and not heard, but we just don't think that transvestites should have all the fun. In our fuck-me dresses and don't-fuck-with-me shoes, we're ready to come out of the closet as the absolutely fabulous females we know we are. We love our lipstick, have a passion for polish, and, basically, adore this armor that we call "fashion." To us, it's fun, it's feminine, and, in the particular way we flaunt it, it's *definitely* feminist.

Recipe

Janice Mirikitani

Round Eyes

Ingredients: scissors, Scotch magic transparent tape,
       eyeliner—water based, black.
       Optional: false eyelashes.

Cleanse face thoroughly.

For best results, powder entire face, including eyelids.
  (lighter shades suited to total effect desired)

With scissors, cut magic tape 1/16" wide, 3/4"–1/2"
long—
depending on length of eyelid.

Stick firmly onto mid-upper eyelid area
  (looking down into handmirror facilitates finding
  adequate surface)

If using false eyelashes, affix first on lid, folding any
excess lid over the base of eyelash with glue.

Paint black eyeliner on tape and entire lid.

Do not cry.

═══════════════════

Who Is the Enemy and What Does He Want? 1994

James William Gibson

Free of the family members who remind him of childish weaknesses, and of the women who seek to entrap him, the warrior is ready to begin his mission and confront the enemy. The enemy is the most important figure in all war mythologies, because without him neither society nor its heroic defenders would exist. In ancient myths, the evil ones are first defeated by the gods. After the Great Battle, the sacred order is founded, and the dark forces are cast outside the boundaries of society. They are still there, always trying as hard as they can to penetrate society and destroy it completely. When societies undergo serious crises, the particular identity of the enemy as well as the location of the symbolic boundaries may change. As sociologist Kai T. Erikson writes, "Boundaries are never a fixed property of any community. They are always shifting as the people of the group find new ways to define the outer limits of their universe, new ways to position themselves on the larger cultural map."[1]

For many Americans in the 1970s and 1980s, the "larger cultural map" wasn't just changing, it was becoming unrecognizable. The New War represented these fears by portraying a world where all symbolic boundaries were weak. Now more than ever, the evil ones were gaining power and threatening to intrude.

In New War movies and novels, the heroes journey beyond the threatened boundaries into primeval chaos. No place embodies anarchic evil more than Vietnam. In *The Deer Hunter*, Robert De Niro finds Saigon not a city, but hell itself, a smoky dungeon in which frantic Asian crowds place bets on drug addicts' games of Russian roulette. In *The Executioner*, volume 123, the pilot who flies Mack Bolan back to Vietnam for a mis-

146

sion in 1989 describes it as "the end of the world, man. Right where civilization stops and the jungle begins."[2]

Soldier of Fortune also strove to take its readers to the edge of chaos. From Africa, Jeff Cooper reported on the civil war in Rhodesia during the mid-1970s; the nation's chromium deposits were so necessary for the manufacture of steel and weapons, he asserted, that "the frontier of civilization of which the United States is a part lies on the Zambezi River."[3] *SOF* also published dispatches from Beirut where "Christian soldiers man the Green Line," the boundary between Christian West Beirut and the barbaric forces of Islam to the east.[4] And from 1979 to 1989 there were literally scores of stories with titles such as "The War on Our Doorstep: *SOF*'s Front-Line Report from Central America."[5]

In these dark regions dwell the enemies of the New War. Since they do not live in civilized society, their fundamental natures are not civilized either. Far from being small-time criminals hustling a living through petty theft, these deeply savage animals are perverts who commit crimes for pleasure. At the most mundane level, the evil ones are driven by greed. . . .

Bad men also lust after women. They always have harems at their disposal. . . .

For bad men, additional sexual pleasures can readily be obtained through rape, torture, and killing. . . .

Even when such villains hunt and kill men, the same perverted desires drive them. Pham, a Communist Vietnamese soldier, rejoices when he hears that his old adversary Mack Bolan is back in town: "Pham could feel the death lust singing inside him as it never had before."[6] Villains are so base that they seem like animals with "wolfish features and cold, merciless eyes." They have "the smell of the beast" about them and an "air of cruelty and brutality."[7] Occasionally the evil ones are not men at all, but aliens from outer space with these same characteristics, like the four-fanged trophy hunters who skin humans for sport in *Predator* (1987) and *Predator 2* (1990).

Bad men are often so evil that they will not grant their victims the mercy of a quick death. Neofascist drug dealers in Argentina burn their victims slowly, while Colombians prefer to lower people inch by inch into vats of acid. Soviet doctors threaten one hero with excruciating torture, administered along with a drug "that will keep you awake, alert, in spite of the pain, so that you can experience it all. There will be no unconsciousness, only an endless burning hell."[8]

Villains also take great pleasure in spreading diseases and drugs. In one World War III scenario, David Alexander's *Dark Messiah*, the Soviets develop biological-warfare diseases that turn the contaminated (called "contams") into "blood-drinking subhumans practically overnight. The contams became cannibals with a voracious appetite for human flesh."[9] *RoboCop 2* (1990) presents an evil drug trafficker—named Cain—working on the most addictive drugs to date, the "Nuke" ensemble: "There's a Nuke for every mood." It isn't money Cain desires, but the thrill of destroying ordinary human feelings with his chemical trances. Frequently, the enemy is himself infected with disease: Niles Barrabas, the counterterrorist leader, looks at the face of his opponent and sees "the glowing eyes of a maniac. Foam gathered at the corner of the terrorist's mouth."[10]

What is so interesting about all these enemies—the drug dealers, the left-wing terrorists, the neo-Nazis, the Soviets, and the Mafia—is how closely they resemble one another. They all commit the same evil crimes for the same perverted reasons. And, in the New War, all of the enemies are connected to each other, no matter how different they may seem at first glance. . . .

Creating chaos is the objective of the evil ones in the New War, just as it was at the beginning of time. Each criminal action furthers the spread of chaos. Every boundary they penetrate—from the geographic borders of good countries like the United States to the physical boundaries of a once-pure body ravaged by rape, torture, and death—leads to the victory of chaos and the destruction of the sacred order. And with each victory the enemies want more; they incarnate what Paul Ricoeur calls "the evil infinite of human desire."[11]

Ultimately, the evil ones can only be satisfied by the collapse of social stability and all moral values. The Mafia wants to corrupt everyone, from the highest political officials to the poorest woman selling her body to pay off her family's debt. The drug dealers want a world so addicted to drugs and the money drugs bring that people will do anything the dealers want. . . .

Since the enemies of the New War are all essentially the same, the New Order they envision looks about the same, too: a totalitarian world that resembles their criminal organizations. At the top stands the supreme leader, be he the Mafia's "boss of bosses," the head of the Soviet KGB, a local gang leader and drug lord, or Carlos the terrorist. The supreme leader is war chief of his tribe; under him are an assemblage of henchmen who do his bidding in return for a share of the spoils. And below the henchmen are the spoils themselves—slaves who labor in the evil ones' factories and drug addicts who buy their wares, men who can be hunted for sport and the women who can be taken and disposed of at will.

The New Order is a world without law or individual rights. There are neither rules nor rituals to give the world rhythm and meaning. Instead there is only the will and desire of the leader. To him, everyone is expendable, especially those who fail to carry out his orders immediately and with success. The New Order that the evil ones so fervently desire is both a form of social organization and a continuation of chaos.

Given the depth of his depravity, the enemy, one might think, poses an obvious danger to society. But oddly enough, in New War narratives this danger is not always immediately apparent. Many times his crimes at first look like ordinary killings, personal tragedies for the victims and their families but not a threat to the entire social order. In order to alert readers and viewers to the true dimensions of the problem, New War stories usually cast their enemies as reincarnations of older, more recognizable enemies of society.

The most obvious and detectable villains look somewhat like Indians. From the dangerous streets of *Death Wish* to the bloody highways of *The Road Warrior*, common street punks, their more organized motorcycle-gang brethren, and the tough leaders of the drug trade all have an Indian look about them. The men have long, wildly flowing hair or fierce Mohawk cuts or Jamaican-style dreadlocks. Either their faces are smeared with dirt and grease that looks like war paint or they actually wear war paint. They are only partially clothed, usually in leather, and their massive arms and chests are always bare. Just as Indian men traditionally wore necklaces, earrings, and other jewelry, so too do their modern-day reincarnations. These Indians can be white men, but more often they are some shade of brown or black. Finally, the new "Indians" show their teeth and shout war cries when they attack, shattering contemporary civilization with frightening echoes from an archaic past.

All of these images can in turn be summoned up by one phrase—"Indian country." During the Vietnam War, "Indian country" showed up time and time again in the everyday language of the troops; it continued to appear in their novels and memoirs later on. In the 1970s, the Indians turned up in Rhodesia, where an American in the Rhodesian Army formed a cavalry unit to ride them down during that country's civil war.[12] A few years later they reappeared in El Salvador. Peter G. Kokalis began one of his many *SOF* reports on the Atlacatl infantry battalion whom *SOF* trainers regularly advised with the dateline: "Indian country—just east of the Rio Lempa in Usulutan Province, El Salvador. The rugged terrain is infested with Communist guerrillas, swarming gnats, tall grass, and choking heat."[13]

When villains don't resemble Indians they may be reimagined as the Nazi and Japanese enemies of World War II. For example, when Rambo returns to Vietnam in *First Blood, Part 2*, he finds Vietnamese who wear World War II Japanese caps and are led by a blond-haired Russian who wears black leather and speaks with a guttural, vaguely Germanic accent. Myth readily substitutes one enemy for another, combining them in ways that make cultural sense: If Russian white men really controlled and directed the yellow Vietnamese, then the U.S. defeat becomes more understandable and belief in white superiority is confirmed.

At the same time, if Vietnamese are only Japanese in disguise, then even the Vietnam War with its murky moral imperative was not that different from a good clean fight like the Second World War. This process of taking what America already "knows" about an old enemy and transferring it to a new enemy has infinite possibilities. If the Vietnamese are simply reincarnations of the bad Japanese, then logically any group or nationality who resemble the Vietnamese in any way (using the AK47 rifle, for instance, or wearing sandals) will have the same evil connotation. By establishing such analogies, myth creates closure, replacing doubts about present conflicts with certainties about the just wars of the past.

Given that so many of the enemies in the New War are not white, one must ask to what extent the New War is about white racism. The notion that all nonwhites are the enemy finds its strongest contemporary expression in the right-wing fundamentalism of Christian Identity theology, which claims that the Anglo-Saxons and the Teutons (Germanic peoples) are the lost tribes of Israel and the true heirs of Abel, the child of Adam and Eve. The Jews are actually the descendants of Cain, who, say Christian Identity theologians, was the son of Eve and the Devil. All nonwhites—"the mud people"—are descendants of the Jews. Hence, they are literally the children of the primordial evil one, the Devil himself.[14]

In 1978, William S. Pierce published a novel informed by this racist philosophy. *The Turner Diaries* tells the story of the white victory in a race war fought in the United States in the early 1990s.[15] The novel is presented as the lost diary of Earl Turner, a low-level white guerrilla who is killed in the war. White historians subsequently find his document and annotate it for the reader. Hence the book appears as the history of the future.

As the diary reveals, two events precipitated armed revolution by whites against the U.S. government, which is called ZOG—the "Zionist Occupational Government." First, the government's ban on guns made it impossible for white men to protect their families from the ever-increasing criminal attacks by nonwhites. At the same time, ZOG also abolished rape as a crime, on the grounds that it was sexist: men can't be raped. Consequently, nonwhite men were free to rape white women, and they did so by the tens of thousands. The last barrier against universal miscegenation had been breached. Only the white revolution could stop the devil's work.

The open contempt for nonwhites, particularly blacks, expressed in *The Turner Diaries* may be found in some pulp novels as well. But in general such blatant racism is rare. Instead, the New War uses several different rhetorical mechanisms to shift attention away from the important fact that the evil ones who cannot control their desires are predominantly nonwhite.

The process of reincarnating old enemies as new ones is one such method. Since the Indian Wars fought over a hundred years ago are presented as the struggle between civilization and savagery (rather than as the aggression of white society against Indian society), any "new" Indian is just another savage. Killing an Indian, then, seems a victory for civilization in general, not whites in particular.

A second, related rhetorical technique that diffuses the racism of the New War involves the avoidance of race as an explicit plot theme; it appears as secondary detail. Movies and novels stress the crimes in question. They give names like terrorist, Communist, and drug dealer to the people who commit these crimes. Few New War stories openly address the racial composition of the enemy, but in the telling of the tale, it

emerges that most of the enemies are not white. Hence the heroes fight drug dealers who just happen to be black.

To make race appear even less of an issue, the heroic warrior tribes are usually shown as integrated. Although white heroes typically head these tribes, there are a few noteworthy exceptions. Rambo is half Apache. Danny Glover, the black costar of the first three *Lethal Weapon* movies, finally gets the star role in *Predator 2*. He leads his elite, racially integrated team of L.A. detectives against Colombian and Jamaican drug gangs and against alien predators from outer space. If the heroes transcend racial differences in their relations with one another, then surely the battles they fight against the evil ones are not racist, either.

Finally, the unity of the various enemies tends to obscure the fact that most of them are not white. Although gangs in the real world have traditionally been racially segregated and are frequently enemies, in the New War white, Latin, and black hoodlums are often bosom buddies who share the same evil pleasures. When they are not buddies, at least they can find a temporary common ground in a mutually beneficial division of labor for their criminal endeavors.

Of course, political terrorism is the greatest glue of all. Soviet KGB agents hand out drug money to black radicals. Bulgarian hangmen do the dirty work in Nicaragua. German terrorists assist their comrades around the Third World in hijackings and assassinations. Establishing links among disparate enemies also makes each one look more dangerous. The local warlord and his handful of minions are a threat to society, because they are potentially connected to all the other enemies. As the counterterrorists of *Phoenix Force* reason, "They were out there somewhere, the vermin, planning murder, plotting revolution. They were everywhere where men knew a measure of freedom. They subscribed to different political faiths, but behind the slogans and the false patriotism they were all the same."[16]

"Against a world infested with terror goons," heroic warriors must be ready to risk their lives to save society.[17] Yet, to their bitter frustration, they have to contend with a different kind of enemy every step of the way—"bleeding heart" liberals and complacent government officials, moral cowards who refuse to fight. Why do these leaders make themselves the enemy of courageous good men?

To answer this troubling question, New War stories point to a deep philosophical flaw in liberalism or what the religious right wing in the 1970s and 1980s called "secular humanism." Although most social and political analysts would say that post-Vietnam America has been decidedly conservative, in the New War a liberal ethos still permeates the leadership. These "practicing" liberals deny some fundamental truths; above all, they refuse to recognize the absolute reality of evil. By insisting that there are no bad men, but only bad social conditions, liberals fail to see that criminals, terrorists, and Communists commit their horrendous acts because they feel pleasure in killing, raping, and kidnapping. They are men who have lost self-control and succumbed to their desires—and their desires are infinite. Infected with evil, criminals can neither be contained nor reformed as liberalism would have it; they must be eliminated. . . .

Liberalism is also associated with serious character defects, moral corruption, and outright cowardice. (In Brian Garfield's *Death Wish,* "A liberal is a guy who walks out of the room when the fight starts."[18]) Often, corruption is linked to greed. Class, too, is a factor. Liberal elites, the graduates of Harvard and other Ivy League schools, are frequently pitted against heroic warriors with working-class origins. . . .

For the warrior, therefore, the official guardians of society are no longer legitimate. And society itself has become suspect. Liberalism has permeated the educational system, the churches, and the news media. Men who fight have been relegated to a "polluted," taboo caste—even though they risk their lives for those who despise them. Indeed, they will be condemned for their violent acts no matter what they do. . . .

Sentenced to hell by the media, unappreciated by most ordinary people, and abused by the power structure, in time the New War warriors are forced to let go of their old allegiances. Instead of being part of the system, they find they have been betrayed by it. So the warriors must always fight on two fronts. They must do battle with the true evil ones and, at a minimum, avoid the representatives of the establishment. To carry on this war, they need to establish bases far removed from the mainstream of society. In *Uncommon Valor* the private commandos train on an isolated Texas ranch. *The Black Berets* have a bunker-like home on a rural Louisiana farm. . . .

In this twilight, the true nature of both the evil ones and the heroes is briefly silhouetted. In the enemy, the hero glimpses himself. The reflection is his mirror image gone bad, a vision of a man who cannot control his desires but has instead surrendered to them completely and thus become evil.

Scenes of doubling or mirror-imaging occur with some regularity in the New War. In *Mad Max*, the Mel Gibson character, Max, and the chief of his highway-patrol unit have an extraordinary conversation after Max's buddy, Goose, has been burned by the outlaws. The chief wants Max to keep fighting because the public needs heroes. Max replies that he is about to lose control. "Look, any longer on that road, then I'm one of them." The chief says it's already too late. "You're hooked, Max, and you know it." . . .

Sometimes heroes find their increasing identification with the evil ones to be unbearable. Vigilante, one of the many comic-book avengers of the 1980s, finally admits that "instead of stopping crime I became the criminal. I was supposed to rid the streets of killers and madmen, wasn't I? I didn't want to die. I couldn't continue to live."[19] To end his pain, he kills himself. Not all heroes have this option—Catholics, for example. At the beginning of *Marked for Death*, a distraught undercover narcotics detective confesses his sins to a priest: "I did whatever I had to do to get the bad guys. I realize that I have become what I once despised. I have lied, slept with informants, done drugs."

But in the end there is really only one way to stop the mirror-imaging of hero and villain. The mirror must be shattered; someone must die. Hence, the mythology of the New War always involves a radical reduction of social conflict to one basic scene: the duel. To create this duel, myth reduces the Indians, the Vietnamese, the Soviets, the Arabs, and all the other collective enemies to a handful of men. Never do these enemies have any political or social or moral reasons for fighting; they have no real historical existence. How they came to be the enemies of America and what they want is never mentioned. As Roland Barthes once said, *"myth is depoliticized speech"*; by depoliticizing the enemy, it avoids "the whole of human relations in their real, social structure, in their power of making the world."[20]

Removed from history, the enemy is transformed by myth into the embodiment of evil: a man who cannot control his desires. Once evil is defined in this way, the struggle between hero and villain can be represented as a psychological conflict within the hero; the villain is but a phantasm, a projection of the hero's own desires, rages, and frustrations. Thus, like most mythological tales, New War stories function on at least two levels: they are simultaneously a vision of a social world—the battlefield—and a journey into the psyche.[21] At the psychological level, the New War narrative appears to be a story about male self-control.

Warriors are men of nearly impeccable self-control, with enemies as well as with women. They begin killing only because they must—to avenge a loved one or to see justice done—and not because they like it. As Pendleton points out, Mack Bolan feels no joy in his killings; only the "psychopathic" villain "wants to go out and slay and see blood flow."[22]

Everyone who has lost self-control, from the American political elite to rapists and murderers, is the warrior's enemy. Since in the New War all human desire is seen as insatiable and thus evil, without self-control every man would rape, murder, and try to become dictator of the world. Hence the hero's recognition of himself in the villain. When Dirty Harry shoots the naked man running wild in the streets with his knife and erection, he in effect shoots every man (including himself).

In the New War, criminal actions appear wonderfully exciting. In doing exactly what he wants to do, the villain moves freely from one kind of pleasure to another; he suffers under no restraints and his only responsibilities are to sustain and increase his pleasure. Upon inspection, though, it becomes clear that the enemy's gratification is derived from a single source—from transgression, from breaking all laws and acting contrary to all moral codes. Even the standard image of hedonism and sensuality—the villain surrounded by his harem—reveals this same pattern. The villain's pleasure comes from neither heightened love nor lust, but from having more than one woman, thus breaking the rule that says a good man gets just one.

In her study of Marquis de Sade, Angela Carter illuminates the nature of this transgressive impulse. Sade's pornography, she argues, has little to do with sexual pleasure per se and everything to do with a compulsive need to defy authority. Hence the characteristic combination in his work of endless scenes of anal, oral, genital, and group sex with incest, abortion, prostitution, patricide, and other more mundane murders—and of course domination and submission. For Sade, Carter says, sex is essentially a criminal act and the libertine's "entire pleasure" is "the cerebral, not

sensual one, of knowing he is engaging in forbidden activity."[23]

By presenting sexuality as a constant and inescapable alternation of domination and submission, Sade removes it from the realm of mutual human relations; since there is no experience of pleasure with equal others, the individual is left alone. At the same time, by presenting sexual desire as "cerebral insatiability," in Carter's words, Sade denies that it can ever be fulfilled: each act of defiance of authority requires yet a greater transgression to provide the same rush of excitement. Eventually, in Sade's works, this compulsive need to break all rules leads the libertines to regress from adulthood to infancy:

Transgression becomes regression and, like a baby, they play with their own excrement . . . The shamelessness and violence of the libertines is that of little children who are easily cruel because they have not learned the capacity for pity which the libertines dismiss as "childish" because the libertines themselves have not grown up enough to acknowledge the presence of others in their solipsistic world.[24]

The New War portrays human desire in much the same way. The evil one always wants more, because what he ultimately desires is to defy the laws of society, and seeking that solitary pleasure takes him down the road of cerebral insatiability toward childish regression. When the hero and his mirror-image villain face off, their confrontation may be seen as the hero's attempt as an adult to control his own regressive childlike nature.

But that isn't what happens. There is tragedy here, not psychological development. The New War, like Sade, eliminates the reality of other people and the good companionship and satisfaction they can give. If the villain in effect is a needy, enraged child who must have everything and everyone at his disposal, the hero is still another kind of child. He is the narcissistic, omnipotent child, the one who says "I need nothing and no one to sustain me." The villain must transgress the parental law to feel that he is alive, while the hero must deny that he ever had parents at all. Both the villain and the hero live in completely self-referential worlds.

The villain's murderous rage is a natural part of his pleasure in transgression, in violating all boundaries—both those of the body and those of society. In contrast, the hero's rage comes from his constant self-denial and personal sacrifice. This rage and self-denial is easy to see on the face of the hero. All the major male stars wear that same hard, mean look of controlled power. The heroic warrior lives for the final confrontation with the evil one. Only his prowess in combat, a form of impeccable self-control, enables him to protect the boundaries of society against threatening intrusions by the insatiable enemy. At the same time, only by killing the enemy can he release the rage accumulated from a life of emotional self-denial.

NOTES

1. Kai T. Erikson, *Wayward Puritans: A Study in the Sociology of Deviance* (New York: Wiley, 1968), 12.

2. Don Pendleton and staff writers, *War Born*, vol. 123 of *The Executioner* (Toronto: Worldwide 1989), 128.

3. Jeff Cooper, "Cooper on Rhodesia: An Alternative View to the State Department Position," *Soldier of Fortune*, Summer 1975, 28.

4. "Beirut: Christian Soldiers Man the Green Line," *Soldier of Fortune*, November 1986, 55.

5. "The War on Our Doorstep: *SOF*'s Front-Line Report from Central America," *Soldier of Fortune*, July 1983, 48.

6. Pendleton et al., *War Born*, 238.

7. Smith, *The Delta Decision*, 226, 203, 67.

8. Sievert, *C.A.D.S.*, 365.

9. David Alexander, *Dark Messiah*, vol. 1 of *Phoenix* (New York: Leisure Books, 1987), 61.

10. Jack Hild, *Firestorm U.S.A.*, vol. 16 of *SOBs: Soldiers of Barrabas* (Toronto: Worldwide, 1987), 186.

11. Paul Ricoeur, *The Symbolism of Evil*, trans. Emerson Buchanan (Boston: Beacon, 1969), 254.

12. Major L. H. "Mike" Williams, "The Cavalry Rides Again," *Soldier of Fortune*, June 1984, 55.

13. Peter G. Kokalis, "Atlacatal Assault: *SOF* in Combat with El Salvador's Elite Immediate Reaction Battalion," *Soldier of Fortune*, June 1984, 55.

14. Sara Diamond, *Spiritual Warfare: The Politics of the Christian Right* (Boston: South End Press, 1989).

15. William S. Pierce (under the pseudonym Andrew Macdonald), *The Turner Diaries* (Arlington, Va.: The National Alliance, 1978; second edition, 1980).

16. Gar Wilson, *The Fury Bombs*, vol. 5 of *Phoenix Force* (Toronto: Worldwide, 1983), 7.

17. Ibid., 5.

18. Brian Garfield, *Death Wish* (New York: McKay, 1972), 68.

19. Paul Kupperberg, "A Life!", *Vigilante*, no. 50 (February 1988), 7, 23.

20. Roland Barthes, *Mythologies*, trans. Annette Lavers (New York: Hill and Wang, 1987), 143.

21. Bruno Bettelheim, *The Uses of Enchantment: The Meaning and Importance of Fairy Tales* (New York: Knopf, 1976), 63.

22. Quoted by Elizabeth Mehren, "Some Dare Call It Romance," *Los Angeles Times*, July 29, 1988, V:2.

23. Angela Carter, *The Sadeian Woman: An Exercise in Cultural History* (London: Virago, 1979), 146–47.

24. Ibid., 147.

The Fight Against Hate
Why we can't—and shouldn't—win it.

1999

Andrew Sullivan

I.

I wonder what was going on in John William King's head two years ago when he tied James Byrd Jr.'s feet to the back of a pickup truck and dragged him three miles down a road in rural Texas. King and two friends had picked up Byrd, who was black, when he was walking home, half-drunk, from a party. As part of a bonding ritual in their fledgling white supremacist group, the three men took Byrd to a remote part of town, beat him and chained his legs together before attaching them to the truck. Pathologists at King's trial testified that Byrd was probably alive and conscious until his body finally hit a culvert and split in two. When King was offered a chance to say something to Byrd's family at the trial, he smirked and uttered an obscenity.

We know all these details now, many months later. We know quite a large amount about what happened before and after. But I am still drawn, again and again, to the flash of ignition, the moment when fear and loathing became hate, the instant of transformation when King became hunter and Byrd became prey.

What was that? And what was it when Buford Furrow Jr., longtime member of the Aryan Nations, calmly walked up to a Filipino-American mailman he happened to spot, asked him to mail a letter and then shot him at point-blank range? Or when Russell Henderson beat Matthew Shepard, a young gay man, to a pulp, removed his shoes and then, with the help of a friend tied him to a post, like a dead coyote, to warn off others?

For all our documentation of these crimes and others, our political and moral disgust at them, our morbid fascination with them, our sensitivity to their social meaning, we seem at times to have no better idea now than we ever had of what exactly they were about. About what that moment means when, for some reason or other, one human being asserts absolute, immutable superiority over another. About not the violence, but what the violence expresses. About what—exactly—hate is. And what our own part in it may be.

I find myself wondering what hate actually is in part because we have created an entirely new offense in American criminal law—a "hate crime"—to combat it. And barely a day goes by without someone somewhere declaring war against it. Last month President Clinton called for an expansion of hate-crime laws as "what America needs in our battle against hate." A couple of weeks later, Senator John McCain used a campaign speech to denounce the "hate" he said poisoned the land. New York's Mayor, Rudolph Giuliani, recently tried to stop the Million Youth March in Harlem on the grounds that the event was organized by people "involved in hate marches and hate rhetoric."

The media concurs in its emphasis. In 1985, there were 11 mentions of "hate crimes" in the national media database Nexis. By 1990, there were more than a thousand. In the first six months of 1999, there were 7,000. "Sexy fun is one thing," wrote a New York Times reporter about sexual assaults in Woodstock '99's mosh pit. "But this was an orgy of lewdness tinged with hate." And when Benjamin Smith marked the Fourth of July this year by targeting blacks, Asians and Jews for murder in Indiana and Illinois, the story wasn't merely about a twisted young man who had emerged on the scene. As The Times put it, "Hate ar-

rived in the neighborhoods of Indiana University, in Bloomington, in the early-morning darkness."

But what exactly was this thing that arrived in the early-morning darkness? For all our zeal to attack hate, we still have a remarkably vague idea of what it actually is. A single word, after all, tells us less, not more. For all its emotional punch, "hate" is far less nuanced an idea than prejudice, or bigotry, or bias, or anger, or even mere aversion to others. Is it to stand in for all these varieties of human experience—and everything in between? If so, then the war against it will be so vast as to be quixotic. Or is "hate" to stand for a very specific idea or belief, or set of beliefs, with a very specific object or group of objects? Then waging war against it is almost certainly unconstitutional. Perhaps these kinds of questions are of no concern to those waging war on hate. Perhaps it is enough for them that they share a sentiment that there is too much hate and never enough vigilance in combating it. But sentiment is a poor basis for law, and a dangerous tool in politics. It is better to leave some unwinnable wars unfought.

II.

Hate is everywhere. Human beings generalize all the time, ahead of time, about everyone and everything. A large part of it may even be hard-wired. At some point in our evolution, being able to know beforehand who was friend or foe was not merely a matter of philosophical reflection. It was a matter of survival. And even today it seems impossible to feel a loyalty without also feeling a disloyalty, a sense of belonging without an equal sense of unbelonging. We're social beings. We associate. Therefore we disassociate. And although it would be comforting to think that the one could happen without the other, we know in reality that it doesn't. How many patriots are there who have never felt a twinge of xenophobia?

Of course by hate, we mean something graver and darker than this kind of lazy prejudice. But the closer you look at this distinction, the fuzzier it gets. Much of the time, we harbor little or no malice toward people of other backgrounds or places or ethnicities or ways of life. But then a car cuts you off at an intersection and you find yourself noticing immediately that the driver is a woman, or black, or old, or fat, or white, or male. Or you are walking down a city street at night and hear footsteps quickening behind you. You look around and see that it is a white woman and not a black man, and you are instantly relieved. These impulses are so spontaneous they are almost involuntary. But where did they come from? The mindless need to be mad at someone—anyone—or the unconscious eruption of a darker prejudice festering within?

In 1993, in San Jose, Calif, two neighbors—one heterosexual, one homosexual—were engaged in a protracted squabble over grass clippings. (The full case is recounted in "Hate Crimes," by James B. Jacobs and Kimberly Potter.) The gay man regularly mowed his lawn without a grass catcher, which prompted his neighbor to complain on many occasions that grass clippings spilled over onto his driveway. Tensions grew until one day, the gay man mowed his front yard, spilling clippings onto his neighbor's driveway, prompting the straight man to yell an obscene and common anti-gay insult. The wrangling escalated. At one point, the gay man agreed to collect the clippings from his neighbor's driveway but then later found them dumped on his own porch. A fracas ensued with the gay man spraying the straight man's son with a garden hose, and the son hitting and kicking the gay man several times, yelling anti-gay slurs. The police were called, and the son was eventually convicted of a hate-motivated assault, a felony. But what was the nature of the hate: anti-gay bias, or suburban property-owner madness?

Or take the Labor Day parade last year in Broad Channel, a small island in Jamaica Bay, Queens. Almost everyone there is white, and in recent years a group of local volunteer firefighters has taken to decorating a pickup truck for the parade in order to win the prize for "funniest float." Their themes have tended toward the outrageously provocative. Beginning in 1995, they won prizes for floats depicting "Hasidic Park," "Gooks of Hazzard" and "Happy Gays." Last year, they called their float "Black to the Future, Broad Channel 2098." They imagined their community a century hence as a largely black enclave, with every stereotype imaginable: watermelons, basketballs and so on. At one point during the parade, one of them mimicked the dragging death of James Byrd. It was caught on videotape, and before long the entire community was depicted as a caldron of hate.

It's an interesting case, because the float was indisputably in bad taste and the improvisation on the Byrd killing was grotesque. But was it hate? The men on the float were local heroes for their volunteer work; they had no record of bigoted activity, and were not members of any racist organizations. In previous years, they had made fun of many other groups and saw themselves more as provocateurs than bigots. When they were described as racists, it came as a shock to them. They apologized for poor taste but refused to confess to bigotry. "The people involved aren't horrible people," protested a local woman. "Was it a racist act? I don't know. Are they racists? I don't think so."

If hate is a self-conscious activity, she has a point. The men were primarily motivated by the desire to shock and to reflect what they thought was their community's culture. Their display was not aimed at any particular black people, or at any blacks who lived in Broad Channel—almost none do. But if hate is primarily an unconscious activity, then the matter is obviously murkier. And by taking the horrific lynching of a black man as a spontaneous object of humor, the men were clearly advocating indifference to it. Was this an aberrant excess? Or the real truth about the men's feelings toward African-Americans? Hate or tastelessness? And how on earth is anyone, even perhaps the firefighters themselves, going to know for sure?

Or recall H.L. Mencken. He shared in the anti-Semitism of his time with more alacrity than most and was an indefatigable racist. "It is impossible," he wrote in his diary, "to talk anything resembling discretion or judgment into a colored woman. They are all essentially childlike, and even hard experience does not teach them anything." He wrote at another time of the "psychological stigmata" of the "Afro-American race." But it is also true that, during much of his life, day to day, Mencken conducted himself with no regard to race, and supported a politics that was clearly integrationist. As the editor of his diary has pointed out, Mencken published many black authors in his magazine, The Mercury, and lobbied on their behalf with his publisher, Alfred A. Knopf. The last thing Mencken ever wrote was a diatribe against racial segregation in Baltimore's public parks. He was good friends with leading black writers and journalists, including James Weldon Johnson, Walter White and George S. Schuyler, and played an underappreciated role in promoting the Harlem Renaissance.

What would our modern view of hate do with Mencken? Probably ignore him, or change the subject. But, with regard to hate, I know lots of people like Mencken. He reminds me of conservative friends who oppose almost every measure for homosexual equality yet genuinely delight in the company of their gay friends. It would be easier for me to think of them as haters, and on paper, perhaps, there is a good case that they are. But in real life, I know they are not. Some of them clearly harbor no real malice toward me or other homosexuals whatsoever.

They are as hard to figure out as those liberal friends who support every gay rights measure they have ever heard of but do anything to avoid going into a gay bar with me. I have to ask myself in the same, frustrating kind of way: are they liberal bigots or bigoted liberals? Or are they neither bigots nor liberals, but merely people?

III.

Hate used to be easier to understand. When Sartre described anti-Semitism in his 1946 essay "Anti-Semite and Jew," he meant a very specific array of firmly held prejudices, with a history, an ideology and even a pseudoscience to back them up. He meant a systematic attempt to demonize and eradicate an entire race. If you go to the Web site of the World Church of the Creator, the organization that inspired young Benjamin Smith to murder in Illinois earlier this year, you will find a similarly bizarre, pseudorational ideology. The kind of literature read by Buford Furrow before he rained terror on a Jewish kindergarten last month and then killed a mailman because of his color is full of the same paranoid loopiness. And when we talk about hate, we often mean this kind of phenomenon.

But this brand of hatred is mercifully rare in the United States. These professional maniacs are to hate what serial killers are to murder. They should certainly not be ignored; but they represent what Harold Meyerson, writing in Salon, called "niche haters": cold-blooded, somewhat deranged, often poorly socialized psychopaths. In a free society with relatively easy access to guns, they will always pose a menace.

But their menace is a limited one, and their hatred is hardly typical of anything very widespread. Take Buford Furrow. He famously issued a "wake-up call" to "kill Jews" in Los Angeles, before he peppered a Jewish community center with gunfire. He did this in a state with two Jewish female Senators, in a city with a large, prosperous Jewish population, in a country where out of several million Jewish Americans, a total of 66 were reported by the F.B.I. as the targets of hate-crime assaults in 1997. However despicable Furrow's

actions were, it would require a very large stretch to describe them as representative of anything but the deranged fringe of an American subculture.

Most hate is more common and more complicated, with as many varieties as there are varieties of love. Just as there is possessive love and needy love; family love and friendship; romantic love and unrequited love; passion and respect, affection and obsession, so hatred has its shadings. There is hate that fears, and hate that merely feels contempt; there is hate that expresses power, and hate that comes from powerlessness; there is revenge, and there is hate that comes from envy. There is hate that was love, and hate that is a curious expression of love. There is hate of the other, and hate of something that reminds us too much of ourselves. There is the oppressor's hate, and the victim's hate. There is hate that burns slowly, and hate that fades. And there is hate that explodes, and hate that never catches fire.

The modern words that we have created to describe the varieties of hate—"sexism," "racism," "anti-Semitism," "homophobia"—tell us very little about any of this. They tell us merely the identities of the victims; they don't reveal the identities of the perpetrators, or what they think, or how they feel. They don't even tell us how the victims feel. And this simplicity is no accident. Coming from the theories of Marxist and post-Marxist academics, these "isms" are far better at alleging structures of power than at delineating the workings of the individual heart or mind. In fact, these "isms" can exist without mentioning individuals at all.

We speak of institutional racism, for example, as if an institution can feel anything. We talk of "hate" as an impersonal noun, with no hater specified. But when these abstractions are actually incarnated, when someone feels something as a result of them, when a hater actually interacts with a victim, the picture changes. We find that hates are often very different phenomena one from another, that they have very different psychological dynamics, that they might even be better understood by not seeing them as varieties of the same thing at all.

There is, for example, the now unfashionable distinction between reasonable hate and unreasonable hate. In recent years, we have become accustomed to talking about hates as if they were all equally indefensible, as if it could never be the case that some hates might be legitimate, even necessary. But when some 800,000 Tutsis are murdered under the auspices of a

Hutu regime in Rwanda, and when a few thousand Hutus are killed in revenge, the hates are not commensurate. Genocide is not an event like a hurricane, in which damage is random and universal; it is a planned and often merciless attack of one group upon another. The hate of the perpetrators is a monstrosity. The hate of the victims, and their survivors, is justified. What else, one wonders, were surviving Jews supposed to feel toward Germans after the Holocaust? Or, to a different degree, South African blacks after apartheid? If the victims overcome this hate, it is a supreme moral achievement. But if they don't, the victims are not as culpable as the perpetrators. So the hatred of Serbs for Kosovars today can never be equated with the hatred of Kosovars for Serbs.

Hate, like much of human feeling, is not rational, but it usually has its reasons. And it cannot be understood, let alone condemned, without knowing them. Similarly, the hate that comes from knowledge is always different from the hate that comes from ignorance. It is one of the most foolish clichés of our time that prejudice is always rooted in ignorance, and can usually be overcome by familiarity with the objects of our loathing. The racism of many Southern whites under segregation was not appeased by familiarity with Southern blacks; the virulent loathing of Tutsis by many Hutus was not undermined by living next door to them for centuries. Theirs was a hatred that sprang, for whatever reasons, from experience. It cannot easily be compared with, for example, the resilience of anti-Semitism in Japan, or hostility to immigration in areas where immigrants are unknown, or fear of homosexuals by people who have never knowingly met one.

The same familiarity is an integral part of what has become known as "sexism." Sexism isn't, properly speaking, a prejudice at all. Few men live without knowledge or constant awareness of women. Every single sexist man was born of a woman, and is likely to be sexually attracted to women. His hostility is going to be very different than that of, say, a reclusive member of the Aryan Nations toward Jews he has never met.

In her book "The Anatomy of Prejudices," the psychotherapist Elisabeth Young-Bruehl proposes a typology of three distinct kinds of hate: obsessive, hysterical and narcissistic. It's not an exhaustive analysis, but it's a beginning in any serious attempt to understand hate rather than merely declaring war on it. The obsessives, for Young-Bruehl, are those, like the Nazis or Hutus, who fantasize a threat from a minority, and obsessively try to rid themselves of it. For them, the very existence of the hated group is threatening. They often describe their loathing in almost physical terms: they experience what Patrick Buchanan, in reference to homosexuals, once described as a "visceral recoil" from the objects of their detestation. They often describe those they hate as diseased or sick, in need of a cure. Or they talk of "cleansing" them, as the Hutus talked of the Tutsis, or call them "cockroaches," as Yitzhak Shamir called the Palestinians. If you read material from the Family Research Council, it is clear that the group regards homosexuals as similar contaminants. A recent posting on its Web site about syphilis among gay men was headlined, "Unclean."

Hysterical haters have a more complicated relationship with the objects of their aversion. In Young-Bruehl's words, hysterical prejudice is a prejudice that "a person uses unconsciously to appoint a group to act out in the world forbidden sexual and sexually aggressive desires that the person has repressed." Certain kinds of racists fit this pattern. White loathing of blacks is, for some people, at least partly about sexual and physical envy. A certain kind of white racist sees in black America all those impulses he wishes most to express himself but cannot. He idealizes in "blackness" a sexual freedom, a physical power, a Dionysian release that he detests but also longs for. His fantasy may not have any basis in reality, but it is powerful nonetheless. It is a form of love-hate, and it is impossible to understand the nuances of racism in, say, the American South, or in British Imperial India, without it.

Unlike the obsessives, the hysterical haters do not want to eradicate the objects of their loathing; rather they want to keep them in some kind of permanent and safe subjugation in order to indulge the attraction of their repulsion. A recent study, for example, found that the men most likely to be opposed to equal rights for homosexuals were those most likely to be aroused by homoerotic imagery. This makes little rational sense, but it has a certain psychological plausibility. If homosexuals were granted equality, then the hysterical gay-hater might panic that his repressed passions would run out of control, overwhelming him and the world he inhabits.

A narcissistic hate, according to Young-Bruehl's definition, is sexism. In its most common form, it is rooted in many men's inability even to imagine what it is to be a woman, a failing rarely challenged by men's control of our most powerful public social institutions. Women are not so much hated by most men as simply ignored in nonsexual contexts, or never conceived of as true equals. The implicit condescension is mixed, in many cases, with repressed and sublimated erotic desire. So the unawareness of women is sometimes commingled with a deep longing or contempt for them.

Each hate, of course, is more complicated than this, and in any one person hate can assume a uniquely configured combination of these types. So there are hysterical sexists who hate women because they need them so much, and narcissistic sexists who hardly notice that women exist, and sexists who oscillate between one of these positions and another. And there are gay-bashers who are threatened by masculine gay men and gay-haters who feel repulsed by effeminate ones. The soldier who beat his fellow soldier Barry Winchell to death with a baseball bat in July had earlier lost a fight to him. It was the image of a macho gay man—and the shame of being bested by him— that the vengeful soldier had to obliterate, even if he needed a gang of accomplices and a weapon to do so. But the murderers of Matthew Shepard seem to have had a different impulse: a visceral disgust at the thought of any sexual contact with an effeminate homosexual. Their anger was mixed with mockery, as the cruel spectacle at the side of the road suggested.

In the same way, the pathological anti-Semitism of Nazi Germany was obsessive, inasmuch as it tried to cleanse the world of Jews; but also, as Daniel Jonah Goldhagen shows in his book, "Hitler's Willing Executioners," hysterical. The Germans were mysteriously compelled as well as repelled by Jews, devising elaborate ways, like death camps and death marches, to keep them alive even as they killed them. And the early Nazi phobia of interracial sex suggests as well a lingering erotic quality to the relationship, partaking of exactly the kind of sexual panic that persists among some homosexual-haters and anti-miscegenation racists. So the concept of "homophobia," like that of "sexism" and "racism," is often a crude one. All three are essentially cookie-cutter formulas that try to understand human impulses merely through the one-dimensional identity of the victims, rather than through the thoughts and feelings of the haters and hated.

This is deliberate. The theorists behind these "isms" want to ascribe all blame to one group in society—the "oppressors"—and render specific others— the "victims"—completely blameless. And they want to do this in order in part to side unequivocally with the underdog. But it doesn't take a genius to see how this approach, too, can generate its own form of bias. It can justify blanket condemnations of whole groups of people—white straight males for example—purely because of the color of their skin or the nature of their sexual orientation. And it can condescendingly ascribe innocence to whole groups of others. It does exactly what hate does: it hammers the uniqueness of each individual into the anvil of group identity. And it postures morally over the result.

In reality, human beings and human acts are far more complex, which is why these isms and the laws they have fomented are continually coming under strain and challenge. Once again, hate wriggles free of its definers. It knows no monolithic groups of haters and hated. Like a river, it has many eddies, backwaters and rapids. So there are anti-Semites who actually admire what they think of as Jewish power, and there are gay-haters who look up to homosexuals and some who want to sleep with them. And there are black racists, racist Jews, sexist women and anti-Semitic homosexuals. Of course there are.

IV.

Once you start thinking of these phenomena less as the "isms" of sexism, racism and "homophobia," once you think of them as independent psychological responses, it's also possible to see how they can work in a bewildering variety of ways in a bewildering number of people. To take one obvious and sad oddity: people who are demeaned and objectified in society may develop an aversion to their tormentors that is more hateful in its expression than the prejudice they have been subjected to. The F.B.I. statistics on hate crimes throws up an interesting point. In America in the 1990's, blacks were up to three times as likely as whites to commit a hate crime, to express their hate by physically attacking their targets or their property. Just as sexual abusers have often been victims of sexual abuse, and wife-beaters often grew up in violent households, so hate criminals may often be members of hated groups.

Even the Columbine murderers were in some sense victims of hate before they were purveyors of it. Their classmates later admitted that Dylan Klebold and Eric Harris were regularly called "faggots" in the corridors and classrooms of Columbine High and that nothing was done to prevent or stop the harassment. This climate of hostility doesn't excuse the actions of Klebold and Harris, but it does provide a more plausible context. If they had been black, had routinely been called "nigger" in the school and had then exploded into a shooting spree against white students, the response to the matter might well have been different. But the hate would have been the same. In other words, hate-victims are often hate-victimizers as well. This doesn't mean that all hates are equivalent, or that some are not more justified than others. It means merely that hate goes both ways; and if you try to regulate it among some, you will find yourself forced to regulate it among others.

It is no secret, for example, that some of the most vicious anti-Semites in America are black, and that some of the most virulent anti-Catholic bigots in America are gay. At what point, we are increasingly forced to ask, do these phenomena become as indefensible as white racism or religious toleration of anti-gay bigotry? That question becomes all the more difficult when we notice that it is often minorities who commit some of the most hate-filled offenses against what they see as their oppressors. It was the mainly gay AIDS activist group Act Up that perpetrated the hateful act of desecrating Communion hosts at a Mass at St. Patrick's Cathedral in New York. And here is the playwright Tony Kushner, who is gay, responding to the Matthew Shepard beating in The Nation magazine: "Pope John Paul II endorses murder. He, too, knows the price of discrimination, having declared anti-Semitism a sin. . . . He knows that discrimination kills. But when the Pope heard the news about Matthew Shepard, he, too, worried about spin. And so, on the subject of gay-bashing, the Pope and his cardinals and his bishops and priests maintain their cynical political silence. . . . To remain silent is to endorse murder." Kushner went on to describe the Pope as a "homicidal liar."

Maybe the passion behind these words is justified. But it seems clear enough to me that Kushner is expressing hate toward the institution of the Catholic Church, and all those who perpetuate its doctrines. How else to interpret the way in which he accuses the Pope of cynicism, lying and murder? And how else either to understand the brutal parody of religious vocations expressed by the Sisters of Perpetual Indulgence, a group of gay men who dress in drag as nuns and engage in sexually explicit performances in public? Or T-shirts with the words "Recovering Catholic" on them, hot items among some gay and lesbian activists? The implication that someone's religious faith is a mental illness is clearly an expression of contempt. If that isn't covered under the definition of hate speech, what is?

Or take the following sentence: "The act male homosexuals commit is ugly and repugnant and afterwards they are disgusted with themselves. They drink and take drugs to palliate this, but they are disgusted with the act and they are always changing partners and cannot be really happy." The thoughts of Pat Robertson or Patrick Buchanan? Actually that sentence was written by Gertrude Stein, one of the century's most notable lesbians. Or take the following, about how beating up "black boys like that made us feel *good* inside. . . . Every time I drove my foot into his [expletive], I felt better." It was written to describe the brutal assault of an innocent bystander for the sole reason of his race. By the end of the attack, the victim had blood gushing from his mouth as his attackers stomped on his genitals. Are we less appalled when we learn that the actual sentence was how beating up "white boys like that made us feel *good* inside. . . . Every time I drove my foot into his [expletive], I felt better?" It was written by Nathan McCall, an African-American who later in life became a successful journalist at The Washington Post and published his memoir of this "hate crime" to much acclaim.

In fact, one of the stranger aspects of hate is that the prejudice expressed by a group in power may often be milder in expression than the prejudice felt by the marginalized. After all, if you already enjoy privilege, you may not feel the anger that turns bias into hate. You may not need to. For this reason, most white racism may be more influential in society than most black racism—but also more calmly expressed.

So may other forms of minority loathing—especially hatred within minorities. I'm sure that black conservatives like Clarence Thomas or Thomas Sowell have experienced their fair share of white racism. But I wonder whether it has ever reached the level of intensity of the hatred directed toward them by other blacks? In several years of being an openly gay writer and editor, I have experienced the gamut of responses to my sexual orientation. But I have only directly experienced articulated, passionate hate from other homosexuals. I have been accused over the years by other homosexuals of being a sellout, a hypocrite, a traitor, a sexist, a racist, a narcissist, a snob. I've been called selfish, callous, hateful, self-hating and malevolent. At a reading, a group of lesbian activists portrayed my face on a poster within the crossfires of a gun. Nothing from the religious right has come close to such vehemence.

I am not complaining. No harm has ever come to me or my property, and much of the criticism is rooted in the legitimate expression of political differences. But the visceral tone and style of the gay criticism can only be described as hateful. It is designed to wound personally, and it often does. But its intensity comes in part, one senses, from the pain of being excluded for so long, of anger long restrained bubbling up and directing itself more aggressively toward an alleged traitor than an alleged enemy. It is the hate of the hated. And it can be the most hateful hate of all. For this reason, hate-crime laws may themselves be an oddly biased category—biased against the victims of hate. Racism is everywhere, but the already victimized might be more desperate, more willing to express it violently. And so more prone to come under the suspicious eye of the law.

V.

And why is hate for a group worse than hate for a person? In Laramie, Wyo., the now-famous epicenter of "homophobia," where Matthew Shepard was brutally beaten to death, vicious murders are not unknown. In the previous 12 months, a 15-year-old pregnant girl was found east of the town with 17 stab wounds. Her 38-year-old boyfriend was apparently angry that she had refused an abortion and left her in the Wyoming foothills to bleed to death. In the summer of 1998, an 8-year-old Laramie girl was abducted, raped and murdered by a pedophile, who disposed of her young body in a garbage dump. Neither of these killings was deemed a hate crime, and neither would be designated as such under any existing hate-crime law. Perhaps because of this, one crime is an international legend; the other two are virtually unheard of.

But which crime was more filled with hate? Once you ask the question, you realize how difficult it is to answer. Is it more hateful to kill a stranger or a lover? Is it more hateful to kill a child than an adult? Is it more hateful to kill your own child than another's? Under the law before the invention of hate crimes, these decisions didn't have to be taken. But under the law after hate crimes, a decision is essential. A decade ago, a murder was a murder. Now, in the era when group hate has emerged as our cardinal social sin, it all depends.

The supporters of laws against hate crimes argue that such crimes should be disproportionately punished because they victimize more than the victim.

Such crimes, these advocates argue, spread fear, hatred and panic among whole populations, and therefore merit more concern. But, of course, all crimes victimize more than the victim, and spread alarm in the society at large. Just think of the terrifying church shooting in Texas only two weeks ago. In fact, a purely random murder may be even more terrifying than a targeted one, since the entire community, and not just a part of it, feels threatened. High rates of murder, robbery, assault and burglary victimize everyone, by spreading fear, suspicion and distress everywhere. Which crime was more frightening to more people this summer: the mentally ill Buford Furrow's crazed attacks in Los Angeles, killing one, or Mark Barton's murder of his own family and several random day-traders in Atlanta, killing 12? Almost certainly the latter. But only Furrow was guilty of "hate."

One response to this objection is that certain groups feel fear more intensely than others because of a history of persecution or intimidation. But doesn't this smack of a certain condescension toward minorities? Why, after all, should it be assumed that gay men or black women or Jews, for example, are as a group more easily intimidated than others? Surely in any of these communities there will be a vast range of responses, from panic to concern to complete indifference. The assumption otherwise is the kind of crude generalization the law is supposed to uproot in the first place. And among these groups, there are also likely to be vast differences. To equate a population once subjected to slavery with a population of Mexican immigrants or third-generation Holocaust survivors is to equate the unequatable. In fact, it is to set up a contest of vulnerability in which one group vies with another to establish its particular variety of suffering, a contest that can have no dignified solution.

Rape, for example, is not classified as a "hate crime" under most existing laws, pitting feminists against ethnic groups in a battle for recognition. If, as a solution to this problem, everyone, except the white straight able-bodied male, is regarded as a possible victim of a hate crime, then we have simply created a two-tier system of justice in which racial profiling is reversed, and white straight men are presumed guilty before being proven innocent, and members of minorities are free to hate them as gleefully as they like. But if we include the white straight male in the litany of potential victims, then we have effectively abolished the notion of a hate crime altogether. For if every crime is possibly a hate crime, then it is simply another name for crime. All we will have done is widened the search for possible bigotry, ratcheted up the sentences for everyone and filled the jails up even further.

Hate-crime-law advocates counter that extra penalties should be imposed on hate crimes because our society is experiencing an "epidemic" of such crimes. Mercifully, there is no hard evidence to support this notion. The Federal Government has only been recording the incidence of hate crimes in this decade, and the statistics tell a simple story. In 1992, there were 6,623 hate-crime incidents reported to the F.B.I. by a total of 6,181 agencies, covering 51 percent of the population. In 1996, there were 8,734 incidents reported by 11,355 agencies, covering 84 percent of the population. That number dropped to 8,049 in 1997. These numbers are, of course, hazardous. They probably underreport the incidence of such crimes, but they are the only reliable figures we have. Yet even if they are faulty as an absolute number, they do not show an epidemic of "hate crimes" in the 1990's.

Is there evidence that the crimes themselves are becoming more vicious? None. More than 60 percent of recorded hate crimes in America involve no violent, physical assault against another human being at all, and, again, according to the F.B.I., that proportion has not budged much in the 1990's. These impersonal attacks are crimes against property or crimes of "intimidation." Murder, which dominates media coverage of hate crimes, is a tiny proportion of the total. Of the 8,049 hate crimes reported to the F.B.I. in 1997, a total of eight were murders. Eight. The number of hate crimes that were aggravated assaults (generally involving a weapon) in 1997 is less than 15 percent of the total. That's 1,237 assaults too many, of course, but to put it in perspective, compare it with a reported 1,022,492 "equal opportunity" aggravated assaults in America in the same year. The number of hate crimes that were physical assaults is half the total. That's 4,000 assaults too many, of course, but to put it in perspective, it compares with around 3.8 million "equal opportunity" assaults in America annually.

The truth is, the distinction between a crime filled with personal hate and a crime filled with group hate is an essentially arbitrary one. It tells us nothing interesting about the psychological contours of the specific actor or his specific victim. It is a function primarily of politics, of special interest groups carving out particular protections for themselves, rather than a serious response to a serious criminal concern. In such an endeavor, hate-crime-law advocates cram an entire world of human motivations into an immutable, tiny box called hate, and hope to have solved a problem. But nothing has been solved; and some harm may even have been done.

In an attempt to repudiate a past that treated people differently because of the color of their skin, or their sex, or religion or sexual orientation, we may merely create a future that permanently treats people differently because of the color of their skin, or their sex, religion or sexual orientation. This notion of a hate crime, and the concept of hate that lies behind it, takes a psychological mystery and turns it into a facile political artifact. Rather than compounding this error and extending it even further, we should seriously consider repealing the concept altogether.

To put it another way: violence can and should be stopped by the government. In a free society, hate can't and shouldn't be. The boundaries between hate and prejudice and between prejudice and opinion and between opinion and truth are so complicated and blurred that any attempt to construct legal and political fire walls is a doomed and illiberal venture. We know by now that hate will never disappear from human consciousness; in fact, it is probably, at some level, definitive of it. We know after decades of education measures that hate is not caused merely by ignorance; and after decades of legislation, that it isn't caused entirely by law.

To be sure, we have made much progress. Anyone who argues that America is as inhospitable to minorities and to women today as it has been in the past has not read much history. And we should, of course, be vigilant that our most powerful institutions, most notably the government, do not actively or formally propagate hatred; and insure that the violent expression of hate is curtailed by the same rules that punish all violent expression.

But after that, in an increasingly diverse culture, it is crazy to expect that hate, in all its variety, can be eradicated. A free country will always mean a hateful country. This may not be fair, or perfect, or admirable, but it is reality, and while we need not endorse it, we should not delude ourselves into thinking we can prevent it. That is surely the distinction between toleration and tolerance. Tolerance is the eradication of hate; toleration is co-existence despite it. We might do better as a culture and as a polity if we concentrated more on achieving the latter rather than the former. We would certainly be less frustrated.

And by aiming lower, we might actually reach higher. In some ways, some expression of prejudice serves a useful social purpose. It lets off steam; it allows natural tensions to express themselves incrementally; it can siphon off conflict through words, rather than actions. Anyone who has lived in the ethnic shouting match that is New York City knows exactly what I mean. If New Yorkers disliked each other less, they wouldn't be able to get on so well. We may not all be able to pull off a Mencken—bigoted in words, egalitarian in action—but we might achieve a lesser form of virtue: a human acceptance of our need for differentiation, without a total capitulation to it.

Do we not owe something more to the victims of hate? Perhaps we do. But it is also true that there is nothing that government can do for the hated that the hated cannot better do for themselves. After all, most bigots are not foiled when they are punished specifically for their beliefs. In fact, many of the worst haters crave such attention and find vindication in such rebukes. Indeed, our media's obsession with "hate," our elevation of it above other social misdemeanors and crimes, may even play into the hands of the pathetic and the evil, may breathe air into the smoldering embers of their paranoid loathing. Sure, we can help create a climate in which such hate is disapproved of—and we should. But there is a danger that if we go too far, if we punish it too much, if we try to abolish it altogether, we may merely increase its mystique, and entrench the very categories of human difference that we are trying to erase.

For hate is only foiled not when the haters are punished but when the hated are immune to the bigot's power. A hater cannot psychologically wound if a victim cannot psychologically be wounded. And that immunity to hurt can never be given; it can merely be achieved. The racial epithet only strikes at someone's core if he lets it, if he allows the bigot's definition of him to be the final description of his life and his person—if somewhere in his heart of hearts, he believes the hateful slur to be true. The only final answer to this form of racism, then, is not majority persecution of it, but minority indifference to it. The only permanent rebuke to homophobia is not the enforcement of tolerance, but gay equanimity in the face of prejudice. The only effective answer to sexism is not a morass of legal proscriptions, but the simple fact of female success. In this, as in so many other things, there is no solution to the problem. There is only a transcendence of it. For all our rhetoric, hate will never be destroyed. Hate, as our predecessors knew better, can merely be overcome.

The Outsiders

1999

Adrian Nicole LeBlanc

The fight takes place in the bright light of adult view—on a weekday afternoon, on a tree-lined residential street, within sight of the police station and a block from the middle school. The smaller boy, about 12, waits until there is a safe distance between himself and the other boy, about 13. Then he sends a curse. It lands. He waits. No response. He follows with a homophobic slur. His opponent—a chubby boy nicknamed Sex Machine—finally turns around.

A freckled friend of Sex Machine's loops around him on his bicycle, lazily doing doughnuts. He prods Sex Machine chirpily: "You gonna take that? He's a punk!" Halfheartedly, Sex Machine blusters back a retort. More friends appear and cajole him, challenging him to at least pretend that he has nerve.

"C'mon, Sex Machine!" one shouts, then whispers to another, alarmed: "Look at him. He keeps backing up!"

Whatever started the fight is irrelevant. The friends clamber up a nearby wire fence to get a good view, hyper spiders clinging to the mesh.

Sex Machine is frightened. Despite his oversize T-shirt, you can see the rise and fall of his heaving chest. A man's voice chimes in and shouts encouragement to the smaller boy from the driveway.

"That's his father!" a boy says. "Can you believe it? He's telling him to fight!"

"That's not right," says a girl.

Borrowing from the man's confidence, the smaller boy rushes forward and swings. Sex Machine stumbles backward as he tries to duck. A woman leans out from the second-floor window of a ranch house and says, "Come in, come in," without sounding as though she means it, a weary Juliet.

Sex Machine looks desperate, flailing his arms frantically, trying to flag down a car. Luckily, one stops. Apparently, it's his mother. All the tension and fear that his body has been holding bursts into punctuated sobs. He storms around the car to the passenger side. His freckled friend, who had been cheering within inches of the action, cycles over and dismounts to say goodbye. With all the fury raging inside him, Sex Machine bellows, *"You didn't help me!"* then shoves him to the ground.

Antrim, New Hampshire, where the fight took place, is a long way away from Littleton, Colo., as well as from Conyers, Ga., where a 15-year-old boy shot six classmates at his high school in May. It is one of nine towns whose regional high school, ConVal, sits in Peterborough, N.H., the setting that inspired Thornton Wilder's "Our Town." But what it shares with those other places, and with countless others across the country, is a brutally enforced teen-age social structure.

Boys at the bottom of the pyramid use different strategies to cope—turning inward and outward, sometimes in highly destructive ways. (There has been a fivefold jump in the homicide and suicide rates of boys in the last 40 years, a rise some experts attribute to increasing male depression and anger as well as access to guns, among other factors.) Most boys live through it, suffer, survive. But the journey may be especially deadly now because, as the avalanche of new "male identity" literature demonstrates, the old prescriptions for behavior no longer hold, and the new ones are ambivalent. Today's young males may be feminism's children, but no one is comfortable with openhearted or vulnerable boys.

ConVal is in some ways progressive. There are about 900 students and an administration that consciously works to minimize the ultramacho sports culture that dominates many schools. Says Bob Marshall, the head of the social studies department, who founded the football program in 1992: "We had to cre-

ate a football culture. People didn't know when to cheer. We didn't even have a school song."

Even so, the traditional hierarchies operate: the popular kids tend to be wealthier and the boys among them tend to be jocks. The Gap Girls-Tommy Girls-Polo Girls compose the pool of desirable girlfriends, many of whom are athletes as well. Below the popular kids, in a shifting order of relative unimportance, are the druggies (stoners, deadheads, burnouts, hippies or neo-hippies), trendies or Valley Girls, preppies, skateboarders and skateboarder chicks, nerds and techies, wiggers, rednecks and Goths, better known as freaks. There are troublemakers, losers and floaters—kids who move from group to group. Real losers are invisible.

Bullying, here as elsewhere, is rampant. Even in small-town, supposedly safe environments like Peterborough, a 1994 study found, the vast majority of kids from middle school up are bullied by their peers. The shaming is sex-based, but the taunting is more intense for boys—an average high-school student, according to another study, hears 25 antigay slurs a day.

To be an outcast boy is to be a "nonboy," to be feminine, to be weak. Bullies function as a kind of peer police enforcing the social code, and ConVal's freaks are accustomed to the daily onslaught. The revenge-of-the-nerds refrain—which assures unpopular boys that if they only hold on through high school, the roster of winners will change—does not question the hierarchy that puts the outcasts at risk. So boys survive by their stamina, sometimes by their fists, but mainly, if they're lucky, with the help of the family they've created among their friends.

A good day for Andrew, 14, occurs when R., a boy who torments him, is absent from school, like when he was suspended for ripping the hearing aid out of another classmate's ear. R., 15, weighs more than 200 pounds. Andrew, a small boy with straight, dirty-blond hair and glasses, takes care to note R.'s better days—say, when Andrew helps him with an assignment, when he's in a good mood or distracted by harassing someone else.

The trouble started long before the appearance of R. "First people harassed me because I was really smart," Andrew says, presenting the sequence as self-evident. "I read all the time. I read through math class." Back then, in middle school, he had the company of Tom Clancy and a best friend he could talk to about anything. He says things are better now; during school, he hangs out with the freaks. Yet the routine days he describes sound far from improvement—being body-slammed and shoved into chalkboards and dropped into trash cans headfirst. At a school dance, in the presence of chaperones and policemen, R. lifted Andrew and ripped a pocket off his pants. "One day I'll be a 'faggot,' the next day I'll be a 'retard,' " Andrew says. One girl who used to be his friend now sees him approaching and shouts, "Oh, get out of here, nobody wants you!"

Andrew joined the cross-country team but the misery trailed him on the practice runs. He won't rejoin next year although he loves the sport. Recently he and some other boys were suspended for suspected use of drugs. According to Andrew, he used to earn straight A's; now be receives mostly C's and D's. He does not draw connections between the abuse and the changes in his life.

He also does not expect help from the adults around him. He suspects they have their reasons—some don't care, while others worry only about physical attack. When I point out that he's being physically attacked, he imagines that the teachers think it's horsing around, although he does wonder why the teachers can see the same kid pushing other kids every day and don't just tell the kid to stop. "Maybe have a talk with him or do something," he says. "One little push isn't that much, but when it's every day, it's something." He only wishes that someone had helped in middle school, before the contagion grew. "When it first starts to happen, there's definitely something you can do," he says. "But you can't turn a whole school."

Neither does Andrew tell his parents. He believes they think he is popular. "If I try to explain it to my parents," he says, "they'll say: 'Oh, but you have plenty of friends.' Oh, I don't *think* so. They don't really get it." His outcast friends, however, do.

One of them is Randy Tuck, a 5-foot-4-inch sophomore with a thick head of hair and cheeks bright red with acne. He rescued Andrew from a "swirly" (two boys had him ankle up, and headed for the toilet bowl).

Randy moved from Alaska to New Hampshire almost three years ago. To his frustration, his classmates called him Eskimo Boy. Art is his solace, along with the occasional cigarette. He loves to draw. He used to sketch Ninja Turtles and now, with the help of an art teacher, he's studying anatomy. He associates with the freaks during school mainly because they let him. He says, "They are friendly, but not welcoming."

Classmates debate with Randy about his atheism, but he refuses to believe a God could arrange a life as unlucky as his. Andrew blames himself. Randy says, "Andrew's vulnerable and small and weak and R. takes advantage of that." Randy utilizes "verbal bashing" as a defense, although he admits that its powers don't prevent physical attack. R. surprised him one day in the hallway. He passed Randy, then turned around and punched him in the spine. But Randy also notes that R. can be funny. "When he's not in a bad mood, he can be very entertaining."

Andrew says that the ostracizing "does build up inside. Sometimes you might get really mad at something that doesn't matter a lot, kinda like the last straw." He could understand the Columbine killers, Dylan Klebold and Eric Harris, if their misery had shown no signs of ending, but Andrew remains an optimist. After all, there are some people who have *no* friends. "Things are not going up really fast, but they are getting better," he says. "I might have a week where they get worse, but overall they are getting better, definitely."

The quips ricochet around the bedroom like friendly-fire darts. Myles Forrest, 16, a sophomore with baby fat and sweet eyes, is one of George Farley's closer friends. George, also 16, is a floater. He has set up camp with ConVal's freaks for now. George sees weakness everywhere—in women who look for milk cartons with the latest expiration date at the store where he works; in the unemployed drunk who receives an allowance from his working wife; in white girls who think they are cool because they date guys who are black. Softness arouses his contempt. He is no more gentle with himself. The volleying with Myles, who wears his Y2K T-shirt—"01-01-00"—relieves George of the clearly burdensome obligation of having so much edge.

"The end of Myles's life," George starts.

"The end of life as we know it," Myles says. The phone rings. George lifts the receiver. "Myles Forrest, loser," he announces, and so the afternoon begins.

Myles and George provide sustenance between insults. Myles fiddles with his computer—one of two—as George peers out over the street. "What's up with the dress?" George asks, spotting an exchange student from ConVal.

"What? He's Hindu," says Myles.

"I said, What's up with the dress?"

"It's like a cult thing," Myles says, somewhat sharply.

"That's a dress," George says, losing steam.

"It's like a cult thing. It's like a kilt."

"You know I'm messing with you, don't go getting all politically correct with me." (Later on, Myles will explain the theory of equal opportunity hatred: "You ever notice that you can't hate a particular group, but if you generally hate everybody nobody seems to mind?") The sarcasm slows when the Quake competition begins.

It strikes me as I watch them in front of the famously violent video game that it is one way for the boys to enjoy closeness without it being threatening. The violence of the game, the state-of-siege mentality, the technical expertise required, supplant the macho expectations and give the boys a rest from the relentless one-upmanship. Rather than insult each other, they can attack the game. Soon enough, they are allies in the search for snacks, rushing down the stairs. They amble past the locked gun case behind the door leading through the playroom, to the kitchen. George sticks his head in the fridge.

"How about some of these worms?" he asks, holding a baggie of bait. "Fishing is like alcoholism. It's an excuse to drink. Or maybe they're trying to level the playing field. How hard can it be to outsmart a fish?"

"Catching it is kinda fun—" Myles tries.

"Now ice fishing—alcoholism in the extreme," George continues. "Cold, boring, worry about falling through the ice. Hey, my girlfriend dumped me. She dumped my slacker [expletive]."

"I thought you were gonna give her the—" Myles tries.

"Yeah, but she surprised me."

"Irony of ironies. So, technically, you're the loser."

"Shut up," George says, sounding sad.

"To the winner goes all the spoils of war," Myles appeals.

"Shut up," George says, relocating to the sun room. He lifts Fido, Myles's lizard.

"Watch out, George," Myles says protectively. George presses Fido into the aquarium to make the wood chips fly.

"That's cruel, stop it," Myles says, retrieving his lizard, as George moves on to to his lectern, the Stairmaster.

"That cat is wishing for a tail," George says, observing Myles's tailless cat.

"To the victor goes the spoils of war," Myles sighs, mock ruefully.

"Stop defending your tailless cat," says George. "Anyways, so Colleen broke up with me."

"You already told me that," Myles says. He glances at his buddy. "I thought that's what you wanted."

"I did," George says, sounding far from sure. Now that he has been rendered single, what will come of the flirtation he lost his girlfriend for? The new girl, a computer skateboarder chick, likes to spar. George says, "We're both the same person, but it's hard when you have two sarcastic people making fun of each other, and then they get worse and worse until—"

"Until there's no place you can go," Myles says knowingly.

"Shut up, you slack [expletive]," George says, knowing, too.

Teen-agers find heroes among their friends. Tyler Snitko, 17, pulls other outcasts in, functioning as a kind of human insulation for the freaks. To each taunt he quips, "Thank you." He booms, "These are my people," opening his arms, his fingernails polished black, to embrace his fellow freaks at lunch time in what has been labeled Mutant Hall. In the presence of someone like Tyler, more vulnerable teen-agers are less likely to be picked on, and they intuitively know this.

Tyler's hero is his grandfather. Not only did the old man give him advice that he often quotes ("Sometimes there are going to be rat bastards in life, and you have to deal with them"), but he also backed up the talk with action: he gave Tyler his first set of weights.

Tyler kept his strategy secret, taking long, midnight runs because he did not want to jeopardize his affiliation with the freaks, who were supposed to be "all skinny and pale." He soon discovered that his best friend, Toffer, 17, studied jujitsu to control the anger building in himself.

Toffer knew what it was like to be excluded. His isolation began in elementary school, and only in high school, through his friendship with Tyler and with his girlfriend, Anne Baker, did the fog begin to lift. Through the worst of the ostracization, the boys had each other. Says Tyler: "Other people turned me away, like I'd bring the whole house down. He stood by me."

Toffer, whose name is Christopher Eppig, is a senior who looks very much like Jesus. He survived the solitary years by not showing emotion. He shows very little emotion now. "I think it was the fact that I couldn't completely control myself that scared me," he says flatly. "I didn't like myself because I didn't have anything. No athletics, no grades. The only thing that kept me going was that I hated them more than I hated myself.

"Before, all I knew was what people were telling me about myself, and it wasn't a positive image, and I wasn't interested in who I was," he continues. "Jujitsu gave me something else that I was, that was better and more believable."

The friendship with Tyler created elbow room. They joined the wrestling team. They formed a band named Gawd. It helps that Tyler's parents encourage his use of their renovated colonial as a social center, and that his dad quit his job as an executive to stay home full time. His parents call the arrangement a luxury, a decision they made around the time when Tyler's mother was promoted to assistant principal of a middle school. Then Tyler had the great good fortune of several growing spurts, which, at last measure, topped six feet to match the hard-earned bulk.

His upbeat personality may defuse hostility, but his physical presence is a moat. A friend who has known Tyler since childhood, who will only give his on-line name, Bladerunner, says: "He is just really nice and he sticks up for people."

Bladerunner, 17, has had his own troubles. A boy he'd met in the hospital after a suicide attempt wanted to beat him up, and for months, the tranquil New Hampshire town became a minefield for him. Bladerunner stopped visiting the park and dreaded school. The restaurant where he washes dishes was the only place he anticipated with some pleasure because his boss treats him "like a person." Otherwise, he met Tyler at the Incubator, a room where students go when they have a free period. They would get passes to the weight-lifting room.

Bladerunner didn't stick with the weights, but it mattered that Tyler encouraged him. Recently, Tyler invited Bladerunner to be a vocalist for Gawd. "I realized I was walking around people on eggshells, because I'm always afraid of what's going to happen to me, or what people are going to think," Bladerunner says. "I am going to try to take what I am afraid of and look it in the face, as much as it might physically hurt."

Even as it helps in the day-to-day of high school, bodily renovation perpetuates the hierarchy. Bulking up—or being near someone who does—just means the pyramid starts lower down. Tyler sees similarities between R. and himself. "He gets respected because he throws his weight around. I get respected because I don't have to." He also recognizes how the pressure to prove his masculinity drove him to objectify girls. "I treated my girlfriends really bad," he says. "I admit it. I was like, Oh, there's a pair of boobs, I'll go stand next to it. I think I'll go talk to it."

Of course, trivializing girls is a most likely result of a pecking order in which girls represent "femininity," the perceived threat to conventional masculinity, the mix of which leaves boys so confused these days. The fear of feminizing boys is embedded in the hierarchy of the social cliques: winner-loser, popular-outcast, boy-girl. "This fear of sissifying boys," says Olga Silverstein, author of "The Courage to Raise Good Men," "I think it's going to be the last prejudice to go."

The danger signs are everywhere, but only if you want to see. Banning trench coats, installing metal detectors and security guards—the quick-fix solutions to the problem of seemingly rampant boy violence—"becomes a weird kind of McCarthyism," says Russell Novotny, a 1999 ConVal graduate. "The only way to get kids not to hurt each other is to get kids not to want to hurt each other," a process he compares to a road. "It's the whole little-step thing. You take a little step and suddenly you are in the woods. How did I get here? We are so far into the woods. For every mile you walk, you have to walk a mile back. You can't look too far ahead or you trip over what's in front of you." Or you look at what's in front of you, a boy like J., and you don't really see him.

J., who doesn't want his name to be used, ranks as a loser. He finds temporary refuge with the burnouts, but his precarious welcome depends upon their mood and whether or not he has weed. His greatest flaw seems to be his willingness to try anything to fit in.

"That kid does whatever you tell him to do," says Josh Guide, a classmate. Past instructions are rumored to include wading knee-high in a running brook, with his sneakers and socks on, fetching sticks. He doesn't fight back when people shake him down for money. He claims to get high when a classmate sells him oregano with chives. He falls off his bicycle when the other boys are done using it and ignores the bleeding, which, during a game of basketball, stains another boy's new Tommy Hilfiger shirt.

"Now I have AIDS," the boy says, disgusted. J.'s distress is so apparent that the boy says, "I'm kidding," but his hostility is clear. This particular afternoon, J., who has ragged black hair and a crumpling smile, opens his mouth as if to speak, but doesn't. He saves his mouth for his teachers.

The week after the shootings in Littleton, Colo., ConVal High School held an assembly about school safety. J. recounts what happened in his class next period. "I said, 'I wish those kids would come over here and blow away the teachers,'" especially an assistant principal, with whom J. had a long history. J. says, "I am always in trouble, every day, for my attitude."

According to J., the classroom teacher said, "I'm kind of concerned about you."

"Nothing to be concerned about," J. replied. "Everyone hates him anyway."

"Do you want to go to the office?" she asked.

"Hell, no," he said. Then she sent him there.

Ordinarily, J. would have been sent home for cursing. He knew the drill. This time, however, he waited for the Peterborough police, who, he says, searched his knapsack and escorted him to the station, where he was charged in juvenile court with disorderly conduct. (ConVal officials cannot comment on J.'s case because he is a juvenile and because it is pending.)

That night, the police appeared at the homes of members of J.'s family with a search warrant and collected handguns and sporting rifles. The next day, news cameras greeted ConVal students in the parking lot. The print media continued the story, and J. became known as a copycat in a wider world. "It's retarded," he says. "I shouldn't have got in trouble. If it was some good kid that did it, they wouldn't have gotten in trouble." Many students feel that the administration overreacted, less because of Columbine than for the fact that even if he had meant what he said, he was an unlikely candidate to carry out that particular kind of plan. Says one parent, sighing, summing up a typical adult response, "That's just J. being J. again."

Being J., according to J., is as inevitable as his difficulty in school, which he compares to his unhappiness in his family life. He says: "I try not to spend much time at home. It's like I'm a failure. My sister is a straight-A student and everything." He doesn't get along with his stepfather. Right now, his relationship with his mother isn't good. "Whenever I get in trouble, she yells at me for 10 minutes, then she stops," J. says. "They yell nonstop, then they forget what they

are yelling for. They don't even punish me. It's like a habit with them."

J. spends his days watching television. In the afternoons, he goes to the nearby basketball court. His mother tracks him down. (She declined to comment for this story.) J. says, "Then she yells at me all the way home, then I fall asleep and get up and do it all over again."

More upsetting to J. than his threat to an assistant principal—and more memorable to many ConVal students—was an event for which he was suspended earlier. He stepped into a bathroom to smoke a joint. It wasn't getting high, or even getting high during school, that was so problematic to the other students, but that he had selected a bathroom without ventilation that led directly into the hall where a teacher stood. J. heard the teacher but still kept smoking. "I just finished cuz I knew I was gonna get caught," he says.

"How stupid can you get?" George asks. "He just proved to everyone that he's the [expletive] everyone thinks he is."

Andrew ventures, "Not to be mean to J., but that's plain old stupid."

Even Tyler, who tried to defend what was left of J.'s eroding reputation, admits: "That was the stupidest thing I ever heard of. I don't even know why I tried to protect that kid."

Drugs—at least temporarily—blur the social lines. Boys and girls from different groups get high together; says George: "Polar opposites—they are bound together by drugs." James Key-Wallace, a 1999 graduate, attributes the social leveling to limited distribution: "The drugs come from the same half-dozen sources. You're going to come in contact on grounds that demand respect." Says Hayden Draper, who also just graduated: "Popular kids do drugs. Unpopular kids do drugs. Everyone has their own place to get high." J., however, was all alone.

Since Columbine, the Safe School Committee at ConVal has undergone a renaissance. The Peterborough police have stationed an officer at the entrance. But many of the students believe that a shooting spree like that of Klebold and Harris's could happen anywhere. Says Toffer: "It certainly didn't happen because of the lack of a safe-school committee. Their problem was, they weren't accepted, and they weren't going to be accepted, and that's the way that our society is. There are always people that are going to be cast out and people that are cast in."

Colleen, George's ex, a slim girl with short straight hair and an easy smile, grew up down the street from J. He's generally annoying, she says. He used to sing Christmas carols on the bus in June, but he is not cruel. Everyone, she says, has their days. What J. hates is people talking down to him, so she takes care not to do that. She feels the same way when people talk down to her because she is a girl. "There are times I can talk to him about things, without it being weird and without him being a pervert," she says. It's all relative. When you are close to the bottom, there's not much room left to fit. She recalls J. at his happiest during a class he described to her, in the high school's on-site preschool, how content he felt playing among the little kids.

Youth Violence

In the first two sections of this text, we have presented a variety of disciplinary and interdisciplinary conceptualizations of the etiology of violence as well as multiple perspectives regarding the construction of masculinities, femininities, and the "Other." Those two sections lay the foundation for our present exploration into how issues of violence and gender are related to a variety of contemporary topics, including youth violence, the subject of this third section. While youth violence is a topic that can be quite broadly defined, we have chosen to concentrate on two distinct areas of inquiry—gangs and school violence. We have chosen these two areas for concentrated study because much of the media coverage around youth violence centers around gangs and school violence; thus, it is important for us to examine these phenomena critically and to form our own judgments about them. Moreover, it is imperative to consider the role of gender in these violent incidents by youth, since mainstream media seldom highlight this component of the problem.

This section begins with a book chapter, written by psychologists Daniel J. Flannery, C. Ronald Huff, and Michael Manos, that provides a developmental perspective on youth gangs. Providing this framework for understanding what gangs are and why adolescents become gang members is valuable because an understanding of developmental issues can better inform our prevention and intervention efforts. After all, as the authors note, there is not one standardized, commonly accepted definition of a gang. Typical characteristics, however, include a formal organizational structure, identified leaders and positions of leadership, a territory or turf, and members who interact with each other relatively frequently and who sometimes engage in criminal and/or delinquent behavior. In other words, gangs, by most of the above criteria, are simply another adolescent group. Do most people unfairly— or accurately—view gangs as dangerous groups, with a specific gang style in the use of gang symbols such as clothing, tattoos, and graffiti (Miller, 1995)? What are some of the reasons why youth, both boys and girls, join gangs? What are the risk factors at the individual, family, peer, and community-levels that are associated with delinquency, violence, and gang activity in adolescence? How does gang membership place young boys and girls at risk for a variety of negative outcomes? Only when we understand the risk factors and outcomes associated with gang involvement and activity can we begin to consider the needs of youth and design effective programs that aim both to help those who are engaged in gang activity cease their involvement and to prevent them from initially becoming involved.

The second selection in this section also provides an overview about who joins gangs so that readers can compare and contrast this research with the images and stereotypes that they may have previously held. The chapter by the sociologist Irving Spergel titled, "Gang Member Demographics and Gang Subcultures," taken from his book, *The Youth Gang Problem: A Community Approach*, is an overview about how factors such as age, sex, race, ethnicity, and class are related to gang membership, subcultures, and social contexts. In particular, it is valuable to consider young girls and women as gang members. Spergel asserts that "the youth gang problem in its violent character is essentially a male problem" (p. 58). Considering both of these opening selections, we ask that you think about females as gang members and gang offenders. Do only "bad girls" who flaunt their sexuality join gangs, while "good girls" reject gang culture (Campbell, 1991)? Are female gang members increasingly involved in serious gang violence or not? If not, why do the media portray them as such? It is also important to consider the roles of race, ethnicity, and class. Are the community-level risk factors cited in the chapter written by Flannery and his colleagues supported by the information presented about gang membership, subcultures, and social contexts? Spergel also raises concerns about how white delinquents are less likely to be stereotyped, labeled, and feared as gang members than ethnic minority youth. How does this fact play into some of the theories of violence as introduced in the first section and into the social construction of the "Other," as studied in Section II of the book?

The next article in this section shifts from describing gang member demographics, risk factors, and subcultures to thinking more concretely about solutions that have been put forward to address the problem of youth gangs and specifically their violent behavior. One of the biggest public policy debates, particularly after the 1999 school shootings at Columbine High School in Littleton, Colorado, has been over gun control. While we will address the issue of gun control more comprehensively in the final section of this book, the next selection, "Kids, Guns, and Violence: Conclusions and Implications," introduces some key concepts that will lay the foundation for our later study. This chapter by the sociologists, Joseph Sheley and James Wright, is taken from their book, *In the Line of Fire: Youth, Guns, and Violence in Urban America*. Specifically, it examines whether attempting to regulate the flow of guns to youth is a viable approach to reducing youth violence, or whether society should, rather, be addressing the conditions that contribute to gun-related behaviors—reminding us, once again, of some of the fundamental theories of violence presented in the first section of this book. In order to answer these questions, Sheley and Wright interviewed both criminally active juveniles currently incarcerated in state detention facilities and inner-city youth in ten urban cities. As you consider their arguments, think about their research participants. Does the choice of whom they interviewed impact how you view their findings and in what ways? The answers to questions about how best to provide a sense of an attainable future for our youth are complex and vary according to one's philosophical and moral positions. We urge you to consider your beliefs and positions carefully as we move toward the end of the readings on youth gangs.

The final reading pertaining to youth gangs is a poem, "Race Politics," by Luis Rodriguez. As you read the poem, think about the intentions of the young brothers. What are the barriers with which they are faced? In what ways do you observe socially constructed notions of masculinity influencing their decisions and behavior? What connections to Sheley and Wright and to the other articles can you make?

We shall now shift our focus from youth gangs to school violence. While there is some overlap between these two topics, clearly not all incidents of school violence involve members of gangs, and not all incidents of gang violence occur on school property. The first selection on this topic is a report by the U.S. Departments of Education and Justice that presents an overview of the extent to which students across the country experience violent crime or theft of their property at school. Moreover, the report highlights changes between 1989 and 1995. One of the most promising findings of the report is that there has been little or no change in the percentage of students reporting *any* victimization at school or *property* victimization at school between these years. Unfortunately, there was an increase in the percentage of students reporting *violent* victimization at school. This finding is quite disturbing given current students' fears about experiencing violence in their schools. The report also presents students' perceptions about the presence of guns, drugs, and street gangs at their schools. As you read the research report, consider what it suggests about any sex-related trends. What age differences were found; in other words, who is more likely to experience violent victimization at school? What were the findings across different ethnicities and household incomes? These questions are important to consider as we reflect on the school violence that has been given the most visible media attention—those school shootings that have occurred in predominantly white, middle-class, suburban neighborhoods.

Related to this issue is the next article, entitled "Supremacy Crimes," written by the feminist journalist and co-founder of *Ms* magazine, Gloria Steinem, soon after the school shootings that took place at Columbine High School. Steinem's thesis is that "senseless killings" in the United States—which includes serial murders, hate crimes, and the recently covered school shootings—are disproportionately committed by white, non-poor males who are "hooked on the drug of superiority" (p. 46). She defines this drug as one which naturalizes and codifies a male-dominant, overly materialistic, and homophobic culture that falsely elevates whiteness. As you reflect on her argument, you might think about why the vast majority of school shootings are perpetrated by boys and why the media coverage has not acknowledged that youth violence is primarily a male phenomenon? Steinem also provides ideas about how to reduce the number of violent Americans and how to change our violent culture in the raising of children. We ask that you consider what you might add to or take away from the list that she provides. Are we, for example, raising children in a consumer culture in which they are promised a high level of agency (e.g., active power) and autonomy and yet actually experience far less?

Steinem implies that when this violence has occurred in communities of color, it has hardly been described in the media as a national tragedy. This bias is the principal focus of Tonya Maria Matthews' poem, "I Prayed for More Gun Control and Got Better Background Checks." The poem also explores how prejudice, stereotyping, and ignorance misinform our views of who is dangerous and who is not (refer back to the section on the "Other" and to Spergel on gang demographics), as well as how the media shape our beliefs and attitudes—a topic we cover later in this book.

In reading the selections in this section, think about possible links to the two previous sections of this book. How might our constructions of masculinities, femininities, and the "Other" influence who joins gangs and what types of criminal offenses are committed by gang members? Is there a relationship between the rise of white gangs, the construction of the "Other" or of an enemy, and incidents of hate crimes as discussed in Section II? What support is there in the readings presented here for different theories of violence?

REFERENCES

CAMPBELL, A. (1991). The praised and the damned. In *The Girls in the Gang* (pp. 4–32). New York: Basil Blackwell.
MILLER, J. (1995). Struggles over the symbolic: Gang style and the meanings of social control. In J. Ferrell & C. R. Sanders (Eds.), *Cultural Criminology* (pp. 213–234). Boston: Northeastern University Press.

Youth Gangs

A developmental perspective

Daniel J. Flannery
C. Ronald Huff
Michael Manos

1998

Adolescence as a developmental period is characterized by significant changes and transformations in family and peer relationships (Montemayor & Flannery, 1990; Paikoff & Brooks-Gunn, 1991; Steinberg, 1989). Peers often gain influence during adolescence, usually at the expense of parents. Youth seek out more time with their peers and report a high degree of satisfaction from their peer relations (Larson & Richards, 1989). For some youth, spending time with peers has a positive influence on socialization, providing opportunities to become more involved in community organizations and activities like Boy Scouts, school band, athletics, or church activities. For others, spending time with peers becomes a mechanism for opportunity to engage in deviant behavior such as truancy, substance use, theft, or assault (Gottfredson & Hirschi, 1990).

For better or worse, peers are an important influence in adolescence, affecting development in multiple domains. The purpose of this chapter is to provide an overview of one specific form of peer group relationship, the youth gang, and to provide a developmental framework for understanding what gangs are, why adolescents in particular may become gang members, and how developmental issues can inform prevention and intervention efforts. We begin by providing a general definition of gangs. This is followed by a discussion of different kinds of gang activity, including recent data on the role of drugs in gangs. We then examine gangs from a developmental perspective, focusing on reasons why some kids may join gangs (including risk factors), the developmental needs that gangs may meet for some youth, and the role of parents and families in gang activity. Where pertinent, we discuss the role of gender and ethnicity in gangs and gang-member activity. We also provide a brief overview, within a developmental framework, of factors associated with successful prevention and intervention programs, and we discuss programs that have shown iatrogenic effects. Finally, we review some of the macrosocial or individual factors that appear to preclude youth involvement in prosocial

settings or prohibit attachment to school and other institutions, and why socially appropriate groups have lost their appeal to many youth.

DEFINING GANGS

As Howell (1994) and Klein (1995) state, no accepted standard definition of a gang currently exists. State and local jurisdictions tend to develop their own definition and form policies based on those local criteria. However, several common criteria are typically used to define gangs: (a) There exists a formal organizational structure; (b) the group has an identified leader or leadership hierarchy; (c) the group is usually, but not always, identified with a specific territory or turf; (d) there exists recurrent interaction among the members of the group; and (e) the members of the group engage in delinquent or criminal behavior. The last criterion, participating in delinquent or criminal behavior, is the characteristic that distinguishes gangs from other, more prosocially focused adolescent groups. Curry, Ball, and Fox's (1994) law enforcement survey for 1991 estimated that there were 4,881 gangs in the United States with 249,324 members.

Who belongs to a gang? Gang members typically range in age from 14 to 24, with the peak age of gang membership around age 17, although in some cities the gang members are somewhat older. Evidence exists that children as young as 8 are gang involved or gang "wannabes" (Embry, Flannery, Vazsonyi, Powell, & Atha, 1996; Huff, 1996). To some degree, gang membership depends on where one lives. In established gang cities such as Los Angeles or Chicago, the majority of gang members tend to be adults, whereas in cities reporting recent or emerging gang problems, up to 90% of gang members are estimated to be juveniles. Certainly not every youth is involved in gang activity. Most reports estimate that between 5% and 8% of youth are at high risk for engaging in violent, gang-

172

related activities (Tolan & Guerra, 1994). Although no reliable national data exist, a recent Denver study estimated that 7% of inner-city, high-risk juveniles were gang involved (Esbensen & Huizinga, 1993).

Based on research in Colorado, Florida, and Ohio, Huff (1996) identified a developmental progression from "hanging out" with the gang (being a gang "wannabe") to joining the gang and getting arrested. Gang members responded that they first began associating with the gang at about age 13 and joined, on average, about 6 months later. They were then arrested for the first time at about age 14, 1 year after beginning to associate with a gang and about 6 months after joining. Arrests for property crimes peaked 1 to 2 years before arrests for either drug offenses or violent offenses. Rather than gang membership providing protection, Huff found that a high percentage of gang leaders' declining arrest rates was due to incarceration and homicide. The gang lifestyle places individuals at much higher risk than would normally be expected.

Gangs are also appearing in more and more cities, particularly smaller communities (Maxson & Klein, 1996). Curry et al. (1994) reported that more than 90% of the nation's largest cities report youth gang problems, up from about 50% in 1983. This increase is mostly due to family migration and local gang genesis rather than to relocation, suggesting that gang formation is not due solely to the recruitment of youth to "other city" gangs. Even very young children report exposure to gang activity at school (Embry et al., 1996). In Tucson, 42% of youth in Grades K through 5 reported seeing gang activity at school in a given week (Embry et al., 1996). This trend among young people is of concern because the Tucson data were collected from self-contained elementary schools, limiting the possibility that youth were reporting gang activity of older peers, or, conversely, suggesting that older peers were coming to elementary schools to recruit younger members.

The racial and ethnic composition of gangs is rapidly changing. Until the mid-1900s, the majority of gangs in the United States were white and composed of various European backgrounds. By the 1970s, an estimated 80% of gang members were either African American or Hispanic, and in the past few years, Asian groups have been emerging rapidly. The ethnic composition and social class position of gang members has remained fairly constant, with gangs comprised of recently migrated youth and those of lower socioeconomic status (Howell, 1994; Miller, 1982; Spergel, 1991).

Female gang membership is also increasing (Chesney-Lind, Sheldon, & Joe, 1996), although girls still account for a relatively small percentage of gang-involved youth (3.5% to 6%; Curry et al., 1994). In 1992, 40 cities reported female gangs with an estimated 7,205 members (Curry, Fox, Ball, & Stone, 1992). Historically, the stereotype of girls in gangs and delinquent girls in general was that these girls were either tomboys or sex objects (Campbell, 1990) or a form of male property (Jankowski, 1991). Girls' delinquency was viewed as interpersonal and sexual, whereas boys' offending was viewed as aggressive and more criminal in nature (Chesney-Lind & Sheldon, 1992). Recent data on girls' participation in gangs, their activities, and their motivations for joining are discussed below.

ACTIVITY: WHAT DO GANGS AND GANG MEMBERS DO?

In this section, we provide an overview of gang member activity, including the social role of the gang and the role of firearms and drugs in gangs. Huff (1996) recently completed several studies of current and former gang-involved youth compared to at-risk youth in Cleveland, metropolitan Denver, and south Florida. He used detailed, semistructured, individual interviews conducted by graduate students and youth workers. For the Cleveland sample, Huff found that gang-involved youth were, on average, younger when first arrested (age 14 for gang members vs. never arrested for most nongang members) and had been arrested more often than their at-risk peers (median of three arrests for gang members vs. zero for nongang youth). Gang-involved youth were significantly more likely to have guns or knives in school, carry a concealed weapon, use or sell drugs, and engage in theft and property crimes. These trends also held for comparisons of the collective criminal behavior of gangs and nongang peer groups (Huff, 1996). These results reflect the criminogenic nature of gangs and the powerful socializing influence of the peer group in a gang member's life.

The Social Role of Gangs

Joe and Chesney-Lind's (1995) interviews with gang members in Hawaii show the social role of the gang for young people. They identified two primary mechanisms for group solidarity through gangs, particularly in disorganized and chaotic neighborhoods. First, boredom with lack of resources and high visibility of crime in neglected communities create the conditions for turning to others who are similarly situated, that is, peer groups that offer a social outlet. Second, the stress on families from living in marginalized areas combined with financial struggles create tension and, in many cases, violence at home. Patterson and his colleagues have demonstrated the role of economic stress and violence on disrupted family management practices that lead to school failure and delinquency (Patterson, DeBaryshe, & Ramsey, 1989). In these families, high levels of physical and sexual abuse and assault, particularly among siblings (Finkelhor & Dziuba-Leatherman, 1994), exist. The group or gang, then, is perceived by both girls and boys as providing safe refuge and a surrogate family.

With respect to "normative" adolescent activities, Huff's recent data shed some light on what gang members and nongang members have in common and how they differ (Tables 1 and 2). The only activity that is more common for nongang members is involvement in sporting activities. Although varying proportions of nongang youth engage in these activities, gang members are significantly more likely to "party"; attend musical concerts; "hang out"; "cruise" for the opposite sex; engage in fighting, drinking, drug use, and drug sales; and put up and cross out graffiti. These data illustrate how the activities of youth gang members are in some respects very similar to activities of non-gang-member youth.

Table 2 Comparison of Gang and Nongang Member Criminal Behavior

Crime	Gang (%)	Nongang (%)	p
Shoplifting	30.4	14.3	n.s.(.058)
Check forgery	2.1	0.0	n.s.
Credit card theft	6.4	0.0	n.s.
Auto theft	44.7	4.1	***
Theft (other)	51.1	14.3	***
Sell stolen goods	29.8	10.2	*
Assault rivals	72.3	16.3	***
Assault own members	30.4	10.2	*
Assault police	10.6	14.3	n.s.
Assault teachers	14.9	18.4	n.s.
Assault students	51.1	34.7	n.s.
Mug people	10.6	4.1	n.s.
Assault in streets	29.8	10.2	*
Bribe police	10.6	2.0	n.s.
Burglary (unoccupied)	8.5	0.0	*
Burglary (occupied)	2.1	2.0	n.s.
Guns in school	40.4	10.2	***
Knives in school	38.3	4.2	***
Concealed weapons	78.7	22.4	***
Drug use	27.7	4.1	**
Drug sales (school)	19.1	8.2	n.s.
Drug sales (other)	61.7	16.7	***
Drug theft	21.3	0.0	***
Arson	8.5	0.0	*
Kidnap	4.3	0.0	n.s.
Sexual assault	2.1	0.0	n.s.
Rape	2.1	0.0	n.s.
Robbery	17.0	2.0	*
Intimidate/assault victims or witnesses	34.0	0.0	***
Intimidate/assault shoppers	23.4	6.1	*
Drive-by shooting	40.4	2.0	***
Homicide	15.2	0.0	**

$*p < .05; **p < .01; ***p = .001$; n.s. = not significant.

Table 1 Comparison of Gang and Nongang Member Activities

Activity	Gang (%)	Nongang (%)	p
Dances, parties	89.4	66.0	**
Sports, events	46.7	77.8	**
Concerts	61.7	40.0	*
"Hang out"	100.0	87.5	*
"Cruise"	86.4	54.5	**
Fighting	93.6	20.5	***
Drinking	87.0	31.8	***
Drug use	34.0	7.0	**
Drug sales	72.3	9.1	***
Put up graffiti	95.7	46.9	***
Cross out graffiti	89.1	46.9	***

$*p < .05; **p < .01; ***p < .001.$

Activities of Boys Versus Girls

Recent analyses of arrest patterns have shown consistently that for boys suspected of gang activity, the most common arrest was "other assaults," mostly fighting with other males (Federal Bureau of Investigation, 1994). Boys also report engaging in frequent drinking, cruising, and looking for trouble (Huff, 1996). Female suspected gang members tend to be chronic, but not serious, offenders who are arrested most commonly for larceny theft, followed by status offenses such as running away. Serious violent offenses (murder, sexual assault, robbery, and aggravated assault) accounted for 23% of the most serious offenses of boys suspected of gang membership, but none of the girls' most serious offenses. Girls are three times more likely than boys to be involved in "property offenses," an important consideration given Huff's (1996) recent findings that property offenses are often a major precursor of more serious gang activity. In jurisdictions that track female gang activity, girls accounted for 13.6% of gang-related property offenses, 12.7% of the drug crimes, but only 3.3% of the crimes of violence (Curry et al., 1994). Joe and Chesney-Lind (1995) report that, if anything, the presence of girls in a gang tends to depress the occurrence of violence. They quote one 14-year-old Filipino boy: "If we not with the girls, we fighting. If we not fighting, we with the girls" (Joe & Chesney-Lind, 1995, p. 424).

In 1994, girls accounted for about 25% of all arrests of youth in the United States (Federal Bureau of Investigation, 1995). As with boys, arrests of girls for violent crimes have increased steadily and significantly in the past decade. From 1985 to 1994, arrests of girls for murder were up 64%, robbery arrests were up 114%, and aggravated assault arrests were up 136%. Similar to males, however, serious crimes of violence represent a small proportion of all girls' delinquency: 2.3% in 1984 and 3.4% in 1993. Girls are more likely to fight with a parent or sibling, for example, whereas boys are more likely to fight with friends or strangers.

For girls, fighting and violence are part of their life in the gang but not necessarily something they seek out. In qualitative interviews, girls consistently mention protection from neighborhood and family violence as major reasons why they join gangs (Chesney-Lind et al., 1996). Chesney-Lind and her colleagues assert that, in general, female gang activity is not an expression of "liberation," nor are female gang members the hyperviolent, amoral individuals portrayed in popular media accounts. Rather, gang membership reflects the attempts of young women to cope with a bleak and harsh present as well as a dismal future. This sense of hopelessness about the future and need to cope with the here and now permeate both male and female gang activity and youths' motivations for membership.

Use of Firearms

Gangs and gang members are engaging in more violent offenses, experiencing more serious injuries, and using more lethal weapons in the commission of delinquent and criminal acts. Sheley and Wright (1993) recently surveyed male incarcerated offenders and males in 10 inner-city high schools about their use of and access to firearms. Although their findings cannot be generalized to other populations, they were somewhat sobering. Approximately 83% of inmates (average age 17) and 22% of students said that they possessed guns, and more than half of the inmates said that they had carried guns all or most of the time in the year or two before being incarcerated. This compared to 12% of high school students who reported regularly carrying guns to school; nearly one in four reported that they did so "now and then." Perhaps even more disconcerting was the ease with which both incarcerated and high school males reported they could acquire a gun. Only 13% of inmates and 35% of high school males said they would have a lot of trouble getting a gun; nearly half of all respondents indicated that they would "borrow" one from family or friends, more than those who said they would get one "off the street" (54% of inmates and 37% of students). The most frequently endorsed reason for owning or carrying a gun was self-protection. These inner-city youth were convinced they were not safe in their neighborhoods and their schools.

Although not a primary focus of their study, Sheley and Wright (1993) identified members of the incarcerated and student cohorts who reported being in quasi-gangs, unstructured gangs, and structured gangs. Especially for the inmates but to some extent for students, moving from nongang member to gang member was associated with increased frequency of possessing and carrying guns. For members of both structured and unstructured gangs, the most commonly owned weapon was a revolver. Ownership of military-style weapons among gang-affiliated inmates was high, averaging 53% across gang types. In the street environment inhabited by these juvenile offenders, owning and carrying guns were virtually universal behaviors (Sheley & Wright, 1993). Furthermore, the inmate respondents reported that they regularly experienced both threats of violence and violence itself. A total of 84% reported that they had been threatened with a gun or shot at during their lives; 45% of the student sample reported being threatened or shot at on the way to or from school. The researchers also found that firearms were a common element in the drug business; 89% of inmates and 75% of students who dealt drugs carried guns regularly.

Drug Use and Gang Activity

Recent research has demonstrated that although some gang members are involved in the distribution and sale of drugs, and although some gangs have evolved specifically for the purpose of drug distribution, drug trafficking is not a primary gang activity (Klein, Maxson, & Cunningham, 1991; Huff, 1996). Furthermore, most of the homicides involving gang members are over turf battles, not drug violence. In a study conducted in two smaller cities outside Los Angeles, Klein et al. (1991) found that gang members were involved in about 17% of arrests for cocaine sales and about 12% of arrests connected to other drug sales. Firearms were involved in only about 10% of the cases, and violence was present in only about 5% of the incidents. Block and Block's (1994) Chicago study of the city's four largest and most criminally active street gangs found only 8 out of 285 gang-motivated homicides between 1987 and 1990 to be related to drugs. Approximately 90% of violent crimes, including homicides, involving youth gangs in the Boston area between 1984 and 1994 were unrelated to drug dealing or drug use.

Drugs and Firearms

The combination of drugs and firearms appears to contribute a great deal to both the contextual and situational determinants of violence and gang activity. Youth involved in gangs who carry weapons for self-protection and status seeking and who also may be involved with drugs are at high risk for violence. These youth are often impulsive and frequently lack the cognitive problem-solving skills to settle disputes calmly. Fistfights turn into more lethal confrontations because guns are present. This "sequence" can be exacerbated by the socialization problems (e.g., poor parental monitoring) associated with extreme poverty, the high proportion of single-parent households, educational failures, and the pervasive sense of hopelessness about one's life and economic situation (Blumstein, 1995). The number of murders by adolescents, gun-related homicides by 10- to 17-year-old offenders, the homicide arrest rates for 14- to 17-year-old males, and the number of drug arrests have all increased significantly in the past decade.

Huff (1995, 1996) found a significant disparity in profit from drug selling between gang and nongang youth. The typical gang member was much more likely than his at-risk peers to be selling drugs, usually on a daily basis. At-risk youth who sold drugs also did so on a daily basis. However, gang members reported, on average, nearly 50% more in earnings per week ($1,000 vs. $675) with far fewer customers (30 vs. 80 per week). Thus, the average earnings per transaction for gang members was $33.33 compared to $8.44 for nongang/at-risk youth. Gang membership has high potential for profit making and presents an additional motivation for remaining in a gang.

Wilkinson and Fagan (1996; Fagan, 1996), using detailed individual interviews with incarcerated and at-risk youth, have found alcohol to be present in nearly 40% of violent incidents, with subjects reporting that the use of alcohol prior to conflict increased the chances of the conflict being handled violently. Respondents also characterized violent events as "shocking" life experiences, where alcohol "juiced up" a seemingly harmless situation into a physical assault. Furthermore, problematic alcohol use predicted involvement in violent behaviors for both males and females, regardless of gang involvement (Fagan, 1990).

In addition to alcohol use, other situational factors significantly affect the onset, escalation, desistance, and injury outcomes of assaults (Sampson & Lauritsen, 1993). Third parties, for example, are important to how a situation is handled. In Fagan's (1996) recent work, individuals explained how disputes that could have been "squashed" or "deaded" were continued by third parties who would provoke combatants with comments like "don't let him play you like that," appealing to courage, respect, and power as reasons to fight back. Even if events were squashed one day, disputes were often continued at school or in the neighborhood at a later time.

DEVELOPMENTAL PERSPECTIVE

A developmental perspective of youth gangs needs to ground itself in understanding what is normal for children and adolescents as a framework for understanding how normal development may have gone "awry." Recent advances in research on adolescent violence show promise in this regard. Specifically, the study of individual risk factors has focused recently on understanding the cognitive underpinnings of antisocial behavior (e.g., attitudes, beliefs, and information-processing skills; Kendall & Hollon, 1979) and has moved from a dependence on static, simplistic definitions of outcome to an articulation of the sequence of behaviors that mark increasing risk for chronic and serious antisocial behavior (Loeber & Hay, 1994). An emphasis on how developmental sequences are altered rather than a focus on changing static behavioral outcomes has helped advance our thinking about prevention and intervention (Kellam & Rebok, 1992). Furthermore, there has been a growing recognition of the impact of context on individual risk (Tolan & Loeber, 1993), particularly with emphases on family factors in the etiology of antisocial behavior and how family factors interact with and unfold in specific cultural and community contexts (Henggeler & Borduin, 1990).

There are many developmental tasks and transformations for adolescents that may influence whether a young person joins a gang. For most youth, delinquent and violent behavior does not suddenly emerge in adolescence. Although risk for gang membership is multifactored, multifaceted, and complex in its etiology, there are several factors that exert a great deal of influence on determining who is at highest risk for gang involvement. We briefly review some of the risk factors at the individual, family, and neighborhood levels. Individual risk includes exposure to and victimization from violence. Under family risk, we include a discussion of peer group influence. Macrosocial risk factors are also examined. Gang membership and gang-related violence are strongly associated with local economic, school, and peer group factors that need to be taken into account (Klein, 1995; Spergel, 1991, 1995). Several excellent reviews of risk for youth violence and delinquency are available (Earls, 1994; Fraser, 1996; Reiss & Roth, 1993; Yoshikawa, 1994).

Individual-Level Risk Factors

At the individual level, those youth who exhibit an antisocial personality at an early age are most at risk for becoming delinquent adolescents and antisocial adults (Elliott, 1994; Farrington et al., 1993). Aggressive behavior in kindergarten and first grade is an important predictor of delinquency in adolescence (Huesmann, Eron, Leftkowitz, & Walder, 1984; Tremblay, Masse, Leblanc, Schwartzman, & Ledingham, 1992), and, in one longitudinal study, this relationship persisted until the age of 30 (Eron & Huesmann, 1990). A child's early aggressive behavior interacts

with family factors to place young children at high risk for delinquency and gang membership. Children who have histories of coercive, intimidating social relations from a very early age experience limited social opportunities with other children and adults (Kupersmidt & Coie, 1990). Of course, not all aggressive children end up becoming delinquent or gang-involved adolescents (Tolan, Guerra, & Kendall, 1995).

Young children who suffer from a combination of a mood disorder (e.g., major depression, bipolar disorder), conduct disorder, and associated attention deficit hyperactivity disorder are at particularly high risk for criminal offending, school failure, and incarceration as adolescents and young adults (Farrington, 1991; Loeber, 1982). In the longitudinal studies that have followed young children through adolescence and into adulthood, low verbal intelligence has been shown to be the best predictor of aggressive behavior at age 8 (as rated by both teachers and parents), delinquent behavior in adolescence, and violent criminal offending in late adolescence (Huesmann et al., 1984). The effects of IQ on later delinquency remain even after controlling for the effects of socioeconomic status on delinquent behavior. There is also growing evidence of prenatal factors being associated with adolescent delinquency. Low birth weight, being small for gestational age, and anoxia at birth have all been associated with adolescent delinquency and violence (Kandel & Mednick, 1991).

One cannot discuss gangs from an individual developmental perspective without mentioning the significant link between exposure to violence, victimization from violence, and risk for violence perpetration (Martinez & Richters, 1993; Richters & Martinez, 1993), particularly among African American youth (DuRant, Cadenhead, Pendergrast, Slaven, & Linder, 1994; Fitzpatrick & Boldizar, 1993). The developmental impact of chronic exposure to violence and victimization by violence can be significant for children and adolescents (Flannery et al., 1996). In general, males are more likely than females to be victims of assault and violence and to witness violent acts. Furthermore, symptoms of posttraumatic stress are commonly reported among children and adolescents exposed to violence (Bell & Jenkins, 1991; Garbarino, Durbrow, Kostelny, & Pardo, 1992; Singer, Anglin, Song, & Lunghofer, 1995).

Family conflict and assault also have been linked to increases in interpersonal assaultive behavior among youth. Sibling assault is one of the most commonly reported forms of youth victimization (Finkelhor & Dziuba-Leatherman, 1994). Coupled with high family conflict and poor parental management, violence between siblings creates a home environment with high potential for child victimization and exposure to violence, and for learning interaction styles that lead to further violent behavior (Cicchetti & Lynch, 1993). Other family factors related to victimization and violent youth behavior include poor parental monitoring (Patterson et al., 1989; Steinberg, 1987) and accessibility of firearms in the home (Ropp, Visintainer, Uman, & Treloar, 1992).

Research over the past few years has shown consistently that intentional injury victimization increases one's risk of subsequently perpetrating violence. Prothrow-Stith (1995), in her book *Deadly Consequences*, discusses her experience as a young emergency department physician in Boston. She was often faced with young patients who told her that the person who injured them would soon be at the hospital for treatment of his own injuries, usually involving the use of firearms. The consensus is that advances in emergency medical care keep the homicide rates among young people from skyrocketing beyond their already epidemic proportions.

Several theories have been advanced about why individuals sometimes alternate between the role of offender and victim. Singer (1981) argues that victims of crime may become offenders because of norms that justify retaliation. Conversely, offenders may become victims because they hold values that support the initiation of violence to resolve disputes (i.e., "victim precipitation"). Sparks (1982) suggested that offenders make ideal victims because they are likely to be viewed by other offenders as vulnerable targets who are unlikely to call police, as compared to nonoffender victims. Gottfredson (1984) supported the victimogenic potential of offending by showing the relationship between victimization and self-reported criminal behavior.

In their most recent work, Rivara, Shepherd, Farrington, Richmond, and Cannon (1995) examined criminal records of males ages 10 to 24 treated for injuries in emergency departments compared to males treated for unintentional injury. They found that assault patients were significantly more likely in the past to have been formally warned or convicted of a violent crime. In addition, they found that differences between injury groups was most pronounced for males 10 to 16 years old, who had significantly different and less extensive criminal histories than did their older counterparts. Rivara et al. (1995) did find, however, that all of their 10- to 16-year-old offenders had convictions in the year following treatment of an injury. This showed that the incident in which they were injured did not deter them from further criminal activity and supports the risk for an intentional injury victim subsequently perpetrating violence and assault against others.

The relationship between victimization and assault perpetration is particularly salient for gang-involved youth. Huff (1996) found that gang-involved youth in Cleveland were significantly more likely to assault rivals (72% vs. 16%) and to be victims of assault (34% vs. 0%) than were their nongang peers. Furthermore, gang members were more likely to be assaulted by other members of their own gangs than their at-risk peers were of being assaulted by their peers. The notion that gang membership somehow protects a member from being victimized by violence or from perpetrating assault against others is a dangerous falsehood for young people to endorse. Sanchez-Jankowski (1991) showed that the longer a gang remains viable, the greater the potential for criminal victimization to occur for its members. Savitz, Rosen, and Lalli (1982) also found that membership in a fighting gang was related to increased chances of victimization. Finally, it should be noted that Huff's interviews in Cleveland, south Florida, and Denver consistently revealed that youth are far more likely to be assaulted if they join a gang (as part of the initiation and thereafter) than if they politely refuse to join (Huff, 1995, 1996).

Family-Level and Peer-Related Risk

Patterson and his colleagues have a model of early versus late starters in delinquent activity that incorporates child antisocial behavior as a precursor to early childhood behavior problems and poor parent management. These lead to school failure and rejection by peers, precursors of adolescent delinquency and violence. According to Patterson and Yoerger (1993), there exist two primary routes to delinquency, each with a different set of determinants and long-term outcomes. The critical determinant is age at first arrest. If a child is arrested prior to age 14, he or she is considered an early starter. If arrested after the age of 14, the child is considered to be a late starter. The primary assumptions of both models is that disrupted parenting practices directly determine a child's antisocial behavior, and that these, in turn, place a child at risk for early arrest (Patterson et al., 1989). Second, it is assumed that the majority of adult criminal offenders are early starters. This latter assumption is consistent with the evidence for the chronicity and stability of aggressive, violent behavior shown across longitudinal studies (Eron & Huesmann, 1990; Farrington, 1991; Patterson, Reid, & Dishion, 1992).

Several other findings and assumptions that underlie their coercion model are important to mention. First is the assumption that, as the frequency of antisocial behavior increases, the severity shifts from the trivial to more severe acts (Patterson & Bank, 1989). Second, Patterson and colleagues have found that parents of antisocial children are noncontingent in many of their interactions with their children. They are essentially ineffective disciplinarians who punish frequently, inconsistently, and ineffectively, and they tend to ignore or fail to reinforce prosocial behaviors. Patterson et al.'s model focuses on five parenting constructs shown to be important predictors of antisocial and delinquent child behavior: discipline, monitoring, family problem solving, involvement, and positive reinforcement (Patterson et al., 1992).

Their program of research has demonstrated how child antisocial behaviors directly determine school failure, rejection by peers, and involvement with deviant peers and indirectly determine depressed mood and substance use. All of these factors place youth at greater risk for gang involvement. In the coercion model, child antisocial behavior is viewed as merely the first step in a long-term dynamic process resulting in adolescent delinquency and adult antisocial behavior. What is crucial, from a developmental perspective, is understanding that early childhood behavior is the marker for who is at risk for early adolescent gang involvement and for participation in the aggressive, criminal, and violent behavior characteristic of many gang-involved youth.

The influence of peers on gang involvement and activity is significant. Goldstein (1991) asserts that establishing a stable sense of identity and striving for peer acceptance are two central features of adolescent development fostered by gang involvement. Contacts with deviant peers are readily available to most adolescents. Cairns and Cairns (1991) showed that most adolescents develop support networks of some kind. For most adolescents, the peer group provides at least one of those social networks. For some adolescents, the gang becomes the primary support network, made up mostly of other deviant peers and rejected youth who are not attached to school or home, and who live in families where parents are not interested in or are unable to monitor effectively who they are with and what they are doing. In their struggle to establish an identity, the gang can provide a context for establishing a system of values, beliefs, and goals.

Physical, emotional, cognitive, and social developmental tasks merge during early and middle adolescence, forcing young people to cope with many issues, expectations, and responsibilities that they may not yet be capable of handling on their own. For gang-involved youth, it is the peer group that provides both girls and boys with a safe refuge and a surrogate family. Patterson and others have shown that the most antisocial youth are those most committed to a deviant peer group. Being relatively free from adult supervision and free from any attachment to school, religion, or family, hanging out with other rejected youth provides a great deal of opportunity to engage in delinquent activity (Gottfredson & Hirschi, 1990; O'Donnell, Hawkins, & Abbott, 1995). The sooner the antisocial child is out on the streets, the more exposed he or she is to higher levels of antisocial behavior and violence and the more opportunities he or she has to perpetrate criminal acts.

Macrosocial/Community-Level Risk

Several macrosocial or community-level factors contribute to gang membership, gang activity, crime rates, and violence. Examples of macrolevel risk factors include neighborhood resident mobility, levels of disorganization, population density, heterogeneity, unemployment, and income inequality (e.g., the spatial proximity of middle class and poor). Each of these has been related to higher levels of gang activity, crime, and violence (Coulton, Korbin, & Su, in press; Sampson & Lauritsen, 1993). A major dimension of social disorganization relevant to violence is the ability of a community to supervise and control teenage peer groups, particularly gangs (Sampson & Groves, 1989). There is much evidence that adolescent delinquency is most often a group activity, and thus the capacity of the community to control group-level dynamics is a key theoretical mechanism linking community characteristics with crime and gang activity (Sampson & Lauritsen, 1993).

Skogan (1986) reviews some of the "feedback" processes that may further increase levels of crime and gang activity in a community. These include (a) physical and psychological withdrawal from community life, (b) weakening of the informal social control processes that inhibit crime, (c) a decline in the organizational life and mobilization capacity of the neighborhood, (d) deteriorating business conditions, (e) the importation and domestic production of delinquency and deviance, and (f) further dramatic changes in the composition of the population. So, if people shun their neighbors and withdraw from their community, there will be fewer opportunities to form friendship networks that may help provide appropriate adult supervision of youth group activity (Sampson & Lauritsen, 1993).

IMPLICATIONS FOR ADOLESCENT DEVELOPMENT

During adolescence, multiple developmental tasks converge to make this an important time for gang activity and involvement. Gangs can be an attractive alternative to an at-risk youth struggling to fulfill unmet needs and resolve emerging developmental issues. Gang membership jeopardizes adolescent psychosocial development in general and particularly threatens the adequate resolution of primary adolescent developmental tasks, including achieving effective relations with peers of both genders, achieving a masculine or feminine social role, achieving an appropriate body image and becoming competent in using the body, achieving emotional autonomy, preparation for marriage and family life, preparing for an economic career, developing a value-based ideology, and aspiring to participate responsibly in the community (Straus, 1994). Gang membership, which may substitute for an adolescent's desire to be a member of an accepting and supportive social network, cannot replace the support and adequate supervision that a parent can provide. Furthermore, membership in a social network that tolerates and approves of violence is a strong predictor of violent behavior (Callahan & Rivara, 1992; Webster, Gainer, & Champion, 1994). This is a particular irony for those youth who initially join a gang for

protection. Females who join a gang for protection from abusive parents have, in most cases, simply placed themselves at greater risk (although perhaps different) for sexual and physical victimization (Portillas & Zatz, 1995). Because victimization leads to an increased risk for perpetrating violence, the attainment of any "normative" developmental tasks in adolescence is problematic at best.

Gang membership places young people at risk for a variety of negative outcomes. Gang membership is highly associated with earlier onset of delinquency and victimization from violence (Widom, 1989). For both genders, gang involvement has been associated with earlier onset of sexual intercourse, unsafe sex, and early pregnancy or the fathering of a child (Morris et al., 1996). Gang members also more frequently report suicidal ideation and suicide attempts, often involving heavy substance abuse.

Recently, researchers have begun to specifically examine outcomes for gang-involved females. Moore and Hagedorn (1996) assert that no matter what the cultural context, and no matter what the economic opportunity structure, there appears to be one constant in the later life of women in gangs. Most of them have children, and children have more effect on women's lives than on men's. For women, but rarely for men, the new responsibilities associated with child rearing may speed up the process of maturing out of the gang. As Chesney-Lind and Brown (in press) point out, in an environment of extreme poverty and deprivation, developmental tasks are subordinate to the imperatives of short-term survival on the streets. There is little hope for the future, especially for females in this environment: Recent data suggest that the future awaiting gang girls is bleak indeed; 94% will go on to have children, and 84% will raise them without spouses. One third of them will be arrested, and the vast majority will be dependent on welfare (Campbell, 1990).

PREVENTION AND INTERVENTION

As the developmental and criminological literature illustrates, child aggressive, antisocial behavior is highly predictive of adolescent delinquency, violence, and gang involvement. To systematically prevent adolescent gang activity, we endorse a primary prevention approach with the goal of reducing child aggressive and antisocial behavior (Tolan et al., 1995). By the early elementary school years, aggression is predictive of later aggressive and antisocial behavior. This suggests that interventions should begin by the first grade, especially given the significant increase in aggression between the first and second grades (Tremblay, Kurtz, Masse, Vitaro, & Phil, 1995). It is important to note, however, that postintervention aggression scores are typically lower than developmentally expected increases and not lower than preintervention scores. Similar results were found for high-risk K through 5 children in Tucson (Flannery et al., 1996). These findings for aggression highlight the need to use normative developmental information as a measuring stick for intervention effectiveness (Kendall & Grove, 1988).

Tolan et al. (1995) point out that even among aggressive children, less than half continue to engage in high rates of aggressive behavior, and relatively few go on to escalate their involvement in serious antisocial behavior. We need to identify multiple-risk pathways that may contain different combinations of risk factors or may be differentiated by the relative influence of risk factors common to pathways. Especially needed are studies of how intervention components affect the risk of children who differ by gender, ethnicity, socioeconomic status, and other major demographic markers. Evidence also exists for the significant influence of social-cognitive factors on delinquency and violence and their legitimacy as a focus of intervention efforts. The work of Dodge (Crick & Dodge, 1994) and of Guerra and her colleagues (Guerra, Huesmann, & Hanish, 1994; Guerra, Huesmann, Tolan, Acker, & Eron, 1995) demonstrates the link between attributional bias, social information-processing skills, and individual beliefs with aggressive and antisocial behavior. Each of these is a potentially modifiable skill through preventive interventions. For example, Guerra et al. (1995) reported that normative beliefs supporting the legitimacy of aggression predict aggression during elementary school, and O'Donnell et al. (1995) showed that attitudes toward substance use and aggression predicted involvement in both behaviors for adolescents. Family variables, particularly communication skills and management practices, are also increasingly the focus of both prevention efforts with young children and interventions with adolescents (Dishion & Andrews, 1995).

The influence of peers has been a major focus of this chapter. Given the impact of association with anti-social peers, peer rejection, and the support network provided by peers in a gang, peer relations has become a major focus of prevention and intervention efforts. Successful interventions are not merely exercises in teaching youth to cope with peer pressure to engage in antisocial acts. Lack of effective social skills and social problem solving are critical elements in the escalation of minor conflicts into serious altercations (Dodge, 1993). The tendency of delinquent youth to interpret ambiguous or neutral events as reflective of hostile intent is problematic in the classroom, at home, and on the streets. Many gang-involved youth speak about the necessity of retaliation for being "disrespected" or "dissed" because of how someone else looked at them or their girlfriend, for example.

One of the dangers of peer-focused interventions is attempting to conduct group therapy with all antisocial youth. A social network effect was described by O'Donnell, Manos, and Chesney-Lind (1987) in programs such as the Juvenile Awareness Project at Rahway State Prison in New Jersey and the Group Guidance Project (Klein, 1971). These programs were associated with an increase in delinquency, gang membership, and cohesiveness of gangs because they brought fringe members into contact with active gang members who recruited them. Activities of programs that promote prosocial affiliation or disrupt existing affiliations do so by creating opportunities for youth to participate meaningfully within different networks. The Ladino Hills Project (Klein, 1971), for example, offered employment as an alternative to gang membership. Although the number of offenses per gang member did not change, follow-up data indicated decreases in gang membership, gang cohesiveness, and in the total number of gang offenses. In a sense, interventions with a focus on social networks emphasize forming more gangs. But these gangs are of a different nature. Developing prosocial networks that bring youth into contact with others who can provide what the gang provides holds promise for prevention efforts and takes advantage of a developmental task that is a powerful influence in the lives of children and youth. It is imperative that prosocial peers be included in group settings for long-term gain (Tremblay et al., 1995). Moreover, Goldstein and Glick (1994) report some success in implementing aggression replacement training with New York City gangs.

But even programs that alter social networks are likely to be ineffective if they do no more than attempt to control behavior or translate competitive entrepreneurial initiative (e.g., drug trafficking) into low-level job opportunities (Jankowski, 1991). A pervasive sense of hopelessness about the future in a prosocial world drives many youth to seek the power and opportunity that gang membership affords. A young person with low bonding to school and family, with unlikely access to higher education, with fewer opportunities to enter the legal labor market, and with little likelihood of being socioeconomically mobile will tend to continue gang involvement into adulthood (Wilson, 1987). For some youth, economic, political, and social forces compel gang membership. Although it is beyond the scope of this chapter to pursue such issues, until these forces are successfully redirected, the developmental tasks confronted by some youth will require that gangs persist.

Clearly, many demographic variables, including gender, ethnicity, family composition, and neighborhood disorganization, affect entrance into a gang, how long a youth stays in a gang, and how and why he or she leaves a gang. Most research to date on aggressive and delinquent behavior has focused on white, middle-class youth, whereas research on gang-involved youth has focused on ethnic minority youth. There is little work that spans the developmental literature on aggression and delinquent behavior and the sociological/criminological work on gangs. Huff's (1995, 1996) recent studies directly comparing gang-involved and at-risk youth highlight the need to begin examining the continuum of aggressive behavior, delinquency, gang involvement, and antisocial behavior for both groups of adolescents. Factors that predict which youth will go from being at risk to being involved in a gang are not yet well understood beyond a descriptive level. The relative influence of normative beliefs, stress, poverty, exposure to violence and victimization, and ethnicity may all contribute differentially to this process. The relative effectiveness of any preventive intervention also may vary tremendously depending on which factors are pertinent for a particular adolescent or group.

Finally, all of the research to date on youth at risk for engaging in aggressive, delinquent behavior and gang activity points to the need for multicomponent, multicontext interventions. To date, those that have shown the most promise include a focus on the individual (e.g., attitudes about aggression), the influence of close interpersonal relations (e.g., problem solving,

peer pressure, family conflict), and the contexts within which development takes place (e.g., home, school, peer group). Promising programs include aggression replacement training with delinquent youth (Goldstein & Glick, 1994), multisystemic family therapy (Henggeler, Melton, & Smith, 1992), the Seattle Social Development Project (Hawkins et al., 1992), and the Peace Builders youth violence prevention project (Embry et al., 1996; Flannery et al., 1996). Each of these approaches takes into account a combination of intrapersonal, interpersonal, and contextual factors in attempting to reduce delinquency, violent behavior, or gang involvement. Certainly, the relative importance of environmental risk factors, compared with individual risk factors, may vary with age and by context. This has been demonstrated quite well by Finkelhor in his model of "developmental victimology" for children exposed to and victimized by violence (Finkelhor, 1995). Young children may be more affected by context (e.g., persistent family violence) than adolescents, who may have more resources to avoid becoming victims of violence.

MACROSOCIAL ISSUES THAT DELIMIT INTERVENTION

Gang activity and violence are likely to be fostered by the same macrostructural factors at the community level that have been linked to other forms of deviance and negative child and adolescent outcomes (Huff, 1993). For example, highly mobile communities have been shown to have lower density of acquaintanceships, which limits their ability to control crime, socialize their youth, and care for members with special needs (Freudenburg, 1986). There exists considerable evidence that the density of friendship networks, parental control over teen peer groups, and participation in voluntary organizations—all aspects of community organization—are good predictors of rates of crime and delinquency within a community (Figueira-McDonough, 1991). Rates of delinquency are related to the community instability that develops in neighborhoods that experience significant population turnover (Bursik & Webb, 1982). Durkin, Davidson, Kuhn, O'Connnor, and Barlow (1994) found that high census tract proportions of low-income households, single-parent families, non-high school graduates, and unemployment were significant predictors of violence and delinquency among children younger than 17 years of age. These findings are consistent with those of Coulton, Korbin, Su, and Chow (1995), who showed that impoverishment, population instability, child care burden (e.g., ratio of children to adults), and geographic/economic isolation (i.e., whether a neighborhood had a contiguous census tract with at least 40% poor residents) were all related to increased risk of child victimization and delinquency.

In a recently completed study, the RAND Corporation examined the cost-effectiveness of several crime-prevention strategies that involve early intervention in the lives of people at risk of pursuing a criminal career (Greenwood, Model, Rydell, & Chiesa, 1996). Focusing on California, RAND contrasted California's "three-strikes" policy, which guarantees extended sentences for repeat offenders, with four different approaches: (a) home visits by child care professionals, beginning before birth and extending through the first 2 years of childhood, followed by 4 years of day care; (b) parent training for families with aggressive or acting-out children; (c) 4 years of cash and other graduation incentives for disadvantaged high school students; and (d) monitoring and supervision of high school-age youth who have already exhibited delinquent behavior. All of the examined programs, with the exception of home visits and day care, were appreciably more effective at reducing serious crimes than was the three-strikes policy. Graduation incentives for disadvantaged youth proved the most cost-effective approach, averting nearly $260 million from serious crimes compared to about $60 million for the three-strikes option. These findings have serious implications for policymakers who believe that increased incarceration time for juvenile offenders will systematically and over time reduce the youth crime rate.

SUMMARY

In this chapter, we have provided an overview of youth gangs from a developmental perspective and presented social and criminological literature integrated with research on development and risk to underscore the importance of including multiple disciplines in our prevention and intervention strategies. Gang membership increases in adolescence because adolescence is a developmental transition period in which peers take on a significant support and influence role, and this is done often at the expense of parents and families. The gang can provide a vehicle for identity formation and a setting where an at-risk youth can find acceptance and reinforcement for rejecting social norms and engaging in deviant, delinquent, and sometimes violent behavior. Adolescence is a transitional period when the need to meet multiple developmental tasks makes the gang an attractive alternative to at-risk youth.

Although the challenges are complex and long-term systematic change difficult to achieve, the cost of doing nothing is too high. We know that if we start early and identify at-risk youth in the early elementary years, we can promote prosocial competence and reduce the incidence of aggressive, antisocial behavior. Gang violence is not an insurmountable social malady. Youth seek out gang involvement typically to meet normal developmental tasks and to fulfill needs that all adolescents and all individuals have. Prothrow-Stith is fond of saying that children will eventually get our time, our money, our attention, and our resources. It is up to us, as parents, researchers, educators and advocates, to decide when that will be. Will it be when children are young, eager to learn, and perhaps not yet exposed to high levels of violence and victimization? Or will it be later, after our children reach adolescence, have failed at school, and have chosen to meet their needs through gangs? Before systems can change, individuals must take action and make their choices.

REFERENCES

Bell, C., & Jenkins, E. (1991). Traumatic stress and children. *Journal of Health Care for the Poor and Underserved, 2,* 175–185.

Block, C. R., & Block, R. (1994). *Street gang crime in Chicago* [Research in brief]. Washington, DC: U.S. Department of Justice, Office of Justice Programs, National Institute of Justice.

Blumstein, A. (1995). Violence by young people: Why the deadly nexus? *National Institute of Justice Journal,* pp. 2–9.

Bursik, R. J., & Webb, J. (1982). Community change and patterns of delinquency. *American Journal of Sociology, 88,* 24–41.

Cairns, R. B., & Cairns, B. D. (1991). Social cognition and social networks: A developmental perspective. In D. J. Pepler & K. H. Rubin (Eds.), *The development and treatment of childhood aggression* (pp. 249–274). Hillsdale, NJ: Lawrence Erlbaum.

Callahan, C. M., & Rivara, F. P. (1992). Urban high school youth and hand-guns. *Journal of the American Medical Association, 267,* 3038–3042.

Campbell, A. (1990). Female participation in gangs. In C. R. Huff (Ed.), *Gangs in America* (pp. 163–183). Newbury Park, CA: Sage.

CHESNEY-LIND, M., & BROWN, M. (in press). Girls and violence: An overview. In D. Flannery & R. Huff (Eds.), *Youth violence: Prevention, intervention, and social policy.* Washington, DC: American Psychiatric Press.

CHESNEY-LIND, M., BROWN, M., LEISEN, M. B., PERRONE, P., KWASCK, D., MARKER, N., & KATO, D. (1996). *Perspectives on juvenile delinquency and gangs: An interim report to Hawaii's state legislature.* Honolulu: University of Hawaii at Manoa, Center for Youth Research, Social Science Research Institute.

CHESNEY-LIND, M., & SHELDON, R. G. (1992). *Girls, delinquency and juvenile justice.* Pacific Grove, CA: Brooks/Cole.

CHESNEY-LIND, M., SHELDON, R., & JOE, L. K. (1996). Girls, delinquency and gang membership. In C. R. Huff (Ed.), *Gangs in America* (pp. 185–204). Thousand Oaks, CA: Sage.

CHICCHETTI, D., & LYNCH, M. (1993). Toward an ecological/transactional model of community violence and child maltreatment: Consequences for children's development. *Psychiatry, 56,* 96–118.

COULTON, C., KORBIN, J., & SU, M. (in press). Measuring neighborhood context for young children in an urban area. *American Journal of Community Psychology.*

COULTON, C., KORBIN, J., SU, M., & CHOW, J. (1995). Community level factors and child maltreatment rates. *Child Development, 66,* 1262–1276.

CRICK, N. R., & DODGE, K. A. (1994). A review and reformulation of social information-processing mechanisms in children's social adjustment. *Psychological Bulletin, 115,* 74–101.

CURRY, G. D., BALL, R. A., & FOX, R. J. (1994). *Gang crimes and law enforcement recordkeeping* [Research in brief]. Washington, DC: U.S. Department of Justice, National Institute of Justice, Office of Justice Programs.

CURRY, G. D., FOX, R. J., BALL, R. A., & STONE, D. (1992). *National assessment of law enforcement anti-gang information resources* [Draft 1992 Final Report]. Morgantown: West Virginia University, National Assessment Survey.

DISHION, T. J., & ANDREWS, D. W. (1995). Preventing escalation in problem behaviors with high-risk young adolescents: Immediate and 1-year outcomes. *Journal of Consulting and Clinical Psychology, 63,* 538–548.

DODGE, K. A. (1993). Social-cognitive mechanisms in the development of conduct disorder and depression. *Annual Review of Psychology, 44,* 559–584.

DURANT, R., CADENHEAD, C., PENDERGRAST, R., SLAVEN, G., & LINDER, C. W. (1994). Factors associated with the use of violence among urban black adolescents. *American Journal of Public Health, 84,* 612–617.

DURKIN, M., DAVIDSON, L., KUHN, L., O'CONNOR, P., & BARLOW, B. (1994). Low-income neighborhoods and the risk of severe pediatric injury: A small area analysis in Northern Manhattan. *American Journal of Public Health, 84,* 587–592.

EARLS, F. J. (1994). Violence and today's youth. *Critical Issues for Children and Youth, 4,* 4–23.

ELLIOT, D. E. (1994). Serious violent offenders: Onset, developmental course, and termination. *Criminology, 32,* 1–21.

EMBRY, D., FLANNERY, D., VAZSONYI, A., POWELL, K & ATHA, H. (1996). PeaceBuilders: A theoretically driven, school-based model for early violence prevention. *American Journal of Preventive Medicine, 12,* 91–100.

ERON, L. D., & HUESMANN, R. (1990). The stability of aggressive behavior—Even unto the third generation. In M. Lewis & S. M. Miller (Eds.), *Handbook of developmental psychopathology* (pp. 147–156). New York: Plenum.

ESBENSEN, F. A., & HUIZINGA, D. (1993). Gangs, drugs, and delinquency in a survey of urban youth. *Criminology, 31,* 565–589.

FAGAN, J. (1990). Social processes of delinquency and drug use among urban gangs. In C. R. Huff (Eds.), *Gangs in America* (1st ed., pp. 183–223). Newbury Park, CA: Sage.

FAGAN, J. (1996). Gangs, drugs and neighborhood change. In C. R. Huff (Ed.), *Gangs in America* (2nd ed., pp. 39–74). Thousand Oaks, CA: Sage.

FARRINGTON, D. P. (1991). Antisocial personality from childhood to adulthood. *The Psychologist, 4,* 389–394.

FARRINGTON, D. P., LOEBER, R., ELLIOT, D. S., HAWKINS, J. D., KANDEL, D. B., LEIN, M. W., MCCORD, J., ROWE, D. C., & TREMBLAY, R. E. (1993). Advancing knowledge about the onset of delinquency and crime. In B. B. Lahey & A. E. Kazdin (Eds.), *Advances in clinical child psychology* (Vol. 12, pp. 283–342). New York: Plenum.

FEDERAL BUREAU OF INVESTIGATION. (1994). *Crime in the United States—1993.* Washington, DC: U.S. Department of Justice.

FEDERAL BUREAU OF INVESTIGATION. (1995). *Crime in the United States.* Washington, DC: U.S. Department of Justice.

FIGUEIRA-MCDONOUGH, J. (1991). Community structure and delinquency: A typology. *Social Service Review, 65,* 69–91.

FINKELHOR, D. (1995). The victimization of children: A developmental perspective. *American Journal of Orthopsychiatry, 65,* 177–193.

FINKELHOR, D., & DZIUBA-LEATHERMAN, J. (1994). Victimization of children. *American Psychologist, 49,* 173–183.

FITZPATRICK, K., & BOLDIZAR, J. (1993). The prevalence and consequence of exposure to violence among African American youth. *Journal of the American Academy of Child and Adolescent Psychiatry, 32,* 424–430.

FLANNERY, D. J., VAZSONYI, A., EMBRY, D., & ATHA, H. (1996). *Longitudinal follow-up of PeaceBuilders violence prevention program* (Centers for Disease Control and Prevention, Cooperative Agreement #U81/CCU513508-01).

FRASER, M. W. (1996). Aggressive behavior in childhood and early adolescence: An ecological-developmental perspective on youth violence. *Social Work, 41,* 347–361.

FREUDENBURG, W. R. (1986). The density of acquaintanceship: An overlooked variable in community research. *American Journal of Sociology, 92,* 27–63.

GARBARINO, J., DURBROW, N., KOSTELNY, K., & PARDO, C. (1992). *Children in danger: Coping with the consequences of community violence.* San Francisco: Jossey-Bass.

GOLDSTEIN, A. P. (1991). *Delinquent gangs: A psychological perspective.* Champaign, IL: Research Press.

GOLDSTEIN, A. P., & GLICK, B. (1994). *The prosocial gang: Implementing aggression replacement training.* Thousand Oaks, CA: Sage.

GOTTFREDSON, M. (1984). *Victims of crime: The dimensions of risk* (Home Office Research Study #81). London: Her Majesty's Stationery Office.

GOTTFREDSON, M., & HIRSCHI, T. (1990). *A general theory of crime.* Stanford, CA: Stanford University Press.

GREENWOOD, P. W., MODEL, K. E., RYDELL, P., & CHIESA, J. (1996). *Diverting children from a life of crime: Measuring costs and benefits.* Santa Monica, CA: RAND.

GUERRA, N. G., HUESMANN, L. R., & HANISH, L. (1994). The role of normative beliefs in children's social behavior. In N. Eisenberg (Ed.), *Social development* (pp. 140–158). Thousand Oaks, CA: Sage.

GUERRA, N. G., HUESMANN, L. R., TOLAN, P. H., ACKER, R., & ERON, L. F. (1995). Stressful events and individual beliefs as correlates of economic disadvantage and aggression among urban children. *Journal of Consulting and Clinical Psychology, 63,* 518–528.

HAWKINS, J. D., CATALANO, R. F., MORRISON, D. M., O'DONNELL, J., ABBOTT, R. D., & DAY, L. E. (1992). The Seattle Social Development Project: Effects of the first four years on protective factors and problem behaviors. In J. McCord & R. Tremblay (Eds.), *The prevention of antisocial behavior in children* (pp. 139–161). New York: Guilford.

HENGGELER, S. W., & BORDUIN, C. M. (1990). *Family therapy and beyond: A multi-systemic approach to treating the behavior problems of children and adolescents*. Pacific Grove, CA: Brooks/Cole.

HENGGELER, S. W., MELTON, G. B., & SMITH, L. A. (1992). Family preservation using multisystemic therapy—An effective alternative to incarcerating serious juvenile offenders. *Journal of Consulting and Clinical Psychology, 60*, 953–961.

HOWELL, J. C. (1994). Recent gang research: Program and policy implications. *Crime & Delinquency*, 40, 495–515.

HUESMANN, L. R., ERON, L. D., LEFTKOWITZ, M. M., & WALDER, L. O. (1984). Stability of aggression over time and generations. *Developmental Psychology, 20*, 1120–1134.

HUFF, C. R. (1993). Gangs and public policy: Macrolevel interventions. In A. P. Goldstein & C. R. Huff (Eds.), *The gang intervention handbook* (pp. 463–475). Champaign, IL: Research Press.

HUFF, C. R. (1995). *Final report to the National Institute of Justice regarding the criminal behavior of gang members*. Columbus: Ohio State University Press.

HUFF, C. R. (1996). The criminal behavior of gang members and nongang at-risk youth. In C. R. Huff (Ed.), *Gangs in America* (2nd ed., pp. 75–102). Thousand Oaks, CA: Sage.

JANKOWSKI, M. S. (1991). *Islands in the street: Gangs and American urban society*. Berkeley: University of California Press.

JOE, K. A., & CHESNEY-LIND, M. (1995). Just every mother's angel: An analysis of gender and ethnic variations in youth gang membership. *Gender & Society, 9*, 408–430.

KANDEL, E., & MEDNICK, S. A. (1991). Perinatal complications predict violent offending. *Criminology, 29*, 519–529.

KELLAM, S. G., & REBOK, G. W. (1992). Building developmental and etiological theory through epidemiologically based preventive intervention trials. In J. McCord & R. E. Tremblay (Eds.), *Preventing antisocial behavior: Interventions from birth through adolescence* (pp. 62–195). New York: Guilford.

KENDALL, P. C., & GROVE, W. (1988). Normative comparisons in therapy outcome. *Behavioral Assessment, 10*, 147–158.

KENDALL, P. C., & HOLLON, S. D. (1979). *Cognitive-behavioral interventions: Theory, research, and procedures*. New York: Academic Press.

KLEIN, M. (1971). *Street gangs and street workers*. Englewood Cliffs, NJ: Prentice Hall.

KLEIN, M. (1995). *The American street gang: Its nature, prevalence, and control*. New York: Oxford University Press.

KLEIN, M. W., MAXSON, C. L., & CUNNINGHAM, L. C. (1991). "Crack," street gangs, and violence. *Criminology, 29*, 623–650.

KUPERSMIDT, J. B., & COIE, J. D. (1990). Preadolescent peer status, aggression, and school adjustment as predictors of externalizing problems in adolescence. *Child Development, 61*, 1350–1362.

LARSON, R., & RICHARDS, M. H. (EDS.). (1989). The changing life space of early adolescence [Special issue]. *Journal of Youth and Adolescence, 18*(6).

LOEBER, R. (1982). The stability of antisocial and delinquent child behavior: A review. *Child Development, 53*, 1431–1446.

LOEBER, R., & HAY, D. F. (1994). Developmental approaches to aggression and conduct problems. In M. Rutter & D. F. Hay (Eds.), *Development through life: A handbook for clinicians* (pp. 288–316). Boston: Blackwell Scientific.

MARTINEZ, P., & RICHTERS, J. E. (1993). The NIMH community violence project: II. Children's distress symptoms associated with violence exposure. *Psychiatry, 56*, 22–35.

MAXSON, C. L., & KLEIN, M. W. (1996). Defining gang homicide: An updated look at member and motive approaches. In C. R. Huff (Ed.), *Gangs in America* (2nd ed., pp. 3–20). Thousand Oaks, CA: Sage.

MILLER, W. B. (1982). *Crime by youth gangs and groups in the United States*. Washington, DC: U.S. Department of Justice, Office of Juvenile Justice and Delinquency Prevention.

MONTEMAYOR, R., & FLANNERY, D. (1990). Making the transition from childhood to early adolescence. In R. Montemayor, G. Adams, & T. Gullotta (Eds.), *Advances in adolescent development, Vol. 2: From childhood to adolescence: A transitional period?* (pp. 291–301). Newbury Park, CA: Sage.

MOORE, J. W., & HAGEDORN, J. M. (1996). What happens to girls in the gang? In C. R. Huff (Ed.), *Gangs in America* (2nd ed., pp. 205–220). Thousand Oaks, CA: Sage.

MORRIS, R. E., HARRISON, E. A., KNOX, G. W., ROMANJHAUSER, E., MARQUES, D. K., & WATTS, L. L. (1996). Health risk behavioral survey from 39 juvenile correctional facilities in the United States. *Journal of Adolescent Health, 117*, 334–375.

O'DONNELL, C., MANOS, M., & CHESNEY-LIND, M. (1987). Diversion and neighborhood delinquency programs in open settings: A social network interpretation. In E. Morris & C. Braukman (Eds.), *Behavioral approaches to crime and delinquency: Application, research and theory* (pp. 251–271). New York: Plenum.

O'DONNELL, J., HAWKINS, J. D., & ABBOTT, R. D. (1995). Predicting serious delinquency and substance use among aggressive boys. *Journal of Consulting and Clinical Psychology, 63*, 529–537.

PAIKOFF, R. L., & BROOKS-GUNN, J. (1991). Do parent-child interactions change during puberty? *Psychological Bulletin, 110*, 47–66.

PATTERSON, G., DEBARYSHE, B., & RAMSEY, B. (1989). A developmental perspective on antisocial behavior. *American Psychologist, 44*, 329–335.

PATTERSON, G. R., & BANK, L. (1989). Some amplifying mechanisms for pathologic process in families. In M. R. Gunner & E. Thelem (Eds.), *Systems and development: The Minnesota symposia on child psychology* (Vol. 22, pp. 167–210). Hillsdale, NJ: Lawrence Erlbaum.

PATTERSON, G. R., REID, J. B., & DISHION, T. J. (1992). *A social learning approach: IV. Antisocial boys*. Eugene, OR: Castalia.

PATTERSON, G. R., & YOERGER, K. (1993). Developmental models for delinquent behavior. In S. Hodgins (Ed.), *Mental disorders and crime* (pp. 140–172). Newbury Park, CA: Sage.

PORTILLAS, E., & ZATZ, M. S. (1995, November). *Not to die for: Positive and negative aspects of Chicano youth gangs*. Paper presented at the annual meeting of the American Society of Criminology, Boston.

PROTHROW-STITH, D. (1995). *Deadly consequences*. New York: HarperCollins.

REISS, A. J., JR., & ROTH, J. (1993). *Understanding and preventing violence*. Washington, DC: National Academy Press.

RICHTERS, J., & MARTINEZ, P. (1993). The NIMH community violence project: I. Children as victims of, and witnesses to violence. *Psychiatry, 56*, 7–21.

RIVARA, F., SHEPHERD, J., FARRINGTON, D., RICHMOND, P. W., & CANNON, P. (1995). Victim as offender in youth violence. *Annals of Emergency Medicine, 26*, 609–615.

ROPP, L., VISINTAINER, P., UMAN, J., & TRELOAR, D. (1992). Death in the city: An American childhood tragedy. *Journal of the American Medical Association, 267*, 2905–2910.

SAMPSON, R. J., & GROVES, W. B. (1989). Testing social-disorganization theory. *American Journal of Sociology, 94*, 774–802.

SAMPSON, R. J., & LAURITSEN, J. (1993). Violent victimization and offending: Individual, situational, and community-level risk factors. In A. J. Reiss, Jr., & J. A. Roth (Eds.), *Understanding and preventing violence. Vol. 3: Social influences* (pp. 1–114). Washington, DC: National Academy Press.

SANCHEZ-JANKOWSKI, M. (1991). *Islands in the street: Gangs and American urban society*. Berkeley: University of California Press.

SAVITZ, L., ROSEN, L., & LALLI, M. (1982). Delinquency and gang membership as related to victimization. *Victimology, 5*, 152–160.

SHELEY, J. F., & WRIGHT, J. D. (1993). *Gun acquisition and possession in selected juvenile samples.* Washington, DC: U.S. Department of Justice, National Institute of Justice, Office of Juvenile Justice and Delinquency Prevention.

SINGER, S. (1981). Homogenous victim-offender populations: A review and some research implications. *Journal of Criminal Law and Criminology, 72,* 779–788.

SINGER, M., ANGLIN, T., SONG, L., & LUNGHOFER, L. (1995). Adolescents' exposure to violence and associated symptoms of psychological trauma. *Journal of the American Medical Association, 273,* 477–482.

SKOGAN, W. (1986). Fear of crime and neighborhood change. In A. J. Reiss & M. Tonry (Eds.), *Communities and crime* (pp. 203–229). Chicago: University of Chicago Press.

SPARKS, R. (1982). *Research on victims of crime.* Washington, DC: U.S. Government Printing Office.

SPERGEL, I. A. (1991). *Youth gangs: Problem and response.* Washington, DC: U.S. Department of Justice, Office of Juvenile Justice and Delinquency Prevention.

SPERGEL, I. A. (1995). *The youth gang problem: A community approach.* New York: Oxford University Press.

STEINBERG, L. (1987). Familial factors in delinquency: A developmental perspective. *Journal of Adolescent Research, 2,* 255–268.

STEINBERG, L. (1989). Pubertal maturation and family relations: Evidence for the distancing hypothesis. In G. Adams, R. Montemayor, & T. Gullotta (Eds.), *Advances in adolescent development* (Vol. 1, pp. 71–97). Newbury Park, CA: Sage.

STRAUS, M. (1994). *Violence in the lives of adolescents.* New York: Norton.

TOLAN, P., & GUERRA, N. (1994). *What works in reducing adolescent violence: An empirical review of the field.* Boulder, CO: Center for the Study and Prevention of Violence.

TOLAN, P. H., GUERRA, N. G., & KENDALL, P. C. (1995). A developmental perspective on antisocial behavior in children and adolescents: Toward a unified risk and intervention framework. *Journal of Consulting and Clinical Psychology, 63,* 579–584.

TOLAN, P. J., & LOEBER, R. (1993). Antisocial behavior. In P. H. Tolan & B. J. Cohler (Eds.), *Handbook of clinical research and practice with adolescents* (pp. 307–331). New York: John Wiley.

TREMBLAY, R. E., KURTZ, L., MASSE, L. C., VITARO, F., & PHIL, R. O. (1995). A bimodal preventive intervention for disruptive kindergarten boys: Its impact through adolescence. *Journal of Consulting and Clinical Psychology, 63,* 560–568.

TREMBLAY, R., MASSE, B., LEBLANC, M., SCHWARTZMAN, A. E., & LEDINGHAM, J. E. (1992). Early disruptive behavior, poor school achievement, delinquent behavior, and delinquent personality: Longitudinal analyses. *Journal of Consulting and Clinical Psychology, 60,* 64–72.

WEBSTER, D. W., GAINER, P. S., & CHAMPION, H. R. (1994). Weapon carrying among inner-city junior high school students: Defensive behavior vs. aggressive delinquency. *American Journal of Public Health, 83,* 1604–1608.

WIDOM, C. S. (1989). The cycle of violence. *Science, 244,* 160–166.

WILKINSON, D. L., & FAGAN, J. (1996). Understanding the role of firearm violence: The dynamics of gun events among adolescent males. *Law and Contemporary Problems, 59,* 55–90.

WILSON, W. J. (1987). *The truly disadvantaged: The inner city, the underclass and public policy.* Chicago: University of Chicago Press.

YOSHIKAWA, H. (1994). Prevention as cumulative protection: Effects of early family support and education on chronic delinquency and its risks. *Psychological Bulletin, 115,* 28–54.

Gang Member Demographics and Gang Subcultures

1995

Irving A. Spergel

skip for now

This chapter continues the discussion of the gang problem, but in specific sociodemographic and related subcultural terms. The analysis of age, gender, and especially race/ethnic, gang characteristics suggests that there are distinctive gang subcultures, and therefore distinctive intervention approaches are required. These subcultures must be understood and their causes and special characteristics addressed through particular policy emphases. Large-scale social, economic, cultural, and political as well as local forces generate different patterns of poverty and social disorganization. These together, interactively, create distinctive subcultures. These forces, at both the national and the local level, must be addressed if the delinquent norms and behaviors of gang youth are to be prevented, modified, and controlled.

In the following pages I describe first the dimensions of age, gender, and race/ethnicity as correlates of different gang systems and patterns of gang behavior.

Race/ethnicity or minority status is a key dimension that conditions gang patterns and the policy responses developed, but race/ethnicity per se does not generate gang subcultures. The discussion in this chapter becomes a basis for understanding the problem and for prescribing policies that are sensitive to particular communities, organizations, and cultures in later chapters.

DEMOGRAPHICS

Age

Gang activity is still perceived as primarily or almost exclusively a teenage, if not a juvenile, phenomenon. Recent scholarly work continues to convey this incorrect perception. For example, Covey, Menard and Franzere's 1992 text is titled *Juvenile Gangs*. (Legislation and criminal justice policy has been less likely to make this mistake in recent years.) Researchers and analysts in the 1950s and 1960s often made this assumption because they largely used youth samples derived from agency streetwork programs. Youth work programs then and even today do not generally address the interests and needs of older adolescents and young adults. Before the 1980s juvenile or youth units of police departments usually dealt with gang problems. Many of these units have been transformed into gang, street-gang, or organized crime units over the last decade or two.

As in pre-World War II days, there is recognition at the present time that gang membership extends well into young adulthood—certainly into the early and mid-20s, and to some extent into the 30s, 40s, and even 50s. Thrasher's (1936) gang members of the 1920s ranged in age from 6 to 50 years old, but were concentrated in two groups: "earlier adolescent," 11 to 17 years old, and "later adolescent," 16 to 25 years old. Whyte's (1943) street-gang members were in their 20s. While the gang literature of the 1950s and 1960s focused on teenage gangs, there were also young-adult street gangs and even significant numbers of young adults in so-called teenage gangs. Many case histories (New York City Youth Board 1960; Yablonsky 1962; Spergel 1964; Klein 1971) provide ample evidence of the presence and influence of young adults in street gangs of that era. There may, however, have been relatively fewer older teenagers and young adults associated with gangs in the 1950s and 1960s than appears to be the case today.

By the early 1970s, it was already clear—at least in New York City—that the age range of gang members was broader "at the top and the bottom than in the fighting gangs of the 1950s. The age range in some gangs starts at 9 years old and elevates as high as 30 years old" (Collins 1979, pp. 30–40). On the basis of New York City police data of the 1980s, Chin estimated that the age range of Chinese gang members was 13 to 37 and that their mean age was 22.7 years (Chin 1990b, p. 130). A report of San Diego's gang problem indicated that the age range of gang members was 12 to 31 years and the median age was 19 years (San Diego Association of Governments 1982). The Honolulu Police Department estimated that as of November 1991, approximately 77 percent of the 1,020 persons it suspected of being gang members were legally adults (18 years of age and over) (Chesney-Lind et al. 1992, p. 19).

Some analysts have continued to insist that the "traditional" age range of gang members in most cities was 8 to 21 or 22 years (W. Miller 1975, 1982). Miller (1982), for example, found, from a small data sample (N=121), that no gang offenders or victims in Chicago were 23 years of age or older. Spergel (1986), however, found, on the basis of 1982–1984 Chicago police data on 1,699 offenders and 1,557 victims, that the age range for offenders was 8 to 51 years, and for victims was 3 to 76 years. Miller's mean age categories were 16 and 17 years; Spergel's mean age for offenders was 17.9 years and for victims was 20.1 years. On the basis of analysis of Chicago Police Department case reports for 1987 and the first half of 1988, Bobrowski (1988) concluded that the average age of the male offender was 19.4 years and of the female offender was 15 years. For victims, the average age was 22.1 years, although the modal or most frequently arrested group was 17 years (p. 40).

The age period during which most gang homicides occur is late adolescence and young adulthood. The mean age of the gang homicide offender in Los Angeles city and county in the 1980s was 19 and 20 years, respectively (Maxson, Gordon, and Klein 1985; see also Torres 1980 and Horowitz 1983). Spergel's (1983) gang homicide offender data in Chicago for 1978–1981 indicated major age category percentages as follows: 14 years and under, 2.2 percent; 15 to 16 years, 17.6 percent; 17 to 18 years, 32.4 percent; 19 to 20 years, 21.7 percent; 21 years and older, 25.9 percent. The percentages for these age categories are approximately the same for a 1982–1985 analysis of gang homicides in Chicago (Spergel 1986; see also Klein, Maxson, and Cunningham 1991). Analysis of gang homicides in Chicago for the years 1985, 1989, and 1990 again indicates average ages identical to those in the late 1970s and early 1980s: gang homicide offenders, 19 years or 20 years; victims, 20 or 21 years.

Females and Gangs

There appears to be considerable confusion about the relation of number and proportion of females who are gang members to their participation in serious or violent crimes. An assumption is often made that increasing numbers of young females are "participating in youth gangs and [in] their violent illegal activities" (Candamil 1990, p. 1). The U.S. Department of Health and Human Services, Administration for Children and Families currently refers to evidence that there are "more adolescent females actively participating in gangs and illegal drug activities than previously estimated" [but does not cite specific data sources or evidence] (Federal Register 1992, p. 9869).

Good data on the percentage of females in gangs are difficult to obtain; data on females known to the police as gang offenders, however, are somewhat more available. In this regard it is important to distinguish the sources of data on female gang membership: arrest records, self-reports, or field observations. Bernard Cohen (1969a, p. 85) indicated that 6.3 percent of delinquent group members arrested in Philadelphia in the early 1960s were females but that only 1.4 percent of juvenile gang members arrested were females. Tracy (1982, pp. 10–11) found that 17 percent of violent delinquents in the 1958 Philadelphia cohort study were females and that most of those were arrested for non-gang-related offenses.

Focusing on females as gang members rather than as gang offenders, Collins (1979, p. 51) estimated that males outnumbered females by a margin of 20 to 1 in New York City. He also reported that half of all street gangs in New York City had female chapters or auxiliaries. Walter Miller (1975) reported that females made up 10 percent of gang members. Campbell (1984b) and Lee (1991) estimated that about 10 percent of gang members are girls. On the other hand, some analysts, using self-reports or field observations, have estimated the proportion of female gang members to be as high as 33 percent (Fagan 1990; Moore 1991). Knox found, in a 1991 survey of forty-five short- and long-term juvenile correctional facilities, that 46.4 percent of confined males and 42.2 percent

of confined females "self-reported" gang membership (Knox 1991c, pp. 4–5). What the respondents referred to as gangs and what their behavior was in such gangs are not indicated.

Despite media reports, field research findings, and youth agency warnings about the large and increasing proportion of female gang members and their reported involvement in serious gang crime, police data corroboration is not available. In fact, police data suggest that a relatively small amount of serious gang crime is committed by females and that this proportion has probably not changed over the past two decades. In a study of four police districts in Chicago between 1982 and 1984, 95 to 98 percent of the offenders in 1,504 gang incidents were males (Spergel 1986). In a more recent Chicago police study that used citywide data covering a year and a half between January 1987 and July 1988, 12,602 males but only 685 females (2% of the total) were arrested for street gang crimes (Bobrowski 1988, p. 38). Of 2,984 offenders arrested for felony gang assaults over the same period, only 94 (3.2%) were females (ibid., Table 18a).

Harris claimed, on the basis of a small ethnographic sample study, that female gang members were engaged in "vandalism, narcotics, assault, battery, rape, burglary, extortion, robbery, and murder" (Harris 1988, p. 11). She reported that of the twenty-one female gang members she interviewed, two spoke of using drugs and three declared they were drug dealers (pp. 132–133). Harris provided no direct observational or police record confirmation of these statements; we also do not know how typical the gang and gang members were whom she interviewed. Again, it should be noted that self-reported gang member data are particularly suspect because of the tendency of gang youths to exaggerate their delinquent, especially gang-related, activity.

There is evidence that the number of females arrested for serious crimes has been increasing. "In New York City, the number of girls arrested for felonies increased 48 percent over four years, from 7,340 in 1986 to 10,853 last year [1990]. In New Jersey the number of girls arrested for violent crimes like robbery and aggravated assault increased 67 percent from 1980 to 1990" (Lee 1991). But as yet there is no clear evidence that female gang members are increasingly involved in serious gang violence.

The most reliable gang crime data regarding females are based on gang homicide incidents. In a study of 345 gang homicide offenders in Chicago between 1978 and 1981, only 1 was a female; of 204 gang homicide victims for this period, 6 were female (Spergel 1983). In a more recent analysis of 286 gang homicide offenders in Chicago, between 1988 and 1990, only 2 were females; of 233 gang homicide victims for this later period, 3 were females. From these data, females appear not to be significantly involved in serious criminal gang incidents as offenders or victims, nor does the situation appear to have changed over the past several decades. The youth gang problem in its violent character is essentially a male problem.

Several researchers have recently concluded that females are increasingly involved in street-gang or street-clique drug operations, either with male counterparts or on their own, as much for social and emotional support as for profit:

It was their introduction to crack sales in the mid-1980's by gang affiliated boyfriends that precipitated the formation of this independent group. Extremely dissatisfied with the division of profits and labor from these drug ventures, they decided to enter into business themselves. . . .

The importance of this association goes beyond the immediate financial benefits. Their own family ties were weak at best prior to their involvement in the gang. The group fills a void in the lives of its members. . . . This group is not merely a bunch of drug dealing deviants. For them, it is a family, a sisterhood.

Many of these women made it clear, however, that, given their present circumstances, no other opportunities were available to raise their children. . . . All noted that, in time, they would prefer another lifestyle, particularly one more legitimate. (Lauderback, Hansen, and Waldorf 1992, pp. 69–70; see also Taylor 1993).

Race/Ethnicity and Class

Race/Ethnicity. Race and ethnicity have played a role in the development of the urban gang problem, especially since World War II, but in more complex ways than is ordinarily indicated. Blacks and Hispanics have constituted the largest numbers of youths arrested for gang offenses. In his first national survey, Walter Miller (1975) estimated that 47.6 percent of gang members in the six largest cities were black, 36.1 percent Hispanic, 8.8 percent white, and 7.5 percent Asian. A few years later (1982), Miller found, in a more extensive survey of all gang members in nine of the largest cities, that 44.4 percent were Hispanic, 42.9 percent black, 9 percent white, and 4.0 percent Asian. He speculated that illegal Hispanic immigrants, especially from Mexico, may have played a large role in the increasing numbers of gangs in California and in their spread to smaller cities and communities in that state (ibid., chap. 9).

In their 1989 and 1990 survey of the gang problem and organized programs to deal with it in forty-five cities and six special jurisdictions, Spergel and Curry found a similarly high proportion of African-Americans and Hispanics as gang members. The race/ethnic composition of gang members was also, to a considerable extent, dependent on who was doing the defining or perceiving. The majority of gang members contacted (or arrested) by law enforcement agencies were blacks (53%), considerably more than Hispanics (28%). On the other hand, grass-roots organizations and social agencies in the same cities reported contact with relatively fewer black (46%) and relatively more Hispanic (30%) gang members. Law enforcement agencies were defining and contacting blacks more often as gang members than were other justice agencies (Spergel and Curry 1990, p. 64).

The dominant proportions of blacks and Hispanics identified as gang members based on police reporting seem hardly to have changed, although the numbers have significantly increased in the past twenty years. The analysis by Curry et al. of the ethnic composition of gang members remains predominantly black (48 percent) and Hispanic (43 percent). The black groups comprised primarily African Americans but also included some blacks from other countries, particularly the Caribbean area. There was, however, some evidence of a relative increase of Hispanic gang members compared to black gang members from 1990 to 1991 (1994, p. 9).

Whites and Asians comprised a very small proportion of youth gang members reported by either law enforcement (2.2% and 1.6%, respectively) or non-law enforcement organizations (4.2% and 2.2%, respectively) (Spergel and Curry 1990, p. 65). Whites were the most numerous racial group in most of the cities surveyed. Why contacts with or arrests of white gang members were so much smaller is not entirely clear. Part of the answer is the relatively smaller numbers of risk-age youths in the white population. Part of the answer also may be matters of perception and definition. Youthful white delinquents or nondelinquents are simply less likely to be stereotyped, labeled, or feared as gang members. Also, what one racial or ethnic community or group of youths considers a gang may not necessarily be what another racial or ethnic community or group of youths considers a gang. Nevertheless, Curry, Ball, and Fox's recent survey of 79 large city police departments between 1990 and 1991 reported a greater rate of increase of white and Asian gang members than of blacks and Hispanics, although from a much smaller base (1994, p. 9).

The largest variety of youth gang types by race/ethnicity probably occurs on the West Coast, particularly in Southern California, and increasingly in Texas, New Mexico, Colorado, Utah, and Florida, based on recent population settlements or migrations. Asian and Pacific Island youth gangs are reported in many states and communities, but particularly in Los Angeles, Denver, and Salt Lake City. American Indian gangs have been active in Minneapolis and in several southwestern states. Mixed-race and ethnic gang membership patterns are not uncommon in many localities, although black gangs tend to be all black. The relation of black American gangs to Jamaican gangs ("posses") is unclear; ethnicity may be both a stronger basis for bonding and gang conflict than race.

Hispanic gangs tend to be predominantly Mexican-American or Puerto Rican, with increasing numbers of Central and South Americans. Asian and Pacific Island youth gangs include Korean, Thai, Cambodian, Hmong, Japanese, Samoan, Tongan, Filipino, and Chinese with origins in Hong Kong, Taiwan, and Vietnam. White gangs can be predominantly second and third generation or of mixed Italian, Irish, Polish, or middle-European origin, situated in inner-city "defensive" enclaves, suburban areas, or small towns. Recent first-generation Russian, Jewish, and Albanian youth gangs have been identified in certain neighborhoods of New York City. The more entrepreneurial gangs, regardless of race or ethnicity, tend to travel more often and have weak territorial identifications. Jamaican posses, some black drug gangs, and white motorcycle gangs roam widely.

In general, gang violence tends to be intraracial or intraethnic. Exceptions occur during periods of competition and conflict by different ethnic groups over local resources (Thrasher 1936) and rapid community race/ethnic population change. Local gangs, often acting out the anxiety of adults in the neighborhood, become organized to defend against newcomers, who in turn establish themselves—protectively at first—as gangs to ward off the hostility and aggression of the established low-income youth population. The most serious and long-term gang conflicts, however, arise and are sustained within and across adjacent neighborhoods with quite similar racial/ethnic populations.

Class. Contemporary youth gangs are located primarily in lower-class, slum, ghetto, barrio, or working-class changing communities, but it is not clear that either class, poverty, culture, race or ethnicity, or social change per se primarily accounts for gang problems. A variety of social and economic factors mainly must interact with each other.

The gangs of the early part of the century in urban areas like Chicago were usually first-generation youths born of Irish and German, and later Polish, Russian, and Italian, parents who lived in areas of transition or first settlement (Thrasher 1936). Gang neighborhoods more often than not represent lower-class population concentrations in the city. Nevertheless, delinquent and somewhat violent youth gangs do occasionally arise in middle-class neighborhoods but are less prevalent; they are also of different character from lower-class gangs (Myerhoff and Myerhoff 1976; see also Muehlbauer and Dodder 1983). At the same time, the most serious gang problems, at least in their violent manifestations, are not necessarily concentrated or most prevalent in the poorest urban neighborhoods (Spergel 1984). Furthermore, gang members do not necessarily come from the poorest families in these low-income communities. Although delinquency and crime rates are generally associated with poverty or class, this relationship is less strong for gang-related than for non-gang-related crime (Curry and Spergel 1988).

The assumption that poverty, low socioeconomic status, or lower-class lifestyle are highly or singularly related to the prevalence of violent youth gangs has been questioned in various studies. The communities in which black gangs flourished in the early 1960s were generally below city averages in housing standards and employment rates, but not below city average unemployment rates (Cartwright and Howard 1966). Gang members often came from low median family-income census tracts in Philadelphia, but not from the lowest (B. Cohen 1969a). The members of conflict groups in New York City were not drawn necessarily from the poorest families of the slum town areas (Spergel 1964). Many of the street gangs of New York City in the 1970s "emerged from a lower-middle-class lifestyle" (Collins 1979). Hispanic fighting gangs in East Los Angeles were not limited to the lowest-income areas of the city (Klein 1971).

Also, the spread of gangs in Los Angeles County and other suburban areas around the country reportedly is due in part to the movement of upwardly mobile families with gang youths to middle-class suburban areas (Los Angeles County Sheriff's Department 1985). Violent and criminal motorcycle gangs are reportedly composed of mainly lower-middle-class, white, older adolescents and young adults (Roger Davis 1982a, b). White youth gangs in suburban communities, "Punks," "Stoners," "White Supremacists," "Satanics," and others, seem to come from lower-middle-class and middle-class communities (Deukmajian 1981; Dolan and Finney 1984). The class identity of the newly developing Asian gangs is not clearly established: gang members may come from two working parent families, where there is inadequate supervision of the youth rather than insufficient access to income (Sung 1977; Chin 1990b). Issues of family and neighborhood disorganization as well as class must be considered as variables in the explanation of the development of the gang problem.

GANG SUBCULTURES AND SOCIAL CONTEXTS

Gangs are quasi-organized component elements of communities, in which youths and young adults are only partially integrated with the general or dominant interests, resources, needs, and customs of local residents. Gang structures and activities, especially violence, vary by race and ethnicity conditioned by class, access to legitimate and illegitimate opportunities, social isolation, and community stability or instability, as well as particular history of gang culture or subculture. These factors can be interrelated and analyzed for policy purposes, using two general causal dimensions—*poverty*, or limited access to social opportunities, and *social disorganization*, or the lack of integration of key social institutions including youth and youth groups, family, school, and employment in a local community.

Violent youth gang subcultures or social subsystems have persisted in inner-city African-American and Hispanic communities at least since World War II. More recently these subcultures and systems have developed not only in central cities but in smaller cities and suburban areas where social, family, economic, and educational supports are increasingly inadequate. Furthermore, in inner-city African-American communities, limited criminal opportunity systems have evolved at gangs partially change from status-oriented conflict groups to more rational but predatory organizations, with special interests in drug trafficking and other criminal gain. Violent gang subcultures may develop when poor immigrants arrive in urban communities. Some blue-collar, white, low- or middle-class communities, subjected to severe economic pressures and consequent social or cultural changes, may also spawn youth gangs or deviant youth groups, such as Satanic, Stoner, punk rocker, hate, neo-Nazi, or racist Skinhead groups, characterized by perverse, negative, or violent behaviors including vandalism, drug use, homosexual assaults, and sometimes homicides (Spergel 1992a, pp. 3–5). This section describes particular gang subcultures and systems in somewhat greater detail.

Black Gangs

In no other community are legitimate opportunities more thoroughly blocked than in the urban African-American community. More limited systems of illegitimate opportunity have evolved, based pervasively on street-gang structures, than is the case for any other racial or ethnic group. Black youths in these communities tend to maintain gang connections longer than nonblack youths in other communities. Because of persistent poverty associated with racism, black male youths also become overidentified as gang members. Anderson, in his study of the black ghetto in Philadelphia, states

Many disadvantaged young blacks living in the ghetto of Northton find themselves surrounded by a complex world that seems arbitrary and unforgiving. Major changes in the regular economy . . . combined with the massive influx of drugs into the local community—have exacerbated social breakdown . . . All of this has undermined traditional social networks that once brought youths into the world of legitimate work and family life. . . . (Anderson 1990, pp. 109–111)

Sullivan, in his study of a public housing project in Brooklyn's black ghetto, observes

Projectville youths had the fewest family and neighborhood connections to jobs . . . Projectville youths left school early because they were about to become fathers and wanted to find full-time jobs to support their new families . . . [compared to Hispanic and white neighborhoods] Projectville youths suffered from the most joblessness. . . . Their neighborhood's physical isolation from centers of employment limited the work opportunities of residents. . . . (Sullivan 1989, pp. 43, 55, 104)

Distrust, estrangement, segmentation, and social distance characterize many inner-city impoverished black communities. Gangs and crime touch a great many households. Everyone seems vulnerable to "assault and incivilities" almost any time of the day or night. The perpetrator of a crime—whether a drive-by shooting, burglary, or drug deal—might be a nephew, a best friend, or the young man down the block. Anderson observes that "new role models are being created." The currently respected gang member or gang-related drug dealer who is out to make fast money does not look forward to an unskilled or semiskilled job that may not be available to him, anyway. "He is out to beat the next fellow" (Anderson 1990, pp. 78, 103).

A process of destructive socialization occurs: youths who have insufficient social support at home from separated, alienated, or unemployed parents receive inadequate and minimal attention at school where they consequently fail or are inadequately educated. Furthermore, youth or community agencies no longer have the resources or capabilities to reach out to these now more socially detached and disorganized young people. Youths must learn to survive on the streets through attachment to a variety of semi-organized illegitimate structures and criminal and status-providing activities. Unsupervised black youths in inner-city areas are reported to become, in sequence, "scavenger" groups, turf gangs, and even corporate drug gangs (Anderson 1990; Taylor 1990a). Access to earlier socially compensatory legitimate routes (e.g., Job Corps, the Army, special education and training programs) has been increasingly closed off. A few roles and systems, for example drug trafficking, more and more offer some social status and personal satisfaction necessary to achieve even limited economic and social success. Taylor observes that "cocaine and crack cocaine have provided goals, jobs, and economic realities that African-American communities in Detroit had never seen before" (1990a, p. 98).

Taylor claims also that America's drug habit

has created the economic boom needed to trigger gang imperialism. . . . African-Americans have moved into the main-

stream of major crime. Corporate gangs . . . are part of organized crime in America. Drugs, as a commodity, have become the same unifying economic force for gangs today (adult and juvenile) as alcohol during prohibition. . . . Detroit gangs are using drugs as this vehicle for social mobility. . . . (Taylor 1990a, pp. 97, 103, 112)

Taylor has probably exaggerated the success of black gang members moving into corporate crime.

Hispanic Gangs

Parallels—within limits—can be made between the emergence of Latino (Hispanic) and black street gangs. Some observers claim there are similarities, for example, in Southern California between the

origins of Cholo gangs in the mid-to-late forties and the rise of the CRIPS and Bloods a generation later. . . . Both were products of communities only recently arrived in Los Angeles. Neither group was truly new, of course. Just as there had been a significant Mexican-American community in Los Angeles long before the 20s, so the black presence long predated the population surge around World War II. But like the great Mexican migration which preceded it, the wave of black migrants during and after the war, all but submerged the older community. . . . (Reiner 1992, pp. 4–5)

Much of the writing on Latino or Hispanic gangs in the past several decades has focused on Mexican-American groups in Southern California and the Southwest. However, Hispanic gangs, including Mexican-American, Puerto Rican, Dominican, and Salvadoran groups, have been a major problem also in the Midwest, on the East Coast, and in Texas. Nevertheless, the longest continuous Mexican-American or Chicano gang tradition has probably developed in the Los Angeles area. Some Latino street gangs in Southern California have existed within particular localities as extended families or clans for three or more generations, although the families of gang members often arrived in the area at different times. "Parents and in some cases even grandparents were members of the same gang. There is a sense of continuity of family identity" (Jackson and McBride 1985, p. 42).

Each new wave of Mexican-American immigrants and more recently low-income Nicaraguans, Salvadorans, and other Central Americans provides a new generation of poorly schooled and partially acculturated youths around which gangs seem to organize or perpetuate themselves. Vigil and Long claim, particularly in reference to Mexican-Americans, "the gang subculture is embedded in and representative of the larger cholo (marginalized) subculture to which large numbers of Chicano youths (especially urban youths) subscribe . . ." (Vigil and Long 1990, p. 56). *Cholo* refers to the poorest of the poor marginalized immigrants. These are persons who were marginal to Spanish culture and are now marginal to "the more recent European culture" in America (Vigil 1990, p. 116). Vigil believes the cholozation process becomes "more intensified in the third generation, within which a subculture of the streets has become institutionalized . . . youths with particularly problematic, traumatic family and personal experiences . . . are forced into the streets" (ibid., p. 124).

However, not all or even a significant minority of poor Mexican-American youths become gang members in East Los Angeles or elsewhere. First- and second-generation Mexican-Americans in substantial numbers move out of barrios and become integrated into the larger society. Many rise from the lower economic stratum (see Moore 1978, 1991). This is not to deny that Hispanic gangs, particularly Chicano gangs, are probably the most turf oriented and most expressive of gangs in terms of "street styles of dress, speech, gestures, tatoos, and graffiti" (see Vigil 1988b, p. 2). But such patterns also vary considerably among Mexican-American gangs in different parts of the country, and within particular localities over time (Hutcheson 1993). Bobrowski (1988) noted differences between Hispanic, white, and black gangs in Chicago. Symbolic property crime (graffiti) is more common among Hispanic than black gangs (p. 19). The ratios of personal crime to property crime (mainly graffiti) for Hispanics and whites are 3 to 1 and 4 to 1, respectively, while for blacks it is 8 to 1 (Bobrowski 1988, p. 21).

Mexican-Americans and other Hispanic youths are also more likely than African-Americans to be integrated into multiethnic/racial gangs, in large measure, because they more often reside in less racially or ethnically segregated communities. Further, not all low-income and/or recently settled Hispanic or black communities necessarily or consistently produce violent gangs in a particular city. For example, although there was a tradition of gang formation and gang violence in Philadelphia's innercity neighborhoods in the 1970s, that did not happen in Puerto Rican enclaves or in Mexican-American low-income enclaves in a number of other cities. Nevertheless, Duran (1987, p. 2)

observed that while Chicano gangs in certain parts of East Los Angeles have declined in membership, immigrant gangs from Mexico and Central and South America are on the increase; the tradition of Hispanic gangs that fight, kill, and risk their lives for turf and "respect" remains dominant.

White Gangs

White lower-class youths have the longest (recorded) history of street gang activity in the United States. . . . They have been far less visible and in fact considerably less violent than black and Hispanic gangs in recent decades. There were more white than black gangs in Boston in the 1950s and 1960s, and there was more violence among white gangs than among black gangs (however, the level of violence among Boston gangs may have been lower than among black or white gangs in other cities (W. Miller 1976b). In Chicago, white gangs, comprising youths of a somewhat higher class origin than black gangs, were reported in the late 1950s and early 1960s to be rowdier, more rebellious, more openly at odds with adults, and more into drinking, drug use, and sexual delinquency than black gangs (Short and Strodtbeck 1965). White gangs in Philadelphia in the middle 1970s were less territorially bound, less structured, and therefore more difficult to identify and consequently to label than black gangs (Friedman, Mann, and Adelman 1976).

White gangs come in many varieties. Not unlike black and Hispanic gangs, some are concerned with protecting turf or territory, less often with expanding it. They may be in coalition with certain Hispanic or black gangs. White gangs have at times been suppliers of weapons (often stolen in home burglaries) and certain types of drugs to black and Hispanic gangs, or in turn have sought out dealers in black and Hispanic gang territories in order to buy drugs. White gangs or deviant groups have been identified as Stoners, freaks, heavy-metal groups, satanic worshipers, bikers, Skinheads, and copy-cat gangs, involved in a greater range of delinquent activities, but generally of a less violent character, than have black or Hispanic gangs in recent years.

White gangs have been generally better integrated into the life of their particular communities than black or Hispanic gangs, and thereby have better access both to legal and illegal opportunities. They have probably been more exposed to adult social constraints (Sullivan 1989, p. 46). To the extent that white communities are fearful and insecure about interacting with "invading" minority (especially low-income) newcomers to the local culture, youth gangs assist directly and indirectly in the defense and protection of their neighborhoods, often by aggressive or violent means (Suttles 1968). White gangs also do not have to resort to violent or street level criminal acts as extensively to achieve status or income. For younger adolescents, "illegal sources of income often . . . supplement rather than substitute for wages, but these sources were drug selling and drug errands for local adult organized crime figures rather than the high-risk, low-return thefts so prevalent among minority youths" (Sullivan 1989, p. 179; see also Cloward and Ohlin 1960; Spergel 1964).

In certain communities, whites—at least those recently arrived from certain European countries—become the newcomers. In a series of violent gang attacks on other youths, police in the Bronx, New York, reported:

Some of the [Albanian] cliques . . . also include black, Hispanic and other white teenagers as well, often friends they met in elementary school.

Albanian immigration began with political refugees during the 1960s, followed by a record wave from Kosovo in the early 1970s. Estimates of their numbers in the region range from 75,000 to 150,000, with about a fifth of those in the Williamsbridge neighborhood of the Bronx. Many of them started in blue-collar jobs, with a sizable number attaining a measure of success in residential real estate and small businesses. (Gonzalez 1992)

The Albanian Boys or Albanian Bad Boys were described as loosely knit groups of teenagers who often gathered near a mural that took up an entire wall of a building. It contained an epitaph to a youth killed in a gang fight. " 'Rest in peace' is written flamboyantly on one side and a blood-red Albanian flag flank[s] the other" (ibid.). The area is considered turf for the group of perhaps several dozen youths who hang out, "raising cain and eagerly taking on all they perceive as interlopers. . . . Sometimes an odd look or a casual remark would trigger a confrontation" (ibid.). Much of the fighting was to earn or maintain a reputation.

Increasing numbers of white youths who become gang or pseudo gang members seem to come from disorganized and disrupted or recently unemployed, working, and middle-class families. Many no longer live at home and are regarded as throwaways. To sur-

vive, they turn to ephemeral forms of antisocial gang activity, sometimes closely identified with a particular neighborhood, sometimes not (see Dunston 1990, p. 20). Stoners originally were groups made up of persistent drug or alcohol abusers, sometimes with heavy-metal rock music as a common bond. One of the special early traits of Stoner groups in Southern California was satanism, including grave robbing and the desecration of churches and human remains. Stoner groups have been known to mark off territory with graffiti. They may adopt particular dress styles (Jackson and McBride 1985, pp. 42–55). Stoner youth gangs ("taggers," graffiti groups, or "tag bangers") have been present in Hispanic communities, such as Los Angeles, alongside and sometimes interacting with or converting to violent gangs (Ayres 1994). Taggers may interact with and/or become gang bangers.

Various middle- and upper-income communities, particularly on the West Coast, have reported white youth gangs forming in imitation of certain Hispanic and black gangs. Justice agencies have reported these groups, sometimes ephemeral, as a kind of "dalliance" or flirtation that may be "as innocent as a fashion statement or as deadly as hard-core drug dealing and violence. . . . [Certain white youths] are joining established black . . . gangs like the CRIPS or Bloods; others are forming what are sometimes called copy-cat or mutant yuppie gangs" (Office of Criminal Justice Planning 1990, p. 11).

Some Skinhead groups are neo-Nazi youth gangs, originally modeling themselves after punk rockers and Skinheads in England. They may have ties to racist or Nazi adult groups, such as the Ku Klux Klan, the American Nazi Party, and the National Socialist White Workers Party. The SWP (Supreme White Pride) young adult gang has recently spread from the prisons to the streets. Racist and violent Skinheads have been identified in major cities on the West Coast, in the Midwest, and in the South. Some law enforcement officials of Southern California believe the Skinhead movement may be a reaction by white youths in certain middle-class neighborhoods to a sudden increase in the number of black, Hispanic, and Asian residents. Skinhead group structure and style fit the gang pattern: a gang name, colors, tattooing, distinctive dress, drug use, and criminal behavior (Coplon 1988, p. 56; see also Jackson and McBride 1985; Anti-Defamation League 1986, 1987; and Donovan 1988).

A report of the Florida state legislature (Reddick 1987) noted that the Skinheads in Florida started in Jacksonville and are now uniformly found in major urban areas all over the state. They profess to being "anti-black, anti-Jew, and anti-homosexual, while promoting their pro-God, pro-white American ideology." Their activities in Florida have been "primarily harassment, violence, fighting, and provoking riots and racial incidents." Often, parents of these youths are either unaware of their activities or support them (Reddick 1987, p. 9). Some of these loosely knit groups and their members drift from one city to another. Coplon (1988, p. 56) claimed that Skinhead ranks swelled throughout the United States from 300 in 1986 to 3,500 in 1988. The Anti-Defamation League has noted that Skinhead membership has stabilized at about 3,000 to 3,500 nationally (Anti-Defamation League 1990, p. 3; Applebome 1993). The League observed in 1993 that the number of Skinhead anti-Semitic homicide incidents had risen in recent years. Attacks on "blacks, Jews, homosexuals, immigrants, and members of other minority groups . . . have resulted in 28 deaths since 1987, 22 of them since 1990" (Applebome 1993).

Another type of white gang is the criminal biker or motorcycle gang. Some Hispanic and black motorcycle gangs and groups also exist. They may have elaborate rituals, signs, symbols, and tattoos and complex organizational structures—including written constitutions—with chapters of the larger gangs in Canada and Europe, as well as in many states. Some are white supremacists. They consist mostly of working-class young adults, sometimes from rural areas, with limited education. They have engaged in a wide range of illegal activity, including the sale and use of drugs, extortion, disorderly conduct, vandalism, theft, prostitution, white slavery, and hijacking (Commission de Police du Quebec 1980). They have been, in some cases, connected to major criminal organizations and syndicates, particularly in the transport or sale of drugs. In 1986 the Drug Enforcement Administration estimated that "outlaw" motorcycle gangs were responsible for manufacturing over 40 percent of the methamphetamine sold on the streets (Lyman 1989, p. 70).

Asian and Pacific Island Gangs

Increasing numbers of criminal and violent Asian youth gangs were reported in the 1970s, 1980s, and early 1990s. In the 1970s, Walter Miller (1982) estimated that the number of Asian youth gangs almost equaled the number of white gangs on the West Coast. In the 1980s, Duran believed that Asian youth gangs were almost twice as numerous as white gangs (Duran 1987). The gangs have "spread" from the West and East coasts to inland American cities. Several factors have especially contributed to the current development of Asian and Pacific Island gangs in the United States. First, the expansion of immigration quotas during the Kennedy and Johnson administrations provided an influx of immigrants from various countries, particularly from Southeast Asia. Large pools of immigrant youths began to collect in various parts of the country, especially in the West Coast, but also in several cities on the East Coast. In some cases they found existing gangs of the same or a related ethnicity; in other cases they formed their own distinctive ethnic gangs or later became integrated into older established gangs, particularly Chinese.

Second, the communities in which these groups settled, mainly white but also black and Hispanic, have sometimes failed to accept the new Asian immigrants and have either isolated or attacked them. The communities were not prepared to provide for the special cultural, social, and legal learning needs of the new immigrants. Asian immigrants also have been viewed by resident minority black or Hispanic communities as competitors for limited existing resources. A great deal of tension and animosity may develop, which leads to or encourages the creation of youth gangs as defensive groups to protect against the hostility of the established youth groups or gangs.

Asian youth gang members tend to be more secretive than non-Asian members. They are also less apparently interested in status, honor, or reputation, and more involved in criminal-gain activities such as extortion, burglary, and narcotics selling. Asian youth gang members are sometimes used by adult criminal organizations as "enforcers" (Breen and Allen 1983). They are difficult to detect because most police units lack Asian language facility or the confidence of Asian communities. However, significant numbers of Vietnamese, Cambodian, and other Asian youth gangs are reported to be typical street gangs: they protect turf, are involved in street violence, dress alike, take gang names, use graffiti, and have affiliate girl groups.

Third, each type of ethnic Asian or Pacific Island gang may have distinctive characteristics. Japanese,

Taiwanese, and Hong Kong youth gangs are reported to be the better organized, and perhaps more secretive. Vietnamese street gangs may be particularly mobile. Some Samoan gang youths manifest tattoos and particular gang dress, use graffiti, have reputations for violence, and are reported to have become assimilated into black gangs. Violent acts are said to be relatively more likely among Vietnamese, Chinese, Cambodian, and Laotian compared with Khmer or Hmong youth gangs. Filipino gang members in California are reported to be older, ranging in age from 20 to 40 years. While they may adopt black or Hispanic gang violent behavioral characteristics, they engage mainly in property crime activities (auto theft, extortion, burglary, drug trafficking) (Donovan 1988).

Some of the Asian youth gangs are found in expanding business communities. For example, Chinese youth or street gangs may be found in communities that are economically robust. They may be connected to Tongs—certain businessmen's associations—which may in turn be closely related to Triad criminal societies. Tongs may recruit or enjoy the allegiance of particular youth gangs. "The fear that gangs inspire in merchants is enormously useful to the Tongs which govern the community through intimidation" (Dannen 1992, p. 77). Chinese youth gangs in New York City were reported engaged in economically rewarding criminal ventures, especially heroin trafficking. With the new waves of Chinese immigrants, however, established street-gang and criminal or legitimate adult business relationships have been disrupted. Violence by competing street gangs, Tongs, and Triad groups has periodically escalated (see Chin 1990b). Dannen notes also that Chinese youth gangs in New York's Chinatown have a distinctive subculture: "a bizarre mixture of traits borrowed from the Hong Kong Triads (secret criminal societies) and the clichés of American and Chinese gangster movies. Gang members dress all in black and have their chests and arms tattooed with dragons, serpents, tigers, and sharp-taloned eagles" (Dannen 1992, p. 77).

CONCLUSION

Age, gender, and culture as well as economics and community structure affect the character and development of the youth gang problem. Youth gangs—as they concern the larger community—comprise mainly male adolescents and young adults. The gang problem, however, is distinctive in particular racial, ethnic, and cultural, often lower-class, contexts. Not only poverty but social disorganization, especially population change and movement, are key conditions or pressures for the development of gang systems and subcultures. The way the factors of poverty and criminal opportunity, family, and neighborhood disorganization interact and combine with racial and ethnic cultural traditions creates the basis for certain patterns of gang crime behavior. Certain gang subcultures, for example, Hispanic tend to be characterized by greater identification with turf and violence; black gang systems appear to be shifting toward an emphasis on economic survival and development of criminal opportunities, especially through street-level drug trafficking. Asian groups tend to be more interested in property crime, and in some cases are more integrated into adult crime and/or business organizations. White youth gangs are less violent but more varied in their structures and patterns of criminal behavior.

REFERENCES

ANDERSON, E. (1990). *Street wise.* Chicago: University of Chicago Press.

ANTI-DEFAMATION LEAGUE. (1986, June). Extremism targets the prisons: A special report. New York: Anti-Defamation League of B'nai B'rith, Civil Rights Division.

ANTI-DEFAMATION LEAGUE. (1987, November). Shaved for battle. Skinheads target American youth: A special report. New York: Anti-Defamation League of B'nai B'rith, Civil Rights Division.

ANTI-DEFAMATION LEAGUE. (1990). Neo-Nazi skinheads: A 1990 status report. An ADL Special Report. New York: Anti-Defamation League of B'nai B'rith, Civil Rights Division.

APPLEBOME, P. (1993, July 18). Skinhead violence grows, experts say. *The New York Times,* p. 18.

AYRES, B. D., JR. (1994, March 13). In a city of graffiti, gangs turn to violence to protect their art. *The New York Times,* p. 8.

BOBROWSKI, L. J. (1988, November). Collecting, organizing, and reporting street gang crime. Chicago Police Department, Special Functions Group.

BREEN, L., & ALLEN, M. M. (1983). Gang behavior: Psychological and law enforcement implications. *FBI Law Enforcement Bulletin 52(2):* 19–24.

CAMPBELL, A. (1984a). Girls' talk: The social representation of aggression by female gang members. *Criminal Justice and Behavior, 1(1),* 139–156.

CAMPBELL, A. (1984b). *The girls in the gang.* Oxford, United Kingdom: Basil Blackwell.

CANDAMIL, M. T. (1990). Female gangs. U.S. Department of Health and Human Services, Administration for Children, Youth, and Families. Washington, DC. (Unpublished paper.)

CARTWRIGHT, D. S., & HOWARD, K. I. (1966). Multivariate analysis of gang delinquency I: Ecological influence. *Multivariate Behavioral Research 1(3),* 321–337.

CHESNEY-LIND, M., MARKER, N., RODRIGUEZ STERN, I., YAP, A., SONG, V., REYES, H., REYES, Y., STERN, J., & TAIRA, J. A. (1992). *Gangs and delinquency in Hawaii.* Center for Youth Research, Social Science Research Institute, University of Hawaii at Manoa, January 3.

CHIN, K-L. (1990a). Chinese gangs and extortion. In C. R. Huff (Ed.), *Gangs in America* (pp. 129–145). Newbury Park, CA: Sage Publication.

CHIN, K-L. (1990b). *Chinese subculture and criminality. Non-traditional crime groups in America*. New York: Greenwood Press.

CLOWARD, R. A., & OHLIN, L. E. (1960). *Delinquency and opportunity: A theory of delinquent gangs*. Glencoe, IL: Free Press.

COHEN, B. (1969). The delinquency of gangs and spontaneous groups. In T. Sellin & M. E. Wolfgang (Eds.), *Delinquency selected studies* (pp. 61–111). New York: John Wiley & Sons.

COLLINS, H. C. (1979). Street gangs: Profiles for police (pp. 14–55). New York: New York City Police Department.

COMMISSION DE POLICE DU QUEBEC. (1980). *Motorcycle gangs in Quebec*. Quebec: Ministere des Communications.

COPLEN, B. R. (1988). Field interview. *National youth gang suppression and intervention project*. University of Chicago, School of Social Service Administration and the U. S. Office of Juvenile Justice and Delinquency Prevention.

CURRY, G. D., & SPERGEL, I. A. (1988). Gang homicide, delinquency and community. *Criminology, 26(August)*, 381–405.

CURRY, G. D., FOX, R. J., BALL, R. A., & STONE, D. (1992). *National assessment of law enforcement anti-gang information resources*. (Draft, 1992, Final Report). Morgantown, WV.

CURRY, G. D., BALL, R. A., & FOX, R. J. (1994). Gang crime and law enforcement recordkeeping. *Research in brief*. National Institute of Justice. Office of Justice Programs, U. S. Department of Justice, August.

DANNEN, F. (1992). Revenge of the green dragons (pp. 76–09). *The New Yorker*, November 16.

DAVIS, R. H. (1982a). Outlaw motorcyclists: A problem for police (Part 1). *FBI Law Enforcement Bulletin 51(10)*, 12–17.

DAVIS, R. H. (1982b). Outlaw motorcyclists: A problem for police (Part 2). *FBI Law Enforcement Bulletin 51(11)*, 16–22.

DEUKMAJIAN, G. (1981, June). *Report on youth gang violence in California*. Sacramento, CA: Department of Justice, State of California.

DOLAN, E. F., JR., & FINNEY, S. (1984). *Youth gangs*. New York: Julian Messner.

DONOVAN, J. (1988, August). An introduction to street gangs. A paper prepared for Senator John Garamemdi's Office, Sacramento, CA.

DUNSTON, L. G. (1990). *Reaffirming prevention*. Report of the Task Force on Juvenile Gangs. Albany, NY: New York State Division for Youth, March 1.

DURAN, M. (1987). Specialized gang supervision program (SGSP) progress report. Los Angeles County Probation Department.

FAGAN, J. (1987). Neighborhood education, mobilization, and organization for juvenile crime prevention. *Annuals American Academy of Political and Social Science, 494 (November)*, 55–70.

FAGAN, J. (1990). Social processes of delinquency and drug use among urban gangs. In C. R. Huff (Ed.), *Gangs in America* (pp. 183–219). Newbury Park, CA: Sage Publications.

FEDERAL REGISTER. (1987). Juvenile gang suppression and intervention program. Office of Juvenile Justice and Delinquency Prevention (OJJDP), Justice. Vol. 52, No. 133, July 13, pp. 26254–26259.

FEDERAL REGISTER. (1989). Availability of FY 1989 funds and request for applications. Youth gang drug prevention program. Administration on Children, Youth, and Families (ACYF), Office of Human Development Services (OHDS), U.S. Department Health and Human Services, Vol. 54(71), Friday, April 14, pp. 15108–15129.

FEDERAL REGISTER. (1992). Youth gang drug prevention program; Availability of funds and request for applications; Notice. Administration on Children, Youth, and Families (ACYF), U.S. Department of Health and Human Services, Vol. 57(55), Friday, March 20, pp. 9865–9897.

FRIEDMAN, C. J., MANN, F., & ADELMAN, H. (1976). Juvenile street gangs: The victimization of youth. *Adolescence 11(44)*, 527–533.

GONZALEZ, D. (1992, January 16). Teenagers send a message of hate. *The New York Times* (p. A16).

HARRIS, M. G. (1988). CHOLAS, *Latino girls and gangs*. New York: AMS Press.

HOROWITZ, R. (1983). *Honor and the American dream*. New Brunswick, NJ: Rutgers University Press.

HUTCHESON, R. (1993). Blazon nouveau: Gang graffiti in the barrios of Los Angeles and Chicago. In S. Cummings & D. Monti (Eds.), *Gangs: The origins and impact of contemporary youth gangs in the United States*. New York: State University New York Press.

JACKSON, R. K., & MCBRIDE, W. D. (1985). *Understanding street gangs*. Costa Mesa, CA: Custom Publishing Company.

KLEIN, M. W. (1968). From association to guilt: The group guidance project in juvenile gang intervention. Los Angeles, CA: Youth Studies Center, University of Southern California and the Los Angeles County Probation Department.

KLEIN, M. W. (1971). *Street gangs and street workers*. Englewood Cliffs, NJ: Prentice Hall.

KLEIN, M. W., MAXSON, C. L., & CUNNINGHAM, L. C. (1988, May). Gang involvement in cocaine 'rock' trafficking. Project summary/Final report, Center for Research on Crime and Social Control, Social Science Research Institute, University of Southern California. Los Angeles.

KLEIN, M. W. (1991). 'Crack,' street gangs, and violence. *Criminology 29(4)*, 623–650.

KNOX, G. W. (1991). Personal communication. August 26.

KNOX, G. W. (1991). Findings from the 1991 National Survey of Juvenile Corrections. A preliminary report. Gang Crime Research Center, Chicago State University, Department of Corrections and Criminal Justice.

LAUDERBACK, D., HANSEN, J., & WALDORF, D. (1992). 'Sisters are doin' it for themselves': A black female gang in San Francisco. *The Gang Journal, 1(1)*, 57–72.

LEE, F. R. (1991, November 11). For gold earrings and protection, more girls take violence. *The New York Times* (pp. A1, 16).

LOS ANGELES COUNTY SHERIFF'S DEPARTMENT. (1985). Testimony. California State Task Force on Youth Gang Violence.

LYMAN, M. D. (1989). *Gangland: Drug trafficking by organized criminals*. Springfield, IL: Charles C. Thomas.

MAXSON, C. L., GORDON, M. A., KLEIN, M. W. (1985). Differences between gang and nongang homicides. *Criminology, 23*, 209–222.

MILLER, W. B. (1958). Lower class culture as a generating milieu of gang delinquency. *The Journal of Social Issues, 14(3)*, 5–19.

MILLER, W. B. (1975). Violence by youth gangs and youth groups as a crime problem in major American cities. National Institute for Juvenile Justice and Delinquency Prevention, U. S. Department of Justice. Washington, DC: U. S. Government Printing Office.

MILLER, W. B. (1976). Youth gangs in the urban crisis era. In J. F. Short, Jr. (Ed.), *Delinquency, crime, and society* (pp. 91–128). Chicago: University of Chicago Press.

MILLER, W. B. (1982). Crime by youth gangs and groups in the United States. National Institute for Juvenile Justice and Delinquency Prevention, Office of Juvenile Justice and Delinquency Prevention, U. S. Department of Justice. Washington, DC: Office of Juvenile Justice and Delinquency Prevention.

MOORE, J. W. (1978). *Homeboys*. Philadelphia, PA: Temple University Press.

MOORE, J. W. (1991). *Going down to the barrio*. Philadelphia, PA: Temple University Press.

MUEHLBAUER, G., & DODDER, L. (1983). *The losers: Gang delinquency in an American suburb*. New York: Praeger.

MYERHOFF, H. L., & MYERHOFF, B. G. (1976). Field observations of middle class 'gangs'. In R. Giallombardo (Ed.), *Juvenile delinquency* (pp. 295–304). New York: John Wiley & Sons.

NEW YORK CITY YOUTH BOARD. (1960). *Reaching the fighting gang*. New York: New York City Youth Board.

OFFICE OF CRIMINAL JUSTICE PLANNING QUARTERLY NEWSLETTER. (1990). Copycat gangs: Phenomenon among the wealthy. *Newsline, 5(2)*, 11.

REDDICK, A. J. (1987, October). Issue paper: Youth gangs in Florida. Committee on youth, Florida House of Representatives.

REINER, I. (1992, May). Gangs, crime and violence in Los Angeles. Los Angeles, CA: Office of the District Attorney of the County of Los Angeles.

SAN DIEGO ASSOCIATION OF GOVERNMENTS. (1982, June). Juvenile violence and gang-related crime. San Diego, CA: Association of State Governments.

SHORT, J. F., JR. (1963). Introduction to *The gang: A study of one thousand three hundred thirteen gangs in Chicago*, by F. Thrasher. Chicago: University of Chicago Press.

SHORT, J. F., & STRODTBECK, F. L. (1965). *Group process and gang delinquency*. Chicago: University of Chicago Press.

SPERGEL, I. A. (1964). *Slumville, racketville, haulburg*. Chicago: University of Chicago Press.

SPERGEL, I. A. (1983). *Violent gangs in Chicago: Segmentation and integration*. Chicago: University of Chicago, School of Social Service Administration.

SPERGEL, I. A. (1984). Violent gangs in Chicago: In search of social policy. *Social Service Review, 58*.

SPERGEL, I. A. (1986). The violent gang in Chicago: A local community approach. *Social Service Review, 60*.

SPERGEL, I. A. (1992, January). Community mobilization. Technical Assistance Manual. Chicago: University of Chicago, School of Social Service Administration.

SPERGEL, I. A., & CURRY, G. D., WITH R. E. ROSS AND R. L. CHANCE. (1990, April). Survey of youth gang problems and pro-grams in 45 cities and 6 sites. Chicago: University of Chicago, School of Social Service Administration.

SULLIVAN, M. L. (1983). Youth crime: New York's two varieties. *New York Affairs. Crime and Criminal Justice, 8(1)*, 31–48.

SULLIVAN, M. L. (1989). *'Getting paid': Youth crime and work in the inner city*. Ithaca, NY: Cornell University Press.

SUNG, B. L. (1977). Gangs in New York's Chinatown. New York: Department of Asian Studies, City College of New York, Monograph No. 6.

SUTTLES, G. D. (1968). *The social order of the slum*. Chicago: University of Chicago Press.

TAYLOR, C. S. (1988). Youth gangs organize for power, money. *School Safety* (Spring), 26–27.

TAYLOR, C. S. (1993). *Girl gangs, women and drugs*. East Lansing, MI: Michigan State University Press.

THRASHER, F. M. (1927, 1936). *The gang* (2nd Ed.). Chicago: University of Chicago Press.

TORRES, D. M. (1980). Gang violence reduction project evaluation report. Sacramento: California Youth Authority.

TRACY, P. E. (1982). Gang membership and violent offenders: Preliminary results from the 1958 cohort study. Philadelphia: Center for Studies in Criminology and Criminal Law, University of Pennsylvania.

VIGIL, J. D. (1988a). Street socialization, locura behavior, and violence among Chicano gang members. In J. Kraus & A. Morales (Eds.), *Violence and homicide in Hispanic communities*. Washington, DC: National Institute of Mental Health.

VIGIL, J. D. (1988b). *Barrio gangs: Street life and identity in Southern California*. Austin: University of Texas Press.

VIGIL, J. D. (1990). Cholos and gangs: Culture change and street youth in Los Angeles. In C. R. Huff (Ed.), *Gangs in America* (pp. 116–128). Newbury Park, CA: Sage Publications.

VIGIL, J. D., & LONG, J. M. (1990). Emic and etic perspectives on gang culture: The Chicano case. In C. R. Huff (Ed.), *Gangs in America* (pp. 55–70). Newbury Park, CA: Sage Publications.

WHYTE, W. F. (1943). *Street gang society*. Chicago: University of Chicago Press.

YABLONSKY, L. (1962). *The violent gang*. New York: MacMillan.

Kids, Guns, and Violence

Conclusions and implications

1995

Joseph F. Sheley and James D. Wright

The contemporary discussion of juvenile crime is dominated by the imagery of guns, drugs, gangs, and wanton violence. As the rates of crime and violence committed by and against juveniles have increased, the imagery has become progressively more alarmist and terrifying. The "troubled teens" of a decade or two ago have been transformed in media and scholarly accounts into roving bands of well-armed marauders spraying bullets indiscriminately at all who venture near. For all the media copy these themes and images command, there has been relatively little previous research concerning where, how, and why juveniles acquire, carry, and use guns. The research reported here was designed to provide some reliable, quantitative information on these topics.

Our assessment has centered on two critical groups: criminally active juveniles currently incarcerated in state reformatories and inner-city youth in ten urban high schools. Both these groups represent extreme cases. The average criminally active juvenile is probably not nearly as active or as violent as were the juveniles who are now incarcerated for their crimes; and likewise, students in ten of the nation's more troubled urban high schools are certainly not "representative" of high school students in general or even of central-city public high school students in particular. Thus, the depiction of youth crime and violence that emerges from our study is doubtlessly more ominous than it would be had we surveyed a nationally representative sample of inner-city teens.

Still, while ours is not a probability sample of juveniles or of criminally active juveniles, we think it is a fair sampling of the juvenile violence *problem*. Our findings are not radically at odds with those of other studies of the topic; also . . . problems that only a few years ago were concentrated in "troubled" inner-city high schools have begun to spread noticeably into once-safe neighborhoods and communities. Thus, while the results we have reported do not generalize in the statistical sense to larger or wider populations, they may well be pointing to what is to come for those larger populations.

Among the many findings reported here, which ones are most relevant to public policy issues? First, we have learned that owning and carrying guns were fairly common behaviors in both our samples. About nine of every ten inmates had owned a gun at some time. Fifty-five percent had carried a gun routinely before being incarcerated. One in five male students possessed a gun during the period of our survey; one in three had access to a gun; 12 percent carried guns routinely. Thus, while these behaviors are by no means universal, least of all among the student sample, neither are they unusual. In the inner-city neighborhoods from which our respondents are drawn, firearms seem to have become part of the landscape, one among the many cheerless realities of daily existence.

The evident implication of these findings is that the problem of juvenile violence seems not to be confined to a small group of deviant "bad apples." Violence and the means by which it is perpetrated, rather, have come to be widespread in the impoverished inner city and may be spreading outward. Indeed, a leading concern voiced by many observers of the contemporary urban scene is that violent behavior has become culturally *normative* in the context of underclass life (Auletta 1983; Devine and Wright 1993; Harrington 1984; Jencks and Peterson 1991; Rose and McClain 1990; Wilson 1987). We are left, then, pondering whether we should attempt to control the flow of guns to juveniles or to attack the conditions producing gun-related behaviors. Controlling the flow of guns—"cracking down" on guns is the colloquial phrase—is a euphemism for enacting stricter gun control laws, increasing penalties for juveniles caught carrying guns, and disrupting the flow of arms traffic among youth. Policy discussions of conditions that generate violence generally focus attention on drugs and gangs as youth problems and on the larger issue of poverty and the underclass in this country. Let us consider gun control efforts first.

CONTROLLING GUNS

Much of the recent policy debate over firearms has concerned the wisdom of banning ownership or sales of military-style combat rifles to the general public and, as a matter of fact, sales of many of these weapons were banned federally by provisions of the 1994 Crime Bill. (Several states had already enacted bans on the ownership of these kinds of firearms.) Just as the small, cheap Saturday Night Special once was thought to be the "weapon of choice" for criminals (but turned out not to be), assault weapons are now commonly said to be the weapons of choice for drug dealers, youth gangs, and juvenile offenders of the sort studied here. There is practically no systematic evidence to support such an assertion. The fraction of guns confiscated from criminals by police that could be called assault weapons, even using liberal definitions, is not more than 1 or 2 percent (Kleck 1991:73).

For all the attention these assault weapons have received, it is worth stressing that, whether a matter of accessibility or preference, the most likely owned gun of either sample was a hand weapon (automatic or not) of at least .357 caliber. This is not to say they are uninterested in military-style equipment; more than one-third possessed a military-style assault rifle at the time of their incarceration. Still, these are highly specialized weapons that are generally ill suited for the day-to-day business of urban thuggery (or for protecting oneself against that thuggery). Outfitted with high-capacity magazines or clips, these weapons are bulky, relatively hard to handle, and impossible to conceal, and it would be a rare circumstance indeed that would require the firepower such weapons represent. For most offensive *and* defensive purposes, hand weapons are much better suited and, indeed, are far more commonly owned in both of our samples, as among the gun-owning public at large.

The recurrent emphasis in policy circles on specific *types* of guns (whether today's emphasis on military-style guns or the earlier emphasis on small, cheap handguns) is generally misplaced (Kleck 1991:Ch. 3). There may well be good reasons to restrict the availability of certain types of guns, but the attention now being given to military-style weapons illustrates what Kleck has called "searching for 'bad' guns," the persistent hope among gun control advocates that if we can just find a way to ban "bad guns" and leave "good guns" alone, we will reduce the level of crime and violence but not infringe on the rights of legitimate gun owners. Yet, since the "goodness" or "badness" of a gun surely inheres in the motivations and intentions of its user, not in the features of the gun itself, this approach, although commonly urged, is likely to be unproductive.

Turning from the issue of gun type to motivation, perhaps the most striking feature of our findings on juveniles' gun ownership is the *quality* of the firearms they possess. Theirs are not lesser weapons, Saturday Night Specials, homemade zip guns, or anything of the sort. Rather, they are mostly well made, easy to shoot, accurate, reliable firearms with considerable firepower. Many of the incarcerated juvenile felons we surveyed were as well armed as the police. Given the apparently pervasive atmosphere of violence and desperation (certainly given the *perception* of such an atmosphere by our respondents), the preference for high-quality, high-firepower small arms hardly comes as a surprise. Whether the intention is to protect what one has or to take by force what one wants, success depends on being adequately armed. The inner logic of an "arms race" seems altogether too apt. No street criminal (whether juvenile or adult) would willingly carry anything other than the best small arms he could

lay hands on; neither would anyone seeking protection from those criminals. Given the evidently heavy flow of firearms of all sorts through the neighborhoods in question, the natural process of selection obviously favors large, well-made, highly lethal guns among both perpetrators and their possible victims, which is to say, among nearly everybody.[1]

The national alarm over youth and violence has been accompanied by insistent demands for "tough," "new" gun control legislation of one or another sort. We think there is probably some merit in increasing criminal penalties for the unlawful transfer of firearms to juveniles; if nothing else, this would give the police and the courts an extra plea-bargaining chip. But it is a sobering lesson that most of the methods used by juveniles to obtain guns already are against the law. Consider: It is already illegal for juveniles to purchase handguns through normal retail channels, pawnshops included. Likewise, it is already illegal to cross state lines to obtain guns. Theft of guns from homes, cars, and shipments is against the law; transferring or selling stolen property is also illegal. Transferring a firearm to a person with a criminal record is against the law. Possession of guns by persons with histories of alcohol or drug abuse is against the law. Street sources and friends who deal firearms to or make proxy purchases for juveniles are surely contributing to the delinquency of minors and are probably in violation of other laws as well.

Likewise, nearly everything juveniles do with their guns is already against the law. Unlicensed carrying of firearms is illegal everywhere; discharging firearms within city limits is illegal almost everywhere; bringing a gun onto school property is unlawful in most jurisdictions; assaults, robbery, murder, and other acts of violence are unlawful in every jurisdiction. Since we are not deterring juveniles from engaging in these behaviors in the first place, it is doubtful that increased threats regarding procurement of the tools to engage in the behaviors will accomplish much. The problem, it seems, is not that the appropriate laws do not exist. The problem instead is that the laws that do exist either are not or cannot be enforced due to the enormity of the problem and the lack of sufficient resources, and that the persons who are involved in firearms transactions with juveniles clearly are not concerned in the least with the legality of the transaction.

Informal commerce in small arms involving purchases, swaps, and trades among private parties is inherently difficult or impossible to regulate, is heavily exploited by juveniles as well as adults to obtain guns, and successfully subverts the legal apparatus we have erected to prevent guns from falling into the wrong hands (that is, controls imposed at the point of retail purchase). That much of the illicit commerce involves informal buys, swaps, and trades poses strict and obvious limits on the effectiveness of gun controls enacted at the point of retail sale, for example, the recently enacted Brady Law, which establishes a national five-day waiting period for handgun purchases. Since most "bad guys," adult and juvenile, do not obtain guns through normal retail channels, a five-day waiting period will not affect their firearms acquisitions. So far as juveniles specifically are concerned, retail sale of handguns is already illegal for persons under the age of twenty-one and retail sale of rifles and shotguns illegal for persons under age eighteen.

If retail sales are not the source of firearms for juveniles, then the illegal gun supply merits attention. It is fairly obvious that theft is the ultimate (if not proximate) source of many or most of the firearms that now circulate in the informal street market; otherwise, prices presumably would be higher. Theft erodes the distinction between legitimate and illegitimate firearms (or between "right hands" and "wrong hands"), since any firearm that can be legally possessed by a legitimate owner can be stolen from that owner and thus enter the illicit street commerce in guns. We feel there is merit in a national campaign to encourage responsible firearm ownership and to persuade legitimate firearm owners to store their weapons in such a way as to discourage theft. However, so long as guns are available to *anyone*, they will also be available to any *juvenile* or any *felon* with the means and motives to steal one or to exploit the informal network of family and friends to obtain a gun stolen by someone else. Surveys dating to the 1950s confirm that half the households in the United States possess one or more guns, and so on the average, a gun is available to be stolen in every second home.[2]

Seeing little hope in deterring juveniles from stealing legitimately owned guns, some gun control advocates reason that if guns were generally more difficult to obtain by the public at large, then there would be fewer guns available to steal. This in turn would reduce the number of guns circulating in the street market and thus decrease the number that fall into the "wrong hands." It seems to us that the "restricted-mar-

ket" model is an example of reasoning from a correlation to a cause in exactly the wrong direction. If there were many fewer guns available to steal from the general gun-owning public, the street market in guns would not magically disappear; rather, more organized street sources would obtain the requisite supply of firearms from other sources. The general lack of organized supply at the moment is mostly a function of the relatively low profit associated with selling guns to juveniles: the supply is just too great. Even if we could halt the entire domestic production of firearms, which is very unlikely, and also confiscate the larger share of the two hundred million or so firearms currently in circulation in the United States (Wright et al. 1983; Kleck 1991), even less likely, there is little we could do to prevent the manufacture of firearms elsewhere in the world or their illegal importation into this country. If it is possible to organize a system of commerce to bring hundreds of tons of cocaine from Colombia and get it into the hands of people on the streets of our cities, it is certainly possible to organize a system that will bring hundreds of tons of small arms from Israel or Switzerland or the Czech Republic or Brazil and supply a street market in firearms as well.

We have no evidence in the present study to suggest that an international illicit market in small arms already exists (at least not as a supplier to our kind of respondent). That is because theft is a *convenient* way to obtain firearms for street sale in the current regulatory and gun ownership environment. It does not follow that if we could eliminate that convenience by reducing household stockpiles, we would therefore shut down the street market entirely. More generally, if a demand for some commodity exists, be it guns, drugs, pornography, or whatever, then satisfying that demand will be a profitable enterprise. The commodity will be supplied through an illegal network of smuggling and distribution if no other market mechanism is available. Bans on otherwise desired commodities will sometimes affect their price but generally not their availability to anyone willing to pay the price. And if, as we have suggested, guns may now be a bargain at any price (standing as the last line of defense against predation, intimidation, or death), then efforts to deal with the violence problem through restrictions on the potential supply of firearms are bound not to be very effective. A juvenile who "must have a gun" now can easily steal enough money to purchase one on the street; that same juvenile likely will work somewhat harder to steal more money to obtain the more expensive weapon.

Recognizing that prohibition of retail gun sales to juveniles has generally not prevented young people from arming themselves, many jurisdictions are currently contemplating the passage of legislation that would make it illegal for juveniles even to possess guns. Presumably, the point of such legislation is to give the police a reason to arrest a young person found to be carrying a gun. But unlicensed carrying of guns is already illegal for juveniles and adults alike; more generally, it is hard to believe that the police could not find a legitimate reason to arrest virtually any juvenile they thought to be carrying a gun in the absence of a legal prohibition against juvenile firearms possession. Thus it is difficult to see the exact point of this sort of legislation. As in many other cases involving "gun control," the point seems more symbolic than practical; the intent is more to strike a posture of concern about the problem of juvenile violence than to provide police or the courts with legislative tools necessary to do their job.

DISRUPTING THE ILLEGAL GUN MARKET

Assuming that little can be done to alter the number of guns circulating in this country, some have suggested harassing the sellers of guns to the point that it is just too difficult to do business profitably. Reiss and Roth (1993), for example, argue for centralized and street-level tactics to disrupt illegal gun sales, like those now used to intervene in illegal drug markets. Such tactics might include

> buy-bust operations, high-priority investigation and prosecution of alleged unregulated gun dealers, the development of minors arrested in possession of guns as informants against gun sources, phony fencing operations for stolen guns, high priority investigations and prosecutions of burglaries and robberies in which guns are stolen, and high mandatory minimum sentences for those who steal or illegally sell guns. (p. 280)

On the one hand, it is hard to imagine a "war on guns" that borrows tactics from a fairly obviously failed "war on drugs" (Inciardi 1992). On the other, according to researcher David M. Kennedy (1994), a disruption experiment in Tampa, Florida, seems to have had a noticeable impact on drug dealing in that

city. A heavy and directed police presence around known dealing sites forced drug dealers to move around more than they wished. "Reverse stings" (in which buyers were arrested by police posing as dealers) frightened potential customers. Dealers' drug stashes were located and seized. Dealers' places of business (abandoned houses, shops, etc.) were closed or torn down. Local ordinances were employed to clear crowds from known trafficking sites. The power of such harassment lay in its multiple attacks on the free functioning of the drug market. In Kennedy's estimation, six months of concentrated disruption virtually eliminated dealers from public activity.

Can such tactics be applied to the suppliers of guns on the illegal market? Kennedy sees possible parallels. By way of illustration, he suggests that police could cultivate informants who could identify persons with stockpiles of guns and could offer juveniles caught with guns plea bargains based on giving up their suppliers. They could press for state laws making those who sell guns to juveniles jointly liable for crimes committed with those guns. They could mount reverse sting operations and coordinate drug and firearm offensives so that drug dealers who also profit from gun sales would view the police attention to guns as bad for the drug business. Stores, bars, and other businesses that front for those selling guns to juveniles could be shut down through civil or licensing proceedings. In short, there seem to be a number of means by which to make the sale of firearms to juveniles more difficult and less profitable.

Until such tactics are evaluated experimentally, their potency is uncertain. Undoubtedly, they will have *some* positive effect. Overall, though, there are some serious issues to be addressed. First, the cost of prolonged concentration of police resources to the level of harassment in question may be prohibitive for many communities. Second, Kennedy argues that the goal of harassment of drug dealers is the absence of public drug dealing, and thus the public perception of community disorder. Clearly, highly visible, public gun transactions can and should be discouraged. But most illegal gun transactions are not so blatant; most citizens have observed drugs being sold at one time or another, but few have seen firearms peddled. While the public feels better when drug transactions are driven underground, the issue regarding guns is not transactions but uses of guns. Harassment of gun dealers may disrupt sales, but will they influence gun use patterns?

Third and related, though juveniles appear interested in new and better guns, the fact remains that a given juvenile only needs *one* firearm. Here the interest in acquiring firearms differs from that associated with acquiring drugs. Drugs disappear when used, and stocks must be replenished. Guns need only be reloaded.[3] In the final analysis, disruption of the gun market likely will have two results: guns will cost more but interested youth will raise the funds to make the one purchase they see as necessary; they will then hold onto that one gun for a longer period before "trading up." The accuracy of this gaze into the crystal ball, of course, is as open to refutation as are any of the potential disruption possibilities Kennedy suggests.

DRUGS AND GUNS

If controlling guns and disrupting gun sales is not likely to reduce firearm-related violence, where then do we turn? As we have suggested, the key to understanding the problem of juveniles and guns lies not in the trigger that is being pulled but in the juvenile's perceived need and evident willingness to pull that trigger. In short, we need to explore the juvenile's motivation for carrying and using firearms if we are to devise strategies to reduce such activities.

Much has been made in the media of the role that drugs play in gun-related violence among juveniles. Our findings do not belie these understandings, but they do suggest greater complexity to the relationships than is ordinarily assumed. We note, first, that it is not wholly clear that drug activity drives gun activity today as it may have some years ago. Street gang homicide in Chicago, for example, has had relatively little to do with drugs in recent years (Block and Block 1993; see also Klein, Maxson, and Cunningham 1991). We believe that ten years ago the average urban juvenile with a gun likely had some connection to drug trafficking. Picture such youths as lying at the core of a series of concentric circles. Those in the circle immediately adjacent to the core, only marginally involved in drugs, nonetheless felt endangered by the youth at the core and responded by carrying guns. Those in the next ring then were threatened and followed suit. Ultimately, the problem rippled to urban areas (and, if our data concerning suburban gun use are generalizable, beyond urban areas) once considered immune to it. And with that spread came a shift in the mean use of a gun. The norm no longer appears drug related, but protection or dispute related.

Second, it is abundantly clear that to the extent drug use of *any* kind increases, so also do criminal behavior, gun possession, and gun use. Drug *dealing* at any level is also linked to higher levels of crime and gun-related activity. Nonetheless, the majority of both inmate and student respondents did not use hard drugs and few who did used regularly (i.e., more than a few times a year). The popular image of inner-city youth and, especially, criminally involved inner-city youth as drug addicts one and all finds little support here. Substantial numbers of non-users among our respondents had committed serious crimes and had significant levels of gun-related activities.

Our interpretation of these findings is that drug activity is less a precipitant of crime and gun use than one crucial element in the new subculture of inner-city underclass youth. That is, the drug epidemic in the inner cities has certainly worsened the problems of crime and violence, but it is misleading to think that drugs per se are their ultimate or final cause (Wright and Devine 1994). The primal attraction of drugs is that they provide immediate gratification; they give a sense of euphoria or well-being *right now*. Arguments against using drugs—that one might *become* an addict or *eventually* destroy one's physical health—all require an orientation toward the future, a concern, in short, about tomorrow's consequences of today's behaviors. And this is precisely the sort of orientation, we argue below, that the structural conditions of the inner city have destroyed among many of its youth.

In this sense, drugs are not the cause of crime and violence so much as they are indicative or symptomatic of a more general unraveling of social norms, values, and expectations that otherwise constrain behavior. What has arisen in the inner city is a subculture where anything goes, a subculture that is essentially defined by estrangement from—indeed, hostility to—the norms and conventions of the larger society. That this subculture is rejected and even despised by the majority of inner-city residents does not exempt the majority from the need to live with and deal with its consequences.

When all is said and done, the drug epidemic has become a convenient scapegoat for many of the ills of the inner city. This, however, mistakes a symptom for a cause. Three-quarters of our juvenile inmates have fired a gun at someone. Most did *not* do so because they were high on drugs or because they were strung out and needed more drugs; most did so because they live in a moral universe that ascribes no particular value to a human life, that counsels no hesitance in pulling the trigger, that promotes immediate gratification for the very simple reason that tomorrow may never come. Inner-city juveniles (or more accurately put, that minority of inner-city juveniles whose anomic and antisocial behavior now defines the conditions of life in the cities) own and carry guns, use and deal drugs, and perpetrate crimes and violence all for the same reasons: because they have little or no discernible future to which they can aspire and therefore nothing much better to do.

GANGS AND GUNS

What has just been said about drugs and guns can also be said about gangs and guns. The public image linking youth gangs with urban violence is not wholly supported by our findings. On the one hand, youth who are involved in gang activities also show higher levels of gun possession and use; the more structured the gang involvement, the stronger these tendencies. Yet, one-third of our inmate respondents claimed no prior affiliation with a gang. Only 22 percent of the student sample were affiliated with a gang. Thus, judging from our findings, a sizable percentage of criminally active youth and a very large percentage of inner-city high school students have no gang involvements. Gun possession and usage is far more common than is gang membership.

Like drugs, the gang has become an all-purpose scapegoat for the afflictions of the inner city. As a form of social organization, gangs exist for some purpose and reason. In the context of the contemporary urban underclass, gangs exist because there is safety in numbers and because they provide some degree of organization and control in what are otherwise disorganized, out-of-control neighborhoods. In many cases, urban gangs have assumed the "social control" function that the customary agents of social control can no longer adequately provide. They also give estranged youth something meaningful to which to belong, a source of identity that is otherwise lacking. Gangs express the pathology of inner-city underclass life and the new urban culture of violence, but are the

consequence of these developments more than the cause.

URBAN STRUCTURE AND CULTURE

It is probably true that every major U.S. city could make a substantial short-term dent in its crime and violence problems by incarcerating several hundred of its high-rate juvenile offenders; mandatory and severe sentencing is yet another commonly urged approach to the juvenile violence problem. But all else equal in terms of extant social environment, there will soon be several hundred new high-rate juvenile offenders to take their place. Shall we continue this process until we have incarcerated an entire class of the urban population?

There is a useful analogy to be drawn between the violence problem and the yellow fever problem that plagued many southern cities in the nineteenth century. The vector for the yellow fever infection was eventually found to be the mosquito; once that essential fact was learned, it became possible to control yellow fever by eradicating the conditions under which mosquitoes bred. No one suggested that the solution to yellow fever was to wander through the swamps of Louisiana removing the mouthparts of mosquitoes with little tweezers, so they could no longer bite people and thereby spread the infection. Guns, we suggest, are the "mouthparts" of our contemporary epidemic of violence; as such, "gun control" has no better chance of solving the violence problem than "proboscis control" had to solve the yellow fever problem.

Daniel Polsby (1994) offers a similarly useful analogy, in this instance between the population of violent offenders and the population of game animals such as deer. His essential insight is that the size of the herd is determined strictly by the carrying capacity of the habitat, not by annual efforts to cull it, for example, through hunting. Imprisoning violent juvenile offenders is very much like culling the herd; the measure will result in a short-term reduction in herd size but the herd will quickly breed back up to the carrying capacity limit. The opportunities and motivations to commit crime, and therefore the number of crimes that are committed, are features of the urban habitat. Over any sufficiently long period, therefore, the number of offenders and offenses will not be affected by the rate of incarceration. In the absence of attention to the defining features of the urban habitat, proposals to control juvenile crime through increased incarceration are doomed.

To this point, our search for policy to reduce gun-related violence has focused on attempts to keep firearms out of the hands of juveniles. We see little hope in this vein. As well, we have examined the presence of drug and gang activities as central features of the violent social environment and have found them implicated in but not wholly explicative of urban violence. Strictly speaking, the nature of our data on juveniles and guns permits exploration of little else. However, two findings surely point toward contemporary urban structure and culture as the source of gun-related activity among youth and as the necessary target of change in the level of that activity. First, there are simply too many juveniles in possession of and carrying guns to indicate that the cause and cure lie with individual carriers or even with social phenomena like gangs and drugs. Second, our findings indicate dramatically that, for the majority of inner-city youth, inmates and students alike, self-protection in a hostile, violent, and dangerous world is the chief reason to own and carry guns. By default, these findings indicate the need to reduce the *demand* for guns, which implies addressing the inner-city problems (beyond drugs and gangs) for which guns have become the perceived solution.

It is erroneous to depict every poor neighborhood in every large city as a killing field or to suggest that all residents of the inner city now go about their daily business armed. At the same time, it is also a mistake to understate the levels of violence and fear of violence that now pervade inner-city life. In the past few years, homicide rates in nearly every major city have reached record highs. Arrests for drug offenses have swollen jail and prison populations beyond capacity; most cities of which we are aware find themselves plagued by increasingly violent youth gangs. Surveys of young children in inner cities report astonishingly high percentages who say they have seen someone shot or seen a dead body in the streets. In circumstances such as these, possession of a firearm provides a necessary if otherwise undesirable edge against the uncertainty of police protection and the daily threat of intimidation or victimization.

The pervasive atmosphere of violence extends from the streets into the schools. Male and female respondents to our survey alike viewed their schools as relatively violent places. Fourteen percent of the males and 15 percent of the females described themselves as scared in school most of the time. Just under 50 percent of each group knew schoolmates at whom shots had been fired. The level of violent victimization among the students was exceptionally high. Twenty percent of the males and 6 percent of the females had been shot at in or on the way to or from school. Ten percent of the males and 7 percent of the females had been stabbed. Both reacting to and promoting this violence, 3 percent of the males and 1 percent of the females carry a gun to school all or most of the time.

The perception that so many people are armed presumably combines with the reality of frequent victimization and with routine transit through precarious places (including schools) and involvement in dangerous activities (such as drug deals, gang ventures, and crimes) to create what amounts to a siege mentality among individuals and a subculture of fear for inner-city youth in the aggregate. More than two-thirds of the inmates we surveyed, for example, said they had fired guns in self-defense. Among the activities that increase the likelihood of gun possession and use are gun dealing and drug dealing (nearly half of the inmates had dealt guns, more than 80 percent had dealt drugs). Gun and drug dealers are considerably more likely to engage in serious criminal activity as well. In general, the more dangerous the environment and activities of juveniles, the more likely they are to own and carry firearms.

The apparent implication of these findings is that our juveniles are strongly, not weakly, motivated to own and carry guns; these behaviors appear, in our findings at least, to be largely utilitarian reactions to life in neighborhoods ruled more and more by predation, that is, neighborhoods where the police can*not* be counted on to protect life and property. Surely, when people have concluded that their very ability to survive depends on the protection and power that having a gun affords, then arguments against owning and carrying guns become unpersuasive. That many of our juveniles seek protection from one another does not diminish the point; if the issue is indeed survival, then weapons are a bargain at nearly any price.

It is not necessary to review here *all* the various social, economic, and structural conditions that have created this emergent underclass culture. In brief, the national poverty rate has been generally increasing since about 1980, and so the sheer number of the poor has increased, especially in the central cities. Even more troubling, the rate of *chronic* poverty has increased (Devine, Plunkett, and Wright 1992). At the same time, the poverty of the poor has deepened as the gap between affluence and poverty has widened; the proportion of total national income going to the poorest quintile now stands at the lowest point in the twentieth century. Simultaneously, nearly all central cities have been losing population for the past two decades as more affluent middle-class families, black and white, leave for the suburban fringe. The net result of these economic and demographic developments is an increasing concentration of increasingly poor people in inner-city areas and a substantially reduced tax base to provide the revenues required to respond to the increasingly deeper needs of the population that remains. The neighborhoods are deteriorating, infested with dealers, addicts, criminals, and other vermin, both human and otherwise (Skogan 1990). City services range from pathetic to nonexistent; no one tends to public spaces or collects the trash and litter. Many areas are essentially unpoliced, their perimeters defined more or less officially as the boundaries of free-fire zones within which anything goes.

Other developments have exacerbated the resulting problems. Critically, the proportion of young people among the inner-city poor has also sharply increased (Wilson 1987:36–37). Public schools are generally in disarray, dropout rates are high and increasing, joblessness among young central city nonwhite males now routinely exceeds 40 or 50 percent, and vast numbers of entry-level manufacturing jobs have exited the urban areas for the suburbs or abroad (Kasarda 1985). The consequence is an increasingly large cohort of impoverished young people without adequate educations and with little or no prospects for decent jobs—a cohort to whom, in essence, conventional routes of upward mobility have been closed off. Many of these youth have a much better chance of going to prison than going to college, a better chance of becoming homeless or addicted than of becoming stably employed.

Within African-American communities, the exodus of successful, upwardly mobile persons from the inner city has left the young with fewer and fewer role models; the steady deterioration of the inner-city economic structure has created joblessness and underemployment on a vast scale; the decline of indigenous community organizations such as black churches and black-owned businesses has further reduced the presence of successful lives to emulate and respect. "Thus, in such neighborhoods the chances are overwhelming that children will seldom interact on a sustained basis with people who are employed or with families that have a steady breadwinner" (Wilson 1987:57). The role models that remain are the drug dealers, pimps, and thugs who play by a different set of rules and, within the context, prove relatively successful at it.

Lacking an attainable future, or at least the belief in one, and absent models of deferred gratification and conventional success, it is all too easy to see how life can quickly become a quest for the immediate gratification of present impulses, a moment-to-moment existence where weighing the consequences of today's behavior against their future implications is largely pointless. Given, too, a larger culture that increasingly defines personal worth in terms of one's ability to consume, and a social and economic situation wherein one's ability to consume often depends on being able to take what one wants, the sense of personal merit or self-esteem easily comes to imply being stronger, meaner, and better armed than others.

Much is written these days about "empowerment" as the nearly universal solution to the problems of the disenfranchised. The point is well taken in that the powerless are forever at the mercy of others. And certainly, poor urban minority youth must be counted as among the most disadvantaged and least powerful groups in American society. Imagine, then, the empowerment that results when inner-city teenagers wrap their fingers around firearms. In that act, they suddenly become people to be feared, whose wishes must be respected, whose bidding must be done. With so much of the day-to-day reality of existence clearly beyond their control, they can at least decide where to point the gun and when to pull the trigger. It is very clearly agency of a high order.

To avoid misunderstanding, it must be stressed that underclass culture is *not* a majority culture among the inner-city poor, not even among the poor inner-city youth represented (for example) by our high school respondents. It should go without saying that the majority of poor people in the inner cities remain hard-working, law-abiding people. The concern, rather, is that the culture of the underclass has become (or is becoming) the *defining* aspect of the inner city, such that even those who reject it in entirety must

tipping point

nonetheless organize their lives around the reality it represents. In exactly this sense, Wilson (1987:38; see also Rose and McClain 1990) posits a "critical mass" of disaffected and hostile youth that, once exceeded, can literally explode into a "self-sustaining chain reaction" of crime, violence, addiction, and predation, a relatively small group whose influence on the life of the inner city is all out of proportion to its actual numbers.

Against this backdrop, what do our findings and interpretations suggest about the ongoing policy debate concerning juveniles and violence? Many of the terms of debate—drugs, gangs, even guns themselves—prove to be essentially epiphenomenal. They provide a method of restating the problem but do not and cannot suggest a solution. Guns, drugs, gangs, crime, and violence are all expressions of a pervasive alienation of certain inner-city youth from the conventions of larger society. We can seek to impose our will, pass new legislation to outlaw that of which we disapprove, and insist on harsher punishments for those who defy our rules. Ultimately, however, convincing inner-city juveniles (or adults) not to own, carry, and use guns requires convincing them that they can survive in their neighborhoods without being armed, that they can come and go in peace, that their unarmed condition will not cause them to be victimized, intimidated, or slain. Until we attend to the conditions that promote insecurity and fear and that breed hostility, estrangement, futility, and hopelessness, the perception that firearms are necessary to survival in the inner city will endure.

NOTES

1. In this vein consider the description of firearms given by one Los Angeles central city youth to another who just got out of prison: "[L]et me explain what fullies do. They don't blow you up, they don't shoot you, they *spray* you. . . . Sprays are permanent. They ain't no joke. We got shit that shoots seventy-five times. . . . The latest things out are fullies, body armor, and pagers. Offense, defense, and communication. . . . I got a Glock model seventeen that shoots eighteen times. It's a hand strap. Bro, this is the real world" (Scott 1993:366–67).

2. It should not be assumed that guns owned by adults and stored in homes and cars were purchased legally, i.e., not "hot," on the black market. In short, juvenile demand may be only one element driving an illegal gun market; the problem of illegal access to guns may involve more citizens of more ages than we think.

3. There is considerable attention now being given to the issue of control of ammunition supplies as a form of gun control (see Moynihan 1993). It is doubtful that such a tactic will produce large-scale results. Ammunition is even easier to produce and export into the United States than are guns. For that matter, black market demands for ammunition likely will foster the creation of domestic cottage industries to produce bullets.

REFERENCE

AULETTA, K. (1983). *The underclass.* New York: Viking.
BLOCK, C., & BLOCK, R. (1993). *Street gang crime in Chicago.* Washington, DC: U.S. Department of Justice.
DEVINE, J., & WRIGHT, J. (1993). *The greatest of evils.* Hawthorne, NY: Aldine de Gruyter.
DEVINE, J., PLUNKETT, M., & WRIGHT, J. (1992). The chronicity of poverty. *Social Forces, 70,* 787–812.
HARRINGTON, M. (1984). *The new American poverty.* New York: Holt, Rinehart and Winston.
INCIARDI, J. (1992). *The war on drugs II.* Mountain View, CA: Mayfield.
JENCKS, C., & PETERSON, P. (1991). *The urban underclass.* Washington, DC: Brookings.
KASARDA, J. (1985). Urban change and minority opportunities. In P. Peterson (Ed.), *The new urban reality* (pp. 33–67). Washington, DC: Brookings.
KENNEDY, D. (1994). Can we keep guns away from kids. *American Prospect, 18,* 74–80.
KLECK, G. (1991). *Point blank: Guns and violence in America.* Hawthorne, New York: Aldine de Gruyter.
KLEIN, M., MAXSON, C., & CUNNINGHAM, L. (1991). 'Crack,' street gangs, and violence. *Criminology, 29,* 623–50.
POLSBY, D. (1994). The false promise: Gun control and crime. *Atlantic Monthly, 273,* 57–70.
REISS, A., ROTH, J. (1993). Understanding and preventing violence. Washington, DC: National Academy Press.
ROSE, H. M., & McCLAIN, P. D. (1990). *Race, place, and risk: Black homicide in urban America.* Albany, NY: SUNY Press.
SKOGAN, W. (1990). *Disorder and decline.* New York: Free Press.
WILSON, W. J. (1987). *The truly disadvantaged: The inner city, the underclass, and public policy.* Chicago: University of Chicago Press.
WRIGHT, J., & DEVINE, J. (1994). *Drugs as a social problem.* New York: Harper Collins.
WRIGHT, J., ROSSI, P., & DALY, K. (1983). *Under the gun.* Hawthorne, NY: Aldine.

'Race' Politics

Luis J. Rodriguez

My brother and I
—shopping for *la jefita*—
decided to get the "good food"
over on the other side
    of the tracks.

We dared each other.
Laughed a little.
Thought about it.
Said, what's the big deal.
Thought about that.
Decided we were men,
not boys.
Decided we should go wherever
we damn wanted to.

Oh, my brother—now he was bad.
Tough dude. Afraid of nothing.
I was afraid of him.

So there we go,
climbing over
the iron and wood ties,
over discarded sofas
    and bent-up market carts,
over a weed-and-dirt road,
into a place called South Gate
—all white. All American.

We entered the forbidden
narrow line of hate,
imposed,
transposed,
supposed,
a line of power/powerlessness
full of meaning,
meaning nothing—
those lines that crisscross
the abdomen of this land,
that strangle you
in your days, in your nights.
When you dream.

There we were, two Mexicans,
six and nine—from Watts no less.
Oh, this was plenty reason
to hate us.

Plenty reason to run up behind us.
Five teenagers on bikes.
Plenty reason to knock
the groceries out from our arms—
    a splattering heap of soup
    cans, bread and candy.

Plenty reason to hold me down
on the hot asphalt; melted gum
    and chips of broken
    beer bottle on my lips
    and cheek.

Plenty reason to get my brother
by the throat, taking turns
    punching him in the face,
    cutting his lower lip,
    punching, him vomiting.
Punching until swollen and dark blue
he slid from their grasp
like a rotten banana from its peeling.

When they had enough, they threw us back,
dirty and lacerated;
back to Watts, its towers shiny
across the orange-red sky.

My brother then forced me
to promise not to tell anybody
how he cried.
He forced me to swear to God,
to Jesus Christ, to our long-dead
Indian Grandmother—
keepers of our meddling souls.

Students' Reports of School Crime: 1989 and 1995

Kathryn A. Chandler
Christopher D. Chapman
Michael R. Rand
Bruce M. Taylor, Ph.D.

INTRODUCTION AND BACKGROUND

This report is the first focusing on data collected in the 1995 School Crime Supplement (SCS), an enhancement to the National Crime Victimization Survey (NCVS). The NCVS is an ongoing household survey that gathers information on the criminal victimization of household members age 12 and older. While this report does not cover all of the items in the dataset, it covers those pertinent to school crime. These include: victimization at school, drug availability at school, street gangs at school, and guns at school. In this report, victimization is in terms of prevalence as opposed to counts of events. In other words, the report focuses on the percent of students who have been victimized one or more times.

To put the 1995 estimates in context, data from the 1989 SCS are also presented. Key findings include:

- There was little or no change in the percent of students reporting any (violent or property) victimization at school (14.5 percent versus 14.6 percent), or the percent of students reporting property victimization at school (12.2 percent versus 11.6 percent) between 1989 and 1995 (table 1). However, there was an increase in the percent of students reporting violent victimization at school (3.4 percent versus 4.2 percent) between the two years.

- In 1989, most students, 63.2 percent, reported that marijuana, cocaine, crack, or uppers/downers were available at school (either easy or hard to obtain; table 2). This number increased somewhat to 65.3 percent in 1995.

- The percent of students reporting street gang presence at school nearly doubled between 1989 and 1995, increasing from 15.3 percent to 28.4 percent (table 4).

- In 1995, a series of questions was asked about guns at school.[1] Almost no students reported taking a gun to school (less than one half of one percent), 5.3 percent reported seeing another student with a gun at school, and 12.7 percent reported knowing another student who brought a gun to school.

The supplements were fielded in January through June of their respective years to nationally representative samples of approximately 10,000 students. Eligible respondents to the supplements had to be between the ages of 12 and 19, and had to have attended school at some point during the six months preceding the interview. Respondents were only asked about crimes that had occurred at school during the six months prior to the interview. "At school" was defined as in the school building, on school grounds, or on a school bus.

Readers should be aware that the 1989 SCS estimates on victimization at school shown in this report do not match the estimates presented in the first analysis of the 1989 SCS.[2] In both the 1989 and 1995 SCS collections, persons 12 to 19 years of age were asked to respond to the NCVS and the SCS, and victimization information was captured in both questionnaires. The earlier authors elected to use the victimization information reported in the NCVS, rather than the SCS, in the development of their estimates. Because of a redesign of the NCVS in 1992, the 1995 victimization estimates from the NCVS cannot readily be compared to those developed before 1993.[3] Therefore, the authors of this report elected to reanalyze the 1989 data to compare estimates of victimization in 1995 to 1989 using the SCS data in both cases. Undoubtedly, the redesign of the NCVS also had implications on responses to the SCS. Unfortunately, it is not possible to measure the extent of the impact. (More information about the redesign and a comparison of SCS versus NCVS estimates of victimization can be found in the methodology section of this report.)

This report presents estimates for two points in time, six years apart. Readers should not assume that the time points represent a stable trend between 1989

---

[1] A similar series of questions was not included in 1989.

[2] See L. Bastian and B. Taylor. *School Crime: A National Crime Victimization Survey Report*, NCJ-131645 (U.S. Department of Justice, Bureau of Justice Statistics, Washington, D.C.: 1991).

[3] C. Kindermann, J. Lynch, and D. Cantor. *Effects of the Redesign on Victimization Estimates*, NCJ-164381 (U.S. Department of Justice, Bureau of Justice Statistics, Washington, D.C.: 1997).

and 1995. In fact, if estimates had been developed for the intervening years, many changes might be seen.

In this report, each topic is covered in a two- or three-page presentation that consists of bullets and figures. Comprehensive tables on each of the topics can be found after the body of the report. A methodology section, which describes the data collections and the analysis approach, follows the tables. Shown in appendix A are tables containing standard errors of the estimates, and shown in appendix B are the 1989 and 1995 School Crime Supplement questionnaires.

Again, this report does not exhaustively cover all of the data available in the 1989 and 1995 data sets. Readers can obtain the 1989 SCS data through the National Archive of Criminal Justice web site at "http://www.icpsr.umich.edu/NACJD/" (study number 9394), and the 1995 SCS data…[are study number 6739]. A SCS, jointly developed by the Bureau of Justice Statistics (BJS) and the National Center for Education Statistics (NCES), will continue to be fielded as a supplement to the NCVS every few years.

STUDENT VICTIMIZATION

FIGURE 1   Percent of students ages 12 through 19 who reported experiencing various forms of victimization at school: 1989 and 1995.

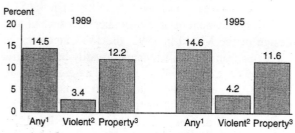

Student reports of victimization

[1]Any victimization is a combination of reported violent and property victimization. If the student reported an incident to either, he or she is counted as having experienced any victimization. If the respondent reported having experienced both, he or she is only counted once under "Any victimization".
[2]Violent victimization includes physical attacks or taking property from the student directly by force, weapons, or threats.
[3]Property victimization includes theft of property from a student's desk, locker, or other locations.

SOURCE: U.S. Department of Justice, Bureau of Justice Statistics, School Crime Supplement to the National Crime Victimization Survey, spring 1989 and 1995.

• The overall level of victimization in schools in 1995, 14.6 percent, was similar to that in 1989, 14.5 percent. There was an increase in the percentage of students reporting violent victimizations, however, increasing from 3.4 percent to 4.2 percent.

FIGURE 2   Percent of students ages 12 through 19 who reported experiencing violent victimization at school, by gender: 1989 and 1995

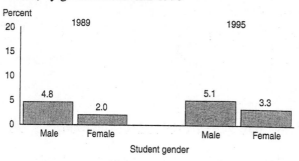

NOTE: Violent victimization includes physical attacks or taking property from the student directly by force, weapons, or threats.

SOURCE: U.S. Department of Justice, Bureau of Justice Statistics, School Crime Supplement to the National Crime Victimization Survey, spring 1989 and 1995.

• In 1995, male students (5.1 percent) were more likely than female students (3.3 percent) to have experienced violent victimization at school. A similar relationship also existed between violent victimization and gender in 1989.

• While the percent of male students who reported having experienced violent victimization at school was about the same in 1989 as it was in 1995, there was an increase in the percent of female students who reported such victimization.

FIGURE 3   Percent of students ages 12 through 19 who reported experiencing violent victimization at school, by age: 1989 and 1995

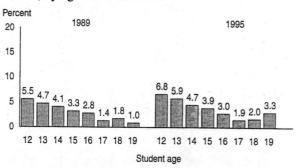

Student age

NOTE: Violent victimization includes physical attacks or taking property from the student directly by force, weapons, or threats.

SOURCE: U.S. Department of Justice, Bureau of Justice Statistics, School Crime Supplement to the National Crime Victimization Survey, spring 1989 and 1995.

• Younger students were more likely to experience violent victimization than were older students in both 1989 and 1995.

FIGURE 4 Percent of students ages 12 through 19 who reported experiencing violent victimization at school, by student reports of street gang presence at school: 1989 and 1995

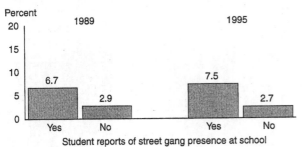

NOTE: Violent victimization includes physical attacks or taking property from the student directly by force, weapons, or threats.

SOURCE: U.S. Department of Justice, Bureau of Justice Statistics, School Crime Supplement to the National Crime Victimization Survey, spring 1989 and 1995.

- In 1995, only 2.7 percent of students who reported no street gang presence at school experienced violent victimization compared to 7.5 percent who reported street gang presence at school. Similar results occurred in 1989. (See figure 9 and table 4 for reported prevalence of street gangs at school.)
- Between 1989 and 1995, the percent of students reporting that they were violently victimized at school did not noticeably change among students who reported street gang presence at school, nor did it noticeably change among students who reported no street gang presence at school.

FIGURE 5 Percent of students ages 12 through 19 who reported experiencing various forms of victimization at school, by student reports of seeing a student with a gun at school: 1995

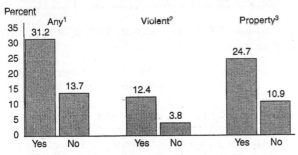

[1]Any victimization is a combination of reported violent and property victimization. If the student reported an incident to either, he or she is counted as having experienced any victimization. If the respondent reported having experienced both, he or she is only counted once under "Any victimization".
[2]Violent victimization includes physical attacks or taking property from the student directly by force, weapons, or threats.
[3]Property victimization includes theft of property from a student's desk, locker, or other locations.

NOTE: Students were not asked about seeing other students with guns at school in the 1989 SCS.

SOURCE: U.S. Department of Justice, Bureau of Justice Statistics, School Crime Supplement to the National Crime Victimization Survey, spring 1995.

- Of those students who reported seeing a student with a gun at school, 12.4 percent reported being victims of violent crime at school compared to 3.8 percent of those who had not. (See figure 5 for student reports of seeing a student with a gun at school.)

Additional findings about student reports of victimization at school:

- Student reports of having experienced violent victimization at school were relatively uniform across the different places of residence in 1995 when 4.7 percent of students residing in central cities, 4.4 percent of those residing in suburbs, and 3.5 percent of students residing in non-metropolitan areas reported such victimization. The same was true in 1989.
- Public school students were more likely to report having experienced violent victimization (4.4 percent) than were private school students (2.3 percent) in 1995. However, public (3.5 percent) and private school students (2.9 percent) were about as likely to report having experienced violent victimization in 1989.
- In 1995, students who reported that drugs were available at school were more likely to report having been violently victimized than students who reported that no drugs were available (4.7 percent v. 3.0 percent). Similar results occurred in 1989. (See figure 6 and table 2 for student reports of drug availability at school.)

AVAILABILITY OF DRUGS

FIGURE 6 Percent of students ages 12 through 19 who reported that drugs were available at school, by grade: 1989 and 1995

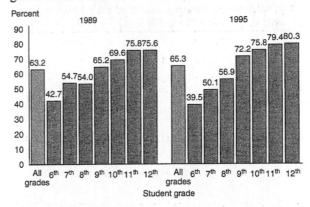

NOTE: In the 1989 and 1995 SCS, students were asked about the availability of marijuana, cocaine, crack, and uppers/downers. If the students reported any of these to be easy or hard to obtain at school, they are considered having reported that drugs were available at school.

SOURCE: U.S. Department of Justice, Bureau of Justice Statistics, School Crime Supplement to the National Crime Victimization Survey, spring 1989 and 1995.

- Though the increase was small, the percentage of students reporting that drugs were available rose from 63.2 percent in 1989 to 65.3 percent in 1995.
- Students in higher grades were more likely than students in lower grades to report that drugs were available at school in both 1989 and 1995.

FIGURE 7   Percent of students ages 12 through 19 who reported that drugs were available at school, by school type: 1989 and 1995

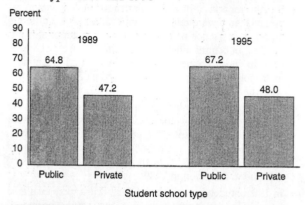

Student school type

NOTE: In the 1989 and 1995 SCS, students were asked about the availability of marijuana, cocaine, crack, and uppers/downers. If the students reported any of these to be easy or hard to obtain at school, they are considered having reported that drugs were available at school.

SOURCE: U.S. Department of Justice, Bureau of Justice Statistics, School Crime Supplement to the National Crime Victimization Survey, spring 1989 and 1995.

- In 1995, students in public schools were more likely to report that drugs were available in their schools than were students in private schools (67.2 percent v. 48.0 percent). Similar results occurred in 1989.
- A higher percent of public school students reported that drugs were available at school in 1995 than in 1989. However, the percent of private school students who reported that drugs were available at school was about the same in 1995 as it was in 1989.

FIGURE 8   Percent of students ages 12 through 19 who reported that drugs were available at school, by student reports of violent victimization at school: 1989 and 1995

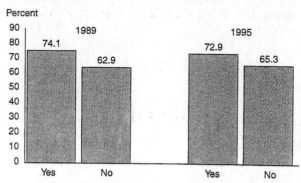

Student reports of violent victimization at school*

*Violent victimization includes physical attacks or taking property from the student directly by force, weapons, or threats.

NOTE: In the 1989 and 1995 SCS, students were asked about the availability of marijuana, cocaine, crack, and uppers/downers. If the students reported any of these to be easy or hard to obtain at school, they are considered having reported that drugs were available at school.

SOURCE: U.S. Department of Justice, Bureau of Justice Statistics, School Crime Supplement to the National Crime Victimization Survey, spring 1989 and 1995.

- In both 1995 and 1989, students who reported that they had experienced violent victimization at school were more likely to report that drugs were available at school than were students who reported that they had not been violently victimized at school.
- Among students who reported that they had experienced violent victimization at school, the percent of students reporting that drugs were available in 1989 was similar to the percent of students reporting that drugs were available in 1995.

Additional findings about student reports of drug availability at school:

- Older students were more likely than younger students to report that drugs were available at school in both 1989 and 1995.
- In 1995, students who reported that street gangs were present at their schools were more likely to indicate that drugs were available (79.5 percent) than were those who did not report that street gangs were present (61.0 percent). The same results occurred in 1989.
- Among students reporting that street gangs were present at school, reports that drugs were available increased by 6 percentage points between 1989 and 1995. Among students reporting that gangs were not present, reports that drugs were available are similar between the two years.

- The percent of students reporting that marijuana was easy to obtain at school increased between 1989 and 1995, rising from 30.5 percent to 36.4 percent.
- In 1995, more students reported that marijuana was easy to obtain than any other drug. The same result was true in 1989.

STREET GANGS AT SCHOOL

FIGURE 9   Percent of students ages 12 through 19 who reported that street gangs were present at school, by race/ethnicity: 1989 and 1995

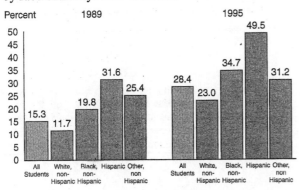

SOURCE: U.S. Department of Justice, Bureau of Justice Statistics, School Crime Supplement to the National Crime Victimization Survey, spring 1989 and 1995

- Students in 1995 were much more likely to report that street gangs were present in their schools than were students in 1989 (28.4 percent v. 15.3 percent).
- In 1995, Hispanic students were more likely than either white or black students to report the existence of street gangs in their schools (49.5 percent v. 23.0 percent and 34.7 percent, respectively). A similar set of relationships existed in 1989.

FIGURE 10   Percent of students ages 12 through 19 who reported that street gangs were present at school, by household income: 1989 and 1995

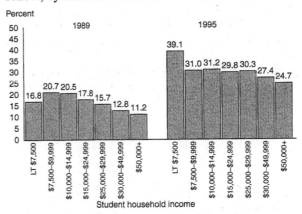

SOURCE: U.S. Department of Justice, Bureau of Justice Statistics, School Crime Supplement to the National Crime Victimization Survey, spring 1989 and 1995

- In 1989 and 1995, students living in households with higher incomes were less likely to report that street gangs were present at school than were students in households with lower incomes.

FIGURE 11   Percent of students ages 12 through 19 who reported that street gangs were present at school, by place of residence: 1989 and 1995

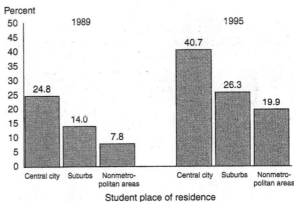

SOURCE: U.S. Department of Justice, Bureau of Justice Statistics, School Crime Supplement to the National Crime Victimization Survey, spring 1989 and 1995

- Students in central cities were more likely to respond that there were street gangs at their schools (40.7 percent) than were suburban students (26.3 percent) or students in nonmetropolitan areas (19.9 percent) in 1995. Similar results occurred in 1989.
- Between 1989 and 1995, reports of gang presence increased in all three categories of student place residence.

FIGURE 12 Percent of students ages 12 through 19 who reported that street gangs were present at school, by school type: 1989 and 1995

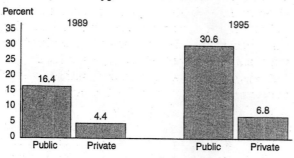

SOURCE: U.S. Department of Justice, Bureau of Justice Statistics, School Crime Supplement to the National Crime Victimization Survey, spring 1989 and 1995

- Students in public schools were more likely to report that street gangs were present at school than were students in private schools in both years. In 1995, 30.6 percent of students in public schools reported that street gangs were present compared to 6.8 percent in private schools. The 1989 percents were 16.4 and 4.4, respectively.
- Public school students were more likely to report that street gangs were present at school in 1995 than in 1989, while private school students were about as likely to report that street gangs were present in both years.

GUNS AT SCHOOL

FIGURE 13 Percent of students ages 12 through 19 who reported knowing a student who brought a gun to school, by age: 1995

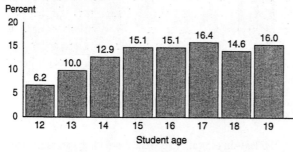

SOURCE: U.S. Department of Justice, Bureau of Justice Statistics, School Crime Supplement to the National Crime Victimization Survey, spring 1995.

- In 1995, older students were more likely than younger students to report knowing a student who brought a gun to school.

FIGURE 14 Percent of students ages 12 through 19 who reported the presence of guns at school, by student reports of street gang presence at school: 1995

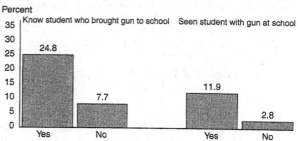

SOURCE: U.S. Department of Justice, Bureau of Justice Statistics, School Crime Supplement to the National Crime Victimization Survey, spring 1995

- Street gang presence at a student's school was related to knowing another student who brought a gun to school (24.8 percent v. 7.7 percent). In addition, street gang presence at a student's school was related to seeing another student with a gun at school (11.9 percent v. 2.8 percent).

FIGURE 15 Percent of students ages 12 through 19 who reported the presence of guns at school, by student reports of drug availability at school: 1995

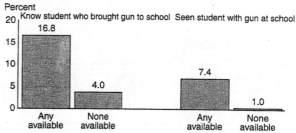

NOTE: In both the 1989 and 1995 SCS, students were asked about the availability of marijuana, cocaine, crack, and uppers/downers. If students reported any of these to be easy or hard to obtain at school, they are included in the "Any available" category. If they said each is impossible to obtain, they are counted in the "None available" category.

SOURCE: U.S. Department of Justice, Bureau of Justice Statistics, School Crime Supplement to the National Crime Victimization Survey, spring 1995.

- Students who reported that drugs were available at school were more likely to have known another student who brought a gun to school (16.8 percent), and to have seen another student with a gun at school (7.4 percent) than were students who reported that drugs were not available (4.0 percent and 1.0 percent, respectively).

Additional findings about student reports of guns at school:

- In 1995, almost no students reported taking a gun to school (less than one half of one percent), 5.3 percent reported seeing another student with a gun at school, and 12.7 percent reported knowing another student who brought a gun to school.
- Black, non-Hispanic students were more likely than white, non-Hispanic students to report knowing another student who brought a gun to school (15.5 percent versus 12.3 percent). Black, non-Hispanic students were also more likely to report seeing another student with a gun at school than were white, non-Hispanic students (8.7 percent v. 4.4 percent).
- Students residing in central cities were more likely to report knowing another student who brought a gun to school (15.0 percent) than were students from suburban areas (12.3 percent) or students from nonmetropolitan areas (11.1 percent). Similarly, students from central cities were more likely to report seeing another student with a gun at school (6.8 percent) than were suburban or nonmetropolitan area students (each 4.8 percent).
- Public school students were more likely to report knowing another student who brought a gun to school than were students attending private schools (13.6 percent v. 4.4 percent). Public school students were also more likely to report seeing another student who brought a gun to school than were students attending private schools (5.7 percent v. 2.0 percent, respectively).

SUMMARY

This report presents the first published findings from the 1995 School Crime Supplement (SCS) to the National Crime Victimization Survey (NCVS) in addition to findings from a reanalysis of the 1989 SCS. Because of the issue's obvious importance to students, parents, educators, and policymakers, this first report focuses on the reported prevalence of crime in America's schools. More specifically, it explores student reports of victimization, drug availability, street gang presence, and gun presence at school.

One important finding that emerged from comparing estimates from the two time points was that more students were exposed to certain problems at school in 1995 than in 1989. As compared to students in 1989, students in 1995 were more likely to report that they had experienced violent victimization, could obtain drugs, and were aware of street gangs at school.

A second key finding was that various types of problems tended to co-exist. For instance, student reports of drug availability, street gang presence, and gun presence at school were all related to student reports of having experienced violent victimization at school. Reports of having experienced violent victimization were higher among students who reported that drugs were available than among students who reported that they were not. In addition, students who reported that street gangs were present were more likely than students who reported that they were not present to say that they had been violently victimized. Finally, students who reported seeing another student with a gun were more likely to say that they had experienced violent victimization than students who had not seen another student with a gun.

Because of the exploratory nature of this report, the crime variables were studied using bivariate analyses only. Future research will apply multivariate approaches to the data to help better understand possible interactions and patterns. Also, because the report focused on the important issues of school crime, it did not exhaustively cover all of the topics addressed by the data bases. Such topics as safety measures taken by schools to prevent crime, student avoidance of places in or near school because of fear of attack, and student perceptions of rule enforcement at school will form the basis of future work. It is the intent of both NCES and BJS to continue what has been a successful collaborative effort to conduct some of this research.

Supremacy Crimes

Gloria Steinem

From domestic violence to sexual harassment, naming a crime has been the first step toward solving it. But another crime is hiding in plain sight. You've seen the ocean of television coverage, you've read the headlines: "How to Spot a Troubled Kid," "Twisted Teens," "When Teens Fall Apart."

After the slaughter in Colorado that inspired those phrases, dozens of copycat threats were reported in the same generalized way: "Junior high students charged with conspiracy to kill students and teachers" (in Texas); "Five honor students overheard planning a June graduation bombing" (in New York); "more than 100 minor threats reported statewide" (in Pennsylvania). In response, the White House held an emergency strategy session titled "Children, Violence, and Responsibility." Nonetheless, another attack was soon reported: "Youth With 2 Guns Shoots 6 at Georgia School."

I don't know about you, but I've been talking back to the television set, waiting for someone to tell us the obvious: it's not "youth," "our children," or "our teens." It's our sons and "our" can usually be read as "white," "middle class" and "heterosexual."

We know that hate crimes, violent and otherwise, are overwhelmingly committed by white men who are apparently straight. The same is true for an even higher percentage of impersonal, resentment-driven, mass killings like those in Colorado; the sort committed for no economic or rational gain except the need to say, "I'm superior because I can kill." Think of Charles Starkweather, who reported feeling powerful and serene after murdering ten women and men in the 1950s; or the shooter who climbed the University of Texas Tower in 1966, raining down death to gain celebrity. Think of the engineering student at the University of Montreal who resented females' ability to study that subject, and so shot to death 14 women students in 1989, while saying, "I'm against feminism." Think of nearly all those who have killed impersonally in the workplace, the post office, McDonalds.

White males—usually intelligent, middle class, and heterosexual, or trying desperately to appear so— also account for virtually all the serial, sexually motivated, sadistic killings, those characterized by stalking, imprisoning, torturing, and "owning" victims in death. Think of Edmund Kemper, who began by killing animals, then murdered his grandparents, yet was released to sexually torture and dismember college students and other young women until he himself decided he "didn't want to kill *all* the coeds in the world." Or David Berkowitz, the Son of Sam, who murdered *some* women in order to feel in control of *all* women. Or consider Ted Bundy, the charming, snobbish young would-be lawyer who tortured and murdered as many as 40 women, usually beautiful students who were symbols of the economic class he longed to join. As for John Wayne Gacy, he was obsessed with maintaining the public mask of masculinity, and so hid his homosexuality by killing and burying men and boys with whom he had had sex.

These "senseless" killings begin to seem less mysterious when you consider that they were committed disproportionately by white, non-poor males, the group most likely to become hooked on the drug of superiority. It's a drug pushed by a male-dominant culture that presents dominance as a natural right; a racist hierarchy that falsely elevates whiteness; a materialist society that equates superiority with possessions, and a homophobic one that empowers only one form of sexuality.

As Elliott Leyton reports in *Hunting Humans: The Rise of the Modern Multiple Murderer*, these killers see their behavior as "an appropriate—even 'manly'— response to the frustrations and disappointments that are a normal part of life." In other words, it's not their life experiences that are the problem, it's the impossible expectation of dominance to which they've become addicted.

This is not about blame. This is about causation. If anything, ending the massive cultural cover-up of supremacy crimes should make heroes out of boys and men who reject violence, especially those who reject the notion of superiority altogether. Even if one believes in a biogenetic component of male aggression, the very existence of gentle men proves that socialization can override it.

Nor is this about attributing such crimes to a single cause. Addiction to the drug of supremacy is not their only root, just the deepest and most ignored one. Additional reasons why this country has such a high rate of violence include the plentiful guns that make killing seem as unreal as a video game; male violence in the media that desensitizes viewers in much the same way that combat killers are desensitized in training; affluence that allows maximum access to violence-as-entertainment; a national history of genocide and slavery; the romanticizing of frontier violence and organized crime; not to mention extremes of wealth and poverty and the illusion that both are deserved.

But it is truly remarkable, given the relative reasons for anger at injustice in this country, that white, non-poor men have a near-monopoly on multiple killings of strangers, whether serial and sadistic or mass and random. How can we ignore this obvious fact? Others may kill to improve their own condition—in self-defense, or for money or drugs; to eliminate enemies; to declare turf in drive-by shootings; even for a jacket or a pair of sneakers—but white males addicted to supremacy kill even when it worsens their condition or ends in suicide.

Men of color and females are capable of serial and mass killing, and commit just enough to prove it. Think of Colin Ferguson, the crazed black man on the Long Island Railroad, or Wayne Williams, the young black man in Atlanta who kidnapped and killed black boys, apparently to conceal his homosexuality. Think of the Aileen Carol Wuornos, the white prostitute in Florida who killed abusive johns "in self-defense," or Waneta Hoyt, the upstate New York woman who strangled her five infant children between 1965 and 1971, disguising their cause of death as sudden infant death syndrome. Such crimes are rare enough to leave a haunting refrain of disbelief as evoked in Pat Parker's poem "jonestown": "Black folks do not / Black folks do not / Black folks do not commit suicide." And yet they did.

Nonetheless, the proportion of serial killings that are not committed by white males is about the same as the proportion of anorexics who are not female. Yet we discuss the gender, race, and class components of anorexia, but not the role of the same factors in producing epidemics among the powerful.

The reasons are buried deep in the culture, so invisible that only by reversing our assumptions can we reveal them.

Suppose, for instance, that young black males—or any other men of color—had carried out the slaughter in Colorado. Would the media reports be so willing to describe the murderers as "our children"? Would there

be so little discussion about the boys' race? Would experts be calling the motive a mystery, or condemning the high school cliques for making those young men feel like "outsiders"? Would there be the same empathy for parents who gave the murderers luxurious homes, expensive cars, even rescued them from brushes with the law? Would there be as much attention to generalized causes, such as the dangers of violent video games and recipes for bombs on the Internet?

As for the victims, if racial identities had been reversed, would racism remain so little discussed? In fact, the killers themselves said they were targeting blacks and athletes. They used a racial epithet, shot a black male student in the head, and then laughed over the fact that they could see his brain. What if *that* had been reversed?

What if these two young murderers, who were called "fags" by some of the jocks at Columbine High School, actually had been gay? Would they have got the same sympathy for being gay-baited? What if they had been lovers? Would we hear as little about their sexuality as we now do, even though only their own homophobia could have given the word "fag" such power to humiliate them?

Take one more leap of the imagination: suppose these killings had been planned and executed by young women—of any race, sexuality, or class. Would the media still be so disinterested in the role played by gender-conditioning? Would journalists assume that female murderers had suffered from being shut out of access to power in high school, so much so that they were pushed beyond their limits? What if dozens, even hundreds of young women around the country had made imitative threats—as young men have done—expressing admiration for a well-planned massacre and promising to do the same? Would we be discussing their youth more than their gender, as is the case so far with these male killers?

I think we begin to see that our national self-examination is ignoring something fundamental, precisely because it's like the air we breathe: the white male factor, the middle-class and heterosexual one, and the promise of superiority it carries. Yet this denial is self-defeating—to say the least. We will never reduce the number of violent Americans, from bullies to killers, without challenging the assumptions on which masculinity is based: that males are superior to females, that they must find a place in a male hierarchy, and that the ability to dominate *someone* is so important that even a mere insult can justify lethal revenge. There are plenty of studies to support this view. As Dr. James Gilligan concluded in *Violence: Reflections on a National Epidemic,* "If humanity is to evolve beyond the propensity toward violence . . . then it can only do so by recognizing the extent to which the patriarchal code of honor and shame generates and obligates male violence."

I think the way out can only be found through a deeper reversal: just as we as a society have begun to raise our daughters more like our sons—more like whole people—we must begin to raise our sons more like our daughters—that is, to value empathy as well as hierarchy; to measure success by other people's welfare as well as their own.

But first, we have to admit and name the truth about supremacy crimes.

I Prayed for More Gun Control and Got Better Background Checks

2002

Tonya Maria Matthews

I.

I was called out of work today
by my son's principal.
I flew across town in a panic
near despair
only to find that woman had yanked my son
   out of class because
he had braids in his hair
   my God, my God
    keep me from knocking this woman to the floor.
    somehow Holy Spirit lead me
    quietly out the front door
but later that evening
on News Channel 4
two young boys in Denver
have assassinated twelve of their classmates.
I don't know who to pray for anymore.

II.

Another white kid bites the dust
society's upper crust is confused
not used to charging these
blonde-haired, blue-eyed criminals
thanks to six o'clock news subliminals.

So they claim the perpetrators are monsters
clearly not their children
then one of those mass murder high school shootings
happens again
to the parents chagrin
this time bombs were being made
in their own basement

but no amazement coming out of the ghettosphere
we watched society hatch them chickens
knew they had to roost somewhere

out there La La Land is singing a new song.
that tune won't last long
though tomorrow's headlines read
New Public Enemy Number One . . . The NRA
that's just a platform for Election Day.
A couple hundred thousand dollars in political PACs
congressmen tend to let stuff slide
even though this time
they're taking their own babies along for the ride.

III.

Suburban body count rises
folks wanna ask how? why? what? but

you can't throw rocks in glass houses
and expect your children won't get cut.

Lady Liberty becomes society's highest paid slut
as long as those gunslingers pay her bill
she will continue to yank Uncle Sam's chain.

this is a sick, sick game

As the fallout from this political particulating
hits the safest of places
Uncle Sam laughs in our faces
his minions pass a resolution
suggesting the solution:

Better Background Checks.

IV.

But I did some checking on my own and found

   7 out of 10 of us Americans think that the Black
Panther party has more members than the Ku Klux
Klan and
   7 out of 10 of us Americans think that the Black
Muslims hide more guns than right white militias and
   7 out of 10 of us Americans think that hip hop's
attitude incites more violence than rock music's mania
and so

with our inclinations
negro affiliations
all we'll be checking for.
7 out of 10 gives the political majority moral superiority
adding morbidity to stupidity until
black boys can't wear braids to school
without being accused of gang-related transgression
while black lipstick spiked hair trench coats
in the dead of summer
is nothing but self-expression.

Before we finish prioritizing criteria for this bogus
background check

check into gilded alabaster family trees
cuz I done sees the enemies
they don't wear oversized FUBU jeans Malcolm X tees
these well-armed juvenile assassins are sporting
Abercrombie caps and Gap khakis.

VI.

Raised kids to think Judgement Day is a movie
but take no responsibility
callous self-denial
leaves our babies cold
fiscally tainted gun control measures, ridiculous.

Be bold.

Stop checking backgrounds
start checking souls.
Reason the death of our children
at society's very core:

better background checks are irrelevant
if we don't know what we're checking for.

V.

Half of these first-degree murderers
below the age of reason.
.38 caliber birthday gift marked the dawn
of his killing season
by age 10 has sharp shooter's aim
has learned life is nothing more than a metaphor
for hunting wild game.
A federal judge sentences another child to death
   or worse
believing the evil he displayed is inherent.
Blame the music, the video games, the child himself
but never, never the parent.
America claims that to be a murderer
one must pull the trigger
gives her citizens an excuse not to look in the mirror.

The Violation of Body Space

This fourth section of the book moves toward several social issues that often dominate inquiries and discussions related to violence and gender: domestic violence, sexual assault, and child abuse. Internationally, at least one woman in every three has been beaten, coerced into sex, or otherwise abused in her lifetime (Heise, Ellsberg, & Gottemoeller, 1999). Far from being an international leader in eradicating such abuse, the United States is similarly plagued by high rates of domestic violence, sexual assault, and child abuse, as will be seen in the readings included in this section. Heise et al. note that the abuse of women and girls is best understood within a gender framework because it is often a function of women's and girls' subordinate social status. However, it is also true that gender frameworks help us to understand the violence that some men experience, as will be discussed later in this section. Further, as was noted in the second section on the construction of femininities, masculinities, and the "Other," the dominant cultural norm linking aggression and masculinity is also important to consider.

The first reading in this section is a review article by the psychologists, Lisa Goodman, Mary Koss, and Nancy Felipe Russo, titled, "Violence Against Women: Physical and Mental Health Effects. Part I: Research Findings." This article remains one of the most comprehensive literature reviews that presents the definitions of physical abuse and sexual assault, the prevalence of violence, the physical health consequences of battering and sexual assault, and the mental health consequences—both short- and long-term—of experiencing sexual assault and battering. As you read, consider the effects of battering and other violence, including rape, on women. What do you think of the suggestions for health-care professionals presented at the end of the article? Are they feasible? Can you think of ways to adapt these recommendations for professionals in other fields?

With that brief background as an introduction, the second selection is a chapter titled "Violence in Intimate Relationships: A Feminist Perspective" from the book, *Talking Back: Thinking Feminist, Thinking Black*, by the scholar and "public intellectual," bell hooks. This more personal, introspective examination of having been hit by someone she loved raises a number of important issues and questions. It is particularly important to note how complex a phenomenon battering really is, and hooks's difficulty in predicting her own reaction to being hit—". . . I had always thought that I would never allow any man to hit me and live" (p. 85)—is surely evidence that people cannot assume that they know how they would react if they were hurt by someone they love. Hooks also raises concerns about the potential relationships among hitting children to discipline them, child abuse, and the acceptance of battering as an adult. Do you find her argument persuasive: that children who have accepted violence from a loved one as a child are at-risk for accepting violence from a loved one as an adult? Do you believe that our cultural notions of romantic love contribute in any way to the phenomenon of battering? Finally, consider her discussion of the term, "battered woman." What are some of the problems associated with its use?

Bell hooks may question the use of the term "battered woman" for the potential impact that it has on individual women, but she also acknowledges that having such a term has helped to address violence against women more broadly. Ann Jones, a feminist journalist and authority on violence against women and on violent women, echoes those gains in her essay, "Battering: Who's Going to Stop It?" The battered women's movement has created numerous positive changes in services, legislation, public policy, and law enforcement on behalf of women. Despite these gains, however, statistics show that women are still being battered in extraordinary numbers. A 1998 survey by The Commonwealth Fund found that nearly one-third of American women (31 percent) report having been physically or sexually abused by a husband or boyfriend at some point in their lives. Moreover, as Jones notes, our youth are experiencing dating violence in frighteningly high proportions. How can we help women and young girls free themselves of violence in their relationships? What do you think should be done in schools, on university campuses, and in communities to prevent and intervene in dating and domestic violence? Jones argues that acting out the "macho myth" leads boys to abuse their girlfriends. To what extent do you think that dominant cultural notions of masculinity and femininity impact individuals in battering relationships?

Considering these issues will also be important as you read the poem, "Healthy Choices," by Janice Mirikitani. Why has she titled the poem in such a way? The spacing of this poem on the page is also particularly important. How does it impact on your reading and interpretation of the poem?

Clearly, domestic violence affects a tremendous number of women and girls; however, sexual assault is another critical issue to bear in mind as we explore the violation of body space. The statistics are quite sobering, particularly given that sexual violence remains a dramatically underreported crime, with an estimated fewer than 50 percent of rapes reported in the United States (Dupre, Hampton, Morrison, & Meeks, 1993). Research has shown that at least 20 percent of adult women in the United States have been sexually assaulted in some form during their lifetime (Koss, 1988) and that 61 percent of victims are under the age of eighteen (National Victim Center, 1992). The National Victim Center has also reported that every minute in America there are 1.3 rapes of women and that 1,871 women in America are forcibly raped each day. Not surprisingly, the problem also surfaces on U.S. college and university campuses, with research indicating that one in four women college students have been victims of rape or attempted rape (Koss, Gidycz, & Wisniewski, 1987; Finley and Corty, 1993). What many people do not realize, however, is that rape is more likely to be committed against women by someone known to them than by a stranger. Victims of rape and sexual assault report that in nearly three out of four incidents, the perpetrator was not a stranger (Greenfeld, 1997).

The phenomenon of acquaintance rape is the focus of the essay by the journalist and writer on issues of women and sexuality, Paula Kamen, titled "Acquaintance Rape: Revolution and Reaction." In this reading, Kamen reflects on the shifts that have taken place in rape prevention activism and the type of attention that these shifts have generated in the media. In particular, she comments on the antifeminist media backlash and "date-rape hysteria," a term that was created in the early 1990s by conservative critics to suggest that acquaintance rape is a bogus social problem created by feminists. One of the most active proponents of this term, Katie Roiphe, who authored the book, *The Morning After: Sex, Fear, and Feminism on Campus*, goes as far as to deny the existence of acquaintance rape and suggests that in reality it represents nothing more than normal, unpleasant sexual experiences. Kamen presents the data that are in dispute by the antifeminist and feminist camps and demonstrates how antifeminists like Roiphe have misrepresented the data to the public. This article debunks many of the myths that have been given more than their share of media attention over the past decade. As you read this essay, consider why this backlash occurred. Whose interests are served, and whose are not, by denying the existence of acquaintance rape? Obviously, definitions of consent can be a murky area: What is freely consenting sex? How does the fact that some of the most vocal antifeminist critics are women who play into this debate? What responsibility do the media have in this debate?

What the media do not report very often are incidents of male-on-male rape. The preface and a chapter from Michael Scarce's book, *Male on Male Rape: The Hidden Toll of Stigma and Shame*, underscore the growing awareness on the part of rape prevention activists that men are raped and in need of services. As Scarce notes from his review of the literature, estimates from research studies indicate that 5 to 10 percent of men are rape survivors. Further, male victims of sexual assault experience the same reactions as women, as well as an increased sense of vulnerability, damaged self-image, and emotional distancing. These reactions are often a result of the cultural belief that a male should be capable of defending himself. Consequently, males often blame themselves for the attack (National Victim Center, 1992). Despite these similarities to women's experiences of victimization, there are also important differences, which Scarce examines in his book. In his preface, Scarce shares his story of sexual victimization by another man. The chapter, "An Assault on Sexual Identity," then explores how homophobia plays a central role in the stigma that is attached to male rape. As you read this chapter, consider how homophobia might create a culture supportive of violence. From where do our ideas about who can and cannot be raped come? To what extent do our beliefs about masculinity and femininity influence these ideas? What similarities and differences between acquaintance rape in heterosexual versus gay relationships did you find?

We now move our inquiry from sexual assault to child abuse. Child abuse is a phenomenon that includes physical, sexual, and emotional abuse, as well as neglect. In her chapter, hooks raised questions about the relationship between experiencing physical punishment as a child and subsequent experiences of violence from an intimate partner. In fact, research has demonstrated explicit connections between child abuse and domestic violence. In a national survey of more than two thousand American families, approximately 50 percent of the men who frequently assaulted their wives also frequently abused their children (Straus & Gelles, 1988). However, other research reports that the perpetrators of physical child abuse are nearly equally women and men (Barnett, Miller-Perrin, & Perrin, 1997). What might account for the relatively high proportion of female perpetrators of physical child abuse compared to other types of violence studied thus far?

While it is important to be aware of child abuse in all of its forms, we focus our inquiry here on child sexual abuse. The next selection is an article by Kathleen Kendall-Tackett, Linda Meyer Williams, and David Finkelhor, all of the Family Research Laboratory at the University of New Hampshire, titled, "Impact of Sexual Abuse on Children: A Review and Synthesis of Recent Empirical Studies." This review article demonstrates that children who have been sexually abused exhibit more symptoms—such as fears, posttraumatic stress disorder, and behavior problems to name a few—than children who were not sexually abused. The authors also present the most prevalent symptoms across a variety of age groups of child sexual abuse survivors and discuss the factors that impact the degree of symptomatology that children may experience. Understanding the impact of childhood sexual abuse is particularly relevant given the recent uncovering of child sexual abuse by members of the clergy. Although almost certainly an underestimate of true incidence, statistics have shown that in 1994, 11 percent of all child abuse and neglect reports in the United States involved child sexual abuse (McCurdy & Daro, 1995). Moreover, a review of methodologically strong self-report studies concluded that at least 20 percent of women and 5 to 10 percent of men have experienced some form of sexual abuse as children (Finkelhor, 1994). Research has also suggested that 90 percent or more of perpetrators are male (Finkelhor & Hotaling, 1984). As you read this article, what finding(s) did you find most surprising and why? What similarities did you note between some of the effects of child sexual abuse discussed here and the symptoms experienced by rape survivors discussed in the Goodman, Koss, and Russo article? What do you make of this apparent link between masculinity and sexual predation? Based on your readings for this section thus far, what areas for intervention and prevention would you recommend?

The final selections in this section are two poems that relate directly to child abuse, both physical and sexual. The first is a poem by Bruce Weigl, titled "The Impossible." In this poem, the speaker recalls how s/he was forced into oral sex with an older man at the age of seven. Before and after reading the poem, reflect on why you think the poet chose this title. What is the impact of each of the two stanzas on you as a reader? The second poem is written by Toi Derricotte and is simply titled "Abuse." In Derricotte's poem, how many different forms of abuse or violence can you identify? Why do you think that in both poems the poets chose to run the words and sentences together? How do such brief poems manage to convey such powerful and disturbing images?

REFERENCES

BARNETT, O. W., MILLER-PERRIN, C. L., & PERRIN, R. D. (1997). Physical child abuse. In *Family Violence across the Lifespan*. Thousand Oaks, CA: Sage Publications.

THE COMMONWEALTH FUND (May 1999). Health Concerns Across A Woman's Lifespan: The Commonwealth Fund 1998 Survey of Women's Health.

DUPRE, A. R., HAMPTON, H. L., MORRISON, H., & MEEKS, G. R. (1993). Sexual assault. *Obstetrical and Gynecological Survey, 48*(9), 640–648.

FINKELHOR, D. (1994). The international epidemiology of child sexual abuse. *Child Abuse & Neglect, 18*(5) 409–417.

FINKELHOR, D. & HOTALING, G. T. (1984). Sexual abuse in the National Incidence Study of Child Abuse and Neglect: An appraisal. *Child Abuse & Neglect, 8*(1), 23–32.

FINLEY, C. & CORTY, E. (1993). Rape on campus: The prevalence of sexual assault while enrolled in college. *Journal of College Student Development, 34*(2), 113–117.

GREENFELD, L. A. (1997). *Sex offenses and offenders: An analysis of data on rape and sexual assault.* (NCJ Publication No. 163392). Washington, DC: U.S. Department of Justice.

HEISE, L., ELLSBERG, M., AND GOTTEMOELLER, M. (December 1999). Ending Violence Against Women. *Population Reports*, Series L, No. 11. Baltimore: Johns Hopkins University School of Public Health, Population Information Program.

KOSS, M. P. (1988). Hidden rape: Sexual aggression and victimization in a national sample of students in higher education. In A. W. Burgess (Ed.) *Rape and sexual assault.* New York, NY: Garland Publishing.

Koss, M. P., Gidycz, C. A., & Wisniewski, N. (1987). The scope of rape: Incidence and prevalence of sexual aggression and victimization in a national sample of higher education students. *Journal of Consulting & Clinical Psychology, 55*(2), 162–170.

McCurdy, K. & Daro, D. (1994). Child maltreatment: A national survey of reports and fatalities. *Journal of Interpersonal Violence, 9*(1), 75–94.

National Center for Victims of Crime and Crime Victims Research and Treatment Center. (1992). Rape in America: A report to the nation (pp. 1–16). Arlington, VA.

Straus, M. A. & Gelles, R. J. (1988). How violent are American families?: Estimates from the National Family Violence Resurvey and other studies. In G. T. Hotaling & D. Finkelhor (Eds.), *Family abuse and its consequences: New directions in research*. Newbury Park, CA: Sage Publications.

Violence Against Women

1993

Physical and mental health effects.
Part I: Research findings

Lisa A. Goodman
Mary P. Koss
Nancy Felipe Russo

ABSTRACT

Interpersonal violence is a ubiquitous source of fear, distress, and injury in the lives of women in the United States, crossing lines of age, race, ethnicity, and economic status (Coley & Beckett, 1988; Frieze & Browne, 1989; Koss, 1988; Straus, Gelles, & Steinmetz, 1980). In recent years, the public health community has become increasingly aware that "this violence is a serious public health problem . . . [and that] nonfatal interpersonal violence has far-reaching consequences in terms of morbidity and quality of life" (Center for Disease Control, 1985, p. 739). This article reviews the physical and mental health effects on adult women of physical abuse and sexual assault, and describes their implications for mental health research and practice.

Key words: Violence, Abuse, Physical assault, Sexual assault, Rape, Trauma.

Violence against women takes many forms including physical abuse and sexual assault. The term physical abuse includes acts of violence likely to cause injury—ranging from slight pain to murder—although an injury does not have to occur (Gelles, 1988). Common forms of physical violence include hitting, pushing, punching, choking, slapping, throwing objects, biting, kicking, and threatening with or using a lethal weapon (Straus et al., 1980).

The term sexual assault encompasses a broad range of acts ranging from unwanted petting to rape (Russell, 1986). Although definitions vary by state, statutes often define rape as the "nonconsensual sexual penetration of an adolescent or adult obtained by physical force, by threat of bodily harm, or when the victim is incapable of giving consent by virtue of mental illness, mental retardation, or intoxication" (Bohmer, 1990; Koss & Harvey, 1991; Searles & Berger, 1987).

Both physical and sexual assault can be perpetrated by strangers or by intimates (in heterosexual or homosexual relationships). Forms of male violence against women in intimate relationships include acquaintance rape, date rape, marital rape, courtship violence, dating violence, and battering. Acquaintance rapes are assaults by anyone who is not a complete stranger to the victim. Courtship or dating violence includes act of physical violence perpetrated by someone who has some level of romantic relationship with the victim. Partner violence encompasses both marital rape and wife battering and refers to assaults by adult men against adult women with whom they share or have previously shared a marriage or cohabiting relationship.

Although psychological violence will not be discussed in detail in this article, it is important to note its frequent occurrence, particularly within marital relationships. Psychological violence may include coercion, degradation, intimidation, and humiliation. A perpetrator may attempt to control his victim by threatening to beat her, to harm her pets, to take away or hurt her children, or to commit suicide (Schechter, 1982; Walker, 1979). Violence against a women's property may also be used to display a perpetrator's potential for destruction (Soakin, Martin, & Walker, 1985). Given the power of psychological abuse, physical or sexual violence need not be constant or severe to perpetuate an environment of unremitting terror. The effects of the *threat* of violence can be psychologically devastating.

This article reviews the physical and mental health effects on adult women of physical abuse and sexual assault (particularly rape) with special attention to intimate violence. As health-care providers, policy

---

The order of authorship is alphabetical.

225

makers, and the public have become increasingly aware of the prevalence and consequences of violence against women in our society, they have come to recognize the importance of identifying and treating victims of violence. Mental health professionals have important roles—as researchers, service providers, and policy advocates—in educating and training service providers in all health-care professions to identify, treat, and refer victims of violence. The goal of this article is to help equip psychologists for these roles by stimulating a more sophisticated, research-based understanding of the mental and physical health effects of male violence on women.

THE PREVALENCE OF VIOLENCE

Sexual and physical violence against women in the United States is widespread. According to prevalence estimates from several large community samples, one in five women has been the victim of completed rape (Bagley et al., 1984; Kercher & McShane, 1984; Russell, 1982, 1983; Wyatt, 1985). A woman reports a rape to the police every 5–6 minutes (Uniform Crime Reports, 1989).

Most sexual assaults are committed by perpetrators who are known to their victims (Koss, 1988). Indeed, women are more likely to be assaulted, killed, or raped by a current or former male partner than by all other categories of assailants combined (Browne & Williams, 1989; Finkelhor & Yllö, 1985; Koss, 1985; Koss, Woodruff, & Koss, 1991; Russell, 1982). Furthermore, over 80% of sexual assaults reported by college-age and adult women are perpetrated by an acquaintance (Koss, 1985, Koss, Dinero, Seibel, & Cox, 1988; Russell, 1983); nearly half of the aggravated assault and completed rapes identified in a recent criminal victimization survey were perpetrated by men with whom the victims were romantically involved (Kilpatrick et al., 1987); of the physical and sexual assaults reported by psychiatric patients, 90% are perpetrated by family members (Carmen, Reiker, & Mills, 1984).

Sexual assaults, particularly rape, are underreported, and when women are raped by acquaintances, friends, or partners, they are even less likely to report the experience (Finkelhor & Yllö, 1983; Gelles, 1979; Pagelow, 1984; Russell, 1983); an estimated one-third of stranger rapes and 13% of acquaintance rapes are reported (Koss et al., 1988). Yet rape by an intimate produces mental health effects that are at least as severe as rape by strangers (Browne, 1992). Chances of injury appear particularly great for marital rape, possibly due to its link to wife battering (Pagelow, 1984).

Research indicates that between one-quarter (Straus & Gelles, 1990; Straus, Gelles, & Steinmetz, 1980) and one-half (Stark & Flitcraft, 1988) of all wives are physically battered by their husbands. More than 2 million women experience severe assault—being punched, kicked, choked, hit with an object, beaten up, or threatened with a knife or gun—during an average 12-month period in the United States (Langan & Innes, 1986; Straus & Gelles, 1990; Straus et al., 1980). The rate of severe intimate violence in cohabitating or dating partners appears to be increasing (Browne & Williams, 1989) and now reaches the rate for married couples (Center for Disease Control, 1989).

Although some studies have reported that men and women commit acts of physical violence in roughly equal numbers (see, e.g., Straus et al., 1980), the form, severity, and consequences of that violence differ between the sexes. Women's physical violence is almost always in self-defense and is much less severe in consequences than men's violence (Saunders, 1986).

THE PHYSICAL CONSEQUENCES OF VIOLENCE

Experiences of physical assault and sexual assault (particularly rape) result in acute medical conditions and are associated with lowered self-perceptions of health and increased self-reported symptomatology across nearly all body systems (except eyes and skin), higher levels of injurious health behaviors such as smoking or failure to use seat belts, and greater utilization of medical services (Fellitti, 1991; Koss & Heslet, 1992; Koss, Koss, & Woodruff, 1991). A high prevalence of physical or sexual victimization appears in a variety of patient populations, including patients diagnosed with chronic pelvic pain, other chronic pain syndromes, premenstrual syndrome, and alcoholic liver disease (Cunningham, Pearce, & Pearce, 1988; Drossman et al., 1990; Golding, Stein, Siegel, Burnam, & Sorenson, 1988; Koss & Heslet, 1992; Sedney & Brooks, 1984).

In addition, abuse may be the most important precipitating factor in female suicide. An estimated one in four female suicide attempts is preceded by physical violence (Stark et al., 1981) and suicidal ideation is reported in 33–50% of rape victims (Ellis, Atkeson, & Calhoun, 1981; Koss, 1988; Resick, Jordan, Girelli, Hutter, & Marhoefer-Dvorak, 1989). During the posttraumatic period of rape recovery, victims are nine times more likely than nonvictims to attempt suicide (Kilpatrick, Saunders, Veronen, Best, & Von, 1987).

Physical or sexual violence may also result in mild to moderate head injuries that can underlie symptoms of physical and psychological distress. Head injuries can lead to changes in cognition, affect, motivation, and behavior that are similar to those found in individuals suffering from a dementia or clinical depression (Kwentus, Hart, Peck, & Kornstein, 1985). Such injuries may remain undetected because of lack of overt neurological distress or failure to obtain medical attention (McGrath, Keita, Strickland, & Russo, 1990).

Sexual Assault

Among rape victims, 39% report sustaining a nongenital physical injury including abrasions about the head, neck, and face; the extremities; and the trunk region; of these, 54% seek medical treatment (Beebe, 1991). Severe injuries include multiple traumas, major fractures, and major lacerations (Geist, 1988). Posttrauma skeletal muscle tension is reflected in fatigue, tension headaches, and sleep disturbances. Gastrointestinal irritability is also frequent and includes stomach pains, nausea, no appetite, and inability to taste food.

Nearly one-third of rapes involve oral or anal penetration in addition to vaginal contact, and one-half of rape victims seen in trauma centers have vaginal and perineal trauma (Geist, 1988; Woodling & Kossoris, 1981). Fifteen percent of raped women have significant vaginal tears, and 1% require surgical repair (Cartwright & The Sexual Assault Study Group, 1987). Anorectal injuries may be produced by penetration of the penis as well as of digits, hands, blunt objects, or foreign bodies into the rectum. They include disruption of anal sphincters, retained foreign bodies, mucosal lacerations, and transmural perforations of the rectosigmoid (Chen, Davis, & Ott, 1986; Elam & Ray, 1986).

The physical aftermath of rape may also include any one of 15 different sexually transmitted diseases (Koss & Heslet, 1992), estimated to occur in 3.6–30% of victims (Beebe, 1991; Forster, Estreich, & Hooi, 1991; Lacey, 1990; Murphy, 1990). Gonorrhea, chlamydia, trichomonal infections, and syphilis are the most common, but there is also the life-threatening risk of hepatitis B and human immunodeficiency virus infection.

Rape results in pregnancy in about 5% of cases (Beebe, 1991; Koss et al., 1991). Rape victims who are already pregnant when assaulted have vulvar, oral, and anal penetration in proportions similar to those found in nonpregnant women: 95, 27, and 6%, respectively (Satin, Hemsell, Stone, Theriot, & Wendel, 1991). No catastrophic effects of rape on pregnancy have been identified.

Current statistics on the physical consequences of sexual assault may severely misrepresent the nature and underestimate the scope of effects. Only those with relatively severe injuries may seek trauma center care. Effects on victims who are not asked about the origin of their injuries, those who saw private physicians, and those who sought no treatment in the immediate posttrauma period, only to present themselves to the medical system later with delayed consequences of violence, are unknown (Koss & Heslet, 1992). One longitudinal study found that adult victims of sexual assault sought help from physicians twice as frequently as other women (Koss et al., 1991), most often in the second year following victimization. Frequency of physician visits increased 56% in the 2nd year following victimization compared to increases of 2% during the same period among nonvictimized women. The single most powerful predictor of total yearly physician visits and outpatient costs was severity of victimization, exceeding the predictive power of age, ethnicity, self-reported symptoms, and morbidity-related injurious health behaviors (Koss & Heslet, 1992).

Battering

An estimated 1 million women each year seek medical assistance for injuries resulting from wife battering (Stark & Flitcraft, 1988). One fifth to one third of women seen in emergency services, regardless of their stated presenting complaint, have symptoms directly linked to battering (Council on Scientific Affairs, 1987; Goldberg & Tomlanovich, 1984; Stark, Flitcraft, & Frazier, 1979), accounting for more injuries than automobile accidents, muggings, and rapes combined.

The most extreme physical consequence of violence is, of course, death. More women are killed by their male partners than by all other categories combined (52% of all murders of women are by male partners). Black women are more likely then white women to be killed by their spouse (Plass & Strauss, 1987).

For women that survive, physical injuries associated with partner violence most often involve multiple injuries to the face, head, neck, breast, or abdomen (Randall, 1990). Additionally, common presenting symptoms of such victims include evidence of past injury (Burge, 1989), chronic headaches, abdominal pain, sexual dysfunction, joint and muscle pain, sleeping and eating disorders, and recurrent vaginal infections (Randall, 1990, 1991).

Battering and Pregnancy

Women are at highest risk for battering in young adulthood, during their most active childbearing years (Gelles, 1988). The rate of husband-to-wife violence experienced by pregnant women is 35% higher than that experienced by nonpregnant women; if only severe violence is considered, the rate is 60% higher. In addition, women with a history of being battered are three times more likely to be injured during pregnancy than nonbattered women; those reporting current abuse, then, are clearly at risk for future abuse (Helton, McFarlane, & Anderson, 1987; Hillard, 1985; Stark & Flitcraft, 1988).

The abdomen is targeted twice as frequently in pregnant women as compared to nonpregnant victims (Berenson, Stiglich, Wilkinson, & Anderson, 1991). Physical assault during pregnancy may result in premature labor, rupture of the membranes, placental separation, antepartum hemorrhage, fetal fractures, and rupture of the uterus, liver, or spleen (Saltzman, 1990). Women battered during pregnancy are more likely than nonbattered women to experience negative pregnancy outcomes including miscarriages and stillbirths and delivery of low-birthweight infants (Bullock & McFarlane, 1989; Helton et al., 1987; McFarlane, 1989; Satin et al., 1991). The Surgeon General has recommended that all pregnant women be evaluated for battering as part of routine prenatal assessments (Surgeon General's Workshop on Violence, 1985).

THE MENTAL HEALTH CONSEQUENCES OF VIOLENCE

Victims of rape and battering experience a wide range of emotional and cognitive sequelae. Research has yet to delineate the relationships between particular types of violence and specific psychological outcomes; numerous overlapping factors can shape a victim's posttrauma response, including the frequency, severity, form, and duration of the violence, the age of the victim when it occurred, the relationship between the victim and the perpetrator, a prior history of abuse, and other sources of life stress (Browne & Finkelhor, 1986; Kilpatrick et al., 1987; Koss, 1988; Russell, 1986). An individual's particular psychological resources and coping ability prior to the violence and the nature of the recovery environment also exert important influences on a victim's posttrauma adaptation (Green, Wilson, & Lindy, 1985). Thus, although women of diverse circumstances experience physical and sexual assault, those who live under high stress and have few coping resources—including women living in poverty (Belle, 1990) and homeless women (Goodman, Saxe, & Harvey, 1991)—are at especially high risk for negative psychological sequelae.

Rape

Immediate impact. Rape victims are likely, during and just after the assault, to focus on physical and emotional survival. Initial responses may include talking with, or fighting, the perpetrator in an effort to escape, remaining calm so as not to provoke more severe violence, praying, and attempting to remember advice on how to deal with rape (Burgess & Holmstrom, 1979a, 1979b; Gelles & Straus, 1988). If escape is perceived to be impossible, victims may attempt to dissociate (Burgess & Holmstrom, 1979a, 1979b).

Shock, intense fear, numbness, confusion, extreme helplessness, and/or disbelief may follow the experience (Burgess & Holmstrom, 1974, 1979a, 1979b; Kilpatrick, Veronin, & Resick, 1979; Koss & Harvey, 1991). Women may fear that their rapist will return and harm them further, particularly if they contact the police. Victims of rape by intimates or acquaintances may be stunned that someone they trusted could attack them (Browne, 1992). Indeed, when women are raped by a partner, their shame and humiliation may be so intense that it becomes impossible for them to disclose the experience to anyone, even when anonymity is guaranteed (Finkelhor & Yllö, 1983; Gelles, 1979; Pagelow, 1984; Russell, 1982; Walker, 1984).

For some victims, overall symptom elevation subsides by the third month, but approximately one-quarter of rape victims go on to experience severe and long-term symptoms (Hanson, 1990). Although research suggests that mental health status at the end of the third month is a good indicator of long-term adjustment (Burgess & Holmstrom, 1974; Roth & Lebowitz, 1988), for some women symptomatology disappears temporarily and then returns several months after the assault (Forman, 1980). At this time the woman may seek help for these symptoms without informing service providers about the rape experience underlying them (Browne, 1992).

Long-term Impact. Victims of sexual assault may suffer from a wide variety of disturbing long-term psychological aftereffects (Browne, 1992; Koss & Harvey, 1991). Victimization is an "overwhelming assault" on the survivors "world of meaning" (Conte, 1988, p. 325; Janoff-Bulman, 1992). A woman whose body is violated, particularly by someone she knows, may cease believing that she is secure in the world, that the world has order and meaning, and that she is a worthy person (Janoff-Bulman, 1992; Janoff-Bulman & Frieze, 1983). Such perceptions may lead to feelings of vulnerability and loss of control (Burgess & Holstrom, 1979a, 1979b; Kilpatrick, Vernonen, & Best, 1985; Resick, Calhoun, Atkeson, & Ellis, 1981).

Furthermore, cultural myths about rape, including notions such as the victim provoked the assault, she enjoyed it, only promiscuous women get raped, and raped women are "damaged goods," can shape the victim's perceptions of the event and create feelings of guilt, shame, and self-blame (Roth & Lebowitz, 1988).

The most common psychiatric sequelae of sexual assault include anxiety and fear, depression, sexual dysfunction, substance abuse, and posttraumatic stress disorder (PTSD). Victims of sexual assault have reported heightened fear and anxiety even long after the attack (Ellis et al., 1981; Ellis, Calhoun, & Atkeson, 1980; Kilpatrick, Resick, & Veronen, 1981). Fear may be triggered by stimuli directly associated with the attack itself, by potential consequences of the rape such as testifying in court or contracting a sexually transmitted disease, or by situations that appear to pose a new threat of attack (Kilpatrick et al., 1981). Even in the absence of specific triggers, anxiety can become

generalized, leading to "jumpiness" (Burgess & Holmstrom, 1979a, 1979b), sleep disruptions (Burgess & Holmstrom, 1979a, 1979b; Ellis et al., 1981; Nadelson, Notman, Zackson, & Gornich, 1982), lack of concentration (Nadelson et al., 1982), and distrust or fear of men (Finkelhor & Yllö, 1985).

A variety of depressive symptoms have been noted in victims of sexual assault (Becker, Skinner, Abel, Axelrod, & Treacy, 1984), including sleep and appetite disturbance, loss of interest in normal activities, and decreased concentration (Frank & Stewart, 1984; Frank, Turner, & Duffy, 1979). They may exhibit symptoms such as nightmares, catastrophic fantasies, and feelings of alienation and isolation (Koss & Harvey, 1991). Rape victims may withdraw from people and activities, becoming virtually immobile (Burgess & Holmstrom, 1979b). Even when they continue their activities, many sexual assault victims report less enjoyment and satisfaction with their daily lives (Ellis et al., 1981). Self-blame is common and often severe (Burgess & Holmstrom, 1979a, 1979b; Frieze, 1979), and many rape victims develop major depressive disorders (Burnam et al., 1988; Frank et al., 1979). Among women in the community not in treatment, almost one in five rape victims have attempted suicide (Kilpatrick et al., 1985; Resick et al., 1989).

Victims of sexual assault may suffer from a variety of sexual dysfunctions including fear of sex, arousal dysfunction, and decreased sexual interest (Becker et al., 1984; Becker, Skinner, Abel, & Cichon, 1986; Ellis et al., 1980). Such dysfunction may result from victims' increased insecurities concerning sexual attractiveness, lowered sexual self-esteem, and negative feelings about men (Koss & Harvey, 1991; McCahill, Meyer, & Fischman, 1979). Rape victims are also more likely than nonvictims to receive diagnoses of alcohol abuse/dependence and drug abuse/dependence, even several years postassault (Burnam et al., 1988).

Finally, the diagnosis PTSD encompasses many of the preceding symptoms and can be applied to a large proportion of rape victims. Indeed, rape victims are thought to be the largest single group of PTSD sufferers (Foa, Olasov, & Steketee, 1987). In a prospective study of hospital-referred rape victims, 94% met full criteria for PTSD at initial assessment, a mean of 12 days after the assault (Rothbaum, Foa, Riggs, Murdock, & Walsch, in press), and the lifetime prevalence of PTSD in a national sample of rape victims was 31% (National Victims Survey, 1992). The hallmark of

PTSD is intrusive reexperiencing of the trauma. Recollections are in the form of daytime memories or nightmares and are accompanied by intense psychological distress including reactivation of the emotions and physiologic sensations experienced during the attack. To reduce the distress of reexperiencing, trauma victims often go to great lengths to avoid reminders of the trauma, which results in phases of diminished responsiveness to the external world.

Predictors of response to sexual assault. Income and education do not appear to be related to type or severity of symptoms exhibited by adult victims of sexual assault (Becker, Skinner, Abel, & Tracey, 1982; Kilpatrick & Veronen, 1984; Kilpatrick et al., 1985; Ruch & Leon, 1983), but being elderly (Atkeson, Calhoun, Resick, & Ellis, 1982; Burgess & Holmstrom, 1974; Frank & Stewart, 1984; Ruch & Chandler, 1983), married (McCahill et al., 1979), or Asian or Mexican American (Ruch & Chandler, 1983; Ruch & Leon, 1983; Williams & Holmes, 1981) has been linked to greater postassault distress. Women with preexisting psychological distress are also at higher risk for negative mental health consequences following sexual assault (Atkeson et al., 1982; Ellis et al., 1981; Frank & Anderson, 1987; Frank, Turner, Stewart, Jacob, & West, 1981; Gidycz & Koss, 1990; Lurigio & Resick, 1990).

Prior victimization has a complex relationship to post-assault distress. First-time victims usually show more distress immediately following the rape, whereas prior victims have increased distress over time, ultimately becoming more distressed than first-time victims (Ruch & Leon, 1983; Ruch, Gartrell, Amedeo, & Coyne, 1991; 1991b). Women who are raped more than one time are more likely to abuse substances (Ruch et al., 1991) and have a lifetime diagnosis of depression (Kilpatrick et al., 1987). Having experienced other negative life stressors, including crimes other than rape or loss of a spouse, is also linked to greater postassault stress among victims (Burgess & Holmstrom, 1979c; Glenn & Resick, 1986; Kilpatrick et al., 1985).

The nature of the attack itself can affect postassault psychological functioning as well: Assault variables predictive of symptoms include number of assailants, physical threat, injury requiring medical care, and medical complications (Sales, Baum, & Snor, 1984).

Interestingly, the absence of violence may also lead to enhanced postassault distress (McCahill et al., 1979). This association is particularly strong when the sexual assault included fondling and caressing. The victim of such an assault may confuse subsequent displays of physical affection with the coerced caresses of the rapist, leading to the emergence of anxiety and other symptoms (McCahill et al., 1979).

Finally, evidence suggests that women who have been sexually assaulted by acquaintances or family members suffer serious psychological aftereffects equal to those suffered by women assaulted by strangers (Koss et al., 1988). Women assaulted in environments that seemed safe, such as at home or with a trusted person, may suffer especially serious symptoms of depression and fear (Burge, 1989; Frank & Stewart, 1984).

Marital rape. Although marital rape can occur in the absence of other forms of violence, it is most frequent in relationships marked by ongoing physical abuse (Frieze, 1983; Russell, 1982; Walker, 1984). Of women physically assaulted by partners, 33–46% report sexual assault as well (Frieze & Browne, 1989). In severely physically abusive relationships, forcible rape can occur several times a month (Browne, 1992). Furthermore, battered women who are raped by their partners are likely to experience more severe nonsexual attacks than other battered women (Bowker, 1983; Browne, 1987, 1992; Shields & Hanneke, 1983).

Sexual relations have been traditionally viewed as a means to express love and trust among partners. Women can lose their capacity for intimacy and trust when sexual relations with their partner become coerced or violent. Also, because the experience of marital rape is shameful and humiliating, its victims may have difficulty sharing their distress with others and become especially isolated (Finkelhor & Yllö, 1985; Russell, 1982; Shields & Hanneke, 1983). In addition to experiencing the typical aftereffects of physical battery (see the following section), victims of marital rape may experience terrifying flashbacks and nightmares, an aversion to sex, and a general inability to trust men, leading, in some cases, to total withdrawal from contact with men, including strangers and nonstrangers (Finkelhor & Yllö, 1985). Thus, the long-term effects of wife battering may be especially pronounced in women who have also been sexually abused by their partners.

Battering

Immediate impact. During and immediately after a physical attack by a partner, women are likely to focus on their own survival and the safety of their children. Victims' behavior might include crying, yelling and cursing at the perpetrator, using arms, legs, and feet to protect the body, or attempting to escape (Bowker, 1983; Gelles & Straus, 1988). As with sexual assault, after the initial attack, reactions such as shock, numbing, and intense fear are common. The fear of future violence continues and can be expressed in a variety of psychological and somatic symptoms even if no further physical violence occurs.

Long-term impact. The long-term effects of battering include depression, fear and anxiety, social isolation, and PTSD (Browne, 1992; Hilberman & Munson, 1977–1978; Walker, 1984). Battered women's feelings of vulnerability, loss, betrayal, and hopelessness are compounded by the fact that someone they love, trust, and depend on is their attacker (Browne, 1992) Violence in the home, a place traditionally conceived as a haven of safety and comfort, undermines women's sense of security and trust as well as confidence in their ability to judge another individual. Victims also may fear for the safety of their children or feel ashamed and humiliated by abuse that occurs in front of their children.

Of all the psychological sequelae associated with battery, the most prominent are symptoms of depression (Hilberman & Munson, 1977–1978; McGrath et al., 1990; Walker, 1984). Specific depressive symptoms noted in the literature include blunted affect, numbed responsiveness (Douglas, 1986; Hilberman, 1980; Hilberman & Munson, 1977–1978), reduced social involvement (Hilberman, 1980), feelings of worthlessness (Gelles & Straus, 1988; Mitchell & Hodson, 1983), self-blame, guilt (Walker, 1979, 1983), and self-hatred, often expressed actively through self-destructive behaviors and suicide attempts, some of which are successful (Hilberman, 1980; Stark et al., 1979).

Victims experience high levels of anxiety (Stark et al. 1979; Walker, 1984) and feelings of terror in anticipation of future violence (Hilberman, 1980; Hilberman & Munson, 1977–1978). Anxiety reactions may become particularly acute in response to environmental cues that serve to remind victims of the battering event (Douglas, 1986; Hilberman, 1980; Hilberman & Munson, 1977–1978). Symptoms of anxiety might include sleeping and eating difficulties, a heightened startle reaction, concentration difficulties (Douglas, 1986), and agitation and hypervigilance (Hilberman, 1980; Hilberman & Munson, 1977–1978).

Being battered often leads to a dramatic shift in women's interpersonal interactions. Battered women may socialize less with neighbors, decrease their contacts with friends, join voluntary organizations less frequently, and cease going out with their husbands over the course of their abusive relationships (Dobash & Dobash, 1979; Walker, 1984). Explanations for the increased social isolation of battered women vary. Some suggest that batterers isolate their wives to keep them dependent and helpless (Hilberman & Munson, 1977–1978); others suggest that battered women feel helpless and thus fail to reach out (Walker, 1984), or that friends, neighbors, and relatives respond negatively to the experience of battering (Mitchell & Hodson, 1983). Some people may blame battered women for failing to extricate themselves (Lerner, 1980; Ryan, 1971) or perceive them as "losers" (Bard & Sangrey 1979). Still others perceive victims as depressed and therefore unpleasant to be with (Coates, Wortman, & Abbey, 1979). These negative, unsympathetic reactions can confirm and amplify victims' subjective feelings of isolation. In the absence of companionship, women may attempt to ameliorate their psychological pain by substance abuse, especially with prescription drugs (Hilberman & Munson, 1977–1978; Stark et al. 1979). They may also minimize or even deny the danger and personal loss they have experienced for reasons of shame, fear, or psychological self-protection (Bard & Sangrey, 1979; Douglas, 1986).

Recently, high rates of PTSD have been documented among battered women. Sixty percent of battered women at an outpatient clinic (Cimino & Dutton, 1991) and 89% of those living in a battered women's shelter (Kemp, Rawlings, & Green, 1991) were diagnosed with PTSD; studies of community samples remain to be done. As with sexual assault, the PTSD diagnosis encompasses many of the negative psychological sequelae of physical battery, thereby creating a clearer and more comprehensive understanding of battered women's postassault responses.

Predictors of response to partner violence. Battered women do not form a homogeneous group and the effects of spouse abuse are by no means uniform. Recent research indicates that the number and severity of symptoms that battered women suffer may be associated with frequency of abuse, adherence to traditional sex role values, the presence of emotional abuse, and victim perception of the violence as potentially lethal (Cimino & Dutton, 1991; Follingstad, Brennan, Hause, Polek, & Rutledge, 1991). A history of abuse in childhood also predicts greater psychological distress in the aftermath of physical battery or sexual assault by a partner (Cimino & Dutton, 1991). This last finding is buttressed by a growing body of research suggesting that childhood trauma can have a damaging and enduring effect on subsequent personality functioning and cause vulnerability to a variety of subsequent trauma (Van der Kolk, 1987, 1988).

IMPLICATIONS FOR MENTAL HEALTH-CARE PROVIDERS

These research findings have a number of general implications for mental health research and practice. Of highest priority is the need to identify victims of violence in health-care delivery systems, because neither physical nor mental health problems of victims of violence can be appropriately addressed and resolved without identifying and addressing underlying etiology. Intimate violence in particular is repetitive and cross-generational. Ignoring it may cause a client to return repeatedly for multiple physical and mental health problems and enhances the potential for members of the patient's family to become future victims/clients (Koss, 1998; Koss & Heslet, 1992).

Although violence against women is widespread and has serious consequences, it remains largely undetected in health-care settings. Victims are naturally reluctant to discuss their victimization experiences. The process of labeling oneself a victim of violence is difficult and becomes especially complicated when the experience has occurred within the family or if the actions were ambiguous (Browne, 1991). Inadequate identification on the part of service providers compounds the problem by communicating a lack of permission to discuss victimization.

Diagnostic assessments should always include taking a history of sexual and physical violence. Because of the struggle to avoid the devaluation inherent in being a victim, women who have experienced violence do not often label their experience with words such as rape, incest, molestation, child abuse, battering, wife beating, or domestic violence. Health-care providers conducting screenings or diagnostic assessments can be more effective in identifying violence if they avoid such terms and focus on describing the behaviors involved. For example, clients could be asked "When you were growing up, did a parent or relative or anyone older make you do sexual things?" "As a teenager or adult did anyone make you have sex when you didn't want to by using force?" and "Are you currently being physically hurt by anyone?" Positive responses should be followed up to assess the client's present danger by asking questions such as "Is there anyone at home you are afraid of?" "Do you have plans for getting help if he hurts you again?" and "How can I help?" It is essential that screening for violence, whether in person or by checklist, take place under circumstances that provide privacy and the safety to implicate intimates. A family member who accompanies an abused client may be the perpetrator.

Many victims, particularly those who have experienced sexual violence, have never told anyone about their experiences. The simple act of disclosing their secret trauma may have a significant impact on their health status. Even in the context of a safe and private space and supportive interviewer, it can be painful and retraumatizing to discuss the details of physical and sexual abuse. Difficulties are compounded by the fact that repression and dissociation are common survival strategies in response to trauma. Detailed information, however, is important because symptoms may have a symbolic value that cannot be ascertained unless the entire picture of the victimization experience is revealed. Time, patience, and persistence are needed to screen and treat victimized clients (McGrath et al., 1990).

In their roles as educators, trainers, and consultants, knowledgeable psychologists can increase the ability of health and mental health service delivery providers to screen and refer victims of violence to appropriate physical and mental health treatment. In particular, emergency room personnel, family practitioners, obstetrician-gynecologists, pediatricians, and psychiatrists need to be informed about the causes, prevalence, and physical and mental health consequences of violence. The American Medical Association has recently taken steps to encourage its members to seek such knowledge (Browne, 1992), and psychologists in hospitals and clinics have special roles to play in training medical students and providing continuing education to medical practitioners. They are also in special positions to build partnerships to facilitate referrals so that physical and psychological health interventions can be coordinated in treatment planning.

Psychologists must begin, however, by educating themselves about male violence against women—not only about its nature and effects, but also about the multiple and complex factors that cause and perpetuate it, and potential avenues toward reducing its prevalence. The ubiquity of violence against women demands an urgent response, and psychologists are in ideal positions to provide it.

REFERENCES

ATKESON, B., CALHOUN, K. S., RESICK, P. A., & ELLIS, E. (1982). Victims of rape: Repeated assessment of depressive symptoms. *Journal of Consulting and Clinical Psychology, 50,* 96–102.

BAGLEY, C., ALLARD, H., McCORMIER, N., PROUDFOOT, P., FORTIN, D., OGILVIE, D., RAE-GRANT, Q., GELINAS, P., PEPIN, L., & SUTHERLAND, S. (1984). *Committee on sexual offenses against children and youth: Vol. I. Sexual offenses against children.* Ottawa: Canadian Government Publication Center.

BARD, M., & SANGREY, D. (1979). *The crime victim's book.* New York: Basic Books.

BECKER, J. V., SKINNER, L. J., ABEL, G. G., AXELROD, R., & TREACY, E. C. (1984). Depressive symptoms associated with sexual assault. *Journal of Sex and Marital Therapy, 10*(3), 185–192.

BECKER, J. V., SKINNER, L. J., ABEL, G. G., & CICHON, J. (1986). Level of post-assault sexual functioning in rape and incest victims. *Archives of Sexual Behavior, 15,* 37–49.

BECKER, J. V., SKINNER, L. J., ABEL, G. G., & TREACY, E. C. (1982). Incidence and types of sexual dysfunction in rape and incest victims. *Journal of Sex and Marital Therapy, 8,* 65–74.

BEEBE, D. K. (1991). Emergency management of the adult female rape victim. *American Family Physician, 43,* 2041–2046.

BELLE, D. (1990). Poverty and women's mental health. *American Psychologist, 45,* 385–389.

BERENSON, A. B., STIGLICH, N. J., WILKINSON, G. S., & ANDERSON, G. A. (1991). Drug abuse and other risk factors for physical abuse in pregnancy among white non-Hispanic, black, and Hispanic women. *American Journal of Obstetrics and Gynecology, 164,* 1491–1499.

BOHMER, C. (1990). Acquaintance rape and the law. In A. Parrot (Ed.), *Acquaintance rape.* New York: John Wiley.

BOWKER, L. H. (1983). *Beating wife-beating.* Lexington, MA: Lexington Books.

BROWNE, A. (1987). *When battered women kill.* New York: Lexington Books.

BROWNE, A. (1991). The victim's experience: Pathways to disclosure. *Psychotherapy, 28,* 150–156.

BROWNE, A. (1992). Violence against women: Relevance for medical practitioners. *Journal of the American Medical Association, 267,* 23, 3184–3187.

BROWNE, A., & FINKELHOR, D. (1986). Impact of child sexual abuse: A review of the research. *Psychological Bulletin, 99,* 66–77.

BROWNE, A., & WILLIAMS, K. R. (1989). Exploring the effect of resource availability and the likelihood of female-perpetrated homicides. *Law and Society Review, 23,* 75–94.

BULLOCK, L. F., & McFARLANE, J. (1989). The birth weight-battering connection. *American Journal of Nursing, 89,* 1153–1155.

BURGE, S. K. (1989). Violence against women as a health care issue. *Family Medicine, 21*(September—October). 368–373.

BURGESS, A. W., & HOLMSTROM, L. L. (1974). Rape trauma syndrome. *American Journal of Psychiatry, 131,* 981–986.

BURGESS, A. W., & HOLMSTROM, L. (1979a). Adaptive strategies and recovery from rape. *American Journal of Psychiatry, 136,* 1278–1282.

BURGESS, A. W., & HOLMSTROM, L. (1979b). *Rape: Crisis and recovery.* Bowie, MD: Robert J. Brady.

BURGESS, A. W., & HOLMSTROM, L. (1979c). Rape: Sexual disruption and recovery. *American Journal of Psychiatry, 133* (49), 648–657.

BURNAM, M. A., STEIN, J. A., GOLDING, J. M., SIEGEL, J. M., SORENSON, S. B., FORSYTHE, A. B., & TELLES, C. A. (1988). Sexual assault and mental disorders in a community population. *Journal of Consulting and Clinical Psychology, 56,* 843–850.

CARMEN, E. H., RIEKER, P. P., & MILLS, T. (1984). Victims of violence and psychiatric illness. *American Journal of Psychiatry, 141,* 378–383.

CARTWRIGHT, P. S., & THE SEXUAL ASSAULT STUDY GROUP. (1987). Factors that correlate with injury sustained by survivors of sexual assault. *Obstetrics and Gynecology, 70,* 44–46.

CENTER FOR DISEASE CONTROL, U.S. DEPARTMENT OF HEALTH AND HUMAN SERVICES. (1985), December 13). Adolescent sex offenders—Vermont, 1984. *Morbidity and Mortality Weekly Report, 34*(49), 738–741.

CENTER FOR DISEASE CONTROL. (1989). Education about adult violence in U.S. and Canadian Medical Schools: 1987–88. *Morbidity and Mortality Weekly Report, 38,* 17–19.

CHEN, Y. M., DAVIS, M., & OTT, D. J. (1986). Traumatic rectal hematoma following anal rape. *Annals of Emergency Medicine, 15,* 122–124.

CIMINO, J. J., & DUTTON, M. A. (1991). *Factors influencing the development of PTSD in battered women.* Paper presented at the 99th annual convention of the American Psychological Association, San Francisco.

COATES, D., WORTMAN, C. B., & ABBEY, A. (1979). Reactions to victims. In I. H. Frieze, B. Bar-Tal, & J. S. Carroll (Eds.), *New approaches to social problems: Applications of attribution theory.* San Francisco: Jossey-Bass.

COLEY, S. A., & BECKET, J. O. (1988). Black battered women: A review of empirical literature. *Journal of Counseling and Development, 66,* 266–270.

CONTE, J. R. (1988). The effects of sexual abuse on children: Results of a research project. *Annals of the New York Academy of Sciences, 528,* 311–326.

COUNCIL ON SCIENTIFIC AFFAIRS. (1987). Elder abuse and neglect. *Journal of the American Medical Association, 257,* 966–971.

CUNNINGHAM, J., PEARCE, T., & PEARCE, P. (1988). Childhood sexual abuse and medical complaints in adult women. *Journal of Interpersonal Violence, 3,* 131–144.

DOBASH, R. E., & DOBASH, R. P. (1979). *Violence against wives.* New York: Free Press.

DOUGLAS, M. A. (1986). The battered woman syndrome. In O. J. Sonkin (Ed.), *Domestic violence on trial: Psychological and legal dimensions of family violence* (pp. 39–54). New York: Springer.

DROSSMAN, D. A., LESSERMAN, J., NACHMAN, G., LI, Z., GLUCK, H., TOOMEY, T. C., & MITCHELL, M. (1990). Sexual and physical abuse in women with functional or organic gastrointestinal disorders. *Annals of Internal Medicine, 113*, 828–833.

ELAM, A. L., & RAY, V. G. (1986). Sexually related trauma: A review. *Annals of Emergency Medicine, 15*, 576–584.

ELLIS, E. M., ATKESON, B. M., & CALHOUN, K. S. (1981). An assessment of long-term reactions to rape. *Journal of Abnormal Psychology, 90*, 263–266.

ELLIS, E. M., CALHOUN, K. S., & ATKESON, B. M. (1980). Sexual dysfunctions in victims of rape: Victims may experience a loss of sexual arousal and frightening flashbacks even one year after the assault. *Women and Health, 5*, 39–47.

FELLITTI, V. J. (1991). Long-term medical consequences of incest, rape, and molestation. *Southern Medical Journal, 84*, 328–331.

FINKELHOR, D., & YLLÖ, K. (1983). Rape in marriage: A sociological view. In D. Finkelhor, R. J. Gelles, G. T. Hotaling, & M. A. Straus (Eds.), *The dark side of families: Current family violence research* (pp. 119–131). Beverly Hills, CA: Sage.

FINKELHOR, D., & YLLÖ, K. (1985). *License to rape: Sexual abuse of wives.* New York: Holt, Rinehart & Winston.

FOA, E. B., OLASOV, B., & STEKETEE, G. S. (1987, September). *Treatment of rape victims.* Paper presented at the conference State of the Art in Sexual Assault, Charleston, SC.

FOLLINGSTAD, D. R., BRENNAN, A. F., HAUSE, E. S., POLEK, D. S., & RUTLEDGE, L. L. (1991). Factors moderating physical and psychological symptoms of battered women. *Journal of Family Violence, 6*, 81–95.

FORMAN, B. (1980). Psychotherapy with rape victims. *Psychotherapy: Theory, research, and practice, 17*, 304–311.

FORSTER, G. E., ESTREICH, S., & HOOI, Y. S. (1991). Screening for STDs [Letter to the editor]. *Annals of Emergency Medicine, 324*, 161–162.

FRANK, E., & ANDERSON, B. P. (1987). Psychiatric disorders in rape victims: Past history and current symptomatology. *Comprehensive Psychiatry, 28*, 77–82.

FRANK, E., & STEWART, B. D. (1984). Depressive symptoms in rape victims: A revisit. *Journal of Affective Disorders, 7*, 77–85.

FRANK, E., TURNER, S. M., & DUFFY, B. (1979). Depressive symptoms in rape victims. *Journal of Affective Disorders, 1*, 269–297.

FRANK, E., TURNER, S. M., STEWART, B. D., JACOB, J., & WEST, D. (1981). Past psychiatric symptoms and the response to sexual assault. *Comprehensive Psychiatry, 22*, 479–487.

FRIEZE, I. H. (1983). Investigating the causes and consequences of marital rape. *Signs, 8*, 532–553.

FRIEZE, I. H., & BROWNE, A. (1989). Violence in marriage. In L. Ohlin & M. H. Tonrey (Eds.), *Crime and justice—An annual review of research. Family violence.* Chicago: University of Chicago Press.

GEIST, R. F. (1988). Sexually related trauma. *Emergency Medical Clinics of North America, 6*, 439–466.

GELLES, R. (1979). *Family violence.* Beverly Hills, CA: Sage.

GELLES, R. (1988). Violence and pregnancy: Are pregnant women at greater risk for abuse. *Journal of Marriage and the Family, 50*, 841–847.

GELLES, R., & STRAUS, M. (1988). *Intimate violence: The definitive study of the causes and consequences of abuse in the American family.* New York: Simon and Schuster.

GIDYCZ, C. A., & KOSS, M. P. (1990). A comparison of group and individual sexual assault victims. *Psychology of Women Quarterly, 14*, 325–342.

GLENN, F., & RESICK, P. A. (1986). *The effects of family violence on coping ability to a later victimization.* Unpublished manuscript, University of Missouri–St. Louis.

GOLDBERG, W. G., & TOMLANOVICH, M. C. (1984). Domestic violence victims in the emergency department. *Journal of the American Medical Association, 251*, 3259–3264.

GOLDING, J. M., STEIN, J. A., SIEGEL, J. M., BURNAM, M., & SORENSON, S. B. (1988). Sexual assault history and use of health and mental health services. *American Journal of Community Psychology, 16*, 625–644.

GOODMAN, L., SAXE, L., & HARVEY, M. (1991). Homelessness as psychological trauma: Broadening perspectives. *American Psychologist, 46* (11), 1219–1225.

GREEN, B. L., WILSON, J. P., & LINDY, J. D. (1985). Conceptualizing post-traumatic stress disorder. A psycho-social framework. In C. R. Figley (Ed.), *Trauma and its wake: The study of post-traumatic stress disorder* (pp. 53–69). New York: Brunner/Mazel.

HANSON, R. K. (1990). The psychological impact of sexual assault on women and children: A review. *Annals of Sex Research, 3*, 187–232.

HELTON, A., McFARLANE, J., & ANDERSON, E. (1987). Battered and pregnant: A prevalence study. *American Journal of Public Health, 77*, 1337–1339.

HILBERMAN, E. (1980). Overview: The "wife-beater's wife" reconsidered. *American Journal of Psychiatry, 137*, 1336–1347.

HILBERMAN, E., & MUNSON, K. (1977–1978). Sixty battered women. *Victimology: An International Journal, 2*, 460–471.

HILLARD, P. J. (1985). Physical abuse in pregnancy. *Obstetrics and Gynecology, 66*, 185–190.

JANOFF-BULMAN, R. (1992). *Shattered assumptions: Towards a new psychology of trauma.* New York: Free Press.

JANOFF-BULMAN, R., & FRIEZE, I. H. (1983). A theoretical perspective for understanding reactions to victimization. *Journal of Social Issues, 39*, 1–17.

KEMP, A., RAWLINGS, E. I., & GREEN, B. L. (1991). Post-traumatic stress disorder (PTSD) in battered women: A shelter example. *Journal of Traumatic Stress Studies, 4*(1), 137–148.

KERCHER, G., & McSHANE, M. (1984). The prevalence of child sexual abuse victimization in an adult sample of Texas residents. *Child Abuse & Neglect, 8*, 495–502.

KILPATRICK, D. G., RESICK, P. A., & VERONEN, L. J. (1981). Effects of a rape experience: A longitudinal study. *Journal of Social Issues, 37*, 1050–1121.

KILPATRICK, D. G., SAUNDERS, B. E., VERONEN, L. J., BEST, C. L., & VON, J. M. (1987). Criminal victimization: Lifetime prevalence, reporting to police, and psychological impact. *Crime and Delinquency, 33*, 478–489.

KILPATRICK, D. G., & VERONEN, L. J. (1984). *Treatment of fear and anxiety in victims of rape* (Final Rep., grant No. ROI NG29602). Rockville. MD: National Institute of Mental Health.

KILPATRICK, D. G., VERONEN, L. J., & BEST, C. L. (1985). Factors predicting psychological distress among rape victims. In C. R. Figley (Ed.), *Trauma and its wake: The study and treatment of post-traumatic stress disorder* (pp. 113–141). New York: Brunner/Mazel.

KILPATRICK, D. G., VERONEN, L. J., & RESICK, P. A. (1979). Assessment of the aftermath of rape: Changing patterns of fear. *Journal of Behavioral Assessment, 1*, 133–148.

KILPATRICK, D. G., VERONEN, L. J., SAUNDERS, B. E., BEST, C. L., AMICK-McMULLAN, A., & PADUHOVICH, J. (1987). *The psychological impact of crime: A study of randomly surveyed crime victims* (Final Rep. on grant No. 84-IJ-CX-0039). Submitted to the National Institute of Justice, Washington DC.

KOSS, M. P. (1985). The hidden rape victim: Personality, attitudinal, and situational characteristics. *Psychology of Women Quarterly, 9*, 193–212.

KOSS, M. P. (1988). Women's mental health research agenda: Violence against women. *Women's Mental Health Occasional Paper Series.* Washington, DC: National Institute of Mental Health.

KOSS, M. P., DINERO, T. E., SEIBEL, C., & COX, S. (1988). Stranger, acquaintance, and date rape: Is there a difference in the victim's experience? *Psychology of Women Quarterly, 12*, 1–24.

KOSS, M. P., & HARVEY, M. (1991). *The rape victim: Clinical and community approaches to treatment.* Lexington, MA: Stephen Greene Press.

KOSS, M. P., & HESLET, L. (1992). *Medical consequences of violence against women.* Unpublished manuscript.

KOSS, M. P., KOSS, P. G., & WOODRUFF, W. J. (1991). Deleterious effects of criminal victimization on women's health and medical utilization. *Archives of Internal Medicine, 151*, 342–347.

KOSS, M. P., WOODRUFF, W. J., & KOSS, P. G. (1991). Criminal victimization among primary care medical patients: Incidence, prevalence, and physician usage. *Behavioral Science and the Law, 9*, 85–96.

KWENTUS, J. A., HART, R. P., PECK, E. T., & KORNSTEIN, S. (1985). Psychiatric complications of closed-head trauma. *Psychosomatics, 26*, 8–14.

LACEY, H. B. (1990). Sexually transmitted diseases and rape: The experience of a sexual assault centre. *International Journal of STD and AIDS, 1*, 405–409.

LANGAN, P. A., & INNES, C. A. (1986). *Preventing domestic violence against women.* Washington, DC: U.S. Department of Justice, Bureau of Justice Statistics.

LERNER, M. J. (1980). *The belief in a just world.* New York: Plenum Press.

LURIGIO, A. J., & RESICK, P. A. (1990). Healing the psychological wounds of criminal victimization: Predicting postcrime distress and recovery. In A. J. Lurigio, W. G. Skogan, & R. C. Davis (Eds.), *Victims of crime: Problems, policies, and programs* (pp. 51–67). Newbury Park, CA: Sage.

MCCAHILL, T. W., MEYER, L. C., & FISCHMAN, A. M. (1979). *The aftermath of rape.* Lexington, MA: D. C. Health & Co.

MCFARLANE, J. (1989). Battering during pregnancy: Tip of an iceberg revealed. *Women and Health, 15*, 69–84.

MCGRATH, E., KEITA, G. P., STRICKLAND, B. R., & RUSSO, N. F. (EDS.). (1990): *Women and depression: Risk factors and treatment issues.* Washington, DC: American Psychological Association.

MITCHELL, R. E., & HODSON, C. A. (1983). *Battered women: The relationship of stress, support, and coping to adjustment.* Paper presented at the meeting of the American Psychological Association, Washington, DC.

MURPHY, S. M. (1990). Rape, sexually transmitted diseases and human immunodeficiency virus infection. *International Journal of STD and AIDS, 1*, 79–82.

NADELSON, C., NOTMAN, M., ZACKSON, H., & GORNICH, J. (1982). A follow-up study of rape victims. *American Journal of Psychiatry, 139*, 1266–1270.

NATIONAL VICTIMS CENTER (1992, April 23). *Rape in America: A report to the nation.* Arlington, VA: Author.

PAGELOW, M. D. (1984). *Woman-battering: Victims and their experiences.* Beverly Hills, CA: Sage.

PLASS, P. S., & STRAUSS, M. A. (1987). *Intra-family homicide in the United States: Incidence, trends, and differences by religion, race, and gender.* Paper presented at the Third National Family Violence Research Conference, University of New Hampshire, Durham, NC.

RANDALL, T. (1990). Domestic violence begets other problems of which physicians must be aware to be effective. *Journal of the American Medical Association, 264*, 940–943.

RANDALL, T. (1991). Hospital-wide program identifies battered women; offers assistance. *Journal of the American Medical Association, 266*, 1177–1179.

RESICK, P. A., CALHOUN, K., ATKESON, B., & ELLIS, E. (1981). Adjustment in victims of sexual assault. *Journal of Consulting and Clinical Psychology, 49*, 704–712.

RESICK, P. A., JORDAN, C., GIRELLI, S., HUTTER, C., & MARHOEFER-DVORAK, S. (1989). A comparative outcome study of behavioral group therapy for sexual assault victims. *Behavior Therapy, 19*, 385–401.

ROTH, S., & LEBOWITZ, L. (1988). The experience of sexual trauma. *Journal of Traumatic Stress Studies, 1*(1), 79–107.

ROTHBAUM, B. O., FOA, E. B., RIGGS, D. S., MURDOCK, T., & WALSH, W. (in press). A prospective examination of post-traumatic stress disorder in rape victims. *Journal of Traumatic Stress.*

RUCH, L. O., & CHANDLER, S. M. (1983). Sexual assault trauma during the acute phase: An exploratory model and multivariate analysis. *Journal of Health and Social Behavior, 24*, 174–185.

RUCH, L. O., GARTRELL, J. W., AMEDEO, S., & COYNE, B. J. (1991). The sexual assault symptom scale: Measuring self-reported sexual assault trauma in the emergency room. *Psychological Assessment, 3*, 3–8.

RUCH, L. O., & LEON, J. J. (1983). Sexual assault trauma during the acute phase: An exploratory model and multivariate analysis. *Journal of Health and Social Behavior, 24*, 174–185.

RUSSELL, D. E. H. (1982). *Rape in marriage.* New York: Macmillan.

RUSSELL, D. E. H. (1983). The prevalence and incidence of forcible rape and attempted rape of females. *Victimology: An International Journal, 7*, 81–93.

RUSSELL, D. E. H. (1986). *The secret trauma: Incest in the lives of girls and women.* New York: Basic Books.

RYAN, W. (1971). *Blaming the victim.* New York: Basic Books.

SALES, E., BAUM, M., & SHORE, B. (1984). Victim readjustment following assault. *Journal of Social Issues, 37*, 5–27.

SALTZMAN, L. E. (1990). Battering during pregnancy: A role for physicians. *Atlanta Medicine, 64*, 45–48.

SATIN, A. J., HEMSELL, D. L., STONE, I. C., THERIOT, S, & WENDEL, G. D. (1991). Sexual assault in pregnancy. *Obstetrics and Gynecology, 77*, 710–714.

SAUNDERS, D. G. (1986). When battered women use violence: Husband abuse or self-defense? *Victims and Violence, 1*, 47–60.

SCHECTER, S. (1982). *Women and male violence: The visions and struggles of the battered women's movement.* London: Pluto Press; and Boston: South End Press.

SEARLES, P., & BERGER, R. J. (1987). Factors associated with a history of childhood sexual experience in a nonclinical female population. *Journal of the American Academy of Child Psychiatry, 23*, 215–218.

SEDNEY, M. A., & BROOKS, B. (1984). Factors associated with a history of childhood sexual experience in a nonclinical female population. *Journal of the American Academy of Child and Adolescent Psychiatry, 23*, 215–218.

SHIELDS, N. M., & HANNEKE, C. R. (1983). Battered wives' reactions to marital rape. In D. Finkelhor, R. J. Gelles, G. T. Hotaling, & M. A. Straus (Eds.), *The dark side of families: Current family violence research* (pp. 131–148). Beverly Hills, CA: Sage.

SONKIN, D. J., MARTIN, D., & WALKER, L. E. A. (1985). *The male batterer: A treatment approach.* New York: Springer.

STARK, E., & FLITCRAFT, A. (1988). Violence among intimates: An epidemiological review. In V. B. Van Hasselt, R. L. Morrison, A. S. Bellack, & M. Hersen (Eds.), *Handbook of family violence* (pp. 293–318). New York: Plenum Press.

STARK, E., FLITCRAFT, A., & FRAZIER, W. (1979). Medicine and patriarchal violence: The social construction of a "private" event. *International Journal of Health Services, 9*, 461–493.

STARK, E., FLITCRAFT, A., ZUCKERMAN. D., GREY, A., ROBINSON, J., & FRAZIER, W. (1981). Wife abuse in the medical setting: An introduction for health personnel. *Domestic Violence Monograph Series,* No. 7. Rockville, MD: National Clearinghouse on Domestic Violence.

STRAUS, M. A., & GELLES, R. S. (1990). *Physical violence in American families*. New Brunswick, NJ: Transaction Publishers.

STRAUS, M. A., GELLES, R. S., & STEINMETZ, J. K. (1980). *Behind closed doors: Violence in the American family*. Garden City, NY: Anchor/Doubleday.

SURGEON GENERAL'S WORKSHOP ON VIOLENCE. (1985). *Response, 9*. 19–21.

UNIFORM CRIME REPORTS. (1989). Washington, DC: Department of Justice.

VAN DER KOLK, B. A. (ED.) (1987). *Psychological trauma*. Washington, DC: American Psychiatric Press.

VAN DER KOLK, B. A. (1988). The trauma spectrum: The interactions of biological and social events in the genesis of the trauma response. *Journal of Traumatic Stress, 1*, 273–290.

WALKER, L. E. (1979). *The battered woman*. New York: Harper & Row.

WALKER, L. E. (1983). The battered woman syndrome study. In D. Finkelhor, R. J. Gelles, G. T. Hotaling, & M. A. Straus (Eds.), *The dark side of families: Current family violence research* (pp. 31–48). Beverly Hills, CA: Sage.

WALKER, L. E. (1984). *The battered woman syndrome*. New York: Springer.

WILLIAMS, J. E., & HOLMES, K. A. (1981). *The second assault: Rape and public attitudes*. Westport, CT: Greenwood Press.

WOODLING, B. A., & KOSSORIS, P. D. (1981). Sexual misuse: Rape, molestation, and incest. *Pediatric Clinics of North America, 28*, 481–499.

WYATT, G. E. (1985). The sexual abuse of Afro-American and White-American women in childhood. *Child Abuse & Neglect, 9*, 507–519.

Violence in Intimate Relationships

A feminist perspective

bell hooks

I

We were on the freeway, going home from San Francisco. He was driving. We were arguing. He had told me repeatedly to shut up. I kept talking. He took his hand from the steering wheel and threw it back, hitting my mouth—my open mouth, blood gushed, and I felt an intense pain. I was no longer able to say any words, only to make whimpering, sobbing sounds as the blood dripped on my hands, on the handkerchief I held too tightly. He did not stop the car. He drove home. I watched him pack his suitcase. It was a holiday. He was going away to have fun. When he left I washed my mouth. My jaw was swollen and it was difficult for me to open it.

I called the dentist the next day and made an appointment. When the female voice asked what I needed to see the doctor about, I told her I had been hit in the mouth. Conscious of race, sex, and class issues, I wondered how I would be treated in this white doctor's office. My face was no longer swollen so there was nothing to identify me as a woman who had been hit, as a black woman with a bruised and swollen jaw. When the dentist asked me what had happened to my mouth, I described it calmly and succinctly. He made little jokes about, "How we can't have someone doing this to us now, can we?" I said nothing. The damage was repaired. Through it all, he talked to me as if I were a child, someone he had to handle gingerly or otherwise I might become hysterical.

This is one way women who are hit by men and seek medical care are seen. People within patriarchal society imagine that women are hit because we are hysterical, because we are beyond reason. It is most often the person who is hitting that is beyond reason, who is hysterical, who has lost complete control over responses and actions.

Growing up, I had always thought that I would never allow any man to hit me and live. I would kill him. I had seen my father hit my mother once and I wanted to kill him. My mother said to me then, "You are too young to know, too young to understand." Being a mother in a culture that supports and promotes domination, a patriarchal, white-supremacist culture, she did not discuss how she felt or what she meant. Perhaps it would have been too difficult for her to speak about the confusion of being hit by someone you are intimate with, someone you love. In my case, I was hit by my companion at a time in life when a number of forces in the world outside our home had already "hit" me, so to speak, made me painfully aware of my powerlessness, my marginality. It seemed then that I was confronting being black and female and without money in the worst possible ways. My world was spinning. I had already lost a sense of grounding and security. The memory of this experience has stayed with me as I have grown as a feminist, as I have thought deeply and read much on male violence against women, on adult violence against children.

In this essay, I do not intend to concentrate attention solely on male physical abuse of females. It is crucial that feminists call attention to physical abuse in all its forms. In particular, I want to discuss being physically abused in singular incidents by someone you love. Few people who are hit once by someone they love respond in the way they might to a singular physical assault by a stranger. Many children raised in households where hitting has been a normal response by primary caretakers react ambivalently to physical assaults as adults, especially if they are being hit by someone who cares for them and whom they care for. Often female parents use physical abuse as a means of control. There is continued need for feminist research that examines such violence. Alice Miller has done insightful work on the impact of hitting even though she is at times anti-feminist in her perspective. (Often in her work, mothers are blamed, as if their responsibility in parenting is greater than that of fathers.) Feminist discussions of violence against women should be expanded to include a recognition of the ways in which women use abusive physical force toward children not only to challenge the assumptions that women are likely to be nonviolent, but also to add to our understanding of why children who were hit growing up are often hit as adults or hit others.

Recently, I began a conversation with a group of black adults about hitting children. They all agreed that hitting was sometimes necessary. A professional black male in a southern family setting with two children commented on the way he punished his daughters. Sitting them down, he would first interrogate them about the situation or circumstance for which

they were being punished. He said with great pride, "I want them to be able to understand fully why they are being punished." I responded by saying that "they will likely become women whom a lover will attack using the same procedure you who have loved them so well used and they will not know how to respond." He resisted the idea that his behavior would have any impact on their responses to violence as adult women. I pointed to case after case of women in intimate relationships with men (and sometimes women) who are subjected to the same form of interrogation and punishment they experienced as children, who accept their lover assuming an abusive, authoritarian role. Children who are the victims of physical abuse—whether one beating or repeated beatings, one violent push or several—whose wounds are inflicted by a loved one, experience an extreme sense of dislocation. The world one has most intimately known, in which one felt relatively safe and secure, has collapsed. Another world has come into being, one filled with terrors, where it is difficult to distinguish between a safe situation and a dangerous one, a gesture of love and a violent, uncaring gesture. There is a feeling of vulnerability, exposure, that never goes away, that lurks beneath the surface. I know. I was one of those children. Adults hit by loved ones usually experience similar sensations of dislocation, of loss, of new found terrors.

Many children who are hit have never known what it feels like to be cared for, loved without physical aggression or abusive pain. Hitting is such a widespread practice that any of us are lucky if we can go through life without having this experience. One undiscussed aspect of the reality of children who are hit finding themselves as adults in similar circumstances is that we often share with friends and lovers the framework of our childhood pains and this may determine how they respond to us in difficult situations. We share the ways we are wounded and expose vulnerable areas. Often, these revelations provide a detailed model for anyone who wishes to wound or hurt us. While the literature about physical abuse often points to the fact that children who are abused are likely to become abusers or be abused, there is no attention given to sharing woundedness in such a way that we let intimate others know exactly what can be done to hurt us, to make us feel as though we are caught in the destructive patterns we have struggled to break. When partners create scenarios of abuse similar, if not exactly the same, to those we have experienced in childhood, the wounded person is hurt not only by the physical pain but by the feeling of calculated betrayal. Betrayal. When we are physically hurt by loved ones, we feel betrayed. We can no longer trust that care can be sustained. We are wounded, damaged—hurt to our hearts.

Feminist work calling attention to male violence against women has helped create a climate where the issues of physical abuse by loved ones can be freely addressed, especially sexual abuse within families. Exploration of male violence against women by feminists and non-feminists shows a connection between childhood experience of being hit by loved ones and the later occurrence of violence in adult relationships. While there is much material available discussing physical abuse of women by men, usually extreme physical abuse, there is not much discussion of the impact that one incident of hitting may have on a person in an intimate relationship, or how the person who is hit recovers from that experience. Increasingly, in discussion with women about physical abuse in relationships, irrespective of sexual preference, I find that most of us have had the experience of being violently hit at least once. There is little discussion of how we are damaged by such experiences (especially if we have been hit as children), of the ways we cope and recover from this wounding. This is an important area for feminist research precisely because many cases of extreme physical abuse begin with an isolated incident of hitting. Attention must be given to understanding and stopping these isolated incidents if we are to eliminate the possibility that women will be at risk in intimate relationships.

Critically thinking about issues of physical abuse has led me to question the way our culture, the way we as feminist advocates focus on the issue of violence and physical abuse by loved ones. The focus has been on male violence against women and, in particular, male sexual abuse of children. Given the nature of patriarchy, it has been necessary for feminists to focus on extreme cases to make people confront the issue, and acknowledge it to be serious and relevant. Unfortunately, an exclusive focus on extreme cases can and does lead us to ignore the more frequent, more common, yet less extreme case of occasional hitting. Women are also less likely to acknowledge occasional hitting for fear that they will then be seen as someone who is in a bad relationship or someone whose life is out of control. Currently, the literature about male violence against women identifies the physically abused woman as a "battered woman." While it has been important to have an accessible terminology to draw attention to the issue of male violence against women, the terms used reflect biases because they call attention to only one type of violence in intimate relationships. The term "battered woman" is problematical. It is not a term that emerged from feminist work on male violence against women; it was already used by psychologists and sociologists in the literature on domestic violence. This label "battered woman" places primary emphasis on physical assaults that are continuous, repeated, and unrelenting. The focus is on extreme violence, with little effort to link these cases with the everyday acceptance within intimate relationships of physical abuse that is not extreme, that may not be repeated. Yet these lesser forms of physical abuse damage individuals psychologically and, if not properly addressed and recovered from, can set the stage for more extreme incidents.

Most importantly, the term "battered woman" is used as though it constitutes a separate and unique category of womanness, as though it is an identity, a mark that sets one apart rather than being simply a descriptive term. It is as though the experience of being repeatedly violently hit is the sole defining characteristic of a woman's identity and all other aspects of who she is and what her experience has been are submerged. When I was hit, I too used the popular phrases "batterer," "battered woman," "battering" even though I did not feel that these words adequately described being hit once. However, these were the terms that people would listen to, would see as important, significant (as if it is not really significant for an individual, and more importantly for a woman, to be hit once). My partner was angry to be labelled a batterer by me. He was reluctant to talk about the experience of hitting me precisely because he did not want to be labelled a batterer. I had hit him once (not as badly as he had hit me) and I did not think of myself as a batterer. For both of us, these terms were inadequate. Rather than enabling us to cope effectively and positively with a negative situation, they were part of all the mechanisms of denial; they made us want to avoid confronting what had happened. This is the case for many people who are hit and those who hit.

Women who are hit once by men in their lives, and women who are hit repeatedly do not want to be placed in the category of "battered woman" because it is a label that appears to strip us of dignity, to deny that there has been any integrity in the relationships we are in. A person physically assaulted by a stranger or a casual friend with whom they are not intimate may be hit once or repeatedly but they do not have to be placed into a category before doctors, lawyers, family, counselors, etc. take their problem seriously. Again, it must be stated that establishing categories and terminology has been part of the effort to draw public attention to the seriousness of male violence against women in intimate relationships. Even though the use of convenient labels and categories has made it easier to identify problems of physical abuse, it does not mean the terminology should not be critiqued from a feminist perspective and changed if necessary.

Recently, I had an experience assisting a woman who had been brutally attacked by her husband (she never commented on whether this was the first incident or not), which caused me to reflect anew on the use of the term "battered woman." This young woman was not engaged in feminist thinking or aware that "battered woman" was a category. Her husband had tried to choke her to death. She managed to escape from him with only the clothes she was wearing. After she recovered from the trauma, she considered going back to this relationship. As a church-going woman, she believed that her marriage vows were sacred and that she should try to make the relationship work. In an effort to share my feeling that this could place her at great risk, I brought her Lenore Walker's *The Battered Woman* because it seemed to me that there was much that she was not revealing, that she felt alone, and that the experiences she would read about in the book would give her a sense that other women had experienced what she was going through. I hoped reading the book would give her the courage to confront the reality of her situation. Yet I found it difficult to share because I could see that her self-esteem had already been greatly attacked, that she had lost a sense of her worth and value, and that possibly this categorizing of her identity would add to the feeling that she should just forget, be silent (and certainly returning to a situation where one is likely to be abused is one way to mask the severity of the problem). Still I had to try. When I first gave her the book, it disappeared. An unidentified family member had thrown it away. They felt that she would be making a serious mistake if she began to see herself as an absolute victim which they felt the label "battered woman" implied. I stressed that she should ignore the labels and read the content. I be-

lieved the experience shared in this book helped give her the courage to be critical of her situation, to take constructive action.

Her response to the label "battered woman," as well as the responses of other women who have been victims of violence in intimate relationships, compelled me to critically explore further the use of this term. In conversation with many women, I found that it was seen as a stigmatizing label, one which victimized women seeking help felt themselves in no condition to critique. As in, "who cares what anybody is calling it—I just want to stop this pain." Within patriarchal society, women who are victimized by male violence have had to pay a price for breaking the silence and naming the problem. They have had to be seen as fallen women, who have failed in their "feminine" role to sensitize and civilize the beast in the man. A category like "battered woman" risks reinforcing this notion that the hurt woman, not only the rape victim, becomes a social pariah, set apart, marked forever by this experience.

A distinction must be made between having a terminology that enables women, and all victims of violent acts, to name the problem and categories of labeling that may inhibit that naming. When individuals are wounded, we are indeed often scarred, often damaged in ways that do set us apart from those who have not experienced a similar wounding, but an essential aspect of the recovery process is the healing of the wound, the removal of the scar. This is an empowering process that should not be diminished by labels that imply this wounding experience is the most significant aspect of identity.

As I have already stated, overemphasis on extreme cases of violent abuse may lead us to ignore the problem of occasional hitting, and it may make it difficult for women to talk about this problem. A critical issue that is not fully examined and written about in great detail by researchers who study and work with victims is the recovery process. There is a dearth of material discussing the recovery process of individuals who have been physically abused. In those cases where an individual is hit only once in an intimate relationship, however violently, there may be no recognition at all of the negative impact of this experience. There may be no conscious attempt by the victimized person to work at restoring her or his well-being, even if the person seeks therapeutic help, because the one incident may not be seen as serious or damaging. Alone and in isolation, the person who has been hit must struggle to regain broken trust—to forge some strategy of recovery. Individuals are often able to process an experience of being hit mentally that may not be processed emotionally. Many women I talked with felt that even after the incident was long forgotten, their bodies remain troubled. Instinctively, the person who has been hit may respond fearfully to any body movement on the part of a loved one that is similar to the posture used when pain was inflicted.

Being hit once by a partner can forever diminish sexual relationships if there has been no recovery process. Again there is little written about ways folks recover physically in their sexualities as loved ones who continue to be sexual with those who have hurt them. In most cases, sexual relationships are dramatically altered when hitting has occurred. The sexual realm may be the one space where the person who has been hit experiences again the sense of vulnerability, which may also arouse fear. This can lead either to an attempt to avoid sex or to unacknowledged sexual withdrawal wherein the person participates but is passive. I talked with women who had been hit by lovers who described sex as an ordeal, the one space where they confront their inability to trust a partner who has broken trust. One woman emphasized that to her, being hit was a "violation of her body space" and that she felt from then on she had to protect that space. This response, though a survival strategy, does not lead to healthy recovery.

Often, women who are hit in intimate relationships with male or female lovers feel as though we have lost an innocence that cannot be regained. Yet this very notion of innocence is connected to passive acceptance of concepts of romantic love under patriarchy which have served to mask problematic realities in relationships. The process of recovery must include a critique of this notion of innocence which is often linked to an unrealistic and fantastic vision of love and romance. It is only in letting go of the perfect, no-

work, happily-ever-after union idea, that we can rid our psyches of the sense that we have failed in some way by not having such relationships. Those of us who never focussed on the negative impact of being hit as children find it necessary to reexamine the past in a therapeutic manner as part of our recovery process. Strategies that helped us survive as children may be detrimental for us to use in adult relationships.

Talking about being hit by loved ones with other women, both as children and as adults, I found that many of us had never really thought very much about our own relationship to violence. Many of us took pride in never feeling violent, never hitting. We had not thought deeply about our relationship to inflicting physical pain. Some of us expressed terror and awe when confronted with physical strength on the part of others. For us, the healing process included the need to learn how to use physical force constructively, to remove the terror—the dread. Despite the research that suggests children who are hit may become adults who hit—women hitting children, men hitting women and children—most of the women I talked with not only did not hit but were compulsive about not using physical force.

Overall the process by which women recover from the experience of being hit by loved ones is a complicated and multi-faceted one, an area where there must be much more feminist study and research. To many of us, feminists calling attention to the reality of violence in intimate relationships has not in and of itself compelled most people to take the issue seriously, and such violence seems to be daily on the increase. In this essay, I have raised issues that are not commonly talked about, even among folks who are particularly concerned about violence against women. I hope it will serve as a catalyst for further thought, that it will strengthen our efforts as feminist activists to create a world where domination and coercive abuse are never aspects of intimate relationships.

Battering

1996

Who's going to stop it?

Ann Jones

"He's fucking going nuts. . . ." Nicole Brown Simpson told a police dispatcher on October 25, 1993. Eight months later, after O. J. Simpson was arrested for the murder of his ex-wife and her friend Ronald Goldman, that 911-call was played and replayed on television and radio, plunging startled Americans into the midst of a typical terrifying incident of what we lamely call "domestic" violence. Previously, both O. J. Simpson and Jon Russo, vice president of the Hertz Corporation, which retained Simpson as its spokesman even after he pleaded no contest to assaulting Nicole in 1989, had described O.J.'s wife beating as a private "family matter" of no significance.

The press calls O. J. Simpson the most famous American ever charged with murder, but he's certainly not the first celebrity to be a batterer, or even to be implicated in homicide. In fact, the list of celebrity batterers from the sports world alone is a long one which includes boxer Sugar Ray Leonard, baseball star Darryl Strawberry, former University of Alabama basketball coach Wimp Sanderson, former heavyweight champ Mike Tyson (cited by then-wife Robin Givens and subsequently convicted of raping Miss Black Rhode Island), California Angels pitcher Donnie Moore (who shot and wounded his estranged wife, Tonya, before killing himself in 1989), and Philadelphia Eagles defensive lineman Blenda Gay (stabbed to death in 1976 by his battered wife, Roxanne, who said she acted in self-defense).

The list of entertainers named as batterers is also lengthy and star-studded. Tina Turner reported in her autobiography that husband Ike abused her for years. Ali MacGraw described the violent assaults of Steve McQueen. Sheila Ryan sued her then-husband James Caan in 1980, alleging that he'd beaten her. Madonna accused Sean Penn, and Daryl Hannah named Jackson Browne. Such incidents make titillating copy for scandal sheets and tabloid TV.

And such incidents continue to be commonplace—as all-American as football—precisely because so many people still think of battering as, in O.J.'s words, "no big deal." But when America listened last June to

that 911-tape, eavesdropping on the private, violent raging of the man publicly known as the cool, affable Juice, anyone could hear that what Nicole Brown was up against was a very big deal indeed. For the first time, Americans could hear for themselves the terror that millions of American women live with every day.

That terror begins with small, private, seemingly ordinary offenses. Take this list of complaints logged in a single week by the security office of one small institution. One woman harassed by "unwanted attention" from a man. One woman "annoyed" at finding "obscene photographs" in her desk. Two women "annoyed" by obscene phone calls from men. One woman sexually assaulted in her living quarters by a male acquaintance. One woman stalked by a man in violation of a restraining order.

Routine offenses? You bet. And they're increasingly common—not just because women are fed up with such behavior and reporting it more often, but because these days there's more and worse to report.

What makes this particular list of complaints noteworthy is that it comes from the security office at a small New England college—the sort of place where old stone buildings surround a quadrangle shaded by ancient trees. The sort of place where parents who can afford it send their daughters to be safe from the dangers of the "real" world, safe from violence and violent men.

These days, however, there seems to be no safe haven. Not in exclusive Brentwood. Not even on the picture-perfect college campus. Violence, which has always struck women of every social class and race, seems to be aimed increasingly at the young.

Last year, at Mount Holyoke College—the oldest women's college in the country—the student newspaper carried the front page headline: "Domestic Violence on the Rise." Reported cases of "domestic" violence were increasing all across the country, according to student reporter Gretchen Hitchner—and on the Mount Holyoke campus as well. "There are five or six students on campus who have obtained stay-away orders," Hitchner reported.

Beyond the boundaries of the campus, the statistics grew much worse. Statewide, in Massachusetts in 1991, a woman was murdered by a current or former husband or boyfriend every twenty days. By 1993, such a murder occurred once every eight days. Among the dead: Tara Hartnett, a twenty-one-year-old senior psychology major at the nearby University of Massachusetts at Amherst. In February 1993, Tara Hartnett had obtained a restraining order against James Cyr, Jr., her former boyfriend and the father of her eleven-month-old daughter. In March, when Hartnett's roommates were away on spring break, Cyr broke in, stabbed Hartnett, set the house on fire, and left her to die of smoke inhalation.

"Incidents" like the murder of Tara Hartnett happen all the time. Every day, in fact, four or five women die in the United States at the hands of their current or former husbands or boyfriends. But recently feminists (like me) who call attention to these crimes have been taking a lot of heat for perpetuating the image of women as "victims." Critics charge that "victim feminists" exaggerate the dangers women face in male violence. Katie Roiphe, for example, suggests in her book *The Morning After* that most alleged cases of date rape involve nothing more than second thoughts by daylight after bad sex the night before. Battering, according to the critics, is nothing that any woman with moderate self-esteem and a bus token can't escape. What prevents women from exercising our full female power and strength, some say, is not male violence but the *fear* of violence induced by fuddy-duddy feminists who see all women as victims.

Could it be true that the apparent crime wave against women, on campus and off, is only a delusion of paranoid radical feminists? Is it real violence that keeps women down, or only feminists' hysterical perceptions that hamper us?

In Canada, where the same questions were raised, Statistics Canada attempted to find out by interviewing 12,300 women nationwide in the most comprehensive study of violence against women ever undertaken. The results were worse than expected. They showed violence against women to be far more common than earlier, smaller scale studies had indicated. They revealed that more than half of Canadian women (51 percent) have been physically or sexually assaulted at least once in their adult lives. And more than half of those women said they'd been attacked by dates, boyfriends, husbands, friends, family members, or other men familiar to them. One in ten Canadian women, or one million, had been attacked in the past year.

These figures apply only to Canada, but considering that the United States is a more violent culture all around, it's unlikely that women in the United States are any safer from attack. In fact, battering alone is now the single leading cause of injury to women in the United States. A million women every year visit physicians and hospital emergency rooms for treatment of battering injuries. The National Centers for Disease Control identify battering as a leading cause of the spread of HIV and AIDS, as countless batterers force "their" women into unprotected sex. The American Medical Association reports that 38 percent of obstetric patients are battered during pregnancy, and studies name battering during pregnancy a cause of birth defects and infant mortality.

Survivors confirm that a man often begins to batter during a woman's first pregnancy, when she is most vulnerable and least able to pack up and move. Marie's husband, a lawyer, beat her so severely during her seventh month that she went into labor. He then ripped out the phone, locked her in a second-floor bedroom, and left the house. She barely survived, and the little boy she bore that day has always been small and frail. Carol miscarried after her husband knocked her down and kicked her repeatedly in the belly. He threatened to kill her if she tried to leave. When she became pregnant again, he beat her again, saying "I'm going to kill that baby and you, too." Instead, she killed him with his own gun and was sentenced to twenty years in prison, where she bore her child and gave it up for adoption. Jean left her husband after he repeatedly punched her in the belly while she was pregnant. Later, when a doctor told Jean that her daughter had epilepsy, he asked if Jean had suffered a fall or an "accident" of any kind during pregnancy. Now that her daughter is in college and still suffering seizures, Jean says, "I only lived with that man for a year, but he casts his shadow over every day of my life, and my daughter's, too."

Millions of women live with such consequences of male violence, but it's not surprising that many choose another way out. Battering is cited as a contributing factor in a quarter of all suicide attempts by women, and half of all suicide attempts by black women. At least 50 percent of homeless women and children in the United States are in flight from male violence.

Only a few years ago the FBI reported that in the United States a man beat a woman every eighteen seconds. By 1989, the figure was fifteen seconds. Now it's twelve.

Some people take those facts and statistics at face value to mean that male violence is on the rise; while others argue that what's increasing is merely the *reporting* of violence. But no matter how you interpret the numbers, it's clear that male violence is not going *down*.

As crime statistics go, homicide figures are most likely to be accurate, for the simple reason that homicides produce corpses—hard to hide and easy to count. Homicide figures all across the country—like those in Massachusetts—indicate so clearly that violence against women is on the rise that some sociologists have coined a new term for a common crime: "femicide." The FBI estimates that every year men murder about three thousand wives and girlfriends. The conclusion is inescapable: male violence against women is *real*. And it is widespread.

Such violence was once thought of as the plague of married women, but battering, like date rape, affects young, single women as well. In its recent study, Statistics Canada found that a disproportionate number of women reporting physical or sexual assault were young. Women ages eighteen to twenty-four were more than twice as likely as older women to report violence in the year preceding the study; 27 percent of them had been attacked in the past year. In the United States, the first study of "premarital abuse," conducted in 1985, reported that one in five college students was the victim of "physical aggression," ranging from slapping and hitting to "more life threatening violence." When a guy who'd had too much to drink offered Sarah a ride home from a fraternity party she turned him down and advised him not to drive. He waited for her outside and beat her up—to "teach the bitch a lesson," he said. Susan went home for her first break from college and told her hometown boyfriend that she wanted to date at school. In response, he deliberately pulled out clumps of her hair, broke her arm, and drove her car into a tree. After Bonnie broke up with a possessive guy she'd been dating at college, he sneaked into her home at night and smashed in her head with a hatchet. Typically, guys like this think they're *entitled* to get their way, by any means necessary. Resorting to violence seems justified to them.

They think they've done nothing wrong—or at least no more than she *asked* for.

Even high school boys are acting out the macho myth. A study of white middle-class high school juniors and seniors found that roughly one in four had some experience of dating violence, either as victim or perpetrator. In another study one in three teenage girls reported being subjected to physical violence by a date. After reviewing many such studies of high school and college students, Barrie Levy, author of *In Love and In Danger: A Teen's Guide to Breaking Free of Abusive Relationships,* reports that "an average of twenty-eight percent of the students experienced violence in a dating relationship. That is more than one in every four students." Male counselors who work with wife beaters confirm that many older batterers first began to use violence as teenagers, against their dates.

That doesn't mean that violence against young women is just "kid's stuff." According to the FBI, 20 percent of women murdered in the United States are between the ages of fifteen and twenty-four. Recently a high school boy in Texas shot his girlfriend for being "unfaithful," and for good measure he killed her best friend, too. Former police officer Barbara Arrighi, who has witnessed increased date rape, battering, and stalking among college students as assistant director for public safety at Mount Holyoke College, bluntly sums up the situation: "Anyone who doesn't believe America has a serious problem with violence against young women," she says, "is living in Lalaland."

Some who've studied dating violence say young women may be more vulnerable to male aggression because they believe so innocently in "true love." Schooled by romance novels and rock videos, which typically mingle sex and violence, they're more likely to mistake jealousy, possessiveness, control, and even physical or sexual assault for passion and commitment. In fact, in some surveys of college dating, about one-third of students interviewed reported that their relationships *improved* after violence—although most of the students who said so were men.

Consider the case of Kristin Lardner who was twenty-one in 1992 when her ex-boyfriend Michael Cartier gunned her down on a Boston street, then later shot himself. Kristin Lardner herself was scared to death of Michael Cartier, a man she had dated for only two months; and she did just what abused women are supposed to do. She stopped dating Cartier the first time he hit her; and when he followed her, knocked her down in the street, and kicked her unconscious, she got a restraining order against him. But even after she was murdered, Lardner's roommate and best friend still bought the "romantic" view of Michael Cartier's violence. She told reporters that Lardner had "cared" about Cartier, and "she was the only one who ever did. That's what pushed him over the edge . . . when he lost her."

Young men, too, buy into this romantic scenario. One of Michael Cartier's male friends commented after the murder: "He loved her a lot and it was probably a crime of passion. He didn't do it because he's nuts," the friend said. "He was in love."

But Cartier's former girlfriend, Rose Ryan, also talked to reporters, and what she had to say put Michael Cartier's "love" in a new light. She had cared about Cartier, too, she said, and for months she had tried to make him happy with love and kindness and Christmas presents, even after he started to abuse her. It didn't work. Finally, after he attacked her with scissors, she brought assault charges against him and got him jailed for six months. Then, after Cartier murdered Kristin Lardner, Rose Ryan spoke about his "lovemaking." "After he hit me several times in the head," she said, "he started to cry." He would say, "I'm so sorry. I always hit people I love." And the clincher: "My mother, she never loved me. You're the only one."

It's a familiar part of the batterer's control technique, that message. And it often works because it appeals at once to a woman's compassion and her power, snaring her in a web of "love" and "violence" as two contradictory concepts become inextricably entwined. It leads some women to reinterpret a boyfriend's violent behavior as passion. It leads some—like Rose Ryan for a while—to forgive and try to help a batterer to change. Attorney Lynne Gold-Birkin, founder of the American Bar Association's Committee on Domestic Violence and chair of the ABA's family law section, recently pointed out on ABC's *This Week with David Brinkley* that many married women subjected to abuse don't walk out at once "because they don't want the marriage to end; they want him to stop beating them." But in the end, as the story of Kristin Lardner shows, even a woman who tolerates no violence at all is not safe from it.

To find an explanation for the high rate of male violence against young women, we have to look to the source: to men. Many people still mistakenly believe that batterers are somehow different from ordinary men—that they are "crazy" men with short fuses who "lose control" of themselves and blow up, especially when under the influence of drink or drugs. But those who counsel batterers say that just the reverse is true: the battering man is perfectly in control of himself—and of the woman he batters. That, after all, is the purpose of battering. A man—of any age—threatens, intimidates, abuses, and batters a woman to make her do what he wants. It works. He gets his way, and as a bonus he gets a heady rush of experiencing his own power. As one reformed eighteen-year-old guy put it: "I enjoyed intimidating people." David Adams, director of Emerge, a Boston counseling program for batterers, points out that the same man who says he "loses control" of his temper with "his" woman will be perfectly calm when the police arrive. "Clearly he knows what he's doing." Adams says. "He's making rational choices about how to act with whom—on the basis of what he can get away with."

It's likely, then, that young women—even young women "in love"—get battered for the same reason older women get battered. Namely, they have minds of their own. They want to do what *they* want. Battered women are often mistakenly thought of as "passive" or "helpless" because some of them look that way *after* they've been beaten into submission and made hostage to terror. Their inability to escape is the *result* of battering, not its cause. According to one study, three out of four battering victims are actually single or separated women trying to get free of men who won't let them go. They are not merely victims; they are the resistance. But they are almost entirely on their own.

How can we help women get free of this violence? That's the question that survivors of battering and their advocates have been grappling with for twenty years. And they've done a phenomenal job. Never before in history has there been such an organization of crime victims united to rescue other victims and prevent further crimes. Although battered women's shelters are still so overburdened that they must turn away more women than they take in, they have provided safe haven over the years for millions of women and their children. Undoubtedly, they have saved thousands of lives.

In addition, the battered women's movement has brought battering out of the private household and into the spotlight of public debate. There it has raised a much harder question: how can we make men stop their violence? To that end, the battered women's movement has pushed for—and achieved—big changes in legislation, public policy, and law enforcement. The Violence against Women Act, passed by Congress in 1994, is only one recent example. This bill correctly considers male violence against women as a violation of women's civil rights and provides a wide range of legal remedies for women.

But what's needed is a national campaign to go after the men at fault. Experts such as Susan Schechter, author of *Women and Male Violence* say that men continue to use violence to get their way *because they can*. Nobody stops them. There's no reason for a man who uses violence to change his behavior unless he begins to suffer some real consequences, some punishment that drives home strong social and legal prohibitions against battering. In the short run, the most effective way to protect women and children, save lives, and cut down violence is to treat assault as the crime it is: to arrest batterers and send them to jail.

Usually, that's not what happens. Right now, most batterers suffer *no* social or legal consequences at all for their criminal behavior. Although police in most states and localities are now authorized to arrest batterers, many police departments still don't enforce the law. If police do make arrests, prosecutors commonly fail to prosecute. And if batterers are convicted, judges often release them—or worse, order them into marital counseling with the women they've assaulted. Many men are required to attend a few weekly sessions of a therapeutic support group where they shoot the breeze with other batterers, after which their crime is erased from the record books. (Counselors like David Adams who lead such groups are the first to say that the groups don't work.) One 1991 study found that among assaultive men arrested, prosecuted, convicted, and sentenced, less than 1 percent (0.9 percent) served any time in jail. The average batterer taken into custody by police is held less than two hours. He walks away laughing at his victim and at the police as well.

Even men convicted of near-fatal attacks upon their girlfriends or wives are likely to draw light sentences or be released on probation with plenty of opportunity to finish the job. The husband of Burnadette Barnes, for example, shot her in the head while she slept, served three months in prison for the offense, and was released to threaten her again. Desperate, Burnadette Barnes hired a man to kill her husband. She was convicted of murder and conspiracy to murder and sentenced to life in prison.

In Michigan, police officer Clarence Ratliff shot and killed his estranged wife, Carol Irons, who incidentally was the youngest woman ever appointed to the Michigan bench. (As a judge she was known to treat domestic violence cases seriously.) When the police tried to arrest Ratliff, he squeezed off a few wild shots before he surrendered. For killing his wife, Ratliff got ten to fifteen years; for shooting at the cops, two life terms plus some additional shorter terms for using a firearm.

Such cases make clear that in the scales of American justice men weigh more than women. Assaulting a man is a serious crime, but assaulting a woman or even killing her—well, that's not so bad.

We can do better. Thanks to the battered women's movement, we now know that any social, economic, or political development that counteracts sexism and promotes sex equality helps in the long run to eliminate violence by reducing the power men hold, individually and institutionally, over women. We now know that all the institutions to which battered women and children are likely to turn for help—hospitals, mental health facilities, social welfare services, child protective services, police departments, civil and criminal courts, schools, churches—must join a *concerted* effort to prevent violence before it occurs and stop it when it does. They must stand ready to defend the constitutional right that belongs to all women (though no one ever speaks of it): the right to be free from bodily harm.

That's where college can set a good example for the rest of society. While public officials often seem to accept violence against women as an inevitable social problem, colleges can't afford to. They're obliged to keep their students safe. Mount Holyoke's Barbara Arrighi says,

We've had to work at safety, but as a closed, self-contained system we have advantages over the big world. If one of our students is victimized, she finds a whole slew of helpers available right away—campus and city police, medical services, housing authorities, counselors, chaplains, academic deans. We'll ban offenders from the campus under trespass orders. We'll make arrests. We'll connect her to the county prosecutor's victim/witness assistance program. We'll go to court with her. We'll help her get a protective order or file a civil complaint. We take these things seriously, we don't try to pin the blame on her, and we don't fool around.

What Arrighi describes is the way the system ought to work in every community.

As things stand now, it's still up to women to make the system respond and too often, on a case-by-case basis. It takes time, money, courage, and determination to get a result that looks like justice. Take the case of Stephanie Cain, for example. A college student, she had dated Elton "Tony" Ekstrom for nine months. Then, during the course of one hour on the night of April 28, 1991, he beat her up. He punched and kicked her repeatedly, leaving her with a fractured nose and a face nearly unrecognizable to those who saw her immediately following the attack. Afterward, she said, she lost confidence and mistrusted people. She suffered seizures and had to drop out of college. Major surgery to reconstruct her nose permanently altered her appearance.

Ekstrom was arrested and charged with assault and battery with a dangerous weapon: his foot. But Stephanie Cain wasn't permitted to tell her story in court, for Ekstrom never went to trial. Instead he was allowed to plead guilty to a reduced charge of assault and battery. The judge gave him a two-year suspended sentence, and Ekstrom walked away—still thinking he'd done nothing wrong.

That result upset Stephanie Cain. Worried that Ekstrom might do the same thing to another woman, she decided to sue him for the damage he'd done. In December 1992, when she was back in college finishing her degree, she finally got her day in court. "The best part," she said, "was looking right at him, knowing I wasn't afraid of him anymore." After hearing her story, the jury awarded Cain and her parents $153,000 in damages for her injuries, medical expenses, and emotional distress. At last Ekstrom was to pay a price for his criminal act, as a civil court jury compensated Stephanie Cain for a crime the criminal court had failed to punish. "Every time I look in the mirror," Cain said, "I'm reminded of what happened. There's no reason he should just forget it."

The victory she won was a victory for all women. But it shouldn't have been that hard. And she shouldn't have had to fight for justice all by herself.

Healthy Choices

Janice Mirikitani

Hold still

Keep quiet.

Get a degree
to learn how to talk
saying nothing.

Catch a good man
by being demure.
the one your mother chooses.

Let him climb you
whenever his urge,
amidst headaches

and menstrual aches
and screaming infants.
And when he bids
quick, turn over.

Hold still.

Make your tongue
a slab of cement
a white stone etched
with your name.
Kill your stories with knives
and knitting needles
and Clorox bleach.

Hide in your mysteriousness
by saying nothing.

Starch your thoughts
with ironed shirts.

Tie your anger
with a knot in
your throat
and when he comes
without concern
swallow it.

Hold still.

Keep desire
hopeless as ice
and sleepless nights
and painful as a pinched eyelid.

Keep your fingers
from the razor,
keep your longing
to sever

his condescension
safely in your douchbag.

Turn the blade
against yourself.
Don't twitch
as your slashed wrists
stain your bathroom tiles.
Disinfect with Pine Sol.

Hold still.

Keep quiet.

Keep tight your lips,
keep dead your dreams,
keep cold your heart.

Keep quiet.

And he will shout
praises
to your
perfection.

Acquaintance Rape *1996*

Revolution and reaction

Paula Kamen

Over the past decade, I have witnessed a startling new brand of sex talk—more disarming, uninhibited, and brazen than anything you would ever hear even on the most bold late-night 900-number party chat line or FCC-challenging radio talk show.

One particular conversation that comes to mind took place on an October evening among all males, not in the expected locker room, but in another distinct Old Spice—laced bastion: a fraternity house at the University of Wisconsin in Madison. The men addressed what had gone previously unspoken within their ivy-covered walls: the *meaning* of sex. Their mysterious, long-haired and heavy-set visitor, Joe Weinberg, was challenging them to think about any pressure they may feel to "score" and become part of the "boys' club." First, Weinberg explored some of the "universal" language men use. He then asked his group to come up with positive words to describe a sexually active female. There were none. Then, the same to refer to a man. The list goes on: "Cassanova, stud, player. . . ."

This type of discussion, which Weinberg has led with men on more than 150 campuses throughout the country since 1986—and has recently expanded to include groups in high schools and prisons—takes rape prevention to new levels.

Here, at the University of Wisconsin, men are addressing men. And, Weinberg's recommendations go beyond the behavior modification steps of going out in groups and not drinking to extremes to actually look at how men perceive women. Not only does this new breed of educator address reducing the *opportunity* for assault, but they also challenge the types of attitudes that lead men to be *motivated* to rape. Instead of preaching or thought policing, as the words "peer educator" may imply, men like Weinberg often lead nonjudgmental discussions, where men are free to express their darkest and most unPC thoughts and fears about women. Weinberg says he doesn't criticize men for what can be perceived as sexist or insensitive comments, which reflect what they personally and naturally have felt as males growing up in our culture.

This radical approach is part of a larger and evolving dialogue on the issue of acquaintance rape, which I have witnessed taking place over the last decade on college campuses and beyond. More men and women are questioning the roots of sexual violence and refining and focusing their critiques.

As testament to their success, young activists are provoking controversy—and a mighty backlash in the media. Critics attest that this activism has only been destructive, that action against acquaintance rape is just "sexual correctness" that is ruining sex and straitjacketing natural human activity with too many protective rules. But I have witnessed a different result of activism, a more liberating one than is most often lamented in the mainstream press. Activists now are assuming a challenge in talking about sex in new terms, with new candor, and demystifying it. They are encouraging women to take more control and men to understand and modify their behavior.

Weinberg, a former carpenter now in his early forties, got interested in this small but telling movement after joining Men Stopping Rape in Madison, one of 100 to 150 campus and community-based men's prevention groups operating in the early 1990s. Other men have become visible doing this work. At Brown University students sponsored a 1989 conference called Men Can Stop Rape Now. That same year, Ithaca Rape Crisis, Inc, surveyed 133 other community centers and found that 118 worked with male volunteers.[1]

Such workshops aren't a panacea to dismantle attitudes about aggression and domination; indeed, most men exposed to such antirape messages don't reach instant feminist epiphany, question fundamentals of their patriarchy-induced identity, and then devote their weekends to volunteering on the rape crisis lines. But, at least for a start, many young men are becoming more aware about sexual assault between acquaintances. For men my age and younger, in their teens and twenties, rape among people who know each other has at least become *an issue,* a legitimate topic in public debate—not simply dismissed as a night of bad sex or a private dare or joke as in the past.

Indeed, "acquaintance rape" is a bona fide term, now used regularly in mainstream society. It has been a heading in the *Reader's Guide to Periodical Literature* since 1992 ("date rape" since 1987), and a topic discussed at college orientations and even fraternity meetings nationwide for the past decade. In a recent *Chicago Tribune* report about one local student orientation, readers can see how date rape has become a standard issue in campus life.

In a residence hall lounge at Northwestern, a campus official read to about 60 students the university's definition of sexual assault.

The students also watched a campus-produced video on sexual assault, and afterward, the official led a discussion. Consent must be given clearly and unmistakably to avoid a charge of assault, she said. (James 1994: 2: 7)[2]

I have seen this movement to examine men's behavior evolve slowly. In 1985, when I was a freshman at the Big Ten giant, the University of Illinois in Urbana-Champaign, about the only rape prevention education offered throughout the country was directed exclusively toward women, warning them about strangers. But in the next few years I witnessed the university develop a model program for prevention and education that targets men. More and more university programs across the country have also evolved to look at acquaintance rape, and many schools are including a component to examine men's attitudes and responsibilities. This focus is radical because it takes the exclusive and historical burden of responsibility off women's shoulders. "It's acknowledging that men are the ones committing rape," said Barb Gilbert, an architect of my campus program, in a 1989 interview. "And the only role that women have is to the extent that we can prevent opportunity and prevent the effectiveness [protect ourselves]."

Men's antirape activism is part of a broad, hardly recognized, slowly developing sexual revolution of this generation. While the sexual revolution of the 1970s was largely about women saying yes (to *really* prove themselves liberated), a new movement is empowering them to *also* say no, *along with when, where, and how.* As a result, women are more closely examining what turns them off—and also what turns them on. They are daring to study and even critique what happens to them in bed. Young women are not content with the rules of the old 1970s sexual revolution, which have collapsed under the weight of their own rigidity—and stupidity. That movement, which was liberating mostly for men, has saddled women with too much old patriarchal baggage, including a continuing double standard for women, which discourages communication and honesty from both sexes. Activists are striving for a new model and new freedoms that offer pleasure and freedom from absolute rules, as well as self-respect, autonomy, and responsibility. Their movement is parallel to others I have seen become increasingly visible on college campuses, including efforts to gain reproductive freedom, fight sexual harassment, and secure rights for gays and lesbians.

ANTIFEMINIST BACKLASH

Yet, in the past few years, I have also seen the antifeminist skeptics eclipse all others in the popular press and in slick upscale magazines. While feminists come in all ideological shapes and sizes, the most "wacky" ones have always made the best copy. Most magazine articles addressing acquaintance rape in 1993 and 1994 take the angle that date rape is mostly hype, and seriously question the extent and even the existence of the problem.[3]

A variety of critics, from lofty newspaper columnists to the writers of *Saturday Night Live,* have taken easy aim at "feminist antisex hysteria" by making fun of the extreme Antioch College guidelines, first widely publicized in 1993. The sexual offense policy from this small Ohio liberal arts college has come to represent feminists' supposedly overpowering rhetorical invasion of the minds of college students. The eight-page policy states that students must give and

get verbal consent before "each new level of physical and/or sexual contact/conduct." "Sexual contact" includes the touching of thighs, genitals, buttocks, the pubic region, or the breast/chest area. The policy spells out six categories of offenses: rape, sexual assault, sexual imposition, insistent and/or persistent sexual harassment, nondisclosure of sexually transmitted diseases (STDs), and nondisclosure of positive HIV status. Complaints against violators can be brought before the campus judicial board.

Many conservative critics, including seemingly unlikely allies such as Camille Paglia and George Will,[4] employing every defense mechanism on a psychiatrist's diagnostic chart, reason that militant feminists have invented the problem of "acquaintance rape" and use this term at random to describe bad sex or an encounter that one regrets in the morning. Since the topic of date rape is no longer sexy because of its last few years of exposure in the press, this related topic—date-rape hysteria—has come in vogue. In 1993, "exposés" of date-rape hysteria have appeared as cover stories in *Newsweek* (in an article about "sexual correctness" [Crichton 1993]), *New York* magazine (Hellman 1993), and the *New York Times Magazine* (Roiphe 1993a).[5] Christina Hoff Sommers reiterates many of these claims in *Who Stole Feminism?* (1994), boosted by three right-wing foundations that provided grants of at least $164,000 between 1991 and 1993 (Flanders 1994: 8).

A major leader of the date-rape hysteria charge was twenty-five-year-old Katie Roiphe, author of *The Morning After: Sex, Fear, and Feminism on Campus* (1993b). She says such feminist discussion confuses young women into mislabeling a wide array of normal, often unpleasant, sexual experiences as rape. Her thesis is that the battle against date rape is a symptom of young women's general anxiety about sex. They allegedly displace their fear of sex onto a fear of rape. Roiphe reasons that since some cases are false, *all* claims of acquaintance rape are unfounded; if one is against rape, one must also be against sex. Those that speak out against rape are nothing but malleable dupes of feminists or hysterics, liars, or prudes.

A major gripe of Roiphe and others is that educators are putting an undue burden on men by advising them to obtain articulated mutual consent. "With their advice, their scenarios, their sample aggressive male, the message projects a clear comment on the nature of sexuality: women are often unwilling participants,"

Roiphe writes in her book (Roiphe 1993b: 61). Indeed, rape educators do admit that women have been forced to have sex against their will by people they know. In contrast, Roiphe portrays an idealized, "post-feminist" reality that places men and women in a vacuum, untouched by social attitudes and pressures.

The greatest threat of Roiphe's distortions is that they push acquaintance rape back in the closet. Roiphe is characteristically narrow in her definition of what constitutes a "real" rape—incidents of violence that can never be confused with "bad sex." In her *New York Times Magazine* article, she gives as examples of rape brutal assaults by strangers, such as those of Bosnian girls and "a suburban teen-ager raped and beaten while walking home from a shopping mall" (Roiphe 1993a: 28). To back up her argument, Roiphe takes liberties with data. Her "findings" that discredit date-rape prevention work are often based on out-of-context, secondhand, false examples of radical feminist rhetoric and flimsy "evidence" that questions the validity of professionally scrutinized scientific studies.

A central target of Roiphe and others is a major, influential 1985 survey by a University of Arizona Medical School professor, Mary Koss, sponsored by the Ms. Foundation and financed by the National Institute of Mental Health. One of the study's major findings was that 27.9 percent—or, as most often quoted, "one in four"—of the college women surveyed reported being the victim of a rape or attempted rape since the age of fourteen, with a majority having known the assailants (Koss et al. 1987: 168; Warshaw 1988: 11).

Roiphe, Sommers, and other critics cited here have condemned Koss's findings as invalid without ever contacting Koss to get her side of the story or further information. Roiphe repeats the most commonly waged criticism of Koss: "Seventy-three percent of the women categorized as rape victims did not initially define their experience as rape; it was Mary Koss, the psychologist conducting the study, who did" (Roiphe 1993a: 28). According to Roiphe, "Today's definition has stretched beyond bruises and knives, threats of death or violence to include emotional pressure and the influence of alcohol" (Roiphe 1993b: 52).

However, as all these critics failed to report, Koss makes clear that she used a standard legal definition of rape similar to that used in the majority of states (Koss et al. 1987: 166).[6] Also, contrary to Roiphe's allega-

tions, Koss did not make emotional pressure a variable in her 15.8 percent *completed* rape statistic. She does ask questions about "sexual coercion," but she does not include this group in the 27.9 percent statistic of rape or attempted rape (Koss et al. 1987: 166; Warshaw 1988: 207).

Koss explained to me that she included in her figures women who did not label their experiences as rape because of the prevailing public misconception that the law does not cover such cases of date rape. Also, at the time of the 1985 survey public awareness about the possibility that an attack between acquaintances was legally rape was much lower than it is today.

Koss points out in her writings that the majority of her respondents who reported experiences legally defined as rape still indicated, themselves, that they felt victimized; she did not project this onto them. According to the study, as all these critics fail to mention, of respondents who reported an incident of forced sex (whether or not they called it rape), 30 percent considered suicide afterward, 31 percent sought psychotherapy, and 82 percent said the experience had changed them (Warshaw 1988: 66).

Another major attack on Koss's data is the inclusion of her question, "Have you had sexual intercourse when you didn't want to because a man gave you alcohol or drugs?" Roiphe and Sommers exaggerate the importance of this in distorting her one-in-four statistic (Roiphe 1993b: 53; Sommers 1994: 213). Sommers actually goes on to conclude that "once you remove the positive responses to question eight, the finding that one in four college women is a victim of rape or attempted rape drops to one in nine." But, as Koss writes, without factoring in this question, the victims of rape or attempted rape actually fall from one in four to one in five (Flanders 1994: 6). Sommers took this error out of later printings of her book but still added that when this question is removed and you "subtract from the survey's results all the women who did not believe they were raped, the incendiary 'One in Four' figure drops to between one in 22 and one in 33" (Sommers 1994: 215).[7]

Koss's one-in-four findings reflect those of almost every major, peer-reviewed national and campus study, even though Roiphe and Sommers completely dismiss the existence and validity of this vast body of research.[8] One of the most comprehensive of these studies is a nationwide, federally funded 1992 survey by the National Victims Center. It reported that of the 2,008 respondents contacted randomly over the phone, 14 percent reported a completed rape during their life, excluding cases when they were passed out or otherwise unable to consent. This is comparable to Koss's 15.8 percent statistic of completed rapes.

But, the most convincing evidence of the accuracy of Koss's study comes from the most accurate and comprehensive sex survey in America: the National Health and Social Life Survey (NHSLS) conducted by the National Opinion Research Center. In 1994, it was released in two books, one for a popular and another for an academic audience. The NHSLS found that, since puberty, 22 percent of women were forced by a man to do something sexually, and 30 percent of them were forced by more than one man (Michael et al. 1994, 225; Laumann et al. 1994: 337). And even these numbers underestimate the true level of sexual violence in our society, as the researchers point out: "Because forced sex is undoubtedly underreported in surveys because of the socially stigmatized nature of the event, we believe that our estimates are probably conservative 'lower-bound' estimates of forced sex within the population" (Laumann et al. 1994: 322).

In more than three-quarters of the cases, the perpetrator was someone the woman knew well (22 percent), was in love with (46 percent), or married to (9 percent)—only 4 percent were attacked by a stranger. These forced sexual experiences had an impact on women's lives. Fifty-seven percent of the forced women (versus 42 percent of the rest) had emotional problems in the past year which interfered with sex, and 34 percent (versus 18 percent of those not forced) said sex in the past year was not pleasurable. Twenty percent (versus 12 percent of those not forced) generally said they were sometimes fairly unhappy or unhappy most of the time (Laumann et al. 1994: 226–227).[9]

The NHSLS data strongly confirm Koss's findings. It found that 25 percent of women eighteen to twenty-four had been forced to do something sexually (Laumann et al. 1994: 337). The survey also revealed that most of these attacks probably occurred when women were relatively young, since women eighteen to twenty-four had virtually identical rates of forced sex—about 25 percent. The slightly lower number of responses from older women can probably be accounted

for by a greater reluctance to admit to being forced sexually and by a smaller number of sex partners.

These criticisms of Koss are not original or new. Roiphe and Sommers largely got their critiques of Koss's one-in-four figure secondhand, from Neil Gilbert, University of California, Berkeley, social welfare professor. Though Gilbert has never published anything about rape in a scholarly, peer-reviewed journal, he has written other critiques of Koss's research for the right-wing press. Gilbert's widely cited 1991 *Public Interest* article contains grave inaccuracies regarding Koss's data—falsely charging that Koss included "emotional coercion" as part of the definition of rape, for example (Gilbert 1991b). In Gilbert's 1991 and 1993 *Wall Street Journal* commentaries, his stated goal is to defeat the Violence against Women Act, which deals mainly with street crime and domestic violence and was finally passed after years of debate in August 1994 (Gilbert 1991a and 1993). A 1991 press release issued by the University of California, Berkeley, boasted that "partly as a result of Gilbert's research, Governor Deukmejian last year canceled all state funding for the school-based [child sex abuse] prevention programs."[10]

Despite Gilbert's partisan, nonacademic attacks on Koss's rigorously documented, peer-reviewed research, it is often Gilbert who is considered a scholar in press accounts and Koss who is treated as an ideologue. Even the *Chronicle of Higher Education* used this spin in a 1992 headline on the debate: "A Berkeley Scholar Clashes with Feminists over Validity of Their Research on Date Rape."

In exaggerating feminist "date-rape hysteria," reporters from the popular press have clearly taken the easiest and most superficial route in date-rape coverage. The media has failed to report routinely and in depth about acquaintance rape. Instead, the issue is covered in irregular waves when sensational cases come forth (for example, the Kennedy Smith case) or sexy controversy strikes (Roiphe's "exposé" of statistics). The press has barely broken ground in discussing the complexities, root causes, and influences of the crime of acquaintance rape—along with all issues involving violence against women.

When discussing feminism, as the Sommers and Roiphe coverage shows, reporters flock to "cat fight" angles. They pit an extreme antifeminist against an unwavering profeminist, giving the impression to the public that feminists all think and act alike and perceive the issues as clear-cut. Reporters too often take "scientific" criticism of feminists at face value, neglecting to investigate the supposedly refuted data.

Also missing in today's rape coverage is news about important efforts to curb violence against women. The press hardly mentioned the Senate Judiciary Committee's May 1993 report about the failure of the criminal justice system to recognize and prosecute rape, along with the status and content of the Violence against Women Act. The media rarely investigates the criminal justice system's failure to recognize and prosecute acquaintance rapes. This covers the spectrum from police who label reports of rape among acquaintances as "unfounded" to jurors who dismiss a rape victim because she doesn't look "terrorized enough."

The press also needs to focus its lens beyond the comfortable and familiar middle-class university to the less beautifully and neatly landscaped outside world, populated by the vast majority of young women. Rape and activism do happen outside of college campuses. Gone unrecognized has been community feminist activism and education, which are often concentrated at rape crisis centers. (Indeed, the sensational reports of young nubile coeds from white and middle-class communities are more sexy to viewers and readers.)

However, the level of activism is still often most intense at four-year universities, enclaves that Roiphe, a Harvard graduate and Princeton graduate student, knows well. This is not because women there are brainwashed and trying to grab "very oppressed victim" status, as Roiphe describes; the reality is that they commonly have more time and opportunity to speak out on important issues. They are doing what others would—if given the resources. Instead of scorning the activists as privileged, as Roiphe does, I appreciate them for getting the message out the best way they can. Simply criticizing these feminists for causing the date-rape problem just pins all of the blame and all of the responsibility to stop rape on the same old group: women themselves.

But reporters are only part of the solution to more complex and effective dialogue about acquaintance rape. Those feminists and antifeminists debating these issues publicly have yet to discuss responsibly and realistically the subject of danger in sexual experiences. One side, starring Camille Paglia and Katie Roiphe, describes danger as a natural and unavoidable part of

sexuality and says that women should just do the mature thing and accept it.[11] And feminists, usually the only ones in our society who dare to discuss how women are indeed victimized and advocate for them, too often singularly focus in public debate on the risks of sexual behavior and neglect to focus on the women's movement's historic goal to attain women's sexual freedom and autonomy.

We need to hear more arguments that go a step further: the reality is that danger exists, and women should be aware of the risks. But young people also have the *right* to expect safety. Fighting against date rape can also mean fighting for women's pleasure and sexual agency.

However, in the end, some "rape crisis" critics emerging in the early 1990s could have some positive effects. While Roiphe has egregious blind spots and fails to recognize the real danger and harm of acquaintance rape, she and others are inciting feminists to make definitions of abuse and assault clearer and not overly broad in writing and conversation. While she fails to discuss sexual pleasure, Roiphe may remind feminists to articulate and emphasize their goal for sexual agency. As she points out, the organized and vocal feminists that many young women see in the media and on campus often seem to concentrate solely on the victimization of women. With herself and her readers as examples, Roiphe also illustrates that young women—even we young feminists—aren't willing to blindly follow any party line. Instead of telling us what to think, feminists must encourage us to think critically.

When we hear more voices drawing more careful distinctions, discussing further complexities, and telling their stories, change will take place. But there is only so much women can do; action is still most crucially needed from men, who now comprise a relatively small chorus in the antirape movement. Only then, with both sexes involved in rape prevention, will we really know how it feels to experience a true sexual revolution.

NOTES

1. Parts of this profile of Weinberg are from my book, Kamen 1991: 328–333. For more information about male antirape activism, see Funk 1993.

2. Also see Celis 1992.

3. For example, an interview with Katie Roiphe in Stone 1993: 177 and views of Linda Fairstein and Katie Roiphe in Levine 1993.

4. These charges of "date-rape hype" first appeared in an article in *Playboy* by Stephanie Guttman (1990). Gilbert (1991) took up her critique, which was reiterated by Roiphe (1993a, 1993b). Also see Will 1993: 92 and Paglia 1991: 23.

5. Other publicity includes an excerpt of Roiphe's book in *Cosmopolitan*, "Date Rape: State of Siege" (January 1994): 148–151.

6. Koss describes her use of the specific Ohio state statute, as revised in 1980, to define rape as "vaginal intercourse between male and female, and anal intercourse, fellatio, and cunnilingus between persons regardless of sex. Penetration, however slight, is sufficient to complete vaginal or anal intercourse. . . . No person shall engage in sexual conduct with another person . . . when any of the following apply: (1) the offender purposely compels the other person to submit by force or threat of force, (2) for the purpose of preventing resistance the offender substantially impairs the other person's judgment or control by administering any drug or intoxicant to the other person." (Koss et al. 1987: 166).

7. Criticism made by Wilson 1994b.

8. For an example from a single campus, see Marshall and Miller who report that more than one-fourth of the women (27 percent) and nearly one-sixth of the men (15 percent) surveyed had been involved in forced sexual intercourse while in a dating situation. (Marshall and Miller 1987: 46).

9. Criticism made by Wilson 1994a.

10. Much of this criticism was originally published in my article in *EXTRA!* (Kamen 1993: 10–11).

11. Paglia writes, "Rape is one of the risk factors in getting involved with men. It's a risk factor. It's like driving a car. My attitude is, it's like gambling. If you go to Atlantic City—these girls are going to Atlantic City—and when they lose, it's like 'Oh, Mommy and Daddy, I lost.' My answer is stay home and do your nails, if that's the kind of person you are. My Sixties attitude is, yes, go for it, take the risk—if you get beat up in a dark alley in a street, it's okay. That was part of the risk of freedom, that's part of what we've demanded as women. Go with it" (Paglia 1992: 63).

REFERENCES

CELIS, WILLIAM III. 1992. "Growing Talk of Date Rape Separates Sex from Assaults." *New York Times* (1 January): A 1, B7.

COLLISON, MICHELE N-K. 1992. "A Berkeley Scholar Clashes with Feminists over Validity of Their Research on Date Rape." *Journal of Higher Education* (6 February): 35, 37.

CRICHTON, SARAH. 1993. "Sexual Correctness: Has It Gone Too Far?" *Newsweek* (25 October): 52–58.

FLANDERS, LAURA. 1994. "The 'Stolen Feminism' Hoax." *EXTRA!* (September/October): 6–9.

FUNK, RUS ERVIN. 1993. *Stopping Rape: A Challenge for Men.* Philadelphia: New Society Publishers.

GILBERT, NEIL. 1993. "The Wrong Response to Rape." *Wall Street Journal* (29 June): 19.

———. 1991a. "The Campus Rape Scare." *Wall Street Journal* (27 June): 10.

———. 1991b. "The Phantom Epidemic." *Public Interest* 103: 54.

GUTTMAN, STEPHANIE. 1990. "Date Rape: Does Anyone Really Know What It Is?" *Playboy* (October): 48–56.

HELLMAN, PETER. 1993. "Crying Rape: The Politics of Date Rape on Campus." *New York* (8 March): 33–37.

JAMES, FRANK. 1994. "Collegians Are Enrolled in Real Life." *Chicago Tribune* (16 September): section 2; 1, 7.

KAMEN, PAULA. 1993. "Erasing Rape: Media Hype an Attack on Sexual-Assault Research." *EXTRA!* 6 (November/December): 10, 11.

———. 1991. *Feminist Fatale: Voices from the "Twentysomething" Generation Explore the Future of the "Women's Movement."* New York: Donald I. Fine.

———. 1989. " 'No' Means 'No.' " *Chicago Tribune* (31 December): section 6; 8.

KOSS, MARY, CHRISTINE A. GIDYCZ, and NADINE WISNIEWSKI. 1987. "The Scope of Rape: Incidence and Prevalence of Sexual Aggression and Victimization in a National Sample of Higher Education Students." *Journal of Consulting and Clinical Psychology* 55: 162–170.

KOSS, MARY, LISA GOODMAN, LOUISE FITZGERALD, NANCY RUSSO, GWENDOLYN KEITA, and ANGELA BROWNE. 1994. *No Safe Haven.* Washington, DC: American Psychological Association.

LAUMANN, EDWARD O., JOHN H. GAGNON, ROBERT T. MICHAEL, AND STUART MICHAELS. 1994. *The Social Organization of Sexuality: Sexual Practices in the United States.* Chicago: University of Chicago Press.

LEVINE, JUDITH. 1993. "The Rape Debate." *Harper's Bazaar* (September): 236 and ff.

MARSHALL, JON C., and BEVERLY MILLER. 1987. "Coercive Sex on the University Campus." *Journal of College Student Personnel* (January): 38–42.

MICHAEL, ROBERT T., JOHN H. GAGNON, EDWARD O. LAUMANN, and GINA KOLATA. 1994. *Sex in America: A Definitive Survey.* New York: Little, Brown.

NATIONAL VICTIMS CENTER AND CRIME VICTIMS RESEARCH AND TREATMENT CENTER. 1992. *Rape in America: A Report to the Nation* (23 April). Arlington, VA.

PAGLIA, CAMILLE. 1992. *Sex, Art, and American Culture: Essays.* New York: Vintage.

———. 1991. "Feminists Lead Women Astray on the Threat of Rape." *Philadelphia Inquirer* (15 February): 23.

ROIPHE, KATIE. 1993a. "Date Rape's Other Victim." *New York Times Magazine* (13 June): 26–30, 40, 68.

———. 1993b. *The Morning After: Sex, Fear, and Feminism on Campus.* Boston: Little, Brown.

SENATE, JUDICIARY COMMITTEE. 1993. *Violence against Women: The Response to Rape: Detours on the Road to Equal Justice.*

SOMMERS, CHRISTINA HOFF. 1994. *Who Stole Feminism?: How Women Have Betrayed Women.* New York: Simon and Schuster.

STONE, JUDITH. 1993. "Sex, Rape, and Second Thoughts." *Glamour* (October): 177.

WARSHAW, ROBIN. 1988. *I Never Called It Rape.* New York: Harper and Row.

WILL, GEORGE. 1993. "Sex amidst Semi-Colons." *Newsweek* (4 October): 92.

WILSON, JOHN. 1994a. "Sexless in America?" *The Prism* (28 October): 18, 19.

———. 1994b. "Stolen Feminism?" *Teachers for a Democratic Culture* (newsletter) (fall): 6–8.

YOUNG, CATHY. 1992. "Women, Sex, and Rape: Have Some Feminists Exaggerated The Problem?" *Washington Post* (31 May): C1.

Male on Male Rape

Preface

Michael Scarce

In the autumn of 1989, my friend Tom and I returned from summer break to begin our sophomore year at Ohio State University. We unpacked our belongings and settled into room 332 on the third floor of Bradley Hall, an undergraduate residence hall in the south area of campus. Each of the four floors of Bradley Hall was divided into two wings—one for women and one for men. Every wing had its own bathroom shared by the thirty-some residents living there. The rooms were not air conditioned and the dining hall food was less than stellar, but we were glad to be back on campus. The majority of the 32 men sharing our wing were first-year students, and they were equally as excited to be out on their own for the first time in their lives.

The return of students to campus ushered in a flurry of activity as Welcome Week programs and parties abounded around us. Tom and I had been elected president and vice president, respectively, of the Gay and Lesbian Alliance, our campus gay and lesbian student organization. We held weekly meetings and organized events while striving to increase membership and politicize the organization's activities. As GALA became more visible throughout autumn quarter, the organization and its officers frequently appeared in the local media, promoting GALA and challenging homophobia on campus. As our visibility increased, so did our Bradley Hall floormates' recognition that their two neighbors in room 332 were gay.

The stares and sneers from our 30 floormates began early in the academic year and slowly escalated to verbal abuse, menacing, and death threats. Messages were left on our answering machine, death threat notes were mailed to us, signs saying "Die Faggots" were posted on our door, and as the intensity of the intimidation increased, so did the frequency. Eventually the third floor men's wing became so dangerous for Tom and I that the university was forced to evacuate everyone, relocating the male students and splitting them up across campus before someone was bashed or killed.

Tom and I were moved to a nearby Ramada hotel, where we lived in adjoining rooms for the last few weeks of spring quarter. Both of us were escorted around campus by an armed security guard hired by the university to protect us in the midst of hostility. A protest of over 300 students erupted on campus soon thereafter. Some students applauded the university's relocation decision while others criticized campus officials for "pandering" to gay activists. Still others blamed the university administration for allowing the situation to escalate to a level that necessitated such drastic action. The third floor men's wing of Bradley Hall remained vacant, sealed and empty for the remainder of the academic year. A media frenzy ensued, with coverage from CNN to the *New York Times*. This year was devastating for me as I struggled to survive in such an environment of hostility, humiliation, and degradation. I lived in constant fear and frustration while the weight of the events took its toll on my academic performance, my relationships with family and friends, and my health.

The pain and violation I experienced during those months before the relocation exceeded the incidents of homophobic harassment, however. During winter quarter of that academic year, Tom went home for a weekend visit and I was left alone. I was nervous about what could happen to me, what those men could do to hurt and punish me. It was a weekend in February and I decided to go dancing at a gay bar downtown to get out from under the suffocating weight of it all. I went alone, expecting to meet up with friends. The music was great, the bar was hopping, and I was having a wonderful time. As I danced I noticed a handsome man standing at the edge of the dance floor. He watched me for the duration of several songs, and smiled when I returned his stares. Later we talked and I learned he was from out of town, visiting Columbus on business. After an hour of conversation and heavy flirting, I invited him to return with me to my residence hall to escape the loud music, crowd, and cigarette smoke.

On returning to my room and continuing our conversation, we grew more physically intimate with each other. We were on my bed and began to kiss. Slowly he attempted to unzip my pants, and when I resisted, he became surprisingly rough. The more I pushed his hands away, the more aggressive he became until finally he used force. I asked him to stop, but was too embarrassed to raise my voice for fear that others next door or outside in the hallway would hear what was happening. I was afraid the men who hated me for being gay would use this situation as one more excuse to bash me. After several attempts to unfasten my jeans, he finally succeeded and yanked down my pants and underwear. What happened next is somewhat of a blur. I remember he forced me to lie on my stomach and climbed on top of me. He shoved his penis into me, without lubricant and without a condom. He held me down as I squirmed and fought, suppressing the urge to vomit. The physical pain of the anal penetration worsened as he continued and I began to cry. Soon thereafter I stopped moving in hopes he would just finish and get off me. Eventually he did stop, pulled up his pants, and left without saying a word.

The walls in Bradley Hall were very thin. The air vents in the doors were so large you could hear practically everything through those wide cracks, and many of my neighbors were home that night. One yell, one shout would have attracted the attention I needed to stop what was happening, but I could not bring myself to cry out. What would my floormates think? They already hated me for being queer, so how might they react if they responded to my cries for help and burst in on that lovely scene—a man on top of me, penetrating me? There was nothing I could do except lay there and go numb.

After he left I took a long shower, standing under the water and crying. The smell of him was on my body, his semen was between my legs, and I washed with soap over and over—lathering and rinsing continuously. I endured some minor rectal bleeding for the next day, and remained sore for many more. I did not contact the police or visit the hospital emergency room. I did not seek counseling or formal support, nor did I confide in any of my friends for several years. I was ashamed and embarrassed by what had happened, identifying the experience as a form of bad, regretted sex.

It was not until a year later that I began to make more sense of my experience. Through my academic coursework in OSU's Department of Women's Studies, I took an internship with the university's Rape Education and Prevention Program, where I conducted library research on rape and sexual violence. Gradually I came to terms with the fact that I had physically and mentally resisted that night a year ago in Bradley Hall and that I had been, in fact, raped. I now blame those 30 floormates for my rape as much as I blame the man who assaulted me. They created and shaped a space, both actively and through negligence, in which I was gagged, effectively silenced and unable to resist. Their intimidation weakened my spirit, lowered my self-worth, and forced me to appropriate a victim mentality that impeded me from regaining control of my life.

So very little has been published on the rape of adult males. As I began to search for documentation that resonated with my own assault, I was dismayed at being unable to locate many scholarly articles or even popular, first-person accounts of this form of sexual violence. Slowly, over the last few years, I have collected what scarce writing and research has been published about men raping men. Although I was raped by a gay male acquaintance, I discovered multiple other forms of same-sex rape between men—rape in prison institutions, assault by strangers, gang rape, familial rape, and more.

As my knowledge and understanding of the subject has grown, so has my interest in speaking and educating others about this form of sexual violence. When I speak publicly and conduct sensitivity trainings on male rape, I relate to others the story of my own assault, for it serves as a highly useful illumination of the ways in which homophobia and other forms of oppression create climates that foster and perpetuate rape behavior. My rape in Bradley Hall was simply a microcosm of the broader rape culture we all live in, a culture that encourages and condones sexual violence wielded as a tool for the subordination and control of those with less power in our society. Scores of male survivors have approached me after speaking engagements or contacted me later to share their own rape stories with me.

As I gradually became more involved in antirape work on campus, I began facilitating sexual assault workshops for the Rape Education and Prevention Program in classrooms, residence halls, student organizations, fraternities, and sororities. My involvement continued through graduate school, and after receiving my master's degree I was hired as the full-time coordinator of the program. My transformation from helpless victim to empowered survivor has refashioned my sense of self and purpose in life. The atrocities I have experienced provide a lens through which I am better able to see the complexity of injustices around me, and I have learned to harness the resulting anger in positive and productive ways that fuel my drive for social change. I wonder if the man who raped me realizes what he has created.

An Assault on Sexual Identity

No single factor is more responsible for the stigma attached to male rape than homophobia—the irrational fear and hatred of homosexuality. The cultural confusion of where sex ends and rape begins places sexual preference at the center of insensitivity, injustice, and disbelief directed at survivors of same-sex rape. Every survivor I interviewed for this book expressed some amount of difficulty related to their sexual identity throughout the course of their survival and recovery. The complexity of heterosexuality and how it relates to sexual violence between men and women continues to be explored in depth throughout feminist and other forms of literature. But do these same concepts apply to men raping men, and if not, how can we begin to understand the role that sexual identity plays in same-sex rape? Issues of homophobia and sexual identity are a common thread throughout the chapters of this book, but here I wish to place it in a central focus so as to ask (and possibly answer) such questions as:

- Can the rape of a straight man make him gay?
- Who are raped more, straight or gay men?
- Who are the more common perpetrators of male rape, straight or gay men?
- Where do bisexual men fit into discussions of same-sex rape?
- Is the definition of rape the same for rape between men and women and that between men?

The fear of same-sex rape has historically been used to justify and enact the oppression of gay and lesbian people. Most of us have at some time in our lives heard the stereotype that all gay men are child molesters, for example, and therefore must be medically institutionalized or banned from professions that involve working closely with youth. Aside from this perception of a child molester, homophobia is also bolstered by the popular characterization of gay men as adult male rapists. This is embodied by everything from the classic "Don't drop the soap" jokes to the increasingly used "homosexual panic defense" in courts of law where the sexual advances of a gay man are used to justify his brutal murder.

In a discussion on same-sex rape, Paul Cameron, head of the American Family Association, a right-wing antigay organization, wrote in his 1991 book *The Gay 90s* that "rape at any age is violent and emotionally devastating. But it can also edge victims toward homosexuality"[1] and that "in line with traditional psychiatric opinion, violence goes hand-in-hand with the gay lifestyle."[2] Similar statements of this nature are not uncommon from such hate-mongers. Given that a great deal of homophobia is so firmly rooted in sexual violence mythology, it seems strange that gay and lesbian political movements have thus far appeared to be uninterested in addressing male rape. Even sodomy laws are highly dependent on the notion of sexual consent. In terms of equality for gay and lesbian people, the stakes are incredibly high when it comes to perceptions and reactions to same-sex rape.

Male rape is also one of those instances in which heterosexual men greatly suffer from societal homophobia. The fact that a man has had "sexual" contact with another man, even against his will, is more than enough to call into question his manhood and heterosexuality, and these two traits are often considered one and the same. Sometimes these men are left questioning their own sexual identity and wondering if sexual contact with another man constitutes a homosexual experience. As for heterosexual male rapists, stereotypes also prevail, particularly that there are no heterosexual men who rape other men. Without exception, each time I speak to a group of people about male rape and state that the majority of men who rape other men self-identify as heterosexual, I am met with expressions of surprise and confusion. This reaction often comes from individuals working in the field of rape prevention and treatment, people who are well versed in the "rape is violence, not sex" doctrine.

As this chapter will demonstrate, homophobia plays a key role in setting the stage for some men to be raped. However, homophobia actually *protects* the majority of men from being raped by other men. Male socialization dictates that men should be off-limits to each other sexually, even in sexually violent ways. From the time when males are young boys, they are heavily instructed and encouraged to gear their sexualized attention toward women and girls, and most especially their sexually violent conquest of others. Homophobia actually serves as a social deterrent to men raping men in most instances for this reason of compulsory heterosexuality, but the men who are selected as targets of sexual violence are not chosen at random. While homophobia may prevent the majority of men from raping men, it simultaneously and dramatically increases the likelihood that men who do not conform to traditional notions of manhood will be sexually violated.

BODILY RESPONSES

States of intense pain, anxiety, panic, or fear may cause a spontaneous erection and ejaculation in some men. Many rape survivors who ejaculate during their assault may later question whether or not the rape was actually nonconsensual, as ejaculation is commonly associated with orgasm and sexual pleasure. A clear example of equating rape with sex, this may lead heterosexual victims to question their sexual orientation, wondering why they ejaculated in response to "sexual" contact with another man. One male survivor explained, "I always thought a guy couldn't get hard if he was scared, and when this guy took me off [made me ejaculate] it really messed up my mind. I thought maybe something was wrong with me."[3] Spontaneous ejaculation produces a kind of mind/body split for many men, leaving them confused and wondering, "My mind was saying no, but my body seemed to say yes. Why did my body betray me this way?"

Much of this confusion results from a lack of knowledge and education about sexuality in our culture. Most men are not encouraged to learn about their gender-specific health concerns and bodily functions as many women are. The concept of men's health as a field of study and an area deserving of public health attention has only begun to emerge in recent years. Just as knowledge about the rape of women, both popular and scientific, has advanced a great deal in the past 20 years, an understanding of these male rape dynamics will also take considerable time and exploration.

In his book *Men Who Rape*, psychologist Nicholas Groth investigated the motives behind some rapists' attempts to force their male victims to ejaculate:

Such efforts may serve several purposes. In misidentifying ejaculation with orgasm, the victim may be bewildered by his psychological response to the offense and thus discouraged from reporting the assault lest his sexuality become suspect. Such reaction may serve to impeach his credibility in trial testimony and discredit his allegation of nonconsent. In the psychology of the offender, such reaction may symbolize his ultimate and complete control over his victim's body and confirm the fantasy that the victim really wanted and enjoyed the rape.[4]

Others, including medical personnel, family, friends, and other support people, may be reluctant to believe a man who admits rape when he shares that he had an erection or ejaculated. As male rape is widely thought to be impossible anyway, this extra element of doubt may eliminate what few resources male survivors might access.

T. J., a male survivor in his mid-20s was raped by a date in his dorm room while attending college. The man had torn T. J.'s clothing off, turned him around, and was raping him when T. J.'s roommate, Ted, came home and interrupted the assault. T. J. recalled that during the assault, the man raping him "had reached around and was rubbing me. When I'm scared, I'm usually erect too. It's that adrenaline flow. It [the rape] was really hard to deal with after that." Later that evening as T. J. talked with Ted, he wondered aloud if he had done enough to prevent the rape, or if he had really wanted to have sex. "One of the ways my roommate tried to help me was by saying, 'You know you were not to blame. You didn't have an erection.' and I said, 'No, but I did.'" Ted had made the assumption that T. J. did not experience an erection, and attempted to use that information as a strategy for affirming the validity of the rape. Although Ted remained admirably supportive even after learning of the erection, this situation is a prime example of falsely equating an erection with consent, and lack of erection with violence.

Apart from these involuntary responses, male rape survivors sometimes willfully elect to ejaculate in hopes that it will signify an end to the assault, that if the rapist believes the "sexual" experience is over, he will cease the attack. Jonathan, a survivor I interviewed, explained, "I made myself cum very quickly cause I thought that then he would cum and it would be over and I could leave. I consciously decided that if I did cum that maybe it would bring him over the edge and he would cum and then be too tired." As unlikely as it may seem, ejaculation in cases such as this becomes a self-defense strategy to minimize the duration or intensity of the assault. In Jonathan's situation, unfortunately, his ejaculation did not motivate his attacker to stop the rape in progress.

I wish to discuss one more possible connection between the biology of sexuality and male rape, although the issue has not been explicitly raised in the inter-

[handwritten margin notes: how is this homophobia? It could be a by product of 'Natural' thinking]

views I conducted or the literature I have examined. This connection is the increasingly popular media hype that homosexuality is biologically grounded in the body, and that gay men do not have mental control over what they sexually desire. For almost a century, scientists have searched for the cause of homosexuality. In fact, even the term *homosexual* came from a late 19th-century classification of disease. Since 1990, an abundance of claims have been put forth by scientists who believe they have found anatomical correlates, if not direct causes, of homosexuality in the human body. If we believe that the source of gayness comes from the body (such as a gene, hormone, or brain structure), then how can we refute that a bodily response such as erection or ejaculation to same-sex genital contact (i.e., rape) also indicates homosexuality? As the belief in a biological origin of homosexuality becomes more widespread, so will the confusion between same-sex desire and involuntary physiological responses we label as sexual. This reductive and sensational science—sociobiology—reinforces the mind/body split that many rape survivors experience, declaring that the mind cannot be relied on for the truth, rather that it can only come from the physicality of the body.

Other than these issues related to the penis, penetration of the anus may hold profoundly different cultural meanings for gay men than for heterosexual men. Many gay men consider their anus to be a sexual part of their anatomy, and may feel "sexually" violated if they are anally raped, whereas many heterosexual men may feel that forced penetration of their anus represents participation in an activity that is not necessarily sexual, but "unnatural" or "perverse." (Of course this is a generalization, as some heterosexual men engage in activities that bring them anal pleasure and some gay men find anal sex unappealing.) This leads me to ask the following questions: Are gay men who have previously engaged in consensual, receptive anal intercourse better able to identify forced anal penetration as sexual assault? Overall, are gay men more likely to view forced anal penetration as sexual violence, whereas heterosexual men may view it as some other kind of nonsexual assault? I do not pretend to have answers to these questions, but they do warrant serious consideration if we are to effectively understand the diversity of ways in which men define, or do not define, same-sex rape.

In my interview with T. J., we explored these questions in some detail. But rather than discussing at length the differences between heterosexual and gay male survivors of anal rape, he focused more on a comparison between anal and vaginal rape:

To the women who've been raped that I've talked to, they've been raped vaginally. They have not been exposed to anal rape; it's really weird to them. I think it's something they've not actually thought about. This is something that is so rarely talked about. Even when women get raped anally, often I've found that's not something they're willing to talk about the way they are willing to talk about vaginal rape. I think it comes from very ingrained homophobia.

Despite the lack of consent when women are anally raped, T. J. believes many women are silenced by the taboo of anal penetration that carries the stigma of homophobia. Men also rape women anally in an effort to make the experience of forced penetration as physically painful as possible, and the anal assault may signify a special form of symbolic domination over women that exceeds vaginal rape. Even though heterosexual people engage in anal sex, the act is still very much associated with homosexuality, especially in Western cultures. Having grown up in India, T. J. noted this culturally specific element linking anal sex with gay sex and suggested the taboo is grounded in Judeo-Christian religiosity:

In India, when I talk about it [anal rape] I have not had that same reaction. In India, anal sex is very commonly talked about; it doesn't have that religious marginality. In India, gods have anal sex. It's just like any other form of intercourse. But here in the United States, I find that inculcated religious phobia of anal sex which translates into homophobia.

Building on this devaluation of gay male anal sex, that it is inherently inferior to heterosexual vaginal sex, T. J. theorized that anal rape might be deemed less of a sexual victimization than vaginal rape. With respect to gay men, anal rape may be viewed as even less severe if they have practiced consensual, receptive anal intercourse in the past:

I think some people think anal rape of gay men is less of a violation. Especially less of a violation for people who have had anal sex. It's a kind of blame that since you've opened yourself up to violation, you somehow deserve it. It's that whole dynamic that if women wear something sexy and get raped, it's less of a violation because they chose to open themselves up to it.

T. J. proposed that a history of consensual anal penetration might permanently reduce the innocence, and therefore the tragedy, of the rape of a gay man. A heterosexual analogy to this would be the belief that the rape of a virgin is somehow more of a travesty than the rape of a woman who is sexually experienced—that the context of the act (lack of consent) might be different, but the person has already experienced the physical act, so it's no big deal.

The simultaneous presence of these rationales, that anal rape is both more and less severe than vaginal rape, begins to present something of a self-contradiction. T. J. explained:

On the one hand, it's thought of as really bad, a real invasion because it's not the right place to insert the penis. I think there is that general conception. Some women I've talked to have said if they were to be raped they would prefer it to be vaginal rape. But it's a paradox, that if you experience anal rape, it's not something to shout about as much as vaginal rape. That it's somehow worse, but that you're somehow less of a victim.

The following sections offer some observations and comparisons between the rape of gay men by gay men, straight men by straight men, straight men by gay men, and gay men by straight men. These combinations are only hypothetical illustrations of rape scenarios. In reality, categories of gay and straight relations are somewhat artificial. The ways in which people have sex and think about sex are often less rigid and more fluid than these classifications given that sexual identities and behaviors are not limited to opposites of either heterosexual or homosexual. In fact, some of the men I interviewed and quote here self-identified as bisexual or queer, a more politicized identity with multiple meanings.

As I stated earlier, there is a current consensus among those who research male rape that the majority of men who rape other men are heterosexual. Several published studies demonstrate this belief. Some of these rely on the survivor's perception of his attacker's sexual orientation, such as those conducted by Dr. Richard Hillman of St. Mary's Hospital in London in 1991, P. L. Huckle's 1995 study at the South Wales Forensic Psychiatric Service, and Richie McMullen's work at Survivors, a London-based male rape agency. Others are based on interviews with the rapists themselves and report these men's self-identified heterosexuality, such as Nicholas Groth and Ann Burgess's 1980 study.

Although it remains uncertain, evidence suggests gay men are more likely to be raped than straight men.

Despite the fact that heterosexual men far outnumber gay men in sheer masses, gay men seem to be more at risk, on average, than their heterosexual counterparts. A 1990 study conducted by Dr. David F. Duncan at Southern Illinois University at Carbondale found gay and lesbian college students reported significantly higher lifetime prevalences of sexual victimization than did heterosexual men participating in the same study. He also stated, "It is possible, however, that gay/lesbian students differ from heterosexual students in their openness in reporting experiences of sexual victimization rather than in the frequency with which they have been victimized."[5] In a large-scale study of 930 gay men living in England and Wales, 27.6% reported they had been sexually assaulted at some point in their lives. Sociologists Ford Hickson and his colleagues conducted the survey as part of Project SIGMA, a 6-year nonclinical study of homosexually active men.[6] Gay men's vulnerability to rape is related in part to the fact that they have male sexual partners and are frequently in the company of many men. As with acquaintance rape of women, people are most likely to be raped by members of their own race, class, geographic area, and social relations.

GAY MEN RAPING GAY MEN

Even though same-sex relationships may provide equal footing on grounds of gender, other elements of power may be used by a gay man to rape another gay man (physical, economic, and so on). Rape and domestic violence are frequently not believed to occur within gay and lesbian communities because of these traditional definitions of gender-based violence. Gay men's reluctance to speak openly about violence, especially sexual violence, within their communities is understandable. Drawing any attention to "intracommunity" rape affords numerous opportunities for homophobic critics who would eagerly cry out, "See! We told you they are sexual predators. They even attack each other." Apart from the survivors of this violence, many gay community leaders view highly public discussions of gay men raping gay men as an unnecessary airing of dirty laundry, for this risks a provision of fodder to opportunistic enemies who are anxious for information that demonizes homosexuality when taken out of context. The negative consequence of this protective state of affairs is that gay male survivors feel silenced and predict that if they seek support or provide testimony to their experiences, they will betray their own community. A number of factors play into making this sexual violence both possible and in some situations probable. Some stem from internal aspects of gay culture; others are imposed by outside forces.

Alcohol and Other Drugs

A great deal of gay male interaction has historically centered around bars as social gathering spots, although this is changing over time with the proliferation of opportunities for gay men to meet through emerging organizations and events. Gay bars provide important spaces for gay men to meet, relax, and feel relatively safe with one another, but as important as they are for building and maintaining community, they are still businesses that survive on their patrons' purchase and consumption of alcoholic beverages. Like anyone else, gay men are vulnerable to alcoholism and other forms of substance abuse. This combination of drug-induced impairment and the company of men creates a vulnerability to sexual assault. The use of alcohol and other drugs can create situations where men are unable to effectively define and defend their sexual limits. At the same time, men who are under the influence experience impaired judgments that can lead to misinterpretation or failure to respect another's boundaries.

Domestic Violence

Most discussions of rape between gay men have not addressed these acquaintance rape situations where the men have met in bars, at parties, through friends, or as casual sexual partners; they have focused on sexual violence as a component of domestic violence. In a 1989 study by psychologist Caroline Waterman and her colleagues at the University of Albany, 12% of 34 men in gay relationships "reported being victims of forced sex by their current or most recent partner."[7] David Island and Patrick Letellier, the authors of *Men Who Beat the Men Who Love Them*, estimate that some 500,000 gay men are victims of domestic violence every year.[8] The National Coalition of Anti-Gay Violence Programs released a 1996 report of information compiled from data for San Francisco, Chicago, New York, San Diego, Minneapolis, and Columbus, Ohio. The data indicated domestic violence may be no less common among gay couples than heterosexual couples, but the victims face even more

intimidation in seeking the support they need. Gloria McCauley, executive director of the Buckeye Region Anti-Violence Organization in Ohio, told the *Columbus Dispatch*, "I think it's a terrifically high number, particularly because our (gay and bisexual) communities are not recognizing domestic violence. . . . Most of the people who are involved in abusive or violent relationships don't know that they have any resources, don't know what to do. They feel trapped."[9]

As with sexual violence, not everyone sympathizes or recognizes the victimization of same-sex domestic violence. In the December 10, 1996, issue of the *Chicago Tribune*, columnist Mike Royko described his lack of concern for gay men who are battered by their partners because he believes men should have the power and privilege to simply walk away from an abusive relationship, regardless of the circumstances:

It seems to me that if Bill lives with Joe and Joe makes a practice of pummeling Bill, then Bill would have the good sense to just pack a suitcase and get the heck out of there. It should be easier for a man to walk away from an abusive relationship than for a woman since men don't get pregnant and have babies.[10]

Royko continued by saying that if a battered partner chooses to stay with his partner, for any reason, "that is his choice and I respect it—so long as he is not my neighbor and doesn't scream for help or pound on my door at night."[11] Clearly more work must be done to sensitize the public on domestic violence issues generally and same-sex domestic violence specifically.

The dialogue about gay men raping gay men, although valuable, has been shortsighted in that most of the research and writing within this context involves partners who either live together or are in a serious, long-term romantic relationship. If gay communities do not begin to expand recognition of the varied ways that rape can happen, it could result in gay men's inability to name their experience as rape if it occurs outside such an established relationship. This would be similar to interpretations of heterosexual acquaintance rape where women easily put a name to rape if they are attacked by a stranger, but seem to define rape by an acquaintance as just "regretted sex" or a "bad experience."

Camille's Ideal

Expanding the definition of rape in this way, beyond the scenarios of a battering partner or a deranged stranger leaping out from behind the bushes to sexu-

the author gives Paglia a lot of authority

ally attack his unsuspecting victim, has generated controversy and disagreement. For example, some people hold the opinion that if a woman gets drunk and accompanies a man upstairs to his apartment, she is as responsible for her rape as the rapist himself. Cultural critic Camille Paglia puts forth this argument consistently, stating in so many words that women who are stupid enough to be date-raped deserve no sympathy. To support her argument, she holds gay men up as the ideal standard to which heterosexual women should aspire, saying that gay men are "too mature" to whine about a nonconsensual sexual encounter. This takes the form of backlash by depicting feminist definitions of rape to be infantile and childish, not warranting sympathy, attention, or legal action. She paints a worldview where gay men possess a high level of sophistication and maturity whereas heterosexual women who cry rape are hysterical, naive, and overly sensitive. In an interview with Charlie Rose, Paglia elaborated, "I'm using the gay male attitude, okay? Gay men are adults about these things. For thousands of years they have been, okay? . . . gay men don't, in the middle of a sex act, suddenly go, 'I've changed my mind!' "[12] In such a sweeping generalization she positions gay men as unrapeable by their sexual partners with the assumption that gay men do not reserve the right to end a sexual act once in progress.

Okay, life is filled with dangers, like I say. Gay men know this. Gay men understand the dangers of the street. They, they're cruising in parks, do you understand? They get beat up, they get killed. Okay, for thousands of years this has been going on. I'm sick and tired of women behaving this overprotective kind of infantilized condition, okay, where sort of like, "That poor middle-class white girl. Look what happened to her." I'm tired of that.[13]

Paglia makes all gay men out to be hardened, worldly risk-takers who casually accept homicide as an everyday possibility. This serves her purposes by creating a demanding yardstick by which heterosexual women are measured, and the warped reality she imposes on gay men once again serves to silence and invalidate male rape survivors.

Unfortunately, Paglia has had more to say about male rape in her antifeminist tirades. In her book *Vamps and Tramps* she writes:

The dishonesty and speciousness of the feminist rape analysis are demonstrated by its failure to explore, or even mention, man-on-man sex crimes. If rape were really just a

process of political intimidation of women by men, why do men rape and kill other males?[14]

The answer to Ms. Paglia's question, simply put, is that rape is an act of power and control. Such acts of power, or more specifically, overpowerment, often occur in highly gendered ways, as in the case of men raping women. Frequently, however, rape is enacted as part of racist hate crimes, gay and lesbian bashings, assaults on the homeless, and more. Political power manifests itself not only through a lens of gender, but also race, class, age, sexual identity, physical ability, and more. These forms of power do not operate independently, but in a complex and interwoven system that supports a multiplicity of oppression and violence. Rape is but one of the consequences of such power dynamics. Numerous feminist activists and writers, from Andrea Dworkin to Susan Brownmiller, *have* discussed male rape, although it has not been given equal consideration as feminist work has concentrated, understandably, on the rape of women.

Later in *Vamps and Tramps*, Paglia invokes the gay male epitome once again. She recounts a conversation occurring near a New York City pier on the Hudson River where gay men seek out anonymous sex with each other:

This is what I'm always saying about the feminist problem with date rape, okay? . . . I've learned so much from gay men. I mean, I love the gay male attitude, which is to go out into the dark, have anonymous sex. . . . You may get beaten up. That's one of the thrills.[15]

First off, not all gay men have public or anonymous sex. And certainly not all those who participate in anonymous sex do so for the "thrill" of being physically attacked (if there is such a thrill). If gay men are homophobically stereotyped as hypersexual beings always having or wanting to have sex, then theoretically gay men cannot be raped. The old adage, "You can't rape the willing" describes this mentality. In that respect, gay men are culturally designed to be unrapeable, unable to be violated sexually on any level, as it supposedly feeds their self-destructive wish to be brutalized.

The false belief in pleasure derived from violence is sometimes mistakenly equated with sadomasochism—sexual practices involving the infliction of pain. Talking of desire and violence as being one in the same is an oxymoron. If we can agree that desire implies consent, and violence is a lack of consent, then how can one want to be raped? There is quite a difference between rape and sadomasochistic acts, which are typically regulated by a complex system of explicit communication and negotiation of consent. At the same time, violence and pain are not necessarily the same thing. Pain is a physical sensation that most people find unpleasurable, but some individuals find pain to be sexually stimulating and actually enjoy the feeling. A gay male rape survivor I spoke with, Jonathan, engages in consensual sadomasochistic sex. He described how the man who raped him misused this as a venue for violent behavior: "I think he had misrepresented himself and what he was interested in. He wasn't interested in a consensual experience, he was interested in being violent. He wasn't interested in expanding my limits or making me feel something intense. He was mostly interested in beating up on someone."

The Rape Victim Wannabe

The recurring theme that gay men want to be raped recently surfaced in an opinion piece published in the gay literature magazine *Christopher Street*. In his article, "Male Rape: Tragedy, Fantasy, or Badge of Honor?" William Gordon declared the status of rape victim to be trendy among gay men, that they fabricate rape stories to appear desirable in the eyes of others:

Only women are sexy to men? Okay . . . I'll be like a woman, a really attractive woman, not a real woman, of course, just a 'B' movie type-o-gal, the one who gets manhandled wherever she goes, call me Gina Lollabrigida, call me Marilyn Monroe, call me frail, helpless, call me sex kitten, call me rape victim.[16]

His profile extends to the status of "wannabe," a copycat syndrome of people who imitate trends to an excessive degree, saying, "Just when you think you've met every kind of wannabe in the world, you find a new one: the rape victim wannabe."[17] Once again the claim is made that gay men aspire to some sexual status of "good enough to be raped." In the article, William Gordon describes the night a friend revealed he had been raped, remarking, "I doubt he'd admit it, but I'm sure he told it [his rape experience] to entice me."[18] With the rarity of information and reporting on male rape in the gay press, these insensitive characterizations of sexual violence as meaningless, casual, and seductive can do untold damage as the last word, unchallenged by a body of balanced literature.

The Coming-Out Process

For men who are just beginning the process of "coming-out" as gay or bisexual, rape can be a devastating setback in the development of their sexual identities. Several of the men I interviewed spoke about the disruption of rape as a pivotal moment that influenced their future relationships with both women and men. Marcus recalled:

It happened in the course of my coming-out and I was just starting to think about my attraction to men as well as my attraction to women and coming-out as a bisexual man. It really made that process so much more difficult for me. I had this huge distrust of men while wanting to be close to them, and a very deep anger toward men.

The attraction and repulsion to men after rape is a common feeling for many gay and bisexual male survivors. Many of these men want to begin exploring their same-sex attraction, but harbor such distrust and anger toward men that it prevents them from building and sustaining healthy relationships.

For T. J., the aftermath of rape became a catalyst for self-reflection as he sought involvement in campus student organizations that addressed issues of sexism and homophobia. Through his growing investment in feminist politics, he slowly developed integrated identities of "rape survivor" and "queer." He told me, "Then I started going to GLA [Gay and Lesbian Alliance] meetings. My rape consciousness began going hand in hand with my queer consciousness." For T. J., the lines between oppressions of race, sexual identity, and gender began to bleed over into each other, and he realized that his rape was grounded in a larger set of power relations that were social forces beyond the scope of his individual circumstance.

The toll of sexual violence on sexual identity development in gay and bisexual men has only begun to be realized by many therapists and counselors who assist these men in their struggle to come to terms with their life's realities. Susan Wachob, a psychotherapist in San Francisco who specializes in working with male survivors of sexual abuse, explains:

The gay survivor, who may have grown up keeping his sexual orientation a secret, is already skilled at hiding important facets of himself. When a sexual assault takes place, he is already primed for how to treat yet another experience of himself that he has been taught is private, shameful, and unacceptable.

like heterosexual female rape survivors
who alter their relations c/ men

The closets in which gay male rape survivors hide, those of rape-related shame and sexual identity, often collapse into one terrifying feat of pretense. Balancing a high degree of internal pain with an outward performance of normative wellness eventually takes a heavy toll on those men who live in the closet.

Some sexually inexperienced men may perceive rape to be the norm of same-sex relations and drive them deep into the closet even if they were already "out," either fearing or denying their desire for men. Others may normalize rape and sexual brutality as if it is an inherent part of gay culture and come to expect violent interactions with other men. The internalization of this violence can also have drastic effects, leaving gay and bisexual men feeling as if they somehow deserved to be raped as a punishment for their same-sex attraction.

Altered Sex Practices

Even for men who have acknowledged their sexual identity and established a firm sense of self with respect to their sexuality, the experience of rape can force a change in the ways that male survivors engage in sexual activity. Marcus commented:

It didn't change my sexuality, although it made the process of coming-out more painful and I still feel the repercussions of that. Most of my sex partners are women and all of my romantic partners have been women. In terms of sex practices, I felt a much stronger need for safety and also a much greater concern for my partner's feeling of safety. Sometimes that causes problems, especially if I'm involved with a survivor. Because then we both sense the other person putting out boundaries and it's made it more difficult sometimes to have sex. For a while I had less sex.

Some survivors may have less sex after their rape, whereas others may have more sex in an attempt to reestablish a normalcy of sexual experience. Rape trauma syndrome also enters the picture here, when even consensual sex can trigger flashbacks, panic attacks, impotence, and other negative effects. The man who raped Jonathan severely beat him in the face while anally penetrating him, and Jonathan vividly described to me the residual impact of this attack:

I remember talking to people who I was going to have sex with and said, "Don't touch my face. It freaks me out too much." It doesn't bother me anymore, it was for two years

afterward. Initially, for a few months afterward, it would have been anytime. For another year and a half, it was just during sex. I would pull away or snap my head back if men touched my face with their hands.

Jonathan's reaction became an involuntary reflex as he was psychologically conditioned to defend himself against a possibly similar assault in the future. This kind of response is normal and to be expected as part of postraumatic stress disorder in those who suffer from rape trauma syndrome.

In T.J.'s case, this sexual behavior change is especially evident in that he goes to great lengths to monitor his partner's ongoing intentions. T.J. was first raped when he was 12 years old, assaulted from behind while showering in the barracks of his youth military service. He never saw the person who raped him, and was sure that if he had turned around to look, his attacker would have killed him. The man never spoke to him. Ever since he was raped a second time as an adult, he now requires a heightened level of communication with his partner during sex:

With men, there have been lots of repercussions. For a long time I really, really had a phobia of being entered anally. Primarily because most of the time I couldn't see what was happening. I eventually got over that with lots of techniques. I use mirrors, so I can see their face. That's really, really important to me—that I can see their face and their expression. I also started asking my sexual partners to talk to me more during sex.

T.J. has developed a need for consistent reassurance during sexual activity, which he obtains by assessing his partner's facial expressions, viewing exactly what is happening between his and his partner's bodies, and discerning his partner's temperament. The mirrors provide a literal window for T.J. to view the scene from a distanced perspective, enabling observation from outside the sexual activity to ensure ongoing consent.

The rape that occurs among gay and bisexual male populations can have a myriad of negative effects on both individual and collective well-being. Efforts to prevent and treat sexual violence between gay men must continue to develop with a strong cultural competence that takes into consideration the factors of societal homophobia, individual identity, a diversity of gay culture, and the needs of bisexual men.

heterosexual male rape need not be a contradiction; sexuality is defined by action, not partner

GAY MEN RAPING HETEROSEXUAL MEN

Men who rape tend to do so within their own social, cultural, and economic group, or rape those they have power over in society. For these reasons it is not surprising that the incidence of gay men raping heterosexual men is relatively low. This form of violence is possible, however, and does occur, but the fears typically associated with gay on straight rape are greatly exaggerated. As demonstrated throughout this book, many male rape myths are grounded in irrational fears and hatred of homosexuality. The pervasive belief that a gay man will sexually assault a heterosexual man if given the opportunity has been transformed from a possibility into a stereotyped norm. However, one exception to this myth that male rape usually involves gay men assaulting heterosexual men also stems from homophobia. Some people may believe that gay men could not possibly rape straight men because all gay men are supposedly feminine and physically weak, thus unable to overpower a "real man." On a similar note, Ford Hickson and his colleagues at London's Project SIGMA stated, "folk wisdom tells us that it is easy for gay men to find casual sexual partners, so they have no need to force themselves on other men."[19] This folk wisdom is also based on a confusion between rape and sex, assuming that (1) all gay men are promiscuous, (2) rape behavior is driven by one's libido, and (3) sexual violence serves as a suitable substitute in satisfying gay male sexual desire.

If by chance a heterosexual man reports being raped by a gay man, he may be disbelieved or extremely stigmatized for his inability to defend himself against an effeminate person. (Being gay and possessing feminine traits are often stereotypically synonymous.) In one case of military sexual misconduct in 1995, the question of sexual preference became the center of debate during a trial that involved two Army men. After a night of heavy drinking, one man woke up in his bedroom to find another man had broken in, undressed him, and performed oral sex on him. The victim immediately reported the incident to authorities. Army investigators speculated, however, that the sexual contact was consensual and were unsure whether to press forcible sodomy charges against the alleged attacker or consensual sodomy charges against both men. The *National Law Journal* reported on the assault, and in the commentary was a less than subtle

argument based on the myth of physical size and masculinity as an inherent self-defense to rape: "[The alleged attacker] could pass for a high school student. He is 5 feet 8 inches tall and slight—perhaps 2 inches shorter and 40 pounds lighter than [the alleged victim]. He admitted in testimony that he was not pinned down or threatened."[20] In the legal determination of consent, the alleged victim's heterosexuality was called into question because of the belief that he should have had no problem fending off the sexual advances of a man who is depicted as young and "slight." As one rape survivor expressed from Drs. Mezey and King's 1989 study at the Institute of Psychiatry in London, "something very dirty has happened to you that nobody believes can happen—if you let it happen you must be queer, if you're not a queer it can't have happened."[21]

HETEROSEXUAL MEN RAPING GAY MEN

Heterosexual men sometimes rape gay men, usually as part of hate-motivated gay bashings. In the book *Hate Crimes: Confronting Violence Against Lesbians and Gay Men*, violence expert Joseph Harry described what might at first seem to be an illogical behavior:

Occasionally, gay bashing incidents include forcible rape, either oral or anal. Given the context of coercion, however, such technically homosexual acts seem to imply no homosexuality on the part of the offenders. The victim serves, both physically and symbolically, as a vehicle for the sexual status needs of the offenders in the course of recreational violence.[22]

One might think that if a heterosexual man despises homosexuality to such a degree that he attacks gay men, he would not engage in sexual contact with them, even for the purpose of violence. Gay men, or even men who are simply perceived to be gay, are commonly viewed by society as traitors to masculinity. They may be raped as a form of punishment for relinquishing their traditional manhood, with a rapist mentality of "You want to act like a woman? Then I'll show you what it means to be one." Gay men might also be perceived by rapists as not only the most deserving of rape, but the least likely to have the strength, either physical or emotional, to effectively resist the assault.

Are Gay Bashers Actually Gay Themselves?

Controversies in psychological literature continue to debate the motivation of heterosexual men to commit acts of violence against gay men. Some recent research speculates that a man's latent, unrealized homosexuality causes internalized hatred that eventually surfaces as aggression directed toward gay men. This is thought to be a lashing out against what one most fears within one's self. The most recent reprisal of this theory comes from research conducted by Henry Adams at the University of Georgia, who suggests that men who bash gay men are often repressed gay men themselves. A 1996 article that appeared in the *Irish Times* newspaper reported:

Dr. Art O'Connor, forensic psychiatrist at the Central Mental Hospital in Dublin, believes that some homosexual men only express their homosexuality aggressively, perhaps after drinking. Most likely candidates are those who "in their everyday lives are anti-gay and are trying to cover it up from society."[23]

Although these research findings may have some merit, we must also consider whether it is simply recycling the same old homophobic myths regarding male rape: that even the heterosexual men who rape gay men are really gay inside, therefore male rape is actually homosexual rape.

HETEROSEXUAL MEN RAPING HETEROSEXUAL MEN

Again, given that men tend to rape others similar to themselves, the practice of heterosexual men raping each other seems sensible and likely. Without a methodical look at male rape on a mass scale, however, we will remain blind to the exact prevalence of each of these above four categories. Same-sex rape between heterosexual men is also largely an exertion of power and control through feminizing the other by forcing a man into the sexually submissive, receptive role of female. This may occur between strangers, male family members (especially as elder abuse), acquaintances, colleagues, and so on. Acquaintance rape is most likely in this situation, meaning the victim has some form of prior relationship, however casual, to the man who raped him. Especially in the case of heterosexual stranger rape, the victim may misperceive the rapist to be gay if he has no other knowledge of the attacker, believing the myth that rape is a sexually motivated crime. Categorizations of same-sex rape can be skewed depending on the victim's own homophobia, belief in popular rape mythology, and degree of prior relationship to the rapist.

In contrast, heterosexual male rape survivors may lack many of the support systems that most gay men are able to access. Gay and lesbian community centers are often a first point of contact for gay male rape survivors who need referrals or other assistance. Additionally, more and more organizations dedicated to gay and lesbian antiviolence work have sprung up across the globe. This infrastructure has been built to counteract the effects of societal homophobia, foster a sense of community, and enable gay and lesbian individuals to lead the productive and healthy lives they deserve. Very few, if any, such services are tailored specifically to the needs of heterosexual men, given their comparative position of status within society. Heterosexual male survivors may be directed to gay community services because these organizations are perhaps the only local ones who address same-sex rape. (This has historically been the case with HIV-positive heterosexual people who depended on gay-specific AIDS organizations, for example.) These men may be further stigmatized for their reliance on the gay community, and this may further provoke one's questioning of sexual identity.

RAPE OF TRANSGENDER PEOPLE

Aside from discussions of same-sex rape based on the model of biological sex (male/female), we should also consider those people who do not fit neatly into traditional or stable categories of the opposite sexes. Around the world, the social movement of people who identify as transgender is gaining strength and influence through their defiance of imposed gender identities based on one's biological sex at the time of birth. Quite literally, the term *transgender* represents a movement along any or all of the gendered spectrums of masculine/feminine, man/woman, or male/female. Transgender identity and practice might also constitute a behavior or identity that is neither masculine nor feminine, neither man nor woman, or neither male nor female.

Because of this lack of compliance to gender roles that society deems to be "normal" and "healthy," transgender people are frequently targets of physical abuse, including sexual abuse. Unfortunately, social and legal systems designed to support survivors of sexual violence are usually less than helpful to transgender people. For example, in June 1996, South Korea's highest court ruled that two men who had sexually assaulted a male-to-female transsexual could not be convicted of rape, as South Korean law only recognizes the rape of women. Supreme Court Justice Chong Kwi-ho explained to the court, "Though the victim in this case behaves as a female, the person cannot be recognized as one because, among other things, his chromosomes remain unchanged and he cannot get pregnant."[24] In South Korea, male on male rape is a legal impossibility, and one's sex at birth remains the determinant of gender despite any changes that may later occur to one's body. Instead of being charged with rape, the two men were found guilty of the lesser charge of "sexual assault" and were each sentenced to a jail term of 2 1/2 years.

In December 1996, firemen in Managua, Nicaragua, rescued a transvestite who had spent 8 days trapped at the bottom of an abandoned well. Two men had brutally raped Shakira, the man dressed in women's clothing, attempted to strangle him with a cord tied around his neck, then threw him into the 100-foot-deep well. Shakira fractured his leg in the fall and was unable to climb out to safety. He was eventually found by friends and family who had launched a search party once they discovered him missing.

In the United States, one of the highest profile cases of sexual assault of a transgender person was the 1993 rape and murder of Teena Brandon, a woman who cross-dressed and lived much of her life as a man, and her three friends in a Nebraska farmhouse. Of the two men who committed the violence, one was convicted on three counts of first-degree murder and sentenced to death. The other was convicted on two counts of second-degree murder and is serving a life sentence. Before Brandon was murdered on New Year's Eve of 1993, she reported to the local sheriff that she had been raped by the two men on Christmas day. They warned her that if she reported the rape, they would silence her. Brandon ignored the warning and went to the police. After her death, a family member filed a lawsuit against local law enforcement claiming they did not take the rape report seriously, in part because she was a cross-dresser, and could have prevented her murder days later.

In October 1996, two prison guards were indicted in Evry, France, after ten transsexual prostitutes who had been prisoners stepped forward to report the guards had raped them. The transvestites had been separated from other prisoners and were forced to engage in sexual activity under the threat of worsened prison conditions, including denial of food. Unfortunately, these cases are not infrequent incidents. As the transgender social movement increases in size and visibility, backlash tactics such as sexual violence will most likely increase as well. The need for adequate and sensitive services for these survivors is necessary in the face of dual stigmatization. Transgender rape will also call into question the gender-specific legal definitions of sexual assault, as in the case of South Korea.

GAY HISTORY OR RAPE HISTORY?

At the heart of confusion between homosexuality and same-sex rape lies the question of consent. The question of exactly what constitutes consent bears a great deal of importance in the distinction between male rape and male homosexuality, simultaneously helping to define and distinguish the two. Beyond our present-day concerns of how sexual identity and sexual assault influence and relate to one another, a critical attempt to tease apart consensual sex from forced sexual activity bears strong implications for a growing field of academic inquiry, namely, gay history. In the last few decades, scholars worldwide have undertaken the monumental project of recovering the history of same-sex sexual behaviors and communities. As homosexuality has long been considered taboo in most Western civilizations, this evidence and documentation is rather rare. What little evidence has survived is often vague or filtered through the perspective of legal and religious organizations that document the punishment of homosexuality.

As a field of study, gay history has been deemed important because explorations of this past can help to fortify modern gay community through the establishment of cultural heritage and an understanding of how antigay oppression has evolved over the centuries. Some anxious and eager researchers, however, have recovered evidence of what they call sexual behavior but in context appears to be rape behavior by our contemporary definitions. Usually this identification of historical same-sex rape as "gay history" goes unchallenged, even by the rigorous process of peer review. Psychiatry professor Ivor Jones at Royal Hobart Hospital Clinical School in Australia notes:

In historical accounts, problems of definition abound; they arise in defining sexual assault as opposed to sexual co-operation and this ground can readily be shifted by legislative fiat. Male sexual assault is generally regarded as a subset of homosexual behavior, with implications and thereby problems of definitions extending beyond the genital act to sexual reference.[25]

Even in the interviews that I conducted for this book, a surface reading or excerpt would imply consent between two men when in fact there was none. For example, one survivor I spoke with talked about his communication with the man who raped him shortly after the assault:

He called me the next day to thank me and complimented me on my performance. I was so confused. He kept telling me how good I was, as if I had wanted it to happen. He said he wanted to see me again like I would really want for that to happen all over. I wondered if he thought I wanted it . . . if I sent him the wrong signals, like I was to blame 'cause he misunderstood me somehow.

Marcus recounted a similar experience, only during rather than after the rape. "He repeated over and over again that he loved me. He just said, 'I love you. I love you,' over and over again as I was saying 'No. No.' " This redefinition of reality allows the rapist to foreclose opportunities for the survivor to identify the experience as violence, and also affirms the rapist's own denial as he acts out a fantasy that the experience is in fact consensual. The complexity of these interpretations can be difficult enough when one has firsthand access to a subject's own words and testimonies, let alone having to rely on remnant materials that are decades or centuries old.

On the flip side of this, how can we know that records of same-sex rape are not, in fact, evidence of homosexual behavior? Because of the severity of punishment and social ostracization from being discovered to have participated in sex with someone of the same gender, there is a high likelihood that once one of the individuals was caught, he might have claimed

the act was nonconsensual so as to absolve himself of willing participation in the deviance. Ranging from public shame to death, punitive measures for homosexuality could have been (and may still be) a motivation for one to make a false claim of rape, although I do not wish to assert that this constitutes a significant fraction of male rape reports.

One of the most hotly contested historical elements charged by this debate over rape versus sex has been that of the North American Indian social class known as the "berdache." Although similarities and differences can be found between berdache-like people across the breadth and diversity of native North American nations, they are commonly considered to be a kind of third gender status—neither man nor woman. Some berdache, although biologically male, would adopt pieces of women's attire and women's duties, including sexual activity with males. Because of this gender status and same-sex sexual behavior, gay historians such as anthropologist Will Roscoe and others have closely scrutinized the berdache as a kind of predecessor or counterpart to today's gay, lesbian, and bisexual identities.

There is no consensus, however, regarding the characterization of the berdache in historical context. Ramon Gutierrez, professor of history at the Center for Advanced Study in the Behavior Sciences in Stanford, California, criticizes Roscoe and other gay history scholars for depicting the North American berdache as a social role of pure honor and prestige to serve as a contemporary role model for gay life. He draws distinctions between gender roles that are imposed rather than assumed and differentiates between homosexuality and same-sex rape inflicted for purposes of humiliation and degradation. He believes, "Berdache status was one principally ascribed to defeated enemies. Among the insults and humiliations inflicted on prisoners of war were homosexual rape, castration, the wearing of women's clothes, and performing women's work.[26] In his book *Sex and Conquest: Gendered Violence, Political Order, and the European Conquest of the Americas*, historian Richard Trexler fashions a compelling argument for avoiding the convenient blurring of lines between violence and sex. Similar to Gutierrez, Trexler commented that the berdache, as "important figures are seen more as forerunners of modern liberated gays than as emblems of tribal power and authority, genial artistic types rather than the embodiments of dependence they prove to be in the period of the conquests."[27] His book "argues that, in much of antiquity, males as well as females were born into a world of penetrative penalty. That is, men as well as women were sometimes punished through sexual means."[28]

Although some gay-supportive historians may translate same-sex rape into consensual sexual activity for the purposes of bolstering gay community, a similar slight of hand can be pulled by those who wish to demonize same-sex sexuality. Take, for example, author Scott Lively's book *The Pink Swastika: Homosexuality in the Nazi Party*. In his work, Lively characterizes a number of historical figures as "homosexual sadists" and draws the conclusion that there was a strong and influential homosexual presence within the Nazi party. Much of this "sadism," however, is violent and nonconsensual, and cannot necessarily be equated with consensual relationships between men. Lively puts forth a counterclaim to the belief that gay men were persecuted in Nazi Germany, herded up and exterminated in concentration camps. Instead he purports gay men were a prominent force of fascism, identifiable as gay in part because of their sexually violent behavior:

Nazi anti-homosexual rhetoric was largely hollow and served to deflect public attention from Hitler's perverted ruling clique. "Gay Holocaust" revisionists exploit the Holocaust to legitimize their "victim" strategy for manipulating public sympathies. The truth exposes these "victims" as perpetrators and thus they must suppress it.[29]

Again, competing realities center around the interpretation of sexual contact with respect to consent. Episodes of same-sex rape can be used just as easily by those who wish to substantiate a tradition of homosexual vilification.

These components of power can no longer be ignored in historical investigations of same-sex sexual behavior and same-sex rape, from "pederasty" relationships between men and boys that appear to have been consensual to male transvestites who served as sexual slaves to men in authority. In some versions of Greek mythology, for example, Zeus abducted Ganymede against his will for sexual purposes. In other versions of the same myth, Ganymede is simply "seduced" and becomes a willing partner. In every chronicle of earlier sexual events, historians must begin to ask themselves if same-sex rape should be considered homosexual behavior. If so, what are the modern-day implications of using a past of sexual violence to inform and strengthen today's gay male culture and community?

The intertwining of sex and rape has been extensively explored in feminist scholarship, and the need for similar work with same-sex sexuality and same-sex rape is clear. Sexual behavior, psychological wellness, identity formation, social development, historical analysis, and cultural production are but a few of the areas in which sexual identity and rape overlap and affect each other. Dependent on a set of power relations and belief systems that dictate individual realities, the stigma of homophobia is perhaps the strongest element of taboo with respect to male rape. These issues bear strong implications for all men, whatever their sexual identity or history with sexual violence.

NOTES

1. Paul Cameron, *The Gay 90's* (Franklin, TN: Adroit Press, 1991), p. 50.

2. Ibid., p. 51.

3. Groth, p. 124.

4. Groth, p. 124.

5. David F. Duncan, "Prevalence of Sexual Assault Victimization among Heterosexual and Gay/Lesbian University Students," *Psychological Reports* 66 (1990), p. 66.

6. Ford C. I. Hickson et al., "Gay Men as Victims of Nonconsensual Sex," *Archives of Sexual Behavior* 23.3 (1994), pp. 281–294.

7. Caroline Waterman et al., "Sexual Coercion in Gay Male Relationships: Predictors and Implications for Support Services," *Journal of Sex Research* 26.1 (1989), p. 118.

8. David Island and Patrick Letellier, *Men Who Beat the Men, Who Love Them* (Binghamton, NY: Harrington Park Press, 1991).

9. Scott Powers, "Study Finds Gay Domestic Assault Common," *Columbus Dispatch* 24 October 1996, p. 5C.

10. Mike Royko, "500,000 Gay Men Don't Have to Take Abuse From Partner," *Chicago Tribune* 10 December 1996, p. 3.

11. Ibid.

12. *Charlie Rose*, WNET Educational Broadcasting Company, 30 January 1995.

13. Ibid.

14. Camille Paglia, *Vamps and Tramps: New Essays* (New York: Vintage Books, 1994), p. 33.

15. Ibid., p. 304.

16. William Gordon, "Male Rape: Tragedy, Fantasy, or Badge of Honor?" *Christopher Street* August 1992, p. 9.

17. Ibid.

18. Ibid.

19. Hickson, p. 284.

20. Gail Diane Cox, "A 'Good Soldier' Stands Accused of Assault," *National Law Journal* 26 June 1995, p. A12.

21. Gillian Mezey and Michael King, "The Effects of Sexual Assault on Men: A Survey of 22 Victims," *Psychological Medicine* 19 (1989), p. 208.

22. Joseph Harry, "Conceptualizing Anti-Gay Violence," in Gregory Herek and Kevin Berrill, eds. *Hate Crimes: Confronting Violence Against Lesbians and Gay Men* (Newbury Park, CA: Sage Publications, 1992), p. 115.

23. Joe Armstrong, "Exploding the Myths About Male Rape," *The Irish Times* 14 October 1996, sec. Well and Good, p. 6.

24. "In Korea, Male to Female Transsexuals Cannot Be Raped . . . Or So Government Says," Seoul, South Korea: Reuters Newswire, 15 June 1996.

25. Ivor Jones, "Cultural and Historical Aspects of Male Sexual Assault," in Gillian Mezey and Michael King, eds., *Male Victims of Sexual Assault* (Oxford: Oxford University Press, 1992), p. 104.

26. Ramon A. Gutierrez, "Must We Deracinate Indians to Find Gay Roots?" *OUT/LOOK* Winter 1989, p. 62.

27. Richard C. Trexler, *Sex and Conquest: Gendered Violence, Political Order, and the European Conquest of the Americas* (Ithaca, NY: Cornell University Press, 1995), p. 6.

28. Ibid., p. 7.

29. Scott Lively, "Gays Weren't Nazi 'Victims,'" *Capital Times* 18 April 1996, p. 15A.

Impact of Sexual Abuse on Children   *1991*

A Review and Synthesis of Recent Empirical Studies

Kathleen A. Kendall-Tackett, Linda Meyer Williams, and David Finkelhor

ABSTRACT

A review of 45 studies clearly demonstrated that sexually abused children had more symptoms than nonabused children, with abuse accounting for 15–45% of the variance. Fears, posttraumatic stress disorder, behavior problems, sexualized behaviors, and poor self-esteem occurred most frequently among a long list of symptoms noted, but no one symptom characterized a majority of sexually abused children. Some symptoms were specific to certain ages, and approximately one third of victims had no symptoms. Penetration, the duration and frequency of the abuse, force, the relationship of the perpetrator to the child, and maternal support affected the degree of symptomatology. About two thirds of the victimized children showed recovery during the first 12–18 months. The findings suggest the absence of any specific syndrome in children who have been sexually abused and no single traumatizing process.

Until recently, the literature on the impact of child sexual abuse consisted disproportionately of retrospective studies of adults. For example, the conclusions of a widely cited review (Browne & Finkelhor, 1986) were based on only 4 studies of children, compared with 23 studies of adults. Not surprisingly, most reviews combined studies of both groups, because research focused on children was rare.

Since 1985, however, there has been an explosion in the number of studies that have concentrated specifically on sexually abused children. Some studies have even focused on specific types of child victims, such as preschoolers, boys, or victims of ritualistic abuse. The studies of child victims have been distinct in several important ways from the research on adults. First, researchers studying children have often used different methodologies, many times relying on parents' or

Kathleen A. Kendall-Tackett, Linda Meyer Williams, and David Finkelhor, Family Research Laboratory, University of New Hampshire.

This article is based on a paper presented at the meetings of the American Professional Society on the Abuse of Children, January 1991, San Diego, California. The present research was carried out with funds provided by National Institute of Mental Health Grant T32 MH15161 and National Center for Child Abuse and Neglect Grant 90CA 1406. We thank Elizabeth Royal and Patricia VanWagoner for assistance in preparing the manuscript. We also thank members of the 1991 Family Violence Seminar and the anonymous reviewers for their helpful comments.

clinicians' reports rather than on children's self-reports. In addition, they have often evaluated specifically child-oriented symptoms, such as regressive behavior. These methodologies and the concentration on child-oriented symptoms make this research more relevant to intervention and treatment with children than the research on the effects of sexual abuse on adults, from which the implications for the treatment of children were difficult to extrapolate.

Research on children has allowed for a developmental perspective and included the first efforts at longitudinal studies of sexual abuse victims. This literature also has important relevance to other theory and research concerning how children process trauma, for example, how trauma expresses itself at various developmental stages, its role in the development of later psychopathology, and the mediating effects of important factors such as familial and community support. Therefore, research on the effect of sexual abuse on children is worthy of its own review.

We undertook such a review to (a) bring together literature from a broad spectrum of fields, including medicine, social work, psychology, and sociology; (b) highlight areas where there is agreement and disagreement in findings; (c) draw conclusions that may be useful for clinicians currently working with child victims and researchers studying this problem; and (d) suggest directions for future research and theory.

DOMAIN

In the present review, we included studies of child victims of sexual abuse,[1] in which all subjects were 18 years of age or younger (see Appendix). In all of these studies, quantitative results of at least one of the following types were reported: a comparison of sexually abused children with nonabused children or norms (clinical and/or nonclinical) or the age of victims who manifested some symptom. Certain other studies that did not contain these types of data, yet included other relevant data on intervening variables or longitudinal findings, are not listed in the Appendix but are referenced in the appropriate sections. The majority were published within the past 5 years. Because there has been so much research on this topic in the past few years, we also included some unpublished material (most of the manuscripts are currently under review), located through researchers who specialize in research in this area. Although we undoubtedly missed some articles, we are confident that we were able to locate most of them because of the network of researchers we contacted.

Excluded from the present review were nonquantitative or case studies. We also excluded studies in which all subjects manifested a certain behavior (such as teen prostitution or running away) but only some of them had been sexually abused. (In contrast, in the studies we included in the present review, all subjects had been abused.) Finally, we excluded studies that involved both adult and child victims (e.g., ages 15–45) and combined results from these two groups.

The studies used samples from several different sources, but primarily drew from sexual abuse evaluation or treatment programs. Some investigators recruited from specific subgroups of victims, such as day-care victims. Most investigators combined victims of intra- and extrafamilial abuse. The samples also included a wide variety of ages, covering the entire spectrum from preschool to adolescence. The sample sizes ranged from very small ($N = 8$) to large ($N = 369$), with the majority between 25 and 50 children. Approximately half (55%) the studies included comparison groups, and six had both nonabused clinical and nonabused nonclinical controls. This is a major improvement over studies conducted even 10 years ago. The studies used a variety of sources for assessment, including parent report, chart review, clinician report, and children's self-report.

In reviewing these studies, we first looked at the findings with regard to symptoms and then examined the intervening variables that affected these symptoms. We then paid particular attention to the longitudinal studies undertaken thus far. Finally, we drew conclusions for theory and future research.

---

[1] Note that when we refer to victims, we mean victims who have come to public attention. The findings from the present review cannot be generalized to unreported victims, for whom impact may be substantially different. In a controversial study of unreported victims from The Netherlands, Sandfort (1982, 1984) claimed that certain (primarily adolescent) boys had relationships with adult pedophiles that they described in positive terms and appeared to have no negative effects. Because these boys were nominated for the research by the pedophiles themselves, who were involved in a pedophile advocacy group, it is difficult to know to what group of children such findings could be generalized.

COMPARISON OF ABUSED AND NONABUSED CHILDREN

A wide range of symptoms have been examined in the studies in which sexually abused children have been compared with nonabused clinical or nonclinical children (or norms). Table 1 groups these symptoms together under major headings. As shown in Column 1, by far the most commonly studied symptom was sexualized behavior, often considered the most characteristic symptom of sexual abuse. Sexualized behavior usually included such things as sexualized play with dolls, putting objects into anuses or vaginas, excessive or public masturbation, seductive behavior, requesting sexual stimulation from adults or other children, and age-inappropriate sexual knowledge (Beitchman, Zucker, Hood, daCosta, & Akman, 1991). Other symptoms that appeared in many studies included anxiety, depression, withdrawn behavior, somatic complaints, aggression, and school problems.

Column 2 shows the number of studies in which sexually abused children were more symptomatic than

Table 1 Sexually Abused (SA) Versus Nonsexually Abused (NSA) Children: Nonclinical and Clinical Comparison Groups

	Nonclinical		Clinical			
Symptom	Total no. studies	SA > NSA[a]/ no. studies	No. studies in which SA > NSA[a]	No. studies in which there was no difference	No. studies in which SA < NSA[b]	Total no. studies
Anxiety	14	5/8	1	2	0	3
Fear	6	5/5	1	0	2	3
Posttraumatic stress disorder						
Nightmares	3	1/1	1	—	—	1
General	5	1/1	1	0	0	1
Depression						
Depressed	17	10/11	1	2	2	5
Withdrawn	14	11/11	1	1	3	5
Suicidal	7	0/1	—	—	—	—
Poor self-esteem	11	3/6	—	—	—	—
Somatic complaints	16	9/11	1	3	3	7
Mental illness						
Neurotic	3	2/2	0	2	2	4
Other	12	6/7	0	4	2	6
Aggression						
Aggressive antisocial	15	10/11	0	1	6	7
Cruel	2	2/2	0	1	0	1
Delinquent	7	6/6	0	1	3	4
Sexualized behavior						
Inappropriate sexual behavior	23	8/8	6	2	0	8
Promiscuity	2	—	—	—	—	—
School/learning problems	13	5/6	0	1	2	3
Behavior problems						
Hyperactivity	9	5/7	0	1	4	5
Regression/immaturity	7	2/2	1	0	1	2
Illegal acts	4	—	—	—	—	—
Running away	6	1/1	—	—	—	—
General	5	2/2	—	—	—	—
Self-destructive behavior						
Substance abuse	5	—	—	—	—	—
Self-injurious behavior	4	1/1	—	—	—	—
Composite symptoms						
Internalizing	10	8/8	0	2	1	3
Externalizing	11	7/7	0	1	2	3

Note. The numbers in column 2 do not necessarily add up to the number in column 1 because column 1 includes some studies in which only the percentage of children with symptoms was specified.

[a]SA > NSA = SA children were more symptomatic than NSA children. [b]SA < NSA = SA children were less symptomatic than NSA children.

their nonabused counterparts. The denominator is the number of studies in which this comparison was made. For many symptoms, a difference was found in all of the studies in which such a comparison was made. These symptoms were fear, nightmares, general post-traumatic stress disorder (PTSD),[2] withdrawn behavior, neurotic mental illness, cruelty, delinquency, sexually inappropriate behavior, regressive behavior (including enuresis, encopresis, tantrums, and whining), running away, general behavior problems, self-injurious behavior, internalizing, and externalizing.[3] The symptom with the lowest percentage of studies in which a difference was found (besides suicidal behavior, for which a difference was found in only one study) was poor self-esteem (50%). This may be in part because poor self-esteem is so common and has so many possible causes. It may also be because this symptom was the one most frequently measured by child self-report, a method that may underestimate pathology (see Methodological Issues and Directions for Future Research). Nonetheless, for almost every symptom examined, including self-esteem, in most studies sexually abused children were found to be more symptomatic than their nonabused counterparts.

The comparison between sexually abused children and other clinical, nonabused children (i.e., children in treatment) tells a possibly different story, however (Columns 3–5). For many of the symptoms measured, sexually abused children were actually less symptomatic than these clinical children in the majority of the studies. Sexually abused children showed only two symptoms consistently more often than nonabused clinical children: PTSD (just one study) and sexualized behavior (six of eight studies). Thus, sexually abused children tended to appear less symptomatic than their nonabused clinical counterparts except in regard to sexualized behavior and PTSD. These results must be interpreted very cautiously, especially in the light of two features of the clinical comparison groups with which abused children were often compared. First, most clinical comparison groups of so-called

nonabused children probably actually do contain children whose abuse simply has not been discovered. In this case, the comparison is not a true abused-versus-nonabused comparison. Second, clinical comparison groups generally contain many children who are referred primarily because of their symptomatic behavior. Naturally these children are likely to be more symptomatic than children referred not because of symptoms, but because of something done to them (i.e., abuse). Thus, the lower levels of symptoms in sexually abused children may say more about the clinical comparisons than about the sexually abused children themselves.

For a synthesis of findings such as in Table 1, a comparison of effect sizes would ordinarily be preferable to the so-called simple box score approach we used. Unfortunately, most of the studies we reviewed did not present data in a form amenable to the calculation of effect sizes. We were, however, able to calculate effect sizes (Table 2) for seven symptoms on which enough studies had provided adequate information for a comparison of abused and nonabused nonclinical children (all between-groups comparisons[4]).

Table 2 Average Effect Sizes for Seven Symptoms of Sexual Abuse

| Symptom | No. studies | *Effect sizes* | | |
		Range of η^2	Average η	Average η^2
Aggression	4	.37–.71	.66	.43
Anxiety	3	.01–.28	.39	.15
Depression	6	.06–.68	.59	.35
Externalizing	5	.08–.52	.57	.32
Internalizing	6	.11–.70	.62	.38
Sexualized behavior	5	1.9–.77	.66	.43
Withdrawal	6	.12–.68	.60	.36

[2]In this article, we group posttraumatic stress disorder with symptoms even though we realize that it is a cluster of symptoms comprising a diagnostic category.
[3]Internalizing and externalizing are composite symptoms found on the Child Behavior Checklist (Achenbach & Edelbrock, 1984). Internalizing is withdrawn behavior, depression, fearfulness, inhibition, and overcontrol. Externalizing includes aggression and antisocial and undercontrolled behavior.

[4]The criteria for including a study in this review were as follows: The authors reported an exact *t* value or an *F* value from a univariate analysis of variance; they reported the degrees of freedom, and there was only one degree of freedom in the numerator. Eta allowed us to examine the effects of sexual abuse apart from sample size and therefore provided a standard coefficient by which to compare findings (Rosenthal, 1984). In addition, because eta is comparable to a Pearson *r*, it provided an index of the strength of the relationship between sexual abuse status and manifestation of a symptom. Eta squared indicated how much of the variance was accounted for by the child's sexual abuse status. One needs to be cautious when interpreting results based on a small number of studies and widely ranging effect sizes. Unfortunately, very few investigators have reported results that are amenable to effect size calculations.

The symptoms were anxiety, sexualized behavior, depression, withdrawal, aggression, internalizing, and externalizing.

Table 2 shows that sexual abuse status alone accounted for a very large percentage of the variance for all seven symptoms, with the sexually abused children manifesting significantly more of all these symptoms. The highest effect sizes (etas) were for the acting-out behaviors, such as sexualized behaviors and aggression. Sexual abuse status accounted for 43% of the variance for these two behaviors and 32% of the variance for externalizing. Such a large effect size is less surprising for sexualized behavior than it is for more global symptoms such as aggression and externalizing, which could have a variety of underlying causes.

Sexual abuse status also accounted for a large percentage of the variance (35–38%) for the internalizing behaviors—internalizing, depression, and withdrawal. The smallest percentage of variance accounted for was for anxiety (15%) but even this is a large effect.

Overall, the results of effect size analysis support the conclusion drawn from Table 1 that being sexually abused was strongly related to some symptoms specific to sexual abuse, such as sexualized behavior, as well as a range of more global symptoms such as depression, aggression, and withdrawal. Nonetheless, sexually abused children did not appear to be more symptomatic than were other clinical children, except in the case of PTSD and sexualized behavior.

PERCENTAGES OF VICTIMS WITH SYMPTOMS

Many researchers simply reported whether sexually abused children were more symptomatic than nonabused children. Yet it is also important to know the actual percentage of victims with each symptom. Some symptoms may occur more often in sexually abused than nonabused children but occur so rarely that they are of little concern for the majority of children in treatment. The actual frequency of such symptoms in the population of abused children can be an important guide to clinicians in diagnosis and treatment. Furthermore, this information is helpful for clinicians and researchers who may want to anticipate the consequences of abuse or develop theory about the process of recovery from abuse. In Table 3, we synthesize information about these frequencies.

The range of children with each symptom varied widely from study to study, which is not unusual given the heterogeneity of sources. Therefore, for each symptom we calculated a weighted average across all studies, dividing the total number of children with a symptom by the total number of children in all the studies reporting on that symptom.

Across all studies, the percentage of victims with a particular symptom was mostly between 20% and 30%. It is important to note that, with the exception of PTSD, no symptom was manifested by a majority of victims. However, there have been relatively few studies of PTSD, and half the children included in this calculation were victims of severe ritualistic abuse from Los Angeles-area day-care cases (Kelly, in press-a), thus inflating the percentage. If we exempt these unusually severely abused children, the average percentage of victims with symptoms of PTSD was 32%, near the level of other frequently occurring symptoms such as poor self-esteem (35%), promiscuity (38%), and general behavior problems (37%). Because the Child Behavior Checklist (CBCL; Achenbach & Edelbrock, 1984) was used in a large number of studies, we also calculated the percentage of children in the clinical range (or with "elevated scores") for internalizing and externalizing symptomatology.

Overall, the percentage of victims with the various symptoms may seem low to those with a clinical perspective. Part of the problem with the analysis of these composite percentages was that many of the symptoms did not occur uniformly across all age groups. We therefore reexamined the weighted percentages presented in Table 3, grouped by the age of the child at assessment. Percentages were calculated for preschool-age (approximately 0–6 years), school-age (approximately 7–12 years), adolescent (approximately 13–18 years), and mixed age (e.g., 3–17 years) groups. The ages reported in different studies varied and overlapped a bit from these guidelines but by and large fell within these ranges. From a developmental standpoint, we should emphasize that these were very crude cuts across large developmental periods. Furthermore, they represented age at the time of report, not at the onset or end of molestation. In addition, there was no control for the context in which the abuse occurred or the variables that mediated the effects of that abuse.

The results of this analysis (Table 4) hint at possible developmental patterns. Differentiating the samples on the basis of major age groups appeared to yield more focused and consistent findings than when age groups were mixed.

Table 3 Percentage of Sexually Abused Children With Symptoms

Symptom	% with symptom	Range of %s	No. studies	N
Anxiety	28	14–68	8	688
Fear	33	13–45	5	477
Posttraumatic stress disorder				
Nightmares	31	18–68	5	605
General	53	20–77	4	151
Depression				
Depressed	28	19–52	6	753
Withdrawn	22	4–52	5	660
Suicidal	12	0–45	6	606
Poor self-esteem	35	4–76	5	483
Somatic complaints	14	0–60	6	540
Mental illness				
Neurotic	30	20–38	3	113
Other	6	0–19	3	533
Aggression				
Aggressive/antisocial	21	13–50	7	658
Delinquent	8	8	1	25
Sexualized behavior				
Inappropriate sexual behavior	28	7–90	13	1,353
Promiscuity	38	35–48	2	128
School/learning problems	18	4–32	9	652
Behavior problems				
Hyperactivity	17	4–28	2	133
Regression/immaturity	23	14–44	5	626
Illegal acts	11	8–27	4	570
Running away	15	2–63	6	641
General	37	28–62	2	66
Self-destructive behavior				
Substance abuse	11	2–46	5	786
Self-injurious behavior	15	1–11	3	524
Composite symptoms				
Internalizing	30	4–48	3	295
Externalizing	23	6–38	3	295

For preschoolers, the most common symptoms were anxiety, nightmares, general PTSD, internalizing, externalizing, and inappropriate sexual behavior. For school-age children, the most common symptoms included fear, neurotic and general mental illness, aggression, nightmares, school problems, hyperactivity, and regressive behavior. For adolescents, the most common behaviors were depression; withdrawn, suicidal, or self-injurious behaviors; somatic complaints; illegal acts; running away; and substance abuse. Among the symptoms that appeared prominently for more than one age group were nightmares, depression, withdrawn behavior, neurotic mental illness, aggression, and regressive behavior.

To date, the majority of data on the effects of sexual abuse on children have been collected cross-sectionally, with data obtained only once per child. Nevertheless, from this cross-sectional data it is possible to hypothesize some developmental trajectories of changes in symptomatology. The question remains, however, as to whether these changes in symptomatology occur within a given child at different stages or represent developmental changes in response to sexual abuse at the time of report.

Depression appeared to be a particularly robust symptom across age groups and was also one that appeared frequently in adults molested as children, as two recent reviews have indicated (Beitchman et al., 1992; McGrath, Keita, Strickland, & Russo, 1990). School and learning problems were also fairly prominent in all three age groups, especially school-age children and adolescents. This is a symptom that would not appear in adults but could be parallel to employment difficulties in adults, because both are structured environments to which the person must report every day and both require equivalent types of skills.

Table 4 Percentage of Children With Symptoms by Age Group

Symptom	Preschool	School	Adolescent	Mixed
	% of subjects (No. studies/No. subjects)			
Anxiety	61 (3/149)	23 (2/66)	8 (1/3)	18 (4/470)
Fear	13 (1/30)	45 (1/58)	—	31 (2/389)
Posttraumatic stress disorder				
Nightmares	55 (3/183)	47 (1/17)	0 (1/3)	19 (2/402)
General	77 (1/71)	—	—	32 (3/80)
Depression				
Depressed	33 (3/149)	31 (2/66)	46 (3/129)	18 (2/409)
Withdrawn	10 (1/30)	36 (1/58)	45 (2/126)	15 (3/446)
Suicidal	0 (1/37)	—	41 (3/172)	3 (2/397)
Poor self-esteem	0 (1/25)	6 (1/17)	33 (1/3)	38 (4/438)
Somatic complaints	13 (2/54)	—	34 (1/44)	12 (2/442)
Mental illness				
Neurotic	20 (1/30)	38 (1/58)	24 (1/25)	—
Other	0 (1/37)	19 (1/58)	16 (2/69)	3 (1/369)
Aggression				
Aggressive/antisocial	27 (3/154)	45 (1/58)	—	14 (3/446)
Delinquent	—	—	8 (1/25)	—
Sexualized behavior				
Inappropriate sexual behavior	35 (6/334)	6 (1/17)	0 (1/3)	24 (7/999)
Promiscuity	—	—	38 (2/128)	—
School/learning problems	19 (2/107)	31 (1/58)	23 (2/69)	17 (2/418)
Behavior problems				
Hyperactivity	9 (2/55)	23 (2/75)	0 (1/3)	—
Regression/immaturity	36 (4/159)	39 (2/75)	0 (1/3)	15 (2/389)
Illegal acts	—	—	27 (1/101)	8 (3/469)
Running away	—	—	45 (3/172)	4 (3/469)
General	62 (1/17)	—	—	28 (1/49)
Self-destructive behavior				
Substance abuse	—	—	53 (2/128)	2 (3/658)
Self-injurious behavior	—	—	71 (2/128)	1 (1/369)
Composite symptoms				
Internalizing	48 (1/69)	—	—	24 (2/226)
Externalizing	38 (1/69)	—	—	23 (2/226)

Behavior labeled as antisocial in preschool- and school-age children might be labeled as illegal in adolescents. Similarly, the results of our analysis and a recent review by Beitchman et al. (1991) indicate that sexualized behaviors may be prominent for preschool-age children, submerge during latency (or the school-age period), and reemerge during adolescence as promiscuity, prostitution, or sexual aggression. These same symptoms might manifest themselves as sexual dysfunctions or sex offending in adulthood, although this has yet to be demonstrated empirically.

The results presented in Table 4 suggest that much symptomatology is developmentally specific and that generalizing across large age groups distorts the patterns. Fortunately, this is more a problem of data analysis and presentation of findings than it is of data collection, so future research should be able to address this issue. Developmental theory and suggestions for future research are described in the Discussion section.

PERCENTAGES OF ASYMPTOMATIC VICTIMS

In addition to the percentage of children with specific symptoms, another important statistic is the percentage of children with no symptoms. This figure has important clinical implications for the group of children in whom the impact of abuse may be muted or masked. Unfortunately, few investigators have reported on such asymptomatic children, perhaps out of concern that such figures might be misinterpreted or misused.

Nonetheless, when investigators have made such estimates, they have found a substantial, and perhaps to some surprising, proportion of the victims to be free of the symptoms being measured. For example, Caffaro-Rouget, Lang, and vanSanten (1989) found that 49% were asymptomatic at their assessment during a pediatric examination. Mannarino and Cohen (1986) found that 31% were symptom free, and Tong, Oates, and McDowell (1987) found that 36% were within the normal range on the CBCL. Finally, Conte and Schuerman (1987b) indicated that 21% of their large sample appeared to have had no symptoms at all, even though their assessment included both very specific and broad items such as "fearful of abuse stimuli" and "emotional upset."

There are several possible explanations why so many children appeared to be asymptomatic. The first possibility is that the studies did not include measures of all appropriate symptoms or the researchers were not using sensitive enough instruments. In most individual studies, only a limited range of possible effects were examined. Thus some of the asymptomatic children may have been symptomatic on dimensions that were not being measured.

Another possibility is that asymptomatic children are those who have yet to manifest their symptoms. This could be either because the children are effective at suppressing symptoms or have not yet processed their experiences or because true traumatization occurs at subsequent developmental stages, when the children's victim status comes to have more meaning of consequences for them (Berliner, 1991). We would expect these children to manifest symptoms later on. In one study that supports this interpretation (Gomes-Schwartz, Horowitz, Cardarelli, & Sauzier, 1990), the asymptomatic children were the ones most likely to worsen by the time of the 18-month follow up: 30% of them developed symptoms. To date, no one has replicated this finding, however.

A final explanation is that perhaps asymptomatic children are truly less affected. Research indeed suggests there is a relationship between the seriousness and duration of the abuse and the amount of impact (see Intervening Variables section, below). The asymptomatic children might be those with the least damaging abuse. They may also be the most resilient children, the ones with the most psychological, social, and treatment resources to cope with the abuse.

In fact, all three explanations may be simultaneously correct. Unfortunately, the issue of asymptomatic children has been peripheral until recently. Too few researchers have even mentioned the issue, and fewer still have looked at the correlates of being symptom free. Future studies need to address this issue more fully, not as a sidebar of unusual findings, but as a central topic in its own right.

INTERVENING VARIABLES   *See pg 278*

In many studies (25 of the 46 we reviewed), researchers have tried to account for variations in the children's symptomatology by examining characteristics of the abuse experience. The results for variables with consistent findings are listed in Table 5. Vari-

Table 4 Influence of Intervening Variables

| Variable | No. studies | | Direction of findings |
	With significant difference in impact	Total	
Age of child			
At assessment	7	10	Older children were more symptomatic in five studies.
At onset	1	3	Not clear.
Sex of child	5	8	Patterns of symptoms differed for boys and girls.
Penetration/severity	6	10	Oral, anal, or vaginal penetration was related to increased symptoms.
Frequency	4	6	Higher frequency was related to increased symptoms.
Duration	5	7	Longer duration was related to increased symptoms.
Perpetrator	7	9	Symptoms were increased when perpetrator had close relationship with child.
No. perpetrators	1	3	Not clear.
Lack of maternal support	3	3	Lack of support was related to increased symptoms.
Force	5	6	Use of force was related to increased symptoms.
Time elapsed since last abusive incident	1	3	Not clear.
Child's attitudes and coping style	2	2	Negative outlook and coping style were related to increased symptoms.

ables with contradictory or confusing results are discussed in this section.

Age at the time of assessment has been the most commonly considered intervening variable. The majority of studies indicated that children who were older at the time of assessment appeared to be more symptomatic than those who were younger. However, most of these studies did not control for the effect of duration (those who were older may have had longer molestations), identity of the perpetrator (intrafamilial perpetrators may have been able to continue the abuse for a longer time), or severity of the molestation (older victims may have experienced more severe sexual acts). In three studies, no significant differences related to age at time of assessment were found (Einbender & Friedrich, 1989; Friedrich, Urquiza, & Beilke, 1986; Kolko, Moser, & Weldy, 1988); in one study, younger children were more symptomatic (Wolfe, Gentile, & Wolfe, 1989); and in one study there was a curvilinear relationship between age and symptomatology, with the middle age range being more symptomatic (Gomes-Schwartz, Horowitz, & Sauzier, 1985). Although the data appear to indicate roughly that older children are more negatively affected, these results should be interpreted with cau-

tion because of the lack of control over other relevant variables.

Age of onset is another possible intervening variable. However, age of onset was related to symptoms in only one study, which showed that those with early age of onset were more likely to manifest symptoms of pathology (Zivney, Nash, & Hulsey, 1988). In two other studies no difference was found in level of pathology for early versus late age of onset. By and large, it appears that age of onset must be fit into a total conceptual model of molestation. Research is insufficient to permit any conclusions about whether early versus late age of onset is more likely to lead to greater symptomatology. Age of onset might be related more to other characteristics of the abuse (such as identity of the perpetrator) than to overall number and severity of symptoms. Although the relationship of age of onset to symptomatology in children is not clear at this time, in two recent studies an early age of onset was found to be related to amnesia among adult survivors (Briere & Conte, 1989) and late presentation for treatment (Kendall-Tackett, 1991).

With regard to sex of the subject, consistent differences in the reaction of boys and girls to molestation have been found in only a few studies. The scarcity of these findings is in sharp contrast to the popular belief that boys are likely to manifest externalizing symptoms and girls are more likely to exhibit internalizing symptoms. The absence of consistent gender differences is all the more interesting because girls are more likely to suffer intrafamilial abuse, which has been associated with more severe effects (Finkelhor, Hotaling, Lewis, & Smith, 1990). The lack of more systematic attention to gender differences may be due in part to the small number of male victims in most studies and the possibility that, because of bias in the identification of male victims, only the most symptomatic boys end up in clinical samples. It may also be due to the fact that comparison of boys and girls has produced too few interesting differences to motivate researchers to place it in center focus. Nevertheless, researchers should address the issue of sex of the victims in future reports.

Penetration (oral, anal, or vaginal) did influence the impact of sexual abuse in the majority of studies, but most researchers differed in their definitions of severity of abuse. To further add to the confusion, some of the investigators added together all the sexual acts that a victim experienced, and therefore their indices of severity included the severity as well as the number of sexual acts. Even with all these variations, it appeared that molestations that contained some form of penetration were more likely to produce symptoms than molestations that did not.

The identity of the perpetrator is another factor that has been related to the impact of abuse. The weight of the evidence indicated that a perpetrator who was close to the victim caused more serious effects than one who was less close. To date there does not appear to be a uniform coding scheme for closeness, however. For example, fathers and stepfathers are often coded in the same category. Researchers should try to determine a measure of emotional closeness or degree of caretaking responsibility rather than relying on the kinship label of the perpetrator-victim relationship.

On a similar note, the impact of the number of perpetrators is not clear. The number of perpetrators was positively correlated with number of symptoms in one study, negatively correlated with number of symptoms in another, and not correlated with symptoms in another. Future research should address this issue.

Time elapsed since the last abusive incident and assessment is a variable with intuitive appeal, but it has been examined in very few studies. Only 55% of the articles in the present review even mentioned time elapsed, and it varied from a few days to several years. In only three studies was the possible relationship between time elapsed and the impact of abuse examined. In one study (Friedrich et al., 1986), children became less symptomatic over time, whereas in two other studies (McLeer, Deblinger, Atkins, Foa, & Ralphe, 1988; Wolfe et al., 1989) it made no difference. It appears to be too early to decide whether time elapsed is correlated with the number of symptoms. Therefore, we should find out more about this variable before we assume that it makes no difference.

In summary, the findings of the various studies reviewed indicated that molestations that included a close perpetrator; a high frequency of sexual contact; a long duration; the use of force; and sexual acts that included oral, anal, or vaginal penetration lead to a greater number of symptoms for victims. Similarly, as all the studies that included these variables indicated, the lack of maternal support at the time of disclosure and a victim's negative outlook or coping style also led to increased symptoms. The influence of age at the time of assessment, age at onset, number of perpetrators, and time elapsed between the end of abuse and assessment is still somewhat unclear at the present time and should be examined in future studies on the impact of intervening variables.

It should be kept in mind when interpreting these findings that certain intervening variables are highly correlated. For example, intrafamilial abuse normally occurs over a longer time period and involves more serious sexual activity (i.e., penetration). These natural confounds make it difficult to fully analyze the independent effects of intervening variables. Very few studies have included more than one or two of these variables, and almost no one has statistically controlled for their effects.

LONGITUDINAL STUDIES

Perhaps the most encouraging development in the field has been the appearance of longitudinal studies (Bentovim, vanElberg, & Boston, 1988; Conte, 1991; Everson, Hunter, & Runyan, 1991; Friedrich & Reams, 1987; Gomes-Schwartz et al., 1990; Goodman et al., in press; Hewitt & Friedrich, 1991; Mannarino, Cohen, Smith, & Moore-Motily, 1991; Runyan, Everson, Edelson, Hunter, & Coulter, 1988; Valliere,

Bybee, & Mowbray, 1988; Waterman, in press). Most of these studies have followed children for approximately 12–18 months, with a few ranging from 2 to 5 years (Bentovim et al., 1988; Waterman, in press). These studies allow a perspective on two important issues: (a) What is the course of symptomatology over time, and (b) what contributes to recovery?

The picture provided by the longitudinal studies is tentative, but some generalizations are possible. Overall, symptoms seemed to abate with time. The pattern of recovery was different for different symptoms, and some children actually appeared to worsen.

Abatement of Symptoms

Abatement of symptoms has been demonstrated in at least seven longitudinal studies covering all age groups (Bentovim et al., 1988; Conte, 1991; Gomes-Schwartz et al., 1990; Goodman et al., in press; Hewitt & Friedrich, 1991; Mannarino et al., 1991; Runyan et al., 1988). For example, Gomes-Schwartz et al. (1990) noted substantial diminution of emotional distress in 55% of the victims (mixed age group) over 18 months. In Bentovim et al.'s (1988) study, social workers found improvement in the level of symptoms in 61% of the children. Hewitt and Friedrich (1991) noted that 65% of preschool-age children improved over a period of 1 year. About two thirds of even the ritualistically abused preschoolers, who were initially in the clinical range on the CBCL (Waterman, in press), had moved back into the normal range on follow-up.

Nonetheless, there was a sizable group—anywhere from 10% to 24%—of children who appeared to get worse (Bentovim et al., 1988 [10%]; Gomes-Schwartz et al., 1990 [24%]; Hewitt & Friedrich, 1991 [18%]; Runyan et al., 1988 [14%]). Some of these were children who had none of the symptoms measured at the time of initial assessment (Gomes-Schwartz et al., 1990).

Some investigators also noted a pattern in which symptoms tended to abate. Gomes-Schwartz et al. (1990) found that signs of anxiety (e.g., sleep problems or fear of the offender) were most likely to disappear, whereas signs of aggressiveness (e.g., fighting with siblings) tended to persist or worsen. This was consistent with Mannarino et al.'s (1991) finding of a significant reduction over time in the internalizing but not the externalizing scales of the CBCL. Conversely, some symptoms may increase over time. For example,

one symptom that may increase over time, at least for the under-12 group, is sexual preoccupations (Friedrich & Reams, 1987; Gomes-Schwartz et al., 1990). It is not entirely clear what this symptom abatement implies. Although some symptoms may be more transient than others, it does not necessarily mean that underlying trauma is resolved, but perhaps only that overt manifestations are more easily masked. Moreover, these changes may have less to do with abatement of trauma than developmental changes in symptomatology, with children at each age manifesting different types of symptoms.

There is a long list of correlates of improvement over time, but few of these findings have been demonstrated in more than one study. Age was not found to be strongly correlated with recovery in any study, although Goodman et al. (in press) found that 6–11-year-olds recovered most quickly in the very short term (3 months after the trial). Neither gender (Gomes-Schwartz et al., 1990; Goodman et al., in press), nor race and socioeconomic status (Gomes-Schwartz et al., 1990) have been factors in recovery. Children who were the most disturbed at the time of first assessment were found to make the most recovery (Gomes-Schwartz et al., 1990), but this may have been an artifact.

Family and Treatment Variables

A key variable in recovery was family support, demonstrated by several studies. Children who had maternal support recovered more quickly (Everson et al., 1991; Goodman et al., in press). Maternal support was demonstrated through believing the child and acting in a protective way toward the child. Waterman (in press) found that the least symptomatic children (5 years after disclosure) were those whose mothers were most supportive and whose families had less strain, enmeshment, and expressions of anger.

Interestingly, the effect of long-term therapy has not been extensively examined. In one study (Gomes-Schwartz et al., 1990), all clients received crisis intervention through the research project. The clients who showed the greatest amount of recovery (15% of subjects) were those who received therapy in the specialized program run by the research team. Those who received therapy in the community at large (20% of subjects) did not appear to recover as well. The authors did not elaborate on the type of long-term therapy that clients received either through the researchers' program or in the community at large, however. In contrast, Goodman et al. (in press) found psychological counseling unrelated to improvement. But again, clients sought therapy in the outside community and there was no control for the type or quality of the therapy they received.

Court Involvement

The impact of court involvement and testimony was also a focus of several of the longitudinal studies because of the intense public policy debate surrounding this issue. In one study (Goodman et al., in press), children involved in court proceedings were slower to recover over both a 7- and an 11-month period than children not involved in court. Recovery was particularly impeded among children who had to testify on multiple occasions, who were afraid of their perpetrators, and who testified in cases in which there was no other corroborating evidence. Whitcomb et al.'s (1991) findings echoed Goodman et al.'s. Whitcomb et al. concluded that there were adverse effects for older children who had to undergo numerous, lengthy, or harshly contested courtroom testimony. The outcome of the trial (conviction or acquittal of the perpetrator), or the number of times that the child was interviewed did not relate to symptomatology (Goodman et al., in press).

Runyan et al. (1988) had more mixed findings with regard to the impact of court involvement. The children who had slower recovery in this study were those who were involved in a criminal case that was still not resolved 5 months after the initial evaluation. However, children whose cases had terminated more quickly with a conviction or plea bargain recovered just as quickly as children who had no court involvement at all. In fact, children who testified in juvenile court proceedings recovered more quickly. However, in a follow-up of adolescents from the same study, Everson et al. (1991) found that having to testify on multiple occasions caused negative effects, concurring with the findings of Goodman et al. (in press).

Although the longitudinal studies showed the risks involved in testimony, at least one cross-sectional study (Williams, 1991) confirmed that testimony in protected court settings can mitigate trauma. In this study of victims abused in day care, children who testified via closed-circuit television or videotaped testi-

mony or in closed courtrooms suffered fewer symptoms of maladjustment than did children who testified in open court.

Overall, this small number of studies suggests that criminal court involvement posed risks to children's recovery, at least in the short run. But the risks were specifically associated with certain aspects of court involvement that can be modified or avoided. For example, negative impact can be lessened by resolving cases quickly, by preventing a child from having to testify on multiple occasions, and by not requiring a frightened child to face a defendant. Thus, although the research urges caution, it cannot be interpreted as a categorical argument against the prosecution of sexual abuse.

Revictimization

Follow-up studies lend an important perspective to the question of whether abuse victims are reabused in the year or two after disclosure. Most of the follow-up studies we reviewed showed the rate of reabuse to be between 6% and 19% (Bentovim et al., 1988 [16%]; Daro, 1988 [19%]; Gomes-Schwartz et al., 1990 [6%]), with follow-up ranging from 18 months to 5 years. Daro (1988) pointed out that the reabuse rate for sexually abused children in her study was still substantially lower than the reabuse rate for victims of neglect or emotional abuse.

Summary

In summary, in the first year or year and a half after disclosure, one half to two thirds of all children became less symptomatic, whereas 10–24% become more so. Six to nineteen percent experienced additional sexual abuse. Fears and somatic symptoms abated the most quickly; aggressiveness and sexual preoccupations were the most likely to remain or increase. Children's recovery was clearly assisted by a supportive family environment, and certain kinds of court experiences delayed recovery.

DISCUSSION

The present review confirms the general impression that the impact of sexual abuse is serious and can manifest itself in a wide variety of symptomatic and pathological behaviors. There is virtually no general domain of symptomatology that has not been associated with a history of sexual abuse. Age and a variety of abuse-related factors can affect both the nature and the severity of symptoms. However, some sexually abused children may also appear to have no apparent symptoms. Indeed, approximately one third of sexually abused children in the studies we reviewed fell into this category. These findings have a number of important implications for theory development.

Core-Symptom Theories

The first and perhaps most important implication is the apparent lack of evidence for a conspicuous syndrome in children who have been sexually abused. The evidence against such a syndrome includes the variety of symptoms children manifest and the absence of one particular symptom in a large majority of children. Despite the lack of a single symptom that occurs in the majority of victims, both sexualized behavior and symptoms of PTSD occurred with relatively high frequency. These also appeared to be the only two symptoms more common in sexually abused children than in other clinical groups. Even though they do not occur in all victims, some theorists have forwarded PTSD and sexualized behaviors as the core manifestations of sexual abuse trauma (Corwin, 1989; Jampole & Weber, 1987; Wolfe et al., 1989), so the evidence pertaining to these two symptoms is worth reviewing more carefully.

The frequency of sexualized behavior in sexually abused children (including frequent and overt self-stimulation; inappropriate sexual overtures toward other children and adults; and compulsive talk, play, and fantasy with sexual content) is somewhat difficult to determine. Although it is the most regularly studied symptom, its occurrence varies enormously. Across six studies of preschoolers (the children most likely to manifest such symptoms) an average of 35% exhibited sexualized behavior. Friedrich et al. (1992), using an instrument specially designed to measure such behaviors, detected a somewhat higher percentage. But across all sexually abused children it may be only half of all victims. The lowest estimate (7%) was based on a very large study, including many well-functioning and older children (Conte & Schuerman, 1987b). Besides sample and methodological differences, other variations may well arise because the concept itself can be vague (sometimes it is called inappropriate sexual behavior, and other times it is called sexual acting

out). Furthermore, some forms of sexualization may be quite minor and transitory (e.g., playing with anatomical dolls), whereas others may be deeply etched, even affecting a child's physiology. Putnam (1990; F. Putnam, personal communication, January 10, 1991) detected elevated hormone levels among some sexually abused girls and evidence that onset of puberty was advanced for these girls by as much as 1 year. Although such physiological changes could be the effect of sexualization or, alternatively, one of its sources, it suggests how profound and pervasive the impact of sexual abuse can be.

Although sexualization is relatively specific to sexual abuse (more so than symptoms such as depression), nonsexually abused children may also be sexualized. For example Deblinger, McLeer, Atkins, Ralphe, and Foa (1989) found that 17% of physically (but not sexually) abused children exhibited sexually inappropriate behavior. Although sexualized behavior may be the most characteristic symptom of sexual abuse, and the one that best discriminates between abused and nonabused children, as many as half of victims may not be overtly sexualized, and this symptom does not occur only in sexually abused children. From a clinical point of view, this symptom may indicate sexual abuse but is not completely diagnostic because children can apparently appear to be sexualized for other reasons.

The evidence for PTSD as a central effect of sexual abuse is also its relative frequency (particularly in preschool- and school-age victims) and its higher incidence in sexual abuse victims than in other clinical groups. Although PTSD is relatively common in child sexual abuse victims, it is not a universal reaction. In the two most thorough clinical evaluations of PTSD (according to criteria in the revised third edition of the *Diagnostic and Statistical Manual of Mental Disorders*; American Psychiatric Association, 1987), 48% (McLeer et al., 1988) and 21% (Deblinger et al., 1989) of sexually abused children could be diagnosed as having PTSD. Although many other children have related symptoms, such as fears, nightmares, somatic complaints, autonomic arousal, and guilt feelings, it is not clear whether this is evidence for PTSD dynamics or other symptoms. More importantly, PTSD is not specific to sexual abuse in that many nonsexually abused children suffer from PTSD.

PTSD has served as a focal point for the analysis of sexual abuse trauma in part because it is a well-developed, generalized theory of traumatic processes. Finkelhor (1987), however, has raised some questions about how well the model of PTSD accounts for sexual abuse trauma. Theorists describe PTSD as resulting from experiences that are overwhelming, sudden, and dangerous (Figley, 1986; Pynoos & Eth, 1985). Much sexual abuse, however, lacks these components, especially abuse that occurs through manipulation of the child's affections and misrepresentation of social standards. Thus, although many children may suffer symptoms that are explained by the PTSD model, the theory and the empirical findings do not support PTSD symptomatology as universal to sexual abuse or as the most characteristic pattern.

There is at least one other core-symptom theory about the effect of sexual abuse, one that argues that the central damage is to children's self-image (Bagley & Young, 1989; Putnam, 1990). According to this view, it is the damaged self-image, not the sexual abuse per se, that leads to other difficulties. If this theory were true, disturbed self-esteem should be one of the most consistent, pervasive, and long-lasting effects of sexual abuse. Unfortunately, although many victims do have low self-esteem, researchers (e.g., Mannarino et al., 1991) have had considerable difficulty demonstrating this phenomenon. It is not certain whether poor self-esteem, which has been assessed primarily through self-reports, has been effectively measured. But the evidence to date does little to support the theory that self-esteem is the core element of sexual abuse traumatization.

Multifaceted Models of Traumatization

Overall, the absence of one dominant and consistent set of symptoms argues against these core-domain theories. Rather, these data suggest that the impact of sexual abuse is more complicated because it produces multifaceted effects. Several conceptual models are consistent with such a pattern. Finkelhor and Browne's (1985) model suggests that sexual abuse traumatizes children through four distinctive types of mechanisms, which account for the variety of outcomes. The four mechanisms have been termed (a) traumatic sexualization, (b) betrayal, (c) stigmatization, and (d) powerlessness. Traumatic sexualization includes a variety of processes such as the inappropriate conditioning of the child's sexual responsiveness

and the socialization of the child into faulty beliefs and assumptions about sexual behavior. Betrayal includes the shattering of the child's confidence that trusted persons are interested in and capable of protecting him or her from harm. Stigmatization covers all the mechanisms that undermine the child's positive self-image: the shame that is instilled, the ostracism the child suffers, and the negative stereotypes that are acquired from the culture and immediate environment. Finally, powerlessness comprises PTSD-type mechanisms (intense fear of death or injury from an uncontrollable event) as well as the repeated frustration of not being able to stop or escape from the noxious experience or elicit help from others. These mechanisms are present to varying degrees and in different forms in different abuse scenarios.

In addition, Finkelhor and Browne (1985) propose that certain symptoms are more closely related to certain dynamics. The sexualization symptoms have an obvious connection to the traumatic sexualization processes, self-esteem is connected to stigmatization, and fears and PTSD are connected to powerlessness. Little research has been carried out to confirm the model in part because of its complexity, the variety of different mechanisms posited, and the difficulty of clearly delineating and measuring them.

Other theorists have also adopted a multiple-dynamics approach to account for the seeming variety of sexual abuse symptoms. Briere (1992) has developed such a model whose dynamics include (a) negative self-evaluation, (b) chronic perception of danger or injustice, (c) powerlessness and preoccupation with control, (d) dissociative control over awareness, (e) impaired self-reference, and (f) reduction of painful internal states.

A different model posits sexual abuse as simply a generalized stressor. Although this model has not been specifically developed, it is another way to understand the impact of sexual abuse. In this model, the child is likely to develop problems in whatever area he or she may have had a prior vulnerability. This model predicts a high degree of similarity between the effects of sexual abuse and the effects of other childhood stressors such as parental divorce. There is some evidence to support this view, particularly our finding in the present review of similarity on some symptoms between sexually abused children and other clinical groups. On the other hand, sexually abused children do tend to exhibit some characteristics (e.g. sexualized behaviors) that are much more common among sexually abused children than they are among other clinical groups. These types of effects argue against sexual abuse as merely a generalized stressor.

A third model posits family dysfunction or a general maltreating environment, not the sexually abusive activities per se, as the root of the trauma in most sexually abused children (Clausen & Crittenden, 1991). This model is supported by apparent similarities in the range and types of problems manifested by all abused children. However, certain evidence from the studies included in the present review argues against such a conceptualization. First, the studies showed that nonabused siblings (i.e., children raised in the same dysfunctional families) displayed fewer symptoms than did their abused siblings (Lipovsky, Saunders, & Murphy, 1989). In addition, the review of the 25 studies in which the influence of intervening variables was examined (Table 5) consistently showed strong relationships between specific characteristics of the sexual abuse and the symptomatology in the children (e.g., Newberger, Gremy, & Waternaux, 1990). All of this argues for traumatic processes inherent in the sexual abuse itself that are independent from a generalized family dysfunction or generalized maltreating environment.

This is not to say that prior vulnerabilities, a maltreating environment, and family dysfunction do not contribute to traumatization as well. Research such as Conte and Schuerman's (1987a, 1987b) demonstrates that both abuse-related factors and family dysfunction contribute to children's trauma. And Conte and Schuerman found that over time, the abuse-related factors were less influential than the continuing family processes, such as the amount of family support for the child. This suggests a grand model of sexual abuse trauma that includes effects that are both more and less specific to sexual abuse and that arise from the abusive acts in particular, which also interact with prior vulnerabilities of the child, the health or toxicity of the family environment, and the social response to the discovery of abuse.

Summary

The research to date points to an array of traumatizing factors in sexual abuse, with sexualization and PTSD as frequent, but not universal, processes. The traumatic impact of the abusive acts themselves (e.g.,

their frequency and severity) has been established, as well as the likely contribution of other familial and environmental conditions. The role of disturbance to self-esteem and of a child's prior dispositions or vulnerabilities has not been as well substantiated.

This theoretical discussion has implications for clinicians as well as researchers. The range of symptoms, the lack of a single predominant symptom pattern, and the absence of symptoms in so many victims clearly suggest that diagnosis is complex. Because the effects of abuse can manifest themselves in too many ways, symptoms cannot be easily used, without other evidence, to confirm the presence of sexual abuse. Yet the absence of symptoms certainly cannot be used to rule out sexual abuse. There are too many sexually abused children who are apparently asymptomatic. This finding is especially important for those conducting forensic evaluations.

It may be possible, as Corwin (1989) has argued, to find a combination of symptoms that is extremely diagnostic of sexual abuse, especially in certain subgroups of victims (e.g., preschool children with certain kinds of sexualized behavior and post-traumatic play), and research toward such a screening device may be warranted. But the evidence suggests that such a device would identify only a small percentage of victims and that one could conclude nothing at all from the absence of such symptom patterns.

Although conclusions such as these are useful, we also think this discussion highlights a glaring inadequacy in the literature: a nearly universal absence of theoretical underpinnings in the studies being conducted on this subject to date. Researchers evince a great deal of concern about the effects of sexual abuse but disappointingly little concern about why the effects occur. Few studies are undertaken to establish or confirm any theory or explanation about what causes children to be symptomatic. Rather, most researchers simply document and count the existence of symptoms and some of their obvious correlates. This accounts for one of the main reasons that, in spite of numerous studies since Browne and Finkelhor's (1986) review, there have been few theoretical advances.

Future studies need to turn to the development and confirmation of theory. Those who believe that different mechanisms result in different symptoms need to begin to search for such mechanisms. For example, if dissociation is theorized as an acquired strategy for escaping from unpleasant emotions, then researchers need to document the presence of the cognitive, affective, and physiological underpinnings to this mechanism and relate it to the trauma itself. By contrast, those who see sexual abuse as a generalized stressor need to conduct studies that relate the effects of sexual abuse to preexisting vulnerabilities in coping. The dialogue about variables that mediate the effects of abuse needs to be expanded and ideas forwarded about how to study and test their existence. This process of improving research might be assisted when the sexual abuse researchers join forces with those who study related symptomatology in nonabused children. This has already happened in the work generated by the importation of PTSD theory into the field, and it is only by further developing this cross-fertilization that advances can continue.

METHODOLOGICAL ISSUES AND DIRECTIONS FOR FUTURE RESEARCH

Although the studies we reviewed signal an enormous improvement in methodology, they highlight many major areas where current designs could be improved or refined. Some more specific suggestions for improvement are offered in this section.

Improvement in Measures of Impact

The literature on effects has relied extensively on parent-completed checklists of children's symptomatology, particularly the CBCL. However, two sets of findings have raised concern about the validity of these measures. One shows that mothers' judgments about their children's symptoms are highly related to their own level of distress and willingness to believe their children (Everson, Hunter, Runyan, Edelsohn, & Coulter, 1989; Newberger et al., 1990). A second shows a poor association between parents' and children's own reports (Cohen & Mannarino, 1988; Kelly & Ben-Meir, in press).

It does seem plausible that parents might be biased reporters, especially in the context of a family problem like sexual abuse where parents can experience strong feelings of guilt or ambivalence about a child's disclosure. But other findings suggest that parent reports are nonetheless relatively valid and, in the context of currently used instruments, probably better than their children's reports. For example, although depressed mothers reported more child symptoms than nonde-

pressed mothers on the CBCL, the assessments still differentiated disturbed and nondisturbed children when depression was statistically controlled (Friedlander, Weiss, & Taylor, 1986). Moreover, mothers' ratings tended to be more similar to and correlated better with therapists' and teachers' ratings than with those of their children (Shapiro, Leifer, Martone, & Kassem, 1990; Tong et al., 1987). It appears from several studies (Cohen & Mannarino 1988; Shapiro et al., 1990) that children's self-reports minimize problems like depression or low self-esteem that are noted by parents and therapists. Why this is so is not clear.

One clear implication from this is that researchers should not rely on children's self-reports alone. Ideally, assessments should be obtained from multiple sources, as Waterman, Kelly, McCord, and Oliveri (in press) recently did. In addition, research needs to be undertaken to improve the validity of parent reports and especially, if possible, children's self-assessments.

A second concern, raised in part by the issue of seemingly asymptomatic children, is whether the instruments currently being used are sensitive enough to measure consistently and accurately the trauma of sexual abuse. Several groups of researchers, recognizing particularly the limitations of the CBCL, have branched out in attempts to develop such sensitive measures. Friedrich et al. (1992) have greatly expanded CBCL symptom items in the domain of sexuality. Lanktree and Briere (1991, 1992) have adapted the Trauma Symptom Checklist, highly successful in differentiating sexually abused adults, for use with children. Wolfe et al. (1989) have developed scales to measure more sensitively PTSD-type symptomatology. Such efforts need to be continued and elaborated.

Greater Differentiation by Age and Gender

Many researchers have studied subjects from very broad age ranges (e.g., 3–18 years) and grouped them together to discuss symptoms. Similarly, they have grouped boys and girls together. As shown in Table 4, this grouping together of all ages can mask particular developmental patterns of the occurrence of some symptoms. At a minimum, future researchers should divide children into preschool, school, and adolescent age ranges when reporting the percentages of victims with symptoms. It would be better to provide even more detail on how age at assessment affects the manifestation of symptoms, by looking at smaller age ranges and tying this information into theory about children's social, emotional, and cognitive development during these difficult developmental periods. A parallel effort is needed with regard to gender.

Expanded Analysis of Intervening Variables

The present review confirms that abuse-related variables are associated with outcome and thus should be regularly included in analyses. However, many other factors probably are influential as well, and more emphasis should be placed on understanding their role. These factors include children's intelligence, coping skills, prior adjustment, and cognitive interpretation of the abuse. It also includes children's family and social environment, as well as the actions taken by professionals in response to their disclosures. Another factor that needs to be regularly taken into account is time elapsed since the end of the abuse. In some samples, several years might have elapsed between the end of the abuse and the assessment of the child, and during this time symptoms may have abated.

Longitudinal Research and Developmental Theory

A developmental perspective is one approach that may encourage more theory-driven research. Researchers using a developmental approach may also respond to some of the methodological issues raised here. Current research has tended to focus on assessments of trauma at a specific age or point in time (a snapshot approach), but it would also be helpful to know more about the course of symptomatology and recovery over time. For example, the symptomatology of a 15-year-old molested at age 4 may be different from that of a 15-year-old molested at age 14. Furthermore, symptoms may tend to recur at different developmental stages and asymptomatic children may later become symptomatic. Studies in which data are collected at more than one time point will encourage this developmental approach for studying sexual abuse and may answer many of our questions (see Baltes, 1987; Starr, MacLean, & Keating, 1991). Even in the absence of funding, any research on outcomes should at least pave the way for possible later follow-up by gaining permission to recontact subjects and by recording data that will facilitate such research in the future.

In addition in studying abuse at multiple time points, developmental research means incorporating the multiple dimensions of children's development. Changes occur in children's behaviors, thoughts, and emotions at every developmental stage. Research on the effects of sexual abuse on children tends to focus predominantly on behavioral and emotional symptoms while ignoring the effects of sexual abuse on cognitive and social development.

A number of research questions can be generated by examining sexual abuse within the multiple dimensions of children's development. For example, cognitive development could influence children's interpretations of sexual abuse and the symptoms they subsequently manifest. Specifically, as children mature, their thinking becomes less egocentric. This issue alone generates several possible research questions. For example, are young children more likely to see themselves as responsible for the abuse ("It happened because I was bad") than are less egocentric older children? Furthermore, are children who see themselves as responsible for the abuse more likely to engage in self-abusive or destructive behavior? How do internal attributions affect children's reactions to prosecution of the perpetrator? Are these attributions more likely to increase the children's sense of guilt when the perpetrator is punished?

Along these same lines, children's cognitive development can influence their emotional and social development and their interpretation of the perpetrators' actions. As thinking becomes decentered, children recognize that people can have both positive and negative traits and that they themselves can have both positive and negative feelings toward others. How does the gradual attainment of decentered thinking affect children's interpretations of the perpetrators' actions, their own behaviors, and the abuse itself? This is especially important to understand when the perpetrator is someone whom the child loves and trusts. Are children who can see conflicting traits in others more likely to report abuse because they see it as only one part of their relationship with the perpetrator ("I love him but I want the abuse to stop")?

These are but a few of the types of research questions that can be generated from examining abuse from a developmental and multidimensional perspective. Future researchers could make specific predictions based on developmental theory and clinical research on related topics (e.g., children's reactions to other types of childhood traumas). This type of framework would also allow researchers to incorporate information about intervening variables such as the timing and duration of the abuse and the identity of the perpetrator.

In summary, studies conducted with a developmental and multidimensional framework could readily incorporate the many intervening variables that modify the effects of abuse. In addition, such a framework offers a richer description of why children and adults manifest certain symptoms at each developmental stage and how people cope with psychic trauma. Developmental psychologists and child clinicians could collaborate to develop models of how children at each developmental stage might be affected by their abuse experience. Researchers studying child sexual abuse have looked in isolation at many of the factors related to the impact of abuse. Now it is time for us to combine them into more realistic models. Research of this type would provide helpful theoretical information about the mechanism and processing of psychological trauma in general. It would also provide guidelines on where clinicians can effectively intervene to aid children in their healing process.

REFERENCES

ACHENBACH, T. M., & EDELBROCK. C. S. (1984). *Child behavior checklist*. Burlington VT: University of Vermont.

ADAMS-TUCKER, C. (1982). Proximate effects of sexual abuse in childhood: A report on 28 children. *American Journal of Psychiatry, 139*, 1252–1256.

AMERICAN PSYCHIATRIC ASSOCIATION. (1987). *Diagnostic and statistical manual of mental disorders* (3rd ed. rev.) Washington, DC: Author.

BAGLEY, C., & YOUNG, L. (1989). Depression, self-esteem, and suicidal behavior as sequels of sexual abuse in childhood: Research and therapy. In M. Rothery & G. Cameron (Eds.), *Child maltreatment: Expanding our concept of healing* (pp. 183–209). Hillsdale, MJ: Erlbaum.

BALTES, P. B. (1987). Theoretical propositions of life-span developmental psychology: On the dynamics between growth and decline. *Developmental Psychology, 23*, 611–626.

BASTA, S. M., & PETERSON, R. F. (1990). Perpetrator status and the personality characteristics of molested children. *Child Abuse and Neglect, 14*, 555–566.

BEITCHMAN, J. H., ZUCKER, K. J., HOOD, J. E., DACOSTA, G. A., & AKMAN D. (1991). A review of the short-term effects of child sexual abuse. *Child Abuse and Neglect, 15*, 537–556.

BEITCHMAN, J. H., ZUCKER, K. J., HOOD, J. E., DACOSTA, G. A., AKMAN, D., & CASSAVIA, E. (1992). A review of the long-term effects of child sexual abuse. *Child Abuse and Neglect, 16*, 101–118.

BENTOVIM, A., VANELBERG, A., & BOSTON, P. (1988). The results of treatment. In A. Bentovim, A. Elton, J. Hildebrand, M. Tranter, & E. Vizard (Eds.), *Child sexual abuse within the family: Assessment and treatment* (pp. 252–268). London: Wright.

BERLINER, L. (1991). The effects of sexual abuse on children. *Violence Update, 1*, 1–10.

BRIERE, J. (1992). *Child abuse trauma: Theory and treatment of the lasting effects*. Newbury Park, CA: Sage.

BRIERE, J., & CONTE, J. (1989, August). *Amnesia in adults molested as children: Testing theories of repression*. Paper presented at the 97th Annual Convention of the American Psychological Association, New Orleans, LA.

BROWNE, A., & FINKELHOR, D. (1986). The impact of child sexual abuse: A review of the research. *Psychological Bulletin, 99*, 66–77.

BURGESS, A., HARTMAN, C., McCAUSLAND, M., & POWERS, P. (1984). Response patterns in children and adolescents exploited through sex rings and pornography. *American Journal of Psychiatry, 141*, 656–662.

BURNS, N., WILLIAMS, L., M., & FINKELHOR, D. (1988). Victim impact. In D. Finkelhor, L. M. Williams, & N. Burns (Eds.), *Nursery crimes: Sexual abuse in daycare* (pp. 114–137). Newbury Park, CA: Sage.

CAFFARO-ROUGET, A., LANG, R. A., & VANSANTEN, V. (1989). The impact of child sexual abuse. *Annals of Sex Research, 2*, 29–47.

CLAUSEN, A. H., & CRITTENDEN, P. M. (1991). Physical and psychological maltreatment: Relations among types of maltreatment. *Child Abuse and Neglect, 15*, 5–18.

COHEN, J. A., & MANNARINO, A. P. (1988). Psychological symptoms in sexually abused girls. *Child Abuse and Neglect, 12*, 571–577.

CONTE, J. R. (1991). *Behavior of sexually abused children at intake/disclosure and 12 months later*. Unpublished manuscript.

CONTE, J., & SCHUERMAN, J. (1987a). Factors associated with an increased impact of child sexual abuse. *Child Abuse and Neglect, 11*, 201–211.

CONTE, J., & SCHUERMAN, J. (1987b). The effects of sexual abuse on children: A multidimensional view. *Journal of Interpersonal Violence, 2*, 380–390.

CORWIN, D. L. (1989). Early diagnosis of child sexual abuse: Diminishing the lasting effects. In G. E. Wyatt & G. J. Powell (Eds.), *Lasting effects of child sexual abuse* (pp. 251–270). Newbury Park, CA: Sage.

DARO, D. (1988). *Confronting child abuse: Research for effective program design*. New York: Free Press.

DEBLINGER, E., McLEER, S. V., ATKINS, M. S. RALPHE, D., & FOA, E., (1989). Post-traumatic stress in sexually abused, physically abused, and nonabused children, *Child Abuse and Neglect, 13*, 403–408.

EINBENDER, A. J., & FRIEDRICH, W. N. (1989). Psychological functioning and behavior of sexually abused girls. *Journal of Consulting and Clinical Psychology, 57*, 155–157.

ELWELL, M. E., & EPHROSS, P. H. (1987). Initial reactions of sexually abused children. *Social Casework, 68*, 109–116.

ERICKSON, M. F. (1986, August). *Young sexually abused children: Socioemotional development and family interaction*. Paper presented at the 94th Annual Convention of the American Psychological Association, Washington, DC.

EVERSON, M. D., HUNTER, W. M., & RUNYAN, D. K. (1991, January), *Adolescent adjustment after incest: Who fares poorly?* Paper presented at the San Diego Conference on Responding to Child Maltreatment, San Diego, CA.

EVERSON, M. D., HUNTER, W. M., RUNYAN, D. K., EDELSOHN, G. A., & COULTER, M. L. (1989). Maternal support following disclosure of incest. *American Journal of Orthopsychiatry, 59*, 197–207.

FELTMAN, R. I. (1985). *A controlled correlational study of the psychological functioning of female paternal incest victims*. Unpublished doctoral dissertation.

FIGLEY, C. R. (1986). *Trauma and its wake: Vol. II. Traumatic stress theory, research, and intervention*. New York: Brunner/Mazel.

FINKELHOR, D. (1987). The trauma of child sexual abuse: Two models. *Journal of Interpersonal Violence, 2*, 348–366.

FINKELHOR, D., & BROWNE, A. (1985). The traumatic impact of child sexual abuse: A conceptualization. *American Journal of Orthopsychiatry, 55*, 530–541.

FINKELHOR, D., HOTALING, G., LEWIS, I. A., & SMITH, C. (1990). Sexual abuse in a national study of adult men and women. Prevalence, characteristics, and risk factors. *Child Abuse and Neglect, 14*, 19–28.

FRIEDLANDER, S., WEISS, D. S., & TAYLOR, J. (1986). Assessing the influence of maternal depression on the validity of the Child Behavior Checklist. *Journal of Abnormal Child Psychology, 14*, 123–133.

FRIEDRICH, W., BEILKE, R., & URQUIZA, A. (1987). Children from sexually abusive families: A behavioral comparison. *Journal of Interpersonal Violence, 2*, 391–402.

FRIEDRICH, W. N., BEILKE, R. L., & URQUIZA, A. J. (1988). Behavior problems in young sexually abused boys. *Journal of Interpersonal Violence, 3*, 21–28.

FRIEDRICH, W. N., GRAMBASCH, P., DAMON, L., HEWITT, S. K., KOVEROLA, C., LANG, R., & WOLFE, V. (1992). The Child Sexual Behavior Inventory: Normative and clinical comparisons. *Psychological Assessment, 4*, 303–311.

FRIEDRICH, W. N., & LUECKE, W. J. (1988). Young school-age sexually aggressive children. *Professional Psychology Research and Practice, 19*, 155–164.

FRIEDRICH, W. N., & REAMS, R. A. (1987). Course of psychological symptoms in sexually abused young children. *Psychotherapy, 24*, 160–170.

FRIEDRICH, W. N., URQUIZA, A. J., & BEILKE, R. L. (1986). Behavior problems in sexually abused young children. *Journal of Pediatric psychology, 11*, 47–57.

GALE, J., THOMPSON, R. J., MORAN, T., & SACK, W. H. (1988). Sexual abuse in young children: Its clinical presentation and characteristic patterns. *Child Abuse and Neglect, 12*, 163–170.

GOMES-SCHWARTZ, B., HOROWITZ, J. M., CARDARELLI, A. P., & SAUZIER, M. (1990). The aftermath of child sexual abuse: 18 months later. In B. Gomes-Schwartz, J. M. Horowitz, & A. P. Cardarelli (Eds.), *Child sexual abuse: The initial effects.* (pp. 132–152). Newbury Park, CA: Sage.

GOMES-SCHWARTZ, B., HOROWITZ, J. M., & SAUZIER, M. (1985). Severity of emotional distress among sexually abused preschool, school-age, and adolescent children, *Hospital and Community Psychiatry, 36*, 503–508.

GOODMAN, G. S., TAUB, E. P., JONES, D. P. H., ENGLAND, P., PORT, L. K., RUDY, L., & PRADO, L. (in press), Emotional effects of criminal court testimony on child sexual assault victims. *Monographs of the Society for Research in Child Development.* Chicago: University of Chicago.

HEWITT, S. K., & FRIEDRICH, W. N. (1991, January). *Preschool children's responses to alleged sexual abuse at intake and one-year follow up.* Paper presented at the meeting of the American Professional Society on the Abuse of Children, San Diego, CA.

JAMPOLE, L., & WEBER, M. K. (1987). An assessment of the behavior of sexually abused and nonsexually abused children with anatomically correct dolls. *Child Abuse and Neglect, 11*, 187–192.

KELLEY, S. J. (1989). Stress responses of children to sexual abuse and ritualistic abuse in day care centers. *Journal of Interpersonal Violence, 4*, 502–513.

KELLY, R. J. (in press-a). Overall level of distress. In J. Waterman, R. J. Kelly, J. McCord, & M. K. Oliveri (Eds.), *Behind the playground walls: Sexual abuse in preschools.* New York: Guilford Press.

KELLY, R. J. (in press-b). Effects on sexuality. In J. Waterman, R. J. Kelly, J. McCord, & M. K. Oliveri (Eds.), *Behind the playground walls: Sexual abuse in preschools.* New York: Guilford Press.

KELLY, R. J., & BEN-MEIR, S. (in press). Emotional effects. In J. Waterman, R. J. Kelly, J. McCord, & M. K. Oliveri (Eds.), *Behind the playground walls: Sexual abuse in preschools.* New York: Guilford Press.

KENDALL-TACKETT, K. A. (1991). Characteristics of abuse that influence when adults molested as children seek treatment. *Journal of Interpersonal Violence, 6*, 486–493.

KOLKO, D. J., MOSER, J. T., & WELDY, S. R. (1988). Behavioral/emotional indicators of sexual abuse in child psychiatric inpatients: A controlled comparison with physical abuse. *Child Abuse and Neglect, 12*, 529–541.

LANKTREE, C., & BRIERE, J. (1991, January). *Early data on the Trauma Symptom Checklist for Children (TSC-C).* Paper presented at the meeting of the American Professional Society on the Abuse of Children, San Diego, CA.

LANKTREE, C., & BRIERE, J. (1992, January). *Further data on the Trauma Symptom Checklist for Children (TSC-C): Reliability, validity, and sensitivity to treatment.* Paper presented at the San Diego Conference on Responding to Child Maltreatment, San Diego, CA.

LINDBERG, F., & DISTAD, L. (1985). Survival responses to incest: Adolescents in crisis. *Child Abuse and Neglect, 9*, 521–526.

LIPOVSKY, J. A., SAUNDERS, B. E., & MURPHY, S. M. (1989). Depression, anxiety, and behavior problems among victims of father-child sexual assault and nonabused siblings. *Journal of Interpersonal Violence, 4*, 452–468.

LUSK, R. (in press). Cognitive and school-related effects. In J. Waterman, R. J. Kelly, J. McCord, & M. K. Oliveri (Eds.), *Behind the playground walls: Sexual abuse in preschools.* New York: Guilford Press.

MANNARINO, A. P., & COHEN, J. A. (1986). A clinical-demographic study of sexually abused children. *Child Abuse and Neglect, 10*, 17–23.

MANNARINO, A. P., COHEN, J. A., & GREGOR, M. (1989). Emotional and behavioral difficulties in sexually abused girls. *Journal of Interpersonal Violence, 4*, 437–451.

MANNARINO, A. P., COHEN, J. A., SMITH, J. A., & MOORE-MOTILY, S. (1991). Six and twelve month follow-up of sexually abused girls. *Journal of Interpersonal Violence, 6*, 494–511.

MCGRATH, E., KEITA, G. P., STRICKLAND, B. R., & RUSSO, N. F. (1990). *Women and depression: Risk factors and treatment issues.* Washington, DC: American Psychological Association.

MCLEER, S. V., DEBLINGER, E., ATKINS, M. S., FOA, E. B., & RALPHE, D. L. (1988). Post-traumatic stress disorder in sexually abused children. *Journal of the American Academy of Child and Adolescent Psychiatry, 27*, 650–654.

MIAN, M., WEHRSPANN, W., KLAJNER-DIAMOND, H., LEBARON, D., & WINDER, C. (1986). Review of 125 children 6 years of age and under who were sexually abused. *Child Abuse and Neglect, 10*, 223–229.

MORROW, K. B., & SORELL, G. T. (1989). Factors affecting self-esteem, depression, and negative behaviors in sexually abused female adolescents. *Journal of Marriage and the Family, 51*, 677–686.

NEWBERGER, C. M., GREMY, L, & WATERNAUX, C. (1990). *Mothers and children following sexual abuse disclosure: Connections, boundaries, and the expression of symptomatology.* Unpublished manuscript, Children's Hospital, Boston, MA.

ORR, D. P., & DOWNES, M. C. (1985). Self-concept of adolescent sexual abuse victims. *Journal of Youth and Adolescence, 14*, 401–410.

PUTNAM, F. W. (1990). Disturbances of "self" in victims of childhood sexual abuse. In R. Kluft (Ed.), *Incest-related syndromes of adult psychopathology* (pp. 113–131). Washington, DC: American Psychiatric Press.

PYNOOS, R. S., & ETH, S. (1985). Children traumatized by witnessing acts of personal violence: Homicide, rape, or suicide behavior. In S. Eth & R. S. Pynoos (Eds.), *Post-traumatic stress disorder in children* (pp. 19–43). Washington, DC: American Psychiatric Press.

RIMSZA, M. E., BERG, R. A., & LOCKE, C. (1988), Sexual abuse: Somatic and emotional reactions. *Child Abuse and Neglect, 12,* 201–208.

ROSENTHAL, R. (1984). *Meta-analytic procedures for social research,* Newbury Park, CA: Sage.

RUNYAN, D. K., EVERSON, M. D., EDELSOHN, G. A., HUNTER, W. M., & COULTER, M. L. (1988). Impact of legal intervention on sexually abused children. *Journal of Pediatrics, 113,* 647–653.

SANDFORT, T. (1982). *The sexual aspects of pedophile relations.* Amsterdam: Pan/Spartacus.

SANDFORT, T. (1984). Sex in pedophiliac relationships: An empirical investigation among a nonrepresentative group of boys. *Journal of Sex Research, 20,* 123–142.

SHAPIRO, J. P., LEIFER, M., MARTONE, M. W., & KASSEM, L. (1990). Multimethod assessment of depression in sexually abused girls. *Journal of Personality Assessment, 55,* 234–248.

SIRLES, E. A., SMITH, J. A., & KUSAMA, H. (1989). Psychiatric status of intrafamilial child sexual abuse victims. *Journal of the American Academy of Child and Adolescent Psychiatry, 28,* 225–229.

STARR, R. H., MACLEAN, D. J., & KEATING, D. P. (1991). Life-span development outcomes of child maltreatment. In R. H. Starr & D. A. Wolfe (Eds.), *The effects of child abuse and neglect: Issues and research* (pp. 1–32). New York: Guilford Press.

TONG, L. OATES, K., & McDOWELL, M. (1987). Personality development following sexual abuse. *Child Abuse and Neglect, 11,* 371–383.

VALLIERE, P. M., BYBEE, D., & MOWBRAY, C. T. (1988, April), *Using the Achenbach Child Behavior Checklist in child sexual abuse research: Longitudinal and comparative analysis.* Paper presented at the National Symposium on Child Victimization, Anaheim, CA.

WATERMAN, J. (in press). Mediators of effects on children: What enhances optimal functioning and promotes healing? In J. Waterman, R. J. Kelly, J. McCord, & M. K. Oliveri (Eds.), *Behind the playground walls: Sexual abused preschools.* New York: Guilford Press.

WATERMAN, J., KELLY, R. J., McCORD, J., & OLIVERI, M. K. (in press). *Behind the playground walls: Sexual abuse in preschools.* New York: Guilford Press.

WHITCOMB, D., RUNYAN, D. K., DeVOS, E., HUNTER, W. M., CROSS, T. P., EVERSON, M. D., PEELER, N. A., PORTER, C. A., TOTH, P. A., & CROPPER, C. (1991). *Child victim as witness research and developmental program* (Final report to the Office of Juvenile Justice and Delinquency Prevention, Office of Justice Programs, U.S. Department of Justice). Washington, DC: U.S. Government Printing Office.

WHITE, S., HALPIN, B. M., STROM, G. A., & SANTILLI, G. (1988). Behavioral comparisons of young sexually abused, neglected, and nonreferred children. *Journal of Clinical Child Psychology, 17,* 53–61.

WHITE, S., STROM, G. A., SANTILLI, G., & HALPIN, B. (1986). Interviewing young sexual abuse victims with anatomically correct dolls. *Child Abuse and Neglect, 10,* 519–529.

WILLIAMS, L. (1991). *The impact of court testimony on young children: Use of protective strategies in day care cases.* Unpublished manuscript, Family Research Laboratory, University of New Hampshire.

WOLFE, V. V., GENTILE, C., & WOLFE, D. A. (1989). The impact of sexual abuse on children: A PTSD formulation. *Behavior Therapy, 20,* 215–228.

ZIVNEY, O. A., NASH, M. R., & HULSEY, T. L. (1988). Sexual abuse in early versus late childhood: Differing patterns of pathology as revealed on the Rorschach. *Psychotherapy, 25,* 99–106.

APPENDIX

Studies of the Effects of Sexual Abuse on Children

Author	Victims			Comparison children		
	Age	N	Source	Age	N	Source
Adams-Tucker (1982)	2–16	28	SAT I/E	—	—	—
Basta & Peterson (1990)	6–10	32	I/E	6–10	16	NA—community
Bentovim & Boston (1988); Bentovim, vanElberg, & Boston (1988)	2–16	411	SAT I/E	2–16	362	NA siblings
Burgess, Hartman, McCausland, & Powers (1984)	6–16	46	SAT E[a]	—	—	—
Burns, Williams, & Finkelhor (1988)	2–5	87	SAT/day care/E	—	—	—
Caffaro-Rouget, Lang, & vanSanten (1989)	1–18	240	SAT I/E	2–18	113	NA—community
Cohen & Mannarino (1988)	6–12	24	SAT I/E	—	—	—
Conte & Schuerman (1987a, 1987b)	4–17	369	SAT I/E	4–17	318	NA—community
Deblinger, McLeer, Atkins, Ralphe & Foa (1989)	3–13	29	Inpatient treatment I/E	3–13 3–13	29 29	Physically abused—impatient treatment NA—inpatient treatment
Einbender & Friedrich (1989)	6–14	46	SAT I/E	6–14	46	NA—community
Elwell & Ephross (1987)	5–12	20	SAT I/E	—	—	—
Erickson (1986)	4–6	11	High-risk infant follow-up	4–6	67	NA—same group
Everson, Hunter, & Runyan (1991)	11–17	44	SAT I/E	—	—	—
Everson, Hunter, Runyan, Edelsohn & Coulter (1989)	6–17	88	SAT I/E	—	—	—

Author	Victims			Comparison children		
	Age	N	Source	Age	N	Source
Feltman (1985)	10–17	31	SAT I	10–17	24	NA—outpatient treatment
Friedrich, Beilke, & Urquiza (1987)	3–12	93	SAT I/E	3–12	64	NA—outpatient treatment
					78	NA—community
Friedrich, Beilke, & Urquiza (1988)	3–8	33	SAT I/E	—	—	—
Friedrich & Luecke (1988)	4–11	22	SAT/I/E[b]	—	—	—
	5–13	22	SAT/IE[c]			
Friedrich & Reams (1987)	3–7	8	SAT I/E	—	—	—
Friedrich, Urquiza, & Beilke (1986)	3–12	85	SAT I/E	Norms	—	—
Gale, Thompson, Moran, & Sack (1988)	<7	37	SAT I/E	<7	35	NA—outpatient treatment
					13	Physically abused—outpatient treatment
Gomes-Schwartz, Horowitz, & Sauzier (1985); Gomes-Schwartz, Horowitz, Cardarelli, & Sauzier (1990)	4–18	113	SAT I/E	Clinical and nonclinical norms		
Jampole & Weber (1987)	3–8	10	SAT/NR	3–8	10	NA—community
Kelley (1989)	4–11	32	Day care	4–11	67	NA—day care
		35	Ritualistically abused in day care/E			
Kelly (in press-a, in press-b); Kelly & Ben-Meir (in press); Lusk (in press)	4–14	69	Ritualistically abused in day care/SA/E	5–14	32	NA—day care
		15				
Kolko, Moser, & Weldy (1988)	5–14	7	SA/inpatient treatment/I/E	5–14	44	NA—inpatient treatment
		22	SA and physically abused	5–14	30	Physically abused—inpatient treatment
Lindberg & Distad (1985)	12–18	27	Children's home/I	—	—	—
Lipovsky, Saunders, & Murphy (1989)	M = 12.2	100	SAT I	M = 12.3	100	NA siblings
Mannarino & Cohen (1986)	3–16	45	SAT I/E	—	—	—
Mannarino, Cohen, & Gregor (1989)	6–12	94	SAT I/E	6–12	89	NA—outpatient treatment
					75	NA—community
McLeer, Deblinger, Atkins, Foa, & Ralphe (1988)	3–16	31	SAT I/E	—	—	—
Mian, Wehrspann, Klajner-Diamond, LeBaron, & Winder (1986)	<6	125	Chart review I/E	—	—	—
Morrow & Sorell (1989)	12–18	101	SAT I	—	—	—
Newberger, Gremy, & Waternaux (1990)	6–12	49	SAT I	—	—	—
Orr & Downes (1985)	9–15	20	SAT I/E	9–15	20	NA—emergency room pop
Rimsza, Berg, & Locke (1988)	2–17	72	SAT I/E/chart review	2–17	72	NA—clinic/chart review
Runyan, Everson, Edelsohn, Hunter, & Coulter (1988)	6–17	75	SAT I/E	—	—	—
Shapiro, Leifer, Martone, & Kassem (1990)	5–16	53	SAT I/E	3–16	70	NA—outpatient treatment
Sirles, Smith, & Kusama (1989)	2–17	207	SAT I/E	—	—	—
Tong, Oates, & McDowell (1987)	3–16	49	SAT I/E	3–16	49	NA—community
Valliere, Bybee, & Mowbray (1988)	4–13	34	Day care/E	5–11	136	NA—community Norms
White, Halpin, Strom, & Santilli (1988)	2–6	17	SAT/NR	2–6	23/18	NA—community/neglect
White, Strom, Santilli, & Halpin (1986)	2–6	25	SAT/NR	2–6	25	NA—community
White, Gentile, & Wolfe (1989)	5–16	71	SAT I/E	—	—	—
Zivney, Nash, & Hulsey (1988)	3–16	80	SAT I/E	3–16	70	NA—outpatient treatment

Note. SAT = sexual abuse treatment or evaluation (outpatient unless indicated), I = intrafamilial abuse, E = extrafamilial abuse, NR = data not reported, SA = sexually abused, pop = population.
[a]Children in sex rings. [b]Sexually aggressive victims. [c]Nonsexually aggressive victims.

The Impossible

Bruce Weigl

Winter's last rain and a light I don't recognize
through the trees and I come back in my mind
to the man who made me suck his cock
when I was seven, in sunlight, between boxcars.
I thought I could leave him standing there
in the years, half smile on his lips,
small hands curled into small fists,
but after he finished, he held my hand in his
as if astonished, until the houses were visible
just beyond the railyard. He held my hand
but before that he slapped me hard on the face
when I would not open my mouth for him.

I do not want to say his whole hips
slammed into me, but they did, and a black wave
washed over my brain, changing me
so I could not move among my people in the old way.
On my way home I stopped in the churchyard
to try to find a way to stay alive.
In the branches a red-wing flitted, warning me.
In the rectory, Father prepared
the body and blood for mass
but God could not save me from a mouthful of cum.
That afternoon some lives turned away from the light.
He taught me how to move my tongue around.
In his hands he held my head like a lover.
Say it clearly and you make it beautiful, no matter what.

Abuse

Toi Derricotte

Mama, the janitor is kissing me. Don't tell me that, you make me suffer. You always make me suffer. Mama, father is beating me. Don't tell me that. What do you want me to do? Mama, the janitor is coming in the house and wants to feel me. Well, come here, come see the janitor and say hello. I come in a starched pinafore and she stands at the foot of the stairs as if she is proud. Where were you when a man, a man who could fix a toy, stuck his tongue in my mouth and rubbed his thing on my school uniform? When I flew up the stairs into the arms of the Blessed Mother, where were you? Wanting to bury your head in a tub of warm water, heating dinner in your slip and socks with half a can of flat beer. Where were you when he came with his fists, after nights of "yes suh boss" and "no suh boss," when he knocked us around and threw meat on the table? Mama doesn't care. She puts her little hands in the air and it still comes raining down. Everything's neatly in place—every pin, every needle—but the walls are coming apart. Roaches peek out of the cracks, their feelers trembling; and the little girl is wiped across the floor like a flour sack. She is decorated by love. Her legs have stripes from beating. Later her father sponges her eyes where tears spill like blood. She shuts down like a factory—every thought, a hand without a way to work—or lies in the dark like a whipped dog praying he'll come.

SECTION V

Violence and Sports

Moving from a study of the violation of body space—where incidents of domestic violence, sexual assault, and child abuse can be so hurtful and indeed morbid—to a study of violence and sports may seem like moving from the horrific to the realm of everyday play and games. Yet, the research is sobering. Athletes participate in approximately one-third of sexual assaults on campuses in the United States, and college athletes have higher levels of sexual aggression toward women than nonathletes on college campuses (Messner and Sabo 1994). One 1991 study showed that 55 percent of all admitted acquaintance rapes on a specific campus were committed by athletes who comprised only 16 percent of the male student body (Nelson 1994). Given this information, we begin to understand how some sports are affected by and can themselves affect a culture of violence that is often linked to an individual's behavior.

We begin this section with a view from Great Britain, with Andrew Parker's article, "Sporting Masculinities: Gender Relations and the Body." Starting with a historical view of the development of sports in the nineteenth century and the parallel confirmation of stereotypical views of men and women, Parker explores the relationships among sports, consumer culture, and the body. Do sports foster misogyny and the objectification of women? How do they call into question dominant heterosexual norms?

One of the most respected and frequently cited experts on violence and sports is Michael Messner who, along with the critic, Donald Sabo, has edited a collection of essays, *Sex, Violence, Power in Sports: Rethinking Masculinity*. In one of their essays, "Sexuality and Power," Messner and Sabo present statistics that show that male athletes are more likely than male nonathletes to be involved in sexual assault, rape, and gang rape. They believe that nothing "inherent in sports makes athletes especially likely to rape women. Rather, it is the way sports are organized to influence developing masculine identities and male peer groups that leads many male athletes to rape" (p. 34). Does the culture of male athletes create a problematic hierarchy within the group through sexually aggressive verbal sparring among peers, the denigration of anything considered feminine, and homophobia?

We have already read a chapter from Myriam Medzian's *Boys Will Be Boys* in the first section on conceptualizing violence. In another chapter, Medzian poses the question, "When Winning is the Only Thing, Can Violence Be Far Away?" Basing her arguments on the belief that "sports is an area of life in which it is permissible to suspend usual moral standards" (p. 183), she presents the complexities that athletes face in playing such violent games and yet serving as role models for youth. Is her concern justified given that some male athletes feel a certain need to extend their socially constructed hyper-masculine role-model images from the playing field to their private lives? Medzian also argues that organized sports for youth become detrimental when they place inordinate emphasis on competition and winning and that this emphasis on winning can often prevent some youth from the pleasure of playing the game. Do you agree with Medzian that in order to play sports well, boys must learn to repress empathy? What is the role of the sports' team coach, parents, and fans in this development? And finally, how can we create sports programs that teach pro-social values?

Michael Messner also considers these related issues as he explores "Boyhood, Organized Sports, and the Construction of Masculinities," a fruitful link back to the second section of this book. In this article, Messner explores and interprets the meanings that males attribute to their boyhood participation in organized sports, reviews some of the problems and contradictions with their construction of masculine identities within the institution of organized sports, and asks, perhaps most significantly, in what ways "class and racial differences mediate this relationship and perhaps lead to the construction of different meanings, and perhaps different masculinities" (p. 103). Messner presents research on family influences, the relationship with fathers, competitive structures and conditional self-worth, and socioeconomic, ethnic, and racial status differences as related to a commitment to sports.

Do you agree with his assessment that organized sports are a "gendered institution," one reflecting dominant conceptions of masculinity and femininity? In your view, are organized sports also a "gendering institution"—one that helps to construct and maintain the current gender order? And finally, do you think that his assertion that male athletes develop ambivalence toward intimacy with others is accurate?

If Messner's last statement is accurate, it dovetails statements made by other researchers, as we have seen, that organized sports and certain athletes contribute to a "rape prone" culture and that gang rape among athletes (and others) is at least partially a public performance (Nelson, 1994). Indeed, the next reading in this section presents the case study of several high school athletes in Glen Ridge, New Jersey, who were convicted in the early 1990s of raping a severely mentally challenged young woman. The case study is well documented in the book by the journalist, Bernard Lefkowitz, *Our Guys: The Glen Ridge Rape and the Secret Life of the Perfect Suburb.* Investigating the culture of this suburb in which athletics had become the major focus of the high school and the community at large, Lefkowitz brings up the issues of athletic privilege and entitlement that are accepted and indeed encouraged in family, religious, community, and legal spheres. He returns us to the concept of rape as power, control, and the humiliation of women, as we are asked what punishment best fits this crime.

The final selection in this section is Alicia Ostriker's powerful poem, "The Boys, the Broomhandle, and the Retarded Girl." Clearly written about the Glen Ridge rape case, the poem helps us to visualize the courtroom scene where a mentally challenged young woman explains that she just wanted to be part of the "in crowd" in her neighborhood, that she "cared for them, they were [her] friends" (p. 17). How does this poem allow us to enter into the persona of the female victim in this case? Does the poem offer us the opportunity to understand somewhat better the environment and sports culture that led to such a dreadful crime?

REFERENCES

NELSON, M.B. (1994). Sexual assault as a spectator sport. In *The stronger women get, the more men love football* (pp. 127–158). New York: Harcourt Brace & Co.

Sporting Masculinities

1996

Gender relations and the body

Andrew Parker

INTRODUCTION

Sport means different things to different people. For some it represents the routines of daily work; for others it serves a more cathartic, stress-reducing purpose; for others still, it constitutes little more than fun, games and play. In this chapter I will discuss sport in a very general sense, as something which envelops all of these things. In particular, I will be concerned with the way in which sport might mean different things to different people depending on their biological sex, their gender identity and their ethnicity.

Central here are questions surrounding the way in which male and female bodies are diversely presented within the penetrative channels of consumer culture, and what the role of the sport and leisure industry is within this process. Moreover, I will consider how men in particular are depicted in relation to sporting practice, and how this might influence popular perceptions of the male 'self'.

Whilst raising these issues, this chapter will draw on the work of key theorists within the sociology of sport (and sociology in general) in order to map out the major concepts and debates surrounding both historical and present-day research into sport. It is hoped that an analysis of this kind may, in some way, allow us to develop a more accurate understanding of the social construction of sporting masculinities.

THE DEVELOPMENT OF MODERN SPORT

Many of the common assumptions attached to modern-day sport appear to have originated within the English public schools of the nineteenth century. Here, traditional folk games were transformed by the upper-class codes imposed upon them into more orderly and standardized forms of 'play'. Over time, these activities came to constitute a central element within the public school educational ethos, in that not only were they valued for their competitive and repressive qualities, but in addition, they were seen as a kind of nurturing ground for the attitudes and values imperative to the maintenance of British imperialism (Mangan 1981; Holt 1989).

These male-dominated ideals gained much recognition during the latter part of the nineteenth century, and eventually made the transition into the wider sporting sphere. Graduates of the public schools, for example, spread the games-playing ethos through a variety of societal institutions, thereby enhancing a wider rationalization of sport. In addition, Pierre de Coubertin, the founder of the modern Olympics, also adopted and reinforced the chauvinistic spirit of the English games-playing tradition, and in doing so, publicly promoted sport as a predominantly male concern (Hargreaves 1984).

From these early beginnings, dominant masculine images of sport persisted. The Victorian era witnessed the emergence of commonsense cultural assumptions equating manliness with sporting prowess. Where sport was concerned, women came to be viewed as weak and frail, passive and emotional. They were seen more in terms of their reproductive capacity than in relation to their athletic potential. Rendered ill-suited to vigorous exercise, women became the victims of an unfounded 'scientific' logic which located them as 'biologically' inferior to men. In this way cultural values and attitudes came to determine the limits of female activity, and male superiority within sport became 'the natural order of things'. Men, it seemed, were physically and psychologically 'built' for such pastimes, whereas women were not (Hargreaves 1994).

Of course, vestiges of these beliefs are still evident within society today. Certainly, it is possible that, even within our own lives, we have come across sex and gender differentiation in sport. Research has shown, for instance, that the practices of physical education in schools may well carry spurious gendered inferences towards 'sex-appropriate' sports participation (Scraton 1993). Worse still, these norms may then be reinforced by the blatant processes of female exclusion operational within elite sporting arenas.

Experiences of schooling also tend to show that if children cross over taken-for-granted 'biological sporting boundaries', they may well find themselves the subjects of intense peer group ridicule, particularly in relation to notions of sexuality (Parker 1992). Granted, there are issues of immaturity to consider here. But, at the same time, we must also question how and where such values and ideas originate, and the extent to which they might go on to shape the contours of adult life.

THEORIZING SPORT

Given the pervasive influence of popular belief surrounding the 'biological' and/or 'cultural' differences of men and women, how, we might ask, has sport been theorized?

For many years sport evaded much critical analysis. It was seen as something which was relatively neutral: an area of culture which provided entertainment and enjoyment, whilst remaining separate from wider societal 'contamination'. During the 1960s when analyses of sport became more popular, issues of sex/gender identity and difference failed to be addressed. Instead, an apolitical standpoint was adopted. This constituted part of a broader functionalist approach whereby sport was celebrated as a facilitator of physical well-being and all-round personal development, and as a positive reproductive site for the attitudes, norms and values beneficial to the functioning of society (Loy and Kenyon 1969).

During the 1970s and 80s, however, such perceptions changed. Within this period, sport was recognized as a much more complex cultural sphere, involving entrepreneurial exploitation and profit, nationalistic fervour and ideological bias. In turn, theorists adopted a more critical approach within their writings.

Neo-Marxist critiques emerged, for example, which cited sport as an appendage of bourgeois domination within the context of wider capitalist relations (Vinnai 1973; Brohm 1978; Beamish 1982). According to these accounts, sporting practice mirrored the productive labour demands of industrial capitalism, and therefore served to reinforce the power relations of the workplace. Dismissing the potential of human agency, such analyses cast individuals as the docile recipients of culture, caged by the constraints of sport, and unable to escape its repressive influence.

There were variations along this theme. Similar conclusions, however, were reached in terms of the overall significance of sport and its role within the processes of social reproduction. What is more, although within some aspects of this work issues of sexuality were raised, discussion gravitated towards the sublimation of male desire, and in general the power relations of gender difference were negated.

The advent of the 1980s witnessed the adoption of a more humanistic approach within this area, and one which refuted previously deterministic notions of personal constraint (Gruneau 1983; Hargreaves 1987). Drawing its inspiration from the work of Antonio Gramsci (1971), this body of 'cultural Marxist' thought directed its attention to the way in which those involved in sport might challenge and contest issues of financial exploitation, commercialization and political bias, by means of their own actions.

The focus of this debate was Gramsci's notion of hegemony, which allowed a more intricate exploration of class relations in sport, particularly in terms of the power struggles between dominant and subordinate groups. Yet, although this modified Marxist stance did pave the way for a detailed critique of male domination and gender inequality, such issues again escaped the rigorous scrutiny they deserved.

This is not to say that cultural Marxist contributions have not had a significant impact on more recent analyses of sport. On the contrary, of late, the concept of hegemony has been widely used within an emerging 'sports feminist' tradition in order to create a backdrop against which male domination in sport might be theorized (Hargreaves 1986; Hall 1988). Furthermore, and again in accordance with the broader feminist resurgence, a predominantly male critique of sport has been established around similar theoretical concerns, the specific aim of which has been to evaluate critically the role men might play in their domination of women within sports settings (Sabo and Runfola 1980; Messner and Sabo 1990).

Collectively this critique has used the concept of hegemony in two main ways. First, theorists have indicated that although men dominate within sporting circles (as well as within society at large), this dominance is not total. It is at all times contested and challenged and should therefore be referred to as a position of 'male hegemony'. Second, commentators have also come to recognize that a particular brand of masculinity has emerged as historically dominant in and around sport—the ideals in play here being those associated with white, middle-class, heterosexual males. Individuals who do not meet these criteria (be they male or female) are necessarily marginalized and must, therefore, occupy a subordinate hierarchical position in terms of sex/gender identity.

SPORT, HEALTH AND CONSUMER CULTURE

Although an analysis of the historical development of modern sport provides some clues as to how it has become a male-dominated concern, such evidence scarcely shows how this position of male hegemony is maintained. How does sport perpetuate notions of male superiority amidst the challenge of contemporary contestation? How does it promote images of sex/gender identity? A good starting point, perhaps, is the relationship between sport and the media, and in particular the contemporary marketing techniques of consumer culture.

Consumer culture, Hargreaves (1987: 132) states, is 'that way of life in the modern era, which is organized around the consumption of goods and services for the mass market'. Advertising, of course, has been largely responsible for the ubiquitous development of consumer culture: a culture which has transformed traditional values of thrift and industry into a new spontaneous, life-course outlook celebrating impulsive, credit-fuelled consumption, self-expression and paganism (Featherstone 1991).

The body has been ever-present within the marketing orbits of mass consumption, and has come to represent the central focus of consumer culture today. Its worth rests not in its autonomous development, but in its ability to match popular ideals of youth, health, fitness, and beauty (Shilling 1993).

This physical and bodily emphasis has marked the arrival of sport and leisure into the consumption debate. Indeed, as Hargreaves (1987) has pointed out, sports culture connects so intimately with consumer culture because both employ the body as a central means of expression:

a good deal of the strength of consumer culture resides in its ability to harness and channel bodily needs and desires—for health, longevity, sexual fulfilment and so on . . . Sports culture's stress on play, contest, strength, energy, movement, speed and skill etc., allows such themes to be given a particularly vivid, dramatic, aesthetically pleasing and emotion-

ally gratifying expression. To be sportive, is almost by definition to be desirable, fit, young and healthy.

(p. 134)

Although, as Shilling (1993) has correctly inferred, specific periods in history have witnessed governmental promotions in the direction of health and fitness education, recent unprecedented expansion within this area has been on a more individual and voluntary basis. Because such a vast number of people have become preoccupied with issues of health and physical appearance, once-trivialized notions of 'keep fit' now constitute the cornerstone of a multimillion dollar fitness industry.

MASCULINITY AND THE BODY

But how does the relationship between sport and consumer culture directly affect popular perceptions of masculinity and the body? The extensive use of visual images seems crucial here. As Featherstone (1991: 178) states,

The perception of the body within consumer culture is dominated by the existence of a vast array of visual images. Indeed, the inner logic of consumer culture depends upon the cultivation of an insatiable appetite to consume images.

Through its widespread employment of body imagery, the media makes individuals more conscious and more aware of their bodily state. Satisfaction with outward appearance often appears to dominate inner feeling. The degree to which we measure up to 'the look' has come to represent the currency of social relations, our value within society and our potential for social acceptability (Shilling 1993).

Sport and exercise play a key role within this body/media nexus. To 'look good' we are told, is to 'feel good'. To maintain one's body is to express a desire to lead a healthy lifestyle, to 'enjoy the good things in life', and to appeal to others. Physical fitness and participation in sports and leisure activities represent a sense of pride in oneself, a sense of cleanliness and purification against the evils of alcohol, tobacco, and the bodily abuse of daily life.

To be healthy and diet conscious is to have some kind of sexual attraction over and above those who are not. The enhancement of sexual prowess is paramount. Indeed, as Featherstone (1991) accurately points out, consumer culture explicitly condones such beliefs in so far as within the confines of its discourse exercise and sex are often 'blurred together through neologisms such as "sexercise" and "exersex" ' (p. 182).

The development of the sport/media relationship has had a dramatic impact on the way in which both male and female bodies have been presented and perceived. Men, as well as women, are expected to respond to the influential and pervasive forces of consumer culture. Masculinity is clearly defined within this realm, particularly within the context of sport. Emanating from film, television, videos, books, and magazines, notions of muscularity, strength and power emerge, wrapped up with generous helpings of fearless domination, to produce images of the ideal man (Dyer 1982; Mishkind *et al.* 1986).

Where might these images originate? Take prime-time British television, for example, and the masculine standards it portrays. On a twice-daily basis, popular Australian soap operas clearly equate notions of maleness with muscularity and manliness. ITV's *Gladiators* reputedly attracts 14 million viewers weekly, who watch male (and female) contestants negotiate situations of direct physical combat with muscular bodybuilders, the majority of whom are, to all intents and purposes, professional sportsmen (and women). Just children's entertainment? Perhaps. But in the unlikely event that such masculine (and feminine) norms are entirely discarded by the adult male population, we must remember that children do grow up, ultimately becoming active agents in the social construction of masculinity within any given period.

Besides the more explicit messages which media portrayals of health and fitness promote, other less visible codes and values are also evident in and through the routines of popular sporting activity. Analysed closely, these can be seen to represent commonsense assumptions regarding, for instance, questions of sexuality and ethnicity. Indeed, in highlighting the way in which sport mediates and reinforces particular attitudes towards such issues, I will now attempt to identify more precisely the complexities of male hegemony within contemporary sports practice.

HETEROSEXUALITY, HOMOPHOBIA AND SPORTING RITUAL

Sport offers complex and contradictory portrayals of masculine construction in relation to sexuality. Physical bonding in the name of team spirit, homophobic taboos, blatant misogyny and the objectification of women are all evident within popular forms of male sporting conquest or related social settings. Acceptable too are the practices of intimate celebration, back slapping, bath sharing and 'pseudo-erotic' ritual (Dunning 1986; Kidd 1987). Meaningful, emotional relations with other males, however, are out of the question.

Enter Stonewall FC, Britain's only gay men's football team. Experiencing a modest amount of recent success in London's Wandsworth and District Sunday Football League, this group of amateur players, Troughton (1994: 18) declares, constitutes 'the biggest challenge to the male ego since the vibrator'. Place this isolated example of homosexual acceptance against a media obsession with the macho social exploits of Britain's footballing élite, and what do we have? A sporting tradition, which via the annals of popular media coverage, takes heterosexuality for granted and dismisses as deviant any alternative form of masculine representation.

Association football, of course, is not alone in its adoption of such views and assumptions. On the contrary, various commentators have cited the way in which attitudes throughout sport collectively contribute to the reification of heterosexuality within the sporting world in general (see Pronger 1990; Hargreaves 1994).

As regards women, the pervasiveness of dominant heterosexual norms often calls into question the 'femininity' and sexuality of sports participants, particularly in relation to those activities which contain a more physical and competitive element (Messner 1988). Just as men are often labelled 'wimps' when they fail to measure up to popular images of strength, power and physical prowess, so women who pursue their sporting/leisure goals within competitive spheres are frequently termed 'butch', 'lesboes' or 'lezzies' because they do not fit the 'natural' feminine norms ascribed to them (Gilroy 1989; Hargreaves 1994).

Translating this masculine logic into the complex world of professional sport, Hargreaves (1994) has outlined the way in which some women appear to attract more attention than men in relation to questions surrounding their sex/gender identities. Of particular interest is the case of the women's tennis player Martina Navratilova.

A sporting legend within her own right, the openly gay Navratilova responded critically in late 1991 to the way in which the world's media framed the enforced retirement of the black American basketball star Earvin 'Magic' Johnson. An equally eminent star within US sporting circles, Johnson shocked the athletic fraternity earlier that year by announcing that he had tested HIV positive, and, as a result, would have to leave the game.

At the time of his announcement, Johnson had received a wave of sympathy and support from both the US media and public, even though it was clear that his heterosexual exploits had been far from conservative. Reminiscing over her own media treatment, and the way in which she had been discriminated against on account of her sexuality during the course of her career, such sympathy, Navratilova claimed, would not have come her way under similar circumstances:

If I had the AIDS virus, would people be understanding? No, because they would say I'm gay—I had it coming. That's why they're accepting it with him, because supposedly he'd got it through heterosexual contact. If it had happened to a heterosexual woman who had been with a hundred or two hundred men, they would call her a whore and a slut, the corporations would drop her like a lead balloon and she would never get another job in her life.

(in James 1991: 38)

In retrospect it may be worth considering here the discrepancy between the overall public appeal of the two sports concerned. Having said that, two main issues remain. First, this statement spells out the massive double standards of the media, in its treatment of sportsmen in comparison to sportswomen over matters of sexuality. Second, and more importantly, in terms of a wider media and public response, it illustrates the extent to which heterosexuality is not only condoned, but implicitly glamorized within popular culture and through certain sections of the sporting press.

Hence the implicit message is that not only is it more acceptable to become HIV positive via heterosexual endeavour, it is also more acceptable to lead a sexually promiscuous lifestyle if you are a male élite athlete. If you're famous and you're a man, and you have AIDS, that's just unlucky. But if you're a woman, and/or you're gay, that's different.

SPORT, ETHNICITY AND MASCULINE CONSTRUCTION

The Navratilova/Johnson case offers a clear example of media discrimination based around issues of biological sex and sexuality. But moreover, it serves to raise

poignant issues concerning the hierarchical position occupied by marginalized and subordinated sex/gender identities within our society. How, for example, would the media have reacted if Johnson had been gay or bisexual? What would have been the implicit message if an equally famous white heterosexual male, or a white gay male élite athlete had suffered a similar fate? The permutations multiply in relation to women. Indeed, as well as issues of sexuality, sex and gender, what this scenario also brings to the fore are notions of race and ethnicity, and pinpoints them as imperative within any theoretical discussion surrounding masculine construction.

By and large, the hegemonic masculine norms and values espoused within consumer culture have a tendency to negate issues of ethnicity. In this arena, masculinity is something which is narrowly structured around images of white males. Such practices reflect the severely racist assumptions which continue to permeate our society, via the institutional and personal relations of everyday life.

In terms of the body, the historic development of racism has been littered with images of physicality, sexuality and violence. As Shilling (1993) has pointed out, aside from women in general, traditionally black men have been made to suffer the consequences of white male fears regarding the 'uncontrollable' desires of their own bodies. Viewed as 'dangerous Others', black peoples, it seems, have conventionally represented some kind of uncivilized, animalistic force posing a sexual threat to the white moral order (Westwood 1990; Shilling 1993). In this respect the negative construction of black bodies has located black people as central within a variety of moral panics, particularly those concerning issues of violent crime, sexual deviance, rape, health and disease (Staples 1982; Shilling 1993).

As regards masculine construction, sport is just one part of that society where such prejudicial assumptions have been evident (Westwood 1990). In recent years, for example, the use of racist chants by supporters and the throwing of banana skins have become all-too-familiar features of English professional football matches (Williams 1991).

In the case of adolescent sport in Britain, concerns have also been aired for some time as to the way in which black males have been excessively encouraged to follow a sporting lifecourse by those within educational circles. Prominent here are racist undertones regarding physiological difference, and academic shortfall (Lashley 1980; Cashmore 1982; Mac an Ghaill 1994). Moreover, there is evidence to suggest that Asian children may also be subjected to the uninformed views and attitudes of teachers in school about the physical and sporting preferences of their respective cultures (Flemming 1988).

Such occurrences reflect something of a more typical pattern when set against the historic prevalence of racism within the wider sporting sphere. Indeed, in addition to the contribution sport made to the naturalization of men's superiority over women, its modern-day development, Majors (1990) declares, also carried with it the ideological implication that 'working-class men as well as men of color could not possibly compete successfully with "gentlemen" ' (p. 109).

Representing one of the few analyses of the development of black masculinity in relation to sport, the work of Majors (1990) draws attention to the way in which male athletic roles within the US have come to be dominated by blacks during the period since the Second World War. Witnessing a significant shift away from white, middle-class supremacy, sport, Majors claims, has, allowed blacks to create and display a unique masculine identity by way of their expressive lifestyle behaviours—which collectively constitute what he calls 'cool pose'.

Reiterating some of the earlier observations made by Staples (1982), Majors describes how although many blacks within American society have accepted the norms and values surrounding social definitions of masculinity, they have been unable to put these into practice on account of the racist restrictions which have denied them access to such areas as education, employment and institutional power. Causing widespread status frustration, this situation, it appears, has led many black males to develop strategies of masculine construction within other 'interpersonal spheres':

black men often cope with their frustration, embitterment, alienation and social impotence by channelling their creative energies into the construction of unique, expressive, and conspicuous styles of demeanor, speech, gesture, clothing, hairstyle, walk, stance, and handshake. For the black male, these expressive behaviors . . . offset an externally imposed invisibility, and provide a means to show the dominant culture (and the black male's peers), that the black male is strong and proud and can survive, regardless of what may have been done to harm or limit him.

(Majors 1990: 111)

Citing how a variety of black male elite athletes have adopted such methods of creativity over time, Majors goes on to initiate an analysis of the historic and political development of 'cool pose' in and through sport. What is more, whilst highlighting the individual habits of popular black sporting figures, Majors is also quick to point out that this phenomenon has more recently come to involve college, high school and playground athletes who, by way of their involvement, represent crucial reproductive agents of such fashionable expressive trends.

Although this work implies that as a result of the development of interpersonal strategies, sport has become something which might play a positive role in the lives of black males, we must be careful not to assume that the development of self-expression, and/or the more recent emergence of black male prominence within particular sports, necessarily means that racism is no longer problematic within this cultural sphere. There is ample evidence to suggest, for instance, that even within our own society various sports are still redolent with the politics of 'race' (Westwood 1990; Jarvie 1991). However, as Majors (1990) concludes, what we can be sure of is that these developments do serve a specific purpose in terms of agency. For in facilitating the articulation of black masculine construction, such reactionary measures constitute a form of popular cultural resistance which, in contesting the white male domination of sport, necessarily represent a challenge to the hegemonic ideals in place.

CONCLUSIONS

My aim within this chapter has been to map out some aspects of the relationship between masculinity and sport by drawing specific attention to the influential powers of consumer culture and the bodily images which it mediates.

Whilst notions of biological sex, sexuality and ethnicity have been highlighted in relation to sporting practice, it is important that we consider these issues as part of a more collective societal order in and around which the formation of gender identity takes place. That is to say, that masculine construction is not limited to such spheres. Rather, it surrounds and interweaves these and many other lifestyle areas.

Having said that, an acknowledgement of differing masculine identities is crucial. As Carrigan *et al.*

(1985) have accurately stated, we cannot discuss masculinity as a fixed entity in terms of an all-encompassing male societal role. Instead, we must recognize the existence of a multiplicity of masculinities according to the diverse cultural values in place at any given time. Moreover, what Carrigan *et al.* go on to argue, and what I have put forward here, is that these divergent masculine forms are arranged in terms of hierarchical position, above which specific hegemonic ideals set the masculine agenda. In this sense, what this work has endeavoured to show is that ultimately, sport, via its links with consumer culture, does have a role to play in the promotion and maintenance of such ideals.

ACKNOWLEDGEMENTS

I would like to thank Professor R.G. Burgess, Professor G. Jarvie and Dr. M. Mac an Ghaill for their constructive comments on earlier drafts of this chapter.

REFERENCES

BEAMISH, R. (1982) Sport and the logic of capitalism, in R. Gruneau and H. Cantelon (eds) *Sport, Culture and the Modern State*. Toronto: University of Toronto Press.

BROHM, J.-M. (1978) *Sport: A Prison of Measured Time*. London: Pluto Press.

CARRIGAN, T., CONNELL, R. AND LEE, J. (1985) Towards a new sociology of masculinity, *Theory and Society*, 5(14): 551–602.

CASHMORE, E. (1982) *Black Sportsmen*. London: Routledge and Kegan Paul.

DUNNING, E. (1986) Sport as a male preserve: notes on the social sources of masculine identity and its transformations, *Theory, Culture and Society*, 3(1): 79–91.

DYER, R. (1982) Don't look now, *Screen*, 23(3/4): 61–73.

FEATHERSTONE, M. (1991) The body in consumer culture, in M. Featherstone, M. Hepworth and B.S. Turner (eds) *The Body: Social Processes and Cultural Theory*. London: Sage.

FLEMMING, S. (1988) Asian lifestyles and sports participation, in A. Tomlinson (ed.) *Youth Cultures and the Domain of Leisure*. Brighton: Leisure Studies Association Conference Papers no. 35.

GILROY, S. (1989) The emBody-ment of power: gender and physical activity, *Leisure Studies*, 8: 163–171.

GRAMSCI, A. (1971) *Selections from the Prison Notebooks*. London: Lawrence and Wishart.

GRUNEAU, R. (1983) *Class, Sport and Social Development*. Amherst, MA: University of Massachusetts Press.

HALL, M.A. (1988) The discourse on gender and sport: from femininity to feminism, *Sociology of Sport Journal*, 5: 330–340.

HARGREAVES, J. (1987) *Sport, Power and Culture*. Cambridge: Polity.

HARGREAVES, J.A. (1984) Taking men on at their games, *Marxism Today*, August: 17–21.

HARGREAVES, J.A. (1986) Where's the virtue, where's the grace? A discussion of the social production of gender relations in and through sport, *Theory, Culture and Society*, 3(1): 109–121.

HARGREAVES, J.A. (1994) *Sporting Females*. London: Routledge.

HOLT, R. (1989) *Sport and the British*. London: Clarendon.

JAMES, M. (1991) Martina in Aids protest, *Guardian*, 21 November, 38.

JARVIE, G. (1991) There ain't no problem here, *Sport and Leisure*, Nov/Dec: 20–1.

KIDD, B. (1987) Sports and masculinity, in M. Kaufman (ed.) *Beyond Patriarchy*. New York: Oxford University Press.

LASHLEY, H. (1980) The new black magic, *British Journal of Physical Education*, 11(1): 5–6.

LOY, J. AND KENYON, G. (eds) (1969) *Sport, Culture and Society*. New York: Macmillan.

MAC AN GHAILL, M. (1994) *The Making of Men*. Buckingham: Open University Press.

MAJORS, R. (1990) Cool pose: black masculinity and sports, in M.A. Messner and D.F. Sabo (eds) *Sport, Men and the Gender Order*. Champaign, IL: Human Kinetics.

MANGAN, A.J. (1981) *Athleticism in the Victorian and Edwardian Public Schools*. Cambridge: Cambridge University Press.

MESSNER, M.A. (1988) Sports and male domination: the female athlete as contested ideological terrain, *Sociology of Sport Journal*, 5: 197–211.

MESSNER, M.A. AND SABO, D.F. (eds) (1990) *Sport, Men and the Gender Order*. Champaign, IL: Human Kinetics.

MISHKIND, M.E., RODIN, J., SIBERSTEIN, L.R. AND STRIEGEL-MOORE, R.H. (1986) The embodiment of masculinity, *American Behavioural Scientist*, 29(5): 545–562.

PARKER, A. (1992) 'One of the boys? Images of masculinity within boys' physical education', unpublished MA dissertation. University of Warwick.

Pronger, B. (1990) Gay jocks: a phenomenology of gay men, in M.A. Messner and D.F. Sabo (eds) *Sport, Men and the Gender Order*. Champaign, IL: Human Kinetics.

SABO, D.F. AND RUNFOLA, R. (eds) (1980) *Jock: Sports and Male Identity*. Englewood Cliffs, NJ: Prentice Hall.

SCRATON, S. (1993) *Shaping up to Womanhood: Gender and Girls' Physical Education*. Buckingham: Open University Press.

SHILLING, C. (1993) *The Body and Social Theory*. London: Sage.

STAPLES, R. (1982) *Black Masculinity*. San Francisco: Black Scholar Press.

TROUGHTON, T. (1994) Seems like a nice team, *Mail On Sunday Review (Night and Day)*, 10 April, 18–19.

VINNAI, G. (1973) *Football Mania*. London: Ocean Books.

WESTWOOD, S. (1990) Racism, black masculinity and the politics of space, in J. Hearn and D.H.J. Morgan (eds) *Men, Masculinities and Social Theory*. London: Unwin Hyman.

WILLIAMS, J. (1991) Having an away day: English football spectators and the hooligan debate, in J. Williams and S. Wagg (eds) *British Football and Social Change*. Leicester: Leicester University Press.

Sexuality and Power

Michael Messner
and Donald Sabo

In recent years, the public image of male athletes has been transformed from that of an idealized role model for youth to that of an irresponsible, selfish, and often violent sexual predator. Indeed, from Mike Tyson's rape conviction to the New England Patriots' locker-room harassment of reporter Lisa Olson; from the accusations of sexual assault against members of the Portland Trailblazers pro basketball team to the youthful Spur Posse's tallying of their sexual "conquests" of young women, we have been inundated with stories of individual sexual assaults, gang rapes, and heterosexual promiscuity among male athletes.

Until fairly recently, rapes by athletes were treated as deviant acts by a few sick individuals. But news reporters and the public are now beginning to ask if incidents like Tyson's rape or the Spur Posse's competitive promiscuity are not isolated at all, but rather manifestations of a larger pattern of sexual abuse of women by male athletes. Though no definitive national study has yet been conducted, a growing body of evidence strongly suggests that, at least among college students, male athletes are more likely than male nonathletes to rape acquaintances and to take part in gang rapes. Consider the following:

- Athletes participated in approximately one-third of 862 sexual assaults on United States campuses according to a 1988–1991 survey by the National Institute of Mental Health (Melnick, 1992).
- Of twenty-six gang rapes alleged to have occurred from 1980 to 1990, most involved fraternity brothers and varsity athletes, Chris O'Sullivan, a Bucknell University psychologist discovered (Guernsey, 1993).
- Among 530 college students, including 140 varsity athletes, the athletes had higher levels of sexual aggression toward women than the nonathletes, Mary Koss and John Gaines (1993) found. Koss and Gaines concluded that campus rape-prevention programs should especially target athletic teams.

Compelling as this evidence is, we want to emphasize two points. First, *nothing inherent in men leads them to rape women*. Peggy Sanday, an anthropologist, and other researchers have found that there *are* rapefree societies in the world, and that they tend to be characterized by low levels of militarization, high levels of respect for women, high levels of participation by women in the economy and the political system, and high levels of male involvement in child care. Second, *nothing inherent in sports makes athletes especially likely to rape women. Rather, it is the way sports are organized to influence developing masculine identities and male peer groups that leads many male athletes to rape.*

The articles in this section illustrate several of the social and psychological processes at work in this masculinity-sports dynamic. A fundamental aspect of this dynamic is the fact that the culture of male athletes is often characterized by sexually aggressive verbal sparring among peers. Central to this group dynamic is the denigration of anything considered feminine. And integrally related to this misogyny is homophobia—"faggot" and "blow me" are put downs on a par with "woman." Through these ritual shows of dominance, boys create the boundaries around their in-group ("We are not women or faggots"), and they simultaneously create a hierarchy within the group: the most successful at the verbal sparring are the "men" in the group; the less successful are the feminized subordinates. Through this process, boys learn to talk about—and treat—females (and penetrated males) as dehumanized objects of male sexual aggression. Underlying this aggressive boasting among young males is often a ragged insecurity about their masculinity and their sexuality. Young males' individual insecurity, coupled with group sparring to show sexual dominance, too often translates into male athletes learning to treat women as objects of sexual conquest, and thus into rape and other forms of violence against women.

The culture of male athletes can change. And in some places it has begun to change. Rape prevention and sexual responsibility programs now involve athletes on a growing number of college campuses. For instance, Tom Jackson has worked with the athletic department at the University of Arkansas to develop a mandatory rape-education and prevention program for athletes. In the five years the program has been in place, he says, no athlete who has participated has been implicated in any sexual assault. Sandra Caron, at the University of Maine, has developed a highly successful program called Athletes for Sexual Responsibility and Rape Awareness. Through this program, male and female athletes together are initiating and facilitating dialogues among other students about rape, sexuality, and "safe sex." A similar program for student athletes has recently begun at Northeastern University. Programs like these suggest that male athletes can take an integral role in disentangling the confusing and destructive ways that our culture has interwined sexual pleasure with power and violence, and in the process can help create a world in which sexuality is associated more strongly with pleasure, love, respect, and care.

REFERENCES

MELNICK, MERRILL, 1992. "Male Athletes and Sexual Assault," *Journal of Physical Education, Recreation and Dance*. (May-June) pp. 32–35.

KOSS, MARY P. & JOHN A. GAINES, 1993. "The Prediction of Sexual Aggression by Alcohol Use, Athletic Participation, and Fraternity Affiliation," *Journal of Interpersonal Violence 8* (1) pp. 94–108.

GUERNSEY, LISA, 1993. "More Campuses Offer Rape-Prevention Programs for Male Athletes," *Chronicle of Higher Education* (February 10) p. A37.

Sports

When winning is the only thing, can violence be far away?

1991

Myriam Medzian

Boys are influenced by sports as participants and spectators.

Outstanding athletes like Rickey Henderson, Joe Montana, Wayne Gretzky, and Magic Johnson serve as role models for millions of boys. But the influence of athletes is by no means limited to a few exceptional players. Starting in high school, boys who are good enough to make varsity teams, especially the football team, tend to be highly admired. For many of their peers, male and female, they represent the essence of masculinity. The same is true in college.

When it comes to music or film stars, there is often a generation gap in the taste of adolescents and their parents. But athletes get parents', especially fathers', stamp of approval. In fact, for many American fathers having a son who is neither interested in sports nor athletically inclined is little short of a tragedy.

Athletes also have society's approval and admiration. Many major sports events begin with the playing of our national anthem. The President, or a member of his family, opens the baseball season, and it has become a tradition for him to invite college and professional athletic champions to the White House.

By the time children are three or four years old, they watch about twenty-eight hours of TV a week. Most little boys watch sports on TV, and many are taken to games long before they participate in them. Their earliest image of what sports is all about comes from being spectators rather participants. . . .

I limit myself to the most popular sports viewed by the largest audiences and played by large number of boys across the country: football, baseball, basketball, ice hockey, boxing. The major emphasis is on football because of its enormous popularity and high level of violence.

In his book *Violence and Sport*, Professor Michael D. Smith of Toronto's York University divides sports violence into four types:

Brutal Body Contact: This comprises acts of assault performed in accordance with the official rules of a sport:

"Tackles, blocks, body checks, collisions, legal blows of all kinds"[1] are included. This kind of violence is inherent in sports such as football, boxing, ice hockey, and lacrosse; and to a lesser degree in games like basketball, soccer, and water polo. The game as officially defined cannot be played without it. Knocking your opponent unconscious is the goal of boxing. Tackling or blocking the members of the other team, which in ordinary English means knocking them down to the ground, is at the core of football.

Borderline Violence: This comprises assaults that are prohibited by the formal rules of a sport, but occur routinely. They are more or less accepted by officials, players, and fans. They include the hockey fistfight, late hitting in football, high tackling in soccer, the baseball brushback pitch, and basketball "body language." Referees and umpires sometimes penalize this kind of violence, but the penalties are not usually severe enough to deter. In theory, criminal statutes also apply; in practice, athletes are not prosecuted. So the violence often escalates.

Quasi-Criminal Violence: This frequently leads to serious injury and is usually brought to the attention of top officials. Penalties can range from suspensions to lifetime bans. Civil and criminal suits are becoming more common, but convictions are infrequent. One well-known case was that of Houston Rockets basketball player Rudy Tomjanovich, who was given a severe punch in the head by Kermit Washington of the Los Angeles Lakers during a 1977 game. Tomjanovich suffered a broken jaw and a fractured skull. He sued the Lakers, won, and eventually settled out of court.

Criminal Violence: This takes place before or after a game among fans. An example is the June 16, 1990, killing of eight people as part of the "celebration" in Detroit after the Pistons won the National Basketball Association Championship. One hundred and twenty-four people were treated at a hospital.

From the perspective of influencing young boys, brutal body contact and borderline violence are probably much more important than quasi-criminal and criminal violence. For while the latter are relatively rare and usually evoke outrage and punishment, body contact is intrinsic to the game and borderline violence is widely accepted as unavoidable.

The acceptance of body contact and borderline violence seems to be based on the idea that sports is an area of life in which it is permissible to suspend usual moral standards.

In a study of how college athletes think about morality and how their thinking relates to their moral judgments and behavior, Professor Brenda Jo Bredemeier of the University of California at Berkeley found that athletes commonly distinguish between game morality and the morality of everyday life. A male college basketball player says, "In sports you can do what you want. In life it's more restricted . . ."[2] A football player says, "The football field is the wrong place to think about ethics."[3]

Bredemeier expresses concern about the social implications of this lower moral standard in such an important and influential area. She points out that sports gives us a wealth of metaphors in other activities: the language of sports is often used in discussions of business, politics, and war.

Bredemeier voices concern over the influence of an ethical double standard on adult men, but the influence begins at a much earlier age.

ATHLETES AS ROLE MODELS

We know from research in psychology that young children tend to model their behavior and attitudes on those of adults, particularly adults they admire. Some professional athletes have described the role that their fathers' admiration of athletes played in developing their own interest in sports and their desire to become athletes. Michael Oriard, former Notre Dame and Kansas City Chiefs football player, now a professor of English literature, tells us that "from watching those Sunday football games with my father I learned . . . to associate football with masculinity. Those football players on the TV screen were ideal men, and my father who watched and enjoyed them was doing what a man did. Though my father was a nonathlete himself, the role model he projected included the importance of football."[4] For boys who have little or no contact with their fathers, athletes may well seem like the most widely accepted and applauded male role models. Even Presidents admire them.

Imagine a young boy watching an ice hockey game. In addition to the pushing and shoving which are part of the game, it has become standard for hockey players to regularly hit each other with hockey sticks and get into fistfights.

"I went to a fight and a hockey game broke out" has become a stale joke. But how many boys, or adults, are aware that a majority of hockey players want to abolish this violence?

To spectators, hockey violence is presented as the kind of brawl that men naturally get into when they are in high-intensity competition. But Richard Lapchick, the director of Northeastern University's Center for the

Study of Sport in Society, informs us that in recent years, at annual meetings of the National Hockey Players Association, a major issue has been violence, with players asking owners to impose much stiffer penalties (including expulsion) on those players who persist in violent behavior. Lapchick explains that there are a small number of hockey players who are genuinely violent—"There are eight or ten players in the league who are in fights every night. The Players Association wants those guys out of the League permanently."

But club owners refuse to discourage the violence, because it attracts spectators who come to see "red ice." Players who don't participate in the violence endanger their jobs. For example, when former Los Angeles Kings hockey player Paul Mulvey refused to participate in a fight between his team and the Vancouver Canucks, he was ordered off the team and immediately shipped to the minor leagues.[5]

Imagine a young boy watching football. Normally, running into someone with all your weight and force and knocking that person down with a good chance of injuring him is viewed as bodily assault and could subject a person to arrest. But in football this behavior is called tackling or blocking and is widely admired and respected. If a player can get away with late hitting or spearing—both of which are illegal—he will be considered particularly clever and adept. (Late hitting refers to a blow dealt after the referee's whistle has declared that a play is over. Spearing is when a player uses his head as a primary instrument to spear another player who is already on the ground. In an interview, former Patriots football player Keith Lee told me that he had seen "flagrant spearing" go unpunished on the football field: "Nothing's illegal unless you get caught. That's the rule.") . . .

Why should football players increase the danger to their bodies? The game is intrinsically dangerous enough. Under present-day conditions three hundred thousand football-related injuries per year are treated nationwide in hospital emergency rooms. In the National Football League, an average of sixteen hundred players miss at least two games a year because of serious injuries.[6] A recent survey reveals that 78 percent of retired professional players suffer physical disabilities. The average life expectancy of a former professional football player is about fifty-six years.[7]

Injuries that to most of us would seem quite serious are routine. In his autobiography, *Out of Their League,* Dave Meggyesy points out that "one of the justifica-

tions for college football is that it is not only a character-builder, but a body-builder as well." As he sees it, "this is nonsense . . . Young men are having their bodies destroyed, not developed. As a matter of fact, few players can escape from college football without some form of permanent disability. During my four years I accumulated a broken wrist, separations of both shoulders, an ankle that was torn up so badly it broke the arch of my foot, three major brain concussions, and an arm that almost had to be amputated because of improper treatment. And I was one of the lucky ones."[8] . . .

In football as in hockey there are some brutally violent men. Too often other players are pressured to emulate their behavior. If a football player refuses to "take players out" (i.e., to injure an opponent so badly that he cannot finish the game), or to play while injured, there are plenty of others who won't refuse and are waiting to take his job. And so a game that is intrinsically violent is rendered even more violent.

But to a young boy it all seems natural. Little does he know that the extreme violence he sees often grows more out of the owners' commercial interests than players' inclinations.

Some of this violence—such as brawls between teams—does not appear to be orchestrated by coaches or owners, however. In the case of collegiate sports it often causes embarrassment to school officials. The recent increase in brawls and fistfights may be due in part to the general escalation of violence in our society. Athletes with violent inclinations will tend to feel less social restraint on acting them out. Once they do, it becomes unmanly for their opponents not to respond in kind.

The prevalent view in the United States is that violent sports operate as a catharsis, allowing athletes and spectators to release hostile, aggressive energy in a relatively harmless way, thus cutting down crime, domestic violence, or warfare. Research reveals that the facts are actually quite the reverse.

An exhaustive study of heavyweight prizefights held between 1973 and 1978 and subsequent homicide statistics revealed that U.S. homicides increased by 12.46 percent directly after heavyweight championship prizefights. The increase was greatest after heavily publicized prizefights.[9] . . .

A boy who watches acts of violence committed by thieves, murderers, or sadists in films or on TV knows that society disapproves of these acts. The boy who watches sports knows that athletes' acts of violence are approved of. It makes sense that sports violence would serve as an important role model for boys who tend to be well adjusted socially, while illegal violence on the screen would tend to have a greater influence on the behavior of boys who are more psychologically damaged and/or feel more alienated from society.

Because of the respectability of sport, its language and values permeate other areas of legitimate male endeavor.

When New York University professor Martin Hoffman analyzed studies comparing the moral attitudes and behavior of men and women, he found that the women (who as children participate in contact sports far less than do men and watch less sports both as children and adults) were more concerned with fairness, honesty, and helping others than the men.[10]

There are causes other than sports participation that may explain this discrepancy. Hoffman focuses on the fact that boys more than girls are socialized for egoistic achievement and success. But sports play a major role in reinforcing the concern with success, winning, and dominance. On the sports field these goals *alone* justify illegal and violent acts.

What can we do to change this situation, to curtail the violence in college and professional sports that boys grow up watching? Legislation represents our best hope of curtailing borderline violence. This would change the atmosphere of sports; quasi-criminal and criminal violence would become less frequent. In light of athletes short-lived careers, and the fierce competition to get on professional teams, it seems unlikely that professional sports associations will be able to get owners to agree to curtail the violence.

But what about intrinsic violence, what Smith calls brutal body contact?

The two sports which cause the most concern in this respect are football and boxing. . . .

From the perspective of societal violence, the problem with boxing is the legitimizing of clear-cut physical assault.

Imagine a young boy watching boxing matches. The message is clear: punching someone and knocking him unconscious are acceptable, even admirable goals under certain circumstances. The men who are exceptionally good at it are national heroes like Muhammed Ali or Mike Tyson.

The argument that boxing should be permitted because it gives poor minority males, who represent a large percentage of boxers, a chance to move up in the world is a very weak one. Rates of violence in our inner-city ghettos are extraordinarily high. Boxers as role models further legitimize the use of violence. Besides, as New York University professor Jeffrey Sammons, an African-American historian and boxing expert, points out, the idea that boxing is a way out of the ghetto is false for a vast majority of boxers. Only a tiny percent derive any long-term profit from boxing; many are injured. (The odds of any amateur athlete making it to the professional level are one in twelve thousand.)

Given present-day alternatives, a young boy's involvement in a Police Athletic League boxing program certainly seems more desirable than his involvement in crime and drugs. But even here Sammons has serious doubts. He says, "Those who argue that boxing keeps young men off the street, out of crime, and away from drugs—a questionable argument at best—are not praising a sport but signaling a dismal failure of the American dream for many. For there is little difference between what boxing supposedly helps them to avoid and the tragic option the sport represents."[11]

Boxing, as we know it, should be banned. George Lundberg points out that we no longer allow dueling with sharp swords and with intent to injure or kill, but we do permit fencing as a sport in which dexterity is developed and measured electronically. The same could be done with boxing, which requires considerable dexterity, agility, and other skills. But without the violence, boxing would undoubtedly die out as a spectator sport. That is as it should be.

What about football? If the idea of banning boxing is invariably met with cries of dismay in some quarters, the idea of banning football would in many parts of this country be seen as nothing short of sacrilegious.

When CBS's "60 Minutes" sent Morley Safer to Texas to do a program on junior high and high school football (aired on January 11, 1981), he was told by seventh-grade coach Don Clapp that football is "almost like going to church . . . you do that on Sunday, you play football on Friday nights. It's always been here, and it's been big and it's getting bigger."

Safer concluded that "in this part of Texas and a half a dozen other states, junior high school football is the standard by which both man and boy are judged," and "one thing is certain, football in these parts is much more than football. It ranks up there with academics and is really much closer to a kind of theology."

The major focus of Safer's investigation was the "holdback" phenomenon. "Holdbacks" are boys who are held back in eighth grade at their parents' request so that they will be bigger and better at football by the time they get to high school. The motivating fantasy is often getting a college football scholarship and then making it to the professional leagues.

While football may be akin to religion in some states, throughout the United States it is deeply tied to nationalism, patriotism, and zeal about sending our boys to war.

In his book *Sports in America,* James Michener reminisces about a football game he attended in 1972 "at which a squad of marines, assisted by an army band, raised the flag at the start," and together with Boy Scouts, National Guardsmen and clergymen "assembled at midfield during half time . . . to honor America's participation in the Vietnam war."[12]

Michener also points out that football is the only sport in which players are often led in prayer and blessed by clergymen before games. Many NFL teams carry their own chaplain.

This connection between football, religion, and patriotism, as well as the enormous financial interest of colleges, team owners, and connected enterprises in its continued existence, make the notion of banning football politically unthinkable in any near future.

The growing insurance problems that surround the game offer some hope. Harry E. Figgie, Jr., is the chairman of the company that owns Rawlings Sporting Goods. In an October 9, 1988, *New York Times* op-ed piece he warns that "football may be an endangered American sport." It could be "gaveled into extinction" by injured players' lawsuits. By 1986 the cost of insuring his company against helmet-related lawsuits had rendered the production of football helmets unprofitable. In 1988 the company announced that it would no longer manufacture them. Figgie tells us that school systems, universities, coaches, and medical personnel are also increasingly being sued. As a result some school districts are no longer offering football programs.

Unless economic pressures force the abandonment of large numbers of football programs, I can only see the sport dwindling or withering away as a result of the kinds of changes recommended in this book. As the concept of masculinity moves away from obses-

sive competitiveness, dominance, and toughness, and comes to include empathy, nurturant fathering, and willingness to expose one's vulnerabilities, football will become less and less attractive to young boys and their parents. Some regulations which would help this happen will be discussed in the section below on youth and high school sports.

Until we as a nation outgrow football, the best we can do is to pass legislation banning borderline violence in all sports. . . .

YOUTH AND HIGH SCHOOL SPORTS: "JUST LIKE THE GAME OF LIFE"

Thirty million school-age children are involved in youth sports in the United States. They play twenty-five different sports under the direction of 4.5 million coaches and 1.5 million administrators.[13] Four-year-olds play in Midget Hockey leagues. There are national mini-bike championships for six-year-olds.

Among the most popular youth leagues are Pop Warner Junior League Football for boys eight years and up, and Little League Baseball for boys six years and up. As the result of a successful lawsuit, girls have been allowed to play Little League Baseball since 1974, but most teams are still exclusively male.

Little League is the largest youth sports organization. It was created in 1939 by Carl Stotz, a Pennsylvania lumber company employee. By 1955, Stotz, who did not want the organization turned into a large corporation, was removed from his post as commissioner. He has since described Little League as a "Frankenstein" monster because of its commercialism.

Sociology professor Gary Alan Fine, in *With the Boys,* a study of Little League Baseball, tells us that private, community youth leagues came into being in part because professional recreation directors and educators in the 1930s were convinced that highly competitive sports were harmful to preadolescent development. They refrained from developing professionally directed programs.

There is nothing intrinsically wrong with adult-organized sports programs for young boys. At a time when so many parents both work outside the home, and there are so many single mothers, a seemingly healthy supervised outdoor activity must seem like a blessing to many parents.

It is only when these programs place inordinate emphasis on competition and winning that they become detrimental.* There are undoubtedly youth sports programs across the country that emphasize fun and sportsmanship under the guidance of qualified coaches. But, as recreation and education professionals feared in the 1930s, the creation of private sports leagues has often led to extremely competitive programs for very young children.

Richard Lapchick warns that "most youth sport coaches lack even rudimentary knowledge of the emotional, psychological, social and physical needs of children."[14]

A theme that many athletes get back to again and again is the enormous importance of the coach for a young boy. Meggyesy writes about "the father-son relationship that is football's cornerstone."[15] Michael Oriard tells us, "From the fourth grade into my first year as a professional, I was to look to my coaches as figures of wisdom and authority whose pronouncements were gospel and whose expectations of me were to be met at whatever cost."[16] In a study of elite youth hockey and soccer programs, researcher Gai Berlage found that coaches were universally accepted as authority figures. This deep emotional relationship and respect for the coach's authority facilitates players' transference of moral responsibility from themselves to the coach.

The enormous influence of the coach is not limited to the sports field. "Character building" is commonly given as an important positive effect of playing contact sports. In discussing his high school football experience, Meggyesy tells us that "football represents the core values of the status quo, and coaches and school administrators want players to win adherents to these values, not only on the football field but also in their private lives."[17]

David Blankenhorn, the director of the Institute for American Values, played football for his high school

in Jackson, Mississippi. In an interview with the author, he expressed his conviction that a core idea transmitted by football coaches and fathers is that "playing the game is just like the game of life. The rules you learn will stand you in good stead for the rest of your life."

Some of the rules that are emphasized sound good—teamwork, sacrifice for the common good, never giving up, giving 110 percent of yourself—and in the hands of sensitive, knowledgeable, well-trained coaches they can be used to teach boys valuable habits. But such coaches are far from the rule. Michael Oriard provides us with vignettes of high school coaches whose understanding of what football is all about is, to put it mildly, problematic. There is the Texas coach who had students listen to "hypnotic tape recordings" that whispered, "when you're playing on that football field you have such aggressiveness it's absolutely unreal." There is the Wisconsin coach who after each game would give a "Hit of the Week" award for the most vicious hit he could find on the game film. An Iowa coach "spraypainted a chicken gold to represent the 'Golden Eagles' of a rival team, then threw it onto the field to be kicked around by his players. 'Get the eagle' was the name of the game."[18]

These are extreme examples. The following anecdotes are no doubt more typical. Fred Engh, the founder and president of the National Youth Sports Coach Association, describes his nine-year-old son coming home from playing baseball on a very hot July day in Indiana "looking in the dumps." When Engh asked what the matter was, the boy told him that the coach had decided that "nobody gets a drink of water until we score a run." "We didn't score a run until the fifth inning," his son explained. The boys were all thirsty and mad and "it just wasn't any fun even when we won."[19] . . .

The findings of academic researchers and writers like James Michener indicate that the obsession with winning is far from infrequent in youth and high school sports. After describing and deploring the extreme competitiveness of many junior football leagues, Michener quotes from some of their badges, which contain yells for the rooters. They include: Massacre the Braves, Mangle the Matadors, Destroy the Blue Devils, Slay the Aces. He comments that "after a steady diet of this from age eight through sixteen, it would seem that the boys could only escalate to machine-gunning the opposition high school, atom-

---

*Former athletes are often particularly critical of youth sports. Dave Meggyesy told me that Pop Warner football is "too dangerous; their [boys'] bones haven't grown yet; they're just teaching boys to smack into each other with equipment." In his book *Baseball and Your Boy,* former Cleveland Indians player Al Rosen deplores the fact that some Little League coaches risk serious injury to youngsters' arms by encouraging them to throw curveballs. In *Sports in America,* James Michener reports that many professional athletes have told him they would not allow their sons to enter Little League until relatively late childhood.

bombing Notre Dame and hydrogen-bombing the Dallas Cowboys."[20]

Gary Fine points out that in Little League Baseball, at the beginning of the season coaches often play down the importance of their team's win-loss record and emphasize moral factors. But these statements are often very different from the conduct of the coaches. Eventually, "integrity takes a backseat to the pragmatic concern of *winning* baseball games. Players learn that integrity is a rhetorical strategy one should raise only in certain times and places. The adults involved with Little League tend to be oriented toward winning, losing, and competition."[21] . . .

. . . [O]ne of the major gripes that many boys have with organized sports both at the youth and high school levels [is that] the emphasis on winning deprives them of the pleasure of playing the game. Instead of giving everyone the opportunity to play, coaches leave perfectly decent players sitting on the bench watching top players win games for the team. It is not surprising that American children are among the least physically fit of those in any industrialized democracy. Instead of focusing on enjoying sports, reaping physical benefits, and instilling a lifelong involvement in athletics, too many of our sports programs are geared exclusively toward winning. . . .

While youth sports do not involve much borderline violence, the language and attitudes developed serve as preludes to high school contact sports. There, especially in football, borderline violence is often encouraged.

In an interview, University of New Haven sociology professor Allen Sack reminisced about his experience playing high school football: "The coaches thought it was correct to use techniques of pushing, yelling, dehumanizing" the opposing team. "The way I was coached was destroy the bastards . . . punish people, take people out."[22]

To play the game as violently as this, boys must learn to repress empathy. They work hard at it.

Dave Meggyesy tells us that already in high school "the business of setting up a dividing line between us and our opponents went on the whole week before a game. [Coach] Vogt would call Chagrin Falls, our big rival, 'the boys from across the river,' and Mayfield was a team of 'dumb but tough Wops.' . . . We were really fired up and felt we were going to annihilate 'them.' I particularly didn't want to see their faces, because the more anonymous they were the better it was for me . . . They were a faceless enemy we had to meet."[23]

Sociology professor Michael Messner reports on an interview with former Oakland Raiders football player Jack Tatum, whose fierce, violent "hits"—one of which broke Darryl Stingley's neck and left him a paraplegic—led to his being known as "The Assassin." Tatum told Messner, "When I first started playing, if I would hit a guy hard and he wouldn't get up, it would bother me. [But] when I was a sophomore in high school, first game, I knocked out two quarterbacks, and people loved it. The coach loved it. Everybody loved it . . ."[24]

By the time they play college and professional football, players have received so much reinforcement for concerns with dominance, for playing as violently as they can, that empathy has been largely conquered. Michael Oriard provides us with a perceptive description of playing at Notre Dame. "On play after play I rammed my shoulder and forearm into the shoulders and headgear of the man trying to block me . . . I wanted him to feel an ache at ten o'clock that night and think, 'That sonuvabitch Oriard.' . . . I wanted physically to dominate the offensive players attempting to block me. I wanted to feel contempt for their inability to do so, and satisfaction in knowing I was tougher than they were." He then comments. "I could not have continued to maul someone I had come to *know*—even if only a little. But I did not know them."[25]

Former Canadian Football League player John McMurtry, now a professor of philosophy, writes that "the truly professional attitude is not to think of the opponent as a human being at all—he is a 'position' to be removed as efficiently as possible in order to benefit the team's corporate enterprise of gaining points."[26]

It seems that many of the men who succeed in repressing empathy on the football field do so by "doubling"—a psychological process that psychiatrist Robert J. Lifton describes as compartmentalizing the self. They split up into a "personal life self" and a "football self." . . .

Doubling is facilitated by the legitimacy of the game and the undisputed authority of the coach. Players are just doing what is expected of them by the coach and the public. The moral responsibility for their actions is transferred to the coach and other authority figures.

Learning to endure pain and play with it without complaining, learning to conquer and hide fear, are further conditions of playing football. In his autobiography, Meggyesy tells of being shot up with novocaine for a high school game after he had injured his neck so badly during a drill that he couldn't move his head. Oriard describes his experiences in a game played when he was in fifth grade. When confronted with "repeatedly having to tackle one of the biggest kids in the school . . . I was afraid of him, but my greater fear was to show my fear . . . By not quitting and not flinching from contact I proved my 'courage' to myself . . ."[27]

Life is filled with difficulty, danger, and suffering. The reader may wonder what is wrong with teaching boys and men to overcome their fears, to be courageous, to withstand pain.

There is nothing wrong with it. But when a high school football player is shot up with novocaine in order to play, when he plays with injuries that if aggravated could lead to permanent damage, he is learning much more than to withstand pain. *He is learning to sacrifice his body unnecessarily and to hide all feelings of fear and vulnerability, however warranted they may be. He is also being taught to sacrifice the bodies of others*. For if he is willing to risk serious injury to himself, then why shouldn't he be willing to risk injuring others seriously? If he is not allowed to feel sympathy for himself when he is injured or justifiably frightened, why should he feel empathy for anyone else?

When boys have to hide all feelings of fear and vulnerability in order to be accepted as "real men," they are learning to take unnecessary risks that will endanger their and others' health and lives. These lessons learned at an early age can lead to driving cars at ninety miles an hour, enthusiastically going off to unnecessary wars, or sending others off to war. . . .

The sacrifice of young boys to the gods of football, car racing, or military adventurism represents foolhardiness, not courage. Their willingness to sacrifice themselves has everything to do with proving manhood.

Dave Meggyesy describes how on one occasion his coach accused him of being afraid and told him that he had looked "almost feminine" in making a tackle. Meggyesy comments that "this sort of attack on a player's manhood is a coach's doomsday weapon. And it almost always works, for the players have wrapped up their identity in their masculinity, which is eternally precarious for it not only depends on not ex-

hibiting fear of any kind on the playing field, but is also something that can be given and withdrawn by a coach at his pleasure."[28]

The language of sport is filled with insults suggesting that a boy who is not tough enough, who does not live up to the masculine mystique, is really a girl or homosexual.

Football player David Kopay writes of his high school coach that "like many other coaches, Dillingham [fictitious name] used sexual slurs—'fag,' 'queer,' 'sissy,' 'pussy'—to motivate (or intimidate) his young athletes."[29]

Gary Fine reports on the frequent use of this kind of language in Little League. Boys use expressions like "You're a faggot" or "God, he's gay." One eleven-year-old says of another that he "takes birth [control] pills" (i.e., he is a girl). The term "wuss"—a combination of "woman" and "pussy"—is also used as an insult. Fine tells us that "*each insult means that the target has not lived up to expectations of appropriate male behavior*, and is being sanctioned [my emphasis]."[30]

In a May 16, 1988, *New York Times* article, Ira Berkow reports that Indiana University basketball coach Bobby Knight was known to "put a box of sanitary napkins in the locker of one of his players so that the player would get the point that Knight considered him less than masculine." . . .

As we have seen, it starts much earlier, but from high school on, the concern with dominance, winning, and manhood rather than just enjoying the sport becomes close to all-pervasive. Football in particular affords boys a legitimate opportunity to deal with the self-doubts and insecurities of adolescence by asserting their physical dominance over others. "I loved to dominate my opponents physically in a public arena. Such dominance was a salve for the many wounds my adolescent ego received during my high school years," writes Michael Oriard.[31] If one combines this early reinforcement of physical dominance with the ongoing expression of contempt for girls and women, one can see how the end product, for some of the more angry or disturbed players, may be rape. Some preliminary studies indicate that athletes may well be overrepresented in college sexual assaults. In a study of twenty-four cases of campus gang rape, discussed in her forthcoming book *Nice Boys, Dirty Deeds*, psychologist Chris O'Sullivan found that nine of them were by athletes. *Philadelphia Daily News* sportswriter Rich Hoffman carried out an investigation of sexual assaults on college campuses which included interviewing over 150 campus police departments. In a March 17, 1986, article, he informs us that in the fifty reported incidences brought to his attention, football and basketball players were overrepresented by 38 percent.

Concealing rapes committed by football players has been one of the traditional tasks of many university sports departments, a task that has become more difficult as a result of the women's movement.

In 1976 James Michener wrote: "Many big-time schools designate one coach or faculty member to protect the young athlete from the law . . . Not surprisingly, several of our most famous universities have found themselves involved in ugly scandals when whole segments of a team have engaged in gang-rape, a jovial collegiate version of *jus primae noctis* in which the football hero expects to be accorded seignorial rights while the local sheriff stands guard."[32] . . .

A major justification for our nation's enormous investment in competitive contact sports for young boys is that sports build character, teach team effort, and encourage sportsmanship and fair play.

In a 1978 article, professor George Sage discusses six studies of the effect of organized youth sports on sportsmanship. Three of the studies indicate that boys involved in organized sports show less sportsmanship than those who are not involved. One study found that as the children grew older they moved away from placing high value on fairness and fun in participation and began to emphasize skill and victory as the major goals of sport. In several other studies it was found that adolescent boys who participated in organized sports valued victory more than non-participants, who placed more emphasis on fairness.

Instead of learning fair play and teamwork, too many of our young boys are learning that winning is everything.

It is time to regulate children's sports so that boys will *really* learn the pro-social attitudes and values that they are supposed to learn from sports, instead of the obsessive competitiveness, emotional callousness, and disdain for moral scruples that are so often precursors to violence.

NOTES

1. Smith, *Violence and Sport*, p. 10.

2. B. J. Bredemeier and D. L. Shields, "Values and Violence in Sports Today," *Psychology Today,* October 1985, p. 25.

3. Bredemeier, "Athletic Aggression: A Moral Concern," in *Sports Violence*, edited by J. H. Goldstein, p. 64.

4. Oriard, *The End of Autumn*, p. 11.

5. See J. Bryant and D. Zillman, "Sports Violence and the Media," in Goldstein, op. cit., p. 196.

6. See Richard E. Lapchick, editor, *Fractured Focus*, p. 220.

7. See Michael Messner, "When Bodies Are Weapons: Masculinity and Violence in Sport," *International Review of Sociology of Sport.* August 1990.

8. Meggyesy, *Out of Their League*, pp. 81–82.

9. See David Phillips, "The Impact of Mass Media Violence on U.S. Homicides," *American Sociological Review*, August 1983, pp. 560–568. Phillips's findings persisted after corrections for secular trends, seasonal factors, and other extraneous variables. Four alternative explanations for the findings were tested and found wanting. His homicide statistics were taken from the National Center for Health Statistics.

10. See Hoffman, "The Role of the Father in Moral Internalization," in *The Role of the Father in Child Development*, edited by M. E. Lamb, pp. 373–374.

11. Sammons, "Why Physicians Should Oppose Boxing: An Interdisciplinary History Perspective," *Journal of the American Medical Association*, March 10, 1999, p. 1484–1486.

12. Michener, *Sports in America*, p. 469.

13. Lapchick, op. cit., p. 177.

14. Ibid., p. 178. Lapchick makes these comments in the course of summarizing Bennett J. Lombardo's article "The Behavior of Youth Sports Coaches: Crisis on the Bench," which appears in the same volume.

15. Meggyesy, op. cit., p. 20.

16. Oriard, op. cit., p. 13.

17. Meggyesy, op. cit., p. 23.

18. Oriard, op. cit., pp. 49–50.

19. See Fred Engh's introduction to Pat McInally's book *Moms and Dads and Kids and Sports*, p. xiii.

20. Michener, op. cit., p. 131.

21. Fine, *With the Boys*, p. 74.

22. Sack, interview with the author, 1988.

23. Meggyesy, op. cit., p. 28.

24. Messner, op. cit., p. 7.

25. Oriard, op. cit., pp. 97–98.

26. McMurtry quoted in Michael Smith, *Violence and Sport*, p. 33.

27. Oriard, op. cit., pp. 14–15.

28. Meggyesy, op. cit., p. 181.

29. Kopay and Perry Deane Young. *The David Kopay Story*, p. 58.

30. Fine, op. cit., p. 114.

31. Oriard, op. cit., p. 28.

32. Michener, op. cit., pp. 470–471.

Boyhood, Organized Sports, and the Construction of Masculinities

Michael A. Messner

1990

The rapid expansion of feminist scholarship in the past two decades has led to fundamental reconceptualizations of the historical and contemporary meanings of organized sport. In the nineteenth and twentieth centuries, modernization and women's continued movement into public life created widespread "fears of social feminization," especially among middle-class men (Hantover, 1978; Kimmel, 1987). One result of these fears was the creation of organized sport as a homosocial sphere in which competition and (often violent) physicality was valued, while "the feminine" was devalued. As a result, organized support has served to bolster a sagging ideology of male superiority, and has helped to reconstitute masculine hegemony (Bryson, 1987; Hall, 1988; Messner, 1988; Theberge, 1981).

The feminist critique has spawned a number of studies of the ways that women's sport has been marginalized and trivialized in the past (Greendorfer, 1977; Oglesby, 1978; Twin, 1978), in addition to illuminating the continued existence of structural and ideological barriers to gender equality within sport (Birrell, 1987). Only recently, however, have scholars begun to use feminist insights to examine men's experiences in sport (Kidd, 1987; Messner, 1987; Sabo, 1985). This article explores the relationship between the construction of masculine identity and boyhood participation in organized sports.

I view gender identity not as a "thing" that people "have," but rather as a *process of construction* that develops, comes into crisis, and changes as a person interacts with the social world. Through this perspective, it becomes possible to speak of "gendering" identities rather than "masculinity" or "femininity" as relatively fixed identities or statuses.

There is an agency in this construction; people are not passively shaped by their social environment. As recent feminist analyses of the construction of feminine gender identity have pointed out, girls and women are implicated in the construction of their own identities and personalities, both in terms of the ways that they participate in their own subordination and the ways that they resist subordination (Benjamin, 1988;

Haug, 1987). Yet this self-construction is not a fully conscious process. There are also deeply woven, unconscious motivations, fears, and anxieties at work here. So, too, in the construction of masculinity. Levinson (1978) has argued that masculine identity is neither fully "formed" by the social context, nor is it "caused" by some internal dynamic put into place during infancy. Instead, it is shaped and constructed through the interaction between the internal and the social. The internal gendering identity may set developmental "tasks," may create thresholds of anxiety and ambivalence, yet it is only through a concrete examination of people's interactions with others within social institutions that we can begin to understand both the similarities and differences in the construction of gender identities.

In this study I explore and interpret the meanings that males themselves attribute to their boyhood participation in organized sport. In what ways do males construct masculine identities within the institution of organized sports? In what ways do class and racial differences mediate this relationship and perhaps lead to the construction of different meanings, and perhaps different masculinities? And what are some of the problems and contradictions within these constructions of masculinity?

DESCRIPTION OF RESEARCH

Between 1983 and 1985, I conducted interviews with 30 male former athletes. Most of the men I interviewed had played the (U.S.) "major sports"—football, basketball, baseball, track. At the time of the interview, each had been retired from playing organized sports for at least five years. Their ages ranged from 21 to 48, with the median, 33; 14 were black, 14 were white, and two were Hispanic; 15 of the 16 black and Hispanic men had come from poor or working-class families, while the majority (9 of 14) of the white men had come from middle-class or professional families. All had at some time in their lives based their identities largely on their roles as athletes and could therefore be said to have had "athletic careers." Twelve had played organized sports through high school, 11 through college, and seven had been professional athletes. Though the sample was not randomly selected, an effort was made to see that the sample had a range of difference in terms of race and social class backgrounds, and that there was some variety in terms of age, types of sports played, and levels of success in athletic careers. Without exception, each man contacted agreed to be interviewed.

The tape-recorded interviews were semi-structured and took from one and one-half to six hours, with most taking about three hours. I asked each man to talk about four broad eras in his life: (1) his earliest experiences with sports in boyhood, (2) his athletic career, (3) retirement or disengagement from the athletic career, and (4) life after the athletic career. In each era, I focused the interview on the meanings of "success and failure," and on the boy's/man's relationships with family, with other males, with women, and with his own body.

In collecting what amounted to life histories of these men, my overarching purpose was to use feminist theories of masculine gender identity to explore how masculinity develops and changes as boys and men interact within the socially constructed world of organized sports. In addition to using the data to move toward some generalizations about the relationship between "masculinity and sport," I was also concerned with sorting out some of the variations among boys, based on class and racial inequalities, that led them to relate differently to athletic careers. I divided my sample into two comparison groups. The first group was made up of 10 men from higher-status backgrounds, primarily white, middle-class, and professional families. The second group was made up of 20 men from lower-status backgrounds, primarily minority poor, and working-class families.

BOYHOOD AND THE PROMISE OF SPORTS

Zane Grey once said, "All boys love baseball. If they don't they're not real boys" (as cited in Kimmel, 1990). This is, of course, an ideological statement; In fact, some boys do *not* love baseball, or any other sports, for that matter. There are millions of males who at an early age are rejected by, become alienated

from, or lose interest in organized sports. Yet all boys are, to a greater or lesser extent, judged according to their ability, or lack of ability, in competitive sports (Eitzen, 1975; Sabo, 1985). In this study I focus on those males who did become athletes—males who eventually poured thousands of hours into the development of specific physical skills. It is in boyhood that we can discover the roots of their commitment to athletic careers.

How did organized sports come to play such a central role in these boy's lives? When asked to recall how and why they initially got into playing sports, many of the men interviewed for this study seemed a bit puzzled: after all, playing sports was "just the thing to do." A 42-year-old black man who had played college basketball put it this way:

It was just what you did. It's kind of like, you went to school, you played athletics, and if you didn't, there was something wrong with you. It was just like brushing your teeth: it's just what you did. It's part of your existence.

Spending one's time playing sports with other boys seemed as natural as the cycle of the seasons: baseball in the spring and summer, football in the fall, basketball in the winter—and then it was time to get out the old baseball glove and begin again. As a black 35-year-old former professional football star said:

I'd say when I wasn't in school, 95% of the time was spent in the park playing. It was the only thing to do. It just came as natural.

And a black, 34-year-old professional basketball player explained his early experiences in sports:

My principal and teacher said, "Now if you work at this you might be pretty damned good." So it was more or less a community thing—everybody in the community said, "Boy, if you work hard and keep your nose clean, you gonna be good." Cause it was natural instinct.

"It was natural instinct." "I was a natural." Several athletes used words such as these to explain their early attraction to sports. But certainly there is nothing "natural" about throwing a ball through a hoop, hitting a ball with a bat, or jumping over hurdles. A boy, for instance, may have amazingly dexterous inborn hand-eye coordination, but this does not predispose him to a career of hitting baseballs any more than it predisposes him to a life as a brain surgeon. When one listens closely to what these men said about their early experiences in sports, it becomes clear that their adoption of the self-definition of "natural athlete" was the result of what Connell (1990) has called "a collective practice" that constructs masculinities. The boyhood development of masculine identity and status—truly problematic in a society that offers no official rite of passage into adulthood—results from a process of interaction with people and social institutions. Thus, in discussing early motivations in sports, men commonly talk of the importance of relationships with family members, peers, and the broader community.

FAMILY INFLUENCES

Though most of the men in this study spoke of their mothers with love, respect, even reverence, their descriptions of their earliest experiences in sports are stories of an exclusively male world. The existence of older brothers or uncles who served as teachers and athletic role models—as well as sources of competition for attention and status within the family—was very common. An older brother, uncle, or even close friend of the family who was a successful athlete appears to have acted as a sort of standard of achievement against whom to measure oneself. A 34-year-old black man who had been a three-sport star in high school said:

My uncles—my Uncle Harold went to the Detroit Tigers, played pro ball—all of 'em, everybody played sports, so I wanted to be better than anybody else. I knew that everybody in this town knew them—their names were something. I wanted my name to be just like theirs.

Similarly, a black 41-year-old former professional football player recalled:

I was the younger of three brothers and everybody played sports, so consequently I was more or less forced into it. 'Cause one brother was always better than the next brother and then I came along and had to show them that I was just as good as them. My oldest brother was an all-city ballplayer, then my other brother comes along he's all-city and all-state, and then I have to come along.

For some, attempting to emulate or surpass the athletic accomplishments of older male family members created pressures that were difficult to deal with. A 33-year-old white man explained that he was a good athlete during boyhood, but the constant awareness

that his two older brothers had been better made it difficult for him to feel good about himself, or to have fun in sports;

I had this sort of reputation that I followed from the playgrounds through grade school, and through high school. I followed these guys who were all-conference and all-state.

Most of these men, however, saw their relationships with their athletic older brothers and uncles in a positive light; it was within these relationships that they gained experience and developed motivations that gave them a competitive "edge" within their same-aged peer group. As a 33-year-old black man describes his earliest athletic experiences:

My brothers were role models. I wanted to prove—especially to my brothers—that I had heart, you know, that I was a man.

When asked, "What did it mean to you to be 'a man' at that age?" he replied:

Well, it meant that I didn't want to be a so-called scaredy-cat. You want to hit a guy even though he's bigger than you to show that, you know, you've got this macho image. I remember that at that young an age, that feeling was exciting to me. And that carried over, and as I got older, I got better and I began to look around me and see, well hey! I'm competitive with these guys, even though I'm younger, you know? And then of course all the compliments come—and I began to notice a change, even in my parents—especially in my father—he was proud of that, and that was very important to me. He was extremely important . . . he showed me more affection, now that I think of it.

As this man's words suggest, if men talk of their older brothers and uncles mostly as role models, teachers, and "names" to emulate, their talk of their relationships with their fathers is more deeply layered and complex. Athletic skills and competition for status may often be learned from older brothers, but it is in boys' relationships with fathers that we find many of the keys to the emotional salience of sports in the development of masculine identity.

RELATIONSHIPS WITH FATHERS

The fact that boys' introductions to organized sports are often made by fathers who might otherwise be absent or emotionally distant adds a powerful emotional charge to these early experiences (Osherson, 1986).

Although playing organized sports eventually came to feel "natural" for all of the men interviewed in this study, many needed to be "exposed" to sports, or even gently "pushed" by their fathers to become involved in activities like Little League baseball. A white, 33-year-old man explained:

I still remember it like it was yesterday—Dad and I driving up in his truck, and I had my glove and my hat and all that—and I said, "Dad, I don't want to do it." He says, "What?" I says, "I don't want to do it." I was nervous. That I might fail. And he says, "Don't be silly. Lookit: There's Joey and Petey and all your friends out there." And so Dad says, "You're gonna do it, come on." And in my memory he's never said that about anything else; he just knew I needed a little kick in the pants and I'd do it. And once you're out there and you see all the other kids making errors and stuff, and you know you're better than those guys, you know: Maybe I *do* belong here. As it turned out, Little League was a good experience.

Some who were similarly "pushed" by their fathers were not so successful as the aforementioned man had been in Little League baseball, and thus the experience was not altogether a joyous affair. One 34-year-old white man, for instance, said he "inherited" his interest in sports from his father, who started playing catch with him at the age of four. Once he got into Little League, he felt pressured by his father, one of the coaches, who expected him to be the star of the team:

I'd go O-for-four sometimes, strike out three times in a Little League game, and I'd dread the ride home. I'd come home and he'd say, "Go in the bathroom and swing the bat in the mirror for an hour," to get my swing level . . . It didn't help much, though, I'd go out and strike out three or four times again the next game too [laughs ironically]

When asked if he had been concerned with having his father's approval, he responded:

Failure in his eyes? Yeah, I always thought that he wanted me to get some kind of [athletic] scholarship. I guess I was afraid of him when I was a kid. He didn't hit that much, but he had a rage about him—he'd rage, and that voice would just rattle you.

Similarly, a 24-year-old black man described his awe of his father's physical power and presence, and his sense of inadequacy in attempting to emulate him:

My father had a voice that sounded like rolling thunder. Whether it was intentional on his part or not, I don't know, but my father gave me a sense, an image of him being the

most powerful being on earth, and that no matter what I ever did I would never come close to him . . . There were definite feelings of physical inadequacy that I couldn't work around.

It is interesting to note how these feelings of physical inadequacy relative to the father lived on as part of this young man's permanent internalized image. He eventually became a "feared" high school football player and broke school records in weigh-lifting, yet,

As I grew older, my mother and friends told me that I had actually grown to be a larger man than my father. Even though in time I required larger clothes than he, which should have been a very concrete indication, neither my brother nor I could ever bring ourselves to say that I was bigger. We simply couldn't conceive of it.

Using sports activities as a means of identifying with and "living up to" the power and status of one's father was not always such a painful and difficult task for the men I interviewed. Most did not describe fathers who "pushed" them to become sports stars. The relationship between their athletic strivings and their identification with their fathers was more subtle. A 48-year-old black man, for instance, explained that he was not pushed into sports by his father, but was aware from an early age of the community status his father had gained through sports. He saw his own athletic accomplishments as a way to connect with and emulate his father:

I wanted to play baseball because my father had been quite a good baseball player in the Negro leagues before baseball was integrated, and so he was kind of a model for me. I remember, quite young, going to a baseball game he was in—this was before the war and all—I remember being in the stands with my mother and seeing him on first base, and being aware of the crowd . . . I was aware of people's confidence in him as a serious baseball player. I don't think my father ever said anything to me like "play sports . . . [But] I knew he would like it if I did well. His admiration was important . . . he mattered.

Similarly, a 24-year-old white man described his father as a somewhat distant "role model" whose approval mattered:

My father was more of an example . . . he definitely was very much in touch with and still had very fond memories of being an athlete and talked about it, bragged about it. . . . But he really didn't do that much to teach me skills, and he didn't always go to every game I played like some parents. But he approved and that was important, you know. That was important to get his approval. I always knew that playing sports was important to him, so I knew implicitly that it was good and there was definitely a value on it.

First experiences in sports might often come through relationships with brothers or older male relatives, and the early emotional salience of sports was often directly related to a boy's relationship with his father. The sense of commitment that these young boys eventually made to the development of athletic careers is best explained as a process of development of masculine gender identity and status in relation to same-sex peers.

MASCULINE IDENTITY AND EARLY COMMITMENT TO SPORTS

When many of the men in this study said that during childhood they played sports because "it's just what everybody did," they of course meant that it was just what *boys* did. They were introduced to organized sports by older brothers and fathers, and once involved, found themselves playing within an exclusively male world. Though the separate (and unequal) gendered worlds of boys and girls came to appear as "natural," they were in fact socially constructed. Thorne's observations of children's activities in schools indicated that rather than "naturally" constituting "separate gendered cultures," there is considerable interaction between boys and girls in classrooms and on playgrounds. When adults set up legitimate contact between boys and girls, Thorne observed, this usually results in "relaxed interactions." But when activities in the classroom or on the playground are presented to children as sex-segregated activities and gender is marked by teachers and other adults ("boys line up here, girls over there"), "gender boundaries are heightened, and mixed-sex interaction becomes an explicit arena of risk" (Thorne, 1986; 70). Thus sex-segregated activities such as organized sports as structured by adults, provide the context in which gendered identities and separate "gendered cultures" develop and come to appear natural. For the boys in this study, it became "natural" to equate masculinity with competition, physical strength, and skills. Girls simply did not (could not, it was believed) participate in these activities.

Yet it is not simply the separation of children, by adults, into separate activities that explains why many boys came to feel such a strong connection with sports activities, while so few girls did. As I listened to men recall their earliest experiences in organized sports, I heard them talk of insecurity, loneliness, and especially a need to connect with other people as a primary motivation in their early sports strivings. As a 42-year-old white man stated, "The most important thing was just being out there with the rest of the guys—being friends." Another 32-year-old interviewee was born in Mexico and moved to the United States at a fairly young age. He never knew his father, and his mother died when he was only nine years old. Suddenly he felt rootless, and threw himself into sports. His initial motivations, however, do not appear to be based on a need to compete and win:

Actually, what I think sports did for me is it brought me into kind of an instant family. By being on a Little League team, or even just playing with all kinds of different kids in the neighborhood, it brought what I really wanted, which was some kind of closeness. It was just being there, and being friends.

Clearly, what these boys needed and craved was that which was most problematic for them: connection and unity with other people. But why do these young males find *organized sports* such an attractive context in which to establish "a kind of closeness" with others? Comparative observations of young boys' and girls' game-playing behaviors yield important insights into this question. Piaget (1965) and Lever (1976) both observed that girls tend to have more "pragmatic" and "flexible" orientations to the rules of games; they are more prone to make exceptions and innovations in the middle of a game in order to make the game more "fair." Boys, on the other hand, tend to have a more firm, even [in]flexible orientation to the rules of a game; to them, the rules are what protects any fairness. This difference, according to Gilligan (1982), is based on the fact that early developmental experiences have yielded deeply rooted differences between males' and females' developmental tasks, needs, and moral reasoning. Girls, who tend to define themselves primarily through connection with others, experience highly competitive situations (whether in organized sports or in other hierarchical institutions) as threats to relationships, and thus to their identities. For boys, the development of gender identity involves the construction of positional identities, where a sense of self is solidified through separation from others (Chodorow, 1978). Yet feminist psychoanalytic theory has tended to oversimplify the internal lives of men (Lichterman, 1986). Males do appear to develop positional identities, yet despite their fears of intimacy, they also retain a human need for closeness and unity with others. This ambivalence toward intimate relationships is a major thread running through masculine development throughout the life course. Here we can conceptualize what Craib (1987) calls the "elective affinity" between personality and social structure: For the boy who both seeks and fears attachment with others, the rule-bound structure of organized sports can promise to be a safe place in which to seek nonintimate attachment with others within a context that maintains clear boundaries, distance, and separation.

COMPETITIVE STRUCTURES AND CONDITIONAL SELF-WORTH

Young boys may initially find that sports gives them the opportunity to experience "some kind of closeness" with others, but the structure of sports and athletic careers often undermines the possibility of boys learning to transcend their fears of intimacy, thus becoming able to develop truly close and intimate relationships with others (Kidd, 1990; Messner, 1987). The sports world is extremely hierarchical, and an incredible amount of importance is placed on winning, on "being number one." For instance, a few years ago I observed a basketball camp put on for boys by a professional basketball coach and his staff. The youngest boys, about eight years old (who could barely reach the basket with their shots) played a brief scrimmage. Afterwards, the coaches lined them up in a row in front of the older boys who were sitting in the grandstands. One by one, the coach would stand behind each boy, put his hand on the boy's head (much in the manner of a priestly benediction), and the older boys in the stands would applaud and cheer, louder or softer, depending on how well or poorly the young boy was judged to have performed. The two or three boys who were clearly the exceptional players looked confident that they would receive the praise they were due. Most of the boys, though, had expressions ranging from puzzlement to thinly disguised terror on their faces as they awaited the judgments of the older boys.

This kind of experience teaches boys that it is not "just being out there with the guys—being friends," that ensures the kind of attention and connection that they crave; it is being *better* than the other guys—*beating* them—that is the key to acceptance. Most of the boys in this study did have some early successes in sports, and thus their ambivalent need for connection with others was met, at least for a time. But the institution of sport tends to encourage the development of what Schafer (1975) has called "conditional self-worth" in boys. As boys become aware that acceptance by others is contingent upon being good—a "winner"—narrow definitions of success, based upon performance and winning become increasingly important to them. A 33-year-old black man said that by the time he was in his early teens:

It was expected of me to do well in all my contests—I mean by my coaches, my peers, and my family. So I in turn expected to do well, and if I didn't do well, then I'd be very disappointed.

The man from Mexico, discussed above, who said that he had sought "some kind of closeness" in his early sports experiences began to notice in his early teens that if he played well, was a *winner*, he would get attention from others:

It got to the point where I started realizing, noticing that people were always there for me, backing me all the time—sports got to be really fun because I always had some people there backing me. Finally my oldest brother started going to all my games, even though I had never really seen who he was [laughs]—after the game, you know, we never really saw each other, but he was at all my baseball games, and it seemed like we shared a kind of closeness there, but only in those situations. Off the field, when I wasn't in uniform, he was never around.

By high school, he said, he felt "up against the wall." Sports hadn't delivered what he had hoped it would, but he thought if he just tried harder, won one more championship trophy, he would get the attention he truly craved. Despite his efforts, this attention was not forthcoming. And, sadly, the pressures he had put on himself to excel in sports had taken most of the fun out of playing.

For many of the men in this study, throughout boyhood and into adolescence, this conscious striving for successful achievement became the primary means through which they sought connection with other people (Messner, 1987). But it is important to recognize that young males' internalized ambivalences about intimacy do not fully determine the contours and directions of their lives. Masculinity continues to develop through interaction with the social world—and because boys from different backgrounds are interacting with substantially different familial, educational, and other institutions, these differences will lead them to make different choices and define situations in different ways. Next, I examine the differences in the ways that boys from higher- and lower-status families and communities related to organized sports.

STATUS DIFFERENCES AND COMMITMENTS TO SPORTS

In discussing early attractions to sports, the experiences of boys from higher- and lower-status backgrounds are quite similar. Both groups indicate the importance of fathers and older brothers in introducing them to sports. Both groups speak of the joys of receiving attention and acceptance among family and peers for early successes in sports. Note the similarities, for instance, in the following descriptions of boyhood athletic experiences of two men. First, a man born in a white, middle-class family:

I loved playing sports so much from a very early age because of early exposure. A lot of the sports came easy at an early age, and because they did, and because you were successful at something, I think that you're inclined to strive for that gratification. It's like, if you're good, you like it, because it's instant gratification. I'm doing something that I'm good at and I'm gonna keep doing it.

Second, a black man from a poor family:

Fortunately I had some athletic ability, and, quite naturally, once you start doing good in whatever it is—I don't care if it's jacks—you show off what you do. That's your ability, that's your blessing, so you show it off as much as you can.

For boys from both groups, early exposure to sports, the discovery that they had some "ability," shortly followed by some sort of family, peer, and community recognition, all eventually led to the commitment of hundreds and thousands of hours of playing, practicing, and dreaming of future stardom. Despite these similarities, there are also some identifiable differences that begin to explain the tendency of males from lower-status backgrounds to develop higher levels of commitment to sports careers. The

most clear-cut difference was that while men from higher-status backgrounds are likely to describe their earliest athletic experiences and motivations almost exclusively in terms of immediate family, men from lower-status backgrounds more commonly describe the importance of a broader community context. For instance, a 46-year-old man who grew up in a "poor working class" black family in a small town in Arkansas explained:

In that community, at the age of third or fourth grade, if you're a male, they expect you to show some kind of inclination, some kind of skill in football or basketball. It was an expected thing, you know? My mom and my dad, they didn't push at all. It was the general environment.

A 48-year-old man describes sports activities as a survival strategy in his poor black community:

Sports protected me from having to compete in gang stuff, or having to be good with my fists. If you were an athlete and got into the fist world, that was your business, and that was okay—but you didn't have to if you didn't want to. People would generally defer to you, give you your space away from trouble.

A 35-year-old man who grew up in "a poor black ghetto" described his boyhood relationship to sports similarly:

Where I came from, either you were one of two things: you were in sports or you were out on the streets being a drug addict, or breaking into places. The guys who were in sports, we had it a little easier, because we were accepted by both groups. . . . So it worked out to my advantage, cause I didn't get into a lot of trouble—some trouble, but not alot.

The fact that boys in lower-status communities faced these kinds of realities gave salience to their developing athletic identities. In contrast, sports were important to boys from higher-status backgrounds, yet the middle-class environment seemed more secure, less threatening, and offered far more options. By the time most of these boys got into junior high or high school, many had made conscious decisions to shift their attentions away from athletic careers to educational and (nonathletic) career goals. A 32-year-old white college athletic director told me that he had seen his chance to pursue a pro baseball career as "pissing in the wind," and instead, focused on education. Similarly, a 33-year-old white dentist who was a three-sport star in high school, decided not to play sports in college, so he could focus on getting into dental school. As he put it,

I think I kind of downgraded the stardom thing. I thought it was small potatoes. And sure, that's nice in high school and all that, but on a broad scale, I didn't think it amounted to all that much.

This statement offers an important key to understanding the construction of masculine identity within a middle-class context. The status that this boy got through sports had been *very* important to him, yet he could see that "on a broad scale," this sort of status was "small potatoes." This sort of early recognition is more than a result of the oft-noted middle-class tendency to raise "future-oriented" children (Rubin, 1976; Sennett and Cobb, 1973). Perhaps more important, it is that the *kinds* of future orientations developed by boys from higher-status backgrounds are consistent with the middle-class context. These men's descriptions of their boyhoods reveal that they grew up immersed in a wide range of institutional frameworks, of which organized sports was just one. And—importantly—they could see that the status of adult males around them was clearly linked to their positions within various professions, public institutions, and bureaucratic organizations. It was clear that access to this sort of institutional status came through educational achievement, not athletic prowess. A 32-year-old black man who grew up in a professional class family recalled that he had idolized Wilt Chamberlain and dreamed of being a pro basketball player, yet his father discouraged his athletic strivings:

He knew I liked the game. I *loved* the game. But basketball was not recommended; my dad would say, "That's a stereotyped image for black youth. . . . When your basketball is gone and finished, what are you gonna do? One day, you might get injured. What are you gonna look forward to?" He stressed education.

Similarly, a 32-year-old man who was raised in a white, middle-class family, had found in sports a key means of gaining acceptance and connection in his peer group. Yet he was simultaneously developing an image of himself as a "smart student," and becoming aware of a wide range of nonsports life options:

My mother was constantly telling me how smart I was, how good I was, what a nice person I was, and giving me all sorts of positive strokes, and those positive strokes became a self-

motivating kind of thing. I had this image of myself as smart, and I lived up to that image.

It is not that parents of boys in lower-status families did not also encourage their boys to work hard in school. Several reported that their parents "stressed books first, sports second." It's just that the broader social context—education, economy, and community—was more likely to *narrow* lower-status boys' perceptions of real-life options, while boys from higher-status backgrounds faced an expanding world of options. For instance, with a different socioeconomic background, one 35-year-old black man might have become a great musician instead of a star professional football running back. But he did not. When he was a child, he said, he was most interested in music:

I wanted to be a drummer. But we couldn't afford drums. My dad couldn't go out and buy me a drum set or a guitar even—it was just one of those things; he was just trying to make ends meet.

But he *could* afford, as could so many in his socioeconomic condition, to spend countless hours at the local park, where he was told by the park supervisor

that I was a natural—not only in gymnastics or baseball—whatever I did, I was a natural. He told me I shouldn't waste this talent, and so I immediately started watching the big guys then.

In retrospect, this man had potential to be a musician or any number of things, but his environment limited his options to sports, and he made the best of it. Even within sports, he, like most boys in the ghetto, was limited:

We didn't have any tennis courts in the ghetto—we used to have a lot of tennis balls, but no racquets. I wonder today how good I might be in tennis if I had gotten a racquet in my hands at an early age.

It is within this limited structure of opportunity that many lower-status young boys found sports to be *the* place, rather than *a* place, within which to construct masculine identity, status, the relationships. A 36-year-old white man explained that his father left the family when he was very young and his mother faced a very difficult struggle to make ends meet. As his words suggest, the more limited a boy's options, and the more insecure his family situation, the more likely he is to make an early commitment to an athletic career:

I used to ride my bicycle to Little League practice—if I'd waited for someone to pick me up and take me to the ball park I'd have never played. I'd get to the ball park and all the other kids would have their dad bring them to practice or games. But I'd park my bike to the side and when it was over I'd get on it and go home. Sports was the way for me to move everything to the side—family problems, just all the embarrassments—and think about one thing, and that was sports . . . In the third grade, when the teacher went around the classroom and asked everybody, "What do you want to be when you grow up?," I said, "I want to be a major league baseball player," and everybody laughed their heads off.

This man eventually did enjoy a major league baseball career. Most boys from lower-status backgrounds who make similar early commitments to athletic careers are not so successful. As stated earlier, the career structure of organized sports is highly competitive and hierarchical. In fact, the chances of attaining professional status in sports are approximately 4:100,000 for a white man, 2:100,000 for a black man, and 3:1 million for a Hispanic man in the United States (Leonard and Reyman, 1988). Nevertheless, the immediate rewards (fun, status, attention), along with the constricted (nonsports) structure of opportunity, attract disproportionately large numbers of boys from lower-status backgrounds to athletic careers as their major means of constructing a masculine identity. These are the boys who later, as young men, had to struggle with "conditional self-worth," and, more often than not, occupational dead ends. Boys from higher-status backgrounds, on the other hand, bolstered their boyhood, adolescent, and early adult status through their athletic accomplishments. Their wider range of experiences and life chances led to an early shift away from sports careers as the major basis of identity (Messner, 1989).

CONCLUSION

The conception of the masculinity-sports relationship developed here begins to illustrate the idea of an "elective affinity" between social structure and personality. Organized sports is a "gendered institution"—an institution constructed by gender relations. As such, its structure and values (rules, formal organization, sex composition, etc.), reflect dominant conceptions of masculinity and femininity. Organized sports is also a "gendering institution"—an institution that helps to construct the current gender order. Part of this construction of gender is accomplished through the "masculinizing" of male bodies and minds.

Yet boys do not come to their first experiences in organized sports as "blank slates," but arrive with already "gendering" identities due to early developmental experiences and previous socialization. I have suggested here that an important thread running through the development of masculine identity is males' ambivalence toward intimate unity with others. Those boys who experience early athletic successes find in the structure of organized sport an affinity with this masculine ambivalence toward intimacy: The rule-bound, competitive, hierarchical world of sport offers boys an attractive means of establishing an emotionally distant (and thus "safe") connection with others. Yet as boys begin to define themselves as "athletes," they learn that in order to be accepted (to have connection) through sports, they must be winners. And in order to be winners, they must construct relationships with others (and with themselves) that are consistent with the competitive and hierarchical values and structure of the sports world. As a result, they often develop a "conditional self-worth" that leads them to construct more instrumental relationships with themselves and others. This ultimately exacerbates their difficulties in constructing intimate relationships with others. In effect, the interaction between the young male's preexisting internalized ambivalence toward intimacy with the competitive hierarchical institution of sport has resulted in the construction of a masculine personality that is characterized by instrumental rationality, goal-orientation, and difficulties with intimate connection and expression (Messner, 1987).

This theoretical line of inquiry invites us not simply to examine how social institutions "socialize" boys, but also to explore the ways that boys' already-gendering identities interact with social institutions (which, like organized sport, are themselves the product of gender relations). This study has also suggested that it is not some singular "masculinity" that is being constructed through athletic careers. It may be correct, from a psychoanalytic perspective, to suggest that all males bring ambivalences toward intimacy to their interactions with the world, but "the world" is a very different place for males from different racial and socioeconomic backgrounds. Because males have substantially different interactions with the world, based on class, race, and other differences and inequalities, we might expect the construction of masculinity to take on different meanings for boys and men from differing backgrounds (Messner, 1989). Indeed, this study has suggested that boys from higher-status backgrounds face a much broader range of options than do their lower-status counterparts. As a result, athletic careers take on different meanings for these boys. Lower-status boys are likely to see athletic careers as *the* institutional context for the construction of their masculine status and identities, while higher-status males make an early shift away from athletic careers toward other institutions (usually education and non-sports careers). A key line of inquiry for future studies might begin by exploring this irony of sports careers: Despite the fact that "the athlete" is currently an example of an exemplary form of masculinity in public ideology, the vast majority of boys who become most committed to athletic careers are never well-rewarded for their efforts. The fact that class and racial dynamics lead boys from higher-status backgrounds, unlike their lower-status counterparts, to move into non-sports careers illustrates how the construction of different kinds of masculin*ities* is a key component of the overall construction of the gender order.

REFERENCES

BIRRELL, S. (1987) "The woman athlete's college experience: knowns and unknowns." *J. of Sport and Social Issues* 11: 82–96.

BENJAMIN, J. (1988) *The Bonds of Love: Psychoanalysis, Feminism, and the Problem of Domination.* New York: Pantheon.

BRYSON, L. (1987) "Sport and the maintenance of masculine hegemony." Women's Studies International *Forum* 10: 349–360.

CHEDOROW, N. (1978) *The Reproduction of Mothering.* Berkeley: Univ. of California Press.

CONNELL, R. W. (1987) *Gender and Power.* Stanford, CA: Stanford Univ. Press.

CONNELL, R. W. (1990) "An iron man: the body and some contradictions of hegemonic masculinity," In M. A. Messner and D. F. Sabo (eds) *Sport, Men and the Gender Order: Critical Feminist Perspectives.* Champaign, IL: Human Kinetics.

CRAIB, I. (1987) "Masculinity and male dominance." *Soc. Rev.* 38: 721–743.

EITZEN, D. S. (1975) "Athletics in the status system of male adolescents: a replication of Coleman's *The Adolescent Society.*" *Adolescence* 10: 268–276.

GILLIGAN, C. (1982) *In a Different Voice: Psychological Theory and Women's Development.* Cambridge. MA: Harvard Univ. Press.

GREENDORFER, S. L. (1977) "The role of socializing agents in female sport involvement." *Research Q.* 48: 304–310.

HALL, M. A. (1988) "The discourse on gender and sport: from femininity to feminism." *Sociology of Sport J.* 5: 330–340.

HANTOVER, J. (1978) "The boy scouts and the validation of masculinity." *J. of Social Issues* 34: 184–195.

HAUG, F. (1987) *Female Sexualization.* London: Verso.

KIDD, B. (1987) "Sports and masculinity," pp. 250–265 in M. Kaufman (ed) *Beyond Patriarchy: Essays by Men on Pleasure, Power, and Change.* Toronto: Oxford Univ. Press.

KIDD, B. (1990) "The men's cultural centre: sports and the dynamic of women's oppression/men's repression," In M. A. Messner and D. F. Sabo (eds) *Sport, Men and the Gender Order: Critical Feminist Perspectives.* Champaign, IL: Human Kinetics.

KIMMEL, M. S. (1987) "Men's responses to feminism at the turn of the century." *Gender and Society* 1: 261–283.

KIMMEL, M. S. (1990) "Baseball and the reconstitution of American masculinity: 1880–1920," In M. A. Messner and D. F. Sabo (eds) *Sport, Men and the Gender Order: Critical Feminist Perspectives.* Champaign, IL: Human Kinetics.

LEONARD, W. M. II AND J. M. REYMAN (1988) "The odds of attaining professional athlete status: refining the computations." *Sociology of Sport J.* 5: 162–169.

LEVER, J. (1976) "Sex differences in the games children play." *Social Problems* 23: 478–487.

LEVINSON, D. J. ET AL. (1978) *The Seasons of a Man's Life.* New York: Ballantine.

LICHTERMAN, P. (1986) "Chodorow's psychoanalytic sociology: a project half-completed." *California Sociologist* 9: 147–166.

MESSNER, M. (1987) "The meaning of success: the athletic experience and the development of male identity," pp. 193–210 in H. Brod (ed) *The Making of Masculinities: The New Men's Studies.* Boston: Allen & Unwin.

MESSNER, M. (1988) "Sports and male domination: the female athlete as contested ideological terrain." *Sociology of Sport J.* 5: 197–211.

MESSNER, M. (1989) "Masculinities and athletic careers." *Gender and Society* 3: 71–88.

OGLESBY, C. A. (ed) (1978) *Women and Sport: From Myth to Reality.* Philadelphia: Lea & Farber.

OSHERSON, S. (1986) *Finding our Fathers: How a Man's Life is Shaped by His Relationship with His Father.* New York: Fawcett Columbine.

PIAGET, J. H. (1965) *The Moral Judgment of the Child.* New York: Free Press.

RUBIN, L. B. (1976) *Worlds of Pain: Life in the Working Class Family.* New York: Basic Books.

SABO, D. (1985) "Sport, patriarchy and male identity: new questions about men and sport." *Arena Rev.* 9: 2.

SCHAFER, W. E. (1975) "Sport and male sex role socialization." *Sport Sociology Bull.* 4: 47–54.

SENNETT, R. AND COBB, J. (1973) *The Hidden Injuries of Class.* New York: Random House.

THEBERGE, N. (1981) "A critique of critiques: radical and feminist writings on sport." *Social Forces* 60: 2.

THORNE, B. (1986) "Girls and boys together . . . but mostly apart: gender arrangements in elementary schools," pp. 167–184 in W. W. Hartup and Z. Rubin (eds) *Relationships and Development.* Hillsdale, NJ: Lawrence Erlbaum.

TWIN, S. L. (ed) (1978) *Out of the Bleachers: Writings on Women and Sport.* Old Westbury, NY: Feminist Press.

Our Guys

Bernard Lefkowitz

THE BASEMENT

1

Ros Faber* didn't want to fret about her daughter, but she felt that familiar sense of uneasiness tug at her as she saw Leslie* running down the steps in her sweats. She's home from school ten minutes and she's leaving already, Ros thought.

"Where are you going, Les?" Ros asked.

"Shoot some hoops at the park," Leslie said without stopping as she detoured into the kitchen.

Ros watched her gulp down a glass of milk. She hesitated and finally said, "You know, if you're going to be late, you must call." Leslie was expected home at 5:30 on weekdays. That would give her time to help set the table for dinner.

"Don't worry," Leslie replied impatiently. She was seventeen, and she didn't want to be treated like a little kid. "You know I always get back on time."

Carrying her basketball and portable radio, Leslie opened the front door and started down the pathway to the street. "Bye," Ros called after her, trying hard to sound casual.

It was never easy for Rosalind to let her daughter go out alone. Leslie Faber was retarded.

To someone who didn't know her well, Leslie might appear almost normal: a friendly, outgoing teenager who loved sports. But Ros knew that Leslie's condition had left her impaired in a way that wasn't always visible. A lot of what people said in seemingly straightforward conversations went over her head and she was extraordinarily susceptible to suggestion and manipulation by anyone who seemed to like her.

In a big city, Ros thought, Leslie would have been vulnerable to the predatory stranger. But in 1989 Glen Ridge, New Jersey, retained the gentility of a more tranquil age; it remained a small, picture-perfect suburb where almost everyone knew everyone else. And that's what reassured Ros Faber. Today Leslie would be shooting baskets in the middle of the afternoon in a community playground ground that was a five-minute walk from her house. She had played in this park all her life. The other neighborhood children knew her well. They all came from respectable, well-off families like the Fabers themselves. The homes of many of the Fabers' friends were nearby. Strangers rarely passed through the sheltered streets of Glen Ridge. What could be safer than a couple of hours of healthy recreation in Cartaret Park?

The Fabers had moved to Glen Ridge fifteen years before and had never regretted it. When they learned that Leslie was retarded, it comforted them to know that they lived in the sort of place where the strong didn't prey on the weak. For Leslie needed protection, and the cruel streets of the city could inflict terrible injuries on a defenseless child. The Fabers believed that raising their daughter in Glen Ridge would keep her out of harm's way.

It was, in fact, just the sort of lovely, peaceful suburb many Americans dream about but few can afford. Many of the houses were neat and spacious, the streets were immaculate and picturesque, the schools were good, and the values of the community, Glen Ridgers would say with pride, were solidly planted in family, country, and the free enterprise system. On days when the urban swirl seemed overwhelming, Glen Ridge was the kind of place a New Yorker dreamed of escaping to.

Only 7,800 people lived in Glen Ridge. It was the second-smallest municipality in populous Essex County, consisting of just 1.3 square miles, and you could drive from one end to the other in five minutes. Set at the crest of a gentle slope rising from Newark Bay, the town seemed little changed in 1989 from when it was created in 1895. For the people who lived there, Glen Ridge remained a secure retreat in a contentious world.

A teenager walking the cobblestoned, leafy streets of Glen Ridge couldn't help feeling secure. Tranquility was so highly valued that the entire commercial life was limited to a couple of small stores housed in a

---

*. . . The author has used the real names of people who were involved in the investigation and trial, who held public positions, and who were identified in news stories about the case. The author has used pseudonyms, denoted by an asterisk, to disguise the identity and maintain the privacy of the rape victim and her family, as well as others not centrally involved in the case. Any similarity between these fictious names and those of living persons is coincidental.

single building near the commuter rail station. Indeed, when kids complained that it was boring to live in such a small, unexciting town, parents were quick to tell them that it was precisely the pastoral peacefulness of the suburb that made it a perfect place to raise children.

With her usual exuberance, Leslie trotted the short distance to the park. She was tall for her age, broad-shouldered, and somewhat overweight. Leslie was dressed in her play clothes: a West Orange High School shirt, purple sweatpants, and red-and-white sneakers. She was very proud of the radio she carried. It was about a foot and a half long, with speakers at each end. What made it special was its color—pink. It was a pretty radio, a feminine radio. That's why she had bought it. It was important to her because she had paid for it with her own money that she had earned mowing the lawn and raking leaves for her parents. She had plunked down the $35—her savings—at Crazy Eddie's about a year and a half ago; since then, the pink radio had been her constant companion whenever she went out to play.

Her walk to the park took her along Linden Avenue past the elementary school she had attended through the fourth grade. She walked one long block and turned left onto Cartaret Street, where she entered the playground. She had taken the same walk hundreds of times in her life.

Today the weather was cool and blustery, typical of the first day of March. The park was rectangular, about three hundred feet in length. Leslie headed for the basketball court in the southwest corner. She would remember later that as she walked toward the court, she noticed a stick in the grass. It was about a foot long, smeared with mud and flecked with red paint. She picked it up and threw it a few feet away. It was nicely balanced and carried well. She thought it would make a good "throwing stick" and decided to keep it.

Directly parallel to the basketball court, on the northwest side, was the softball diamond. At the other end of the park, the southeast corner, was the baseball diamond. Six rows of wooden bleachers, where spectators sat during Little League games, looked down on the first-base line.

At the baseball diamond a bunch of high school guys had formed two lines. The boys wore baseball gloves and cleats and trailed baseball bats behind them. Leslie, who was so devoted to athletics that she divided the year by the different sports seasons, knew what was going on. The guys on Glen Ridge's championship baseball team were going to have a preseason practice session, an easy drill without any adult coaches around. Loosen up, look sharp. The stars of the high school's other big-time teams, the wrestlers and the football players, also were there, hanging out, checking out the scene. This was very cool, Leslie thought. When she had left her house a few minutes before, who would have guessed that she was headed for jock heaven?

In a bigger town or in a city, most of these guys would be considered average athletes at best. But in the insulated world of Glen Ridge, they were the princes of the playing field. And that was the only world Leslie had ever known. These were the guys who acted as if they owned the high school. More than once, Leslie overheard girls saying they'd just *die* if the jocks didn't invite them to their parties.

It was a tough call to pick out the leader among all these handsome, popular guys, but Leslie guessed that it was Kyle Scherzer, although he wasn't her personal, true fave. Kyle, everybody said, would probably be picked as the best athlete in the senior class. Kyle was captain of the baseball team. He and his twin brother, Kevin, were co-captains of the football team. The Scherzers lived at 34 Lorraine Street, a white shingled house adjoining the park. From their backyard it was just a step onto the grass of Cartaret. Now, as she stood on the basketball court, Leslie could see Kyle on the back deck of his house, surveying the park as though it were his private kingdom.

Leslie knew that the deck was a pretty special place, although she had never stood on it herself. In whispers interspersed with giggles, her teammates on the girls' basketball and softball teams had explained the significance of being invited to a party on the Scherzers' deck.

For years now, Kyle and Kevin had invited their friends to deck parties after long afternoons of sports. Within the closed circle of jocks their spontaneous parties were famous. This was the closest thing the jocks had to a frat house. Here on the deck the guys celebrated a football or baseball victory, cooled out after a tough practice, or just gathered to goof around. Mostly, it was just the guys, but every once in a while one of the girls who trailed after the jocks would be admitted. The menu was usually soda and potato chips; occasionally, when no adults were around, there would be a few cans of beer. When the weather was cold or nasty, the guys would retreat downstairs to the Scherzers' semifinished basement to watch television or play Nintendo.

Leslie understood: If you got invited, it showed that you belonged. You were part of the gang. You counted. The teenage heroes of the town thought you were worthy of their attention. This honor had never been bestowed on Leslie. It wasn't because she was a newcomer to Cartaret or one of those kids who paid tuition to the high school and lived out of town. No, Leslie was as much a fixture in the park and in the town as the Scherzers.

She pitched for the girls' softball team and played guard for the high school girls' basketball team. She sold Girl Scout cookies door to door. In the spring she was there for the Memorial Day parade and in the winter she was there for the Christmas tree-lighting ceremony. At all times of the year, except when the snow got too deep, she could be seen riding around town on her bike, her brown hair blowing back from her forehead, her shoulders hunched over the handlebars, a big smile brightening her face as she called out "Hi" to all the people she knew and to people she knew not at all.

That was Leslie's special attribute: her buoyant personality. "If you smiled at her, she'd give you the world," said Christine Middleton, who was Leslie's teammate on the basketball team. "All she ever wanted was to be accepted by the other kids, to be part of the gang. And the kids she always admired the most, because she herself was good at sports, were the jocks. She'd see the other girls mooning after them and she'd want to do that, too."

Although she traveled freely throughout the small community, her most frequent destination was Cartaret Park. From the time she was a toddler, Leslie had watched the boys of Cartaret grow up. As a child, Leslie had lived near the eastern boundary of the playground. Then when she was in middle school, her mom and dad moved to their current house a few blocks away.

When Leslie was very young, Rosalind would bring her to the shady incline at the western end of the park where all the other mothers gathered with their babies and preschoolers. Rosalind would push her daughter on the yellow and red swings or watch her clamber in the miniature playhouse constructed of logs.

From Leslie's earliest memories, the Scherzer twins were always around. Whenever she was playing, they were playing. Whenever she was just a kid, not a dutiful daughter or an obedient student, the Scherzers were also being kids. Leslie was generally accurate when she later said of Kyle and Kevin, "I knew them all my life." She knew them, but only from afar. Leslie and the boys had followed separate paths through childhood and adolescence—Leslie friendless and alone, the boys clustered in the most envied and admired teenage clique in the town. Up to that moment, their lives had never converged.

Today didn't seem any different from most of the days of her youth. She played by herself on the basketball court, firing up some three-point bombs from behind the foul circle. Then, avoiding the puddles caused by last night's rain, she practiced her drives to the basket, shooting left-handed and right-handed, just like the pros.

A hundred feet away, the elite teenagers of Glen Ridge reveled in their male camaraderie. How many afternoons had she ended, from her vantage point under the backboards or in the top row of the wooden bleachers, watching Kyle and Kevin and their friends trooping happily toward the Scherzer house? But she was never included in that group. Look at it the way the guys did: If you invited a cute cheerleader, that boosted your romantic reputation. If you invited a not-so-cute brain, that might at least help you pass history and stay academically eligible for athletics. But what was the advantage of befriending a plain-looking retarded girl?

Sure, she played on teams, but she wasn't any star. Sure, she'd been hanging around for a lot of years, but she wasn't part of any popular group in school. In fact, she didn't even go to school in Glen Ridge anymore. The district had transferred her out to West Orange, where she attended a class for retarded kids. No matter how cheerful and friendly she was, no matter how desperately she yearned for one sign of recognition from her heroes, Leslie Faber could never expect to break through this invisible wall that separated her from the coolest kids in the school. She could never imagine being invited to one of the famous parties given by the Scherzer twins. No way. "Up until *that* day, I was never invited to a party at the Scherzer house." Leslie Faber would say later.

During the next half hour the baseball players rapped grounders, pegged bullets at each other, and chased down fly balls. The guys who were on other teams stood nearby in small groups, laughing, jostling each other, throwing mock punches. Guy stuff. They didn't seem to pay any attention to the young woman who was faking out an imaginary Michael Jordan over on the basketball court.

The few patches of blue were obscured by thick gray clouds, the wind picked up, and it looked as if it could rain again. The practice was breaking up. A bunch of the baseball players began walking in the direction of the Scherzers' house. Today was a good day to party. The twins' parents were in Florida all week. Aside from an elderly grandmother, the boys had the run of the house.

From the corner of her eye, Leslie could see five or six of the other boys, who weren't on the baseball team, walking toward the basketball court.

They stopped a few feet away, waving, smiling, all part of one happy group. The one boy who kept coming toward her was Christopher Archer.

Of all the kids who played at Cartaret, Leslie Faber probably knew Chris Archer and his brother, Paul, best. Leslie's parents were friends of the Archers' parents. Leslie would visit, sometimes unannounced, at their house down on lower Ridgewood Avenue. She would stay a while and talk with Chris and Paul when she was selling her Girl Scout cookies door to door.

Although she hadn't spent a huge amount of time with them when she was growing up, she had learned that there was a big difference between the two brothers. Paul had a kind smile and gentle, almost mournful, eyes. Eyes that melted you. He was a reasonably good football player and a captain of the wrestling team. And he was *very* good-looking. With all that, you might think he'd act stuck-up. But sometimes he'd talk to her, mostly about sports, and treat her just like any other girl in town. A few times he could be mean, but mostly he was nice. Paul was a really "cool guy." Chris, who was a year younger than Paul, had steel-cold eyes that always seemed to be looking beyond her. He almost never asked her about her basketball and softball, and he always had that sly grin on his face when he was making conversation with her.

Of the two, she liked Paul better, but it was important for her to please Chris; he might tell Paul she was nice. Chris was her link, her connection to Paul. Leslie never tried to hide her feelings about Paul. "I really liked him," she said later. "He's cute. He's handsome. He was my hero."

Chris chatted her up, his big smile radiating high spirits and camaraderie. He said to her, C'mon over to the Scherzer house, the guys just want to talk to you. C'mon over, we're all going to have a party.

Leslie considered this sudden invitation to attend a party with the most popular guys in town. Then she decided it wasn't such a good idea. No, I don't want to, Leslie said. Chris's invitation raised a question in her mind: Why would they want to take me down to the basement when they always called me retarded?

Chris, never at a loss for a new ploy, kept trying. "He said that his brother, Paul, was there," Leslie remembered later. "Chris told me that Paul would go out with me. I like Paul. So I went with Chris."

Gathering up her belongings—the stick, the radio, and her basketball—Leslie set out on the three-minute walk to the house. On the way to her "date" with Paul, Chris "walked with me, and put his arm around me," Leslie said. "He was like really romantic." When she was asked how Chris made her feel as he accompanied her to the Scherzer house, she replied: "Wonderful."

They passed the rear of the Scherzer house. The molded plastic chairs were stacked in one corner of the redwood deck next to a pile of tie-on canvas seat covers. The beach umbrella had been removed from its hole in the round picnic table and propped against a railing. It was too chilly on the first of March to hold an outside deck party; it would have to be in the semifinished basement.

A group of boys entered 34 Lorraine Street first. Trailing behind them were Chris and Leslie. Chris opened the door to the front entrance of the house. Leslie could feel his hand on her back, prodding gently but insistently. In the hall, just beyond the door, pegs had been set in the wall. The boys took off their red-and-white varsity jackets and hung them on the pegs. What a rush! Leslie could hang her own jacket on a peg, just as if she were also part of the team, just as if she were one of the pretty, effervescent girls who were always hanging around the jocks.

Chris led her forward, toward the stairs to the basement. On the way, she glanced into the kitchen, where she thought she saw the figure of an elderly woman.

Chris guided her down the stairs, past the younger kids who were clustered on the steps. As she reached the bottom, Leslie had a view of the entire basement. This was it: She had arrived. She was entering into the boys' special place, the "clubhouse" of the stars of Glen Ridge.

The room she entered now had a musty, wintry feel. It was lighted by a dim overhead bulb, turning ruddy outdoor complexions into gray pallor. The athletic trophies awarded over the years to Kyle and Kevin and their two older brothers were displayed on wall shelves, along with family photographs. One wall was unfinished, consisting of whitewashed concrete. Leslie would remember that three concrete blocks were piled near the wall. A sofa in the middle of the room could comfortably seat three. An area rug had been placed near the sofa. From the sofa you had a good view of a big-screen television. You could also watch TV from a wooden bench and maybe a half-dozen folding chairs. The entire basement was twenty-seven feet long and nineteen feet wide. There was only one exit, the steps to the front door.

In one alcove there was a refrigerator. Up against the wall, near the refrigerator, was a broom. Leslie, with her excellent memory for details, never forgot the color of the broomstick. She would always remember that it was "fire-engine red." In the back end of the basement, leading to the deck, the room was L-shaped. This area contained a bar, with three or four bar stools. There was a shelf at this end, and under it was a jumble of athletic equipment: basketballs, gloves, and baseballs and bats. Quite a few bats, including even a fungo bat used for practice. From her many years of playing softball, Leslie knew all about fungo bats: they were slightly narrower than a regular bat, but close to regulation-length.

Leslie would later remember that lots of boys were milling about in the basement. When she arrived, five of them, all seniors, were already down there. Among them was the one she adored—Paul Archer. Others joined them, including sophomore and senior baseball players and, of course, one junior, her friend Chris Archer. Some of them sat down or stood on the stairs.

The big attraction in the Scherzer basement in the winter and spring of 1989 was the Nintendo game, which at that time was still something of a novelty. Leslie could see a couple of the boys huddled around it.

Leslie also saw some of the boys arranging folding chairs in front of the couch. To her, it looked like they were getting ready to "watch a movie." A movie in which she was the star.

Chris leads her to the sofa where another senior heart-throb, Bryant Grober, is sitting. Leslie doesn't know him as well as she knows the Archers and Kyle and Kevin, because he lives on the other end of town and went to a different elementary school than she did. He comes to the park from way over on Forest Avenue and he isn't around all that much. She has seen Bryant play football, and she sometimes passes him in the corridors when she goes to Glen Ridge High School for basketball practice. She knows he is popular with the guys. She knows the girls think he is really cute. Sit here, Chris says, the idea man, handing her over to Bryant.

There is the hum of pleasantries exchanged in the basement.

Leslie, how's the basketball team doing?

Leslie, you gonna pitch again for the softball team?

But mostly the boys are talking to each other, chattering excitedly, like a group of kids rehearsing a student play.

After a while, Leslie hears the sound of footsteps on the stairs. She sees the adult she only glimpsed when she came into the house. The boys are saying, That's Kyle and Kevin's grandmother. She will always remember the old woman on the stairs—the presence of an adult makes the party seem normal just before it lurches out of control.

The woman, Leslie notices, has "white hair, sort of going bald." She is skinny and has a cane—"a silver metal cane with a green handle." This elderly woman, leaning heavily on her cane, walks halfway down the flight of steps. She calls out, "Kevin, you have a phone call." Kevin bounds up the steps, passing his grandmother, and disappears into the kitchen to take his call. This reassures Leslie: The boys wouldn't do something really bad, would they, knowing that the Scherzer twins' grandmother was bustling about in the kitchen right above them?

The kids are talking, but talking rather softly. For so many kids in a relatively small space, it is surprisingly quiet. Phil Grant, a senior baseball player, feels a hushed, expectant weight in the room, like the heavy silence before a storm.

Another boy, a fifteen-year-old sophomore, watches Chris Archer leaning over and whispering to Leslie. He sees Leslie sitting in the middle of the couch, Bryant on her right. Bryant pulls off his pants and then his underpants. The sophomore can't hear what Chris is saying to Leslie, but he can see what's going on. The sophomore looks into Leslie's eyes and sees what the others can't or won't see. He sees puzzlement and confusion and skepticism.

Now they have all taken their places—thirteen young men, the pride of Glen Ridge High, and Leslie. Some of the boys are seated on the folding chairs, a few feet away from the sofa. Others are standing to the side and behind the chairs. A few kids are watching from the stairs. For the moment Paul Archer is silent; he doesn't seem to be in any rush to ask Leslie out. Kyle is standing near the line of folding chairs. Kevin, who has returned to the basement after taking his phone call, is sitting on one of the chairs.

As Leslie begins to pull up her shirt, the sophomore who has seen puzzlement and confusion in Leslie's eyes turns to another of the underclassmen and says, "Let's get out of here." They leave together.

Phil Grant, the senior baseball player, also feels queasy as Leslie begins to disrobe. He is thinking, I don't belong here, it's just too weird. Phil exchanges looks with a buddy of his, another senior baseball player. They both start up the stairs together. Then Phil stops and turns and says to his childhood friend Paul Archer, "It's wrong. C'mon with me."

Archer says nothing in reply. He stays where he is, with his brother and his buddies.

At the top of the stairs, Phil hears somebody shouting, "Don't go. Don't miss this." Even though what his friends are doing makes him uncomfortable, he feels obliged to offer an excuse. "I got to go home," he says. "Seeya later."

Six young men have left. Seven young men, six seniors and junior Chris Archer, will remain in the basement with Leslie until they are done with her.

Yes, it is "just like a movie"—she attracting all the attention, the boys staring at her from their chairs, the other boys peering down at her from the stairs. But, as in all memorable movies, certain scenes would stand out. Things she heard, things people did—images that would stay with her no matter how many times she was later questioned by the police, by investigators, by psychiatrists and psychologists, by grand jurors and prosecutors and defense lawyers. Some of what Leslie remembers:

The boys getting up from their chairs, crowding around the sofa, a circle of flushed, excited faces urging her, Go further, go further!

Phil and his friend and the younger kids leaving without saying a word to her.

Leslie left alone with the inner circle of jocks: Kyle and Kevin, Bryant Grober, Paul and Chris Archer, and two of their friends and teammates, Peter Quigley and Richard Corcoran.

Leslie feels a hand on her head. There is a penis in her mouth.

Leslie hears another boy shout, You whore!

The boys are laughing, snickering. How does it feel? a boy asks. Does it make you feel good?

Leslie hears the voice say, Let's play a joke on her.

A neighborhood boy, a boy she has known all her life, is walking toward the 'fridge, reaching for the broom with the bright-red handle.

A boy walks to the back of the basement, fishes through the pile of sports equipment, pulls out a bat.

A voice says, Stop. You're hurting her.

Another voice says, Do it more.

Leslie remembers: Everyone was laughing. I was crying to myself, but I had tears coming out of my eyes.

Leslie remembers: The boys say to her that this all must be our secret. We'll be mad at you if you talk about this, you'll get kicked out of your school, we'll tell your mother if you break our secret.

Then, all in a circle, they clasp one hand on top of the other, all their hands together, like a basketball team on the sidelines at the end of a timeout. Leslie would say: It was just like one-two-three win!

A voice announces: We're not going to tell anybody. This is our little secret.

A voice says to Leslie: Hurry up. Go. Get out of here.

After Leslie left the basement, she waited a while outside the Scherzer house. Then she went into the park. She waited there, walking back and forth between the baseball diamond and the basketball court. She waited and waited for Paul Archer, her dream date, to show up. But he never did.

She walked a few blocks into Bloomfield to visit one of her few friends, Jennifer Lipinski. "She always stuck up for me," Leslie would say later. "I wanted to discuss with her what happened to me." But it was already late in the afternoon, long after she was expected at Jennifer's house. Jennifer had left, so Leslie spent a little time playing ball with Jennifer's brother. Then she went home.

Rosalind Faber was not pleased with her daughter. She had expected Leslie to be home by 5:30. Leslie knew she was supposed to set the table for dinner. That was her one daily chore. Routine provided continuity and structure for Leslie. But the table was not set and Ros's daughter was not there. 6:30. 6:45. Rosalind was getting nervous. It was dark outside. Where was Leslie?

When Leslie showed up at 7 o'clock, her mother did not try to hide her disapproval. "Where were you?" she asked, each word coated with ice. "Why didn't you call?"

"I was at the park, playing basketball," Leslie mumbled.

"I was worried."

"I'm okay," she said, looking down at the floor.

Glancing at the stick Leslie was holding, her mother asked, "What's that?"

"Oh, it's just a stick I found in the park," Leslie said.

"It's dirty. Why don't you put it in the garbage?"

"No, I want to keep it. It's good for throwing."

Rosalind took the stick from her. "All right, I'll keep it for you," she said. She put the stick on the top of the refrigerator, out of sight.

"I'm going up to change my clothes," Leslie said, starting up the stairs.

"I don't want you to do this again," her mother called after her. "You know it upsets me when you're not home when you're supposed to be."

Leslie, already upstairs, already going into her room, didn't answer.

At the dinner table, Leslie appeared distracted and withdrawn. She ate quickly and did not volunteer any information about her day. Her behavior made her parents uneasy. Leslie did not usually start a conversation, but she did join in when her mother and father initiated a discussion. Tonight she was quiet.

Charles Faber,* who was a manager at a large corporation, knew how to draw people out, to find out what was bothering them. But with Leslie he was running into a wall.

"Leslie, what's wrong? Is anything bothering you?"

"Nothing," she said. "I don't know. . . . Nothing's wrong."

Something's not right, Rosalind was thinking. She's trying to send us a signal, Charles was thinking, but what signal? The Fabers knew from experience that when Leslie didn't want to talk about a subject or when she was hiding something, it was not productive to push her. You had to wait for her to open up and then you asked a specific question. If you tried to press her, she would go silent on you or lapse into vagueness: Well, gee, I don't know . . .

Rosalind tried one more time. "Did you run into anybody at the park?"

Her response was sharp. "Why do you want to know?"

"I'm just asking, Leslie. Well, did you?"

"No. Nobody."

When they finished dinner, Leslie gathered up the dishes. Then she went into the living room to watch a rerun of "Gilligan's Island," her favorite TV show. After a while, Leslie said she was tired and went upstairs to get ready to go to bed.

At about 3 A.M. her parents heard Leslie talking in her sleep. Their bedroom was next door to Leslie's and the sounds could be heard through the wall. Words. Then what sounded like a muffled cry or gasp. They knew that when something disturbed Leslie, she would talk in her sleep. But she didn't often cry.

They got up and quietly walked into her room. They tried to make out what she was saying, but the words were indistinct. She was squirming in the bed—and groaning. Rosalind didn't want to wake her, but she was so concerned that she couldn't stop herself.

She shook Leslie. "Les, you're talking in your sleep. What's wrong?"

Leslie rubbed her eyes. "Nothing," she said. "*Nothing's* wrong."

Back in their bedroom, Charles Faber looked at his wife and said: "Something's happened."

That morning Rosalind tried to probe gently. "Leslie, you really had a restless night last night. Is everything okay? What were you talking about in your sleep?"

Leslie answered much as she had at dinner. "I don't remember. . . . Everything's okay. . . . I'm fine."

Months later she would recall that night after she came home from the Scherzers' basement and say, "I was embarrassed. I was too scared to tell my parents. They wouldn't understand."

2

Sheila Byron had just attended Easter Sunday Mass at Sacred Heart Church in Bloomfield, Glen Ridge's next-door neighbor. As she left the church this morning, March 26, her mind was definitely not on her job, which was working as a detective for the Glen Ridge Police Department. Her mind was on the week she had just spent with two girlfriends in Mexico, a Club Med vacation. Her mind was on white sand and turquoise water. As she crossed the street in front of the church, she met her boss, Detective Lieutenant Richard Corcoran.

"Hey, boss, how you doing?" she greeted him. "Was it a good week?"

"Oh, it wasn't a good week at all," he said. "There's something pretty serious going on."

It made sense that Lieutenant Corcoran would turn to Sheila Byron when he caught a tough case. Although she was only twenty-six, she was a rising star on the Glen Ridge police force. First of all, she knew the town well. She had graduated from Glen Ridge High in 1981 and had lived in town most of her life. During her four years on the force, she had handled some delicate cases, including wife battering and child abuse, with intelligence and sensitivity. Her style—direct, calm, and easygoing—was effective in tamping down a barroom fight or coping with the good-natured teasing of her fellow cops.

Sheila Byron stood out, and not only because she was a solid cop. She was a tall woman with sparkling eyes and long, thick hair. She was also a stylish dresser. In social situations she was outgoing and gregarious. In the department and the town, she was admired for her personality, beauty, and brains. During her brief police career, she had moved up from uniformed cop to juvenile officer to detective. One of only two women in the department, she was treated with professional respect by the men she worked with. She would need their respect on this case.

As Corcoran filled her in, the case impressed her as something unusual, something her relatively brief experience as a cop in a small, genteel suburb hadn't prepared her for. Bizarre accusations were floating around the school and the town, involving a bunch of high school guys, including the Scherzer twins, and a retarded girl. There were rumors that some of the guys might have done things to the girl with a bat and a broomstick. The police, Corcoran told her, already had the names of nine boys who might have been in the Scherzer basement on March 1. Maybe there had been a sexual assault. There wasn't enough to go on yet to be sure. One thing was clear, a lot of guys had been there. And the cops also had the name of the possible victim: Leslie Faber.

Byron had seen enough of Leslie Faber over the years to know she was different. But she wasn't sure how different. "The Fabers say they want a woman to talk to Leslie," Corcoran told her. "They were waiting for you to get back. They want to bring Leslie in tomorrow."

"I'll get in early and read the file," Byron said.

When she walked into the squad room the next morning, Sheila felt the tension. She didn't hear the usual wisecracks about who got poured out of the Town Pub on Saturday night. Nobody was asking her if she fell in love with one of the studs at Club Med. When the police chief, Tom Dugan, handed her the paper on the case, he seemed more nervous than usual. Dugan was a real go-by-the-book guy. Make sure you follow procedure. Don't leave anything out. He was always like that, but now he seemed strained. Something was eroding the armor of cop stoicism. Emotions swept across his broad Irish face: sadness, anxiety. And she caught that blink in his eyes; it was as close to fear as she had ever seen. All he said to her was "Get it all on paper. I want everything. I want it all."

She understood his concerns when she finished reading. The slim file began with March 22. That day, Charles Figueroa, a high school senior, told school officials that he had overheard students talking about a sexual encounter involving a number of athletes and a retarded girl. The vice-principal of the high school called the police. Detectives Richard Corcoran and Robert Griffin went to the school. There they interviewed the principal, the vice-principal, and Figueroa. Sheila knew Charlie Figueroa. His family lived near where she had grown up, and he was one of only three black students in the Class of '89. She had seen him play football and remembered that he had also wrestled for the high school.

Detective Griffin wrote in his report that, according to the school administrators, "a complainant who was a seventeen-year-old girl, classified as educable mentally retarded, may have been sexually abused by a group of juvenile males from Glen Ridge High School."

According to the detective's report, Figueroa recalled that the day after the experience in the basement, he had been standing outside the Scherzers' house with a group of other jocks. Figueroa said the boys told him what they did to Leslie, which the detective translated into legal terms: "The complainant was reportedly penetrated . . . by baseball bats, broomsticks, and a musical drumstick." The other jocks also reportedly told Figueroa that "oral sex" occurred during the incident.

Baseball bats, broomsticks, oral sex. The detective's account was shocking. But the next report in the file had even greater impact on Byron. This was Griffin's summary of his interview on March 23 with Margaret Savage, Leslie's swimming coach at West Orange High School. In effect, for the first time Byron was hearing the "victim's" account, albeit in a second-hand version from the swimming coach.

Savage reconstructed for Detective Griffin a conversation she had with Leslie three days after the basement encounter. Savage said Leslie told her that she had been at a "party in the basement with ten boys and they did things to me." According to Savage: "They asked her how many fingers could she put up [her] butt and then put 'something very big into me' and then they asked her to suck their dicks and said they wouldn't like her if she didn't do it and she would 'get into trouble.'"

Savage told the detective: "They [the boys] told her not to tell 'cause . . . they'd be mad and she'd be kicked out of school." Griffin noted: "Complainant told Savage that she was afraid to say 'no' and didn't know what to do." Leslie told the swimming coach that the boys had assured her that what they were doing was "okay," but Leslie wasn't so sure of that because, as she put it: "It hurt a lot."

What she read took Byron's breath away. If the allegations contained in these reports could be verified, you had the elements of a major crime. But that wasn't all. One other report in the file contained a list of nine names culled from the interviews with Figueroa and Savage.

Whoa. Wait a minute. She knew these names. She knew these kids. Archer, Scherzer, Grober, Quigley. They were popular, they came from good families, they were the best athletes in the high school. Some of them had been in a few scrapes with the law. Noisy parties, underage drinking—nothing major. As far as she knew, the worst thing you could say about them was that they were boisterous.

It was strange when you thought about it. These jocks, of all the teenagers in town, probably got along

the best with cops. When she was on duty at sports events or keeping order at a high school dance, the Scherzer twins always made a point of coming over and saying hello. She remembered them as far back as the eighth grade.

The only word of caution came from a patrolman who knew the twins. He had told her, "Watch out for those two. They're pretty wild." But it sounded like nothing more than rowdiness, so she'd put it out of her mind. She had been in high school. She had seen jocks acting as though they owned the place, obnoxious, arrogant. But now they were selling stocks, pushing insurance policies, married with a couple of kids, shouldering a heavy mortgage. You can't apply the same standards to a sixteen-year-old that you apply to an adult. You have to give him a few years to grow up.

Often in a small town, when you hear something bad about a kid, the first thing you do is check out the family. Are the parents big drinkers? Do they beat or abuse their kids? No hint of that with the families on this list.

The Archers? Doug Archer was Mr. Congeniality. A salesman of computer systems by trade, he was a big civic booster, along with his wife, Michaele, a nurse. They lived on Ridgewood Avenue, the town's grandest street, in a brick Colonial-revival house. Genial and outgoing, Doug and Michaele were popular in the upper reaches of Glen Ridge's church, civic, and social circuits, and they were friendly with Leslie Faber's parents.

Whenever Sheila met Doug at a school function or on some town committee, he gave her the big handshake with the simultaneous pat on the back and the ear-to-ear smile. Always, "Sheila, it's great to see you. You're doing a great job with the kids in town." And Michaele Archer, she was as nice as they came. Sweet, thoughtful, a loving mother. A good nurse, too, from what Sheila had heard.

Many parents didn't want to hear anything bad about their children. That wasn't true of the Archers. They had four children, all boys, all athletes, all popular with parents and kids in the community. Michaele was always up-front, telling Sheila, Let us know if the boys are problems; call us if they're at a party where there's alcohol. When Sheila did call, they always acted as if they were glad to hear from her, appreciative, very much the concerned parents.

The Scherzers? Jack, he was Mr. Jock. During the days he was a maintenance supervisor for the Otis Elevator Company in New York City. But after work, every season, every year, he was there for each game his kids played in. He was there even when his kids weren't playing. Lived and died with every pass, every base hit. Now, with Jack, you might not want to criticize his boys, because he seemed to think they were nearly perfect. But so did lots of fathers. When you showed up in the police car at a block party on Lorraine Street, Jack would be the first guy to show you around. Mrs. Scherzer, Geraldine, she was quiet, faded into the background. But a nice lady. Pleasant.

The Grobers? They were quiet people with a lovely house on Forest Avenue in the prosperous north end of town, a couple of streets away from the country club. Nate Grober was a doctor, with an office in East Orange. Sheila had heard that his patients loved him because he really showed concern for them. Bryant was a football player and wrestler; his older brother had also been a popular jock—a wrestler, she remembered. The family probably had some money, but didn't show it off. Bryant's mom, Rosemary, was also a nurse, like Michaele Archer. Easygoing, cheerful. The kids in the neighborhood loved her cookies.

The Quigleys? Not as active on the social-civic-sports scene as some of the other families, but a pleasant, low-key couple. Michael Quigley worked as an accountant; his wife, Mary, had been a staff member at an early-childhood center near Glen Ridge. Mr. Quigley didn't show up for every game the way Jack Scherzer did, but he had coached in the town's preteen sports leagues. Peter had two brothers, one younger and one older, both into sports. Many in the town thought Peter was the most affable of all the boys in the jock circle; the seniors had voted him "best-looking" and "best body." He was also a co-captain of the football team, and if you took a secret vote of his teammates, they would probably pick him as the best pure athlete on the team. Solid family, lived a couple of blocks away from Cartaret Park.

Some of the boys listed in the police report had reportedly been in the basement. Others were rumored to have tried to talk Leslie into coming back a second time. Supposedly, there were even more kids involved, but the police didn't have all the names yet. These were the sons of lawyers, investment bankers, accountants, teachers—people who formed the backbone of the town. They weren't necessarily the old-line aristocrats of Glen Ridge; they didn't all run for public office or belong to the country club, but they

held good jobs, volunteered for time-consuming civic activities, coached the community sports teams, and went to church. Cheez, they didn't just show up on Sunday; they sang in the church choir, they were vestrymen. They defined Glen Ridge; they made it what it was.

Sheila knew that the case could be dynamite. If you were a young cop and you wanted to hold on to your job for a while and maybe even had a secret ambition to become the first woman police chief of Glen Ridge, you'd better go slow. The potential was there for charging some of these boys with first-degree rape. Serious stuff. Putting aside what an accusation like that could do to a kid's future, it could tear a family apart, ruin something that these people had worked their whole adult lives to build. And it wasn't only them as individuals. If any of this was true, it could also savage the entire town. This wasn't about one or two kids going bad. What did you have here, many of the best-known boys in the senior class? The file she held in her hands struck at the heart of the way kids were raised in Glen Ridge, at the basic values of the town. The paper in this manila folder was a ticking bomb.

She wondered how many more names might be added to the list. (Ultimately, as the investigation expanded, the police report would list nineteen names of Glen Ridge High School students.) As the town's juvenile officer, Sheila Byron had a good idea of who belonged to the different adolescent cliques. The guys on the list were all jocks, but one name in the group was missing. She knew he was tight with these boys. They were his best friends. He had played football and had wrestled. He had difficulty in school with his studies and with observing rules. He had the reputation of being something of a loudmouth. But so far nobody had put him in the basement. And, God, she hoped they wouldn't. The last name she wanted to see on the list was that of Richard Corcoran Junior. That would be some wonderful bonus: the son of your immediate boss, the son of Detective Lieutenant Richard Corcoran—a rape suspect.

The yellow light of caution warned her: Go slow, Sheila. Don't rush to judgment. The one consolation this Monday morning was that nothing was certain, nothing had been proved. All they had to go on were the fragments of a conversation reported by one student and what a young woman in a special ed class had *reportedly* told a teacher. Sheila hadn't talked to any of the boys who had been in the basement. And she hadn't talked to the young woman. Who knew? Cases could crumble in a hurry. Maybe when she met Leslie this afternoon she would have a clearer idea of whether any of this would stick.

For Sheila, a key question was: Did the boys force Leslie to perform these acts, or did she go along willingly? The matter of consent is a critical issue in most rape cases, except when the victim is so badly beaten that there can be no question that force was used. When victim and assailant know each other, the consent question can be difficult to answer. In this case, involving a supposedly retarded girl, it would be even more so. Did Leslie give consent or not? So far, the reports Sheila had read made it sound like Leslie had not actively resisted.

But if she hadn't, was it possible that she was incapable of giving consent? Was she too retarded to understand what consent meant? Did she realize what was happening to her in the basement? If she hadn't understood, then what? Was what the boys did a crime—or was it just a crummy thing to do? With Leslie, the detective believed that consent would supersede all the other issues in the case.

Byron finished reading the file. At 4:30 Mrs. Faber brought Leslie into the police station. As soon as Leslie saw Sheila, she walked away from her mom. It was obvious to Byron that Leslie didn't want to talk in front of her mother. Ros Faber seemed to sense that, too. After she introduced Leslie to Byron, she left the room. Ros knew that if Leslie was going to unburden herself, she would have to do it without her parents present. As the detective wrote in her notes concerning that first meeting, "She was very concerned about her mother finding out what happened."

Sheila led Leslie to a small room on the second floor of the Public Safety Building that was used for interviews. The furnishings were austere: a desk, a couple of chairs, walls unadorned except for an old map of Glen Ridge. There was one window, which looked down on a quiet residential street.

Leslie was dressed in play clothes: gym shorts, a sweatshirt, sneakers. She sat in a chair. Sheila sat next to her. For much of the next ninety minutes, Leslie would stare down at the wood floor. Often her remarks would drift off the subject. She'd compliment Sheila on her gold earrings. She'd get up and look out the window.

Byron decided that in this first meeting she would try to keep the conversation informal and relaxed. She wanted Leslie to feel comfortable with her. The detective wanted to gauge her competence, to see how credible she appeared.

She did not take a formal, signed statement from Leslie. It was her practice never to take a signed statement during her first meeting with the victim of a sexual assault. Often the traumatic impact of the experience distorted the victim's memory, confusing the chronology of what happened when and the sequence of who did what. At the second or third meeting, when the victim felt more comfortable, her recollection of the assault would be sharper and more complete.

Getting a complete account of what happened in the basement could wait for another day. For openers this afternoon, Sheila asked Leslie about her dog, her schoolwork, her softball and basketball practice. It was pretty clear from the start that Leslie liked her. She had always expressed an affinity for pretty, intelligent young women who had achieved a lot in a short time. And that described Sheila: a woman who radiated confidence. And probably most important to Leslie, this terrific woman seemed to really enjoy her company.

After about forty-five minutes, the detective eased into the reason why Leslie was at the police station this afternoon: "You know, Leslie, some of the kids at the high school heard these boys saying they did sexual things to you."

Without hesitating, Leslie answered, "Yes, yes, yes. It's true. I did things with the wrestling team because I want them to be my friends."

From the list she had, Byron knew that not all the boys who were in the basement were wrestlers, but she understood why Leslie thought they were all on the team. Some of the guys were wrestlers: the Archer brothers and Bryant Grober. And this had happened on a day when the wrestling championships were going to be held later that evening.

Sheila took notes on a lined sheet of paper while Leslie filled in some of the critical gaps about the hour she spent in the basement. Leslie told Byron that it was Chris Archer who talked her into going to the basement. Leslie estimated that there were between twelve and twenty boys in the basement. She said that a broomstick and a bat, which were covered with bags coated with Vaseline, had been inserted into her. As Leslie described what happened, Byron wrote on the paper: "Vaseline on broomstick." She wrote: "White plastic bag covered whole bat."

When the subject of the broomstick came up, Sheila asked, "Where did he put it, Leslie?" Leslie pointed down at her vagina. "In front," she said. She doesn't know the word, Sheila thought; she doesn't know the word *vagina*.

As the objects were being inserted into her, Leslie recalled, one boy, Kyle Scherzer, said, "Let's stop this. You shouldn't be doing this to her." Leslie mentioned the names of different boys who she said had been in the basement: the Scherzers, the Archers, "Brian" Grober. To Sheila's vast relief, one person Leslie did not place at the scene was Richie Corcoran.

She also told Sheila that on the following day she had been approached by two Glen Ridge seniors who asked her to return to the Scherzer basement—and she refused. Leslie said she told the two boys that she was waiting for a friend, which she acknowledged to Sheila was a lie. The girl didn't cry as she told her story to Sheila Byron. She had no apparent bruises on her face and body. She didn't say that the boys had threatened her with knives or guns. She didn't say that they had tried to beat her up. But to the detective she seemed emotionally battered—fearful and confused.

That fear surfaced whenever Leslie brought up the name of one boy—Chris Archer. She complained that Chris had been bothering her for a while. He had been calling her on the phone, she said, talking dirty. "Chris has been bothering me for a year and a half," she said. He had been asking her to have sex with him at different locations in town, including a shed behind one of the elementary schools. "I tell Chris, 'Leave me alone,' but he says he wouldn't ever leave me alone," Leslie told the detective. "Please tell his mother to make him leave me alone."

As Leslie began to fill in the picture, adding images and details to the flat sentences in the police reports, she was also bringing something more: her personality and the limits of her understanding. She had always wanted to be liked—especially by the popular athletes—and what happened in the basement hadn't changed that. She told Sheila that she still wanted the boys to be her friends. She was saying, in effect, "These guys are my heroes; I don't want to get them in trouble." It's clear, Sheila thought, that she's not going to say, as a normal victim would, "This is what they did to me." She's saying, "This is what I did."

It created a predicament for a detective. The victim was reluctant to blame the victimizers. What kind of witness would Leslie make? Would a jury listening to Leslie ever believe that something criminal had happened in the basement? Unless you were able to find independent corroboration, this was going to be a very tough case to win.

But all through this first meeting, Sheila had to remind herself: This is no ordinary case; Leslie is no ordinary adolescent girl. Her loyalty to these boys, her need to be friends with them after all that has happened to her, makes that clear. For successful prosecution of the boys, one would have to argue that Leslie was retarded, that she did not possess the awareness and maturity to know she had been exploited.

Was she, in fact, retarded? Sometimes in the course of her conversation she appeared unfocused and illogical. But at other times her account was precise and coherent. Sheila had wanted to meet Leslie to size her up. But what was the sum total? What could the detective say—unequivocally and definitively—about this seventeen-year-old woman's intellectual capacity and emotional maturity?

Sheila was asking herself exactly that question when out of nowhere she got her answer. It followed a casual remark that Sheila made just as the interview was ending. Byron asked her, "Les, do you want me to make these boys stop bothering you?"

Not missing a beat, Leslie said, "Yes, Please call their mothers and tell them they're bad boys."

It wasn't that many years ago since Sheila herself was seventeen. She couldn't imagine using those words when she was that age. *Tell their mothers they're bad boys!* That's a child talking, Sheila thought. A kid in kindergarten. A first-grader. There was no way that Leslie Faber had the mental age of a normal seventeen-year-old.

With that answer all the surface layers were peeled away, leaving the core of a mentally retarded, emotionally unguarded child. Sheila had much more to do. She wanted to talk to the main actors in the basement and those boys who had observed them. She needed to talk to the kids who had heard about it in school. And there would be many more conversations with Leslie and her parents. But this was ground zero, the bull's-eye. No matter what Sheila heard later, no matter how many people she spoke to, nothing could shake her conviction that Leslie Faber didn't understand what was being done to her in the basement, and that a gang of boys had cruelly exploited her lack of understanding. That conviction was formed in the interview room of the Glen Ridge police station at 6 P.M. on March 27, 1989.

As Byron got up from her chair to signal that the interview was drawing to an end, she said, "Leslie, these boys are not your friends. You can't let them touch you in any way ever again."

"If anyone touches me, I'll tell you right away," Leslie promised.

She left the room and rejoined her mother. Ros didn't ask the detective what Leslie had told her. She didn't ask her where the investigation was going or whether there would be any arrests. Ros believed that this was a police case now, that it was in the hands of the legal system. She didn't want to interfere with the investigation, and also she couldn't bear hearing what had been done to her daughter in the basement. Silently, mother and daughter left the police station.

Sheila Byron's instincts as a woman and a cop told her that something terrible had been done to Leslie Faber. That helped her to uncloud her mind, bleach out the ambiguity. She knew she needed that confidence because this case wasn't going to be easy. Before it was over, it could get very nasty.

Sheila had never backed away from a challenging investigation. And this case certainly presented a mystery, she thought. More than one, really. The most obvious one had to do with crime and the law. What exactly took place in the basement? Did Leslie say "no" to the boys? Did she have the mental capacity to say "no"? What did the law say: Was this a crime? Was it, in the strictest legal sense, a rape? These questions swarmed around her like angry hornets. Months of investigation might provide the answers.

But there was another mystery, too. It was a deeper, more troubling mystery than the police were either equipped or required to solve. But she couldn't drive it from her mind. The mystery was *why*. Why did such a thing happen? Why in this peaceful little town of all places? Why *these* young men, the most pampered and favored boys in a town filled with pampered kids? Crime or not, what these celebrated young men of Glen Ridge had done was ugly. It was barbaric. It was inhuman. It made Sheila sick. How could they do that to another human being?

She was a cop second, but a human being first. She had been shaped in large degree by her life in Glen Ridge. It wasn't only a place. It was a force that in significant part made her who she was. It was also the force that helped to mold these young men. And there

was the mystery. How could this happen in a beautiful place like Glen Ridge? What made a bunch of friendly, likable boys—boys from fine families, boys with every imaginable advantage—do such a thing? A police investigation was always a whodunit. But the human story here, the living story, was a whydunit. Through more than four years of investigation and trial, Sheila Byron would ponder that mystery. Why did it happen? What went wrong in the perfect suburb? . . .

ACCUSATION AND DENIAL

. . . Why would the most popular boys, leaders in the school and town, do something like this?

To answer that question, it's useful to imagine another privileged community and its leaders—for instance, a community composed of college students. Like Glen Ridge, many college communities adhere to fairly homogeneous, traditional values and share common goals and expectations. And they select as some of their leaders young men who act the way the Glen Ridge young men did.

When the psychologist Chris O'Sullivan studied twenty-four documented cases of alleged gang rape on college campuses from 1981 to 1991, she found that it was the elite group at the colleges that were more likely to be involved. These included football and basketball players and members of prestigious fraternities. Not only were these young men regarded as above suspicion on campus, but their elevated status also discouraged them from moral reflection; it made them feel entitled, she said. In a similar fashion, the respect the Ridger Jocks received at the preppie high school they attended did not motivate them to think twice about their behavior.

Anthropologist Peggy Reeves Sanday writes that counselors report that "gang rape is a regular event on every college campus." In fact, some classmates of the Glen Ridge suspects said that they learned about "pulling train" and other practices associated with gang rape from older friends and brothers and sisters in college. A psychologist, Bernice Sandler, studied 110 cases of gang rapes on college campuses during the 1980s for the Association of American Colleges. Comparing these rapes to the Glen Ridge case, she told the *New York Times,* "I thought, No difference. Same scenario."

Why do people assume that athletes are going to go out and commit sex crimes?

Because in disproportionate numbers they do. That was another characteristic of the Glen Ridge case that was consistent with studies of gang rape. For the Glen Ridge suspects and their friends, life had always been centered around The Team. They played sports in which force and aggressiveness are prized. Bernice Sandler, who found striking similarities in the Glen Ridge allegations to the rape cases she studied in universities, said of these college males: "If they are not involved in a fraternity, they are members of sports teams. And it is team sports—football and basketball. It's never the golfers or swimmers." In 1986 an FBI survey found that football and basketball players were reported to police for sexual assault 38 percent more often than the average male college student.

Around the time of the Glen Ridge case, athletes at a number of universities—including St. John's in New York, the University of Oklahoma, Kentucky State University, the University of Wyoming, and the University of Minnesota—were charged with some form of sexual misconduct.

Researchers disagree over whether the force and aggressiveness required to succeed in some sports nurture a tendency toward the abuse of women who are physically weaker than the athletes. But there isn't any argument that athletes form a special, distinct, and often protected class of adolescents and young men in high school and college, and that some of these men think their status entitles them to do whatever they want to women.

A former football lineman for the New York Giants told the author, "In my sophomore year of college, I never got out of bed. While my roommate went to class, I was sleeping off fucking all night. There were girls we treated like property. They were our 'whores' and the jocks shared them. We could do whatever we wanted with them. Lots of people in the school knew about it, but nobody said a word. We were the jocks and we got what we wanted."

In this athletic hothouse, jocks make friends, shape common values, and circulate their tales of sexual exploits. Dr. Mary Koss, who directed a pioneering study of sexual assault on campus for the National Institutes of Health, found that athletes were involved in approximately one-third of the cases she studied. "My gut feeling about gang rape is that it takes place in front of guys who know each other," she told the *New York Times*. "They live together, have a way that they become bonded together. They need a culture that supports treating women this way."

In Glen Ridge, as in many other American communities, belligerence, physical strength, competitiveness, a sense of superiority, winning above all—these qualities dominated all realms of these boys' childhoods from the nursery school to high school graduation. Males who demonstrated such traits were cherished.

In a more heterogeneous community, youngsters like the Glen Ridge boys might have found alternative models of masculinity—regular guys who enjoyed watching a tightly pitched baseball game but who also demonstrated compassion, fairness, and thoughtfulness. Guys who took more pleasure in appreciating females than in humiliating them. But in Glen Ridge the few public dissenters from the Jock ethic were treated as social pariahs.

Many members of the Jock clique grew up in isolation from girls, and that is often a characteristic of young men who rape in groups. Their families were primarily male: Of the defendants actually charged with first-degree rape, only Bryant Grober had sisters. The rest had only brothers. Their immediate environment did not cultivate great empathy for women. Also, apart from athletics, the Glen Ridge guys engaged in few organized activities in the school and the community—such as the band or volunteer social service efforts—where boys and girls participated together, on an equal footing, where they might have got to know members of the opposite sex as human beings worthy of caring and respect.

The psychologist Chris O'Sullivan reviewed literature about rape in different cultures around the world, and found that rape was more prevalent where the sexes were separated. "In rape-prone societies, the sexes are separated not only physically but also by rigid sex role differentiation in which the male role is more valued. Thus, we might expect gang rapes to be most common among men who not only live apart from women but also perform roles closed to women (e.g., football players and fraternity members)."

As so many young men are, these Ridgers were taught that women's main purpose was to be decorative and to please and praise men. (Who were the young women in their lives but cheerleaders and wannabe cheerleaders?) A girl who resisted this role was treated as one more opponent to be dominated or bullied into submission, the way an opposing team would be treated. Everywhere they looked—at school, in sports, at parties—the Jocks saw evidence that boys were entitled to take what they wanted from girls. It was the norm, not the exception, for the guys to assume the girls would feel honored to be included in the company of the town's exalted males, even if the price of inclusion was abuse.

It doesn't make sense—why would you do something like this in front of a dozen witnesses?

The power that gang rapists feel individually is multiplied many times when they are in their group. The presence of the group heightens the "thrill." Robin Warshaw writes:

Gang rape also carries with it an added dose of humiliation. . . . Even when members of the group do not all participate directly, some may watch the rapes or take photographs or simply know "what's going on in the other room," and do nothing to stop it. . . . Indeed, members usually don't want to stop the rape because it enhances the group's good opinion of itself. The humiliation of the victim continues after a gang acquaintance rape as the group members brag to others who know the woman about their "achievement." And the woman feels horribly betrayed by men she may have to continue to see in her everyday life.

Psychologist Chris O'Sullivan points out that in a group, even fringe members who otherwise would be repelled by their leaders' conduct may lose their sense of compassion for a potential victim. Another group characteristic is the loss of individuality. "Nice guys" are able to forget they are nice. "Wimps" are able to shed their "wimpishness."

These guys were just good buddies; don't make anything more out of their friendship.

The devotion to activities such as circle-jerks, "voyeuring," oral sex performed by one girl on a number of guys, humiliating girls, and watching pornography together may suggest a homoerotic tendency among members of adolescent male groups that become involved in sexual assaults. And in the Glen Ridge group, homoeroticism may have been a factor. But some analysts interpret such adolescent behavior not as homoerotic but as an effort to prove heterosexual dominance and to establish masculine authority within the group. The real goal is overcoming your own insecurities about sex by impressing your friends with your sexual prowess. To achieve that goal, a guy needs an audience to witness his dominating performance. A group of appreciative and responsive buddies is essential to build a reputation for sexual control and domination.

Why would guys who had all these girls fawning after them get pleasure out of sticking a baseball bat into a neighbor's vagina?

Someone who knew the guys well might respond: Because they got a kick out of it. The social philosopher Myriam Miedzian, author of the book *Boys Will Be Boys,* said to *Time* magazine, "Why do a bunch of boys in Glen Ridge . . . think it is fun to shove baseball bats and broom handles into the vagina of a retarded girl? This isn't sex. It is violence." Dr. Miedzian was speaking before the case came to trial, but the ultimate verdict by a jury seemed less important to her than the values of the guys in the basement. "It really doesn't matter what is ultimately decided. What bothers me is why they think that is fun."

Yes, that is troubling, but not very unusual. Gang rapes more often involve elements of humiliation than one-on-one rapes. Robin Warshaw, the author of a book on acquaintance rape, cites a number of studies that find that certain abusive behavior is twice as likely to occur in gang rapes as in individual assaults: urinating on the victim; forced fellatio; pulling, burning, and biting the breasts; demanding that the woman masturbate herself while the rapists masturbate as they watch their victim. In her statements to police, Leslie described being forced to provide oral sex; she said that the boys asked her to put her fingers in her vagina and masturbate herself, and that they asked her to masturbate them.

Susan Brownmiller found in her study of wartime rape that "the ramming of a stick, a bottle, or some other object into a woman's vagina is a not uncommon *coup de grace.*" Citing one study of rapes in Philadelphia, Brownmiller says that in one-quarter of the cases "the victim was subject to some form of extra insult beyond the simple rape. Sexual humiliation ran higher in group rapes than in individual rapes."

Bragging about what they have done completes the ritual of gang rape. It's one more chance to humiliate the victim and demonstrate the victimizer's contempt for the rules and principles that apply to mere mortals. For the Glen Ridge guys, sex was more of a public than a private act. It was a coup to get sexual release while your buddies watched. But it doubled the satisfaction when you could sit in the school lunchroom the next day, as Kevin Scherzer did, and brag about it.

Peggy Reeves Sanday writes that fraternity brothers will refer to women they spent the night with as "gashes," "hosebags," and "heifers." To be accepted within the inner circle of the Jock clique in Glen Ridge, you had to be willing to tell your buddies about your sexual experiences, spicing your stories with lots of humiliating putdowns of the girl. For years the boys bragged about "voyeuring," and "Hoovering." They talked of girls as "pigs" and "animals." They boasted about their Saturday-night "blow jobs" within the hearing of the girl who had submitted to their demands, as well as any other teenager who was interested.

Compare their contempt for women to the comments made by frat members. Boasting about their latest degradation, the frat brothers describe *their* target as an "animal" or a "cunt" or "just disgusting." Because they regard her as barely human, it is one short step to treating her as subhuman.

What was "voyeuring" but a way of advertising sexual conquests and demeaning young women? In her study of fraternity gang rape, Peggy Reeves Sanday describes the practice of "beaching" by frat brothers, in which—by looking through windows from a nearby terrace—they watch another frat member having sex with a young woman. "The girls involved do not know they are being watched," Sanday says. "Usually the male knows that he is being watched, indeed he may communicate his intention to the brothers and leave the light on so as to make it easier for brothers to watch."

Why would they pick on someone who knew them so well and could tell their parents and identify them to the police?

The classic target of the rapist is someone the predator knows. A Justice Department report, studying the years 1992 and 1993, found that 80 percent of the 310,000 rapes occurring each year were committed by someone familiar to the victim. The pattern of "acquaintance rape" is quite distinct: The woman chosen for humiliation is someone the rapists know but is rarely an intimate friend or girlfriend of a group member. Most often she is regarded as an "outsider"—somebody who looks or seems different, who doesn't meet the standards the group sets for female attractiveness or sensuality. That is, they pick somebody like Leslie Faber.

And they pick her just because it's unlikely that she will tell anybody about what happened. She's too ashamed; she's scared that these popular guys will ostracize her; or she just doesn't understand what rape is. To would-be abusers, she seems like a safe bet.

Even if they were looking for someone who would submit to them, why would they pick a retarded woman whom they ridiculed as unattractive?

Maybe they wouldn't have if the issue had been sex. But, of course, it wasn't. The Jocks wanted to experiment, to test their power. Leslie was there for their amusement.

Anthropologist Peggy Reeves Sanday and other analysts have noted that the victim in sexual assault cases is often incapacitated—high on drugs or alcohol or, as in Leslie's case, mentally retarded. As Robin Warshaw notes, "The victim may be unpopular, unattractive, or simply naive and therefore easily flattered by the attention suddenly lavished on her before the assault begins." Leslie Faber got a lot of attention from her "heroes" in Cartaret Park and even more attention when she went with them to the basement.

Is it worth ruining so many lives to punish guys who got carried away for an hour?

Many powerful people in and out of Glen Ridge seem to think it is not. On campuses youths accused of group sexual assaults are rarely punished, researchers have found, and prosecutors are unlikely to prosecute. Often, the first response is not to build a case against the suspects but to cover up the allegations. In colleges or in municipalities, governing bodies and law enforcement agencies often believe that the shame disclosure would bring to the community far outweighs the value of prosecuting the accused.

That's because those who are in charge, in the courtroom or in the town or on the campus, tend to buy into certain myths about rape. For example, in the Bordentown case friends of the Bordentown boys said that the victim "asked to be raped" because she got drunk at a party. In Glen Ridge the guys' friends said Leslie asked for it because she was "flirtatious." Researchers working in different disciplines and in different settings throughout the United States have found that when adolescents and young men are accused of rape, many community members leap to the conclusion that it was up to the victim to regulate and control both her behavior *and* the behavior of her assailants. Blaming the rape victim is a common response—and not only in Glen Ridge.

There are other common responses:

When a girl enters a frat house or a basement with a group of guys, she is seen as complicitous in her own assault. "What was she doing there if she didn't want it?" the boys' friends and family members ask.

Many males, and not always young males, and a substantial number of females—*42 percent*—say they believe that if guys are aroused by the victim, it's legitimate and acceptable behavior to force sex on her, according to a survey by the National Clearinghouse on Marital and Date Rape. In some frat houses and jock dormitories, girls wearing low-cut or tight dresses are considered "fair game" for all the brothers or male residents.

Female friends of the accused rally to their defense, as the Jockettes did in Glen Ridge. What better way to win acceptance in the most popular clique in college or in Glen Ridge High than by defeading the suspects against a young woman considered socially unacceptable?

In its rationalizations, excuses, and obfuscations; its willingness to blame and demonize the victim; its attempts to bury the charges, Glen Ridge was typical. It was special in only one respect: What happened there, what happened to Leslie Faber, could not be hidden. Not this time.

"I would not have said those boys could have done such a thing in a million years. What's happening in the world?" said a neighbor of the Scherzer family.

In this woman's mind, "those boys" were the least likely rapists she could imagine—not because they had such stellar characters but because the town had a stellar character. But the boys didn't live only in Glen Ridge. They also lived in a larger, malignant world. What was happening in that world also formed them.

Since their early teens, and maybe before that, they reveled in reading and watching pornography, activities favored by others who engage in gang rape, according to experts. Like the Glen Ridge clique members, some of the frat brothers Peggy Reeves Sanday interviewed would watch pornography before a party started. Sanday notes that pornography may often constitute a primer on gang rape, because the two main ingredients are "shared titillation and a certain distance between the viewer and the sex. . . . There is a thin line between getting off by proxy on the screen and getting off on a surrogate in the house."

One Glen Ridge senior told a writer for *Rolling Stone*, "They'd all get together [to watch pornographic movies] and they'd just start cheering. They just started fucking going, 'Yeah! Yeah! Yeah, look at that.' " Another student recalled that the Jocks would shout as they watched the movie, "Excellent! Fuck her!"

Some porn movies provide a how-to guide for guys who later commit gang rape: the woman/victim is insatiable in her need for sex; she may resist rape, but once it happens, she loves it; providing blow jobs is an ecstatic experience; the more guys she can have sex with at once, and the more orifices in her body that are penetrated by human parts or fabricated objects, the more exciting and fulfilling the sex is.

The point many analysts make is that a movie doesn't have to have an "X" rating or be labeled as "pornography" to contain themes that depict sexual violence and group rape. Mainstream culture is full of such references. Sociologist Gail Dines-Levy says, "Sex and violence have become inextricably confused in the minds of young people." And psychologist Daniel Linz observes, "The first sexual experience for many boys is a slasher movie."

It's no secret that the blending of sex and violence has become commonplace in American popular culture. A study published in *Ms.* magazine in 1990 found that one out of eight Hollywood movies depicts a rape theme. By the age of eighteen, the average youth has watched 250,000 acts of violence and 40,000 attempted murders on television, according to a study by the U.S. Bureau of Justice Statistics in 1990.

This study did not consider the impact of lyrics of popular rock songs, not to speak of the savage treatment of women in "gangsta" rap or in the misogynistic shticks of comedians like Andrew Dice Clay. The world the Glen Ridge boys moved in was saturated with this stuff. On his drives around town, Chris Archer would chant the rap lyrics from a song about sexual violence committed with a bat. The Beastie Boys' song "Paul Revere" came from the group's album *Licensed to Ill*. In March 1987 the album was number one on *Billboard's* "Top Pop Albums" chart, and the top-selling LP for CBS records.

In the community where they grew up and which celebrated their athletic achievements; in their isolation from women and their evolving attitudes toward girls; in their fascination with voyeurism and pornography and in their actual treatment of young women; and, finally, in their choice of victim—in all these respects, the Glen Ridge Jocks resembled the contemporary profile of other privileged and popular male groups that were accused of committing sexual assaults of women. That's not something most Ridgers, who were unaware of the research into group rapes, would have realized or would have been willing to accept.

The Boys, The Broomhandle, The Retarded Girl

Alicia Ostriker

Who was asking for it—
Everyone can see
The facts in the oak and plaster courtroom,
Beneath the coarse flag draped
There on the wall like something on a stage
Which reminds her of the agony of school
But also of a dress they let her wear
To a parade one time,
Anyone can tell
She's asking, she's pleading
For it, as we all
Plead—
Chews on a wisp of hair,
Holds down the knee

That tries to creep under her chin,
Picks at a flake of skin, anxious
And eager to please this scowling man
And the rest of them, if she only can—
Replies *I cared for them, they were my friends*

It is she of whom these boys
Said, afterward, *Wow, what a sicko,*
It is she of whom they boasted

As we all boast, as we reach
Across that oaken bench to touch for luck the flag
Hung in law's house, and avoid
Touching the girl.

Media Representation of Violence

Whether we want to acknowledge it or not, we are all influenced and even partially formed by the media that surround us every day. We decry the level of violence that permeates the media—television news, television programming, movies, fiction, magazines, video games, popular music—and yet for some reason, many of us continue to be drawn to it. In some sense, we like to be scared; we like to play the role of detective; we are intrigued by images of war, murder, and killers; we are fascinated by the horrors that we read about in newspapers and in news magazines and that, especially, we watch on the television news. Have we become desensitized to violence? Why do we focus so intently on the violence to which children are exposed, when we ourselves often choose to be exposed at even heightened levels? Do the media and their depiction of violence cause some individuals to act out their own angry fantasies? These are some of the issues and questions that we are raising as we explore this section of the Reader.

Let us first return to the work of Michael Messner, this time in collaboration with William Solomon, in their analysis of the Sugar Ray Leonard domestic violence case, "Sin and Redemption: The Sugar Ray Leonard Wife-Abuse Story." The interesting focus of this study centers on the role that the media play in the reporting of violence, and here the violence perpetrated by a famous sports figure. Although Leonard had been arrested for domestic violence, the newspapers reporting the crime almost immediately began to focus on his drug addiction. Slowly, the domestic violence for which he had been arrested took back stage to the drug-addiction story, until the issue of drugs dominated the reports, and domestic violence disappeared from the narratives. Some significant portion of the American public refuses to hear that their athletic role models on the playing field may not be model citizens in their private lives. How do the media foster this public stance? Do we judge people like Sugar Ray Leonard, Mike Tyson, and O. J. Simpson according to different moral standards and according to different socially constructed gender roles? And if so, why? Is there a racial bias to media reporting of such cases?

We move on to an overview article, "Why We Watch," by Jeffrey Goldstein, professor of mass communications and social and organizational psychology. Taking us through several theories on violence and the media, Goldstein states that violent entertainment appeals primarily to males and mostly to males in groups. Girls, on the other hand, must socially demonstrate their sensitivity by being appropriately disturbed, dismayed, and disgusted at violence as portrayed in the media. Why are boys drawn more than girls to violent entertainment? Does this fact, once again, stem from our socially constructed gender roles? Goldstein also addresses why children like grotesque stories that often engage them in taboo subjects and how violent imagery changes over time and across media venues. Finally, he asks if we can do away with violent entertainment. What alternatives might you suggest?

The search for alternatives to violent entertainment, particularly for children, has been spurred in part by research into the effects of exposure to media violence. Sissela Bok, of the Harvard Center for Population and Development Studies, presents these effects in two chapters from her book, *Mayhem: Violence as Public Entertainment*. In "Sizing Up the Effects," she discusses the four effects outlined in the 1993 American Psychological Association report: aggression; fear; desensitization; appetite. Bok questions why children, as consumers, are the most affected by violent entertainment. Are cable channels, slasher and gore video films, and video games more violent than network television programming? Do news programs intensify the fear of violence, greater callousness toward suffering, and more craving for realistic entertainment violence? In her chapter on "Aggression," Bok questions why we have been, in the United States, more accepting of the violent content of media than the sexual. Similarly, she questions why the television industry is more resistant to curtailing the glamorization of violence than of smoking and drunk driving. Bok asks additional difficult and complex questions: how has the violence in media changed over the years? Can we isolate television and other media violence from other factors that potentially influence violent behavior such as poverty, alcohol, drugs, and stress? How can one establish risk factors; in other words, how can one demonstrate precisely when and how exposure to media violence affects levels of aggression?

With research interests focusing on the psychological effects of the mass media and particularly children's emotional and cognitive responses to television, Joanne Cantor, Professor of Communication Arts, along with Amy Nathanson, explores children's attraction to violent television in "Predictors of Children's Interest in Violent Television Programs." In this article, Cantor compares the predictive power of a number of theories relating to the attractions of violence, seeking to provide findings as to why children are willing and even eager to experience violence through television. Although children are often frightened or upset by the violent content that they watch, many continue to expose themselves to such material. Cantor considers individual differences such as sex, age, and aggression in this attraction to violent television and then discusses the appeal of restricted and frightening content. Her findings reveal that we must address the type of violence depicted in order to understand children's attraction to it. Why are boys more attracted to justice-restoring violence, as are anxious and aggressive children of both sexes? Why do more girls in general disdain the depiction of violence but are more accepting of it when it is placed in a humorous context? Why do you think that viewing violence peaks in adolescence? As Cantor has pointed out in later research, it is situation comedies, not violent programs, that attract the largest audiences of children in the United States (Cantor, 1998).

An interesting topic related to the effects of media violence is the depiction of tough and murderous women. "Black widow" (killer) women exist, and yet we are continuously surprised to hear and read about these female crimes, as if the social construction of gender does not allow for tough killer women. How do the media help inform our views on this arena of violence? Sherrie Inness, a scholar of cultural, gender, and film studies, explores the changing representations of women in all forms of popular media and what those representations suggest about shifting social mores in her book, *Tough Girls: Women Warriors and Wonder Women in Popular Culture*.

Focusing on media representations of women who kill, Inness's chapter on "Lady Killers: Tough Enough?" raises many important points. She argues that women in the media who adopt the tough attributes typically associated with men will literally go insane. According to her analysis, killer women are created as sex kittens, since female violence is often perceived as erotic and attractive, although threatening (as we have seen in such depictions by Gibson in Section II). Inness argues that "tough women" are ultimately punished, as they represent men's fears about feminism and violate "society's conventions of how women should act" (p. 74). She also questions assumptions made about aggressive women and lesbianism. Inness asks questions that force us to examine and re-examine our own notions of gender and violence, as influenced by the media. Does the appearance of the tough killer woman in films signify new freedoms for women? How are tough women perceived by Americans today? Do these films caution female viewers against toughness? It is clear that such questions bring us back to discussions in previous sections of the book—and especially to the social construction of gender—and make us realize, once again, how deeply we are formed by our culture, as portrayed in the media.

REFERENCES

CANTOR, J. (1998). Children's attraction to violent television programming. In J. H. Goldstein (ed). *Why we watch: The attractions of violent entertainment.* New York: Oxford University Press.

Sin & Redemption

The Sugar Ray Leonard wife-abuse story

Mike Messner and William Solomon

On March 30, 1991, the *Los Angeles Times* broke a story, based on divorce court documents, that Sugar Ray Leonard had admitted to physically abusing his wife, including hitting her with his fists, and to using cocaine and alcohol over a three-year period while temporarily retired from boxing. Despite the fact that stories of sexual violence, drug abuse, and other criminal activities by famous athletes had become commonplace items in the sports pages, these particular revelations shocked many people, because Leonard had been an outspoken advocate for "just say no to drugs" campaigns and he publicly had traded on his image as a good family man (e.g., by posing with his son in a soft drink TV commercial). Thus, revelations of his violence and drug abuse left him open to charges of hypocrisy, to public humiliation, and to permanent loss of his status as a hero.

FRAMING THE STORY

We decided to explore how this story was "framed" by three major newspapers. By a "news frame," we mean the way the media assign meaning to an event or occurrence, by deciding whether or not to report something, and what details to highlight, ignore, or deemphasize. A news frame is therefore an inherently ideological construct, but it rarely appears so. This is because, although news frames ultimately impose preferred meanings on a story, these meanings are commonly drawn from socially shared (hegemonic) understandings of the world (Solomon, 1992).

We analyzed coverage of the Sugar Ray Leonard story in two national dailies, the *Los Angeles Times* (LAT) and the *New York Times* (NYT), as well as in the now defunct specialized paper the *National Sports Daily* (NSD). We collected all news stories and editorial columns in the three papers until the story "died out" as a major news item. This took nine days, from March 30, 1991, until April 7, 1991. Next, we analyzed the contents of the stories. Our overriding concern was to examine how the story

was framed as a "drug story," a "domestic violence" story, or both.

Our analysis of the three newspapers revealed three stages in the development of the news frame. Stage One was day one, when LAT broke the story. Stage Two was days two and three, when all three papers covered Sugar Ray Leonard's press conference and "reactions" inside and outside of the boxing world. Stage Three was days three through nine, when follow-up stories and editorial commentary discussed the "meanings" of the story.

STAGE 1: THE BREAKING STORY

The LAT broke the story and featured it as the top sports story of the day. The headline read, "Leonard Used Cocaine, His Former Wife Testifies," while the subhead stated that "Sugar Ray confirms he abused her physically, acknowledges drug and alcohol abuse." The accompanying photo, of the couple smiling and about to kiss each other, was captioned, "Juanita and Sugar Ray Leonard, pictured before their divorce, testified about marital violence and substance abuse."

Although the wife-abuse issue clearly was a central part of the story, the headlines and the paragraphs that followed revealed a subtle asymmetry in the coverage of the "drug angle" and the "violence angle." The opening paragraph stated that although Leonard "appeared in nationally televised antidrug public service announcements in 1989 [he] has used cocaine himself. . . ." When Leonard's violence toward his wife was introduced in the third paragraph of the story, we read that Leonard confirmed that "he abused her physically *because of* alcohol and drug abuse" (italics ours). This was a key moment in the initial framing of the story: Leonard admitted to abusing drugs and alcohol, which in turn caused him to abuse his wife.

Now that the story was tentatively framed as one about "drug abuse," several paragraphs of sometimes graphic testimony from Maryland divorce-court records followed. In her testimony, Juanita Leonard said that over a two-year period Sugar Ray Leonard often struck her with his fists, and that he would "throw me around" and "harass me physically and mentally in front of the children." He threatened to shoot himself; he threw lamps and broke mirrors. He once scared her so much that she attempted to leave the house with the children: "I was holding my six-month-old child and [Leonard] spit in my face. He pushed me. He shoved me. . . . I was on my way out the door. He wouldn't let me out. He took a can of kerosene and poured it on the front foyer floor in our house. He told me he was going to burn the house down . . . that he wasn't going to let me leave the house or anything." Sugar Ray Leonard, in his testimony, did not deny any of this. He agreed that he sometimes threatened her and struck her with his fists. Despite the newspaper's initial effort to employ a "drug story" frame, the graphic, emotionally gripping testimony about domestic violence left open the possibility that the story could have developed into one about wife abuse. As the story broke, then, the "drug story" frame was still very much in the making, and potentially open to contest.

STAGE 2: PUBLIC ISSUES & PRIVATE MATTERS

On days two and three, the "drug story" news frame was solidified, and the "wife-abuse story" was rapidly marginalized. On day two, the LAT and NYT ran major articles covering the press conference that Sugar Ray Leonard held to discuss the revelations about his drug abuse and family violence. On day three, the NSD ran a story covering the news conference. The headlines of these stories stated, "Leonard Says He Used Cocaine After Injury" (LAT), "Leonard Tells of Drug Use" (NYT), and "Sugar Ray Tells Bitter Tale of Cocaine Abuse" (NSD). None of the headlines, subheads, or lead paragraphs mentioned wife abuse. The photos that ran with the articles showed a somber Leonard apparently wiping a tear from his cheek as he spoke at the press conference. None of the photo captions mentioned wife abuse.

The first seven paragraphs of the LAT story detailed Leonard's explanations of how and why he began to abuse drugs and alcohol after his eye injury

and retirement, and chronicled his statements that his drug use was "wrong . . . childish . . . stupid." The story also highlighted the fact that "as a role model, he advised that cocaine use is 'not the right road to take,' adding, 'It doesn't work. I'll be the first to admit it. I hope they look at my mistake—and don't use it.'" Finally, in the eighth paragraph, the writer noted that Leonard "declined" to discuss "the physical abuse or suicide threats alleged by his former wife, Juanita, last summer during questioning under oath" before the couple reached a multimillion-dollar divorce settlement. The story did not mention Leonard's corroboration, under oath, of his wife's "allegations" of abuse. Instead, it quoted Leonard's statement at the press conference that he would "be lying" if he were to say that he and his wife never "fought, argued, or grabbed each other," but "that was in our house, between us. Unfortunately, during the proceedings, which are very emotional and very painful, certain things are taken out of context or exaggerated." At this point, the violence issue was dropped from the story for good. For the next eight paragraphs, the story returned to explanations of Leonard's drug abuse. The final six paragraphs chronicled his statements of remorse for his drug abuse ("I stand here ashamed, hurt"), and his statements that his drug abuse is now a thing of the past ("I grew up"). The NYT essentially followed suit in framing this news as a "drug story" and almost entirely ignoring Leonard's abuse of his wife.

The NSD story on the press conference went even farther than the LAT and NYT in framing the story almost exclusively as a "drug story." The first eight paragraphs discussed Leonard's admission of drug and alcohol abuse, and noted that once he came out of his retirement and boxed again, his drug abuse ended. "I was again doing what I loved best—fighting," Leonard stated in the story. "I became a better father and person without the use of a substitute." The only mention of wife abuse was in the ninth paragraph: "He also physically abused his wife, Juanita, according to sealed divorce documents." Immediately following this sentence was an abrupt change of subject as the story continued, "Leonard said he did not go to a treatment center to stop." This jarring switch testifies to the extent to which this story had become almost entirely a "drug story." The writer did not see a need to explain, after mentioning wife abuse, that he was referring to a treatment center not for stopping wife abuse, but rather for stopping drug use. Wife abuse was outside the frame.

STAGE 3: REDEMPTION

During the next week, all three papers ran follow-ups and editorial commentaries on the Sugar Ray Leonard story. The dominant theme of nearly all of these stories was that Leonard's redemption from his drug abuse was another stage in a heroic career. On April 1, the NSD ran an opinion column headlined, "This is the Truth about Sugar Ray: He's Not Perfect, but then Who is?" The column celebrated the "love affair" that the people of the United States had had with Leonard: "In Montreal, he fought for us. . . . We applauded [his] courage and we were intoxicated with inspiration. . . . We loved Leonard. We truly did." The column went on to describe the "shock" that "we" all felt at the revelations of Leonard's cocaine use. But the focus of the column was on Leonard's redemption and our "compassion" for him. When we make heroes of athletes, the writer argued, we set them up to "fall down." Nowhere in the column was there mention of wife abuse.

The next day, the LAT ran an opinion column, by the reporter who originally broke the story, headlined "Act of Courage Didn't Involve a Single Punch." In the column, the writer admiringly recalled Leonard's many "acts of courage" in the ring, and argued that Leonard showed this courage again at his press conference, "under the most difficult of circumstances, when he admitted he had used cocaine." In an almost breathless tone, the writer continually mentioned Leonard's "courage" (nine times), his "bravery" (three times) and his "intelligence." He never mentioned wife abuse. Leonard was more than redeemed in the eyes of this writer. In fact, this "difficult" incident appears to have further elevated Leonard's status, from the reporter's point of view: "The man and his courage. It was a class act." The same day, the NYT ran a similar story, headlined. "Leonard Hears Words of Support," which mentioned wife abuse only in passing. The first paragraph expressed the focus of the article: "The reaction of the boxing world to Sugar Ray Leonard's acknowledgment that he used cocaine and drank heavily in the early 1980s had been mostly sympathetic." The dominant news frame clearly had solidified: in all three

newspapers, "wife abuse" was either completely ignored or marginalized as outside the "drug story" frame.

WITHIN THE FRAME: SIN AND REDEMPTION

By the end of the 1980s, stories about athletes on drugs had become so commonplace that they were seldom thought of as big news. In addition, the sports media had constructed an ideological news frame for jocks-on-drugs stories that turned these stories into moral dramas of individual sin and redemption. The jock-on-drugs drama came to follow a formula:

1. revelations of sin and subsequent public humiliation;
2. shameful confession and promises to never take drugs again;
3. public evangelism to children to "say no" to drugs; and
4. public redemption.

This formula reflects the ideology underlying the Reagan administration's "just say no" to drugs campaigns of the 1980s. These campaigns were largely successful in framing drug problems (and their solutions) as issues of individual moral choice, rather than as social problems resulting from growing poverty, the deterioration of cities and schools, or general alienation and malaise. Sports reporters appear to have uncritically accepted this framework of meaning and adapted it to the otherwise thorny social issue of jocks on drugs. Moreover, athletes quickly learned to act out their prescribed parts in this morality play, as Sugar Ray Leonard's tearful press conference aptly demonstrated.

When the drama is properly played out, within a year or so following the initial public revelation of drug use, the athlete is often reinstated as a sports player (some athletes—such as Steve Howe, a baseball player—have managed to cycle through this drama several times). Leonard was fortunate in that the public revelation of his drug and alcohol abuse occurred several years after his "sins" took place. That he could tearfully (and, we are left to assume, honestly) admit that he committed these sins *in the past* meant that there could be a blurring simultaneity to the movement through the drama's stages. The day after the public revelations, Leonard himself shamefully confessed, apologized, swore that he had not taken drugs for a long time, and evangelized to youths to "say no" to drugs. Within a few days, playing out their own part in the drama, the sports media granted Leonard full redemption from his sins.

OUTSIDE THE FRAME

By the third day of the Sugar Ray Leonard story, wife abuse was so entirely outside the dominant "drug story" frame that several follow-up stories and editorials did not mention it at all. But the details about wife abuse were not entirely forgotten. They continued to appear, albeit always very briefly, in some follow-up stories and commentary. Mention of wife abuse, when it appeared, was couched in language similar to the following sentence from a follow-up NYT story: ". . . his former wife, Juanita, [said] that Leonard used cocaine on occasion and physically mistreated her while under the influence of alcohol." This sentence demonstrates the three ways that the facts of wife abuse were handled when they appeared within the "drug story" news frame:

1. *The violence was presented in neutralizing language*: The graphic descriptions of Sugar Ray Leonard's violence—his threats involving guns and kerosene, his spitting in his wife's face, his hitting her with his fists, and so on—that appeared in the original divorce testimony were replaced with more vague and neutral language: Leonard "physically mistreated" his wife.

2. *Sugar Ray Leonard's admitted acts of violence were presented not as facts but as Juanita Leonard's "claims:"* although Leonard clearly had acknowledged in the divorce testimony that he had committed the acts of violence of which his wife accused him, in nearly all of the follow-up stories these acts were presented as incidents that Juanita Leonard "said," "claimed," or "alleged" had occurred. The writers did not add that Sugar Ray Leonard had acknowledged having committed these acts, thus leaving the impression, perhaps, that these were merely Juanita Leonard's "claims," or "allegations," not "facts."

3. *A causal relationship between drug and alcohol abuse and wife abuse was incorrectly implied:* nearly every mention of the wife abuse incidents in the follow-up commentaries implied that drug and alcohol abuse caused Leonard to act violently against his wife. Most often, the articles did not directly argue this causal relationship ("Drugs made him hit her"); rather, they implied the relationship by always linking any mention of his "mistreatment" of his wife with the observation that he had been abusing drugs. Astonishingly, reporters appear to have relied entirely on the testimony of Sugar Ray and Juanita Leonard to conclude, all too easily and quickly, that the drug and alcohol abuse caused the wife abuse to happen.

The writers apparently never consulted experts on domestic violence, who undoubtedly would have made two important points. First, reports by wife abusers, and by abused wives, on why wife abuse has occurred, are generally suspect (Dobash *et al.* 1992). Wayne Ewing (1982), who works with and studies men who batter women, argues that these couples' relationships are usually characterized by a common "cycle of violence" that includes "the building of tension and conflict; the episode of battering; the time of remorse; the idyllic time of reconciliation." In the stage of remorse, the male batterer typically denies responsibility for the act of battery. As Ewing puts it, "There is no shock of recognition in the cycle of violence. It is not a matter of 'Oh my God, did I do that?' It is a matter of *stating* 'Oh my God, I couldn't have done that,' implying that I in fact did not do it. . . . Remorse, in this model of 'making things right' again literally wipes the slate clean." For the victim who decides, for whatever reason, to remain in a relationship with her batterer, the stage of reconciliation in the cycle of violence often involves at least a partial acceptance of this denial of responsibility: "The man who hit me is not the *real* man I love, and who loves me." Within this context of denial, alcohol or other drugs can become convenient scapegoats: "It was the booze talking" (and hitting), not the man.

Second, research on domestic violence has found no evidence that alcohol abuse causes wife abuse. Numerous studies have shown a statistical correlation between heavy drinking (especially alcoholic binging) and wife abuse. But the "drunken bum" theory of wife abuse is largely a myth: only about one out of four instances of wife abuse involves alcohol (Kantor and Strauss 1987). In fact, in cases where binge drinking and wife abuse occur together, both may result from what researchers have called a frustrated "power motivation" in husbands (McClelland *et al.* 1972). Indeed, research suggests that men who are most likely to commit acts of wife abuse are those most firmly enmeshed in "the cultural tradition which glorifies violence, assumes male dominance, and tolerates violence by men against women" (Kantor and Strauss 1987, 225). This sounds remarkably like a description of the world of men's sports, in general, and of boxing in particular (Gorn 1986; Messner 1992; Sabo 1985).

Similarly, Ewing points to a general culture of male dominance and a "civic advocacy of violence" as the main antecedents of men's violence against women.

He argues that "[w]ith respect to the psychological makeup of the abusive male, there is considerable consensus that these men evidence low self-esteem, dependency needs, unfamiliarity with their emotions, fear of intimacy, poor communication skills and performance orientation." This description of the male batterer sounds quite similar to the psychological profile of recently retired male athletes (Messner 1992).

The sports media apparently never entertained the idea that masculine emotional socialization, including a toleration of violence, along with a loss of self-esteem brought on by an insecure public status might be at the root of both Leonard's misuse of drugs and alcohol and his abuse of his wife. To consider this possibility, of course, would have entailed questioning the system of patriarchal values that underlies institutionalized sports. Moreover, this line of analysis inevitably would invite serious questioning of the role of violence in sports, and the possible links between violence in sports with violence in personal life. Young U.S. males grow up in a society that accepts, even celebrates, violence. Sports such as boxing, football, and hockey are surely conveying a pro-violence message to young males (Messner 1992; Sabo and Panepinto 1990). And, given the misogyny that is built into the dominant subculture of men's sports, the advocacy and celebration of men's athletic violence against each other too often becomes directly translated into violence against women—violence that is often sexualized (Koss and Dinero 1988; Sabo 1986; Warshaw 1988).

In the case of Sugar Ray Leonard, sportswriters might have examined the possible links between two facts: first, here is a man who won fame and fortune by successfully battering other men with his fists; second, once out of the sports limelight, because of what appeared to be a career-ending injury, he turned to battering his own body with drugs and alcohol, and the body of his wife with his fists. This line of reasoning would draw together what Michael Kaufman (1987) has called "the triad of men's violence": violence against other men, violence against one's self, and violence against women.

That these links were never acknowledged illustrates the extent to which newspapers still form a symbiotic economic alliance with organized sports. But it would be wrong to suspect a conscious conspiracy to cover up Leonard's abuse of his wife. The adoption of the "drug story" frame and the marginalization of the "wife abuse" frame are logical results of sports reporters' immersion—probably largely unconscious—in a hegemonic ideology based in corporate and patriarchal relations of power. Denial of men's violence against women, especially that which occurs in families, is still widespread in our society (Kurz 1989). Newspaper sports departments, especially, are still relatively unaffected by feminism. Overwhelmingly male, they have been much slower to admit women than non-sports news departments. The Association for Women in Sports Media estimates that 9,650 of the approximately 10,000 U.S. print and broadcast journalists are men (Nelson 1991).

We wonder how the Sugar Ray Leonard story might have been differently framed if women made up a large proportion of newspaper sports departments. There is some evidence that female sports reporters approach their stories from a more "human," less "technical" point of view than male sports reporters (Mills 1988: 229). But we suspect that simply changing the sex composition of the sports newsroom would not drastically change the relative values placed on men's and women's sports. Indeed, it is difficult to imagine a less sexist sports newsroom in the absence of a feminist revolution throughout the sports world.

REFERENCES

DOBASH, R. P., DOBASH, R. E., WILSON, M., AND DALY, M. 1992. "The Myth of Sexual Symmetry in Marital Violence." *Social Problems* 39: 79–91.

EWING, W. 1982. "The Civic Advocacy of Violence." *M: Gentle Men for Gender Justice* 8: 5–7, 22.

GORN, E. J. 1986. *The Manly Art: Bare-Knuckle Prize Fighting in America.* Ithaca: Cornell University Press.

KANTOR, G. K. AND STRAUS, M. A. 1987. "The 'Drunken Bum' Theory of Wife Beating." *Social Problems* 34: 213–230.

KAUFMAN, M. 1987. "The Construction of Masculinity and the Triad of Men's Violence." In *Beyond Patriarchy: Essays by Men on Pleasure, Power, and Change,* ed. M. Kaufman, 1–29. Toronto: Oxford University Press.

KOSS, M. P. AND T. E. DINERO. 1988. "Predictors of Sexual Aggression among a National Sample of Male College Students." In *Human Sexual Aggression: Current Perspectives, Annals of the New York Academy of Sciences,* ed. R. A. Prentsky and V. Quinsey. 528: 133–146.

KURZ, D. 1989. "Social Science Perspectives on Wife Abuse: Current Debates and Future Directions." *Gender & Society* 3: 489–505.

McCLELLAND, D. C., W. N. DAVIS, R. KALIN, AND E. WARNER. 1972. *The Drinking Man.* New York: The Free Press.

MESSNER, M. A. 1992. *Power at Play: Sports and the Problem of Masculinity.* Boston: Beacon Press.

MILLS, K. 1988. *A Place in the News: From Women's Pages to the Front Page.* New York: Columbia University Press.

NELSON, M. B. 1991. *Are We Winning Yet?: How Women Are Changing Sports and Sports Are Changing Women.* New York: Random House.

SABO, D. 1986. "Pigskin, Patriarchy and Pain." *Changing Men: Issues in Gender, Sex and Politics* 16: 24–25.

SABO, D. AND J. PANEPINTO. 1990. "Football Ritual and the Social Production of Masculinity." In *Sport, Men and the Gender Order: Critical Feminist Perspectives*, ed. M. A. Messner and D. F. Sabo, 115–26. Champaign, IL: Human Kinetics.

SOLOMON, W. S. 1992. "News Frames and Media Packages: Covering El Salvador." *Critical Studies in Mass Communication* 9:56–74.

WARSHAW, R. 1988. *I Never Called It Rape.* New York: Harper and Row.

==========

Why We Watch

Jeffrey Goldstein

1998

What do we know about the appeals of violent imagery, and what gaps remain to be filled? Is it possible to devise nonviolent entertainment that is as appealing as its violent counterparts?

VIOLENT IMAGERY IN PERSPECTIVE

Violent imagery is not a single entity. Maurice Bloch believes it would be a mistake to regard all displays of violence as stemming from the same source or serving the same purposes. Ritual violence, he believes, requires a different explanation than violent entertainment. In rituals the line between participant and spectator is not clear. Furthermore, the barrier between daily life and ritual, Bloch claims, is not as clearly demarcated as the separation between reality and imagery in film, television, literature, and sport. Vicki Goldberg suggests a continuum, with personal experience of violence and death at one extreme and violence as entertainment at the other. In between are ritual violence and violence as news. Meaningful distinctions can also be made among genres of violent entertainment—for example, whether it is animated or whether it purports to be documentary or historically accurate. The type or genre of violent imagery may be an important element in its attractiveness, but genre is given short shrift in many discussions of violent imagery, such as the recent reports on televised violence by Cole (1995) and the National Television Violence Study Council (1996). Finally, it is important to bear in mind that what is regarded as violent imagery changes from time to time and across media.

How Attractive Is It?

While there seems always to have been an audience for violent enactments and portrayals, it is worth remembering that violent entertainment is not as popular as other forms of entertainment, such as comedy. Most popular entertainments are devoid of violent images. A particular violent film or video game with a violent theme may be a best-seller, but the sales of such items are greatly exceeded by the sales of nonviolent fare. Film, television, and video comedies are far more popular than those featuring violence. In Joanne Cantor's research, . . . *Mighty Morphin Power Rangers* was said by 26 percent of parents to be among their children's favorite TV programs, but a sitcom, *Full House*, was the favorite program of 33 percent of the children. War toys and video games with fighting themes account for a small portion of the market. Toy guns account for between 1 and 2 percent of the toy market while best-selling video games include strategy games like Tetris and nonviolent games featuring Sonic the Hedgehog and Super Mario Brothers (Toy Manufacturers of America, *Toy Industry Fact Book, 1995–1996*).

While a great many people seem attracted to—or at least not wholly repelled by—violent imagery, there may be a small audience that demands violent images in its entertainment. For some boys and men, the violence is the thing. But for many, it may be not the violence per se but other satisfactions that are its main attractants. For the majority of consumers of violent imagery, the violence is a means to ends, an acceptable device valued more for what it does than for what it is. Players who like video games with action/adventure or martial-arts themes, for example, are not necessarily attracted by the violence. These games have other features that appeal to players— their engaging fantasy, challenge, and stimulation, scorekeeping, feedback, graphics, and sound effects (Malone, 1981).

The Audiences for Violent Imagery

It is difficult to think of a group of people that is not in some way an audience for violent imagery. Young children, Maria Tatar assures us, like grotesque, violent stories, even though these stories are written by adults to serve their needs and beliefs. Even so, "children find nearly all displays of excess exciting, though not necessarily attractive," she writes.

Every study of the subject finds that boys far more than girls are drawn to violent entertainment. This is true not only in the United States and Europe but elsewhere where it has been studied—India, Japan, the Philippines. It is boys and young men who play with toy guns, fill soccer stadia every Saturday, watch *Faces of Death,* and embrace Beavis and Butt-head. Which young men? Based on research reviewed in several chapters of *Why We Watch,* those who find violent entertainment most attractive have a relatively high level of aggression and high need for physical arousal or excitement.

Not every boy and man finds images of violence enjoyable, and not every female finds them repugnant. Individuals differ in their need for excitement and tolerance for stimulation. Those with a greater need for sensation are apt to find portrayals of violence more enjoyable than those with a lesser need. According to unpublished research by Jo Groebel of the University of Utrecht (the Netherlands), this relationship is not linear. Individuals extremely high in sensation seeking tend to find passive activities, like watching films and television, insufficiently stimulating; they prefer active dangers like skydiving and bungee jumping.

Adolescent boys like violent entertainment more than any other group does, although this does not mean that they like only violent entertainment or that they are the only audience for it. Relative to other children, highly aggressive boys find war toys more appealing than other toys (Watson & Peng, 1992) and prefer violent sports, films, video games, and television programs (Brug, 1994; Cantor & Nathanson, 1997; Russel & Goldstein, 1995; Wiegmann et al., 1995). Even preschool children's choice of fairy tales is related to their degree of aggression. Collins-Standley, Gan, Yu, and Zillmann (1995) found a positive association between children's aggressiveness, as rated by their caretakers, and their preference for violent fairy tales.

When Violence Is Not Attractive

The premise that portrayals of violence are inherently appealing is simply untenable. Depending upon personal dispositions and social conditions, these portrayals are capable of evoking grief, disgust, or elation at extreme levels, say McCauley and Zillmann. From studies using bloody films that viewers found decidedly unappealing, Clark McCauley concludes that violent portrayals can be disturbing, disgusting, and depressing, but that these effects are insufficient to deter viewers.

WHY WE WATCH

. . . [T]he attraction of violence is best explained by analyzing its portrayal and its audience. And we must examine it also on a "macro" level, by considering the context in which it is witnessed and the times in which it is experienced.

In discussions of violent entertainment there is much speculation about morbid curiosity and our baser instincts. But the research and analysis in *Why We Watch* suggest that violent entertainment may have less to do with our "violent nature" and more to do with old-fashioned virtues of morality and justice.

There have been attempts, mostly by film reviewers and literary critics, to explain our fascination with violent entertainment. Stephen King, the popular purveyor of fictional horror, has even written a book, *Danse Macabre* (1981), explaining why his fans like to be horrified. In examining these armchair analyses, researchers Joanne Cantor, Clark McCauley, and Dolf Zillmann could find no support for several popular (and a few truly bizarre) explanations. They have laid to rest many of the speculations regarding violent entertainment. For example, they could find no evidence to support the position that people experience a catharsis of deep-seated fears, such as fear of the dark, or fear of aging, death, AIDS, technology, or the unknown. Likewise, there is little evidence to support the claim that viewers identify with the aggressor. Violent entertainment does not purge us of aggression or the propensity for violence, nor does it provide relief from unpleasant emotions.

"We are told . . . that the atomic bomb created a new climate of fear, and that because people now are more death conscious than ever before, they seek exposure to displays of violence and death to work out their fears." This makes no more sense, Zillmann says, than "the claim that a fear of overpopulation is behind our interest in seeing as much slaughter of humanity as we can muster." Zillmann concludes that violent material "has not been found to provide relief from ill emotions and motivations." Indeed, the best evidence is that the audience is disturbed and disgusted by scenes of violence but continues to watch it anyway.

The forms and appeals of violent imagery are many. Below we consider attractions of violent images as proposed in *Why We Watch*.

Social Identity

Violent entertainment appeals primarily to males, and it appeals to them mostly in groups. People rarely attend horror films or boxing matches alone, and boys do not play war games by themselves. These are social occasions, particularly suitable for "male bonding" and establishing a masculine identity. Boys may be playing violent video games alone in their rooms, but they are certain to talk about them with their peers. They use video games to make friends and gain popularity. Violent entertainment may be experienced alone, but it has a social purpose. The documentary film *Faces of Death,* for example, was regarded by adolescent boys as a sort of rite of passage, where the acceptable reaction was to consider the gore "cool" rather than "gross" ("Echt dood, dat is pas spannend" [Real death, that's exciting], *de Volkskrant,* Amsterdam, Apr. 5, 1995). Even though it is disturbing, boys use violent entertainment to demonstrate to their peers that they are man enough to take it. Perhaps one reason the films used by McCauley in his studies were not attractive to viewers is that they were alone while viewing them. Thus the social value of the films was lost.

I once spent an evening with a group of teenage girls and boys watching horror films, which they themselves had selected. How would these middle-class American youngsters react to the horror of dismemberments and exploding bodies? It was gratifying to see that young people found it difficult to watch the bloody excesses, though boys and girls expressed their distress in different ways. When the music-enhanced story suggested impending bloodshed, the girls would look away from the screen and talk animatedly among themselves about an unrelated topic—school, friends, parties. The boys apparently did not feel free to look away; while still gazing determinedly at the screen, they distanced themselves emotionally from the action by commenting upon the special effects, how they were done, whether the gore looked convincingly real. For a moment they saw the film through the dispassionate eyes of a film critic. When the music gave the "all clear" signal, they resumed their interest in the story.

"Distancing" oneself from the mayhem makes it tolerable. These adolescent boys and girls were able to fine-tune their degree of involvement. I spoke with one young woman who watches horrific films. She makes them palatable by squeezing her leg until it hurts, distracting herself while gazing at the screen. She, too, wants to be "man enough" to take it.

Zillmann describes the process well: "Boys . . . must prove to their peers, and ultimately to themselves, that they are unperturbed, calm, and collected in the face of terror; and girls must similarly demonstrate their sensitivity by being appropriately disturbed, dismayed, and disgusted."

As Hoberman notes of reactions to *Bonnie and Clyde,* people defined themselves by their responses to screen excesses. The violence of the film became a subject of conversation and social posturing, the purposes served by our public responses to all forms of entertainment.

Mood Management

An undeniable characteristic of violent imagery is its emotional wallop. It gives most people a jolt. Not everyone finds this kind of stimulation pleasant, but some do. Furthermore, the occasion of violent imagery can be used to express emotions in ways generally prohibited.

Cantor's research confirms the importance of taking the type of violence into consideration when discussing the attractions of violent entertainment. "Typical violent television series might be characterized as anxiety-reducing, justice-restoring genres that attract anxious, more empathic children, who side emotionally with the 'good guy' over the 'bad guy' and use the programs to control their anxieties. Violence for violence's sake should be considered separately. Children who are attracted by something described only as 'very violent' are more likely to be children with a good deal of exposure to violence in their own lives" and who "enjoy the violence irrespective of moral considerations or outcomes to protagonists." But the basis for their attraction remains unclear: is it because, in contrast to what they witness on the screen, their own lives seem less wretched? Perhaps aggressive youngsters have a greater need for excitement, which underlies both their antisocial behavior and their entertainment preferences. It may be a test of their manliness, or a way to make or maintain friends.

Sensation Seeking and Excitement

Perhaps our attraction to violent imagery is an outcome of the "civilizing process" described by Norbert Elias and Eric Dunning (1986), a way to fill the void left by diminished opportunities to experience the real thing. Certainly the events described by Vicki Goldberg lend credence to this view: As the dying and dead became further removed from immediacy, interest in *images* of death and dying seems to have increased.

Regardless of whether we crave excitement because society is increasingly "civilized" and "unexciting," as Elias and Dunning contend, it is certainly so that some individuals crave excitement more than others. Zuckerman's (1979) concept of sensation seeking, described by McCauley, helps to explain individual differences in attraction to violence. Those who have a high need for sensation (as measured by Zuckerman's scale) find violent films and television programs more appealing than do other individuals.

McCauley reviews research on the role of sensation seeking in the appeal of horror films. "There is little doubt," he writes, "that high sensation seekers like horror movies more than low sensation seekers do. The relationship is not always strong, but it is consistent." Still, McCauley dismisses the importance of such individual differences by questioning whether they can explain the broad appeal of horror and other exceedingly violent films.

Emotional Expression

Guttmann notes that violent sports are occasions for "excitement openly expressed." In this regard, sports are similar to rock concerts and other public spectacles. They not only provide a physiological "kick" for the observer but also serve as social occasions for the expression of intense emotion.

Making airplane, automobile, and shooting sounds is one of the appeals of aggressive games, especially for boys. For men, such aggressive sports as football and boxing provide an opportunity to shout and yell. Perhaps males can overcome the social pressures on them not to be emotional or intimate with other males only in a hypermasculine context, like aggressive games and entertainment.

Commenting on expressive responses of horror audiences, Clover (1992) observes that extravagantly participatory audiences (shouting, throwing things) were the norm in all manner of performances (operatic, dramatic, symphonic) until toward the end of the nineteenth century, when they were silenced and "sacralized":

Audiences express uproarious disgust ("Gross!") as often as they express fear, and it is clear that the makers of slasher films pursue the combination. More particularly: spectators tend to be silent during the stalking scenes (although they sometimes call out warnings to the stalked person), scream out at the first slash, and make loud noises of revulsion at the sight of the bloody stump. The rapid alternation between registers—between something like "real" horror on one hand and a camp, self-parodying horror on the other—is by now one of the most conspicuous characteristics of the tradition. (p. 41)

For the child, there are cognitive, emotional, and social reasons for engagement with taboo subjects. According to Maria Tatar, children's curiosity about the forbidden is satisfied. They learn to manage anxiety and defeat fear by distorting and exaggerating reality. And they bond with others, storytellers and peers, by sharing intense emotional experiences.

People say they like horror films because they are exciting and scary. Does enjoyment have something to do with arousal or fear? McCauley and Zillmann note that negative emotions can be mixed with positive ones. In research by de Wied, Zillmann, and Ordman (1994), those who most enjoyed the film *Steel Magnolias* were those who felt the most sadness during the film. The degree of enjoyment was directly related to the degree of sadness experienced during the film. People may be attracted to violent entertainment but they do not necessarily *enjoy* the gory details.

Why don't negative feelings, such as fear and sadness, make for an unpleasant viewing experience? Perhaps feelings of control mediate this process. Control is one of the factors that players enjoy about video games (Saxe, 1994). With the joystick or remote control in their hands, players can control not only what appears on the screen but, indirectly, what effects it will have on them. A remote control is ultimately a device for self-control, for producing satisfying emotional and physiological states in the user. In a study at the University of Utrecht, students who viewed a violent videotape while merely holding a remote control experienced less distress than those who viewed the same tape without a remote control. Presumably, the feeling of control made the gruesome scenes less unpleasant (Goldstein, Claassen, van Epen, de Leur, & van der Vloed, 1993). . . .

Some see predictability as the most appealing feature of violent entertainment, from cowboy movies to horror films (Britton, 1986). We know that the bad guys will "buy it" in the end, or in the sequel. But this does not account for our interest in blood sports, where the outcome is not known in advance. Perhaps the unpredictability of events like a boxing match is attenuated by the knowledge that there will come another fight, another game. Maybe it isn't over when it's over. Perhaps a rematch is equivalent to a movie sequel. While the outcome of a specific game or match is unpredictable, a subsequent one may provide a sense of closure.

Fantasy

The potential of a book, a film, or a video game to engross one in an imaginary world is one of the most attractive features of entertainment media (Turkle, 1984). For a short time, one becomes totally immersed in an activity, a phenomenon referred to as "flow" by Csikszentmihalyi (1990). Violent entertainment may be enjoyed repeatedly because it lends itself to imaginative experiences and to a temporary loss of self-consciousness (flow). The willing suspension of disbelief, the leap into imaginary worlds, is emphasized in nearly every chapter of *Why We Watch,* whether considering literature, film, television, play, or sport. Although this potential inheres in all entertainment, it helps explain the tolerance for, if not the attraction of, violent imagery. Moreover, the richness of the fantasy may be enhanced by the emotional impact of violent images.

The Importance of Context

Both the context of violent images themselves and the circumstances in which they are experienced play crucial roles in their appeal. Violent images lose their appeal when the viewer does not feel relatively safe. When there are few cues to the unreality of the violence, as in the "disgusting" films studied by McCauley, violent images are not very appealing. If the violent imagery does not itself reveal its unreality, the physical environment may do so. We are aware of holding a book, of sitting in a movie theater or a sports stadium.

People go to horror films in order to experience in safety emotions that are usually associated with danger. Fairy tales that "end tragically in the punishment of likable wrongdoers still can be greatly enjoyed, as children find comfort in the arms of the tale-telling caretaker. The caretaker, by radiating security, constitutes a happy ending of sorts" (Zillmann).

Images of carnage on the nightly news are far more disturbing than exploding bodies in a war film or the worst images from Mortal Kombat. Without background music, awareness of the camera, exaggerated special effects, or film editing, images of violence are unattractive to both males and females, according to McCauley's experiments. In the Scandinavian study cited by Joanne Cantor, preschool children typically showed facial expressions of joy while watching cartoon violence but showed negative emotions while watching realistic physical violence (Lagerspetz, Wahlroos, & Wendelin, 1978).

The Justice Motive

The popularity of violent entertainment may reflect the wish to be reassured that good prevails over evil.

Displays of violence result in distress, which is reduced when the bad guys get their comeuppance. Some might say there would be no wish to see justice restored if people did not watch the injustice on the screen in the first place. But people can bring a sense of generalized injustice in society with them to the theater.

According to Zillmann, negative attitudes about the victims "contribute greatly to the enjoyment of humiliation, disparagement, defeat, and destruction. . . . Observing the audience of any contemporary action film, especially the apparent euphoria of young men upon seeing the bad guys being riddled with bullets and collapsing in deadly convulsions, should convince the doubtful that Western audiences fully exercise their moral right of rejoicing in response to exhibitions of *righteous violence*. . . . There can be little doubt, then, that righteous violence, however brutal but justified by the ends, will prompt gloriously intense euphoric reactions the more it is preceded by patently unjust and similarly brutal violence."

Fictional characters toward whom an audience holds particular dispositions elicit affective responses and emotional involvement similar to real persons toward whom the same dispositions are held, writes Zillmann. These emotions are mediated by moral judgment. Viewers come to have strong feelings and fears regarding protagonists and antagonists, and decide in moral terms what fate they deserve. "[J]ustified hatred and the call for punishment allows us to uninhibitedly enjoy the punitive action when it materializes. *Negative affective dispositions, then, set us free to thoroughly enjoy punitive violence.* As we have morally condemned a villain for raping and maiming, for instance, we are free to hate such a person, can joyously anticipate his execution, and openly applaud it when we finally witness it" (Zillmann). Thus the typical story line of enjoyable entertainment involves the establishment of animosity toward wrongdoers, which makes later violence against them seem justified and hence enjoyable.

The Historical Context

Not only the viewing situation but also the larger social world influences the attractiveness of violence. Interest in violent imagery changes with the times. There are also historical shifts in what violent images are regarded as acceptable or excessive.

Real-life violence influences the desire for violent entertainment. War and war play are not independent of one another, nor are crime and crime entertainment. Real violence activates aggressive associations and images. These, in turn, may heighten the preference for further exposure to violent entertainment. If children first hear aggressive stories, they are more likely to choose toy guns for play (Jukes & Goldstein, 1993). The same relationship is evident in preferences for violent film entertainment (Cantor; Hoberman), war toys and video games (Goldstein . . .), and enjoyment of blood sports (Guttmann). . . . [A]n increase in student patronage of violent films occurred at the University of Wisconsin following the murder of a coed on campus (Boyanowsky, Newtson, & Walster, 1974). Sales of replica missiles increased during the Persian Gulf War (Goldstein, 1994). Public support for military expenditures is correlated with an increase in the sale of war toys and in the prevalence of war movies (Regan, 1994).

Almost Real

An important issue not yet decided regarding the attractions of violent images is the degree to which realism enhances or diminishes their acceptance or appeal. In the discussions of ritual (Bloch), photographic images of death (Goldberg), and spectator sports (Guttmann), a close relationship is said to exist between the apparent realism of violent images and their appeal to their consumers. Zillmann writes that violence in sports is appealing not because of any "blood lust" among spectators but because it is a sign that the participants are willing to take risks for their sport, an indication of their passionate commitment. In other realms, such as film (McCauley), children's television (Cantor), and play (Goldstein), it appears that violent imagery must carry cues to its unreality or it will lose its appeal.

Based on his previous studies of disgusting films and research conducted for this project, McCauley concludes with two possibilities: (1) Emotions elicited by drama are weaker than everyday emotions. Thus, the arousal accompanying fear, disgust, and pity can be experienced as pleasurable. Within a dramatic or protective frame, violent imagery becomes exciting rather than anxiety provoking. (2) The emotions experienced in drama are qualitatively different from their real-life counterparts. "Indeed, this theory would assert that we err in calling dramatic emotions by the same names as everyday emotions; the dramatic emotions are a parallel but different reality." Perhaps when the violence is almost real, so too are the emotions it elicits. Both sides of the equation—the violent images as well as the emotions that result—are recognizably different from the genuine article. We are then able to tolerate both reasonably well, without the distress being too intense to spoil our enjoyment.

Violent Images as Social Control

Gerbner, Gross, Morgan, and Signorielli (1986) report that heavy viewers of violence in the media come to see the world as a frightening and dangerous place. As a result, they lend support to the forces of law and order. In Gerbner's "cultivation theory," media violence is seen to serve as a means of social control in a broad sense. Similarly, Maria Tatar considers children's stories as a form of moral instruction, produced by adults to frighten children into obedience. Do these scary tales with morals produce obedience? Yes, she says, if it is clear what must be done to reduce the jeopardy. Children who disobey their parents, lie, or steal in these tales meet horrific ends. The message is that obedience, truthfulness, and honesty will enable children to avoid these horrible consequences.

Summary

It is obvious that the attractions of violent imagery are many. The audiences for images of violence, death, and dying do not share a single motive—some viewers seek excitement, others companionship or social acceptance through shared experience, and still others wish to see justice enacted. For some, the immersion in a fantasy world is its primary appeal.

Table 1 lists the features that, according to the authors in *Why We Watch,* make violence attractive. These do not fit neatly into a single theory. They illustrate the range of phenomena that any theory would have to explain. An adequate theory must account for sex and personality differences, the social uses to which violent entertainment is put, and the broader cultural roles it plays.

Not all the elements in table 1 seem compatible. Some may even appear to be inherently incompatible. For example, it appears that violent imagery becomes more appealing when signs are present indicating that the violence is not real, yet historical analysis finds heightened interest in violent imagery when war and crime are salient to the audience. And while the real

Table 1   When Violence is Attractive

Subject Characteristics

Those most attracted to violent imagery are
  Males
  More aggressive than average
  Moderate to high in need for sensation or arousal
  In search of a social identity, or a way to bond with friends
  Curious about the forbidden, or interested because of their scarcity
  Have a need to see justice portrayed or restored
  Able to maintain emotional distance to prevent images from being too disturbing
Violent images are used
  For mood management
  To regulate excitement or arousal
  As an opportunity to express emotion

Characteristics of Violent Images that Increase Their Appeal

  They contain clues to their unreality (music, editing, setting)
  They are exaggerated or distorted
  Portray an engaging fantasy
  Have a predictable outcome
  Contain a just resolution

Context

Violent images are more attractive
  In a safe, familiar environment
  When war or crime are salient

violence of war increases interest in violent entertainment, Vicki Goldberg finds increasing images of death and dying precisely when death and dying begin to disappear from sight.

One feature of violent entertainment that presumably enhances its appeal is a predictable outcome. Yet in sports, the outcome is not known in advance. Clearly, other appeals of aggressive sports—perhaps the opportunity they afford for the intense expression of emotions—outweighs their unpredictability.

Emotional expression and control and the ability to distance oneself emotionally from threatening images are not, strictly speaking, subject characteristics. But they are included in table 1 because violent imagery may enable its audience to seek and obtain a level of emotional or social engagement that is personally satisfying.

WHAT WE DON'T KNOW

What we don't know about the attractions of violent entertainment could fill a book. Some of the issues remaining to be explored are considered below. Not only are the data currently available minute in quantity, but even where research on the subject does exist, it is often inadequate. It fails to consider the role of culture or of subcultural groups, fails to adequately define key terms, like "attraction," "entertainment," and "violence."

Do we need a "macro" or a "micro" theory to explain the attractions of violent entertainment? A macro-level explanation would focus on society's changing definitions and wavering opinions of violence and violent entertainment, as well as the relationship between violent imagery and social institutions, like religion, politics, business, and the military. The historical and anthropological chapters in *Why We Watch* (Bloch, Guttmann, Goldstein, Tatar, Hoberman) make just such connections. At the same time, we know from experimental, micro-level research a few features of violent images that make them appealing, and something about the individuals who find them most attractive.

Some explanations are very difficult to put to the test, but worth considering nonetheless. For example, violent imagery may be attractive to humans in general because we, alone among creatures, know that we will die but, except in rare cases, we do not know when or how. Hence, we may be motivated by morbid curiosity. Violent images may be compelling in part because we are tantalized by images of mortality.

Individual Differences

Aside from sex, sensation seeking, and individual differences in aggressiveness, we know little about characteristics of the audiences for different forms of violent entertainment. Who likes professional wrestling? Do they share traits or experiences with those who read detective fiction or watch slasher films? Why don't females find this material as appealing as men do? Is it because men have different needs than women (for arousal, for example), or because women have alternative means of satisfying the same needs (for example, expressing emotion more openly)?

Context

Except for Maurice Bloch's contribution to this volume, there has been virtually no cross-cultural or cross-national analysis of the extent, appeal, or functions of violent imagery. In Japan, extraordinarily violent images are the bases of countless comic books read by both men and women. Does such graphic violence appeal to the Japanese for the same reasons that Arnold Schwarzenegger films appeal to Westerners?

Can the future course of violent entertainment be predicted? The violence in some media, like fairy tales, has been toned down over time, while the violence in others, like Hollywood films, has increased. What is technologically feasible will almost inevitably be tried. Are the exploding bodies of Hollywood only a test of the limits of new technology? If so, we can expect increasingly realistic shoot-'em-ups as virtual reality and other new technologies evolve.

ALTERNATIVES TO VIOLENT ENTERTAINMENT

Violent entertainment did not suddenly arrive on the scene, and it is not likely any time soon to depart it. Zillmann's analysis suggests that people become acclimated to the arousal generated by violent images but that they have a continuing need for excitement. "Does this mean that we shall have to accept an ever increasing utilization of violence and terror for entertainment purposes?" he asks. "[I]t would appear to be so, indeed."

It is worth remembering that violent entertainment is the preferred form of entertainment only for a minority of the general audience. Most viewers appear to prefer comedies and sitcoms to violent entertainment. These attract large audiences of all ages and of both sexes. When violent entertainment is preferred, it is often not for the violence itself; for many males, it is a means toward an end—to achieve a desired level of stimulation, to help establish a masculine identity, or to be accepted by peers.

Is there something that meets the requirements and serves the purposes of violent entertainment without relying on the violence? Are there effective substitutes for violent entertainment? People use all forms of entertainment to achieve a desirable level of excitement or relaxation. Nonviolent but equally stimulating entertainment satisfies many of the same needs as violent entertainment. Arousal from visual media can be generated through editing and special effects. Hitchcock's famous shower scene in *Psycho,* while bloody, showed little direct violence.

Some essential features of attractive entertainment are an engaging fantasy, an unpredictable path toward a predictable end, the restoration of justice and the depiction of morality, and opportunities for arousal and its reduction. These attributes would seem to be present in most of the violent fare discussed in *Why*

We Watch. Other features that may make violent images more attractive are the presence of humor, appealing graphics, and sound effects.

Can we do away with violent entertainment? Social and historical circumstances influence its popularity. During times of war, or when violence permeates our neighborhoods, it gains in popularity. Violent entertainment may be as inevitable as violence in society.

It is up to the image makers to put violence in perspective—to emphasize, as they still do, the unacceptability of random, arbitrary, anarchistic, and plain sadistic violence, and to applaud violence that ultimately serves justice and the good of humanity. The public can and does influence the determination of what are acceptable and what are unacceptable displays of violence. There is opposition to "ultimate fighting," and even the future of boxing is in doubt because of growing public discontent with its crippling injuries. Eventually it might suffer the fate of smoking. The portrayal of violent action is inevitable; nevertheless, the limits we place on it, the manner in which we consume it, and the ways we respond to it help to define a culture.

REFERENCES

BLOCH, M. (1998). The presence of violence in religion. In J. H. Goldstein (Ed.), *Why we watch: The attractions of violent entertainment* (pp. 163–178). New York: Oxford University Press.

BOYANOWSKY, E. O., NEWTSON, D., & WALSTER, E. (1974). Film preferences following a murder. *Communication Research, 1,* 32–43.

BRITTON, A. (1986). Blissing out: The politics of Reaganite entertainment. *Movie, 31/32,* 1–7.

BRUG, H. H. VAN DER (1994). Football hooliganism in the Netherlands. In R. Giulianotti, N. Bonney, & M. Hepworth (Eds.), *Football, violence, and social identity*. London: Routledge.

CANTOR, J. R. (1998). Children's attraction to violent television programming. In J. H. Goldstein (Ed.), *Why we watch: The attractions of violent entertainment* (pp. 88–115). New York: Oxford University Press.

CANTOR, J. R. (1994). Fright reactions to mass media. In J. Bryant & D. Zillmann (Eds.), *Media effects: Advances in theory and research*. Hillsdale, N. J.: Lawrence Erlbaum Associates.

CANTOR, J., & NATHANSON, A. I. (1997). Predictors of children's interest in violent television programs. *Journal of Broadcasting and Electronic Media, 41,* 155–167.

CLOVER, C. J. (1992). *Men, women, and chainsaws: Gender in the modern horror film*. Princeton, N. J.: Princeton University Press.

COLE, J. (1995). *The UCLA television violence monitoring report*. Los Angeles: University of California, Center for Communication Policy.

COLLINS-STANDLEY, T., GAN, S., YU, H. J., & ZILLMANN, D. (1995). Choice of romantic, violent, and scary fairy-tale books by preschool girls and boys. Unpublished manuscript, University of Alabama, Tuscaloosa.

CSIKSZENTMIHALYI, M. (1990). *The flow experience*. San Francisco: Jossey-Bass.

DEWIED, M., ZILLMANN, D., & ORDMAN, V. (1994). The role of empathic distress in the enjoyment of cinematic tragedy. *Poetics, 23,* 91–106.

ELIAS, N., & DUNNING, E. (1986b). *Quest for excitement*. Oxford: Blackwell.

GERBNER, G., GROSS, L., MORGAN, M., & SIGNORIELLI, N. (1986). Living with television: The dynamics of the cultivation process. In J. Bryant & D. Zillmann (Eds.), *Perspectives on media effects*. Hillsdale, N. J.: Lawrence Erlbaum Associates.

GOLDSTEIN, J. H. (1998). Immortal Kombat: War toys and violent video games. In J. H. Goldstein (Ed.), *Why we watch: The attractions of violent entertainment* (pp. 53–68). New York: Oxford University Press.

GOLDSTEIN, J. H. (1994). Sex differences in toy play and use of video games. In J. Goldstein (Ed.), *Toys, play, and child development*. New York: Cambridge University Press.

GOLDSTEIN, J. H., CLAASSEN, C., VAN EPEN, E., DE LEUR, W., & VAN DER VLOED, G. (1993). Preference for violent films and the search for justice. Unpublished manuscript, University of Utrecht, the Netherlands.

GUTTMANN, A. (1998). The appeal of violent sports. In J. H. Goldstein (Ed.), *Why we watch: The attractions of violent entertainment* (pp. 7–26). New York: Oxford University Press.

HOBERMAN, J. (1998). "A test for the individual viewer": *Bonnie and Clyde's* violent reception. In J. H. Goldstein (Ed.), *Why we watch: The attractions of violent entertainment* (pp. 116–143). New York: Oxford University Press.

JUKES, J., & GOLDSTEIN, J. H. (1993). Preference for aggressive toys. *International Play Journal, 1,* 93–103.

KING, S. (1981). *Danse macabre*. New York: Berkley.

LAGERSPETZ, K. M., WAHLROOS, C., & WENDELIN, C. (1978). Facial expressions of preschool children while watching televised violence. *Scandinavian Journal of Psychology, 19,* 213–222.

MALONE, T. (1981). Toward a theory of intrinsically motivating instruction. *Cognitive Science, 4,* 333–369.

MCCAULEY, C. (1998). When screen violence is not attractive. In J. H. Goldstein (Ed.), *Why we watch: The attractions of violent entertainment* (pp. 144–162). New York: Oxford University Press.

NATIONAL TELEVISION VIOLENCE STUDY COUNCIL. (1996). *National television violence study*. Studio City, CA: Mediascope.

REGAN, P. M. (1994). War toys, war movies, and the militarization of the United States, 1900–1985. *Journal of Peace Research, 31,* 45–58.

RUSSELL, G. W., & GOLDSTEIN, J. H. (1995). Personality differences between Dutch football fans and non-fans. *Social Behavior and Personality, 23,* 199–204.

SAXE, J. (1994). Violence in videogames: What are the pleasures? International Conference on Violence in the Media, St. John's University, New York, October.

TATAR, M. (1998). "Violent delights" in children's literature. In J. H. Goldstein (Ed.), *Why we watch: The attractions of violent entertainment* (pp. 69–87). New York: Oxford University Press.

TOY MANUFACTURERS OF AMERICA. (1996). *Toy industry fact book, 1995–96*. New York: Toy Manufacturers of America.

TURKLE, S. (1984). *The second self*. New York: Simon and Schuster.

WATSON, M. W., & PENG, Y. (1992). The relation between toy gun play and children's aggressive behavior. *Early Education and Development, 3,* 370–389.

WIEGMANN, O., VAN SCHIE, E., KUTTSCHREUTER, M., BOER, H., BREEDIJK, A., & WIEDIJK, C. (1995). *Kind en computer-spelletjes* [Children and computer games]. University of Twente,

Enschede, the Netherlands: Center for Communications Research.

ZILLMANN, D. (1998). The psychology of the appeal of portrayals of violence. In J. H. Goldstein (Ed.), *Why we watch: The attractions of violent entertainment* (pp. 179–211). New York: Oxford University Press.

ZUCKERMAN, M. (1979). *Sensation seeking: Beyond the optimal level of arousal.* New York: Wiley.

Sizing up the Effects

1998

Sissela Bok

A great deal of research has been conducted to sort out the kinds and amounts of violence in the media and to learn how exposure to media violence affects viewers, and especially children. There have also been many meta-analyses, or studies *of* existing studies[1] Focusing primarily on television, they all confirm the common-sense observation that the screen is a powerful teaching medium, for good and for ill, when it comes to violent as to all other material.

There is general agreement that children ought neither to be insulated from gradual acquaintance with the treatment of violence in art and in the media nor assaulted by material they cannot handle. The "*catharsis* theory" put forth in the 1960s and 1970s, to the effect that violent material can help young people live out their aggressive impulses vicariously so that their day-to-day conduct becomes less aggressive, has been abandoned by almost all scholars in the field today. The debate suffers, however, from the fact that different studies concern persons of different ages with different levels of understanding of the nature of violence and of distinctions between real and fictitious events. It seems reasonable to suppose that screen violence offers some viewers a chance for strictly vicarious role-playing and an outlet for aggressive fantasies, just as others are more easily frightened or mesmerized or incited by what they view. But scholars increasingly dismiss as unfounded any categorical claims that the average heavy viewer of media violence is somehow less likely to be aggressive than someone without such exposure.

Instead, the vast majority of the studies now concur that media violence can have both short-term and long-term debilitating effects. In 1993, the American Psychological Association published a report by a commission appointed to survey and review existing studies. According to this report,

There is absolutely no doubt that higher levels of viewing violence on television are correlated with increased acceptance of aggressive attitudes and increased aggressive behavior. . . . Children's exposure to violence in the mass media, particularly at young ages, can have harmful lifelong consequences. Aggressive habits learned early in life are the foundation for later behavior. Aggressive children who have trouble in school and in relating to peers tend to watch more television; the violence they see there, in turn, reinforces their tendency toward aggression, compounding their academic and social failure. These effects are both short-term and long-lasting: A longitudinal study of boys found a significant relation between exposure to television violence at 8 years of life and anti-social acts—including serious violent criminal offenses and spouse abuse—22 years later. . . . In addition to increasing violent behaviors toward others, viewing violence on television changes attitudes and behaviors toward violence in significant ways. Even those who do not themselves increase their violent behaviors are significantly affected by their viewing of violence in three [further] ways:

- Viewing violence increases fear of becoming a victim of violence, with a resultant increase in self-protective behaviors and increased mistrust of others;
- Viewing violence increases desensitization to violence, resulting in calloused attitudes toward violence directed at others and a decreased likelihood to take action on behalf of the victim when violence occurs (behavioral apathy); and
- Viewing violence increases viewers' appetites for becoming involved with violence or exposing themselves to violence.[2]

The report, like most of the research it surveys, speaks of viewing violence as correlated with effects rather than as directly causing them. And it specifies a number of risk factors capable of contributing to the first of these effects—increasing aggression. Among these risk factors, some, such as access to firearms, substance abuse, and experience of abuse as a child, doubtless play a larger role than media violence.[3] But it is on the screen that, as in no earlier generation, today's children, including those not subject to the other risk factors, become familiar with them all and with graphic depictions of every form of mayhem.

Commentators have spoken of the four effects specified in the report as increased aggression, fear, desensitization, and appetite.[4] Psychologist Ronald Slaby, a member of the APA commission, has named them "the aggressor effect, the victim effect, the bystander effect, and the appetite effect."[5] Not all of these effects, he suggests, occur for all viewers; much depends on how they identify themselves in relation to the violence they see and on their ability to evaluate programs critically.

Without taking such variations into account, it is natural to ask, as does critic John Leonard, "How, anyway, does TV manage somehow to *desensitize* but also *exacerbate*, to *sedate* but also *incite*?"[6] As with other stimuli, individuals react to media violence in different ways. While many people experience the quite natural reactions of fear and numbing when exposed to repeated depictions of assault, homicide, or rape, fewer will ever come close to feeling incited by them, much less to engaging in such acts. But among those who do cross that line, the combination of a surge of aggression and numb pitilessness is surely not unusual. Psychiatrist James Gilligan, in a study of homicidally violent men, takes it as a precondition for their being able to engage in violent behavior that ordinary human responses are absent: "What is most startling about the most violent people is how incapable they are, at least at the time they commit their violence, of feeling love, guilt, or fear."[7] In such a state, Macbeth's words are anything but incongruous:

> I am in blood
> Stepp'd in so far that, should I wade no more,
> Returning were as tedious as go o'er.[8]

As research evidence accumulates about the effects linked to media violence, it reinforces the common-sense view that violent programming influences viewers at least as much as the advertising directed at them for the express purpose of arousing their desire for candy and toys. Both types of exposure affect children most strongly to the degree that they are more suggestible and less critical of what is placed before them, and have more time to watch than most. The American Academy of Pediatrics, the American Medical Association, and the National PTA are among the many organizations signaling such effects and calling for reduced levels of television violence and greater parental involvement with children's viewing.

In the early 1990s, researchers frequently mentioned the estimate that the average child leaving elementary school has watched 8,000 murders and more than 100,000 acts of violence.[9] Because network television was for decades the primary source for screen violence in most homes, its role has been especially carefully charted in this regard. In recent years, growing access to numerous cable channels has brought in considerably more violent fare and made it available at all hours. By now, the vast assortment of slasher and gore films on video contribute to a climate of media violence different from that studied over the past four decades. So does the proliferation of video games offering players the chance to engage in vicarious carnage of every sort. These sources bring into homes depictions of graphic violence, often sexual in nature, never available to children and young people in the past. Because videos and interactive games also provide opportunities to play sequences over and over, they add greatly to the amount of violence to which viewers now have access. As a result, it may well be necessary to revise the earlier figures sharply upward.

Although most of the public's concern has been directed primarily toward the first of the four effects noted by researchers—increased levels of aggression—the other three may have a more widespread and debilitating impact on adults as well as children. After all, even in a high-crime society such as ours, the vast majority of citizens will never commit violent crimes; but many are still affected to the extent that the prominence of violence in news and entertainment programs brings an intensified fear of crime, greater callousness toward suffering, and a greater craving for ever more realistic entertainment violence.

In examining studies of the four types of effects, I shall therefore first take up those having to do with fear, desensitization, and appetite, before considering what we know about any links to aggression; and ask under what conditions each may inhibit the development of four basic moral characteristics—resilience, empathy, self-control, and respect for self and others—indispensable for human thriving.

NOTES

1. See Jeffrey Cole, *The UCLA Television Monitoring Report* (Los Angeles: UCLA Center for Communications Policy, 1995); Dietz and Strasburger, "Children, Adolescents, and Television"; Edward Donnerstein, "Mass Media Violence: Thoughts on the Debate," *Hofstra Law Review*, vol. 22 (1994), pp. 828–832; James T. Hamilton, *Channeling Violence: The Economic Market for Violent Television Programming* (Princeton, N.J.: Princeton University Press, 1998). Levine, *Viewing Violence*, ch. 3; Myriam Miedzian, *Boys Will Be Boys* (New York: Doubleday, 1991), chs. 12–13. John P. Murray, "Media Violence and Youth," in Joy D. Osofsky, ed., *Children in a Violent Society* (New York: Guilford Press, 1997), pp. 72–96; National Television Violence Study: Scientific Papers 1994–1995 (Studio City, Calif.: Media-Scope 1996); and Haejung Paik and George Comstock, "The Effects of Television Violence on Anti-Social Behavior: A Meta-Analysis," *Communication Research*, vol. 21, no. 4 (August 1994), pp. 516–46. See also the account and bibliography in Russell G. Geen, "Television and Aggression: Recent Developments in Research and Theory," in Dolf Zillmann et al., eds., *Media, Children, and the Family: Social Scientific, Psychodynamic, and Clinical Perspectives* (Hillsdale, N.J.: Lawrence Erlbaum Associates, 1994), pp. 151–161.

2. American Psychological Association Commission on Youth and Violence, *Violence and Youth: Psychology's Response*, Washington, DC.: The American Psychological Association, 1993.

3. For efforts to chart the different risk factors, see Mark L. Rosenberg and Mary Ann Fenley, *Violence in America: A Public Health Approach* (Oxford: Oxford University Press, 1991), pp. 24–33; and National Research Council, *Understanding and Preventing Violence* (Washington, D.C.: National Academy Press, 1995), p. 20.

4. Some have stressed three of these effects. The 1996 National Television Violence Study proposes three substantial risks from viewing television violence: "learning to behave violently, becoming more desensitized to the harmful consequences of violence, and becoming more fearful of being attacked." Levine sees most of the research to date as attempting to answer three questions: "Does media violence encourage children to act more aggressively? Does media violence cultivate attitudes that are excessively distorted, frightening, and pessimistic? Does media violence desensitize children to violence?" in *Viewing Violence*, pp. 16–17.

5. Ronald G. Slaby, "Combating Television Violence," *Chronicle of Higher Education*, vol. 40, no. 18 (January 5, 1994), pp. B1–2.

6. John Leonard, *Smoke and Mirrors: Violence, Television, and Other American Cultures* (New York: Free Press, 1997).

7. James Gilligan, *Violence: Our Deadly Epidemic and Its Causes* (New York: G. P. Putnam's Sons, 1996), p. 113.

8. William Shakespeare, *Macbeth*, III, 4. For commentary linking this passage to desensitization in media violence and in real life, see Martin Amis, "Blown Away," in Karl French, ed., *Screen Violence* (London: Bloomsbury, 1996), p. 13.

9. David Hamburg, *Today's Children* (New York: Times Books, 1992) p. 192.

Aggression

Sissela Bok

Even if media violence were linked to no other debilitating effects, it would remain at the center of public debate so long as the widespread belief persists that it glamorizes aggressive conduct, removes inhibitions toward such conduct, arouses viewers, and invites imitation. It is only natural that the links of media violence to aggression should be of special concern to families and communities. Whereas increased fear, desensitization, and appetite primarily affect the viewers themselves, aggression directly injures others and represents a more clear-cut violation of standards of behavior. From the point of view of public policy,

therefore, curbing aggression has priority over alleviating subtler psychological and moral damage.

Public concern about a possible link between media violence and societal violence has further intensified in the past decade, as violent crime reached a peak in the early 1990s, yet has shown no sign of downturn, even after crime rates began dropping in 1992. Media coverage of violence, far from declining, has escalated since then, devoting ever more attention to celebrity homicides and copycat crimes. The latter, explicitly modeled on videos or films and sometimes carried out with meticulous fidelity to detail, are never more relentlessly covered in the media than when they are committed by children and adolescents. Undocumented claims that violent copycat crimes are mounting in number contribute further to the ominous sense of threat that these crimes generate.[1] Their dramatic nature drains away the public's attention from other, more mundane forms of aggression that are much more commonplace, and from the other three harmful effects of media violence.

Media analyst Ken Auletta reports that, in 1992, a mother in France sued the head of a state TV channel that carried the American series *MacGyver,* claiming that her son was accidentally injured as a result of having copied MacGyver's recipe for making a bomb.[2] At the time, Auletta predicted that similar lawsuits were bound to become a weapon against media violence in America's litigious culture. By 1996, novelist John Grisham had sparked a debate about director Oliver Stone's film *Natural Born Killers,* which is reputedly linked to more copycat assaults and murders than any other movie to date.[3] Grisham wrote in protest against the film after learning that a friend of his, Bill Savage, had been killed by nineteen-year-old Sarah Edmondson and her boyfriend Benjamin Darras, eighteen: after repeated viewings of Stone's film on video, the two had gone on a killing spree with the film's murderous, gleeful heroes expressly in mind.[4] Characterizing the film as "a horrific movie that glamorized casual mayhem and bloodlust," Grisham proposed legal action:

Think of a film as a product, something created and brought to market, not too dissimilar from breast implants. Though the law has yet to declare movies to be products, it is only a small step away. If something goes wrong with the product, either by design or defect, and injury ensues, then its makers are held responsible. . . . It will take only one large verdict against the likes of Oliver Stone, and his production company, and perhaps the screenwriter, and the studio itself, and then the party will be over. The verdict will come from the heartland, far away from Southern California, in some small courtroom with no cameras. A jury will finally say enough is enough; that the demons placed in Sarah Edmondson's mind were not solely of her own making.[5]

As a producer of books made into lucrative movies—themselves hardly devoid of violence—and as a veteran of contract negotiations within the entertainment industry, Grisham may have become accustomed to thinking of films in industry terms as "products." As a seasoned courtroom lawyer, he may

have found the analogy between such products and breast implants useful for invoking product liability to pin personal responsibility on movie producers and directors for the lethal consequences that their work might help unleash.

Oliver Stone retorted that Grisham was drawing "upon the superstition about the magical power of pictures to conjure up the undead spectre of censorship."[6] In dismissing concerns about the "magical power of pictures" as merely superstitious, Stone sidestepped the larger question of responsibility fully as much as Grisham had sidestepped that of causation when he attributed liability to filmmakers for anything that "goes wrong" with their products so that "injury ensues."

Because aggression is the most prominent effect associated with media violence in the public's mind, it is natural that it should also remain the primary focus of scholars in the field. The "aggressor effect" has been studied both to identify the short-term, immediate impact on viewers after exposure to TV violence, and the long-term influences such as those studied by Dr. Eron and his colleagues in Hudson, New York. There is near-unanimity by now among investigators that exposure to media violence contributes to lowering barriers to aggression among some viewers. This lowering of barriers may be assisted by the failure of empathy that comes with growing desensitization, and intensified to the extent that viewers develop an appetite for violence—something that may lead to still greater desire for violent programs and, in turn, even greater desensitization.

When it comes to viewing violent pornography, levels of aggression toward women have been shown to go up among male subjects when they view sexualized violence against women. "In explicit depictions of sexual violence," a report by the American Psychological Associations Commission on Youth and Violence concludes after surveying available research data, "it is the message about violence more than the sexual nature of the materials that appears to affect the attitudes of adolescents about rape and violence toward women.[7] Psychologist Edward Donnerstein and colleagues have shown that if investigators tell subjects that aggression is legitimate, then show them violent pornography, their aggression toward women increases. In slasher films, the speed and ease with which "one's feelings can be transformed from sensuality into viciousness may surprise even those quite conversant with the links between sexual and violent urges."[8]

Viewers who become accustomed to seeing violence as an acceptable, common, and attractive way of dealing with problems find it easier to identify with aggressors and to suppress any sense of pity or respect for victims of violence. Media violence has been found to have stronger effects of this kind when carried out by heroic, impressive, or otherwise exciting figures, especially when they are shown as invulnerable and are rewarded or not punished for what they do. The same is true when the violence is shown as justifiable, when viewers identify with the aggressors rather than with their victims, when violence is routinely resorted to, and when the programs have links to how viewers perceive their own environment.[9]

While the consensus that such influences exist grows among investigators as research accumulates, there is no consensus whatsoever about the size of the correlations involved. Most investigators agree that it will always be difficult to disentangle the precise effects of exposure to media violence from the many other factors contributing to societal violence. No reputable scholar accepts the view expressed by 21 percent of the American public in 1995, blaming television more than any other factor for teenage violence.[10] Such tentative estimates as have been made suggest that the media account for between 5 and 15 percent of societal violence.[11] Even these estimates are rarely specific enough to indicate whether what is at issue is all violent crime, or such crimes along with bullying and aggression more generally.

One frequently cited investigator proposes a dramatically higher and more specific estimate than others. Psychiatrist Brandon S. Centerwall has concluded from large-scale epidemiological studies of "white homicide" in the United States, Canada, and South Africa in the period from 1945 to 1974, that it escalated in these societies within ten to fifteen years of the introduction of television, and that one can therefore deduce that television has brought a doubling of violent societal crime:

Of course, there are many factors other than television that influence the amount of violent crime. Every violent act is the result of a variety of forces coming together—poverty, crime, alcohol and drug abuse, stress—of which childhood TV exposure is just one. Nevertheless, the evidence indicates that if, hypothetically, television technology had never been developed, there would today be 10,000 fewer homicides each year in the United States, 70,000 fewer rapes, and

700,000 fewer injurious assaults. Violent crime would be half of what it now is.[12]

Centerwall's study, published in 1989, includes controls for such variables as firearm possession and economic growth.[13] But his conclusions have been criticized for not taking into account other factors, such as population changes during the time period studied, that might also play a role in changing crime rates.[14] Shifts in policy and length of prison terms clearly affect these levels as well. By now, the decline in levels of violent crime in the United States since Centerwall's study was conducted, even though television viewing did not decline ten to fifteen years before, does not square with his extrapolations. As for "white homicide" in South Africa under apartheid, each year brings more severe challenges to official statistics from that period.

Even the lower estimates, however, of around 5 to 10 percent of violence as correlated with television exposure, point to substantial numbers of violent crimes in a population as large as America's. But if such estimates are to be used in discussions of policy decisions, more research will be needed to distinguish between the effects of television in general and those of particular types of violent programming, and to indicate specifically what sorts of images increase the aggressor effect and by what means; and throughout to be clearer about the nature of the aggressive acts studied.

Media representatives naturally request proof of such effects before they are asked to undertake substantial changes in programming. In considering possible remedies for a problem, inquiring into the reasons for claims about risks is entirely appropriate. It is clearly valid to scrutinize the research designs, sampling methods, and possible biases of studies supporting such claims, and to ask about the reasoning leading from particular research findings to conclusions. But to ask for some demonstrable pinpointing of just when and how exposure to media violence affects levels of aggression sets a dangerously high threshold for establishing risk factors.

We may never be able to trace, retrospectively, the specific set of television programs that contributed to a particular person's aggressive conduct. The same is true when it comes to the links between tobacco smoking and cancer, between drunk driving and automobile accidents, and many other risk factors presenting public health hazards. Only recently have scientists identified the specific channels through which tobacco generates its carcinogenic effects. Both precise causative mechanisms and documented occurrences in individuals remain elusive. Too often, media representatives formulate their requests in what appear to be strictly polemical terms, raising dismissive questions familiar from debates over the effects of tobacco: "How can anyone definitively pinpoint the link between media violence and acts of real-life violence? If not, how can we know if exposure to media violence constitutes a risk factor in the first place?"

Yet the difficulty in carrying out such pinpointing has not stood in the way of discussing and promoting efforts to curtail cigarette smoking and drunk driving. It is not clear, therefore, why a similar difficulty should block such efforts when it comes to media violence. The perspective of "probabilistic causation," mentioned earlier, is crucial to public debate about the risk factors in media violence.[15] The television industry has already been persuaded to curtail the glamorization of smoking and drunk driving on its programs, despite the lack of conclusive documentation of the correlation between TV viewing and higher incidence of such conduct. Why should the industry not take analogous precautions with respect to violent programming?

Americans have special reasons to inquire into the causes of societal violence. While we are in no sense uniquely violent, we need to ask about all possible reasons why our levels of violent crime are higher than in all other stable industrialized democracies. Our homicide rate would be higher still if we did not imprison more of our citizens than any society in the world, and if emergency medical care had not improved so greatly in recent decades that a larger proportion of shooting victims survive than in the past. Even so, we have seen an unprecedented rise not only in child and adolescent violence, but in levels of rape, child abuse, domestic violence, and every other form of assault.[16]

Although America's homicide rate has declined in the 1990s, the rates for suicide, rape, and murder involving children and adolescents in many regions have too rarely followed suit. For Americans aged 15 to 34 years, homicide is the second leading cause of death, and for young African Americans, 15 to 24 years, it is *the* leading cause of death.[17] In the decade following the mid-1980s, the rate of murder committed by teenagers 14 to 17 more than doubled. The rates of injury suffered by small children are skyrocketing, with the number of seriously injured children nearly quadrupling from 1986 to 1993; and a proportion of these injuries are inflicted by children upon one another.[18] Even homicides by children, once next to unknown, have escalated in recent decades.

America may be the only society on earth to have experienced what has been called an "epidemic of children killing children," which is ravaging some of its communities today.[19] As in any epidemic, it is urgent to ask what it is that makes so many capable of such violence, victimizes so many others, and causes countless more to live in fear.[20] Whatever role the media are found to play in this respect, to be sure, is but part of the problem. Obviously, not even the total elimination of media violence would wipe out the problem of violence in the United States or any other society. The same can be said for the proliferation and easy access to guns, or for poverty, drug addiction, and other risk factors. As Dr. Deborah Prothrow-Stith puts it, "It's not an either or. It's not guns or media or parents or poverty."[21]

We have all witnessed the four effects that I have discussed in this chapter—fearfulness, numbing, appetite, and aggressive impulses—in the context of many influences apart from the media. Maturing involves learning to resist the dominion that these effects can gain over us, and to strive, instead, for greater resilience, empathy, self-control, and respect for self and others. The process of maturation and growth in these respects is never completed for any of us; but it is most easily thwarted in childhood, before it has had chance to take root. Such learning calls for nurturing and education at first; then for increasing autonomy in making personal decisions about how best to confront the realities of violence.

Today, the sights and sounds of violence on the screen affect this learning process from infancy on, in many homes. The television screen is the lens through which most children learn about violence. Through the magnifying power of this lens, their everyday life becomes suffused by images of shootings, family violence, gang warfare, kidnappings, and everything else that contributes to violence in our society. It shapes their experiences long before they have had the opportunity to consent to such shaping or developed the ability to cope adequately with this knowledge. The basic nurturing and protection to prevent the impairment of this ability ought to be the birthright of every child.

NOTES

1. See, for example, Gil Bailie, *Violence Unveiled: Humanity at the Crossroads* (New York: Crossroad, 1995), p. 90. By contrast, sociologist Todd Gitlin, in "Imagebusters: The Hollow Crusade Against TV Violence" (*American Prospect*, Winter 1994, p. 45), estimates that an exceedingly high estimate of the deaths resulting from copycat crimes might be one hundred per year that would not otherwise have taken place: "These would amount to 0.28 percent of the total of 36,000 murders, accidents, and suicides committed by gunshot in the United States in 1992."

2. Ken Auletta, "The Electronic Parent," *New Yorker*, November 8, 1993, p. 74.

3. Michael Shnayerson, "Natural Born Opponents," *Vanity Fair*, July 1996, pp. 98–105, 141–144.

4. John Grisham, "Natural Bred Killers," in French, ed., *Screen Violence*, pp. 226–239, excerpted from *Oxford American*, Spring 1996.

5. Ibid., p. 235.

6. Oliver Stone, "Don't Sue the Messenger," in French, ed., *Screen Violence*, p. 237.

7. American Psychological Association, *Violence and Youth*, p. 34.

8. Edward Donnerstein et al., *The Question of Pornography: Research Findings and Policy Implications* (New York: Free Press, 1987), p. 118.

9. Paik and Comstock, in "Effects of Television Violence on Antisocial Behavior," identify fifteen types of situations for which research data most clearly support the conclusion that violent programs have an effect on behavior. See another list of fifteen factors in Edward Donnerstein and Daniel Linz, "The Media," in James Q. Wilson and Joan Petersilia, eds., *Crime* (San Francisco: Institute for Contemporary Studies Press, 1995), pp. 244–245.

10. Elizabeth Kolbert, "Despair of Popular Culture," *New York Times*, August 20, 1995, sec. 2, pp. 1, 23.

11. Edward Donnerstein suggests that correlational data indicate that early childhood viewing of mass media violence contributes 5 to 10 percent to adult aggressive behavior, in "Mass Media Violence: Thoughts on the Debate," *Hofstra Law Review*, vol. 22 (1994), p. 829. George Gerbner puts the figure at "at most five percent," in "The Hidden Side of Television Violence," in George Gerbner et al., *Invisible Crises* (Westview Press, 1996), p. 27. Karl Erik Rosengren, reporting on a 20-year study of Swedish school children in "Stor Fara med TV-våld," *Dagens Nybeter*, January 30, 1995, p. 5, holds that 10–20 percent of aggression in schools and neighborhoods can be "explained as direct or indirect effects of TV violence." For a view holding that such effects are slight or nonexistent, see Jonathan Freedman, "Television Violence and Aggression: A Rejoinder," *Psychological Bulletin*, vol. 100, 1986, pp. 372–378.

12. Brandon S. Centerwall, "Television and Violent Crime, *Public Interest*, Spring 1993, pp. 63–64. Unlike those who have studied media violence in particular or examined amounts of viewing by different groups, Centerwall's research concerns the mere presence of television in communities.

13. Brandon S. Centerwall, "Exposure to Television as a Risk Factor for Violence," *American Journal of Epidemiology*, vol. 4 (1989), pp. 643–652.

14. See, for example, Kevin W. Saunders, *Violence as Obscenity: Limiting the Media's First Amendment Protection* (Durham, N.C.: Duke University Press, 1996), pp. 35–37; and Franklin E. Zimring and Gordon Hawkins, *Crime Is Not the Problem: Lethal Violence in America* (New York: Oxford University Press, 1997), pp. 132–133, 237–243. Zimring and Hawkins, focusing strictly on lethal violence, speculate that because time spent by large numbers of people with the media is time not spent by the most violent persons committing murder, the media may actually prevent thousands of acts of lethal violence a year (p. 128).

15. Schauer, "Causation Theory and the Causes of Sexual Violence," p. 753.

16. Jean-Claude Chesnais, "The History of Violence: Homicide and Suicide Through the Ages," *International Social Science Journal*, May 1992, pp. 217–234.

17. William H. Foege, Mark L. Rosenberg, and James A. Mercy, "Public Health and Violence Prevention," *Current Issues in Public Health*, vol. 1 (1995), pp. 2–9, at 3.

18. *Child Maltreatment 1994: Reports from the States to the National Center on Child Abuse and Neglect* (Washington, D.C.: U.S. Department of Health and Human Services, 1996).

19. Foege et al., "Public Health," p. 3; C. Everett Koop and G. D. Lundberg, "Violence in America: a Public Health Emergency: Time to Bite the Bullet Back," *Journal of the American Medical Association*, vol. 271 (1992), pp. 3075–3076; Donna Shalala, "Addressing the Crisis of Violence," *Health Affairs*, vol. 12, no. 4 (Winter 1993), pp. 30–33. See also Garbarino, *Raising Children in a Socially Toxic Environment*.

20. Analogies with "epidemics" and "toxic social environments" should not tempt investigators to "medicalize" violence to the point of abstracting from personal responsibility. Being felled by gunshot and by cholera cannot be equated from a moral point of view any more than from a law enforcement point of view. See Mark Moore, "Violence Prevention: Criminal Justice or Public Health?" *Health Affairs*, vol. 12, no. 4, pp. 34–45.

21. Deborah Prothrow-Stith, quoted in Neil Hickey, "Violence on Television," *TV Guide*, 1992. See also Deborah Prothrow-Stith, with Michaele Weissman, *Deadly Consequences* (New York: HarperCollins, 1993).

Predictors of Children's Interest in Violent Television Programs

1997

Joanne Cantor and Amy I. Nathanson

Children's attraction to violent television was explored by comparing the relative contributions of seemingly important predictors. A random sample of 285 parents of children in kindergarten, second, fourth, and sixth grades was interviewed about their children's television viewing habits. Analyses revealed that interest in classic cartoons, which typically display violence for violence's sake, was predicted by grade, whereas attraction to typically justice-restoring violent fare was predicted by grade, gender, aggression, and fright reactions to television.

The bulk of research on children's relationship with violent media has focused on imitative responses to content and increased aggressive tendencies. Most of this work has assumed that children are passive recipients of content rather than active and purposive viewers. Many researchers assert, however (e.g., Dorr, 1986; Rubin, 1979), that children "use" television for specific purposes and that hence, investigations of the antecedents of children's selective exposure to violent content is warranted. This paper explores young children's attractions to violent content and compares the predictive power of a number of theories relating to the attractions of violence. Our goal is to provide preliminary findings relating to why children are willing—even eager—to experience violence through television.

Research shows that children regularly watch television that features violence. According to Wober (1988), young viewers are more likely to attend to violent programs than older viewers, with the heaviest violence viewing occurring between the ages of seven and nine. In addition, violent shows typically earn the highest Nielsen ratings on Saturday mornings, a time slot targeted at children (Stipp, 1995).

Interestingly, children are often frightened or upset by the violent content they watch. Popular movies such as *The Wizard of Oz* and series such as *The Incredible Hulk* have been shown to evoke fright reactions in preschool children (Cantor & Sparks, 1984; Sparks, 1986). Older children, however, tend to experience fright reactions to more realistic portrayals (Cantor, 1994) and programs that feature the threat of violence (Cantor & Sparks, 1984; Sparks, 1986). Not only do children experience fear while watching these portrayals, but they also often report symptoms that persist well beyond exposure (Harrison & Cantor,

1996; Palmer, Hockett, & Dean, 1983), with a few extreme cases diagnosed as "post-traumatic stress disorder" (Simons & Silveira, 1994).

Given the prevalence of these reactions, why do children selectively expose themselves to violent material? A number of reasons have been offered to explain children's attraction to violent programming. One set of explanations focuses on individual differences in viewers; a second set focuses on differences in violent portrayals.

INDIVIDUAL DIFFERENCES IN ATTRACTION TO VIOLENT TELEVISION

Gender differences. Many theorists propose that gender differences in aggressive behavior account for the fact that males are more interested than females in violent television. Debates over whether this difference is due to biology (e.g., Goldstein, in press) or socialization pressures have been plentiful (e.g., Frodi, Macaulay, & Thome, 1977). Whatever the origin of these differences, males are usually more aggressive than females and are taught that violence is, to some degree, acceptable for them (Baron, 1977; Johnson, 1972; Zillmann, 1979).

These gender differences have also been demonstrated among children (Bruce, 1995). Male children have been shown to like and choose violent media more than female children (Donohue, 1975; Lyle & Hoffman, 1972). In addition, little boys express greater interest than little girls in a variety of violent materials including violent toys (Goldstein, in press), cartoons (Lyle & Hoffman, 1972), fairy tale stories (Collins-Standley, Gan, Yu, & Zillmann, 1995), and television shows (Atkin, Greenberg, Korzenny, & Mc-Dermott, 1979). Consistent with past research on gender differences, we expected that:

H$_1$: Male children will be more interested than female children in violent television shows.

Age. A viewer's age may also play an important role in determining how attractive violent media are. Twitchell (1989) states that an interest in vicarious participation in violence peaks for males during adolescence. He argues that adolescence is the time when boys must struggle to bring their aggressive urges under control and to ready themselves for the biological responsibilities that go along with being an adult male. In essence, Twitchell argues that gender and age interact to predict interest in media violence.

However, it is also possible that preschool children (both boys and girls) undergo somewhat similar socialization struggles involving the control of aggressive impulses as they experience the new-found freedom associated with their developing strength and ability to move about independently. Given this uncertainty, we posed a research question that asked:

RQ: What is the relationship between age and interest in violent television programming and does it vary by gender?

Aggression. Another perspective suggests that viewers' own aggressive tendencies predispose them to select violent media. According to this approach, television violence does not lead to viewer violence; instead, viewers who are already aggressive select violent messages to watch. Feningstein (1979) claims that "aggressive thoughts or actions set in motion certain psychological processes, such as the need to understand one's behavior" (p. 2308). Other researchers argue that aggressive people want to witness other people behaving violently to justify their own actions and to perceive them as more typical.

Many studies have demonstrated positive relationships between aggressive behavior and preference for or enjoyment of violent media. Although much of the research has implicated aggressive males in the attraction to violent content (e.g., Bryant, 1989; Diener & DeFour, 1978), other studies have also found that aggressive women enjoy violent media content more than non-aggressive women (Blanchard, Graczyk, & Blanchard, 1986) and that verbally aggressive girls

watch more verbally aggressive television than other girls (Atkin et al., 1979). We thus expected that:

H$_2$: There will be a positive relationship between children's aggression level and their interest in violent television shows.

VIOLENT CONTENT

The appeal of restricted content. Explanations of the attraction of violence can be based on characteristics of the content itself. For example, the "forbidden fruit" hypothesis (Christenson, 1992) suggests that violent television shows are attractive to children because parents often restrict access to them. This hypothesis is based on Brehm's (1972) theory of psychological reactance, which states that when people believe their freedom is threatened or restricted, they become motivated to assert their freedom by performing the restricted behavior. Violent television is often made less accessible to children via advisories and parental restrictions. Children may thus become more attracted to violent content because of its taboo nature.

There is not much evidence on the merits of the forbidden fruit hypothesis with regard to television violence. Herman and Leyens (1977) found that movies broadcast in Belgium with a sex or violence advisory had larger adult audiences than those broadcast without advisories. This study, however, confounded the effects of advisories with the effects of the type of content that co-occurs with advisories. A recent experiment revealed that some advisories, such as "parental discretion advised," and the MPAA ratings "PG-13" and "R" made programs and movies more attractive, especially to boys (Cantor & Harrison, 1996). To test the forbidden fruit hypothesis, the following prediction was advanced:

H$_3$: Children whose parents restrict access to violent television shows will be more interested in violent television shows than children whose parents do not restrict their access to these shows.

The appeal of frightening content. Another explanation based on media content characteristics focuses on the fright-inducing nature of violent depictions. Orbach, Winkler, and Har-Even's (1993) "repetition-compulsion hypothesis" contends that children who are frightened by stories are motivated to select similarly frightening stimuli in order to gain control and master their unpleasant emotions.

Most rationales linking the attraction of violence to anxiety reduction assume that reassuring outcomes to the violent episode are essential (e.g., Goldstein, 1986). Zillmann (1980) suggests that apprehensive individuals selectively expose themselves to suspenseful (usually violent) programming because the typical plot of such televised fare involves the restoration of order and justice. He argues that anxious individuals may be undergoing a self-administered desensitization procedure when they expose themselves to dramatic depictions of suspenseful, violent presentations which portray a just resolution. Bryant, Carveth, and Brown (1981) found support for this explanation among college students.

The following hypothesis explored the repetition compulsion hypothesis' prediction that fright reactions to television will be linked to attractions to violent material:

H$_{4a}$: Children who have been frightened by television will show greater interest in violent programs than children who have not been frightened by television.

To explore the appeal of justice-restoring violence for reducing anxiety, a subsequent hypothesis that distinguished *types* of violent fare was also advanced:

H$_{4b}$: Children who have been frightened by television will show greater interest in justice-restoring violent programs than children who have not been frightened by television.

In summary, this study explored the viability of various explanations for children's attraction to violent media. Our goal was to identify the most important predictors and to compare their relative efficacy in explaining children's interest in this type of content.

METHOD

Respondents

Respondents included 285 parents of kindergarten, second-, fourth-, and sixth-grade children in the Madison, WI Metropolitan School District.[1] The sample was drawn by obtaining lists of the names and addresses of parents of children in the district who were attending these grades during the 1993-94 academic year. Specific names were selected for inclusion in the study at random. Of the 285 parents in the survey, 68.3% were

mothers. This sample reported on 74 kindergartners, 73 second-graders, 69 fourth-graders, and 65 sixth-graders. Slightly over half of the children (53.7%) were boys.

Procedures

Data were collected via telephone interviews. The interviewers told the parent or guardian of the child in the expected grade that they were doing a research project on children and television. The ensuing questionnaire took approximately 15 minutes and contained questions on a variety of topics related to television. Of the phone calls in which an eligible respondent was reached, there was a 73% response rate.

Parents were first asked to provide information about their regulation and guidance of their child's television viewing. They were also asked to estimate the number of hours their child watched television per day ($M = 1.7$, $SD = 1.0$). They were then asked about their child's fright reactions to television. Subsequent sections of the questionnaire asked about their child's interest in violent programming and their child's aggression level. These questions were interspersed among other questions about television viewing, the results of which are reported elsewhere (Cantor & Nathanson, 1996).

Predictor Variables

Aggression. Parents rated their child's aggression level on a five-point scale (1 = not at all aggressive, 5 = extremely aggressive); $M = 1.66$, $SD = .79$.[2]

Parental restriction of television violence. Parents were asked if they forbid their child to watch any particular programs. Affirmative answers to this question received a code of "1" (negative responses received a "0"), and were then probed to reveal the restricted shows. Parents were then asked for their major concerns about these programs and why they wanted to restrict them. Seventy-seven percent ($n = 220$) of the parents said there was at least one show that they forbid their child to watch. The reasons parents provided for restricting shows were then categorized by two independent coders (Cohen's kappa = .93) for violence (1) or no violence (0). Forty-four percent of the sample said that the presence of violence was the major reason why they restricted their children's access to programs.

Fright reactions to television. Parents were asked if television had ever disturbed, upset, or frightened their child to the extent that the effect endured after the program was over. Affirmative answers were coded as "1" and negative responses received a code of "0". Forty-two percent of the parents ($n = 119$) reported that their child had been frightened or upset by television.

Criterion Variables

Attraction to violent content. Parents were asked to estimate their child's level of interest in four types of violent programming. On a four-point scale, parents reported their child's level of interest (1 = not at all interested, 4 = extremely interested) in classic cartoons (e.g., *Bugs Bunny, The Roadrunner*), action cartoons (e.g., *Teenage Mutant Ninja Turtles, GI-Joe*), live-action programs (e.g., *Mighty Morphin Power Rangers*), and reality-based action shows (e.g., *Cops, Rescue 911*). Mean scores for interest in classic cartoons, action cartoons, live-action programs, and reality-based action shows were 2.7, 2.1, 2.3, and 2.2, respectively. Respective standard deviations were .95, 1.16, 1.28, and 1.19.

An "attraction to justice-restoring violence" scale was created by averaging scores for action cartoons, live-action shows, and reality-based action shows ($\alpha = .50$).[3] Action cartoons and live-action dramas have well delineated "good guys" and "bad guys" and feature the heroes triumphing in the end. Reality-action shows exhibit a similar tendency by grossly over-representing both the occurrence of violent crimes and the proportion that are solved (Oliver, 1994). In contrast to these genres, classic cartoons typically portray a series of aggressive activities and pratfalls, with no concepts of "good guys" and "bad guys," and no provision of justice or of good triumphing over evil.

RESULTS

Because the hypotheses for this study use the same criterion variables, the correlations between all of the predictor variables and the criterion variables were computed. These are presented in Table 1. Hierarchical regression equations were then built to examine the relative contributions of each predictor to the criterion variables.

Correlational Analyses

Hypothesis One predicted that male children (coded as "2") would be more interested in violent

Table 1   Correlations Among Predictor and Criterion Variables

	Criterion Variables Interest in...				
	Classic cartoons	Action cartoon	Live-action	Reality shows	Justice restoring*
Gender@	−.01	.37***	.25***	.03	.30***
Grade	−.13*	−.26***	−.27***	.18**	−.18**
Aggression	.06	.37***	.21***	.07	.30***
Violence restrict	.03	.01	−.01	.08	.03
TV-fright	.09	.17**	.12*	.14*	.20***

$p < .05$; $**p < .01$; $***p < .001$
@ females coded 1, males coded 2

television programming than female children (coded as "1"). As Table 1 shows, this prediction was upheld with two of the four dependent variables. There was a positive relationship between gender and interest in both action cartoons ($r = .37, p < .001$) and live-action shows ($r = .25, p < .001$), suggesting that parents of male children were more likely to believe that their child was interested in these two genres of violent programming than parents of female children.

The research question asked how the relationship between age and interest in violent programming would manifest itself. Using grade as a surrogate for age, we found a negative correlation between age and interest in classic cartoons ($r = -.13, p < .03$), action cartoons ($r = -.26, p < .001$), and live-action shows ($r = -.27, p < .001$). In contrast, interest in reality shows increased across grade levels ($r = .18, p < .01$).

Inspection of each grade's mean interest in the four genres revealed a quadratic (inverted U-shaped) relationship between age and classic cartoons. In fact, this quadratic trend was found to explain 4% more variance than the linear trend (adjusted $R^2 = .05$ and .01 for the quadratic and linear trends, respectively). Linear relationships accounted for the most variance in attraction to action cartoons, live action, and reality-based shows as a function of age (adjusted $R^2 = .06, .06$, and .03, respectively).

To test Twitchell's notion of an interaction between gender and age, a two-factor analysis of variance was conducted on the four criteria. We found a significant interaction only in the case of reality shows, $F(3,272) = 3.72, p < .01$. Boys' interest in this genre increased across the grades, while girls' interest followed a U-shaped quadratic trend. Thus, our analyses supported Twitchell in just one case. Contrary to his argument, both boys' and girls' interest in action cartoons and live-action shows decreased across the grades and showed a curvilinear relationship regarding classic cartoons.

The second hypothesis predicted a positive relationship between children's aggression and their interest in violent television. This prediction was supported in two cases. There was a significant positive correlation between the child's aggression score and his or her interest in both action cartoons ($r = .37, p < .001$) and live-action shows ($r = .21, p < .001$). Thus, more aggressive children were more interested in shows that featured cartoon or fantastic action than their less aggressive counterparts.

We found no support for the forbidden fruit hypothesis. No significant relationships were found between parents' tendency to forbid violent shows and the child's interest in any of the four violent genres.

Hypothesis 4a was a test of the repetition compulsion theory and predicted that children who have been frightened or upset by television would be more interested in violent television than children who had not been frightened by television. Significant positive relationships were found between children's fright reactions and their interest in action cartoons ($r = .17, p < .01$), live-action shows ($r = .12, p < .05$), and reality shows ($r = .14, p < .05$), but not classic cartoons ($r = .09$).

An even stronger relationship was observed when the average of the three justice-restoring shows were correlated with children's television-induced fright. Consistent with Hypothesis 4b, children who were upset by television were more interested than other youngsters in violent shows that typically feature justice-restoration ($r = .20, p < .001$).

Regression Analyses

To examine the relative contributions of each predictor variable to the dependent measures, two hierarchical regression analyses were performed: one used interest in classic cartoons as the dependent variable, and one used interest in justice-restoring violent genres as the dependent measure. We believed it was important to segment our analyses in this fashion for several reasons. First, interest in action cartoons, live-action shows, and reality-based action shows are theo-

retically related to one another (i.e., they all represent an interest in justice-restoration); hence, multiple tests performed on each variable separately may provide redundant information and increase the chance of committing Type 1 error. Further, the correlational analyses showed that these variables yield similar patterns of relationships with the predictor variables.[4] Hence, we considered the classic cartoon's violence for violence's sake to be a different type of violent depiction than justice-restoring violence. We should expect, then, that interest in these different types of violence depictions will be predicted by different variables.

Because it is possible that children's interest in violent shows may simply reflect a general tendency toward heavy television viewing, the child's amount of viewing in general (the average number of hours watched per day) was entered in the first block in the analysis of classic cartoons. After this control block, predictor variables were entered in the following steps: (1) both gender and grade, (2) the quadratic function of grade,[5] (3) whether or not the parent restricted violent programming, and (4) both whether the child had had a fright reaction to television and the child's aggression level. This ordering of variables was selected to reflect a possible time-line during which children acquire these characteristics or these events occur. Hence, demographics were entered first, followed by restrictions imposed by parents and finally, responses or characteristics that children develop over time. In this analysis, only grade was a significant predictor. Interest in classic cartoons was negatively related to grade ($\beta = -.17, p < .05$), contributing nearly 3% of the variance. However, as expected from previous analyses, the quadratic function contributed a significant increment in variance (R^2 change $= .03, p < .05$), indicating that this trend best explains the data.

The second analysis used the attraction to justice-restoring violence scale as the dependent measure. The predictors were entered into the regression equation in the same order as the previous analysis (excluding the quadratic function of age). The results revealed that tv viewing contributed nearly 4% of the variance ($\beta = .19$). Next, gender and grade contributed significantly to the variance in attraction to these genres, with gender ($\beta = .31$) accounting for about 10% and grade ($\beta = -.22$) explaining nearly 5% of the variance. Entered on the third step, parental restriction

Table 2   Predicting Children's Interest in Justice-Restoring Television Programs

Step	Variable	Beta R	Mult. R²	Delta R²	Total F sig*
1.	TV viewing	.19*	.19	.04*	.04	.05
2.	Gender	.27**	.42	.14**	.18	.001
	Grade	−.19**				
3.	Violence restricted	−.01	.42	.00	.18	.001
4.	TV-fright	.19**	.48	.06**	.24	.001
	Aggression	.15*				

Note. Betas refer to the standardized coefficients when all variables are included *p < .01; **p < .001

of violent television was not a significant predictor. However, on the fourth step, both fright (β = .19) and aggression level (β = .15) were positively and significantly related to interest, and contributed significantly even after all the other variables were accounted for (R^2 change = .06, $p < .001$). In sum, all of the predictors together accounted for 24% of the total variance in attraction to justice-restoring violence. Table 2 shows the betas for all of the variables at the final step of the analysis, as well as the contributions each block added in the hierarchical analysis.

These findings suggest differential patterns of attraction to violent content depending on the nature of the content. In the case of classic cartoons, grade was the only important predictor. However, interest in justice-restoring violent content was influenced by grade, gender, aggression level, and previous fright reactions to television. At the last step of the regression (see Table 2), it is evident that the variable contributing the most unique variance was gender, followed by grade, TV viewing and fright reactions, and finally, aggressiveness.

DISCUSSION

The results of this study suggest that analyses of children's attraction to violent programming should consider the type of violence depicted. That is, it is not enough to say that all types of violent depictions will be equally attractive to all children. Instead, we must consider how the violence is portrayed in order to select proper predictor variables and draw meaningful theoretical conclusions. In these data, it was evident that children's attraction to violent classic cartoons

displayed a different pattern from interest in violent shows that feature justice restoration.

Specifically, children's attraction to classic cartoons varied as a function of the child's age. Although Twitchell (1989) believes that older males are more attracted to violence than younger children, a quadratic trend best explained the relationship between grade and interest in classic cartoons for both boys and girls. This genre of violence is unique in that it seems to portray violence for violence's sake—in fact, the story-lines of these shows typically center on one character's attempt to hurt another character. The simplicity and predictability of this slapstick may allow younger children to understand and appreciate these shows.

Programs in which violence is used by characters in struggles between "good guys" and "bad guys" may be attractive to different children for different reasons. In these shows, violence is used to achieve retribution—a more complex theme than violence for violence's sake. In our data, we found a distinct pattern of results when data were analyzed on justice-restoring genres of television violence.

Before a discussion of our findings regarding justice-restoration ensues, it is important to keep in mind that we had no direct measure of justice-restoration. As a result, it is quite possible that there are other reasons why this cluster of genres was appealing to certain children. We propose that the presence of justice-restoration is one plausible reason for these relationships and we urge future work to more systematically explore this hypothesis.

The prediction that males would be more attracted to violence than females was upheld for justice-restoring violent programming. Taken with the results of the parallel analysis of interest in classic cartoons, we see that there may be something particularly appealing about justice-restoring violence for males. Rather than liking all types of violence (as most theories of gender differences assume), male children seem to be attracted to shows in which violence is used to accomplish larger goals. This finding suggests that observed differences between males and females in attraction to violence may really be a function of their interest in the theme of justice-restoration.

An alternative explanation for the failure to find gender differences in attraction to classic cartoons is that girls are taught to disdain violence but learn to make an exception for violence that occurs in the context of humor. In fact, our data showed that across the four genres of violent television, girls were most interested in classic cartoons, with a mean interest of 2.7 compared to means of 1.6, 1.9, and 2.2 for interest in action cartoons, live-action shows, and reality shows, respectively. This suggests that the humorous depiction of violence in classic cartoons may be equally acceptable to both boys and girls, and that significant gender differences emerge when violence is depicted in a more serious fashion.

Interest in justice-restoring violent programming was also shown to decrease with grade. However, interest in reality shows increased as male children got older. This is the one finding that was consistent with Twitchell's notion that adolescent males are the primary audience for media violence.

This study also revealed that justice-restoration may be particularly attractive to children who have been frightened by television. As Zillmann (1980) suggested, perhaps fear motivates exposure to violent programming in order to achieve desensitization. Based on our data, we can speculate that the most soothing and therapeutic form of content is that which depicts justice restoration.

It should be made clear, however, that these results do not lead us to suggest that children who suffer from pronounced anxiety levels should watch more violent television. In a study of children in Milwaukee, Bruce (1995) found a negative relationship between severe anxiety symptoms (e.g. hypervigilance, nightmares, recurring disturbing thoughts) and attraction to violent television. Highly anxious children also reported feeling more intensely negative emotions while watching violence than other children. For such children, the effects of viewing violence may be harmful rather than soothing.

Finally, we found a significant positive relationship between children's aggression level and their interest in justice-restoring genres. Perhaps children who are aggressive are not simply attracted to violent content because they can "relate" to the action; instead, it could be that aggressive children are more motivated to see aggression as an instrument for achieving a goal or that which is "justified," allowing them to put their own behavior in a more acceptable light.

We must remind readers that our study is based on parental perceptions of children's responses to television. Therefore, our conclusions are speculative and must be followed up with additional research that can more directly assess children's interests. We urge future work to follow up this exploratory study with more systematic research so that these issues can be addressed. Specifically, we recommend that future research interview children directly about their viewing interests, and that the theme of justice-restoration be either manipulated experimentally, or asked about specifically so that this potentially important variable can be explored further.

In conclusion, these data suggest that media violence is not a unidimensional construct. The way that violence is portrayed may attract different viewers for different reasons. Given that the explanations advanced are only speculative, a systematic exploration of these ideas is needed before any firm conclusions are drawn. In the end, we may discover that programming that satisfies justice-restoration via non-violent means is just as attractive to some children as violent solutions.

NOTES

1. Although research suggests that parents sometimes underestimate the negative effects of media on their children, relative to self-reports (Cantor & Reilly, 1982), findings from surveys of parental perceptions have been consistent with findings of experiments assessing children's responses directly (Cantor, 1994).

2. The fact that parents were asked to provide estimates of their children's aggression may account for the "floor effect" in these data. In the interest of social desirability, parents may have underestimated their child's aggression. It is also possible that parents only perceive aggression when it is enacted in socially inappropriate ways that demand disciplinary action and that the child's sanctioned aggression goes unnoticed (e.g., during play, especially for boys). Perhaps more objective reports of children's aggression would have allowed this measure more variability.

3. Because this alpha coefficient is low, any correlations it shares with other variables will be attenuated (Cohen & Cohen, 1983). We suspect, then, that the true correlations are larger than those observed in this study. We recommend that any findings involving this measure be replicated to instill more confidence in our results.

4. Individual regression analyses for each of the three criteria comprising the justice-restoration scale were also inspected. The results revealed highly similar patterns of predictors across each criterion (each genre was preferred more by boys, aggressive children, and frightened children). The only inconsistency was found in the relationship between grade and interest in the three genres. Whereas younger children were more interested in action cartoons and live action shows, older children were more interested in reality shows. Theoretically, however, fright should be most strongly related to justice restoration; in fact, of the five predictors in our study, children's fright held the strongest relationships with interest in each of the genres. Given the similar patterns of predictors for each criterion, and the especially strong and consistent relationships they held with fright, the use of the justice-restoration scale seems warranted.

5. Because the correlation analysis revealed that a quadratic trend better explained the relationship between grade and interest in classic cartoons, the quadratic function of age was entered into the regression equation after the linear trend to examine if it made a significant contribution to the variance in the criterion (Cohen & Cohen, 1983).

REFERENCES

ATKIN, C., GREENBERG, B., KORZENNY, F., & MCDERMOTT, S. (1979). Selective exposure to televised violence. *Journal of Broadcasting, 23,* 5–13.

BARON, R. A. (1977). *Human aggression.* New York: Plenum Press.

BLANCHARD, D. C., GRACZYK, B., & BLANCHARD, R.J. (1986). Differential reactions of men and women to realism, physical damage, and emotionality in violent films. *Aggressive Behavior, 12,* 45–55.

BREHM, J. (1972). *Responses to loss of freedom: A theory of psychological reactance.* Morristown, NJ: General Learning Press.

BRUCE, L. R. (1995, May). *Interpretive activities of traumatized children in response to violent television fare.* Paper presented at the annual meeting of the International Communication Association, Albuquerque, NM.

BRYANT, J. (1989). Viewers' enjoyment of televised sports violence. In L.A. Wenner (Ed.), *Media, sports, and society,* (pp. 270–289). Newbury Park, CA: Sage.

BRYANT, J., CARVETH, R. A., & BROWN, D. (1981). Television viewing and anxiety: An experimental examination. *Journal of Communication, 31* (1), 106–119.

CANTOR, J. (1994). Fright reactions to mass media. In J. Bryant & D. Zillmann (Eds.), *Media effects: Advances in theory and research* (pp. 213–245). Hillsdale, NJ: Erlbaum.

CANTOR, J., & HARRISON, K. (1996). Ratings and advisories for television programming. Report for the National *Television Violence Study.* Los Angeles: Mediascope.

CANTOR, J., & NATHANSON, A. I. (1996). Children's fright reactions to television news. *Journal of Communication, 46*(4), 139–152.

CANTOR, J., & REILLY, S. (1982). Adolescents' fright reactions to television and films. *Journal of Communication, 32,* 87–99.

CANTOR, J., & SPARKS, G. G. (1984). Children's fear responses to mass media: Testing some Piagetian predictions. *Journal of Communication, 34*(2), 90–103.

CHRISTENSON, P. (1992). The effects of parental advisory labels on adolescent music preferences. *Journal of Communication, 42* (1), 106–113.

COHEN, J., & COHEN, P. (1983). *Applied multiple regression/correlation analysis for the behavioral sciences.* Hillsdale, NJ: Erlbaum.

COLLINS-STANDLEY, T., GAN, S., YU, H. J., & ZILLMANN, D. (1995). *Choice of romantic, violent, and scary fairy-tale books by preschool girls and boys.* Unpublished manuscript.

DIENER, E., & DEFOUR, D. (1978). Does television violence enhance program popularity? *Journal of Personality and Social Psychology, 36,* 333–341.

DONOHUE, T. R. (1975). Black children's perceptions of favorite TV characters as models of anti-social behavior. *Journal of Broadcasting, 19,* 153–167.

DORR, A. (1986). *Television and children: A special medium for a special audience.* Beverly Hills: Sage.

FENINGSTEIN, A. (1979). Does aggression cause a preference for viewing media violence? *Journal of Personality and Social Psychology, 37,* 2307–2317.

FRODI, A., MACAULAY, J., & THOME, P. (1977). Are women always less aggressive than men? A review of the experimental literature. *Psychological Bulletin, 84,* 64–66.

GOLDSTEIN, J. H. (in press). Immortal Kombat: War toys and violent videogames. In J. H. Goldstein (Ed.), *Why we watch.*

GOLDSTEIN, J. H. (1986). *Aggression and crimes of violence.* (2nd edition). New York: Oxford University Press.

HARRISON, K., & CANTOR, J. (1996, May). *Tales from the screen: Long-term anxiety reactions to frightening movies.* Paper presented at the annual meeting of the International Communication Association, Chicago, IL.

HERMAN, G., & LEYENS, J. P. (1977). Rating films on TV. *Journal of Communication, 27*(4), 48–53.

JOHNSON, R. N. (1972). *Aggression in man and animals.* Philadelphia: W.B. Saunders Company.

LYLE, J., & HOFFMAN, H. R. (1972). Children's use of television and other media. In E. A. Rubinstein, G. A. Comstock, & J. P. Murray (Eds.), *Television and social behavior* (Vol. 4, pp. 129–256). Washington, DC: U.S. Government Printing Office.

ORBACH, I., WINKLER, E., & HAR-EVEN, D. (1993). The emotional impact of frightening stories on children. *Journal of Child Psychology and Psychiatry, 34,* 379–389.

PALMER, E. L., HOCKETT, A. B., & DEAN, W. W. (1983). The television family and children's fright reactions. *Journal of Family Issues, 4,* 279–292.

RUBIN, A. M. (1979). Television use by children and adolescents. *Human Communication Research, 5,* 109–120.

SIMONS, D., & SILVEIRA, W. R. (1994). Post-traumatic stress disorder in children after television programmes. *British Medical Journal, 308,* 389–390.

SPARKS, G. G. (1986). Developmental differences in children's reports of fear induced by the mass media. *Child Study Journal, 16,* 55–66.

STIPP, H. (1995, May). *Children's viewing of news, reality-shows, and other programming.* Paper presented at the Convention of the International Communication Association, Albuquerque, NM.

TWITCHELL, J. B. (1989). *Preposterous violence.* New York: Oxford University Press.

WOBER, M. (1988). The extent to which viewers watch violence-containing programs. *Current Psychology: Research and Reviews, 7,* 43–57.

ZILLMANN, D. (1979). *Hostility and aggression.* Hillsdale, NJ: Erlbaum.

ZILLMANN, D. (1980). Anatomy of suspense. In P.H. Tannenbaum (Ed.), *The entertainment functions of television* (pp. 133–163). Hillsdale, NJ: Erlbaum.

Lady Killers

Tough Enough?

Sherrie A. Inness

1999

In China in the early 1990s, "Dagger Ladies" became all the rage with the affluent, who could afford to shell out the 1000 yuan ($172) monthly salary to support one. Dagger Ladies—female body guards who fetch the mail, answer the phone, and perform other such office tasks, but who can also throw a mean right hook when necessary—are trained by a number of specialized schools. One school bragged that it instructed its seventy trainees not only in "shooting, parachute jumping, judo and boxing but also in law, psychology, etiquette and foreign languages." Dagger Ladies caught on to such an extent that three thousand women applied for the 130 openings in a Dagger Lady training course. The Dagger-Lady-wannabes did not seem put off that the class cost 3,500 yuan ($620), which represented three-and-a-half months of the earnings they could expect as Dagger Ladies. The *Chicago Tribune* article about this phenomenon was quick to reassure readers that a Dagger Lady would not lose her femininity: "She's a devil with a dagger and a whiz in martial arts. She often wears high-heel shoes and mini-skirts." As the title of the article informed readers, a Dagger Lady was "tough as steel, but still a lady" (Schmetzer 6).

Though not training to be Dagger Ladies, American women, too, have shown a new interest in learning how to fight, flocking to classes with names like Cardio Combat, Aerobox, and Executive Boxing—exercise classes that teach fighting skills along with providing a workout. Cardio Combat features "chops, punches and kicks" (Eller 124), while Aerobox and Executive Boxing introduce boxing, a sport generally considered off limits to women. If women choose to concentrate on self-protection, a variety of classes are offered that teach them to fight back. Krav Maga is a "technique used by the Israeli Army" that instructs assault victims to lash out at the attacker's groin, kneecap, or eyes (Eller 125). Other classes offered include Model Mugging, in which women learn to fight back by attacking and attempting to disable a male instructor posing as a mugger (Eller 125).

Today, tough, aggressive fighting women are all the rage in Hollywood.[1] One writer observes, "In re-cent years, the rampaging female has become a new cliché of Hollywood cinema, stabbing and shooting her way to notoriety" (Birch 1). Another comments, "Hollywood has long been fascinated by women who kill. In the last ten years, however, deadly dolls have filled the screen. Willingly, even gleefully, they pick up the rocket launcher, the gun, the knife, the fork" (Holmlund 127).[2] Yet another writer, Julie Baumgold, discusses the growing numbers of what she refers to as "killer women" in such films as *Thelma & Louise* and *La Femme Nikita*. She writes, "They have borrowed the competence of the Fonda-Streep women and turned it to killing. They are no longer molls and helpers, no longer love puppies who commit crimes of passion; they are combat-trained outlaws" (26). What explains the increasing prevalence of the tough killer woman in films from the 1980s and 1990s?[3] Does her appearance signify new freedoms for women? What does she reveal about how tough women are perceived by Americans today? This chapter seeks to answer these questions by exploring the depiction of the killer woman in popular films, showing how her presence perpetuates the notion that women who adopt the tough attributes typically associated with men will literally go insane.[4]

. . . [T]his chapter is concerned with tracing the myriad ways that society seeks to limit the threat of toughness in women by showing that women are only pseudo-tough, lacking the "true" toughness of men. In the last two chapters, we discovered how toughness in women was repeatedly toned down by emphasizing the connection between women, sexuality, and femininity. This chapter demonstrates another way that toughness in women is controlled: killer-women films often depict women who are clearly insane or over the edge because they have become too aggressive, too masculine, or too tough. These women, the films show, must be punished for their aggressive gender-bending behavior. Punishment, however, is not the only tactic for dealing with such socially transgressive females. Killer women can be depicted as sex kittens under their tough demeanors, as were the Angels.

They also can be presented as less tough than the boys. We shall find that films about killer women rely on these three tactics to assure viewers of the stability of the patriarchal order.

Despite the increasing number of killer women in recent films, this character type is by no means a new invention but one with deep roots in Hollywood. Notable predecessors include the scheming, manipulative women of *film noir*, such as Phyllis Dietrichson (Barbara Stanwyck) in *Double Indemnity* (1944) and Gilda (Rita Hayworth) in *Gilda* (1946). In the 1960s, the killer woman took different forms. As Ma Barker, Lurene Tuttle was a killer in the film *Ma Barker's Killer Brood* (1960). Bonnie Parker (Faye Dunaway) was also a killer in *Bonnie and Clyde* (1967). The killer woman has been a staple of James Bond films for decades. A beautiful femme fatale lurks around every corner in Agent 007's world. In *For Your Eyes Only* (1981), Melina (Carole Bouquet) is an expert with a crossbow and does not hesitate to kill the man who murdered her parents. Fatima Blush in *Never Say Never Again* (1983) is a sadistic murderer who would do anything to kill Agent 007. Grace Jones plays the sinister May Day in *A View to a Kill* (1985). In *Golden-Eye* (1995), Xenia Onatroop (Famke Janssen) delights in murdering the men with whom she makes love, often squeezing them to death between her muscular thighs.

Obviously, killer women are a recurring motif in Hollywood. However, contemporary killer women are growing in number and have become far more aggressive—changes indicative of altering cultural values. In her book *Spectacular Bodies: Gender, Genre and the Action Cinema* (1993), Yvonne Tasker writes about women in action-adventure films, "There is a whole range of determinants informing the production of the woman as action heroine in recent cinema. Her appearance can be seen to signal, amongst other factors, a response to feminism and the exhaustion of previous formulae" (152). Tasker's words are applicable to killer-women films in which the killer enacts society's worst fears about feminism: strong women prove to be not only career women, but also murderous harpies. In this way, these films offer viewers an extreme scenario about what happens when women usurp roles that have been long considered the province of men.

We can better understand how killer-women films offer an opportunity to enact cultural fantasies about the excesses of feminism in light of Alice Jardine's theory of male paranoia. In "'She Was Bad News': Male Paranoia and the Contemporary New Woman" (1981), Amelia Jones describes how male paranoia operates:

The new woman's films are structured by what Alice Jardine has called "male paranoia"—the fearful response of patriarchy to the loss of boundaries endemic to the condition of subjectivity in contemporary, so-called postmodern, American life. . . . Male paranoia is a defense aimed at rebuilding the subject/object dichotomy that threatens to dissolve as more and more women (and men, for that matter) take on both masculine and feminine roles. (297)

Jones argues that the films "represent patriarchy's last-ditch efforts to rebuild or shore up the tottering ramparts by which the masculine is assured a dominant socio-economic position in social relations" (298). She suggests that the new woman's films "repeatedly attempt to pose resolutions to the problem of gender identity by reinscribing women in traditional roles or eliminating deviant women to remove their threat to the family structure" (315). Jones's thoughts are germane to killer-women films that reassure viewers that women who display too many tough, masculine characteristics will get their just rewards, usually ending up in prison or being killed. In this fashion, the films serve to shore up the gender status quo and to warn women that adopting tough attributes is still unacceptable.

But there are other reasons for the current success of the killer-woman film. It offers a new thrill at a time when Hollywood is searching for the sensation-of-the-year in order to sell more films to jaded viewers. As Baumgold notes, "In part, the male-mogul motive is commercial. To appeal to women repulsed or bored by male action movies, they have created these warrior women. . . . There are contradictions in this new woman. She may wear her heavy jacket with something flimsy. She is hard but breakable" (29). Producers might wish to attract a broader audience to action-adventure films, but, at the same time, they do not wish to stray too far from the gender stereotypes that have served them well in the past. What they create are women killers who might wield a knife or shoot a gun but still remember the importance of appearing feminine and physically desirable to men. Because the sexual allure of killer women is frequently stressed in Hollywood films, these films present images of women and femininity that are less subversive than might initially appear to be the case.

THE KILLER WOMAN AS SEX KITTEN

The threat posed by the killer woman is mitigated in part because she is commonly portrayed as very sexually appealing to men. Christine Holmlund observes, "the murderesses in [killer women] films are, to a woman, white, lithe and lovely, because Hollywood sees female violence as erotic and defines 'erotic' within narrow parameters" (128). Holmlund points out that Hollywood takes the dangerous toughness of many killer women and limits its potential threat to the social order by suggesting that women might be killers, but they are still attractive to men. Often the association between women and violence only heightens their sexual appeal. As we have already discovered, the same connection between women and danger is used in *Charlie's Angels* to heighten the sexual appeal of the show's stars.

By making the women sexually desirable and stressing that they are attracted to men, the films assure viewers that women are sexual objects. Laura Mulvey discusses the objectification of women in the cinema in her essay "Visual Pleasure and Narrative Cinema" (1975): "Traditionally, the woman displayed has functioned on two levels: as erotic object for the characters within the screen story, and as erotic object for the spectator within the auditorium" (11–12). Mulvey's words provide an apt description of the killer woman. She might be a killer, but this does not interfere with how the film portrays her as an erotically appealing object for the pleasure of men. Moreover, killer-women films show not only sexually appealing women, but also women who display a keen interest in sexual relations with men, demonstrating that their tough attitudes and actions fail to interfere with their primary role as sex objects for men.

Throughout the past two decades, the sexually voracious killer woman has become a common character. *Prizzi's Honor* (1985, director John Huston) tells the story of Charley Partanna (Jack Nicholson) and Irene Walker (Kathleen Turner) who fall madly and impetuously in love, knowing nothing about each other's past lives. Irene turns out to be a hired assassin, and her new husband works for the Mafia as a hitman. As a married couple, Irene and Charley continue their careers as assassins. The film emphasizes Irene's sexuality and heterosexual desirability. She is a stunning blonde, and she and her husband have torrid sex every chance they get. The couple is often filmed kissing or hugging or with their arms around each other. The message is clear: Irene might be an assassin but this does not prevent her from being the perfect wife and sexual partner, stereotypically feminine roles that detract from her tough self-presentation.

In other films, the sex-kitten nature of women is emphasized. The image of the woman who kills without a qualm, yet, in reality, is little more than a *Playboy* pinup come to life appears everywhere in the media, especially in the movie theater. Few films make the connection between sexual exploitation and the woman killer more apparent than *No Contest* (1994, director Paul Lynch), a low-budget movie in which the star, Shannon Tweed, was advertised as Playmate of the Year. She is a sex goddess, whose primary purpose is to be drop-dead gorgeous in the various skimpy outfits she wears. Although she takes on a veritable army of men who have captured the participants of a beauty pageant, and, of course, wins the pageant, it is difficult to watch this film and think of Tweed as anything other than a well-endowed woman for teenage boys to ogle. Her character development is obviously less significant than her status as Playmate of the Year.

The notion that killer women are sex kittens first and killers second is stressed in many films, even in 1990s movies that seem to offer tougher images of womanhood than *No Contest*. For example, in the film *Mortal Kombat* (1995, director Paul Anderson), the heroine appears to be as tough as her male compatriots, until we discover that she is really more sex object than warrior. This movie, based on the best-selling video game by the same name, features three martial arts experts who must defeat a host of evil creatures from an alternative universe who are trying to take over the world. One of the three heroes, Sonya Blade (Bridgette Wilson), is a woman.[5] She starts off tough, independent, and self-assured, but during the film her image undergoes a transformation. She is repeatedly viewed in a sexual light by the male fighters. For instance, the lead bad guy, a sorcerer, reveals that he has plans for the "beautiful Sonya." His lascivious intentions are clear. Tough men do not face the kind of sexual threat that tough women face constantly (think of Ripley in the *Aliens* series). The repeated sexualizing of tough women affirms the woman's role as sexual object; no matter how tough she might appear on the surface, she still can be subjected to the ultimate indignity of rape.

Sonya's tough image is also weakened in other ways. Despite her toughness, she lacks any unusual musculature, which is particularly evident when her body is compared with the well-muscled physiques of the men whom she encounters. In *Spectacular Bodies,* Tasker observes that well-developed muscles serve as a visible sign of an action heroine's vulnerability, demonstrating her need to protect herself from some threat (152). But muscles also serve as an important signifier of strength and power in our culture. Showing a tough woman with no bulging biceps is one way to make her appear less masculine, less threatening, and less tough, even if she is a crack shot or a champion kick boxer. Yet another way that Sonya is made to seem less of a threat than her two male comrades is that she appears in only one fighting match with the villains, while the two men engage in many; the men are still very much center stage.

Sonya is finally "put in her place" when she is kidnapped by the evil sorcerer, and her two friends must save her. At this point, Sonya's credibility as a tough hero is entirely destroyed, and her role as a sex kitten is made overt. Even though she had been depicted earlier as independent and in control, when she is kidnapped she does not put up a fight. When she is rescued, she is, for some unknown reason, dressed in a skirt (rather than the no-nonsense uniform she had on earlier) and wearing makeup. Her hair, rather than being pulled back into a sleek ponytail, is a teased mane (I do not know how she managed to work in a trip to the beauty parlor). And suddenly we find that she has fallen in love with one of her two male friends. Sonya's toughness has been entirely deconstructed; at the end, she does not appear to be much of a threat to anyone; she looks more like a model who might appear in *Cosmopolitan* or *Vogue.* The final message of the film is not that women *can* be tough, but that they *cannot* be tough; ultimately, they fail and need to be rescued by men. A woman's primary purpose is to be a sexual creature for the men who are doing the "real" fighting. Thus, we see how deceptive the depiction of tough women can be in the popular media; a woman might start out tough, but she does not end up that way—her "true nature" eventually emerges.

The Killer Woman as Insane Harpy

Another insidious way to portray tough women is to suggest that such women are insane and deserve punishment.[6] In this fashion, a film might allow a woman an unusually tough role, but often only so that she meets with the punishment that, the film suggests, she deserves for transgressing society's dictates about acceptable behavior for women.

Interestingly enough, the women who are portrayed as being so wild and out of control that they appear insane are almost always femme fatales, meaning that they are highly sexually appealing to men and often seem to be perfect mates—until they reveal a seriously flawed personality. In her book *Femmes Fatales: Feminism, Film Theory, Psychoanalysis* (1991), Mary Ann Doane provides a description of the femme fatale's role: "The femme fatale is the figure of a certain discursive unease, a potential epistemological trauma. For her most striking characteristic, perhaps, is the fact that she never really is what she seems to be. She harbors a threat which is not entirely legible, predictable, or manageable" (1). Doane points out some of the reasons that the femme fatale is such a threatening character. At the same time, however, there is something reassuring about the femme fatale because she adheres to various feminine stereotypes; for instance, she is always glamorous and extremely feminine. Thus, the femme fatale simultaneously subverts stereotypical notions of womanhood and upholds them. The femme fatale's danger is a fleeting one because, as Doane observes, she is punished:

> The femme fatale is situated as evil and is frequently punished or killed. Her textual eradication involves a desperate reassertion of control on the part of the threatened male subject. Hence, it would be a mistake to see her as some kind of heroine of modernity. She is not the subject of feminism but a symptom of male fears about feminism. Nevertheless, the representation—like any representation—is not totally under the control of its producers and, once disseminated, comes to take on a life of its own. (2–3)

As we shall find, Doane's words are an appropriate description of what happens to the femme fatales who are featured in killer-women films. The threat they pose to the social order is rarely allowed to last beyond the film's conclusion. Also, the femme fatale is typically shown to be insane, suggesting that her tough attributes are not "normal" for women but signs of a pathological condition.

Many films show that the toughness displayed by femme fatales is just one sign of their insanity. These movies became particularly popular in the late 1980s and 1990s. *Black Widow* (1987, director Bob Rafelson) was enormously popular when it first appeared, leading to a spate of copycat films. In the movie Debra Winger plays Alexandra, a dowdy, drab federal agent who is so wrapped up in her work that she does not take time off from her work even to go on a Friday night date. Everything changes when she starts to track down Catharine (Theresa Russell), a mysterious, beautiful, wealthy woman who marries rich husbands and then murders them. Catharine changes her look and image to attract each man she marries. She is a chameleon, able to change her style to appeal to any man. She fulfills the fantasy of each man she marries and then murders him, coldly and ruthlessly. Although she is a sexy blonde temptress, she is marked as tough and masculine because of her active sexual desire (particularly her desire for Alexandra), which is frequently emphasized in the film. As Lynda Hart observes, "Masculinity is as much verified by active desire as it is by aggression" (x). Thus, *Black Widow* and other femme fatale films typically depict feminine women, but what is often assumed to be their innate masculine toughness is betrayed, revealing that these are by no means "normal" women.

The Black Widow is doubly marked as evil because she is obsessed not only with money but with killing men. Undertones suggest that Catharine is lesbian or bisexual, such as when she gives Alexandra a kiss on the lips at her own wedding. The Black Widow has much closer relationships with women—even with Alexandra, whom Catharine knows is trying to capture her—than with men. The show implies that an erotic obsession exists between the two women that has gotten out of control. Catharine says that their sexually charged relationship is one that she will always remember, even when Catharine's schemes cause Alexandra to be imprisoned for a murder she did not commit.

The connection between lesbianism and women's aggression is explored in Lynda Hart's book *Fatal Women: Lesbian Sexuality and the Mark of Aggression* (1994), in which she discusses the history of the presumed connection between the lesbian and the female criminal. According to Hart, "one ghost in the machine of heterosexual patriarchy is the lesbian who shadows the entrance into representation of women's aggression" (iv). She comments that the lesbian is "the silent escort of the violent woman" (x). This is true in *Black Widow* and in many other killer-women films,

one of the most notorious being *Basic Instinct* (1992, director Paul Verhoeven), in which Catherine Tramell (Sharon Stone) is a cold-hearted bisexual murderer whose weapon of choice is an ice pick. These films and others often imply that the femme fatale's violence stems from her lesbianism, which rarely goes unpunished. As a murderess and a potential lesbian or bisexual, Catherine is not allowed to escape punishment: at the film's conclusion, her plans are exposed and she is held by the police—presumably to be tried for her crimes. Thus *Basic Instinct* reveals that any woman, like Catherine, who transgresses gender boundaries by becoming a killer, must be punished.

The pattern in *Black Widow* and *Basic Instinct* recurs in other movies. *Double Impact* (1991, director Sheldon Lettrich) also depicts an insane femme fatale. Kara (Cory Everson), a bodyguard for a corrupt businessman, is a crazed murderer and sadist who delights in killing. Another film with an insane, vicious woman killer is *Romeo Is Bleeding* (1993, director Peter Medak).[7] This film features the steamy sexual relationship that develops between a policeman, Jack Grimaldi (Gary Oldman), and a hired killer, Mona Demarkov (Lena Olin). Mona is a classic femme fatale—with long nails, plunging neckline, bright red lipstick, and spiked heels. A husky-voiced siren who uses sex to control and manipulate men, she is also a sadistic killer who cares for no one and laughs hysterically when trying to strangle Jack. She is so vicious and so uncaring, that when Jack murders her at the end of the film one feels a sense of relief that this vicious woman has died. She was out of control—insane, wild, and vengeful.

All of these femme fatale films demonstrate that women who are too tough will be punished. The films also show that such women are literally insane. Femme fatale films depict tough women, but only to show what the films suggest are the women's pathological conditions. Moreover, as Amelia Jones points out, the films confirm male paranoia: tough women are basically psychotic and must be punished in order to uphold society's conventions about how women should act.

TOUGH, BUT NOT AS TOUGH AS THE BOYS

In another version of the lady killer film, the woman is revealed to be less tough than her male companions. In

The Professional (1994, director Luc Besson), Matilda (Natalie Portman) is an adolescent girl whose family has been killed by corrupt police. The family is so dysfunctional that Matilda hardly sheds a tear (except for her baby brother), so she is free to get down to business: she befriends Leon (Jean Reno), a professional hit man *par excellence,* to learn how to become a professional killer. . . . She learns how to shoot a rifle, how to load a gun, and other tricks of the assassin's trade, but Matilda is still completely overshadowed by Leon, the true professional, who must rescue Matilda repeatedly.[8] The film emphasizes Matilda's soft side. For instance, she is shown carrying around a stuffed animal and watching Saturday morning cartoons. In other words, she is just a normal everyday girl underneath her tough veneer and poses little threat to Leon's male power. In *The Professional* and other films, it is apparent that tough women maintain rather than challenge the status quo.

The belief that women are not as tough as men is also apparent in *La Femme Nikita* (1990, director Luc Besson), a French film that was popular in the United States. Nikita (Anne Parillaud) is a ruthless, vicious female junkie. She is wildly out of control and faces life imprisonment after killing a policeman, but she is given a second chance by a French secret police agency that coerces her into working for it. She is taught how to shoot guns and how to be an assassin, but she is also taught how to be a seductive femme fatale. . . . She is literally rebuilt, reminding us of the way Henry Higgins rebuilds the cockney flower girl Eliza Doolittle in *My Fair Lady.* In both cases—*My Fair Lady* and *La Femme Nikita*—the intervention of a man is necessary to socialize a young working-class woman. Nikita is redesigned through her constant interactions with a man known only as "Bob" and an unnamed older woman. Both train Nikita for three years; she is never allowed to leave the police compound during that time. Nikita, like Eliza, is taught how to pass in upper-class society. Nikita moves from sporting a studded black leather jacket and heavy boots to wearing slinky dresses and high heels. Not surprisingly, one of the skills she learns is how to apply makeup. She goes from looking like a street punk to looking like an elegant and sophisticated young lady. But she is also a killer. She embodies the ultimate male threat—a seductive, attractive woman who lures men to their deaths with her feminine wiles.

After Nikita is released from the training facility, she leads a happy "normal" life with her newfound boyfriend. During the day, she is an assassin for the mysterious agency for which she works. Ultimately, her lover reveals he knows about her clandestine career and explains that it makes no difference to him. At this point, Nikita is obviously distraught by the viciousness of her profession and wants out. At the film's conclusion we assume she has fled in order to escape the agency and its employees. Nikita's actions at the end reveal the artificiality of her tough pose; the film demonstrates that Nikita only thought she was tough. When the "right" man came along, she was suddenly transformed into a "normal" woman, far more interested in concocting a tasty meal for her lover than plotting her next assassination. Patricia Mellencamp describes the message of *La Femme Nikita* as "tough but tamed by femininity" (*Fine* 116).

Mellencamp's words are also an appropriate description of the dynamics of *The Quick and the Dead* (1995, director Sam Raimi), one of several Westerns that appeared in the mid-1990s starring women in what were traditionally roles for tough guy actors like John Wayne and Clint Eastwood. Rather than being a transgressive redepiction of the Western, *The Quick and the Dead* confirms that women are not capable of holding onto the tough guy roles long played by men.

The film begins with a scene showing a man firing at a woman on horseback, a woman we later discover is Ellen (Sharon Stone). The man thinks he has killed her, but she gets up, slugs him, manacles him to his wagon, and then mounts her horse, leaving him to swear and curse as she rides off. Already, the woman is being set up in the image of the lone gunslinger. We have to remember, however, that the woman playing the role of the gunslinger is Sharon Stone—one of the top sex symbols of Hollywood. . . . It is impossible for Stone to escape her reputation, which Stacey Lassally, TriStar Pictures' president of production, admits the studio promotes when she comments that Stone's character "has very wide appeal . . . [because she] has sex appeal and she also kicks ass" (quoted in Jordan D5). The film further bolsters Stone's status as a sex symbol by having her appear in a very chic Western outfit, never looking dirty or sweaty, whether she has been riding for hours in the hot sun or has just killed a desperado. Stone always looks like a model first and a gunslinger second.

Ellen rides into a small Western town where she and other gunslingers are competing in a shooting contest for a $123,000 prize, which goes to the contestant still alive at the end of the contest. The prize money is offered by the despicable John Herod (Gene Hackman), a cruel gunman who owns the town and runs it with the aid of his henchmen. It is clear that Ellen has a personal vendetta against Herod, which she tries to resolve by entering the contest in which he will also participate. When Ellen states that she wants to sign up for the contest, Herod sneers, "There's no rule against ladies, except women can't shoot for shit." The lines are drawn. Ellen's fight is going to prove not only her skills as a gunfighter, but also that women are just as tough as men. Before this point she has shown her toughness repeatedly in the film by coolly avoiding the sexual advances of several men and doing some fancy shooting that prevents a man from being hung. Yet, just the fact that Ellen has to handle a number of sexual advances from men functions to establish her as a very different character from the traditional tough hero of the Western, who rarely fears sexual attention.

But Ellen's tough character is strongly modified as the film continues; the film's director is obviously not intent upon making Stone into an Eastwood or a Wayne. Instead, her femininity is stressed again and again. For instance, at one point she wakes up in the morning in the company of a handsome young gunslinger known as the Kid; although the film does not show whether the two had sex, the implication is clear. Stone is also constantly depicted as less sure of herself than the men. She shows a great deal more emotion on her face, reminding viewers that, despite her gunslinging talent and ability to slug out a man, she is still a woman and therefore emotional.

Ellen's femininity becomes even more obvious as the film continues. After Herod kills a bragging gunfighter, Ellen looks terrified. Shortly afterward, she has a dream flashback in which she is a little girl, complete with doll and long dress, remembering her father being killed. We later learn that Herod murdered her father. Thus, she becomes a gunslinger only because of her obsessive desire to kill her father's killer. Her toughness is depicted as something that is forced upon her—something, we are led to assume, she would not have adopted if she had been able to avoid the trauma in her childhood.

Ellen's femininity is again emphasized when Herod invites her to dinner. She is shown taking an ornate silk bustier from her dresser. When she goes out for dinner, she wears a long dress with a low neckline and looks every inch a "lady." Here, viewers are reminded that Stone is a sex symbol and a woman. When Ellen is eating dinner, we see the gun that hangs by her side, with which she presumably plans to shoot Herod. The toughness associated with having a gun, however, is diminished by the generous glimpse of her garter-belted leg. She fails in her attempt to kill Herod and flees. At this point, she appears to be no more than another scared woman who cannot stand up to a man's toughness.

Eventually, Ellen returns to town and kills Herod, but we see less of her fight than the gunfight between Herod and Court (Russell Crowe), one of Herod's ex-gunfighters who has turned preacher. The two minutes the film devotes to Ellen's battle with Herod are less significant than the many minutes the film devotes to emphasizing that she has been pushed to extreme measures because of her father's death. The film implies that toughness is not a "natural" part of her identity, or the identity of any other woman.

The Quick and the Dead and many other films that feature killer women are intent on demonstrating that women, no matter how tough they might appear, are only superficially tough. In this fashion, the cultural myth is kept alive that women are no match for their male counterparts—a myth that helps to ensure that women are kept out of positions of power in government and industry because they are not sufficiently tough. Killer-women films are only one of myriad popular culture forms that help to support a social class system in which women are still very much second-class citizens.

TOUGHER GIRLS?

I do not suggest that *all* recent killer-women films are solely helping to perpetuate gender norms. Films are complex and carry many meanings, and the films studied in this chapter could be interpreted in different ways. Furthermore, a number of killer-women films have been produced that seem intent on creating tougher, stronger women characters. A classic example is *Thelma & Louise* (1991, director Ridley Scott), which suggests that women can be just as tough as men. One critic describes the appeal of Thelma Dickinson (Geena Davis) and Louise Sawyer (Susan Sarandon): they "grow stronger, tougher and funnier with every mile they drive" (Shapiro 63). However, no matter how tough these women might appear, they die (presumably) at the end of the film. Even though they make the decision to drive off a cliff rather than risk imprisonment, the decision reveals how impossible it is for tough women to survive and thrive in Hollywood.

Other recent films have developed central women characters who appear even tougher than Thelma and Louise. In *Galaxis* (1995, director William Mesa), Brigitte Nielsen plays a superhuman space alien who is searching for a mysterious crystal that means life or death for her people. Following in the footsteps of Superman and other superheroes, she is invincible. This blonde-haired woman, who stands over six feet tall, dwarfs most of the men in the film; however, her superhuman powers are acceptable because she is an alien. No real woman, the movie suggests, would be able to perform Nielson's deeds. Another approach to toughness in women is adopted in *The Demolitionist* (1996, director Robert Kurtzman). In this film, Alyssa Lloyd (Nicole Eggert) is a tough female undercover police agent who is killed by some particularly repugnant punks. After she dies, she is brought back to life as a superhuman crime fighter who takes out whole gangs of bad guys. Wielding two guns and wearing a suit of body armor, she is almost as tough as the Terminator, except for her emotions, which threaten to overwhelm her. The only reason she is allowed to become a killer crime fighter is that she is dead. She is also deeply concerned about romantic issues; she was going to be married before criminals killed her lover—the event that turned her into a vengeful killer. Now she bemoans the lack of romance in her new life. At one point, she looks at a bridal display and then shoots it up, obviously feeling that phase of her life is over.

Despite the ways they break some gender barriers, *Thelma & Louise, Galaxis,* and *The Demolitionist* show a society in which toughness in women makes people uneasy. The depiction of tough women in films is a visible sign of a culture in which gender roles are no longer as stable and fixed as in previous decades, a culture in which women seem increasingly intent on taking over men's roles. One way to control the threat posed by tough women is to demonstrate that they are not as tough as they seem. Killer-women films repeatedly show that the tough and masculine killer is really all woman beneath the façade. This emphasis implies that *all* tough women are not as tough as they appear and therefore pose no significant threat to male hegemony as far as toughness is concerned. Thus, we discover that even films that present apparently tough women often only depict such characters in order to systematically tear down the tough image and reveal the "real" woman underneath.

If women insist on being too tough and aggressive, killer-women films tell us, the transgressors will be punished. This emphasis on punishment is one way that killer-women films help perpetuate gender norms even when the films seem to be undermining such norms by depicting tough, aggressive women. The films also show that such women are too tough and masculine and hint that these are attributes that women in general should avoid. The movies warn female viewers not to become too tough or too strong, or they will be punished, like the women in the films.

When killer-women films are not intent on showing the punishment meted out to killer women, they often demonstrate that such women, despite their apparent aggression, are still primarily sexual objects for men. Paradoxically, tough attributes are used by the mainstream media in a variety of ways to heighten the sexual allure of women. This emphasis on the sexual desirability of tough women, whether in women's magazines or killer-women films, is yet another way that the media diffuse the danger inherent in tough independent women—women who can take care of themselves and do not seem to need any man, not even Rambo. By stressing the sexual desirability of women and showing that they are still at the beck and call of a man to whom they are sexually attracted, the popular media inform their audience that although tough women are aloof and unavailable on the surface, their toughness undergoes a melt-down when, inevitably, they fall for a man.

This chapter . . . [has] explored the various ways that pseudo-tough women are used in the popular media. Initially such women appear to be tough, but upon closer scrutiny, their toughness is usually superficial and does little to disrupt the gendered social order. To find tougher versions of womanhood, I shall look at the characters played by Jodie Foster and Gillian Anderson, two actors who, as FBI agents Clarice Starling and Dana Scully, present much tougher images than is the norm for women and are far tougher than the fashion-obsessed Angels. However, even Starling and Scully, we will find, are portrayed as less tough than their male counterparts.

NOTES

1. Other discussions of the increased prevalence in the 1980s and 1990s of women who kill in films and books include Mitchell Fink, "Actresses Tough It Out"; Charles Fleming, "That's Why the Lady Is a Champ"; Krin Gabbard and Glen O. Gabbard, "Phallic Women in the Contemporary Cinema"; Richard Grenier, "Killer Bimbos"; Brook Hersey, "Word on Movies: Women Fight Back"; Christine Holmlund, "A Decade of Deadly Dolls: Hollywood and the Woman Killer"; Kathi Maio, "Film: Women Who Murder for the Man"; Sonia Murray, "Bad Babes at the Box Office"; Karen Thomas, "Female Roles Are Packing a New Punch"; and Virginia Tiger, "Alice and Charlie and Vida and Sophy—A Terrorist's Work Is Never Done."

2. Other works address women who kill in real life. Eileen MacDonald discusses women who kill for political reasons in *Shoot the Women First*, and Coramae Richey Mann explores the socioeconomic reasons American women kill in *When Women Kill*. Also, see Ann Jones, *Women Who Kill*, and Mark MacNamara, "Can a Woman Kill Like a Man?"

3. The representation of the woman killer is by no means confined to recent decades. Women who kill have been represented for centuries. For instance, Frances E. Dolan discusses women murderers from the 1600s who were written about in numerous "legal treatises, pamphlets, scaffold speeches . . . ballads, and plays" (25). Perhaps one of the reasons for society's long-standing fascination with the killer woman is that she is representative of a culture turned upside down, since "normal" women in Western cultures have long been assumed to be maternal, not murderous. Describing the killer woman's punishment, whether in a seventh-century ballad or a twentieth-century film, is one way to demonstrate to the audience that social order will not be long unbalanced.

4. For more information about the depiction of women who kill, see the collection edited by Helen Birch, *Moving Targets: Women, Murder and Representation*. Also see Rhoda Estep, "Women's Roles in Crime as Depicted by Television and Newspapers."

5. Why is an action-adventure team never composed of more women than men? The few women are always greatly outnumbered by their male counterparts. The relatively rare women who appear in such teams uphold the ideology that tough women are something of an oddity, whether in films, comic books, cartoons, or action figure sets.

6. A film that takes the idea of the insane killer woman to its ludicrous extreme is *Serial Mom* (1994, director John Waters), which stars Kathleen Turner as suburban housewife Beverly Sutphin, a woman who seems to have it all—a loving husband, a lovely suburban home, and two happy children—until she is revealed to be a psychotic killer.

7. For an article that discusses the life of Hilary Henkin, the screenwriter of *Romeo Is Bleeding* and one of the few women who write action-adventure films, see James Greenberg, "One Tough Cookie."

8. The deadly woman terrorist or assassin has become a staple of popular culture. For example, Friday, the main character of Robert Heinlein's science-fiction novel *Friday* (1982), is a highly trained killer with a "hair-trigger kill reflex" (27). But Friday is more sex kitten than killer, and her sexual exploits take up more of the book than her killing pursuits. Also see Deborah Christian, *Mainline;* William Gibson, *Neuromancer;* and John Le Carré, *The Little Drummer Girl*.

REFERENCES

BAUMGOLD, JULIE. "Killer Women." *New York* 29 July 1991: 24+.

BIRCH, HELEN, ED. *Moving Targets: Women, Murder and Representation*. Berkeley: University of California Press, 1994.

DOANE, MARY ANN. *Femmes Fatales: Feminism, Film Theory, Psychoanalysis*. New York: Routledge, 1991.

ELLER, DARYN. "Fighting Fit." *Harper's Bazaar* Aug. 1992: 122–125.

HART, LYNDA. *Fatal Women: Lesbian Sexuality and the Mark of Aggression*. Princeton University Press, 1994.

HOLMLUND, CHRISTINE. "A Decade of Deadly Dolls: Hollywood and the Woman Killer." *Moving Targets: Women, Murder and Representation*. Ed. Helen Birch. Berkeley: University of California Press, 1994. 127–151.

JONES, AMELIA. "'She Was Bad News': Male Paranoia and the Contemporary New Woman." *Camera Obscura* 25–26 (Jan.-May 1991); 297–320.

JORDAN, CATHERINE. "Go Ahead, Make Her Day." *Los Angeles Times* 26 April 1994: D1+.

MELLENCAMP, PATRICIA. *A Fine Romance . . . Five Ages of Film Feminism*. Philadelphia: Temple University Press, 1995.

MELLENCAMP, PATRICIA. *High Anxiety: Catastrophe, Scandal, Age and Comedy*. Bloomington, IN: Indiana University Press, 1992.

MULVEY, LAURA. "Visual Pleasure and Narrative Cinema." *Screen* 16.3 (1975): 6–18.

SCHMETZER, ULI. "Dagger Lady: Tough as Steel, but Still a Lady." *Chicago Tribune* 3 May 1993: 6.

SHAPIRO, LAURA. "Women Who Kill Too Much." *Newsweek* 17 June 1991: 63.

TASKER, YVONNE. *Spectacular Bodies: Gender, Genre and the Action Cinema*. London: Routledge, 1993.

Preventing Violence
and Revisioning the Future

This book has thus far presented many of the ways that violence is and has been conceptualized across the disciplines, as well as many of the theories about how our culture socially constructs femininities, masculinities, and the "Other." Using these theoretical foundations of violence and gender, we have asked you to explore issues of youth violence, the violation of body space, violence and sports, and media representation of violence. Although the task of reducing violence in our society and preventing its occurrence may seem overwhelming, if not impossible, we do have the knowledge and the tools to begin making a difference. Furthermore, while the specific solutions, policies, and resources needed to address the issues raised in each of the sections of this Reader will vary, there is considerable room for integration across the issues presented. The interrelationships here are significant. For example, making changes in our sports culture and removing athletic privilege could arguably reduce violence against women and in our families. Since understanding that violence in the family is a risk factor that could influence youth violence, such changes in sports culture might also *indirectly* decrease youth violence. This final section suggests how to prevent and reduce violence in our society and how our society might change so that we can envision a more peaceful future.

The first reading in this section is a chapter, titled "What Works, and Why?" from *Safe Passage: Making It Through Adolescence in a Risky Society,* by the developmental psychologist Joy Dryfoos. This overview summarizes what researchers and interventionists have learned about successful programs aimed at helping youth safely negotiate their way through adolescence at four different levels: the individual; family; school; and community. Think back to one of the social issues presented in this book that you found particularly intriguing. Then, as you read this chapter, describe what kind of program might have prevented this issue from arising in the first place. How would you address each of the four levels described above in your prevention strategy? As Dryfoos notes, difficult policy questions will emerge as a result of reviewing various programs. What might be the policy implications of the prevention program that you designed? What national, statewide, community, or other policies would need to be implemented to help your program succeed? In addition to identifying components of successful programs, Dryfoos also outlines several of the unresolved issues that might be important to consider in program implementation. She ends her chapter by raising questions about the ability of the media to influence youth's prosocial behavior. After having read both Dryfoos's chapter and Section VI of this book, "Media Representations of Violence," what do you think about the extent to which media exposure can be used to promote *positive* youth development?

The title of Dryfoos's book, *Safe Passage: Making It Through Adolescence in a Risky Society,* implies a prevention approach, that is, building on youths' strengths so that they may avoid the problems inherent in living in a "risky society," including experiencing violence or perpetrating it. When prevention fails and/or we do not implement comprehensive and effective prevention programming, then our attention must turn toward intervening in the lives of youth. Continuing along this train of thought, the second piece in this section is an excerpt from Dwyer, Osher, and Warger's 1998 publication titled, "Early Warning, Timely Response: A Guide to Safe Schools." This guide was produced by the Center for Effective Collaboration and Practice of the American Institutes for Research in collaboration with the National Association of School Psychologists. As a cooperative agreement between the U.S. Department of Education, the Office of Special Education and Rehabilitative Services, and the Office of Special Education Programs, this guide is a direct response to former President Clinton's request that the Departments of Education and Justice publish information so that adults might quickly and effectively reach out to troubled children. The excerpt presented here, "Intervention: Getting Help for Troubled Children," outlines principles underlying intervention and strategies for early intervention with students at-risk for behavioral problems. This excerpt also discusses the importance of schools in providing a foundation to prevent and reduce violent behavior and specifically addresses characteristics of safe physical environments and characteristics of schoolwide policies that support responsible behavior. As you read this selection, you might consider whether or not you think it is reasonable for schools to be expected to provide any or all of these services. What responsibilities do parents and families, school systems (school boards, principals, teachers, and counselors), and communities have in working to achieve safe schools? What types of government support do you think are required or desirable to implement these programs?

Prevention and intervention strategies aimed at youth, including incarceration of violent youth as a last resort, are some of the most widely accepted ideas for reducing the amount of violence in our society. However, not all ideas for reducing violence meet with such a wide network of support. Indeed, one of the most controversial policy issues in the United States is that of gun control. Given the long-standing debates over the effectiveness of gun control, the fact that such debates shall almost certainly remain in the public eye for the foreseeable future, and the potential of various gun control policies to reduce violence in the United States, a discussion of this important issue belongs in this last section on preventing violence. Philip Cook and Mark Moore's chapter, "Guns, Gun Control, and Homicide: A Review of Research and Public Policy," from the book, *Homicide: A Sourcebook of Social Research,* presents a review of empirical research and identifies the conflicting values concerning the relationship between individual, community, and state that further fuel the controversy over various gun control policies. What are the conflicting values that Cook and Moore identify? Do you think that the right to bear arms is not absolute but is subject to reasonable restrictions, carrying with it certain civic responsibilities? Why or why not? Should citizens be willing to relinquish some of their rights in the interest of achieving a safer society? What are your reactions to the actions suggested in this reading at the federal, state, municipal, community, and household levels?

A second controversial issue related to the desire and need to lessen violence in our society has generated both debate and dialogue: that of censorship. Much of this controversy has been framed in the context of pornography—dividing, for example, First Amendment, pro-pornography feminists like Nadine Strossen and anti-pornography feminists like Catharine MacKinnon (see Strossen, 1995; MacKinnon, 1987). However, a more general and extensive discussion of censorship raises significant questions about political systems and power, artistic expression, and the social equality of people of all religions, races, ethnicities, genders, and sexual orientations. An ardent defender of one's right to free speech is the (in)famous performance artist, Karen Finley, who while not condoning violence against women and children, is driven by her belief in the right of all American citizens to speak, write, perform, paint, and otherwise artistically represent their views on any subject and in any form. One of several artists whose work was initially funded by the National Endowment for the Arts but whose funding was subsequently withdrawn because senators such as Jessie Helms of North Carolina categorized her work as obscene, Finley has written a powerful and poetic performance piece, "It's Only Art," about the dangers of censorship. Taking aim at Senator Helms and others of his ilk who want to censor anything that even vaguely hints at sexuality, body parts, and bodily functions, Finley paints a depressing picture of what the United States would look like if art were suppressed to such an extent. Is there a way to uphold the First Amendment of the U.S. Constitution and not allow particular expressions of art deemed harmful to certain segments of our population? If so, who is to determine those standards? Karen Finley does not believe that we can institute any form of censorship and maintain our freedom of speech, since for her, all forms of art are inevitably reflections of our lives, our dreams, and our fears and cannot be silenced. Other individuals believe that we must censor some materials, even if only applied to certain age groups, in order to curtail the violence that so many women, children, and men in our society experience.

All of the above pieces are related to how we might address the issue of violence in society, primarily based on empirical research and the theories of some of the top experts in their fields, as well as on artistic experience and opinion. One of our primary concerns, however, and the impetus for assembling this Reader, is that for all the insight and expertise available in these bodies of literature, notions of masculinity, femininity, and the "Other" are often conspicuously absent. The premise of this Reader is that in order to understand violence fully and to prevent it or reduce its occurrence, cultural constructions of masculinities, femininities, and the "Other" must also be recognized and altered. Dr. Terry Kupers's book, *Revisioning Men's Lives: Gender, Intimacy, and Power,* continues to explore these issues. The final chapter in his text is entitled "Conclusion: Redefining power." As you read, what connections can you draw between this chapter and what you learned about the construction of masculinities and femininities? Kupers, a psychiatrist, presents Kenneth Boulding's theory of the three dimensions of power. How are these three dimensions of power related to gender? Kupers argues for a redefinition of power for both men and women in order to attain a healthier and less violent society. How do issues of race/ethnicity, class, socioeconomic status, and sexual orientation and preference fit into this discussion? What are some of the ways we can find to be powerful without oppressing anyone and in the process redefine power, heroism, and masculinity?

We close with a broad-based essay by James Gilligan—whose earlier work opened our text. In "How to Create Less Violent Societies," a chapter from his 2001 book, *Preventing Violence,* Gilligan states simply that in order to prevent violence, people must "discontinue the individual and social practices and behaviors that have been shown to cause violence. Once we stop causing violence, it will disappear by itself" (p. 81). He continues his thesis by suggesting certain goals that, in his view, we must work toward if we are to reduce violence in the world: social and political democracy; guaranteed employment; reduction in the artificial and exaggerated polarization of gender roles and the irrational fear, hatred, and contempt expressed toward homosexuality; the elimination of legally permitted violence against children; the restriction of media violence; gun control; universal access to free higher education. Clearly, these are not simple goals. In your view, are they attainable? Are they desirable as means to reduce violence in our society? Gilligan goes on to state that that structural violence—the economic structure of our society and its division into rich and poor—is not only the main form of violence, but also the main cause of violence. Do you agree with his assessment? Is it too simplistic, or does it encompass much of what we have been studying through the selections in this Reader?

Our thoughts and beliefs about the answers to all of these questions—and the actions we take as a consequence—will determine our nation's future. The goal of this Reader has been to show how violence and gender are interrelated in many facets of our lives. Many of us have not stopped to examine critically the intersections of violence and gender, largely because they seem so "normal" to us and because they are such a part of America's historical legacy, as Richard Slotkin and James William Gibson assert. Based on all you have learned about the juxtaposition of violence and gender, what steps do we need to take—as individuals, as community members, and as a nation—to reduce violence and violent behavior?

REFERENCES

MacKinnon, C. (1987). Frances Biddle's sister: Pornography, civil rights, and speech. In *Feminism unmodified: Discourses on life and law* (pp. 163–195, 274–301). Cambridge, MA: Harvard University Press.

Strossen, N. (1995). The sex panic and the feminist split. In *Defending pornography: Free speech, sex, and the fight for women's rights* (pp. 17–35). New York: Anchor Books.

What Works, and Why?

Joy Dryfoos

We are now going to look at what works to help young people overcome the barriers to Safe Passage. This chapter summarizes all that we have learned about program components and compiles those factors that successful programs appear to have in common. I have organized the factors at four different levels: individual, family, school, and community.

If we are to design an effective and comprehensive "package" of services, what pieces should we include? Admittedly, youth development people do not know all the answers. So in this chapter, I also lay out a number of unresolved issues and ambiguities relating to how these programs are implemented and how they may be replicated. Remember that I said the test of a program design was whether it could be reproduced by someone other than the program designer. While we must understand the components of successful programs, we also need to know how to expand the network of excellence—and widely replicate what works.

SUCCESS FACTORS AT THE INDIVIDUAL LEVEL

Early Intervention

Everybody knows intuitively that early intervention is a must. In this book, I have presented further evidence of the long-term effectiveness of early intervention on social behavior and school achievement. The Parents as Teachers program and the Primary Mental Health Model are two examples of services—along with many other programs, such as Head Start—that have demonstrated the importance of preschool interventions. Schools of the 21st Century incorporate these components and extend the approach back to birth and forward to age 12.

Questions have been raised about the efficacy of early intervention if the program simply ends when the child enters school. A review of early childhood programs by Dale Farran substantiates the importance of extending support beyond preschool; "Improvement in the educational program provided for low-income children in the first 4 years of elementary school [is] more effective than simply providing 1 year of preschool."[1]

Based on the results of classroom-based interventions designed to change behaviors, programs are moving down to earlier grades on the theory that once behavior sets in, it is far more difficult to change. Yet you must believe that it is not impossible to change the life scripts of older children. Many of the programs described here do just that—for example, effective community schools at the middle school level can change the course for students along with improving the outlook for their families. Having made a pitch for early intervention, I would be unhappy if that statement were construed as an argument against programs for middle and high school age youth. We should be wary of setting up a competition for resources between different age groups or different kinds of target populations. Consistent attention is necessary at every level. Programs must be age appropriate and based on a sound understanding of youth development.

One-on-One Attention: Creative Shepherding

The critical importance of individual attention as a means of helping young people achieve Safe Passage is verified in a variety of programs: use of trained specialists, child aides, case managers, cross-age tutors, teacher advisors. We observed in the Quantum Opportunities Program how the counselors wrapped themselves (literally and figuratively) around the participants. The Children at Risk Program relies heavily on case managers to help young people cope with family problems and deal with the social welfare system. Recall the words from Robert Slavin that one had to "relentlessly stick with every child until that child is succeeding."

Marion Pines, a pioneer in dropout prevention, summed up her experience:

We have learned that no single system can adequately address complex and interrelated challenges. What we are learning is that continuity of effort makes a difference. Dropping in and dropping out of a kid's life does not work. A sustained and caring adult contact makes a tremendous difference.[2]

The documented success of the Big Brothers/Big Sisters program has given a big boost to mentoring as an intervention, but the research shows that the volunteer mentors must be carefully screened, well-matched to the client, and regularly supervised by paid staff in order for the program to work. From my years of research and observation, I am convinced that young people have to be attached to a caring adult. Without that attachment and bonding, most of these young people will never make it.

One experience in my own life always comes to mind when I think about this subject. About a decade ago, I went to Nepal with my son Paul, and we arranged our own private trek in the lower Himalayas accompanied by several Sherpas, indigenous people who serve as guides for climbers. It was pretty steep and rocky, and I know that I couldn't have made it up the mountain without the support and encouragement of my Sherpa. And that is exactly what is needed by these at-risk children. Joe Klein's characterization in *Newsweek* of Leon Dickerson is revealing: "His official title [at a program called Choice] is team coordinator but a more accurate job description might be shepherd."[3]

Developmentally Appropriate

The most effective programs relate to teenagers according to where the young people are "at," instead of where the professional staff think they ought to be. For example, youth workers have to be very careful how they approach the virtues of abstinence when dealing with a group of sexually active teens. As one youth worker told me, "I try to tell it like it is but not overdo it."

Youth Empowerment

Certain phrases emerge from visits with youth workers around the country. Many feel that what they are doing is "empowering youth," giving them the skills and motivation they need to make it. Others talk about having high expectations for their young people. El Puente has a very strong youth leadership ethos: Students are expected to get involved in solving community problems now and in the future. You can see the growing involvement of young people in the planning, design, and implementation of programs. Ernest McMillan, director of the comprehensive Fifth Ward Enrichment Program in the Houston inner city, recounts:

. . . the realities of living in a war zone and actively listening to the various expressions of the youth [who] serve as guides to the program's development. We have consciously tried to shift from operating as a riverfront hospice that plucks the victim from the swift currents to moving upstream and interceding in the battle itself, recruiting youth to become partners in the fight.[4]

As practitioners describe it, they are listening to the voices of youth and how they see their world. But we must be wary here of empty phrases. Evoking the language of empowerment does not always mean that power is shared. It may just indicate familiarity with politically correct language rather than the intention to allow young people really to make decisions for themselves.

SUCCESS FACTORS AT THE FAMILY LEVEL

Parental Involvement

Extensive experience with family programs verifies the importance of frequent home visiting by a trained practitioner as the best method of securing family involvement and offering parent effectiveness training. Parents of high-risk youth will come to schools and community centers if what they are offered is useful and nonthreatening. Community schools have proved that virtually all the parents will come to a community festival celebrating an ethnic event. Many parents will eventually take advantage of educational courses in English as a Second Language, computers, job preparation, and aerobics. Parents will enthusiastically sign up to volunteer or work part-time in schools as teachers' aides or community advocates.

Experience in family resource centers reveals the growing demand for crisis intervention and attention to immediate basic needs, such as food, clothes, shelter, and basic health care. A designated space within a school where parents can hang out and talk to each other over coffee and refreshments is heavily utilized.

Reaching Across Generations

In recent years, much more attention is being directed toward involving senior citizens in youth development programs. Grandparents are being encouraged to participate when parents are not available. Programs that use senior citizens as mentors and tutors have been around for a while, but the new wave of more innovative efforts encourages retired professionals to work as medical consultants, scientific advisors, and other professional endeavors. Referred to as the "other national service program," the federally supported SeniorCorps utilizes the services of more than 60,000 volunteers.[5]

SUCCESS FACTORS AT THE SCHOOL LEVEL

Educational Achievement

As I have stated repeatedly, the enhancement of educational achievement, measured by grades, promotion, and graduation rates, has become a desirable objective of just about every kind of prevention program. School achievement as a goal is often combined with others such as reduction in substance abuse or unprotected sex (although fair methods for measurement of achievement is still a controversial issue).

Many approaches to improving achievement and retention in schools have been documented here and elsewhere.[6] The evidence that cooperative learning techniques are effective continues to grow. The importance of smaller schools, smaller class sizes, and heterogeneous grouping has generally been confirmed. The reorganization of middle schools into small, intimate, thematic academies or houses is apparently productive, creating more stimulating environments and engaged students. Successful classroom behavioral management techniques have been devised and tested. More schools are moving toward extended days and extended years. One observes a rash of experimental schools arriving on the scene that are alternatives, magnets, charters, "visions," or community schools. No two are alike, but they all seem to have in common a consistent attention to ensuring that each student progresses and learns. Many are devising more challenging curricula that contemporary students will find relevant and will broaden their educational options and career horizons.

It is difficult to imagine that any other kind of prevention program will be successful if it doesn't address the acquisition of basic cognitive skills. None of these other components will ensure Safe Passage if the young person is not fully literate and ready to enter the labor force. In my evolving doctrine (it is always evolving), schools become more and more central to the movement to rescue the children. But to be effective, schools must drastically alter the way they operate, incorporating the growing knowledge about youth development and successful interventions.

Effective Principals

The people factor is paramount in the success of programs for assuring Safe Passage. Although many categories of personnel could be cited (nurse practitioners, community aides, classroom teachers), one group carries significant responsibility for the most productive programs. School principals serve as the entry point for the development of comprehensive school-based approaches. According to Don Davies, a leader in school-community partnerships, effective principals have "grasped the meaning of shared responsibilities for children's learning and well-being. They have learned that the school alone simply can't do the job . . . that partnership means reciprocity."[7]

School-Based but not School-operated

Although schools are the sites for many of the programs we have visited, a number are operated by community agencies. In the case of school-based health or mental health clinics, outside practitioners come into the schools to offer direct services. For instance, the Beacons bring community-based agencies into the schools, allowing the buildings to remain open for extended hours, even weekends and summers.

On-site Facilitators

The implementation of complex programs that reorganize schools or establish multicomponent programs is often difficult. Even to ensure successful replication of classroom-based prevention curricula, outside facilitators are needed to train school personnel. For some of the more sophisticated school reorganization projects, such as Success for All or Accelerated Schools, facilitators or coaches may remain on-site for extended periods of time. Apparently, having access to consistent and skilled advisors helps teachers and youth workers to change their modes of operation and to resolve conflicts that can arise in these situations.

Social Skills Training

The role of social influences on changing youth behaviors has been thoroughly explored in recent years and incorporated into prevention programs. More research support has been allocated for testing classroom curricula than for testing the impacts of mentoring or case management or alternative sports and recreational activities. As a result of the strength of the evaluations, I believe that behavioral social skills curricula can have positive effects. Programs such as Life Skills Training can teach social competency, decision making, how to deal with aggressive feelings, and other social relationships. But research also confirms the need to build into these programs additional sessions, booster sessions in subsequent years, and more substantive material in the curriculum that relates to social competency and the family. The key concept here is increased dosage—greater intensity and sustainability.

Recent experience with new curricula show that the messenger may be as powerful as the message. People With AIDS (PWAs) have been more effective than classroom teachers in persuading students to change their sexual behavior. And practicing behavioral skills—using role play to deal with unwanted sexual encounters or with trying to obtain condoms—is a powerful component of prevention programs. Evidence is mounting, that curricula alone do not influence the behaviors of high-risk youth, but they can be very important components of comprehensive programs.

Group Counseling

Effective prevention curricula are based on a sound interpretation of the psychosocial issues related to adolescent development. Many of the participants gain important insights into their lives as a result of these courses. But students don't have the opportunity to talk about their troubles. Group counseling is another approach that is being successfully used in schools and community agencies to deal with problems. You are probably familiar with Children of Alcoholics, or COA groups, that concentrate on issues in such families. Groups have also been organized around suicidal inclinations, grief, asthma control, sexuality, gay and lesbian issues, parents, drug and alcohol use, violence, and just about every subject that comes up in the lives of teenagers. For some teenagers, it is helpful for them to know that other young people share their anguish and have found solutions.

The In Your Face program initiated in the Columbia University School-Based Clinics is a good example of organized group counseling that has met with success. The program targets high-risk students, involves them continuously with group and individual interventions, and helps them confront their problems with sexual issues.

Community Service

The concept of community service has taken hold in the youth development field. Several of the most successful programs, such as Teen Outreach and Quantum, require participants to spend time working in community agencies, childcare centers, and retirement homes. Community schools such as Turner incorporate community placements into the curriculum—students in the Community Health Academy regularly work in a hospital assisting the dieticians and the floor nurses. Programs like El Puente are designed around the concept of community involvement and teaching young people that they are responsible for building the communities of the future.

SUCCESS FACTORS AT THE COMMUNITY LEVEL

Location in the Community

Having stated that almost any program can be run in a school setting, it is equally important to realize that almost any program, including educational interventions, can take place in a community agency. As time goes on, the distinction becomes less clear between types of sites. For example, El Puente started as a community center and became a school, but it is indisputably community based with strong roots in its Hispanic neighborhood. Quantum Opportunities Program is strongly based in the community in order to remediate for the low quality of the schools in the neighborhood. The national youth organizations—Boys and Girls Clubs, Girls Inc., and the Urban League—maintain sites in store fronts, malls, housing projects, and churches, places that are accessible to young people at all hours and that are not associated with school; many high-risk youngsters have an aversion to classrooms because of negative experiences in the past.

Community Outreach

In the poverty programs of the 1960s and 1970s, street outreach work was a highly visible activity, employing thousands of indigenous people to reach out to their neighbors with all kinds of messages about health promotion and poverty reduction. During the 1980s, this component seemed to disappear, only to reemerge recently. Today, an approach that uses street workers and trained community aides to conduct health promotion and disease prevention, or teach conflict resolution and nonviolent behaviors, is being used successfully in HIV- and violence-prevention programs. It is one sure channel for reaching high-risk youth.

Because so many of the neediest young people live in inner cities, much more attention is being paid to working at the street level. To do this, the youth workers have to be able to relate to indigenous youth and gang members, and they have to be able to communicate ideas about prevention in ways that are both understandable and acceptable.

Cultural Responsiveness

These days, many programs derive their strengths from cultural or racial identity. Quantum and El Puente each strive to surround young people with successful role models and expose them to experiences where they can learn about their own cultural traditions. Parents, too, trust programs that can communicate with them in their own languages and respect their culture.

Community Police

Several programs involve local police in innovative arrangements. The Koban, described in Caimito and replicated in several U.S. cities, translates the Japanese model to our country. Specially trained police officers live in the settlement house and are available to work with youth advocates as a team. Community policing efforts are expanding, using police officers as case managers, youth advocates, and recreation leaders. Specially trained police officers and probation personnel have offices in schools, giving them direct daily access to troubled youngsters.

Safe Havens

When participants are asked what they like about many of the programs described here, they say, "It's safe." They feel protected by the people who operate the facility, protected from the dangers of street life and, in some instances, protected from abusive families and disinterested schools. Not only do some of the programs offer a sense of physical safety, the youth who hang out there know that they can rely on the staff to help them with threatening problems. The young people particularly appreciate being in settings where the adults are nonjudgmental.

Incentives and Entrepreneurial Approaches

Financial incentives have been built into successful programs in a variety of ways. The classic model of I Have a Dream offers students a college scholarship if they complete high school. Quantum pays stipends for completion of each task. Valued Youth pays high-risk older students to teach younger students.

Many programs teach participants to set up small businesses. The Turner school in Philadelphia has a health food market and an after-school snack store run by students. There, children learn how to purchase items wholesale, prepare them for purchase, wait on customers, and handle money. By next year, a garden will be established at the school to grow produce for the store.

The Children's Aid Society's Teen Prevention Programs all offer some form of small business experience, either selling foods at sports events or, as in one replication in Akron, running a used clothing store. The Entrepreneurial Academy at IS218 teaches business skills at the middle school level and operates a school store. That school also has a project that recycles bicycles and sells them. On the first day of school, every "entrepreneurial" student is presented with a briefcase that includes an appointment book, watch, small calculator, and other tools of business efficiency.

Multiagency Multicomponent

I have highlighted the call for programs with multiple components that rely on partnerships between schools and community agencies in both the review of existing programs and in summaries of recommendations for future programs. This broader approach is backed up by a theoretical shift in program rationale that is moving us away from focusing on specific behaviors—sex, drugs, and violence—to a more holistic view of teenagers. The new view indicates programming through multiple channels to alter the life of the participant. Children at Risk, Fifth Ward Achievement, Quantum, Children's Aid Society's Teen Pregnancy Prevention Program, and many other efforts have put together packages of activities to wrap around young people.

One rationale for comprehensiveness is the importance of integrating services and creating one-stop centers. Another is that comprehensive centers can provide "controversial" services in broad settings. Counseling on contraception is offered as one voluntary component in a school-based clinic. Mental health treatment is made available in the context of a youth service center featuring recreational facilities. Parents can obtain drug and alcohol treatment in family resource centers that highlight child care and parent education.

Comprehensiveness means more than providing a bunch of services under one roof. To be effective, the different components need to be integrated so that the client perceives the program as "seamless." For example, a student in a full-service community school should view the supportive environment as a whole—what goes on in the classroom has to be consistent with what goes on in the school clinic and in the after-school program.

Food

Experienced youth workers know that young people need a lot of caloric sustenance along with the caring. Many programs offer after-school snacks (pizza and hamburgers are favorites). Extended-day schools serve breakfast, lunch, snacks, and, in a few places, dinner.

Residential Care

One approach to dealing with high-risk youth that we have not touched upon previously is residential care, in which identified troublemakers of all sorts or habitual runaways are removed from their homes and placed in group settings. They generally live in small "houses" with "houseparents," are taught social skills, and are provided educational programs as well as treatment for any physical or mental health problems. While the older models of group homes were therapeutic, more recent homes have been opened as safe havens for molested youth or those who are otherwise homeless. A study by the U.S. General Accounting Office found many interesting models but little evaluation.[8] That agency concluded that these programs had potential and identified characteristics of the most promising efforts (these should be familiar to you by

now): individual attention, caring adults, comprehensive services, social and coping skills training, family involvement, and safe havens. A distinctive part of residential care was that the successful homes introduced routines into the otherwise chaotic lives of the children and enforced discipline. Arrangements were made for these young people after they left residential care to ensure that they had intensive and consistent follow-up from a staff member.

I believe we will hear much more about residential care in the future because, given the option, many of today's rootless youth would choose a safe haven with regular meals, an orderly environment, and caring people over the anarchy of the streets. The most controversial aspect may be the cost, estimated by the GAO at over $40,000 per participant per year.

Intensive and Long-term Involvement in a Program

Many of the programs that have been singled out as exemplary require almost daily attendance by the clients and students over a number of years. This intensity is an important factor in helping young people acquire sufficient skills and change their self-concepts.

POLICY ISSUES

Many difficult policy questions emerge from this review of programs. Some advocates for youth believe that interventions should start at the policy level, and all practitioners agree that you cannot discuss prevention without attention to policies. But I don't believe that there is a lot of agreement about the resolution of these issues at any level, in communities, states, or the nation.

Policies in the substance abuse field have recently received considerable attention. If we look at alcohol abuse, enforcement of drunken driving laws has significantly reduced fatal accidents. Both alcohol and cigarette consumption by youth have been shown to decrease when taxation raised the prices. Hopefully, eliminating cigarette advertising aimed at youth (such as the Joe Camel campaign) will diminish usage. Recent FDA regulations make the sale of tobacco products to anyone under 18 a federal violation.

Violence prevention begins with gun control, clearly a controversial subject. Other policies in the delinquency field affect how juveniles are dealt with in the justice system. The trend is toward more punitive policies, such as treating adjudicated juveniles as adults. Curfews have been proposed as one method for lowering street crime among teenagers although as many crimes are committed by juveniles in the afternoon as at night.

Those who consider the media to be a negative influence on young people's lives have recommended greater controls over the content of television and movies, particularly in the areas of violence and sex. Efforts are underway to control the Internet.

Many policies that relate to pregnancy prevention among adolescents have generated controversy. Barriers to the provision of birth control inhibit the use of contraception. School-based reproductive health programs are only effective when comprehensive services are available, starting with high-quality sexuality education and including on-site distribution of condoms and other birth-control methods, as well as referral for abortion in the case of unwanted pregnancies. Strong support for abstention programs is being articulated despite the lack of evidence that they are effective.

Many policy issues are implicit in the discussion of educational achievement. Such practices as expulsion, suspension, tracking, and grade retention can discourage high-risk students from continuing in school. The debate is in full swing about whether the implementation of national standards will improve educational achievement across the board. Policies are now being set forth to create safe havens and drug-free environments in schools that may employ body or weapons searches and locker checks.

Family policy obviously affects children. No one knows how profound the impact of welfare reform will be, although it is likely that more children will be poor and hungry, especially if they are immigrants. Policies that create more job opportunities and child care spaces are clearly an issue here.

We cannot contemplate creating a Safe Passage Movement for all children in this country without careful consideration of the implications of policies of all kinds. The pendulum swings between tolerance and control affect the lives of many perplexed teenagers at every policy shift.

IMPLEMENTATION ISSUES

While visiting a variety of programs revealed a significant batch of common factors in successful efforts, it also pointed up some common unresolved issues. This section includes broad questions about targeting programs, and replicating and staffing them. I also bring up the subject of mass media—their influence on youth, both negative and positive, and its place in youth development programs.

Targeting Behaviors

Some programs are based on the theory that specific behaviors such as cigarette smoking or early unprotected sexual intercourse must be targeted. The intervention has to be designed with a strong message focusing on that act in order to get the participant to concentrate on it. Other programs are based on the theory that one should try to alter more universal behaviors and work on areas such as decision making and dealing with peer influences. Still other approaches address broader social needs such as education, employment, and housing, predicated on the assumption that until basic needs are met, young people are not amenable to behavioral change.

Targeting High-Risk Youth

Youth experts do not agree on whether programs should be universal or targeted. Some practitioners argue that singling out certain young people and putting them in special programs will make them feel stigmatized. Instead, they say, we should try to create stronger communities and schools that respond to the principles of youth development. Others assert that the main problem is an inequitable distribution of resources. Advantaged youth have enough resources to maintain their advantage and, therefore, we have to use extra resources to launch programs that are targeted at those who need them.

A distinction has to be made between targeting and segregating. Targeting as a social policy has validity if it addresses the equity question. For example, state attempts to equalize educational funding gaps between inner cities and suburbs are of increasing importance around the country. Policies that segregate children by defined criteria may be counterproductive. For example, special education classes for students with behavioral problems have led to the isolation of mainly disadvantaged children, who then fall farther and farther behind.

Adequacy of Replication

The faithful replication of successful program models often referred to as fidelity is a major issue. I have seen many instances of inadequate replication, attributed not only to lack of funds but also to inadequate preparation and lack of involvement by staff (particularly teachers), as well as to nonsupportive administrative personnel. At one replication of a well-known program, I heard all the theory and rhetoric of the founding "guru," but observed a disorganized staff and disorderly participants. An evaluation showed only limited effects on measures of self-esteem and no effects on school or behavioral measures. I have seen two different sites that were trying to replicate programs that included computer-based curricula, but they had been waiting more than a year to obtain the technology and therefore could not implement the program model in its entirety.

Several studies demonstrate the importance of technical assistance in creating a second generation of programs. Almost all of the success stories have technical assistance built in, in the form of university or think-tank–based teams that come into schools or community agencies and facilitate program implementation. The continuing work of the New American Schools initiative will concentrate heavily on providing on-site consultation to school restructuring efforts.

Cookie Cutters Versus Anarchy

How often I have heard community advocates proclaim, "Just give us the funds, we'll know what to do with it." Yet, as we have seen, excellent program models can founder in the absence of structured replication. I believe that practitioners at the local level require considerable guidance in organizing and implementing programs. Michelle Cahill, a youth development expert who has shepherded the New York City Beacons since their initiation, reports, "You can't just hand out materials for new program ideas and expect that the program will work."[9] She attributes the successful replication of the Teen Outreach program in twenty Beacon schools to the high level of training provided by the program distributers.

The experience of the Kentucky Family and Youth Service Centers is revealing on this point. According to evaluator Robert Illback, "Each program represents a 'field experiment' in which coordinators are selected, given broad guidelines, and 'turned loose' to meet identified needs however they can."[10] The result, according to observers, is a set of innovative, complex, and largely untested approaches, with wide variations and the absence of viable controls. In this case, the conceptual model underlying the program structure is still in the process of evolution.

Charismatic Leaders

You have been introduced to a number of dynamic individuals who deserve much of the credit for creating and operating youth programs and running schools. Program visits reveal just how compelling these people are—you definitely can pick up good and bad vibes from on-site observations. In the final chapter I will return to this subject, because these leaders are fundamental to the Safe Passage Movement. But recognition that individuals are important also suggests a major question: Can a program run without these folks? What would happen if they left? Are they replaceable?

The challenge for the youth development field is to document the models and create the training opportunities that will produce new leaders. The successful experience of Public/Private Ventures with the replication of the Summer Training and Employment Program (STEP) in more than 100 communities is telling. Gary Walker and colleagues have observed, "The replication record of STEP should provide hope that operating effective social interventions is not a rare or mysterious talent, but more a matter of adequate resources, defined strategy and content, and guidance and ready assistance regarding concrete implementation issues and problems."[11]

Interdisciplinary Education

Many people who work with youth were trained in traditional roles. Teachers are graduates of educational establishments that have not changed their own curricula to adapt to contemporary needs. They rarely come into schools prepared to manage team teaching or to organize cooperative learning classrooms. Few school pupil personnel—counselors, psychologists, and social workers—have been trained to deal with issues such as sexual abuse and family substance abuse. Youth workers in community-based programs often are trained through in-service programs, but they are not prepared to work in collaborative arrangements with schools. Many of the successful programs we have looked at require personnel who have very strong interpersonal skills, can understand the issues arising in cross-disciplinary efforts, and are strongly committed to seeing results.

Universities and professional organizations that offer interdisciplinary training have come together to create a Network of Networks. As reported by Richard Brandon of the Human Services Policy Center at the University of Washington in Seattle, an initial meeting of major educators and trainers concluded that this new field of collaborative programs embodies an

implicit model of change in the attitudes, skills, and orientations of individuals that lead them to foster changes in the institutions where they work, which in turn leads to changes in the clients served by those institutions. This same model applies whether we are talking about university faculty changing the institutions which train professional students, and thereby affecting the way students practice when they leave the university; or we are talking about how students trained in collaborative practice transform the service institutions where they work, and affect the lives of children and families.[12]

A National Center on School and Community at New York City's Fordham University, directed by Carolyn Denham, acts as a clearinghouse for information on interprofessional education and community schools. Technical assistance and training for in-service or preservice education is coordinated by Hal Lawson and Katherine Hooper-Briar at University of Utah in Salt Lake City. The Human Services Policy Center in Seattle brings together five graduate and professional programs at the university (education, public affairs, public health, nursing, and social work) that work collaboratively with numerous schools and community agencies in two nearby school districts. Students are exposed to both classroom-based and experiential learning.

Wheelock College in Boston is one of the few undergraduate schools that is creating an interdisciplinary program that prepares students to work in service delivery systems that will be preventive, supportive of family development, and appropriate for contemporary children:

We aim to structure professional training in each of the three human service professions of teaching, social work, and child life . . . to both intellectually and experientially transcend current role definitions within those professions.[13]

Training

The Children's Aid Society, having set up a technical assistance center to help people create community schools, finds that the demand is overwhelming, especially for developing collaborative relationships between schools and community agencies. Other ques-

tions frequently raised include: How do the school principal and the support-services coordinator divide up their responsibilities? How can special education programs be integrated into community schools? How can evaluation be conducted so that it produces evidence of success but is not too intrusive or expensive?

One of the most interesting initiatives is in the preparation of police to work in community and youth projects. The program in Caimito has played host to hundreds of police officials, and the Milton Eisenhower Foundation has arranged for networking among other Koban replications in Columbia, South Carolina, Baltimore, and Washington, DC, and police departments around the country. This foundation also facilitates training for community-based organizations in management, evaluation, and communication techniques.

Every field has its own cadre of trainers. In teen pregnancy prevention, the area I know best, Advocates for Youth, Educational Development Corporation, ETR Associates, SEICUS (Sexuality Information and Education Council of the United States), and various regional centers all provide technical assistance and training in prevention interventions.

Staff Turnover

Just when a program is finally up and running, the director gets a better job offer or the case manager moves across country. Staff turnover both in program development agencies and in youth-serving agencies and schools is a major deterrent to program implementation and replication. Pay scales are generally low in community-based organizations, and many staff are pressured by financial concerns to move to better-paying jobs if available. Principal and superintendent turnover creates a frequent barrier to program sustainability.

Unions

In my field visits, unions were sometimes cited as barriers to program development. This was particularly evident in regard to school reorganization programs, where tenure was an issue. Innovative principals found it difficult to put together a new team in situations where no staff changes were possible. In some communities, union rules make it hard to replace ineffective principals.

The National Education Association and the American Federation of Teachers (AFT) have sought to set the record straight on these issues by taking the leadership in many educational reform initiatives. The AFT recently endorsed the concept of charter schools, with the proviso that they preserve employee bargaining rights.[14] (Only eight of the twenty-five states with charter school laws require that teachers be certified.)

Time

The more complex program models may take five to seven years to implement. The need for extended time for planning and communication cannot be overestimated. Meetings can be the bane of any program developer's existence. Yet as more actors come on the scene from different agencies, with different perspectives on clients, more time is required to make joint decisions and to share information.

Many of the people providing that precious individual attention I keep talking about report that they work seventy to eighty hours a week, including weekends. Safe Passage requires just such an enormous commitment of time. No one expects to get paid for all the hours it takes.

Media: A Powerful Influence?

The extent to which media exposure can be used to promote positive behaviors is definitely an unresolved issue in program development. Although most people would agree that salacious and violent television shows are not good for children, it is unclear to what degree educational television and other forms of positive messages can exert a beneficial influence on behaviors.

Public television in New York City produces a show called *In the Mix,* where the material is presented by teenagers, about teenagers, in a style that teenagers say they want. The program covers a range of subjects—education, employment, AIDS, family and peer relationships, going on a date. Substantive sections are interspersed with music videos that teens select. The producer, Sue Gates, developed discussion guides to be used in schools and with community groups showing how to use the films as triggers for group discussions and socials skills exercises. Preliminary research shows that students and teachers find the *In The Mix* videos interesting and stimulating, but compiling evidence on behavioral impacts is almost impossible to obtain. RMC Research Corporation staff joined a group of very high-risk students watching the segment "Teens Talk Violence." They reported:

Students watched the video with riveted attention . . . all wanted to talk about how violence figures in their lives . . . the session became a catharsis, helping them air their anxieties, fears, frustrations, and street smarts at a specially stressful point in time. The principal was astounded at students' reactions, pointing out that this was probably the first time that they were interested in doing better in life and learning new things.[15]

Many people believe that public service messages can influence behavior. Partnership for Drug Free America has been placing full-page ads and media spots for years, yet no research has documented that the ads are effective. ENABL, a teen-pregnancy-prevention approach used in California, had a large media component using billboards, ads, and television, but it had no effect. Youth were aware of the campaign, but they did not abstain from sex. . . . Maryland also launched a media campaign to prevent pregnancy that was initially deemed a success when the rates declined, yet shortly thereafter the rates rose, suggesting that ads may not have influenced the rates one way or the other. Now, a new national initiative focusing on preventing teen pregnancy has announced its intentions of using media as the centerpiece of the strategy. President Clinton also plans to feature media spots in new smoking-prevention initiatives. We have no reason to believe that these new ventures will succeed any better than those cited here.

Advocates for Youth has long been involved in working with media producers to integrate positive youth development messages into soap operas and sitcoms. Awards are given annually for those programs that present sexual issues with honesty and integrity. Networks are under a lot of pressure from parent and youth advocate groups to clean up the airways and act responsibly.

In my view, the most effective potential role of media for changing youth behaviors is to use films as triggers for group discussions. This requires well-thought-out videos as well as trained group discussion leaders who can use the materials to help teenagers learn valuable life lessons and deal with their feelings.

NOTES

1. D. Farran, "Effects of Intervention with Disadvantaged and Disabled Children: A Decade Review," in S. Meisels and J. Shonkoff (eds.), *Handbook of Early Childhood Intervention* (Cambridge, UK: Cambridge University Press, 1990), p. 533.

2. M. Pines, "Programs That Work: Taking Service to Families," Institute for Policy Studies at Johns Hopkins University. n.d.

3. Ibid., p. 28.

4. M. Adams, *Gentlemen, Shall We Begin Again? The Fifth Ward Enrichment Program* (Austin, TX: Hogg Foundation for Mental Health, 1994). p. 17.

5. M. Freedman, "The Aging Opportunity," *American Prospect* (29) 38–43 (1996).

6. Office of Research, *Educational Reforms and Students at Risk: A Review of the Current State of the Art* (Washington, DC: U.S. Department of Education, 1994).

7. D. Davies, "The 10th School Where School-Family-Community Partnerships Flourish," *Education Week,* July 10, 1996, p. 44.

8. U.S. General Accounting Office, *Residential Care: Some High-Risk Youth Benefit, But More Study Needed* (Washington DC: Department of Health and Human Services, GAO/HEHS 94-56, 1994).

9. M. Cahill, Fund for City of N.Y., personal communication, May 12, 1997.

10. R. Illback, *Kentucky Family Resource and Youth Service Centers: Summary of Evaluation Findings* (Louisville, KY: Reach of Louisville, 1996), p. 3.

11. G. Walker and F. Vilella-Velez, *Anatomy of a Demonstration* (Philadelphia, PA: Public/Private Ventures, 1992), p. iv.

12. R. Brandon and M. Meuter, *Proceedings: National Conference on Interprofessional Education and Training* (Seattle, WA: Human Services Policy Center, University of Washington, March 22, 1995), p. 8.

13. P. Hogan, "Transforming Professional Education," unpublished paper, September 20, 1994, p. 5. Hogan is Chief, Professional Studies Department, Wheelock College, Boston, MA.

14. J. Ponessa, "Cautiously, AFT Embraces Charter Schools," *Education Week*, August 7, 1996.

15. J. Dryfoos, *Adolescents at Risk Revisited: Continuity, Evaluation, and Replication*, report to Carnegie Corporation, January 16, 1996.

Early Warning, Timely Response

A Guide to Safe Schools

Keving Dwyer
David Osher
Cynthia Wagner

SECTION 4: WHAT TO DO

Intervention: Getting Help for Troubled Children

Prevention approaches have proved effective in enabling school communities to decrease the frequency and intensity of behavior problems. However, prevention programs alone cannot eliminate the problems of all students. Some 5 to 10 percent of students will need more intensive interventions to decrease their high-risk behaviors, although the percentage can vary among schools and communities.

What happens when we recognize early warning signs in a child?

The message is clear: It's okay to be concerned when you notice warning signs in a child—and it's even more appropriate to do something about those concerns. School communities that encourage staff, families, and students to raise concerns about observed warning signs—and that have in place a process for getting help to troubled children once they are identified—are more likely to have effective schools with reduced disruption, bullying, fighting, and other forms of aggression.

Principles Underlying Intervention

Violence prevention and response plans should consider both prevention and intervention. Plans also should provide all staff with easy access to a team of specialists trained in evaluating serious behavioral and academic concerns. Eligible students should have access to special education services, and classroom teachers should be able to consult school psychologists, other mental health specialists, counselors, reading specialists, and special educators.

Effective practices for improving the behavior of troubled children are well documented in the research literature. Research has shown that effective interventions are culturally appropriate, family-supported, individualized, coordinated, and monitored. Further, interventions are more effective when they are designed and implemented consistently over time with input from the child, the family, and appropriate professionals. Schools also can draw upon the resources of their community to strengthen and enhance intervention planning.

When drafting a violence prevention and response plan, it is helpful to consider certain principles that research or expert-based experience show have a significant impact on success. The principles include:

- **Share responsibility by establishing a partnership with the child, school, home, and community.** Coordinated service systems should be available for children who are at risk for violent behavior. Effective schools reach out to include families and the entire community in the education of children. In addition, effective schools coordinate and collaborate with child and family service agencies, law enforcement and juvenile justice systems, mental health agencies, businesses, faith and ethnic leaders, and other community agencies.
- **Inform parents and listen to them when early warning signs are observed.** Parents should be involved as soon as possible. Effective and safe schools make persistent efforts to involve parents by: informing them routinely about school discipline policies, procedures, and rules, and about their children's behavior (both good and bad); involving them in making decisions concerning schoolwide disciplinary policies and procedures; and encouraging them to participate in prevention programs, intervention programs, and crisis planning. Parents need to know what school-based interventions are being used with their children and how they can support their success.
- **Maintain confidentiality and parents' rights to privacy.** Parental involvement and consent is required before personally identifiable information is shared with other agencies, except in the case of emergencies or suspicion of abuse. The *Family Educational Rights and Privacy Act* (FERPA), a federal law that addresses the privacy of education records, must be observed in all referrals to or sharing of information with other community agencies. Furthermore, parent-approved interagency communication must be kept confidential. FERPA does not prevent disclosure of personally identifiable information to appropriate parties—such as law enforcement officials, trained medical personnel, and other emergency

personnel—when responsible personnel determine there is an acute emergency (imminent danger).

- **Develop the capacity of staff, students, and families to intervene.** Many school staff members are afraid of saying or doing the wrong thing when faced with a potentially violent student. Effective schools provide the entire school community—teachers, students, parents, support staff—with training and support in responding to imminent warning signs, preventing violence, and intervening safely and effectively. Interventions must be monitored by professionals who are competent in the approach. According to researchers, programs do not succeed without the ongoing support of administrators, parents, and community leaders.
- **Support students in being responsible for their actions.** Effective school communities encourage students to see themselves as responsible for their actions, and actively engage them in planning, implementing, and evaluating violence prevention initiatives.
- **Simplify staff requests for urgent assistance.** Many school systems and community agencies have complex legalistic referral systems with timelines and waiting lists. Children who are at risk of endangering themselves or others cannot be placed on waiting lists.

"Tips for Parents"

- **Make interventions available as early as possible.** Too frequently, interventions are not made available until the student becomes violent or is adjudicated as a youthful offender. Interventions for children who have reached this stage are both costly, restrictive, and relatively inefficient. Effective schools build mechanisms into their intervention processes to ensure that referrals are addressed promptly, and that feedback is provided to the referring individual.
- **Use sustained, multiple, coordinated interventions.** It is rare that children are violent or disruptive only in school. Thus, interventions that are most successful are comprehensive, sustained, and properly implemented. They help families and staff work together to help the child. Coordinated efforts draw resources from community agencies that are respectful of and responsive to the needs of families. Isolated, inconsistent, short-term, and fragmented interventions will not be successful—and may actually do harm.
- **Analyze the contexts in which violent behavior occurs.** School communities can enhance their effectiveness by conducting a functional analysis of the factors that set off violence and problem behaviors. In determining an appropriate course of action, consider the child's age, cultural background, and family experiences and values. Decisions about interventions should be measured against a standard of reasonableness to ensure the likelihood that they will be implemented effectively.
- **Build upon and coordinate internal school resources.** In developing and implementing violence prevention and

response plans, effective schools draw upon the resources of various school-based programs and staff—such as special education, safe and drug free school programs, pupil services, and Title I.

Violent behavior is a problem for everyone. It is a normal response to become angry or even frightened in the presence of a violent child. But, it is essential that these emotional reactions be controlled. The goal must always be to ensure safety and seek help for the child.

Intervening Early with Students Who Are at Risk for Behavioral Problems

The incidence of violent acts against students or staff is low. However, pre-violent behaviors—such as threats, bullying, and classroom disruptions—are common. Thus, early responses to warning signs are most effective in preventing problems from escalating.

Intervention programs that reduce behavior problems and related school violence typically are multi-faceted, long-term, and broad reaching. They also are rigorously implemented. Effective early intervention efforts include working with small groups or individual students to provide direct support, as well as linking children and their families to necessary community services and/or providing these services in the school.

Examples of early intervention components that work include:

- Providing training and support to staff, students, and families in understanding factors that can set off and/or exacerbate aggressive outbursts.
- Teaching the child alternative, socially appropriate replacement responses—such as problem solving and anger control skills.
- Providing skill training, therapeutic assistance, and other support to the family through community-based services.
- Encouraging the family to make sure that firearms are out of the child's immediate reach. Law enforcement officers can provide families with information about safe firearm storage as well as guidelines for addressing children's access to and possession of firearms.

In some cases, more comprehensive early interventions are called for to address the needs of troubled children. Focused, coordinated, proven interventions reduce violent behavior. Following are several comprehensive approaches that effective schools are using to provide early intervention to students who are at risk of becoming violent toward themselves or others.

Intervention Tactic: Teaching Positive Interaction Skills. Although most schools do teach positive social interaction skills indirectly, some have adopted social skills programs specifically designed to prevent or reduce antisocial behavior in troubled children. In fact, the direct teaching of social problem solving and social decision making is now a standard feature of most effective drug and violence prevention programs. Children who are at risk of becoming violent toward themselves or others need additional support. They often need to learn interpersonal, problem solving, and conflict resolution skills at home and in school. They also may need more intensive assistance in learning how to stop and think before they react, and to listen effectively.

Intervention Tactic: Providing Comprehensive Services. In some cases, the early intervention may involve getting services to families. The violence prevention and response team together with the child and family designs a comprehensive intervention plan that focuses on reducing aggressive behaviors and supporting responsible behaviors at school, in the home, and in the community. When multiple services are required there also must be psychological counseling and ongoing consultation with classroom teachers, school staff, and the family to ensure intended results occur. All services—including community services—must be coordinated and progress must be monitored and evaluated carefully.

Intervention Tactic: Referring the Child for Special Education Evaluation. If there is evidence of persistent problem behavior or poor academic achievement, it may be appropriate to conduct a formal assessment to determine if the child is disabled and eligible for special education and related services under the *Individuals with Disabilities Education Act* (IDEA). If a multidisciplinary team determines that the child is eligible for services under the IDEA, an individualized educational program (IEP) should be developed by a team that includes a parent, a regular educator, a special educator, an evaluator, a representative of the local school district, the child (if appropriate), and others as appropriate. This team will identify the support necessary to enable the child to learn—including the strategies and support systems necessary to address any behavior that may impede the child's learning or the learning of his or her peers.

Providing Intensive, Individualized Interventions for Students with Severe Behavioral Problems

Children who show dangerous patterns and a potential for more serious violence usually require more intensive interventions that involve multiple agencies, community-based service providers, and intense family support. By working with families and community services, schools can comprehensively and effectively intervene.

Effective individualized interventions provide a range of services for students. Multiple, intensive, focused approaches used over time can reduce the chances for continued offenses and the potential for violence. The child, his or her family, and appropriate school staff should be involved in developing and monitoring the interventions.

Nontraditional schooling in an alternative school or therapeutic facility may be required in severe cases where the safety of students and staff remains a concern, or when the complexity of the intervention plan warrants it. Research has shown that effective alternative programs can have long-term positive results by reducing expulsions and court referrals. Effective alternative programs support students in meeting high academic and behavioral standards. They provide anger and impulse control training, psychological counseling, effective academic and remedial instruction, and vocational training as appropriate. Such programs also make provisions for active family involvement. Moreover, they offer guidance and staff support when the child returns to his or her regular school.

Providing a Foundation to Prevent and Reduce Violent Behavior

Schoolwide strategies create a foundation that is more responsive to children in general—**one that makes interventions for individual children more effective and efficient.**

Effective and safe schools are places where there is strong leadership, caring faculty, parent and community involvement—including law enforcement offi-cials—and student participation in the design of programs and policies. Effective and safe schools also are places where prevention and intervention programs are based upon careful assessment of student problems, where community members help set measurable goals and objectives, where research-based prevention and intervention approaches are used, and where evaluations are conducted regularly to ensure that the programs are meeting stated goals. Effective and safe schools are also places where teachers and staff have access to qualified consultants who can help them address behavioral and academic barriers to learning.

Effective schools ensure that the physical environment of the school is safe, and that schoolwide policies are in place to support responsible behaviors.

Characteristics of a Safe Physical Environment. Prevention starts by making sure the school campus is a safe and caring place. Effective and safe schools communicate a strong sense of security. Experts suggest that school officials can enhance physical safety by:

- Supervising access to the building and grounds.
- Reducing class size and school size.
- Adjusting scheduling to minimize time in the hallways or in potentially dangerous locations. Traffic flow patterns can be modified to limit potential for conflicts or altercations.
- Conducting a building safety audit in consultation with school security personnel and/or law enforcement experts. Effective schools adhere to federal, state, and local nondiscrimination and public safety laws, and use guidelines set by the state department of education.
- Closing school campuses during lunch periods.
- Adopting a school policy on uniforms.
- Arranging supervision at critical times (for example, in hallways between classes) and having a plan to deploy supervisory staff to areas where incidents are likely to occur.
- Prohibiting students from congregating in areas where they are likely to engage in rule-breaking or intimidating and aggressive behaviors.
- Having adults visibly present throughout the school building. This includes encouraging parents to visit the school.
- Staggering dismissal times and lunch periods.
- Monitoring the surrounding school grounds—including landscaping, parking lots, and bus stops.
- Coordinating with local police to ensure that there are safe routes to and from school.

In addition to targeting areas for increased safety measures, schools also should identify safe areas where staff and children should go in the event of a crisis.

The physical condition of the school building also has an impact on student attitude, behavior, and motivation to achieve. Typically, there tend to be more incidents of fighting and violence in school buildings that are dirty, too cold or too hot, filled with graffiti, in need of repair, or unsanitary.

Characteristics of Schoolwide Policies that Support Responsible Behavior. The opportunities for inappropriate behaviors that precipitate violence are greater in a disorderly and undisciplined school climate. A growing number of schools are discovering that the most effective way to reduce suspensions, expulsions, office referrals, and other similar actions—strategies that do not result in making schools safer—is to emphasize a proactive approach to discipline.

Effective schools are implementing schoolwide campaigns that establish high expectations and provide support for socially appropriate behavior. They reinforce positive behavior and highlight sanctions against aggressive behavior. All staff, parents, students, and community members are informed about problem behavior, what they can do to counteract it, and how they can reinforce and reward positive behavior. In turn, the entire school community makes a commitment to behaving responsibly.

Effective and safe schools develop and consistently enforce schoolwide rules that are clear, broad-based, and fair. Rules and disciplinary procedures are developed collaboratively by representatives of the total educational community. They are communicated clearly to all parties—but most important, they are followed consistently by everyone.

School communities that have undertaken schoolwide approaches do the following things:

- Develop a schoolwide disciplinary policy that includes a code of conduct, specific rules and consequences that can accommodate student differences on a case-by-case basis when necessary. (If one already exists, review and modify it if necessary.) Be sure to include a description of school anti-harassment and anti-violence policies and due process rights.

- Ensure that the cultural values and educational goals of the community are reflected in the rules. These values should be expressed in a statement that precedes the schoolwide disciplinary policy.

- Include school staff, students, and families in the development, discussion, and implementation of fair rules. Provide schoolwide and classroom support to implement these rules. Strategies that have been found to support students include class discussions, schoolwide assemblies, student government, and participation on discipline teams. In addition, peer mediation and conflict resolution have been implemented widely in schools to promote a climate of nonviolence.

- Be sure consequences are commensurate with the offense, and that rules are written and applied in a nondiscriminatory manner and accommodate cultural diversity.

- Make sure that if a negative consequence (such as withdrawing privileges) is used, it is combined with positive strategies for teaching socially appropriate behaviors and with strategies that address any external factors that might have caused the behavior.

- Include a zero tolerance statement for illegal possession of weapons, alcohol, or drugs. Provide services and support for students who have been suspended and/or expelled.

Recognizing the warning signs and responding with comprehensive interventions allows us to help children eliminate negative behaviors and replace them with positive ones. Active sharing of information and a quick, effective response by the school community will ensure that the school is safer and the child is less troubled and can learn.

Guns, Gun Control, and Homicide

A Review of Research and Public Policy

Philip J. Cook and Mark H. Moore

In the search for more effective ways to reduce homicide, establishing more stringent controls on gun commerce and use has the broad support of the American public. Guns are the immediate cause of about 15,000 criminal homicides a year (Federal Bureau of Investigation, 1997) and are used to threaten or injure victims in hundreds of thousands of robberies and assaults (Bureau of Justice Statistics, 1997). It makes sense that if we could find a way to make guns less readily available, especially to those inclined toward crime and violence, we could reduce the level and seriousness of crime, including a reduction in homicide.

It is an understatement to say simply that not everyone accepts this perspective on guns. Some people argue that guns are the mere instruments of criminal intent, with no more importance than the type of shoes the criminal wears. If the type of weapon does not matter, then policy interventions focused on guns would have little use. This argument is taken another step by those who argue that although the type of weapon used by the perpetrator does not matter much, the type of weapon available to the victim for use in self-defense matters a great deal. Their conclusion is that measures depriving the public of guns would serve only to increase criminal activity.

This point and counterpoint make it appear as if the debate about gun control is primarily concerned with facts about the role of guns in crime and self-defense. If this were true, one might hope that empirical research would eventually resolve the matter, and the proper choice of gun control measures would become clear. In reality, however, deeply conflicting values are at stake here concerning the proper relationship between the individual, the community, and the state. Even a definitive empirical demonstration that a gun control measure would save lives will not persuade someone who believes that any infringement on the individual right to bear arms is tantamount to opening the door to tyranny. Further, empirical research in this area will never resolve all the important factual issues, so the value conflict will flourish in the face of uncertainty about the consequences of proposed reforms.

The purpose of this chapter is to set out a framework for thinking about the next steps that should be taken in the search for an effective gun control policy. We begin with a review of the more or less noncontroversial facts about trends in gun ownership and use and the reasons why Americans are inclined to arm themselves. A discussion follows of the more controversial issue of whether guns influence levels or seriousness of crime. We then identify the important values at stake in adopting any gun control policy and go on to describe the existing policies and the mechanisms by which they and other such measures have their effect. Finally, we make recommendations about promising next steps.

GUN OWNERSHIP: USE AND MISUSE

Guns are versatile tools with many uses, so their broad appeal is not surprising. They are an especially common feature of rural life, where wild animals provide both a threat and an opportunity for sport. As America has become more urban and more violent, however, the demand for guns has become increasingly motivated by the need for protection against other people.

Patterns of Gun Ownership

The 1994 National Survey of the Private Ownership of Firearms (NSPOF) by the National Opinion Research Center found that 41% of American households included at least one firearm. Approximately 29% of adults say that they personally own a gun. These percentages reflect an apparent *decline* in the prevalence of gun ownership since the 1970s (Cook & Ludwig, 1996).

Although the prevalence of gun ownership has declined, it appears that the number of guns in private hands has been increasing rapidly. Since 1970, total sales of new guns have accounted for more than half of all the guns sold during this century, and the total now in circulation is on the order of 200 million (Cook & Ludwig, 1996). How can this volume of sales be reconciled with the decline in the prevalence of ownership? Part of the answer is in the growth in population (and the more rapid growth in the number of households) during this period; millions of new guns were required to arm the baby boom cohorts. Beyond that is the likelihood that the average gun owner has increased the size of his or her collection (Wright, 1981). The NSPOF estimates that gun-owning households average 4.4 guns, up substantially from the 1970s (Cook & Ludwig, 1996).[1]

One addition for many gun-owning households has been a *handgun*. The significance of this trend toward increased handgun ownership lies in that although rifles and shotguns are acquired primarily for sporting purposes, handguns are intended primarily for use against people, either in crime or self-defense. The increase in handgun prevalence corresponds to a large increase in the relative importance of handguns in retail sales; since the early 1970s, the handgun fraction of new gun sales has increased from one third to near one half (Cook, 1993).

Although the prevalence of handgun ownership has increased substantially during the past three decades, it remains true that most people who possess a handgun also own one or more rifles and shotguns. The 1994 NSPOF (see Cook & Ludwig, 1996, p. 39) found that just 20% of gun-owning individuals have only handguns, 36% have only long guns, and 44% have both. These statistics suggest that people who have acquired guns for self-protection are for the most part also hunters and target shooters. Indeed, only 46% of gun owners say that they own a gun *primarily* for self-protection against crime, and only 26% keep a gun loaded. Most (80%) grew up in a house with a gun.

The demographic patterns of gun ownership are no surprise: Most owners are men, and the men who are most likely to own a gun reside in rural areas or small towns and were reared in such small places (Kleck, 1991). The regional pattern gives the highest prevalence to the states of the Mountain Census Region, followed by the South and Midwest. Blacks are less likely to own guns than are Whites, in part because the Black population is more urban.[2] The likelihood of gun ownership increases with income and age.

That guns fit more comfortably into rural life than urban life raises a question. What will happen to gun ownership patterns as new generations with less connection to rural life come along? Hunting is already on the decline; as revealed in the National Survey of Wildlife-Associated Recreation, the absolute number of hunting licenses issued in 1990 was about the same as in 1970, despite the growth in the population, indicating a decline in the percentage of people who hunt (U.S. Department of the Interior, 1991). This trend may eventually erode the importance of the rural sporting culture that has dominated the "gun scene." In its place is an ever-greater focus on the criminal and self-defense uses of guns.

Uses of Guns Against People

A great many Americans die by gunfire. The gun death counts from suicide, homicide, and accident have totaled more than 30,000 for every year since 1972. In 1994, there were approximately 39,000 firearms deaths, a rate of 15 per 100,000 U.S. residents. All but 2,200 of these deaths were either homicides or suicides (although homicides garner the bulk of the public concern, there were actually 1,200 more gun suicides than homicides). The remaining gun deaths were classified as accidents, legal interventions, or unknown (Violence Policy Center, 1997).

There are different points of reference to make sense of these numbers. For example, for Americans killed, a year of gun killing in the United States is the equivalent of the Korean War. Another familiar reference is highway accidents: Nearly as many Americans die of gunfire as in motor vehicle crashes, with the former showing a strong secular increase, whereas the latter has declined.

Criminal homicide and other criminal uses of guns cause the greatest public concern. Gun accident rates have been declining steadily during the past two decades,[3] and suicide seems a threat only to those whose loved ones are at risk. Homicide rates have varied little since 1970, with the homicide rate per 100,000 fluctuating between 8.1 and 10.6. Of these, 60% to 70% were committed with guns, mostly (80%) handguns. The peak rates, occurring in 1980 and 1991, were about the same magnitude (Federal Bureau of Investigation, 1971–1997).

Homicide is not a democratic crime. Both victims and perpetrators are vastly disproportionately male, Black, and young. With respect to the victims, homicide is the leading cause of death for Black males aged 15 to 34, whose victimization rate (in 1994) was 9.5 times as high as for White males and Black females in this age range and nearly 50 times as high as for White females. (The evidence suggests that most victims in the high-risk category are killed by people with the same demographic characteristics.) About 75% of the homicide victims in this age group were killed with firearms. Thus, we see a remarkable disparity between the demography of gun sports and of gun crime: Sportsmen are disproportionately older White males from small towns and rural areas, whereas the criminal misuse of guns is concentrated among young urban males, especially minorities.[4] Young Black men have suffered the greatest increase in homicide rates since 1985; by 1994, the homicide victimization rate for 15- to 24-year-olds in this group had tripled, reaching 160 per 100,000[5] (Centers for Disease Control and Prevention, 1997).

Of course, most gun crimes are not fatal. For every gun homicide victim, roughly six gun crime victims receive a less than mortal wound (Cook, 1985), and many more are not wounded at all. Indeed, the most common criminal use of guns is to threaten, with the objective of robbing, raping, or otherwise gaining the victim's compliance. Relatively few of these victims are physically injured, but the threat of lethal violence and the potential for escalation necessarily make these crimes serious. According to the 1994 National Crime Victimization Survey (NCVS), 316,000 guns were used in robberies, 727,000 aggravated assaults (of which 94,000 caused injury), and 25,000 rapes in that year, for a total estimated volume of gun crimes of about 1,068,000 (Bureau of Justice Statistics, 1997, Table 66). For each of these crime types, guns are used in only a fraction of all cases, as shown in Figure 1. When a gun is used, it is almost always a handgun, which accounts for upwards of 92% of these crimes.

Gun Use as Self-Defense

Although guns do enormous damage in crime, they also provide some crime victims with the means of escaping serious injury or property loss. The NCVS is generally considered the most reliable source of information on predatory crime because it has been in the field more than two decades and incorporates the best thinking of survey methodologists. From this source, it appears that use of guns in self-defense against criminal predation is rather rare, occurring on the order of 100,000 times per year (Cook, Ludwig, & Hemenway, 1997). Of particular interest is the likelihood that a gun will be used in self-defense against an intruder. Cook (1991), using NCVS data, found that only 3% of victims were able to deploy a gun against someone

FIGURE 1   Personal Crimes of Violence, 1994. SOURCE: Bureau of Justice Statistics (1997, Table 66).

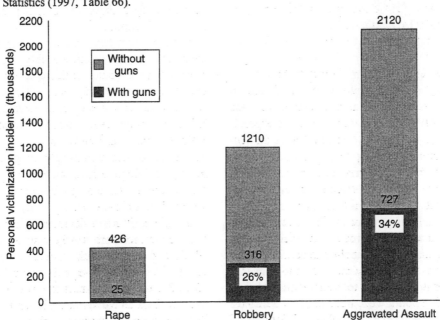

who broke in (or attempted to do so) while they were at home. Remembering that 40% of all households have a gun, we conclude that it is quite rare for victims to be able to deploy a gun against intruders even when they have one available.

Gary Kleck and Marc Gertz (1995) have come up with far higher estimates of 2.5 million self-defense uses each year. Indeed, Kleck and Gertz conclude that guns are used more commonly in self-defense than in crime. Cook et al. (1997) have demonstrated that Kleck and Gertz's high estimate may result from a significant false-positive rate—in short, there is no clear sense of how many shootings were truly justifiable in the sense of being committed in self-defense. It is quite possible that most "self-defense" uses occur in circumstances that are normatively ambiguous, such as chronic violence within a marriage, gang fights, robberies of drug dealers, and encounters with groups of young men who simply *appear* threatening. In one survey of convicted felons in prison, the most common reason offered for carrying a gun was self-defense (Wright & Rossi, 1986); a similar finding emerged from a study of juveniles incarcerated for serious criminal offenses (Smith, 1996). Although self-defense conjures up an image of the innocent victim using a gun to fend off an unprovoked criminal assault, many self-defense cases are not nearly so clear-cut or so commendable.

INSTRUMENTALITY AND AVAILABILITY OF FIREARMS

An overriding issue in the gun control debate is, "Do guns kill people?" or "Do people kill people?" In murder trials, the killer's motivation and state of mind are explored thoroughly, whereas the type of weapon—usually some type of gun—is often treated as an incidental detail. Yet there is compelling evidence that the *type of weapon matters a great deal* in determining whether the victim lives or dies and therefore becomes a homicide victim. This means that depriving potentially violent people of guns probably can save lives, an essential tenet of the argument for restricting gun availability. But then a second question arises: How can we use the law to deprive violent people of guns if such people are not inclined to be law-abiding? The saying "if guns are outlawed, only outlaws will have guns" may ring true.[6] There is also some evidence on

this matter suggesting that some criminals' decisions of what weapon to use are influenced by the difficulty and legal risks of obtaining and using a gun (Wright & Rossi, 1986).

We now explore the evidence on these two issues, designated *instrumentality* and *availability*. The same two issues should also be considered in an assessment of the self-defense uses of guns, and we do so in the next two sections.

Instrumentality

The first piece of evidence is that robberies and assaults committed with guns are more likely to result in the victim's death than are similar violent crimes committed with other weapons. In public health jargon, the *case fatality rates* differ by weapon type. A prime example is robbery, for which the fatality rate for *gun robbery* is 3 times as high as for robberies with knives and 10 times as high as for robberies with other weapons (Cook, 1987). It is more difficult to come up with significant probability estimates for aggravated (serious) assault because the crime itself is in part defined by the type of weapon used. We do know, however, that for assaults in which the victim sustains an injury, the case fatality rate is closely linked to the type of weapon (Kleck & McElrath, 1991; Zimring, 1968, 1972), as is also the case for family and intimate assaults known to the police (Saltzman, Mercy, O'Carroll, Rosenberg, & Rhodes, 1992).

Fatality rates do not by themselves prove that the type of weapon has an independent causal effect on the probability of death. Possibly, the type of weapon is simply an indicator of the assailant's intent, and the intent, rather than the weapon, determines whether the victim lives or dies. In this view, the gun makes the killing easier and hence is the obvious choice if the assailant's intent is indeed to kill. The overriding assumption is that if no gun were available, most would-be killers would still find a way (Wolfgang, 1958; Wright, Rossi, & Daly, 1983).

Perhaps the most telling response to this argument comes from Franklin Zimring (1968, 1972; see also Zimring & Hawkins, 1997), who concluded that there actually is a good deal of overlap between fatal and nonfatal attacks; even in the case of earnest and potentially deadly attacks, assailants commonly lack a clear or sustained intent to kill. Zimring's argument in a nutshell is that homicide is fundamentally a byproduct of violent crime. Although the law determines the seriousness of the crime by whether the victim lives or dies, the outcome is not a reliable guide to the assailant's intent or state of mind. One logical implication of this perspective is that there should be a close link between the overall volume of violent crimes and the number of murders. One study provided confirmatory evidence, finding that an additional 1,000 gun robberies "produces" three times as many extra murders as an additional 1,000 robberies with other weapons (Cook, 1987). The instrumentality explanation for this result is simpler and more persuasive than an argument based on changes in the prevalence of homicidal intent among robbers.

Another study provides further evidence on the importance of reducing gun use in violent homes. In research based on six cities in three crimes, it was found that mandatory sentencing enhancements for those convicted of using a gun in a crime are effective in reducing the homicide rate (McDowall, Loftin, & Wiersema, 1992b).

Zimring's reasoning can also be extended to a comparison of different types of guns. In the gun control debate, the prime target has been the handgun, because handguns are used in most gun crimes. But rifles and shotguns tend to be more lethal than handguns; a rifle is easier to aim, and the bullet travels with higher velocity than for a short-barreled weapon, whereas a shotgun blast spreads and causes a number of wounds when it strikes. To the extent that assailants substitute rifles and shotguns for handguns in response to handgun control measures, the result may be to increase the death rate (Kleck, 1984).[7] Unfortunately, there is little evidence on the question of whether effective handgun control would lead robbers and other violent people to substitute long guns (more lethal) or, in contrast, knives (less lethal).

Other Perspectives on Instrumentality

Instrumentality effects are not limited to differences in case fatality rates among weapons. The type of weapon also appears to matter in other ways. For example, gun robbers are far less likely to attack and injure their victims than are robbers using other weapons and are less likely to incur resistance (Conklin, 1972; Cook, 1976, 1980; Skogan, 1978). We have evidence that aggravated assaults also follow similar patterns (Kleck & McElrath, 1991). The most plausible expla-

nation for this pattern of outcomes is simply that a gun gives the assailant the power to intimidate and gain the victim's compliance without use of force, whereas with less lethal weapons, the assailant is more likely to find it necessary to back up the threat with a physical attack.

The intimidating power of a gun may also help explain the effectiveness of using one in self-defense. According to one study of NCVS data, in burglaries of occupied dwellings, only 5% of victims who used guns in self-defense were injured, compared with 25% of those who resisted with other weapons.[8] Other studies have confirmed that victims of predatory crime who are able to resist with a gun are generally successful in thwarting the crime and avoiding injury (Kleck, 1988; McDowall et al., 1992b). The interpretation of this result, however, is open to some question. In particular, other means of defense usually are attempted after the assailant threatens or attacks the victim, whereas those who use guns in self-defense are relatively likely to be the first to threaten or use force (McDowall et al., 1992b). Given this difference in the sequence of events, and the implied difference in the competence or intentions of the perpetrator, the proper interpretation of the statistical evidence concerning weapon-specific success rates in self-defense is unclear (Cook, 1986, 1991).

In sum, we postulate that the type of weapon deployed in violent confrontations appears to matter in several ways. Because guns provide the power to kill quickly, at a distance, and without much skill or strength, they also provide the power to intimidate other people and gain control of a violent situation. When there is a physical attack, then the lethality of the weapon is an important determinant of whether the victim survives. But when the assailant's purpose is robbery, intimidation, or self-defense, rather than inflicting injury, then a gun appears to be more effective than other weapons in achieving that purpose, and without actual use of violence. These hypothesized effects receive support from the empirical work that has been published in this area, but the current state of that evidence surely leaves room for doubt.

Availability

If the type of weapon transforms violent encounters in important ways, as suggested in the preceding discussion, then the extent to which guns are available to violence-prone people is a matter of public concern.

Availability can be thought of as time, expense, and other costs. Violent confrontations often occur unexpectedly, and in such cases, the weapons that will be used are among those that are close at hand; the relevant question is whether a gun is *immediately* available. Logically, the next question concerns the likelihood that a gun will be present *when* a violent confrontation occurs. In particular, do the costs of obtaining a gun and keeping it handy influence the likelihood of gun use in violence?

Arthur L. Kellermann and his associates (1993, 1992) provide evidence on the importance of the first issue, immediate availability. In case control studies of violent events occurring in the home, they found that the likelihoods of both suicide and homicide are greatly elevated by the presence of a gun in the home. The authors selected each control from the same neighborhood as that in which the killing occurred, and through their matching criteria and use of multivariate statistical techniques, attempted to control for other differences between the suicide/homicide cases and cases used as controls. There is no guarantee that this effort to control for other factors that might be confounded with gun possession was successful, so the proper interpretation of these findings remains controversial.[9] If we accept Kellermann et al.'s interpretation, then two propositions follow.

1. If a member of the household owns a gun, then at-home suicide attempts and armed assaults are more likely to involve a gun than otherwise.
2. A gun is more deadly than other weapons would have been in these circumstances (an instrumentality effect).

Extending these propositions, we can ask whether the extent to which guns are readily available in a community influences the likelihood of weapons used in violent crime (and suicide). A recent cross-national comparison for 11 countries indicates a strong positive correlation (.72) between a country's household prevalence of gun ownership and the proportion of homicides committed with a gun (Killias, 1993). This finding suggests that the overall scarcity (or availability) of guns in a country influences weapon choice in violent events.

Within the American context, however, many commentators have expressed doubt that guns are in any sense scarce, or that anyone (including youths and violent criminals) would find it more difficult to obtain a gun than, say, a kitchen knife. Regional comparisons, however, suggest otherwise. The prevalence of gun ownership differs rather widely across urban areas, from around 10% in the cities of the Northeast to upwards of 50% in the Mountain states. (An obvious explanation for these large differences has to do with the differing importance of rural traditions in these areas.[10]) The overall prevalence of gun ownership has been found to be highly correlated with the percentage of homicides, suicides, and robberies that involve guns in these cities (Cook, 1979, 1985). Therefore, where gun ownership is prevalent in the general population, guns tend to be prevalent in violence.

A natural explanation for this pattern is differences among cities in their *scarcity* of guns. Predatory criminals obtain most of their guns from acquaintances, family members, drug dealers, thefts from homes and vehicles, and other street sources, rather than from licensed dealers (Decker, Pennell, & Caldwell, 1997; Sheley & Wright, 1995; Smith, 1996). The ease of making such a connection will be greater in a city in which guns are prevalent. Further, the black markets for guns, which are the ultimate source for perhaps half or more of the crime guns, will tend to be more active in cities in which gun ownership is prevalent (Moore, 1981; Wright & Rossi, 1986).

It helps in thinking about the availability of guns to realize how frequently they change hands. For youthful criminals, acquiring a gun is typically not a one-time decision. One statistic from a survey of inner-city male high school students helps make the point: 22% said they currently owned a gun, whereas an additional 8% indicated that they had owned one or more guns in the past but did not at the time of the interview. Further, the number who said they carried a gun on occasion exceeded the number who owned one, suggesting loans and other temporary arrangements may be important features of this scene (Wright, Sheley, & Smith, 1992). The thrust of this research certainly suggests that acquiring a firearm poses little challenge to those persons who are motivated to acquire one.

Of course, for a gun to be available for use during a violent encounter, it must also be carried. Because most violent crime occurs away from home, one important aspect of gun availability is the propensity to go armed. The majority of states allow carrying concealed handguns (if the carrier has obtained a license) but do not treat violations as serious offenses. A notable exception is the Bartley-Fox Amendment in Massachusetts, which in 1975 legislated a mandatory 1-year prison sentence for anyone convicted of carrying a gun without a license. This mandatory sentence provision received tremendous publicity at the time it was implemented. The immediate impact was that thousands of gun owners applied for the licenses required to carry a handgun legally. Several studies analyzed subsequent trends in violent crime. Among these, Pierce and Bowers (1981) concluded that the short-term impact was to reduce the fractions of assaults and robberies involving guns and, presumably, as a consequence, to reduce the criminal homicide rate (see also Deutsch, 1979). Apparently, some streetwise people were deterred from carrying a gun; as a result, they were more likely to commit their robberies and assaults, when the occasion arose, with weapons other than guns. Because of the instrumentality effect, the death rate was reduced in these attacks.

It is not just street criminals who carry guns; sometimes, their potential victims do as well. The practice of going armed in public has been facilitated in recent years by changes in state laws governing concealed-carry licensing; by 1997, a majority of states had liberal provisions that enable most adults to obtain a license to carry. A controversial study by two economists (Lott & Mustard, 1997) found evidence that states that liberalized their concealed-carry regulations enjoyed a reduction in violent crime rates, presumably because some would-be assailants feared that potential victims might be armed. Black and Nagin (1998), however, using the same data, conclude that there is no evidence of a deterrent effect (see also McDowall, Loftin, & Wiersema, 1995). Stronger conclusions will have to await better evidence.

One important question remains: Does gun availability influence the overall *volume* of violent crime? The existing evidence provides little reason to believe that robbery and assault rates are much affected by the prevalence of gun ownership (Cook, 1979; Kleck & Patterson, 1993). Consequently, that the United States is such a violent country[11] does not have much to do with guns; that our violent crimes *are so deadly*—and thus, our homicide rate so high—however, has *much* to do with availability and use of guns (see Zimring & Hawkins, 1997, for an extensive argument concerning this aspect of crime in the United States).

GUNS AND PUBLIC POLICY: THE VALUES AT STAKE

Used in the manner of our rural sporting tradition, a gun provides recreation, food, and, arguably, a way of learning a sense of responsibility. When kept behind the counter of a small grocery store in a high-crime neighborhood, a gun may serve as a means of self-defense and even a deterrent to crime. When used in a robbery, gang warfare, or domestic violence, however, a gun becomes part of the nation's nightmare of crime that terrorizes urban residents and cuts short far too many lives.

Guns have many uses, all of which have legitimacy to the people who use them in those ways. Society as a whole, however, values some uses less highly than do the individual owners. The result is a "great American gun war," a continuing debate and political struggle to determine which uses will be protected and which should be sacrificed to achieve some greater social good.

The debate about gun control policy makes broad use of both consequentialist and deontological arguments. A *consequentialist* framework is concerned with ascertaining and valuing the consequences of proposed reform, whereas the *deontological* framework is concerned with how a proposed reform measures up in its assignment of civic rights and responsibilities. Advocates on both sides tend to make use of both sets of claims. For instance, control advocates typically argue their case by pointing to the reductions in fatalities engendered by the proposed reform *and* by insisting that gun owners, as a matter of principle, should be willing to relinquish some of their rights to own guns in the interests of achieving these benefits. The anticontrol advocates argue that gun ownership reduces, rather than increases, crime *and* that it is their constitutional right to own guns.

Much of the rhetoric in the debate stems from three broad perspectives that will be considered in the following sections. Two of these, the public health and welfare economics perspectives, are predominantly consequentialist, whereas the third is primarily deontological.

The Public Health Perspective

The essence of the public health framework is whether a proposed control measure would reduce the incidence of injury and death. There is little concern with the value of sporting uses of guns. From this perspective, the modest pleasures associated with recreational shooting and the dubious benefits from self-defense should yield to society's overwhelming interest in reducing gun deaths. Preserving life is the paramount value in this scheme. (For a highly critical review of the public health literature on firearms and homicide, see Blackman, 1997.)

The Welfare Economics Framework

The welfare economics framework is similar to that of the public health framework but has a wider array of consequences and greater attention to individual preferences. It leads us to view the gun "problem" as the harm inflicted on others, with much less attention to suicides and self-inflicted accidents. The uses seen as socially detrimental are virtually the same as those that are prohibited by law. There is no presumption within this framework, however, that punishing criminal uses is an adequate response; consequently, there remains the possibility that the benefits of preemptive controls on guns, such as a ban on carrying concealed handguns, would outweigh the costs. The costs of such controls include the public costs of enforcement and the private costs of compliance (or evasion) of these regulations.

In this calculus of cost and benefit, where does self-defense fit in? For most gun owners, the possibility that the gun will prove useful in fending off a robber or burglar is one source of its value.[12] Indeed, if guns had no value in self-protection, a ban on possession of guns in the home would quite likely be worthwhile, because sporting uses of guns could be preserved by allowing people to store firearms in shooting clubs and use them under regulated conditions. Given this, the self-defense uses of guns ultimately are more important than sporting uses in assessing the costs of restrictions on home possession and carrying in urban areas.

Some writers have even argued that the private valuation of guns in this respect understates their public value because the widespread possession of guns has a *general* deterrent effect on crime (Kleck, 1991; Snyder, 1993). Indeed, one survey of imprisoned felons found that a paramount concern in doing their crimes was the prospect of meeting up with an armed victim (Wright & Rossi, 1986). We do not know, however, whether the predominant effect on criminal behavior is desisting, displacement to victims who are not likely to be armed, or a change in technique. If the latter two predominate, then the overall impact is negative, rather than positive (Clotfelter, 1993).

The "Rights and Responsibilities" Perspective

The welfare economics framework helps organize the arguments pro and con gun controls and suggests a procedure for assigning values. But for those who believe in the "right" to bear arms, it is not a completely satisfactory approach. The debate about gun control can and should be conducted, at least in part, in the context of a framework that defines the appropriate relationship between the individual, the community, and the state.

Much in the foreground of this debate lies the Second Amendment, which states, "A well regulated militia, being necessary to the security of a free State, the right of the people to keep and bear arms, shall not be infringed." The proper interpretation of this statement has been contested in recent years. The U.S. Supreme Court has not chosen to clarify the matter, having ruled only once during this century on a Second Amendment issue, and that on a rather narrow technical basis.[13] Indeed, no federal court has ever overturned a gun control law on Second Amendment grounds.

For most people, the crucial issue concerns self-defense. Some commentators go so far as to assert that there is a public duty for private individuals to defend against criminal predation now, just as there was in 1789 when there were no police. The argument is that if all reliable people were to equip themselves with guns both in the home and out, there would be far less predatory crime (Polsby, 1993; Snyder, 1993). Other commentators, less optimistic about the possibility of creating a more civil society by force of arms, also stress the public duty of gun owners but with an emphasis on responsible use: storing them safely away from children and burglars, learning how to operate them properly, exercising good judgment in deploying them when feeling threatened, and so forth (Karlson & Hargarten, 1997). In any event, the right to bear arms, like the right of free speech, is not absolute but is subject to reasonable restrictions and carries with it certain civic responsibilities. The appropriate extent of those restrictions and responsibilities, however, remains an unresolved issue.

In conclusion, each of these three perspectives—public health, welfare economics, and civic rights and responsibilities—provides arguments about the public interest that seem familiar and important. Each is well represented in the debate about the appropriate regulation of firearms. In practice, the public health perspective helps focus greater attention on suicide, whereas the perspective that stresses civic rights strengthens the case for protecting self-defense uses of guns. We are not inclined to argue the relative merits of these differing perspectives in the abstract but will have more to say about policy evaluation in the next sections.

ALTERNATIVE GUN CONTROL POLICIES

Commerce in guns and the possession and use of guns are regulated by federal, state, and local governments. To assess the options for reform, it is first helpful to understand the current array of controls and why they fail to achieve an acceptably low rate of gun violence.

The Current Array of Policies

The primary objective of federal law in regulating firearms is to insulate the states from one another, so that restrictive laws adopted in some states are not undercut by the greater availability of guns in other states. The Gun Control Act of 1968 established the framework for the current system of controls on gun transfers. All shipments of firearms (including mail-order sales) are limited to federally licensed dealers who are required to obey applicable state and local ordinances. There are also restrictions on sales of guns to out-of-state residents.[14]

Federal law also seeks to establish a minimum set of restrictions on acquisition and possession of guns. The Gun Control Act of 1968 stipulates several categories of people who are denied the right to receive or possess a gun, including illegal aliens, convicted felons and those under indictment, and people who have at some time been involuntarily committed to a mental institution. Persons with a history of substance abuse are also prohibited from possessing a gun. Dealers are not allowed to sell handguns to people younger than 21 years old or to sell long guns to those younger than 18, although there is no federal prohibition of gun *possession* by youth. These various prohibitions are implemented by a requirement that the buyer sign a form stating that he or she does not fall into any of the proscribed categories.

A number of states have adopted significant restrictions on commerce in firearms, especially handguns. As of 1993, a majority of states require that handgun buyers obtain a permit or license before taking possession of a handgun. All but a few state transfer-control systems are "permissive" in the sense that most people are legally entitled to obtain a gun. In a few jurisdictions, however, it is difficult to obtain a handgun legally. The most stringent is Washington, D.C., where only law enforcement officers and security guards are entitled to obtain a handgun (Jones, 1981). In 1993, Congress adopted the Brady Bill, which requires dealers in states without screening systems for handgun buyers to enforce a 5-day waiting period between the purchase and transfer of a handgun. The dealers are required to notify law enforcement officials shortly after the purchase in order that a background check can be run on the buyer.[15]

State and local legislation tends to make a sharp distinction between keeping a gun in one's home or business and carrying a gun in public. All but a few states either ban concealed weapons entirely or require a special license for carrying concealed weapons (although many states have recently eased the requirements for obtaining a license). Local ordinances typically place additional restrictions on carrying and discharging guns inside city limits.

Some sense of the variety of possibilities here is suggested by this list of recent efforts, proposed or adopted, to extend additional control over firearms commerce and use:

1. Imposing a heavy federal tax on ammunition
2. Banning the sale and possession of assault rifles at the state level
3. Limiting handgun sales to no more than one per month per customer
4. Requiring that gun buyers pass a test demonstrating their knowledge of law and good practice in handling a gun
5. Raising the fees charged to acquire a federal license for gun dealing
6. Trying local drug dealers in the federal courts if they are in possession of a gun at the time of their arrest
7. Offering cash, tickets to sporting events, or even toys in exchange for guns
8. Establishing minimum mandatory sentences for illegally carrying guns
9. Using public education campaigns and the co-operation of the television industry to stigmatize storing unlocked, loaded guns in households
10. Giving the police power to revoke licenses and search intensively for guns in residences for which court restraining orders have been issued against spouses

11. Using magnetometers to keep guns out of schools
12. Developing a "parents' compact" to promote parents' efforts to prevent their children from possessing or carrying guns

Facing such a daunting array of possibilities for legislation, policymakers need guidance on which approaches hold the most promise of reducing firearms violence, and at what cost to legitimate owners. Reliable information is difficult to obtain; still, some evidence is available concerning which general approaches show the most promise. In searching for worthwhile reforms, we find it useful to classify alternative gun control measures into three categories: (a) those designed to affect the supply and overall availability of guns, (b) those designed to influence who has these weapons, and (c) those designed to affect how the guns are used by the people who have them.

On the basis of combined empirical evidence and logic, the generic strengths and weaknesses of each category can be sketched. The result is a rough map of the relevant terrain with some of the details missing, but it is nonetheless a useful guide.

Reducing Overall Supply and Availability

Many gun control measures focus on the supply and availability of the guns themselves (or, in one imaginative leap, on the ammunition that makes them deadly). The basic idea is that if guns (or ammunition) become less readily available, or more expensive to purchase, then some violence-prone people will decide to rely on other weapons instead, and gun violence will be reduced.

Many commentators have suggested that this approach is doomed by the huge arsenal of guns currently in private hands. How can we discourage violence-prone people from obtaining guns when there are already enough in circulation to arm every teenager and adult in the country? In response, we note that the number of guns in circulation is only indirectly relevant to whether supply restrictions can hope to succeed; of direct consequence is the *price* and *difficulty* of obtaining a gun. Our discussion of availability in a previous section helps establish the evidence on these matters—availability *does* seem to matter, even within the current context of widespread private ownership.

Basic economic reasoning suggests that if the price of new guns is increased by amending the federal tax or other means, the effects will ripple through all the markets in which guns are transferred, including the black market for stolen guns (Cook & Leitzel, 1996). If the average prices of guns go up, some people—including some violence-prone people—will decide that there are better uses for their money. Others will be discouraged if, in addition to raising the money price, the amount of time or risk required to obtain a gun increases. Although there are no reliable estimates of the elasticity of demand for guns by youths, we believe that youths, in particular, are likely to be more responsive to price than to more remote costs (such as the possibility of arrest and punishment). Those who argue that youthful offenders will do whatever is necessary to obtain their guns may have some hard-core group of violent gang members and drug dealers in mind, but surely not the much larger group of kids who rarely get into serious trouble (see Sheley & Wright, 1995; Smith, 1996).

At present, a substantial increase in the federal tax on the purchase of firearms is under discussion for the first time in memory. Potentially even more important is the growing possibility of successful tort litigation against manufacturers of cheap concealable handguns, which, if successful, would raise the price of even the cheapest guns (Teret, 1986). Another approach to raising prices, however, is to impose safety requirements on gun manufacturers. Proposals in this area include "childproofing" guns so that they are inoperable by children; requiring that domestically manufactured guns meet the same safety requirements as imports, including protections against accidental discharge; and requiring safety devices such as trigger locks and loaded chamber indicators (Teret & Wintemute, 1993). As it is now, firearms manufacturers are remarkably free of safety regulation, in part because the Consumer Product Safety Commission has no authority over personal firearms. Although such regulations may be welcomed by gun buyers who are seeking some protection against gun accidents, they would have little direct effect on suicide and criminal misuse of firearms. To the extent that complying with such regulations made guns more costly, however, there could be some indirect effect comparable with raising the federal tax (Cook & Leitzel, 1996).

A more far-reaching proposal is to encourage the manufacture of guns that are "personalized," in the sense that they would be equipped with an electronic sensing device that would recognize a ring on the owner's finger, or even the owner's fingerprint. Such devices are currently under development. If they prove reliable, law enforcement agencies may adopt them to protect officers from being assaulted with their own guns. Equipping all new handguns with such devices would gradually reduce the number of gun accidents and reduce the profitability of stealing guns.

Restricting Access

The second broad class of gun control policy instruments includes those designed to influence who has access to different types of weapons. The intuitive notion here is that if we could find a way to keep guns out of the hands of the "bad guys" without denying access to the "good guys," then gun crimes would decrease without infringing on the legitimate uses of guns. The challenges for this type of policy are, first, to decide where to draw the line and, second, to develop effective barriers to prevent guns from crossing this line.

Who should be trusted with a gun? Federal law rules out several large groups, including drug users and illegal aliens, but there are no ready means of identifying those who fall into these categories. Public records provide more information on criminal background, and there is an important debate concerning what sort of criminal record should be disqualifying. Any felony conviction strips an individual of the right to own a gun under federal law, although many felons are able to obtain court orders allowing them to possess guns after they have served their sentences.

A fundamental premise underlying much gun legislation holds that owning a gun is a right granted to all adults[16] unless they do something to disqualify themselves, such as committing a serious crime. A different approach would be to treat gun ownership as a privilege, as is the case, say, with driving a vehicle on public highways. Similar to driving privileges, one eminently sensible requirement for those who seek to acquire a gun is that they demonstrate knowledge of how to use it safely and legally. An intriguing possibility is that such a requirement would engender considerable growth in the National Rifle Association's safety training programs because many of those wishing to qualify for a license would need to enroll in such a course.

Wherever the line is drawn, there is the serious problem of defending it against illegal transfers. That task is currently being done poorly. The major loopholes stem from the widespread abuse of the federal licensing system, the lack of effective screening of those who seek to buy guns from dealers, a vigorous and largely unregulated "gray" market by which used guns change hands, and an active black market supplied by theft, scofflaw gun dealers (those who knowingly violate the terms of their license on a frequent basis), and interstate gunrunning operations.

Federal Licensing System. The U.S. Bureau of Alcohol, Tobacco, and Firearms (ATF) is the agency charged with the regulation of federally licensed gun dealers. It is a small agency whose jurisdiction includes not only regulatory inspections of gun dealers but also criminal investigations of violations of federal gun laws. As well, it is responsible for the regulatory surveillance and criminal investigation of the explosives, alcohol, and tobacco industries. Obtaining a federal dealer's license from ATF was formerly just a matter of paying a small fee and filling out a form, and in 1993, there were 260,000 people who had done so—far more than were genuinely in the business of selling guns to the public. At that time, ATF lacked the authority and resources to screen applicants effectively or to inspect their operations after issuing the license (Violence Policy Center, 1992). In response to this problem, recent changes in application requirements, combined with the hefty increase in fee mandated by the Brady Law, have had the effect of reducing the number of federal licensees to about 100,000 (as of 1997) and of greatly enhancing ATF's ability to serve its regulatory function.

Screening. People who seek to buy handguns from a dealer are required to submit to state permit requirements or, if there are none, a 5-day waiting period required by federal law. If the dealer and purchaser comply with this requirement, there is some chance that disqualified buyers will be identified and screened out. But felons, youths, and others who are not permitted to purchase a gun can ask a qualified friend or relative to make a "straw man" purchase from a dealer on their behalf or find a scofflaw dealer who is willing to sell guns off the books. Most common of all is simply to purchase a gun from a nondealer.

Black and Gray Markets. There is a remarkably active and open market for used guns that is largely unregulated, a market in which buyers and sellers find each other through gun shows, word of mouth, or the classified ads. These transactions are often entirely legal; someone who sells a gun or two on occasion is not subject to any federal requirements except that they not knowingly sell to a felon, illicit drug user, or other person prohibited from possessing a gun.[17]

In considering intervention strategies, it is useful to distinguish between transfers that move guns from the licit to the illicit sectors and transfers within the illicit sector (Koper & Reuter, 1996). In the former category are sales by scofflaw dealers and theft from legitimate owners, whereas the latter includes the active but highly disorganized black market for guns in which kids and criminals frequently buy and sell (Cook, Molliconi, & Cole, 1995; Kennedy, 1994).

Perhaps the best hope for reducing gun trafficking to youths and criminals is a multifaceted enforcement and regulatory effort aimed primarily at reducing the flow of guns from the licit to the illicit sector. On the regulatory side, the main objective is to rein in scofflaw dealers, which most states have left to the ATF. ATF's capacity to act effectively has been strengthened in recent years by the great reduction in the number of licensed dealers resulting from changes in ATF licensing procedures and the increase in the initial license fee from $30 to $200 that was required in the Brady Law. ATF is also beginning to exploit gun tracing data to identify dealers who are frequently involved in selling guns that are used in crime. Further regulatory efforts to discourage gunrunning include the requirement that dealers report multiple purchases and the prohibition adopted by several states on sale of more than one handgun to a customer per month.

Designing policies to reduce theft is conceptually more difficult, yet with an estimated 500,000 guns a year being transferred this way (Cook & Ludwig, 1996), it is just as important. To reduce this source of crime guns, it may be possible to impose some obligation on gun dealers and gun owners to store their weapons securely (as we now do on pharmacists who sell abusable drugs) and to step up enforcement against fences who happen to deal in stolen guns.

Interdicting transfers *within* the illicit sector falls most naturally to local police, although this has been a low-priority mission for most police departments. Because there has been so little experience with local investigations directed at stopping the redistribution of guns among youths, drug dealers, and others in the illicit sector, it is not clear what can be accomplished in

this arena. The analogy to drug enforcement may provide some guidance, but gun markets appear different from heroin and cocaine markets for several reasons, so the effectiveness of similar strategies is open to question (Koper & Reuter, 1996; Moore, 1981).

Considering its various components, the illicit gun market is best seen as a relatively large number of persons engaging in relatively unspecialized enterprises. It is filled with burglars who happen to find some guns next to the household items they wish to steal, some small entrepreneurs who brought a small stock of guns back from the South, gangs who have accumulated an arsenal for their own purposes, and those persons who sometimes are willing to sell a gun to a colleague barred from making a legal purchase. The type of enforcement that would be appropriate in attacking such markets is probably a high-volume "buy and bust" operation (Moore, 1983). Law enforcement agencies may be reluctant to launch an operation of this sort, given the danger inherent in dealing with guns and the legal difficulties in proving that the guns they are buying are actually stolen and being sold illegally. Consequently, the possibilities for choking off supply to the illicit sector appear more promising than attempting to disrupt their activities.

Controlling Uses

The third broad class of gun control policy instruments is concerned with limiting unsafe and criminal uses of guns. Most prominent are provisions for increasing prison sentences when a gun is used in a crime. One clear advantage of this approach as compared with other gun policies is that it does not impinge on legitimate uses of guns. A recent analysis of crime trends in jurisdictions that adopted such sentencing provisions provides evidence that they may be effective in reducing the homicide rate (McDowall, Loftin, & Wiersema, 1992a).

Another and far more controversial tactic is to focus local law enforcement efforts on illegal possession and carrying. As discussed earlier, the potential effectiveness of this approach is suggested by the success of the Bartley-Fox Amendment in Massachusetts. This sort of gun enforcement typically requires proactive police efforts, and there is considerable variation among police departments in how much effort they direct to halting illegal possession and gun carrying (Moore, 1980). The controversy about enforcement stems in part from the concern that police, if sufficiently motivated, may conduct illegal searches in the effort to get guns off the street. More fundamentally, treating illegal carrying as a serious crime puts in jeopardy millions of otherwise law-abiding people who carry guns for self-protection. Nonetheless, gun-oriented patrol tactics appear to have the potential to reduce gun violence (Sherman, Shaw, & Rogan, 1995).

Rather than a general effort to get guns off the streets, a more focused effort can be directed at prohibiting guns in particularly dangerous locations such as homes with histories of domestic violence, bars with histories of drunken brawls, parks in which gang fights tend to break out, and schools in which teachers and students have been assaulted.[18] Often, in seeking to reduce the presence of weapons in these particularly dangerous places, groups other than the police may be mobilized to help make the laws effective. Victimized spouses or their advocates might help enforce rules against guns in violence-prone households, liquor-licensing agencies might be enlisted to help keep guns out of bars, the recreation department might be mobilized to reduce gun carrying in public parks, and so on. The point is that there may be some particular hot spots for gun offenses that could be targeted as places to concentrate gun enforcement efforts much as we focus on keeping guns and bombs out of airplanes.

CONCLUSION: WHAT'S TO BE DONE?

Given the important value conflicts and empirical uncertainties surrounding gun control policies, some caution in recommending public or governmental action is warranted. But recommending caution is far from recommending *inaction*. Indeed, we think that it is time to get on with the business of actively exploring alternative gun control initiatives to develop more effective interventions than those on which we now rely. The goal of gun control policy during the next decade should be to develop and evaluate specific gun control measures that can reduce gun crimes, suicides, and accidents, while preserving as much legitimate use of guns as possible. There is no reason to believe that there is a single best policy. Rather, we should be looking for a combination of policies that address the full array of gun "problems." To some extent, these policies should differ according to local circumstances and values, with an emphasis ranging from suicide prevention in Iowa to street violence in Washington,

D.C. The following suggestions are organized according to the level of government at which the appropriate action should occur.

Action at the Federal Level

The federal government is best positioned to make guns more valuable and harder to obtain while insulating the states from one another's supply of guns. Among the next steps that appear most promising are these:

1. Raise the tax on guns and ammunition to make the cost of acquiring and owning particular types of guns more accurately reflect the social costs and benefits of having them. For instance, we favor converting the current excise tax, which is proportional to the wholesale price, to a flat tax. Cheap handguns do as much damage as expensive ones. On the one hand, we recognize that this tax is regressive and will be particularly burdensome on poorer people who want a gun. On the other hand, the benefit of such a tax, reductions in gun crimes and accidents, will be disproportionately experienced by the poor, who are vastly overrepresented among the victims of gunshot wounds and deaths.

2. Require all gun transfers to pass through federally licensed dealers, with the same screening and paperwork provisions as if the gun were being sold by the dealer.

3. Step up criminal enforcement efforts against gunrunning operations.

4. Provide funding and technical know-how to enhance the quality and completeness of state and federal criminal records files and facilitating access by law enforcement agencies to these files.[19]

5. Enhance cooperation with the local law enforcement efforts in investigating and prosecuting those who deal in stolen guns.

6. Mandating that new guns meet minimum safety requirements to reduce gun accidents, while encouraging research in devices to personalize guns.

The federal government is also in the best position to accumulate the national experience with gun control policy initiatives. For instance, the National Institute of Justice could expedite the search for more effective gun control policies by noting and evaluating the large number of diverse policy interventions that will be launched at different levels of government during the next few years. As well, the surgeon general and attorney general together could use their offices to help create an environment in which local governments, community groups, and private individuals would begin to change their attitudes and behaviors with respect to guns. The message should be clear: Guns are dangerous, particularly in an urban environment, and it is important that owners learn how to store them safely and use them responsibly.

Action at the State Level

The agenda for each state will and should depend on its circumstances. In the past, the states have been the laboratory for instituting a variety of licensing and regulatory programs, as well as establishing different sentencing schemes for use of guns in crime and for carrying illegally. Technology transfer can take place only if these innovations are subjected to careful evaluation.

A battle in the state arena looms over the extent of liability for manufacturers, sellers, and owners of guns when a gun is used to injure someone. Lawsuits based on a variety of liability theories are moving through the courts. The implicit threat posed by these lawsuits is that if manufacturers and sellers are held responsible for the damage done by handguns, the monetary liability would be prohibitive. This possibility is appealing to those who are impatient with the more moderate results achievable through the political process.

Action at the Metropolitan or Municipal Level

Perhaps the greatest opportunities to work on reducing gun violence in the immediate future lie in the cities in which the toll of gun violence is so high. It is there that the scales balancing the competing values of rights to gun ownership on one hand, and the social interest in reducing gun violence on the other, tilt decidedly toward reducing gun violence. Working against effective gun legislation at this level, however, is a persistent fear of crime and the fervent belief by some that a gun will provide protection. Thus, one significant goal of gun control policy at the local level should be not simply to reduce the availability of guns but to find other, less socially costly means that people can use to produce security and reduce fear. In many cities, this is one of the important goals of shifting to a strategy of community policing. To the extent that efforts associated with this strategy help to diminish fear of crime, these measures might also reduce the perceived need for individual gun ownership; with that accomplished, an increase in the range of feasible and desirable gun control policies might become possible.

The particular targets of city efforts against gun violence that seem important to us are these:

1. Reducing gun carrying by offenders on city streets
2. Reducing youth access to and use of all types of weapons[20]
3. Keeping guns out of places that have records of violent conflicts, such as rowdy bars, homes in which domestic violence often occurs, and other community hot spots

Exactly how to accomplish these particular objectives remains unclear, but it is not hard to list particular actions one could imagine police departments undertaking. Indeed, bringing gun crime down is a good exercise in problem solving to turn over to an innovative police agency.

Action at the Community and Household Level

Through the long run, effective gun control may be best achieved by action at the community and household level, rather than at the governmental level. Just as the battles against the costly social consequences of smoking and drinking (and to some degree, drug abuse) are now being advanced through volunteer community initiatives, so may the problem of gun violence be eased as the public demands that individuals become more responsible gun owners. For instance, in particularly risky circumstances, such as continuing domestic violence or if a member of the household is suicidal, neighbors, counselors, and social workers must be prepared to insist that any guns be removed from those premises.

The challenge of implementing effective gun control measures in the United States is daunting in the face of our considerable uncertainty about what works, especially when coupled with the profound national disagreement about which values concerning guns are most important. Still, with continuing attention to the evidence generated by the state and local innovations, and a vigorous public dialogue on the importance of both rights and responsibilities in this arena, there is every hope of doing better. There is little doubt that one of the benefits of such success would be a reduced rate of homicide in the United States.

NOTES

1. Kleck (1991, Appendix 2) offers another explanation, that gun ownership increased during the past couple of decades but that

survey respondents have become increasingly reluctant to admit to gun ownership during this period. We favor our explanation because it is supported by the survey evidence on the number of guns per household as well as by the growth in household disposable income during this period.

2. These patterns are based on surveys and are subject to potential biases induced by the sensitivity of the topic and the difficulty of contacting a representative sample of young urban males.

3. Much has been made of the unintentional firearm deaths of children, but tragic as such cases are, they are quite rare. Between 1985 and 1990, the annual average number of deaths for children less than 10 years old was 94 (Fingerhut, 1993).

4. On the other hand, the demography of gun suicide looks much more like that of gun sports, with victims coming disproportionately from the ranks of older White men.

5. Pierce and Fox (1992) demonstrate that between 1985 and 1991, the homicide arrest rate for males more than doubled for those under age 21, while actually declining for those age 30 and older (see also Blumstein, 1995; Smith & Feiler, 1995).

6. It is, after all, a tautology.

7. Kleck, like Wright et al. (1983), claims that Zimring and others have not succeeded in demonstrating that guns are more lethal than knives but accept with confidence the claim that long guns are more lethal than handguns. See Cook (1991) for a discussion of this paradox.

8. The source is unpublished data provided by the Bureau of Justice Statistics. See Cook (1991) for details.

9. The authors of the case-control study of homicide discuss the possibility that their results are due in part to reverse causation, noting that in a limited number of cases, people may have acquired a gun in response to a specific threat, which eventually led to their murder. They also note that both gun ownership and homicide may be influenced by a third, unidentified factor (Kellermann et al., 1993). From those characteristics that were observed in this study, it is clear that the victims differed from the controls in ways that may have contributed to the likelihood that there was a gun in the house. In comparison with their controls, the cases or the people they lived with were more likely to have a criminal record, to use illicit drugs, and to have a drinking problem.

10. Kleck and Patterson (1993) assert that the intercity differences in the prevalence of gun ownership are influenced by crime rates. Although this may explain some small part of the variance, it could not reasonably be considered the dominant explanation. For one thing, the vast majority of gun owners in the United States are sportsmen, for whom self-defense is a secondary purpose at most.

11. A recent comparison of victim survey estimates found that the U.S. robbery rate was substantially higher than that of England, Germany, Hungary, Hong Kong, Scotland, and Switzerland. On the other hand, Canada's robbery rate was nearly twice as high as that of the United States (Block, 1993).

12. This is true not just for law-abiding citizens but is felt even more keenly by drug dealers and other criminals who are frequently threatened by the bad company they keep (Wright & Rossi, 1986).

13. William Van Alstyne (1994) argues that the Second Amendment has generated almost no useful body of law to date, substantially because of the Supreme Court's inertia on this subject. In his view, Second Amendment law is currently as undeveloped as First Amendment law was up until Holmes and Brandeis began taking it seriously in a series of opinions in the 1920s.

14. The McClure-Volkmer Amendment of 1986 eased the restriction on out-of-state purchases of rifles and shotguns. Such purchases are now legal as long as they comply with the regulations of both the buyer's state of residence and the state in which the sale occurs.

15. On June 27, 1997, the Supreme Court ruled that the federal requirement that local law enforcement agencies conduct background searches on the purchasers of handguns could not be enforced.

16. Although federal law does not prohibit gun possession by youths, a number of states have placed limits on when youths can carry guns in public.

17. A provision of the 1986 McClure-Volkmer Amendments to the Gun Control Act creates a federal criminal liability for individuals who transfer a gun to a person they know or have reasonable cause to believe falls into one of the seven high-risk categories specified in the act.

18. Surprisingly, it is a *federal* crime (under the Gun-Free School Zones Act of 1990) for an individual to carry a gun in a school zone.

19. Upgrading criminal history files will of course have value in a variety of other law enforcement tasks as well.

20. Boston has implemented a comprehensive strategy of this sort. The Boston Gun Project was designed to curb the city's epidemic of youth gun violence and has met with considerable success. See Kennedy, Piehl, and Braga (1996) for a description and analysis of the program.

REFERENCES

BLACK, D., & NAGIN, D. (1998). Do "right-to-carry" laws deter violent crime? *Journal of Legal Studies, 26,* 209–220.

BLACKMAN, P. H. (1997). A critique of the epidemiologic study of firearms and homicide. *Homicide Studies, 1,* 169–189.

BLOCK, R. L. (1993). A cross-section comparison of the victims of crime: Victim surveys of twelve countries. *International Review of Criminology, 2,* 183–207.

BLUMSTEIN, A. (1995). Youth violence, guns, and the illicit-drug industry. *Journal of Criminal Law and Criminology, 86,* 10–36.

BUREAU OF JUSTICE STATISTICS. (1997). *Criminal victimization in the United States, 1994* (NCJ-162126). Washington, DC: Government Printing Office.

CENTERS FOR DISEASE CONTROL AND PREVENTION. (1997). CDC WONDER [On-line]. Available: http://wonder.cdc.gov/WONDER.

CLOTFELTER, C. T. (1993). The private life of public economics. *Southern Economic Journal, 59,* 579–596.

CONKLIN, J. E. (1972). *Robbery and the criminal justice system.* Philadelphia: J. B. Lippincott.

COOK, P. J. (1976). A strategic choice analysis of robbery. In W. Skogan (Ed.), *Sample surveys of the victims of crimes* (pp. 173–187). Cambridge, MA: Ballinger.

COOK, P. J. (1979). The effect of gun availability on robbery and robbery murder: A cross section study of fifty cities. In R. H. Haveman & B. B. Zellner (Eds.), *Policy studies review annual* (Vol. 3, pp. 743–781). Beverly Hills, CA: Sage.

COOK, P. J. (1980). Reducing injury and death rates in robbery. *Policy Analysis, 6,* 21–45.

COOK, P. J. (1985). The case of the missing victims: Gunshot woundings in the National Crime Survey. *Journal of Quantitative Criminology, 1,* 91–102.

COOK, P. J. (1986). The relationship between victim resistance and injury in noncommercial robbery. *Journal of Legal Studies, 15,* 405–416.

COOK, P. J. (1987). Robbery violence. *Journal of Criminal Law and Criminology, 78,* 357–376.

COOK, P. J. (1991). The technology of personal violence. In M. H. Tonry (Ed.), *Crime and justice: A review of research* (Vol. 14, pp. 1–71). Chicago: University of Chicago Press.

COOK, P. J. (1993). Notes on the availability and prevalence of firearms. *American Journal of Preventive Medicine, 9*, 33–38.

COOK, P. J., & LEITZEL, J. A. (1996). Perversity, futility, jeopardy: An economic analysis of the attack on gun control. *Law and Contemporary Problems, 59*, 91–118.

COOK, P. J., & LUDWIG, J. (1996). *Guns in America: Results of a comprehensive national survey on firearms ownership and use.* Washington, DC: Police Foundation.

COOK, P. J., LUDWIG, J., & HEMENWAY, D. (1997). The gun debate's new mythical number: How many defensive gun uses per year? *Journal of Policy Analysis and Management, 16*, 463–469.

COOK, P. J., MOLLICONI, S., & COLE, T. B. (1995). Regulating gun markets. *Journal of Criminal Law and Criminology, 86*, 59–92.

DECKER, S. H., PENNELL, S., & CALDWELL, A. (1997). *Illegal firearms: Access and use by arrestees* (NCJ-163496). Washington, DC: Bureau of Justice Statistics.

DEUTSCH, S. J. (1979). Lies, damn lies, and statistics: A rejoinder to the comment by Hay and McCleary. *Evaluation Quarterly, 3*, 315–328.

FEDERAL BUREAU OF INVESTIGATION. (1971–1997). *Crime in the United States: Uniform crime reports.* Washington, DC: Government Printing Office.

FINGERHUT, L. A. (1993). Firearm mortality among children, youth, and young adults 1–34 years of age, trends and current status: United States, 1985–90. *Advance data from vital and health statistics* (No. 231). Hyattsville, MD: National Center for Health Statistics.

JONES, E. D., III. (1981). The District of Columbia's Firearms Control Regulations Act of 1975: The toughest handgun control law in the United States—or is it? *Annals of the American Academy of Political and Social Sciences, 455*, 138–149.

KARLSON, T. A., & HARGARTEN, S. W. (1997). *Reducing firearm injury and death: A public health sourcebook on guns.* New Brunswick, NJ: Rutgers University Press.

KELLERMANN, A. L., RIVARA, F. P., RUSHFORTH, N. B., BANTON, J. G., REAY, D. T., FRANCISCO, J. T., LOCCI, A. B., PRODZINSKI, J. P., HACKMAN, B. B., & SOMES, G. (1993). Gun ownership as a risk factor for homicide in the home. *New England Journal of Medicine, 329*, 1084–1091.

KELLERMANN, A. L., RIVARA, F. P., SOMES, G., REAY, D. T., FRANCISCO, J. T., BANTON, J. G., PRODZINSKI, J. P., FLIGNER, C., & HACKMAN, B. B. (1992). Suicide in the home in relation to gun ownership. *New England Journal of Medicine, 327*, 467–472.

KENNEDY, D. M. (1994). Can we keep guns away from kids? *The American Prospect, 18*, 74–80.

KENNEDY, D. M., PIEHL, A. M., & BRAGA, A. A. (1996). Youth violence in Boston: Gun markets, serious youth offenders, and a use-reduction strategy. *Law and Contemporary Problems, 59*, 147–196.

KILLIAS, M. (1993). Gun ownership, suicide, and homicide: An international perspective. In A. Del Frate, U. Zvekic, & J. J. M. van Dijk (Eds.), *Understanding crime: Experiences of crime and crime control* (pp. 289–302). Rome: United States Interregional Crime and Justice Research Institute.

KLECK, G. (1984). Handgun-only control: A policy disaster in the making. In D. B. Kates, Jr. (Ed.), *Firearms and violence: Issues of public policy* (pp. 167–199). Cambridge, MA: Ballinger.

KLECK, G. (1988). Crime control through the private use of armed force. *Social Problems, 35*, 1–22.

KLECK, G. (1991). *Point blank: Guns and violence in America.* New York: Aldine de Gruyter.

KLECK, G., & GERTZ, M. (1995). Armed resistance to crime: The prevalence and nature of self-defense with a gun. *Journal of Criminal Law and Criminology, 86*, 150–187.

KLECK, G., & MCELRATH, K. (1991). The effects of weaponry on human violence. *Social Forces, 69*, 669–692.

KLECK, G., & PATTERSON, E. B. (1993). The impact of gun control and gun ownership levels on violence rates. *Journal of Quantitative Criminology, 9*, 249–287.

KOPER, C. S., & REUTER, P. (1996). Suppressing illegal gun markets: Lessons from drug enforcement. *Law and Contemporary Problems, 59*, 119–143.

LOTT, J. R., JR., & MUSTARD, D. B. (1997). Crime, deterrence and right-to-carry concealed handguns. *Journal of Legal Studies, 26*, 1–68.

MCDOWALL, D., LOFTIN, C., & WIERSEMA, B. (1992a). A comparative study of the preventive effects of mandatory sentencing laws for gun crimes. *Journal of Criminal Law and Criminology, 83*, 378–394.

MCDOWALL, D., LOFTIN, C., & WIERSEMA, B. (1992b). *The incidence of civilian defensive firearm use.* Unpublished manuscript, University of Maryland-College Park, Institute of Criminal Justice.

MCDOWALL, D., LOFTIN, C., & WIERSEMA, B. (1995). Easing concealed firearms laws: Effects on homicide in three states. *Journal of Criminal Law and Criminology, 86*, 193–206.

MOORE, M. H. (1980). Police and weapons offenses. *Annals of the American Academy of Political and Social Science, 452*, 22–32.

MOORE, M. H. (1981). Keeping handguns from criminal offenders. *Annals of the American Academy of Political and Social Science, 455*, 92–109.

MOORE, M. H. (1983). The bird in hand: A feasible strategy for gun control. *Journal of Policy Analysis and Management, 2*, 185–195.

PIERCE, G. L., & BOWERS, W. J. (1981). The Bartley-Fox Gun Law's short-term impact on crime in Boston. *Annals of the American Academy of Political and Social Science, 455*, 120–137.

PIERCE, G. L., & FOX, J. A. (1992). *Recent trends in violent crime: A closer look.* Unpublished manuscript, Northeastern University, Boston.

POLSBY, D. D. (1993, October). Equal protection. *Reason, 25*, 35–38.

SALTZMAN, L. E., MERCY, J. A., O'CARROLL, P. W., ROSENBERG, M. L., & RHODES, P. H. (1992). Weapon involvement and injury outcomes in family and intimate assaults. *Journal of the American Medical Association, 267*, 3043–3047.

SHELEY, J. F., & WRIGHT, J. D. (1995). *In the line of fire: Youth, guns, and violence in urban America.* New York: Aldine de Gruyter.

SHERMAN, L., SHAW, J. W., & ROGAN, D. P. (1995). *The Kansas City gun experiment.* Washington, DC: National Institute of Justice.

SKOGAN, W. (1978). *Weapon use in robbery: Patterns and policy implications.* Unpublished manuscript, Northwestern University, Evanston, IL.

SMITH, M. D. (1996). Sources of firearm acquisition among a sample of inner-city youths: Research results and policy implications. *Journal of Criminal Justice, 24*, 361–367.

SMITH, M. D., & FEILER, S. M. (1995). Absolute and relative involvement in homicide offending: Contemporary youth and the baby boom cohorts. *Violence and Victims, 10*, 327–333.

SNYDER, J. R. (1993). A nation of cowards. *The Public Interest, 113*, 40–55.

TERET, S. P. (1986). Litigating for the public's health. *American Journal of Public Health, 76*, 1027–1029.

TERET, S. P., & WINTEMUTE, G. (1993). Policies to prevent firearm injuries. *Health Affairs, 12*(4), 96–108.

U.S. DEPARTMENT OF THE INTERIOR. (1991). *Survey of fishing, hunting, and wildlife-associated recreation.* Washington, DC: Government Printing Office.

VAN ALSTYNE, W. (1994). *The Second Amendment and the personal right to arms.* Durham, NC: Duke University School of Law.

VIOLENCE POLICY CENTER. (1992). *More gun dealers than gas stations.* Washington, DC: Author.

VIOLENCE POLICY CENTER. (1997). *Who dies?* Washington, DC: Author.

WOLFGANG, M. E. (1958). *Patterns in criminal homicide.* Philadelphia: University of Pennsylvania Press.

WRIGHT, J. D. (1981). Public opinion and gun control: A comparison of results from two recent national surveys. *Annals of the American Academy of Political and Social Science, 455,* 24–39.

WRIGHT, J. D., & ROSSI, P. H. (1986). *Armed and considered dangerous: A survey of felons and their firearms.* Hawthorne, NY: Aldine.

WRIGHT, J. D., ROSSI, P. H., & DALY, K. (1983). *Under the gun: Weapons, crime, and violence in America.* Hawthorne, NY: Aldine.

WRIGHT, J. D., SHELEY, J. F., & SMITH, M. D. (1992). Kids, guns, and killing fields. *Society, 30*(1), 84–89.

ZIMRING, F. E. Is gun control likely to reduce violent killings? *University of Chicago Law Review, 35,* 21–37.

ZIMRING, F. E. (1972). The medium is the message: Firearm caliber as a determinant of death from assault. *Journal of Legal Studies, 1,* 97–124.

ZIMRING, F. E., & HAWKINS, G. (1997). *Crime is not the problem: Lethal violence in America.* New York: Oxford University Press.

It's Only Art

Karen Finley

I went into a museum but they had taken down all the art. Only the empty frames were left. Pieces of masking tape were up with the names of the paintings and the artists stating why they were removed. The guards had nothing to guard. The white walls yellowed. Toilets were locked up in museums because people might think someone peeing is art. Someone might think that pee flushing down that toilet is art. Someone might think that the act of peeing is a work of art. And the government pays for that pee flushing down that toilet. There were many bladder infections among those who inspected the museum making sure that there was no offensive art. They might lose their jobs. It's a good life when no one thinks that you ever piss or shit.

In the empty frames were the reasons why art was confiscated.

Jasper Johns—for desecrating the flag.
Michelangelo—for being a homosexual.
Mary Cassatt—for painting nude children.
Van Gogh—for contributing to psychedelia.
Georgia O'Keefe—for painting cow skulls (the dairy industry complained).
Picasso—for urinating, apparently, on his sculptures, with the help of his children, to achieve the desired patina effect.

Edward Hopper—for repressed lust.
Jeff Koons—for offending Michael Jackson.

All ceramicists were banned because working with clay was too much like playing with your own shit.

All glassblowing became extinct because it was too much like giving a blow job.

All art from cultures that didn't believe in one male god was banned for being blasphemous.

We looked for the show of early American quilts, but it had been taken down. One guard said that a period stain was found on one, another guard said he found an ejaculation stain on a quilt from Virginia. In fact, they closed all of the original thirteen states. You can imagine what happened under those quilts at night!

Since the Confiscation of Art occurred, an Art Propaganda Army was started by the government. Last month the national assignment for the army artists was to make Dan Quayle look smart. The assignment for the army writers was to make the stealth bomber as important as the microwave oven. Musicians were asked to write a tune, how the HUD scandal was no big deal, like taking sugar packets from a cafe.

Dancers were to choreograph a dance showing that the Iran-Contra affair was as harmless as your dog going into your neighbors yard. And filmmakers were told to make films about homelessness, poverty and AIDS, saying that God has a plan for us all.

But no art came out.

No art was made.

Newspapers became thin and disappeared because there was no more criticism. There was nothing to gossip about. Schools closed because learning got in the way of patriotism. No one could experiment, for that was the way of the devil.

There was no theory. No academia. No debate teams. No "Jeopardy."

Everyone became old overnight. There was no more reasons for anything. Everything became old and gray. Everyone had blue-gray skin like the color of bones, unfriendly seas and navy bean soup. And then the Punishers, the Executioners, the Judges of creativity grew weary, for there was no creativity left to condemn. So they snorted and they squawked, but they held in their boredom. All that was printed in newspapers, journals and magazines was the phrase, "I don't know."

All actresses and actors were gone from TV except Charlton Heston. Charlton did TV shows twenty-four hours a day (with occasional cameo appearances by Anita Bryant).

One day Jesse Helms was having some guests over from Europe. A dignitary, a land developer and a king. Mrs. Helms asked them where they'd like to go in America. The king said, "Disneyland."

Mr. Helms said, "Oh, that was closed down when we saw Disney's film *Fantasia*."

So the guests said. "Nathan's Hot Dogs on Coney Island."

Mr. Helms answered. "Sorry, but hot dogs are too phallic. In this country we don't eat anything that's longer than it's wide. Nathan's is history. In this country we don't even eat spaghetti. Bananas aren't imported. Tampon instructions are not allowed."

"Well," the guests said. "We'd like to go to the Museum of Modern Art, and if we can't go there, then why come to America?"

Mr. Helms was stuck. He wanted everyone to think he was cool, having Europeans visit him. Then he had an idea. He'd make the art himself to put back into the empty museums. He'd get George Bush and William Buckley and Donald Wildmon and Dana Rohrabacher and Tipper Gore and other conservative allies to come over and make some art on the White House lawn. So he called all of his cronies to come on down and make some art. And everyone came because it was better than watching Charlton Heston on TV.

Mr. and Mrs. Helms looked all over for art supplies. They came up with old wallpaper, scissors and house paint, and laid it all out for their friends to express themselves.

When the friends arrived they were scared to make art because they never had before. Never even used a crayon. But then a child picked up a crayon and drew a picture of her cat having babies. Then she drew a picture of her father hitting her. Then a picture of her alone and bruised. The mother looked at the picture and cried and told the daughter she didn't know that had happened to her. The child screamed out: "DRAW YOUR DREAMS! DRAW YOUR NIGHTMARES! DRAW YOUR FEARS! DRAW YOUR REALITIES!"

Everyone started making pictures of houses on fire, of monsters and trees becoming penises, pictures of making love with someone of the same sex, of being naked on street corners, of pain and dirty words and things you never admitted in real life.

For thirteen days and nights everyone drew and drew nonstop. Some started telling stories, writing poems. Neighbors saw the art-making and joined in. Somehow, pretend was back in. Somehow, expression sprung up from nowhere.

But then the Confiscation Police arrived and they took everyone away. (The father of the child who drew the father hitting the child complained.) Everyone was arrested. They even arrested Jesse Helms, for he was painting his soul out, which was HATE AND ENVY AND CRIME AND DARKNESS AND PAIN. They threw him into the slammer. He was tried for treason and lost. And on his day of execution his last words were: "It was only art."

Conclusion:

Redefining Power

1993

Terry Kupers

Men tend to define power very narrowly as the power to impose one's will over others. In order to enhance his power a man must very early in life begin achieving respect, a reputation, a position of authority, good connections, status, wealth, and the like. And this is connected to our notion of manliness. As long as men believe that they must be concerned above all else with their place in a hierarchy, and that the only choices they have are an ambitious climb to the top or a fall to the bottom of the heap, we will continue to maintain a steady pace, fear dependency, feel isolated from others, compensate for our inadequacies by oppressing women and gays, and continue to be uncertain about our adequacy no matter what heights we attain.

Kenneth Boulding (1990) distinguishes three dimensions of power. *Threat power* is the kind that permits one to get one's way in the face of challenges from others. This is that narrow sense of power, the ability to force opponents to give in for fear of unpleasant consequences. Then there is *exchange power,* the ability to produce and exchange objects of value. And the third is *integrative power,* the ability to achieve what one desires through love, nurturing, loyalty, and other positive forms of connection with people. It is only because men feel that they lack integrative power that they rely so one-sidedly on threat power, for instance beating their wives when they feel unable to attain by any other means the degree of unconditional love and respect they crave.

Steve Smith (1991) applies Boulding's three dimensions of power to the study of masculinity, pointing out that in our society the uses of power are organized along gender lines, men relying more on *threat power* while women rely more on *integrative power.* According to Smith:

If power is exclusively threat power, men are indeed the more powerful sex. But if power includes the ability to bring about any perceived good—including meeting one's own basic needs—then integrative power becomes central to the analysis of power differentials between the sexes. Itself responsible for many of the greatest of human goods, integra-

tive power is frequently exercised more effectively by women. Many men are sadly deficient in integrative power precisely because they have assumed a greater role in the exercise of threat power. They thus become dependent upon women to meet basic human needs, while (in the service of threat power) denying their very dependency. Once we have overthrown the illusion of threat power as all-encompassing, the costs to men are glaringly evident. (p. 25)

There are two aspects of power that warrant redefinition. One involves goals and values, the other involves the actual wielding of power. In terms of goals and values, men traditionally define power in relation to their sense of themselves as "real men." What makes one feel more like a "real man" is what one calls power. Even men who involve themselves fully in the rearing of children or the caring for people who are dying of AIDS sometimes feel they are less a man for it. It is as if a part of these men still buys into the American dream and thinks the most powerful men are the ones who earn huge salaries and sit among the power elite. Then they compare and decide they are relatively less powerful, less successful, and therefore less of a man. If things are to change for the better, we must redefine power so that we can feel powerful while doing tasks that are not traditional for men. Of course, this means men must assign more value to *integrative power* and less to *threat power* and *exchange power*.

An incident from a men's therapy group I conduct illustrates the point. Two group members who regularly spar with each other at meetings begin a dialogue about what it is about the other that rubs each the wrong way. What part of each man is set off by the antics of the other, and what earlier relationship(s) with a man make this combative relationship seem so familiar to each? Both explore earlier relationships with fathers, brothers, and teachers that come to mind. Both say they feel intimidated by the other and find it difficult to open up and be vulnerable in the other's presence. The group confronts the two, demanding to know why they have to be so combative all the time. The group wants this duo to resolve their differences so there can be more trust and openness at meetings.

A few weeks later one of the two men confesses to the group he is feeling very depressed, wonders whether it is worth going on, and has no clue as to the cause of his depression. This degree of vulnerability is quite uncharacteristic for him. The man with whom he usually spars is silent during that session, but at the next weekly meeting says he was quite moved by the other's confession that he did not know the cause of his depression. The group discusses the tendency among men to act intimidating just when they feel vulnerable. At this point a third member asks the man who was depressed whether he really achieves what he wants by being combative. He responds: "Not really. It feels better to be close to you guys, even while I'm feeling miserable, and to be in this conversation right now." In other words; if the goal is to be able to lord it over other men as one does in a business rivalry or legal battle, intimidation and male posturing work; but if the goal is to end one's sense of isolation and feel connected to others, vulnerability and trust make one more effective and powerful.

As a society, should the first priority be the maximization of short-term profit or should it be the creation of a just society in which everyone has a job and a roof over their heads? Should we continue to sink a huge proportion of our tax dollar into the race for global military dominance, or should we shift resources into alternative uses of advanced technology, for instance, figuring out ways to feed everyone and still preserve a livable environment? Would we be less powerful as a nation if we were to put more of our resources into figuring out ways to make the largest number of people in our society happy, but in the process we accumulated less financial and military *threat power* in the international arena? In fact, because the world has changed it is no longer reasonable to expect the United States to dominate the globe economically as it did in the post-World War II era—unless, that is, we attempt to continue our domination by military means, a disastrous course. But if we are to convert our social priorities and embark on a peaceful path of international collaboration, we will have to reconstruct our notion of masculinity, of what it means to be a "real man." We will have to redefine power in a way that permits men to feel powerful while they rear children, care for the ill, develop better quality intimacies, and so forth.

I mentioned that there are two aspects of power that warrant redefining. The second involves the wielding of power. If the men who value their *integrative power* end up giving away their power in the public arena, then control of this society will remain in the hands of the one-dimensional wielders of *threat power* who have succeeded in practically destroying the environment and bringing us to the brink of world war. If men who would change all this redefine power and reorder their priorities, will not that make them, as a group, less powerful in society? Because this has never happened in a modern society, we cannot know the answer. But we can attempt, collectively, to make that answer a resounding no. Men who utilize their *integrative power* as much as their *threat power* can be just as powerful, or more powerful, as those who currently wield power. This must be the case if things are to change for the better.

I believe that men who utilize their *integrative power* can be more powerful as a social force than they would be if they, like traditional men, relied almost exclusively on their *threat power*. Again, the lesson comes from the women's movement. Women were able to improve their situation, their solidarity with other women, and the quality of their lives by refusing to join men in a battle involving *threat power* alone. They insisted the personal was political, and taught us it could be. And in the process they demonstrated how powerful their *integrative power* could make them. For instance, women's friendships and capacity to meet in groups and talk about deeply personal issues make them very effective as organizers for social change. If there is any doubt, consider the way the women's movement has thrown the spotlight on sexual harassment at work, and the greater leverage women now have to put a halt to it. Men must learn that connectedness with others can boost one's power, and that by working together we can be even more powerful, especially if we figure out ways to collaborate without constructing new hierarchies and rivalries.

A large number of men are discovering a new kind of power, the kind that is expressed in having a wonderful circle of intimates and feeling secure because of it, the power that derives from knowing one is living according to one's principles even if that means one does not accumulate all one might, the kind that comes from sharing the burden with others one can respect as equals. In a community of equals a new kind of power can be realized, not the kind where a man stands alone and conquers real and imagined enemies; rather, a man would be able to discuss problems with a network of sympathetic people who might help him devise a collaborative strategy for solving a large array of problems and coping with a variety of threats. When I see men at gatherings celebrating their newfound sense of brotherhood and the relief they feel that they are not as totally alone in the universe as they once felt they were, I know I am part of something that is very powerful and I feel powerful being a part.

Once men begin to expand upon what Boulding terms their *integrative power,* a whole set of connections become obvious. Men who are attuned to the plight of others are not able to ignore sexual harassment at work, homelessness, racism, drastic cutbacks in social welfare programs, inattention to the plight of AIDS sufferers, ecological disasters such as the destruction of the rain forests and the ozone layer, and the threat of war and nuclear annihilation.

Men who get in touch with their feminine side, and begin to value their role as father, friend, and team player, need not give away their power in the public arena. In fact, by working collaboratively with others who share a vision of better gender relations, men will discover a whole new level of power. And, by their example, they will begin to redefine masculinity as well as power.

Vying for power in the public arena involves a large organizational effort. Massive public involvement is needed to win abortion rights, effective affirmative action, decent jobs for men and women, affordable childcare, and so on. I am not ready to propose a specific political program, that will require discussion among a large number of people. But I am saying we need to become more active in social struggles if we are to change anything. Many men's groups as well as individual men have joined women's struggles to "take back the night"; end domestic violence, date rape, and child abuse; and many straights have joined gays in the struggle against AIDS. Men's groups and organizations could also join their blue collar brothers and sisters on picket lines protesting plant closures and joblessness. And men could join their brothers among the minorities in protesting the dismantling of inner city schools, the unavailability of affordable housing and rewarding work opportunities, and the inattention to people of color who are dying of AIDS as well as other diseases.

Changing gender relations is not merely a matter of social struggles. Personal relationships must change as well. As a large number of people engage in collaborative childrearing, our definitions of manliness and power change. Men who work with men who batter are redefining power in the domestic realm, teaching men who feel inadequate that they can feel more powerful on account of caring relationships with women and children (*integrative power*) than they ever would on account of their ability to beat and abuse them (*threat power,* see Sonkin & Durphy, 1982; Kivel, 1992). Black men who go to inner city schools to talk with youths about sex, drugs, and alternatives to enlistment in the military are redefining power for these youngsters, teaching them that a quick buck and the ability to lord it over others is not the only way to feel powerful. There are many other examples of the new kinds of heroes we already have among us.

I began this book with a discussion of men who abhor domination from an early age and support women's struggles for equality, even while they are unable to stand up to the women in their lives and do not accomplish all they might at work for fear of becoming brutes. These men must find ways to stand up for their own rights—in personal relationships, at work, and in the public arena—or else men who have no qualms about the suffering of others will continue to wield most of the power in this society. To the extent men lack a vision of a better society in which one does not have to be a brute to have a voice in the halls of power—a vision that provides a third alternative to the either/or dichotomy of winners and losers in the (*threat*) power game—they settle for lives that are less than fully vital. The challenge that confronts men is to find ways to be powerful without oppressing anyone, and in the process to redefine power, heroism, and masculinity. This is an immense challenge. And men will never meet it in isolation. We need new kinds of bonds among men and between men and women, straight and gay, if we are to construct, collectively, new forms of masculinity and new and better gender relations.

REFERENCES

BOULDING, K. E. (1990). *Three faces of power.* Newbury Park: Sage.

KIVEL, P. (1992). *Men's work: How to stop the violence that tears our lives apart.* Center City, MN: Hazeldon.

SMITH, S. (1991). Men: Fear and power. *Men's Studies Review, 8(4),* 20–27.

SONKIN, D. J., & DURPHY, M. (1982). *Learning to live without violence: A handbook for men.* Volcano, CA: Volcano Press.

How to Create Less Violent Societies

James Gilligan

The first step toward learning how to prevent any health problem is to discover what causes it, so that we know what causes need to be removed or neutralized. . . . Once we know the causes, we can apply that knowledge to the issue of prevention in a very direct way: we can stop causing it. We know how to cause violence: by shaming people. Therefore we know how to prevent it: stop shaming them. That does not mean that we either can or should eliminate shame from the world, for the capacity to experience feelings of shame is as necessary as the capacity to experience physical pain. Just as physical pain signals to us that there is a threat to our physical health, so shame warns us that there is something lacking in our repertoire of social or cognitive skills and knowledge, some failure of development and maturation that needs further work. But unless we provide people with access to the means by which they can develop and mature further, such as education and employment, we leave them with no means other than violence, of protecting themselves from potentially overwhelming and intolerable feelings of shame.

We know how people shame other people, namely, by treating them as inferior, on an individual scale, or by assigning them to an inferior social and economic status on a collective scale. Not everyone who is shamed in these ways will become violent, because most people have enough independent sources of self-esteem and self-respect to withstand even fairly intense disrespect from others. But if the goal is to start a fight, that is the one method that is most guaranteed to work with whoever is vulnerable to becoming violent. Thus, the first steps toward preventing violence consist of not shaming people (as by disrespecting them), and not depriving them of access to the tools they need in order to attain and maintain their self-respect even when they are disrespected by others.

The most important implication this has for the issue of preventing violence is that violence does not occur spontaneously, it occurs only when we cause it; so that the task of preventing violence does not so much require us to do something special, as it requires us to *stop* doing the things we have been doing that cause violence; in other words, to discontinue the individual and social practices and behaviors that have been shown to cause violence. Once we stop causing violence, it will disappear by itself.

That simple statement is not as optimistic as it may sound, however, because it is not at all clear how many of those things people will be willing to stop doing even if they can be convinced that they cause violence. For preventing violence is not the only goal that many people value, and there are many other goals that some value more. As Elliott Currie wrote:

We have the level of criminal violence we do because we have arranged our social and economic life in certain ways rather than others. The brutality and violence of American life are a signal that there are profound social costs to maintaining those arrangements. But by the same token, altering them also has a price; and if we continue to tolerate the conditions that have made us the most violent of industrial societies, it is not because the problem is overwhelmingly mysterious or because we do not know what to do, but because we have decided that the benefits of changing those conditions aren't worth the costs.

(*Confronting Crime*, 1985)

It is very important to note, however, that the only segment of the population for whom changing our social and economic conditions in the ways that prevent violence would exact a higher cost would be the extremely wealthy upper, or ruling, class—the wealthiest one per cent of the population (which in the United States today controls some 39 per cent of the total wealth of the nation, and 48 per cent of the financial wealth, as shown by Wolff in *Top Heavy* (1996). The other 99 per cent of the population—namely, the middle class and the lower class—would benefit, not only from decreased rates of violence (which primarily victimize the very poor), but also from a more equitable distribution of the collective wealth and income of our unprecedentedly wealthy societies. Even on a worldwide scale, it would require a remarkably small sacrifice from the wealthiest individuals and nations to raise everyone on earth, including the populations of the poorest nations, above the subsistence level, as the United Nations *Human Development Report 1998,* has shown. I emphasize the wealthiest individuals as well as nations because, as the U.N. Report documents, a tiny number of the wealthiest individuals actually possess wealth on a scale that is larger than the annual income of most of the nations of the earth. For example, the *three* richest *individuals* on earth have assets that exceed the combined Gross Domestic Product of the *forty-eight* poorest *countries!* The assets of the 84 richest individuals exceed the Gross Domestic Product of the most populous nation on earth, China, with 1.2 billion inhabitants. The 225 richest individuals have a combined wealth of over $1 trillion, which is equal to the annual income of the poorest 47 per cent of the world's population, or 2.5 billion people. By comparison:

It is estimated that the additional cost of achieving and maintaining universal access to basic education for all, basic health care for all, reproductive health care for all women, adequate food for all and safe water and sanitation for all is roughly $40 billion a year. This is less than 4 per cent of the combined wealth of the 225 richest people in the world.

(*U.N.H.D.R.* 1998)

It has been shown throughout the world, both internationally and intranationally, that reducing economic inequities not only improves physical health and reduces the rate of death from natural causes far more effectively than doctors, medicines and hospitals; it also decreases the rate of death from both criminal and political violence far more effectively than any system of police forces, prisons, or military interventions ever invented. My goal in writing this book is simply to make sure that all who read it will learn which choices lead to more violence and which ones to less, so that whatever choices they make will at least be made with full knowledge of the costs and benefits.

It may seem obvious that violence can be caused, but what reason do we have to think that it can be prevented? One reason for believing that is because it is already being prevented, or has been prevented, in all those nations, cultures and periods of history that have lower rates of violence than other nations or epochs.

SOCIAL AND POLITICAL DEMOCRACY

Since the end of the Second World War, the homicide rates of the nations of western Europe, and Japan, for example, have been only about a tenth as high as those of the United States, which is another way of saying that they have been preventing 90 per cent of the violence that the U.S. still experiences. Their rates of homicide were not lower than those in the U.S. before.

On the contrary, Europe and Asia were scenes of the largest numbers of homicides ever recorded in the history of the world, both in terms of absolute numbers killed and in the death rates per 100,000 population, in the "thirty years' war" that lasted from 1914 to 1945. Wars, and governments, have always caused far more homicides than all the individual murderers put together (Richardson, *Statistics of Deadly Quarrels,* 1960; Keeley, *War Before Civilization,* 1996.) After that war ended, however, they all took two steps which have been empirically demonstrated throughout the world to prevent violence. They instituted social democracy (or "welfare states," as they are sometimes called), and achieved an unprecedented decrease in the inequities in wealth and income between the richest and poorest groups in the population, one effect of which is to reduce the frequency of interpersonal or "criminal" violence. And Germany, Japan, and Italy adopted political democracy as well, the effect of which is to reduce the frequency of international violence, or warfare (including "war crimes").

While the United States adopted political democracy at its inception, it is the only developed nation on earth that has never adopted social democracy (a "welfare state"). The United States alone among the developed nations does not provide universal health insurance for all its citizens; it has the highest rate of relative poverty among both children and adults, and the largest gap between the rich and the poor, of any of the major economies; vastly less adequate levels of unemployment insurance and other components of shared responsibility for human welfare; and so on. Thus, it is not surprising that it also has murder rates that have been five to ten times as high as those of any other developed nation, year after year. It is also consistent with that analysis that the murder rate finally fell below the epidemic range in which it had fluctuated without exception for the previous thirty years (namely, 8 to 11 homicides per 100,000 population per year), only in 1998, after the unemployment rate reached its lowest level in thirty years and the rate of poverty among the demographic groups most vulnerable to violence began to diminish—slightly—for the first time in thirty years.

Some American politicians, such as President Eisenhower, have suggested that the nations of western Europe have merely substituted a high suicide rate for the high homicide rate that the U.S. has. In fact, the suicide rates in most of the other developed nations are *also* substantially lower than those of the United States, or at worst not substantially higher. The suicide rates throughout the British Isles, the Netherlands, and the southern European nations are around one-third *lower* than those of the U.S.; the rates in Canada, Australia, and New Zealand, as well as Norway and Luxembourg, are about the same. Only the remaining northern and central European countries and Japan have suicide rates that are higher, ranging from 30 per cent higher to roughly twice as high as the suicide rate of the U.S. By comparison, the U.S. homicide rate is roughly *ten* times as high as those of western Europe (including the U.K., Scandinavia, France, Germany, Switzerland, Austria), southern Europe, and Japan; and *five* times as high as those of Canada, Australia and New Zealand. No other developed nation has a homicide rate that is even close to that of the U.S.

Another reason for concluding that violence can be prevented, and that we know how to do so, can be found by contrasting the effects of the peace settlement that occurred after the First World War with that which followed the Second. As is well known, the Versailles treaty that the Allied powers imposed on Germany following the end of World War I included not only a statement condemning Germany but also a series of financial penalties so punitive that they would have been ruinous had they been fully enforced. The effect of this was to give the right-wing revanchists (of whom Hitler emerged as the leader) an invaluable propaganda tool, namely, the ability to win elections on the campaign promise to 'undo the shame of Versailles,' i.e. the humiliation to which the Allies had subjected Germany. In fact, even before Hitler entered politics, the great British economist John Maynard Keynes, who was a delegate at the peace conference, saw how destructive the terms of the Versailles settlement would be to the prospects for future peace, so he resigned in protest and wrote an angry denunciation of it, *The Economic Consequences of the Peace,* in which he predicted much of what later happened. It goes without saying that neither Keynes's analysis nor mine has anything to do with condoning or justifying any of Hitler's behavior. The point is simply that if one wants peace, then humiliating and punishing one's former enemy is not the way to reach that goal, for, among other things, it only strengthens the hand of people like Hitler who already want revenge and will gladly use any pretext to get it.

Whether we can attribute the very different outcome that followed the end of the Second World War to the sagacity of those who presided over the terms of the peace, as though they had learned from the mistakes made by those who ended World War I, or whether it was merely a fortunate but coincidental byproduct of the Cold War with the Soviet Union, the lesson we ourselves can learn from the difference between the results of the two peace settlements is not only that violence can be prevented, but that the worst form of violence can be prevented—namely, world war. For after the end of World War II, the Allies, far from humiliating the three Axis powers or punishing them financially by ordering them to pay reparations for their war crimes, actually extended financial support to them to help them rebuild their economies after the devastation of the war, and helped them also to establish stable political democratic institutions for the first time. The result has been more than fifty years of unbroken peace on what had been the bloodiest continent in human history during the previous thirty years.

IMMIGRANTS

Another example illustrating both the feasibility and the method of preventing violence is the history of the ethnic groups that have come to the U.S. since the beginning of European colonization, as summarized by Silberman in *Criminal Violence, Criminal Justice* (1978):

The history of ethnic groups in the United States demonstrates that upward mobility is the most effective cure for criminal violence. In the second half of the nineteenth century, most of the people responsible for street crime were Irish- and German-Americans; in the first half of the twentieth century, they were mostly Italian-, Jewish-, Polish-, and Greek-Americans. The James Q. Wilsons of both periods were certain that reducing poverty would have little effect on crime, since (in their view) the "new immigrants," unlike their predecessors, really preferred their dissolute and crime-ridden way of life. But each of these groups moved out of crime as it moved into the middle class. The same will be true—the same is true—of black Americans; involvement in street crime drops sharply as blacks move into the middle class.

Since Silberman wrote those words, they have been abundantly confirmed, as an unprecedentedly large percentage of African-Americans have entered the middle-class professions: law, medicine, academia, and so on. And while crime and violence continue to plague the black community, it is not the black middle class that is committing it. It is, almost entirely, those who have not (yet) made it into the middle class.

GUARANTEED EMPLOYMENT VS. GUARANTEED UNEMPLOYMENT

. . . [U]nemployment tends to stimulate violence. It is noteworthy that, as the rates of unemployment decline, the rates of violence tend to do so as well. Since violence is multi-determined, the effect of any one variable, such as the unemployment rate, can of course be augmented or diminished by the simultaneous effect of other variables (such as the level of unemployment insurance that is provided). Therefore, the high unemployment rates currently seen in many European countries have still not translated into rates of violence remotely as high as those that are seen in the United States because the social "safety net" protecting workers from falling into poverty is so much more secure in Europe than it is in the United States.

But it is not just the effects of unemployment that can be affected by governmental action; so can the rate of unemployment. For example, for many years in the United States, the Federal Reserve Board has intervened to raise the unemployment rate whenever the "danger" arose that it might get too low! Given the effect this can have on the rates of homicide (and suicide), and the efforts of other branches of the government to lower the homicide rate, it is clear that different branches of the government have been working at cross-purposes. One does not have to assume that the Federal Reserve Board was deliberately trying to keep the murder rate as high as possible—and I do not assume that—in order to note that they could hardly have done anything more effective to that end. Conversely, now that the Federal Reserve Board has finally allowed the unemployment rate to reach a thirty-year low, the murder rate has finally fallen slightly below the epidemic levels of the past thirty years. In fact, it is now almost exactly the same as it was at the last time the unemployment rate was this low.

To the extent that we care about the level of violence in our society, however, it is important to do everything in our power to keep the unemployment rate as low as possible—ideally, to provide full employment for everyone able to work (as Roosevelt attempted during the Depression)—and at least not actually cause unemployment. If there is an unavoidable minimum of unemployment, we must try to mitigate the humiliating effects of not being able to find a job, such as providing enough unemployment insurance to prevent poverty.

GENDER ROLES AND HOMOPHOBIA

The discussion of gender roles and homophobia . . . has implications for the prevention of violence that I want to emphasize . . . because I think it has not usually been noticed or acknowledged that decisions we make on these issues can have an impact on the level of violence in our society. The general principle here is clear: anything that will reduce the artificial and exaggerated polarization of gender roles, and the irrational fear, hatred, and contempt felt and expressed toward homosexuals will help to prevent violence, because those are among the main causes of violence—and not only, or even primarily, toward women or gays. In line with my contention that we simply need to stop doing the things we are doing that cause violence, it is relevant to notice that there are now several areas in our public life in which major institutions are actively supporting gender asymmetry and discrimination against homosexuals.

The military still has arbitrary rules that vary people's access to military roles based on their gender or their sexual orientation, rather than on the basis of their individual abilities and wishes. These rules are made by governments (which, in a democracy, means all of us, collectively) and can be repealed by governments. Traditionally, only men were conscripted against their will into the military, and, even after women were allowed to join the military voluntarily, participation in combat was restricted more or less exclusively to men. Both these practices help to maintain the traditional gender-role asymmetries that stimulate and perpetuate violence in society.

Some religious sects restrict access to membership in the clergy, and in some cases to membership in the congregation, based on gender or sexual orientation. While it is not appropriate for the government to repeal these rules, the religious bodies themselves can. Nothing could give more support to the Commandment, "Thou shalt not kill." In debates over these issues it is seldom noticed that they are relevant to the issue of preventing violence.

In my discussion of these issues, I am attempting to focus on actions that could be taken (or rather, violence-provoking policies that could be discontinued) by people in positions of power, in the government, the military, the churches and synagogues and mosques, and so on. I am trying to find the strategic levers in society that influence people's attitudes on a mass scale. The major public institutions of our society serve, as Justice Brandeis said of the government, as the moral teachers of the public: the values that they express through their rules and behaviors cannot help but influence the private behavior of the millions of people who respect those institutions and look to them for guidance as to how to live with other people.

VIOLENCE TOWARD CHILDREN

Among the other policies that would prevent violence, and which it is in the power of governments to adopt, eliminating legally permitted or even mandated violence toward children would be high on my list. It is time for every country on earth to follow Sweden and the other northern European countries in declaring it illegal for an adult to strike a child. Children sometimes need to be physically restrained—for example, if they are running into traffic, or are assaulting another child, and will not respond to words alone. But one never needs to strike a child in order to restrain him, or for any other reason. We know that the more children are hit, the more they hit others, and we know that the more they are disciplined with 'love-oriented' techniques and verbal reasoning the less violently they themselves behave, both as children and as adults. Naturally, it goes without saying that even more extreme forms of physical violence toward children, such as genital mutilation and capital punishment, should not be practiced or permitted. The U.K., like every other Western democracy except the U.S., has abolished capital punishment for all ages. Many other countries prescribe the death penalty for adults, but the U.S. is one of only six nations on earth today that still executes children (as young as sixteen). Clearly, discontinuing this policy would end one practice that is a statement to every parent and child in the country that it is morally and legally permissible to express disapproval of children by killing them.

RESTRICTING MEDIA VIOLENCE

Messages validating violence are also sent to children and adults through the mass media and video games. There is a firm consensus, on the part of the dozens of behavioral scientists and scientific groups who have investigated the effects on children of violence in the media, that it does stimulate violent behavior in those who are, like many children, not merely exposed to it but saturated with it. Major reviews of studies of this subject have been conducted by virtually every major scientific and professional organization and by the Surgeon General's office, and have reached the same conclusion (Bok, *Mayhem*, 1998).

The public policy dilemma is more difficult: how far to go down the road of government censorship. There are other alternatives. One is to encourage parents to protect their children from this influence with the help of "V-chips" programmed to block reception of violent television programs—though that would be least effective with the most vulnerable children, those with the least caring and resourceful parents. Another is to provide "media literacy" classes in schools, to help children learn how to gain some critical distance from the mindless violence to which they are exposed (not to mention the mindless advertisements). A third is for people to boycott the networks and advertisers who bring this material into people's living rooms, to lobby the network executives, and so on.

In Norway, government censors actively monitor programs and films, and block access to those they deem objectionable. Perhaps that works in Norway, and perhaps it would work in the United Kingdom. But based on how I have seen censorship work in the United States and Canada, when it has been tried, I can only worry that government censors might ban the programs and films that were harmless or even worthwhile, and permit the truly violence-provoking material to be shown. For example, after a Canadian law was passed a few years ago forbidding the sale of pornographic books and magazines, the first thing the censors confiscated were newsletters from a lesbian organization that were purely informational and had no sexual content.

It is also important to remember that it is not violence in the media as such that stimulates violent behavior, but rather, the depiction of violence as entertainment rather than as tragedy. There is as much violence in *Hamlet* or *The Bacchae* as there is in any "spaghetti Western," but it is not watching Shakespeare or Euripides that makes children more violent. The difference, apart from the quality of the writing, is that in serious drama there is never any doubt about the gravity of what is happening and the depth of suffering it causes, which is why those plays elicit empathy and compassion rather than the trivialization of violence into a spectator sport. But could government censors be trusted to recognize the difference?

On the other hand, common sense would suggest that some reasonable compromises should be possible here, and that this is an important enough problem to call for a serious discussion of the widest possible range of solutions. One paradox in current censorship is that we are much more active about restricting access to sexual content than to depictions of violence. Apparently there is a consensus that it is acceptable to allow children to see people murdering or assaulting each other in the most brutal fashion, on a daily basis, whereas it would be morally shocking and unacceptable to allow them to see two people making love. I am not arguing that either kind of program or film is appropriate for a child, but the distinction we are making here seems to say that murder as entertainment is acceptable but sex is not. And since we seem to be able to provide some degree of censorship for the films and programs with overt sexual content, I cannot see why violent content cannot also be restricted to hours or television channels less accessible to children, and why violent films could not be restricted to the age groups that might be less vulnerable or suggestible. Why should we allow children to watch violence when we do not allow them to watch erotica? This is especially paradoxical, since most studies of the effects of non-violent erotica have concluded that exposure to it actually decreases people's predisposition to engage in violent behavior.

The ultimate solution to this problem, though it is a long-term one, would be to increase the level and quality of education for the entire population. The definitive end of the production and distribution of this pornography of violence will occur only when people stop wanting to watch it, and that only when they are well educated enough, and emotionally secure and

mature enough, to recognize the difference between mindless mayhem and thoughtful and moving drama.

GUN CONTROL

Great Britain passed a stringent handgun control law not long ago, following the tragic mass shooting at Dunblane in 1996—a very sensible and realistic component, though only one among many, in a national strategy to prevent future violence. If only the United States, which seems to have a new Dunblane of its own every few weeks, could become equally rational. Unfortunately, as most of the rest of the world knows, the United States is in the grip of a national psychosis on the subject of guns—not everyone, but the effective ruling majority. It is a subject on which it is difficult to engage many otherwise reasonable people in a rational discussion. Yet the facts are clear, and there are many that are relevant to this discussion. Incomparably more family members are killed by one of their own family's guns—by accident, suicide, or an impulsive family quarrel—than are killed or even threatened by a criminal's gun. Many people carry guns in order to "protect" themselves; but what the statistics show is that people are much more likely to be killed if they are carrying a gun than if they are not. Between 1984 and 1994 the homicide rate among 14–17-year-olds tripled, and the increase was entirely due to one weapon and one weapon alone—the handgun. The argument that gun ownership by private citizens is either necessary or sufficient to prevent the Federal government from turning into a dictatorship parts company with reality—assault rifles against ballistic missiles, Sherman tanks or hydrogen bombs? Of course people could, and some would, use other weapons if they did not have guns, but that does not undo the fact that fatalities are seven times more likely when the weapon is a gun than when it is a knife.

One of the main obstacles to meaningful gun controls has been the Second Amendment to the U.S. Constitution, which reads in splendid ambiguity. A well regulated militia, being necessary to the security of a free State, the right of the people to keep and bear arms, shall not be infringed. Yet it is not clear why the Second Amendment to the Constitution, ambiguous though it is, continues to be interpreted as forbidding the banning of handguns and assault rifles when it does not stop the government from keeping tanks and machine guns out of private hands. But as long as it continues to be so interpreted, there may be no cure for this national psychosis except to pass a new amendment invalidating it and replacing it with one that will ban guns from private hands. Doing that will not in and of itself stop all violence; if no one had killed anyone with a gun during any recent year, the U.S. would still have had a higher murder rate than any other developed nation because of all the murders that are already being committed by other weapons. Nevertheless, the vast majority of both homicides and suicides in the U.S. are committed by guns, and removing them from circulation would undoubtedly prevent many impulsive shootings, which are much more likely to terminate in death than are impulsive stabbings or beatings. The main problem, however, is that currently an estimated 200 million or more guns are in circulation in the U.S., and it is not clear how it will be possible to confiscate them all, or even just the handguns and assault rifles before the end of the century. On the other hand, it is worth remembering that Boston was remarkably successful in removing handguns from its inner-city youth by concentrating resources on them as well as on the small handful of gun dealers who were supplying most of the guns to criminals. So it is important not to give up.

Nevertheless, it is more important to change people's motives, their wish to harm someone, and to change the culture of violence and death in the U.S. That is precisely what the process of passing a new Constitutional amendment could accomplish—the cohesion of a new set of cultural values that in turn would help to shape people's motives. The values that support the Second Amendment as it is now interpreted are the same values that support violence in all its forms. Repealing it could be the first step toward forging a new set of values that would embody the Biblical command, "Therefore choose life."

UNIVERSAL ACCESS TO FREE HIGHER EDUCATION

Education is one of the most powerful tools for acquiring self-esteem, and since self-esteem is the most powerful psychological force that prevents violence, it is not surprising that level of education is one of the strongest predictors of whether or not a person will be violent.

A few years ago, my colleagues and I conducted a study to determine what programs in the Massachusetts prison system were most effective in preventing recidivism, or reoffending, among prisoners after they are discharged and return to the community. The only one that we found to have been 100 per cent successful, up to that time, was a program of free higher education that enabled prisoners to acquire a college degree. Over a twenty-five-year period, more than 200 inmates, most of whom were serving time for the most serious violent crimes, including murder, rape, and armed robbery, had received a college degree and then left prison, and not one had been returned for a new crime. At first I thought we had made a mistake, and missed someone. Then I discovered that the state of Indiana had found exactly the same result, and so had Folsom State Prison in California—not one prisoner who had acquired a college degree while in prison had been reincarcerated for a new crime.

Now, nothing is 100 per cent forever or under all circumstances, and the success rate for such programs is not that high everywhere. But many surveys have been done throughout the U.S. that have confirmed that higher education reduces rates of recidivism far more than could be due to chance, and far more effectively than any other single program. As a follow-up to our own study, we discovered that, finally, some thirty years after the first inmates were graduated, two have been returned to prison. That is less than a one per cent recidivism rate over a thirty-year period—which compares to national recidivism rates of 65 per cent within three years of leaving prison.

Strictly speaking, free higher education for inmates is an example of what would be called tertiary, not primary, prevention of violence. But I am discussing it in this chapter because I believe the principle it illustrates is relevant to the entire population, not just those who have already become violent.

WHERE DO WE GO FROM HERE?

A century and a half ago, we discovered that cleaning up the water supply and the sewer system was far more effective in preventing physical disease than all the doctors, medicines and hospitals in the world. What we need to learn during the coming century is that cleaning up our social and economic system, by reducing the shame-provoking inequities in social and economic status, will do far more to prevent physical violence than all the police, prisons and punishments in the world, all the prison psychiatrists we could possibly hire, and all the armies, armaments, and Armageddons we could mobilize!

What is at issue here is relative poverty, not absolute poverty. Inferiority is a relative concept. When everyone is poor together, there is no shame in being poor. As Marx said, it is not living in a hovel that causes people to feel ashamed, it is living in a hovel next to a palace. And as he also said, shame is the emotion of revolution, i.e. of violence. But one does not have to be a Marxist, or subscribe to everything he said (and I do not), in order to see how correct his insight was. Adam Smith, Amartya Sen and other non-Marxist economists have seen the same things. In his latest book, Professor Sen in *Development as Freedom* (1999) emphasized how profound the psychological injuries are that are caused by unemployment and by relative poverty. These do not merely cause economic damage to people, they also wound them emotionally. "Among its manifold effects," he points out, "unemployment contributes to social exclusion. . . , to losses of self-reliance, self-confidence, and psychological and physical health." And he reminds us that Adam Smith saw that economic inequality—relative deprivation in terms of income and wealth—can cause absolute deprivation when it exposes people to crippling and disabling intensities of shame. For example, he quotes Smith's comment that leather shoes are not a physical necessity, but they can be a social and psychological one—since anyone would be ashamed to appear in public without them. No one who has seen violent teenagers who will kill each other over a pair of sneakers, as I have, can doubt the importance and validity of what Professor Sen and Adam Smith are talking about. Shakespeare also saw the difference between absolute and relative deprivation, and how devastating the latter can be to a person's sense of his basic human dignity, when he has Lear cry:

O, reason not the need! our basest beggars
Are in the poorest thing superfluous.
Allow not nature more than nature needs,
Man's life is cheap as beast's.

(II. iv. 264–67)

But how can we go about eliminating relative poverty? Clearly, education is relevant and important,

and making it freely available to everyone can only help. But that alone will not solve the problem. I say that because I have worked with the most violent criminals our society produces, and I have heard politicians like John Major in the U.K. and his counterparts in the U.S. say that what we need to do to solve the problem of crime and violence is to teach criminals to learn the difference between right and wrong. In other words, we need to teach them to recognize the difference between justice and injustice, and to pursue the former and eschew the latter. But what the politicians who mouth these sentiments do not realize is that the violent criminals are perfectly aware of the difference between right and wrong, and justice and injustice. They realize that they have been victims of injustice (most of all, from those who preach to them most loudly about it), and they commit their crimes in order to achieve some measure of justice, by taking something back from a society that has subjected them to a degree of deprivation to which it does not subject others. For example, how can we, as a society, say that we have something to teach about justice, when we permit the perpetuation of an economic system in which some people inherit millions of pounds while most people inherit nothing? How can we speak of equality of opportunity under those conditions?

Violent criminals are not violent because they are dumb, out of touch with reality, or unable to recognize hypocrisy, dishonesty, and injustice when they see it. They are violent precisely because they are aware of the hypocrisy, dishonesty, and injustice that surrounds them and of which they have been the victims. That does not mean that they respond to those conditions in a rational or just way, or that we should tolerate and permit their violence—which affects their fellow victims much more often than it does their oppressors. But it does mean that we cannot expect to stop the kind of violence that we call crime until we stop the kind of violence that I have called structural in "Structural Violence" (1999). By this I mean the deaths and disabilities that are caused by the economic structure of our society, its division into rich and poor. Structural violence is not only the main *form* of violence, in the sense that poverty kills far more people (almost all of them very poor) than all the behavioral violence put together, it is also the main *cause* of violent behavior. Eliminating structural violence means eliminating relative poverty.

So how can we do that? There is an old saying that the cure for poverty is money. Since there are two forms of relative poverty—inequities in wealth and in income—we will need to deal with both. Inequities in wealth can be dealt with during the lifetimes of the wealthy by means of a wealth tax, and after their lifetimes, by means of an inheritance or estate tax, with the proceeds in either case distributed to those with less wealth. Inequities in income can be dealt with by means of a negative income tax, in which people whose incomes are below the cut-off point pay no taxes but instead receive money from the taxes paid by those with higher incomes. This strategy has been utilized on a small scale in the U.S., where it has been described by some scholars as being one of the most effective anti-poverty programs in U.S. history (along with the social security system that has lifted many of the elderly and disabled out of poverty). It has several advantages over more traditional welfare systems, of which the one most relevant to our discussion is that it spares the recipients from the humiliation often attendant on visits to welfare offices.

My point here is not that these are the only or even necessarily the best ways to alleviate the inequities in income and wealth that create feelings of injustice, envy, inferiority, and hostility, but simply to point out that there are ways to do it, they have been tried, and some of them seem to work. In principle, there is no limit to the degree to which income and wealth could be equalized. The degree to which we choose to equalize them could be decided on in part by another principle, which is that the more they were equalized, the lower the level of violence we could expect as a result. Ultimately, then, we would be left with the same question with which we started this discussion: how seriously and completely do we want to prevent violence, and how high a price are we willing to pay in order to do so? The choice is ours.

There would, of course, be many objections to such a plan, especially from the wealthy. But there is one objection that might be worth discussing here, namely, that the more we equalized income and wealth, the more we would destroy people's incentives to work. That is an argument which, if you examine it more closely, is applied only to the poor, not to the rich. The traditional defense of class stratification and the existence of a "leisure class," ever since the rise of civilization, from both Plato and Aristotle as well as from more recent social thinkers, is that a leisure class is needed in order to have the time and energy for the specialized intellectual development and technological skills that are necessary preconditions for civilization; and "leisure class" has always meant a group with a *guaranteed income*—i.e. those who did not have to work for a living. Implicit in this argument is the assumption (which I happen to think is correct, as I think the history and development of civilization proves) that when people are freed from the necessity to work—that is, when work is freely chosen rather than slavery or wage-slavery (i.e. "work or starve"), they do not just vegetate in a state of "passivity and dependency." Rather, they engage in much more creative work. Coercion creates an incentive for "passive aggressiveness," because when overpowered and helpless there is no other way to express the minimal degree of autonomy that people need in order to maintain any semblance of self-esteem, dignity, and pride. Furthermore, when work is a means to an end—working in order to eat—then it is, in Marx's terms, "alienated" labor. Labor can only be liberated from alienation when work is an end in itself, entered into freely as the expression of spontaneous and voluntary creativity, curiosity, playfulness, initiative, and sociability—that is, the sense of solidarity with the community, the fulfillment of one's true and "essential" human nature as "social" and "political" animals, to be fulfilled and made human by their full participation in a culture.

In short, the contradiction in the old defense of class stratification is that it defends leisure for the leisure class, but not for the underclass. With reference to the underclass, leisure is said to destroy the incentive to work, leads to slothfulness and self-indulgence, and retards cognitive and moral development. When applied to the leisure class, the concept evokes an image of Plato and Aristotle, whose leisure was based on slave labor, creating the intellectual foundations of Western civilization; or patrician slave-owners like Washington and Jefferson laying the foundations of American civilization; or creative aristocrats like Count Leo Tolstoy or Bertrand, Earl Russell; or, even closer to home, of our own sons and daughters (or of ourselves, when we were young adults) being freed from the stultifying tasks of earning a living until well into our adult years so that we could study in expensive universities to gain specialized knowledge and skills.

As we enter the new millennium, perhaps it is worth reflecting on the fact that this could be a turning-point in the evolution of civilization, for our technologies have evolved to the point where there is no longer a need for an underclass of slaves, serfs, and wage-slaves. This division of society into a hierarchical order of upper and lower social classes did not exist until civilization was invented. The low level of technological development made this necessary to allow a class of specialists (mathematicians, inventors, poets, scientists, philosophers) the leisure for the creative work that is a prerequisite for the creation, maintenance, and further development of civilization. But slaves and underclasses are no longer needed in order to free up enough leisure time and energy for the elite to do work that is creative rather than alienated. Therefore we no longer need social classes and their concomitant, relative poverty and economic inequality, and their concomitant, violence. If we permit ourselves—and by ourselves I mean all of us, all human beings—to enjoy the fruits of the creative labor that has preceded us, we could create a society that would no longer need violence as the only means of rescuing self-esteem.

Implicit in this argument is the idea that money is neither a necessary incentive for creative work, nor the main incentive. The play that infants and children engage in is clearly an inborn, inherent trait of human beings. Play has been called the work that children do, the means by which they acquire the skills and knowledge that enable them to develop and mature into adults. Play has also been described, when applied to adults, as simply another name for work that one enjoys. We could use the word to refer to unalienated labor, creative work, work that is an end in itself. I believe that the wish and the need to engage in this creative work/play is only conditioned out of human beings by the alienating conditions to which the underclass and even the middle class in our society are subjected.

There is a large body of empirical research that is relevant to this. One category consists of psychological experiments, reviewed and summarized by Kohn in "Studies Find Reward" (1987) that call into question the widespread belief that money is an effective and even necessary way to motivate people. Consensus has emerged from major psychology departments throughout the U.S. (e.g. James Garbarino, then at Chicago, now at Cornell; Mark L. Lepper, at Stanford; Edward Deci and Richard Ryan, at Rochester; Teresa Amibile, at Brandeis) that creativity, interest, subjec-

tive satisfaction, persistence, and overall productivity all decline when a task is done for the sake of an external, extrinsic reward. The only sphere in which "material rewards *do* seem to be necessary" is that of the dull jobs "that make very little use of their abilities" (Ryan *Equality*, 1981). But that is precisely the type of work that is much less necessary now that technology has created robots and servomechanisms. The time may have come to ask whether the price we pay in violence and unhappiness is worth the reward of keeping some groups of people in menial jobs that we could easily do without.

Another relevant research program consists of studies investigating the degree of satisfaction or happiness that whole groups of people experience under differing conditions of income distribution. The consensus is that people located at *every* point on the status scale in the unequal income communities—whether at, above, or below the average—reported less personal happiness and subjective satisfaction than those in communities in which income was distributed equally (Furby, "Satisfaction with Outcome Distributions," 1981).

A third field of research has compared productivity in the U.S. with the relatively egalitarian welfare states of western Europe. The consensus has been that "productivity growth since World War II has been much faster in Europe than in the United States" (Schmitt, *New York Times*, 25 August 1999). But, since some would dismiss that finding as showing that it is easier to increase productivity when you start from a lower base (as did Europe after the devastation of the war), it should also be noted that more "recent data show that several European countries, including France, Germany, the Netherlands and Belgium have matched or even exceeded the United States' productivity levels." (Ibid.) And among the O.E.C.D. nations as a whole, Glyn and Miliband in *Paying for Inequality* (1994) have reported that "those with the fastest increases in productivity tend to be those with narrower income differences."

If all we were concerned about was preventing violence, it would not matter whether productivity diminished as wealth and income equalized. We would feel that preventing violence was so important that it was worth the sacrifice of some growth in overall Gross Domestic Product; at least we would all be poor together, and suffer less shame and less violence. But it is relevant, in the real world, to ask how high the price will be to society if we become more egalitarian. Violence is not all that people care about, though if it increases as much in the next century as it did in the last, preventing violence will turn out to be so important as to make all other considerations irrelevant.

The most extreme evidence for that might be the experience of the Third World countries. So as not to shame these states, they are now conventionally referred to as developing countries rather than undeveloped ones; this is little more than a cruel euphemism for many of them. The sad reality is not only that they are not developing, but are actually undeveloping, getting poorer. Is that because they are too egalitarian? On the contrary, by far the greatest degree of both economic inequity and violence in the world is found in the Third World countries, whose populations typically consist of a tiny oligarchy of extremely wealthy rulers, a vast majority of starving peasants and no middle class. In comparison, even the United States looks like a peaceful social democracy. If economic inequity were a prerequisite for economic growth, one would expect these countries to be growing by leaps and bounds. Instead they are regressing. If we look at the group as a whole, we would have to conclude that the higher the degree of economic inequity in a society, the lower its productivity and rate of overall economic growth. Unequal societies are not only the most violent; they are also the least productive.

REFERENCES

Bok, S. (1998). *Mayhem; Violence as public entertainment*. Reading, MA: Perseus Books.

Currie, E. (1985). *Confronting crime: An American challenge*. New York.

Furby, L. (1981). Satisfaction with outcome distributions: Studies from two small communities. *Personality and Social Psychology, 7(2)*.

Gilligan, J. (1999). Structural violence. In R. Gottesman (Ed.), *Violence in America: An encyclopedia*. New York.

Glyn, A. & Miliband, D. (Eds.) (1994). *Paying for inequality*. Concord, MA.

Keeley, L. H. (1996). *War before civilization: The myth of the peaceful savage*. New York.

Kohn, A. (1987, January 19). Studies find reward often no motivator. *Boston Globe*.

Richardson, L. F. (1960). *Statistics of deadly quarrels*. London & Pittsburgh, PA.

Ryan, W. (1981). *Equality*. New York.

Schmitt, J. (1999, August 25). Why Should Europe Follow Our Lead? *New York Times*.

Sen, A. (1999). *Development as freedom*. New York.

Silberman, C. E. (1978). *Criminal violence, criminal justice*. New York.

United Nations Development Program, *United Nations Human Development Report 1998*, New York.

Wolff, E. N. (1996). In *Top Heavy: The increasing inequality of wealth in America and what can be done about it*. New York.

Credits

I CONCEPTUALIZING VIOLENCE

GILLIGAN, J. How to think about violence. From VIOLENCE by James Gilligan, copyright © 1996 by James Gilligan. Used by permission of Grosset & Dunlap, Inc., a division of Penguin Putnam Inc.

MEDZIAN, M. (1991). Boys will be boys. In *Boys will be boys: Breaking the link between masculinity and violence* (pp. 41–76). New York: Anchor Books. Reprinted with permission of the author.

SUSMAN, E. J., & FINKELSTEIN, J. W. (2001). Biology, development, and dangerousness. In G-F. Pinard & L. Pagani (Eds.) *Clinical assessment of dangerousness: Empirical contributions* (pp. 23–46). Reprinted with permission of Cambridge University Press.

RAINE, A., BRENNAN, P., & FARRINGTON, D. P. (1997). Figure: Heuristic biosocial model of violence. From the chapter, Biosocial bases of violence: Conceptual and theoretical issues. In A. Raine, P.A. Brennan, D.P. Farrington, & S.A. Mednick (Eds.), *Biosocial bases of violence.* New York: Plenum. Reprinted with permission.

GLADWELL, M. (1996, June 3). The tipping point. *The New Yorker*, 32–38. Reprinted with permission of the author.

GILLIGAN, J. Shame: The emotions and morality of violence. From VIOLENCE by James Gilligan, copyright © 1996 by James Gilligan. Used by permission of Grosset & Dunlap, Inc., a division of Penguin Putnam Inc.

SLOTKIN, R. The white city and the wild west: Buffalo Bill and the mythic space of American history, 1880–1917. Reprinted with the permission of Scribner, an imprint of Simon & Schuster Adult Publishing Group from GUNFIGHTER NATION by Richard Slotkin. Copyright © 1992 Richard Slotkin.

II SOCIAL CONSTRUCTION OF MASCULINITIES, FEMININITIES, AND "THE OTHER"

LORBER, J. (1994). "Night to his day": The social construction of gender. In *Paradoxes of gender* (pp. 13–36). New Haven, CT: Yale University Press. Reprinted with permission.

TAVRIS, C. Speaking of gender: The darkened eye restored. Reprinted with the permission of Simon & Schuster from THE MISMEASURE OF WOMAN by Carol Tavris. Copyright © 1992 by Carol Tavris.

GIBSON, J. W. (1994). Introduction; Old warriors, new warriors. In *Warrior dreams: Violence and manhood in post-Vietnam America* (pp. 9–12; 17–32). New York: Hill and Wang. Reprinted with permission.

WEIGL, B. (1995). Song of napalm. In C. D. Edelberg (Ed.), *Scars: American poetry in the face of violence* (pp. 187–188). Tuscaloosa, AL: University of Alabama Press. Used by permission of Grove/Atlantic, Inc. Copyright © 1988 by Bruce Weigl.

EHRHART, W. D. "Guerrilla War" is reprinted from *Beautiful Wreckage: New & Selected Poems* by W. D. Ehrhart, Adastra Press. Copyright © 1999, by permission of the author.

EDLEY, N., & WETHERELL, M. (1996). Masculinity, power, and identity. In M. Mac An Ghaill (Ed.), *Understanding masculinities: Social relations and cultural arenas* (pp. 98–113). Buckingham, England: Open University Press. Reprinted with permission.

KILMARTIN, C. (2000). No man is an island: Men in relationships with others. In *The masculine self,* 2nd edition (pp. 263–276). New York: Macmillan. Reprinted with permission of the McGraw-Hill Companies.

GIBSON, J. W. (1994). Black-widow women. In *Warrior dreams: Violence and manhood in post-Vietnam America* (pp. 51–64). New York: Hill and Wang. Reprinted with permission.

III YOUTH VIOLENCE

IV THE VIOLATION OF BODY SPACE

KAMEN, P. (1996). Acquaintance rape: Revolution and reaction. In N. Bauer Maglin & D. Perry (Eds.), *Bad girls good girls: Women, sex, and power in the nineties* (pp. 137–149). New Brunswick, NJ: Rutgers University Press. Reprinted with permission of the author.

SCARCE, M. Preface; An assault on sexual identity. From MALE ON MALE RAPE: THE HIDDEN TOLL OF STIGMA AND SHAME. by MICHAEL SCARCE. Copyright © 1997 by Michael Scarce. Reprinted by permission of Perseus Books Publishers, a member of Perseus Books, L.L.C.

KENDALL-TACKETT, K., WILLIAMS, L. M., & FINKELHOR, D. (1993). Impact of sexual abuse on children: A review and synthesis of recent empirical studies. *Psychological Bulletin, 113 (1)*, 164–180. Copyright © 1993 by the American Psychological Association. Reprinted with permission.

WEIGL, B. (1995). The impossible. In C. D. Edelberg (Ed.), *Scars: American poetry in the face of violence* (p. 41). Tuscaloosa, AL: University of Alabama Press. Reprinted with permission.

DERRICOTTE, T. "Abuse" from CAPTIVITY, by Toi Derricotte, © 1989. Reprinted by permission of the University of Pittsburgh Press.

V VIOLENCE AND SPORTS

PARKER, A. (1996). Sporting masculinities: Gender relations and the body. In Mairtin Mac An Ghaill (Ed.), *Understanding masculinities: Social relations and cultural arenas* (pp. 126–138). Buckingham, England: Open University Press. Reprinted with permission.

MESSNER, M., & SABO, D. (1994). Sexuality and power. In M. Messner & D. Sabo (Eds.), *Sex, violence, power in sports: Rethinking masculinity* (pp. 33–35). Freedom, CA: The Crossing Press. Reprinted with permission.

MEDZIAN, M. (1991). Sports: When winning is the only thing, can violence be far away? In *Boys will be boys: Breaking the link between masculinity and violence* (pp. 181–192, 194–204, 209–210). New York: Anchor Books. Reprinted with permission of the author.

MESSNER, M. (1990). Boyhood, organized sports, and the construction of masculinities. *Journal of Contemporary Ethnography, 18(4)*, 416–444. Copyright © 1990 by Sage Publications. Reprinted by permission of Sage Publications.

LEFKOWITZ, B. (1997). The basement; Accusation and denial. In *Our guys: The Glen Ridge rape and the secret life of the perfect suburb* (pp. 13–40; 278–287). New York: Vintage Books. Reprinted with permission.

OSTRIKER, A. "The Boys, The Broom Handle, the Retarded Girl" from THE LITTLE SPACE: POEMS SELECTED AND NEW, 1968–1998, by Alicia Ostriker, © 1998. Reprinted by permission of the University of Pittsburgh Press.

VI MEDIA REPRESENTATION OF VIOLENCE

MESSNER, M. and SOLOMON, W. (1994). Sin and redemption: The Sugar Ray Leonard wife-abuse story. In M. Messner and D. Sabo (Eds.), *Sex, violence, power in sports: Rethinking masculinity* (pp. 53–65). Freedom, CA: The Crossing Press. Reprinted with permission.

GOLDSTEIN, J. H. "Why We Watch" by Jeffrey Goldstein, from WHY WE WATCH: THE ATTRACTIONS OF VIOLENT ENTERTAINMENT, edited by Jeffrey Goldstein, copyright © 1998 by Oxford University Press, Inc. Used by permission of Oxford University Press, Inc.

BOK, S. Sizing up the effects; Aggression. From MAYHEM: VIOLENCE AS PUBLIC ENTERTAINMENT by SISSELA BOK. Copyright © 1998 by Sissela Bok. Reprinted by permission of Perseus Books Publishers, a member of Perseus Books, L.L.C.

CANTOR, J. and A. NATHANSON (1997). Predictors of children's interest in violent television programs. *Journal of Broadcasting and Electronic Media 41 (2)*, 155–167. Reprinted with permission.

INNESS, S. A. From "Lady Killers: Tough Enough" in *Tough Girls: Women Warriors and Wonder Women in Popular Culture* by Sherrie A. Inness. Copyright © 1999 University of Pennsylvania Press. Reprinted with permission.

VII PREVENTING VIOLENCE AND REVISIONING THE FUTURE

DRYFOOS, J. G. What works, and why? From SAFE PASSAGE by Joy Dryfoos, copyright © 1998 by Oxford University Press, Inc. Used by permission of Oxford University Press, Inc.

DWYER, K., OSHER, D., & WARGER, C. (1998). Early warning, timely response: A guide to safe schools. Washington, D.C.: United States Department of Education, 1998. <www.air.org/cecp/guide/earlywarning.htm>

COOK, P. J., & MOORE, M. H. (1999). Guns, gun control, and homicide: A review of research and public policy. In D. M. Smith & M. A. Zahn (Eds.), *Homicide: A sourcebook of social research* (pp. 277–296). Thousand Oaks, CA: Sage Publications. Reprinted by permission of Sage Publications.

FINLEY, K. (1990). It's only art. In *Shock Treatment* (pp. 69–74). San Francisco. City Lights. Copyright © 1990 by Karen Finley. Reprinted by permission of CITY LIGHTS BOOKS.

KUPERS, T. (1993). Conclusion: Redefining power. In *Revisioning men's lives: Gender, intimacy, and power* (pp. 178–183). New York: Guilford Press. Reprinted with permission by The Guilford Press.

GILLIGAN, J. How to create less violent societies. From *Preventing Violence* by James Gilligan. Copyright © 2001 James Gilligan. Reprinted by permission of Thames & Hudson.